LEARNING AUTOMATA

LEARNING AUTOMATA
AN INTRODUCTION

KUMPATI S. NARENDRA
Yale University

New Haven, Conn.

MANDAYAM A.L. THATHACHAR
Indian Institute of Science

Bangalore, India

Prentice Hall, Englewood Cliffs, New Jersey 07632

Library of Congress Cataloging-in-Publication Data

Narendra, Kumpati S.
    Learning automata : an introduction / Kumpati S. Narendra,
Mandayam A.L. Thathachar.
        p.   cm.
    Bibliography: p.
    Includes index.
    ISBN 0-13-485558-2
    1. Artificial intelligence.   I. Thathachar, Mandayam A. L.
II. Title.
Q335.N37 1989
006.3--dc19   88-36574
                                                         CIP

© 1989 by Prentice-Hall, Inc.
A Division of Simon & Schuster
Englewood Cliffs, New Jersey 07632

Printed in the United States of America

10 9 8 7 6 5 4 3 2 1

ISBN   0-13-485558-2

Prentice-Hall International (UK) Limited, *London*
Prentice-Hall of Australia Pty. Limited, *Sydney*
Prentice-Hall Canada Inc., *Toronto*
Prentice-Hall Hispanoamericana, S.A., *Mexico*
Prentice-Hall of India Private Limited, *New Delhi*
Prentice-Hall of Japan, Inc., *Tokyo*
Simon & Schuster Asia Pte. Ltd., *Singapore*
Editora Prentice-Hall do Brasil, Ltda., *Rio de Janeiro*

To our families

Contents

Preface

Advances in science and technology proceed from empirical observations on controlled experiments to theoretical formulations, that in turn guide the choice of new experiments. The capability and accessibility of modern digital computers, one of the most powerful scientific tools ever invented, have resulted in computer simulations assuming the role of traditional experiments in many areas of scientific investigation. This is particularly true of complex interconnected information systems. Such systems are generally both hierarchical and distributed in structure and contain a large number of decision makers operating in the presence of great uncertainty. Simulations of these systems, under widely different conditions using heuristic assumptions, provide a qualitative understanding of their performance. This in turn has led to a search for new theoretical principles, paradigms, and methods to explain failures and extend successful results. The learning automaton presented in this book is one such paradigm. The rationale underlying the learning approach is based on the desire for adaptive decision making in highly uncertain stochastic environments. The learning automaton achieves this, and in addition, can be implemented in a distributed manner, a critical feature for dealing with large complex systems. Perhaps most important, unlike heuristic techniques, the automaton approach has been developed in a systematic and analytically tractable fashion.

Work on learning automata was started in the 1960s in the Soviet Union by M. L. Tsetlin and his co-workers. However, the term "automaton theory" used by Tsetlin had little in common with the research followed by western automaton theorists and was much closer in spirit to the models of mathematical learning theory and learning machines such as the perceptron. In fact, some of the mathematical models studied intensively by American psychologists in the 1950s could be regarded as the forerunners of the developments in this field. In the 1970s it was realized that similar problems had been independently and extensively investigated in many other fields including statistics and operations research but the common basis of these parallel developments was masked by different terminologies. Although the basic questions are quite similar in the different areas, the viewpoint is conditioned to a great extent by the practitioners. During the past two decades research workers in the systems field in different countries have consistently used the term learning automata to describe systems that improve their performance in random environments. It is this class of systems that is treated in this book.

When the uncertainty encountered in a system is sufficiently small, existing methods can be suitably modified to cope with them. Many of the methods in stochastic identification and control belong to this class and are closely related to their counterparts in deterministic systems. However, when the uncertainty is large, perturbations of existing methods are not adequate and novel methods and tools are needed. This applies both to modeling and control problems. It is for such systems that the methodology developed in this book is most suited. The decision maker or automaton is assumed to operate in a random environment from which it receives only probabilistic feedback regarding the effect of the action taken.

The book is meant to be a self-contained introductory text on the behavior of learning automata. It is intended for a fairly wide audience, since the concepts discussed are appearing with increasing frequency in a wide spectrum of fields including systems theory, operations research, computer science, economics, biology, psychology, artificial intelligence, and robotics. It is recommended for use as a text for a one-semester graduate course. The mathematical level of the book is such that it can be followed relatively easily by a first-year graduate student who has had an introductory course on probability theory, as well as a brief exposure to Markov chains and Markov processes.

The principal theme of the book is how a sequential decision maker with a finite number of choices in the action set would choose an action at every instant, based on the responses of a random environment. Although this aspect, developed in Chapters 3–6, is very close in spirit to the algorithms in mathematical psychology, the thrust of the effort in Chapters 7, 8, and 9 is more toward decentralized decision and control problems and hence closely related to the synthesis of learning systems. Throughout the book, the main ideas are first explained qualitatively and the principal results are presented as theorems. Every effort has been made to include significant results, which are scattered throughout the literature, and rigorous proofs are given wherever possible. Extensive computer simulations are included to complement the theoretical developments.

The book has been in preparation for many years but some of the most important results presented in Chapters 7 and 8 were only published recently.

The book has had an international participation. During almost the entire period the book was being written, one of the authors (K.S.N.) was in New Haven, Connecticut while the other author (M.A.L.T.) was in Bangalore, India. Numerous friends, colleagues, and students in different countries contributed in various ways to the completion of the book. It is with the greatest pleasure that we acknowledge our deep appreciation to all of them. We are particularly indebted to Andrew Barto, S. Lakshmivarahan, Philip Mars, Lorne Mason, David Stern, and Richard Wheeler, Jr. who read various chapters and made constructive suggestions for their improvement. Michael Chrystall, Douglas McKenna, Oleg Nedzelnitsky, Vishu Viswanathan, and Richard Wheeler, Jr. at Yale University and R. Bhakthavathsalam, K. R. Ramakrishnan, and P. S. Sastry at the Indian Institute of Science carried out most of the simulation studies presented here. Our thanks are also due to our doctoral students during the last twenty years who worked in the area of learning automata and contributed greatly to a better understanding of the theory, and to the graduate students of electrical engineering at the two schools who, as captive audiences, were introduced to learning automata theory as presented here.

K.S.N. would like to thank Phil Mars for the many interesting discussions at Aberdeen, Leicester, and Durham. Phil's unwavering faith in the automaton approach to learning was contagious. Lorne Mason's doctoral dissertation introduced K.S.N. to the routing problem in networks. Shiva Tripathi helped in programming network problems in the early days, and Allen Wright provided stimulating discussions on "dynamic routing" long before the term was accepted. Lakshmivarahan was a source of constant assistance. Anu Annaswamy and Dan Koditschek gave encouragement when it was most needed and Kannan Parthasarathy furnished invaluable help in the final stages. Most important, K.S.N. acknowledges with pleasure the enormous help he received from Richard Wheeler, Jr. Richard's untiring help in reading the manuscript, his excellent constructive suggestions, and the innumerable discussions enjoyed together have helped greatly to enrich the book. Many of the results included in Chapter 8 on games of automata were coauthored with Richard while he was a graduate student at Yale.

M.A.L.T. would like to thank all his graduate students who enthusiastically participated in the quest for understanding and extending the field of learning automata. It is heartening to him to note that some of them are continuing to contribute toward enriching the field. He appreciates the liberal academic policies of the Indian Institute of Science, which have enabled him to continue investigations in the area in an uninterrupted manner. The final stages in the preparation of the book were carried out on the beautiful campus of Michigan State University. Thanks are due to Anthony Wojcik and Anil Jain of the Computer Science Department for providing facilities and a congenial environment.

Our sincere thanks also go to the staff of Prentice Hall who were involved in the production of this text. We are particularly grateful to Ed Moura, Engineering Editor, for his enthusiastic support and to Sophie Papanikolaou, Production Editor, for her patience and thoroughness.

Jean Gemmell has untiringly typed numerous versions of the book. If not for her extraordinary efficiency and dedication this book would not have been completed.

Finally, without the encouragement of all members of our respective families and in particular our spouses, Barbara Narendra and Yadu Thathachar, this project could not have been brought to fruition.

K. S. Narendra

M.A.L. Thathachar

LEARNING AUTOMATA

Chapter 1

Introduction

1.1 Introduction

The revolutionary advances in information technology that have been made during the last fifty years may be attributed, to a large extent, to parallel developments in system theoretic methodologies and computer technology. From the time the abstract concept of feedback was introduced in the early 1930s and the term cybernetics was coined by Norbert Wiener (1948) in the 1940s to describe communication and control in man and machine, systems theory has grown into a powerful discipline for the analysis and synthesis of dynamical systems. Its effects are felt throughout the industrial world and the systems that have been generated have become integral parts of our socio–economic environment.

The computer, which only a few decades ago spent its fledgling years as a mere computational tool, has developed into today's supercomplex micro-electronic device responsible for far–reaching changes in processing, storage, and communication of information. Major advances in computer technology have invariably had a profound impact on systems methodology. Even in the initial stages the computer freed the systems theorist from the notion that only closed form solutions were acceptable for practical problems. Mathematical algorithms implemented on a digital computer were recognized as viable substitutes, provided their convergence to the desired state could be established. More recently in the solution of complex problems, where algorithms cannot be developed readily, both specific and general heuristics have been proposed. The availability of microprocessors has also made practical implementation a matter of much less concern to the designer than envisaged earlier and it is only the lack of a well established theory or a good heuristic

1

that has made the realization of practical solutions difficult.

The main objectives of systems theory in the early stages of development concerned the identification and control of well defined deterministic and stochastic systems. Over the decades, interest gradually shifted to systems which contained a substantial amount of uncertainty, since most practical systems belong to this class. Since the ability of living organisms to cope with uncertainty is well known, it is only natural that efforts were also made to incorporate similar features in engineering systems. As a result, a variety of terms borrowed from psychology and biology, such as adaptation, learning, pattern recognition, and self–organization, were introduced into the systems literature and developed into independent disciplines with their own following. The field of adaptive control at present is concerned with the stable control of complex dynamical systems when some uncertainty exists regarding the dynamics of the controlled plant. Learning deals with the ability of systems to improve their responses based on past experience. Pattern recognition, developed mainly for the analysis of cognitive processes, is the methodology for classifying objects into predetermined classes. Self–organizing systems, as the name implies, organize their structures to optimize their performance in uncertain environments. All of these areas are related to the broad field of artificial intelligence (AI), which evolved from the disciplines of computer science, psychology, and cybernetics and which refers to the machine emulation of higher mental functions.

Despite the successes of these different approaches and the large number of publications that have appeared in specialized journals that attest to their vitality, the border–lines between the different areas continue to be less than distinct. Although the sources of the problems treated and the terminologies used are different, many of the difficulties encountered are common to all of them. These include the choice of the analytical or symbolic models used to represent the unknown systems, the nature of information that needs to be obtained, the structure of the decision space, and the performance criterion to be optimized. Hence (while such a prospect is nowhere in sight), any one of the terms "adaptive," "learning," or "AI" could be used generically to describe the various classes of systems treated in these different areas. However, the subdisciplines continue to flourish independently and even to spawn new terms of their own. For example "intelligent control" has been used to characterize the discipline that couples advanced methodologies demonstrating machine intelligence with system theoretic approaches (Saridis, 1979).

The theories and applications presented in this book relate – on a prescriptive level – to all of the areas above. The models, algorithms, and analysis are readily applicable to the design of adaptive or learning systems. However, the basic learning paradigm, discussed in detail in Chapter 2, is also closely related to many of the descriptive learning theories developed over a long period by psychologists. Such theories have been propounded by major schools of psychology, for example, behaviorism, gestalt, and cognitivism; and the names of Thorndike, Pavlov, Guthrie, Hull, Tollman, Skinner, and Estes are associated with them (Bower and Hilgard 1981). In these paradigms, learning is used to explain the processes that are necessary for the occurrence of changes in the behavior of organisms while adjusting to their environments. Since adjustment to complex environments is also desirable on the part of man–made decision makers and controllers, it is not surprising that the same principles were gradually adopted for prescriptive use in their design. In the descriptive learning paradigm as well as the learning automaton model treated in this book, a decision maker operates in a random environment and updates its strategy for choosing actions on the basis of the elicited response. The decision maker, in such a feedback configuration of decision maker (or automaton) and environment, is referred to as a *learning automaton*. The automaton has a finite number of actions and corresponding to each action, the response of the environment can be either favorable or unfavorable with a certain probability. The uses of deterministic and stochastic strategies by which the automaton can achieve different performance objectives are treated in the first few chapters. Methods by which the basic building blocks can be interconnected in a hierarchical or decentralized fashion are described in the chapters that follow. Using the theory of Markov processes, the asymptotic behavior of collectives of automata is stated precisely for different interconnections. The theory presented in the book applies to either a prescriptive or a descriptive viewpoint of the basic learning scenario.

The need for learning in identification or control problems depends on the prior information that is available regarding the system, the characteristics of the noise present, and the constraints that exist on the inputs. For low levels of uncertainty, learning may not be the most effective approach. But for highly uncertain systems it may be essential for adequate system performance. The inverted pendulum or pole balancing problem treated in undergraduate text books on control theory is a simple example of this. The problem is to exert a force on the base of a cart so as to balance a pole that is hinged to it. When the relevant parameters of the system, such as the mass of the cart and the mass and length of the pole are given, the resulting problem is a deterministic one. Well known principles of control theory can be used to balance the pole in such a case. When some of the parameters are unknown, we have an adaptive control problem and the necessary stabilizing input can be generated following the estimation of the unknown parameters, based on repeated trials. When even the dynamic relations are not used to determine the control, the problem becomes significantly more difficult and learning must be invoked. Learning control for this problem has been suggested in the past by many authors including Widrow and Smith (1964), and has been revisited recently in the context of adaptive networks (Barto, Sutton and Anderson, 1983). In the latter approach associations are made between input and output by searching under the influence of reinforcement feedback, which is similar in spirit to the approach used by the learning automaton. Hence, the pole balancing problem can be considered to be qualitatively typical of the class of problems to which the methods developed in the book can be applied.

In more complex systems, the controllers or decision makers are organized in a hierarchical or decentralized fashion and must operate with incomplete information regarding either the structure or parameters of the system. The distributed nature of the system also necessitates that control action be taken using local information. To deal with such systems effectively, an understanding of the principles of adaptation, learning, pattern recognition, artificial intelligence, and self–organization may be necessary, depending on the nature of the problem. For example, pattern recognition based on linguistic and heuristic methods has been used in the classification of speech, images, and information coming through sensory devices in a cognitive system; adaptive control has found wide application in such areas as process control, power systems, and robotics; self–organization has been used in distributed networks requiring a considerable amount of interprocessor communications. Similar ideas are also pertinent in modeling evolution of cooperation in biological populations. In artificial systems one could apply the same notions prescriptively for achieving cooperation among the component subsystems. In all these areas the learning automaton has a distinct potential for application, particularly when the evaluative feedback is of a low quality due to the presence of randomness in the system. Two typical areas where this condition is met are described briefly below.

An example of a complex system exhibiting great uncertainty is a robot that must operate with different levels of imprecise information. It has to organize, coordinate, and execute diverse tasks such as manipulation of arms, obstacle avoidance, path planning, scene analysis, recognition, and tracking. These tasks must be accomplished in real time subject to practical constraints such as a limited number of actuators and sensors. Saridis (1983) has suggested a hierarchical system of control with the lowest level being the most precise and higher levels operating with less precise information and hence requiring an adaptive or learning approach. For example, in different regions of the state space, which of two different motions is preferable, which of two performance criteria is to be used, or even which of two sensors is to be relied upon for accurate information, may have to be learned slowly through experience. This is precisely the type of situation in which the learning automaton can prove most effective. Learning in this case takes place over a time scale that is long as compared with the normal operation of the system.

A second area where learning automata concepts may arise naturally is in distributed processing, dictated in many practical situations both by necessity as well as the need for efficiency. Distributed systems have evolved in modern society due to the distribution of databases, which in turn has called for distributed locations for collecting, processing, and accessing data. In recent years a tremendous growth in distributed communication networks to provide greater computational power to the user community has occurred. The construction of massively expensive systems such as the one described above is bringing into focus the fact that our overall understanding of their behavior is quite sparse and that a general theory of such systems is practically nonexistent. The fact that the collective behavior of a number of automata operating in a distributed fashion can be described analytically using game theory and the theory of Markov processes, as shown in Chapter 8, makes the approach particularly attractive in this context.

Recently there has been a new surge of interest in the artificial intelligence community in simulated neural networks. A number of research groups have begun exploring the use of massively parallel computer architectures in an attempt to avoid the limitations of conventional serial symbolic processing. Since the permanent knowledge in such systems is stored in the weights associated with the connections rather than in memory cells, such architectures are termed *connectionist*. Although part of the interest in the research is in simulating the neural networks of the human cortex, the main motivation is in the hope that it will lead to a practical technology for building intelligent systems. In some of these systems many hypotheses are pursued in parallel in the search for optimal solutions. In others, the connectionist architecture is used to admit a rich distributed representation of patterns. In both cases the aim is to achieve good performance, at high computational rates, using a dense interconnection of simple elements. The network developed by Hopfield and Tank (1985), for instance, has been used as an associative memory and as an approach to some NP-complete optimization problems. In Sejnowski and Rosenberg (1987), a program called NETtalk learns to read written text. Based on the analogy between thermodynamic systems and neural networks, a Boltzman machine has been suggested (Hinton and Sejnowski, 1986) to determine the global optimum of a performance function. An approach to the same problem has also been proposed by Barto (1985) using stochastic search. All these and many more ongoing efforts attempt to bridge the gap between the behavior of networks of neuron–like computing elements and complex forms of behavior that appear at higher levels. In later chapters of this book, substantial focus is placed on this theme of interconnecting simple well understood elements as a means of modeling or analyzing more complex systems. Although the details of the elements and interconnections used in collectives of automata differ from those of connectionist systems, the two areas are very similar in concept and a compelling potential exists for establishing the relationship more precisely.

At present many of the methods above work best in domains free of noise. Most are based on heuristic methods and any analytical basis that can be provided is attractive for the coherence that usually accompanies each method. It is clear that the gradual shift in the future will be towards more robust systems which can perform satisfactorily even with noisy distorted input data. As pointed out by Kleinrock (1985), in contrast to man–made computers that are highly constrained, precisely laid out, not very fault tolerant, largely serial, centralized, deterministic, and minimally adaptive, the brain is massively parallel, densely connected with leaky transmission paths, fault tolerant, self repairing, adaptive, noisy and stochastic, and performs the acts of perception, cognition, and decision making with tremendous efficiency even while using natural processing elements which are orders of magnitude slower than current computer processing elements. All these observations reveal there is much that is unknown in this realm and there is a real need for analytical methods that are applicable to distributed stochastic systems. The learning automaton, which is simple in structure, easily interconnected with other automata, stochastic in nature, and which has been shown to be optimal in hierarchical and distributed structures, appears to have the flexibility and analytical tractability needed for this purpose.

1.2 Learning: Perspectives and Context

In this section we describe many of the ideas related to learning systems that were mentioned in Section 1.1. These ideas are part of an interrelated cluster of concepts that are essential for understanding learning phenomena and which arise in most problems, either implicitly or explicitly. In Section 1.3 we describe learning automata in a qualitative manner and indicate how such automata implicitly use the concepts and satisfy the criteria of learning described below.

1.2.1 Learning in Psychology

In psychology, the process of learning deals with the formation of concepts, thoughts, and images as well as the relationship between experience and the organization of the mind. The major conceptual division within psychological approaches is between empiricism and rationalism. The principal tenets of the former are that experience is the only source of knowledge, all complex ideas are made up of simpler ideas and these complex ideas are connected together through the association of experiences. Philosophers such as Hobbes, Locke, Hume, and Mill have elaborated on empiricism and associationism as explanations of mental phenomena and all learning theories such as those of Thorndike, Pavlov, Guthrie, Ebbinghaus, Hull, Skinner, and Tolman are based on the associationistic framework. The opposing position of rationalism, on the other hand, is that the interrelations among elementary ideas are just as fundamental as the ideas themselves, and raw experience together with associative learning principles are not generally adequate to interpret events. An excellent introduction to the various theories of learning can be found in Bower and Hilgard (1981).

A second division among associationistic theories is the conflict between stimulus–response theories and cognitive theories. The importance of motivation, reward, and punishment in learning and performance received great emphasis in the behavioristic revolution led by Watson in the United States. In the 1930s and 1940s Skinner developed his principles of radical behaviorism and argued that a scientific psychology should deal directly with observable behavior. Although behaviorism made no headway in Europe, most American psychologists were behaviorists until the end of the second World War. Behaviorists argued that a detailed understanding of the internal workings of an organism is not necessary for developing a theory of behavior. Around the 1950s, psychology abandoned the radically behaviorist point of view in what came to be termed the *cognitive revolution*. A critical focus of cognitive psychology is concerned with the collection, transmission, storage, and retrieval of information. The advent of the computer, which had a great influence on the information–processing conception of human cognition, had a natural impact on the development of the new psychology that dealt with such processes as perception, attention, memory, thought, and problem solving. For over two decades behaviorism and cognitive psychology have continued to coexist. However, in recent years, an increasing convergence of these distinct theories of learning has occurred.

The subject of learning has been studied extensively in psychology over the past decades and vast amounts of data have been collected in scientific studies in which an organism is placed in a highly controlled environment that is systematically manipulated to observe changes in behavior. Through the use of controlled experiments, simple and general laws of learning have been established under headings such as expectancy learning, classical conditioning, instrumental conditioning, and operant conditioning. In expectancy learning the subject samples stimulii and notices a stable pattern in the association between two stimulii. Hence the subject expects certain stimulii to follow others. Generally such expectancies become stronger with more often repeated experiments as described in Section 1.2.4 on inductive inference. In classical conditioning, learning involves associating a stimulus with a response. In the famous experiments of Pavlov, an unconditional stimulus such as food is repeatedly presented to a dog with a neutral stimulus like the ringing of a bell. Eventually the neutral stimulus elicits a response like salivation, which prior to conditioning, was elicited only by the unconditioned stimulus. Other examples of responses to unconditional stimulii include heart rate, blood pressure, sweat, dilation of pupil, and so on. In instrumental conditioning the organism's behavior is instrumental in obtaining reward or avoiding punishment. Because instrumental behavior is governed mainly by the events it produces, such behavior can be characterized as goal directed. A variation of instrumental conditioning is operant conditioning. From initial unlearned behavior, responses are learned that are most economically effective. A hungry rat or pigeon placed in a Skinner box can be eventually taught to learn to push a bar or press a button to feed itself. Skinner proposed the concept of an operant as a way of dividing behavior into meaningful and measurable units.

Although the learning process discussed above is based primarily on the study of simple responses, the principles derived from them have been applied to serial learning such as driving an automobile, learning a language, or learning to play a game, all of which involve the coordination of a complicated sequence of responses. The learning of principles differs from response learning and is classified as cognitive learning. Contemporary research in animal cognition includes the processing of various types of information including serial patterns, the learning of concepts, and the training of language in primates. Much of the current work in machine learning in areas like pattern recognition (refer to Section 1.2.6) and AI is closely related to cognitive learning.

Mathematical Learning Theory: A tradition of expressing behavior data in quantitative terms has been in vogue since the nineteenth century when the experimental method for the study of learning in psychology was introduced. Out of this was born mathematical learning theory, which eventually led to a diversity of substantive hypotheses about learning and behavior. Starting with the work of Hull (1943), who forcefully argued for the development of quantitative theories in learning, it later appears in the works of Estes (1959), Burke (1954), Bush and Mosteller (1958), Luce (1959), and Suppes and Atkinson (1960). An extensive literature currently exists based on their work. Much of this concentrates on experimental situations that arise in instrumental conditioning and is in the vein of stimulus–response associationism. According to Estes, a major figure in this field, the development of learning theory for individual organisms is, for the most part, an elaboration of association theory. The associative relations are not merely between elementary stimulii and corresponding responses, but also between complex stimulus and response patterns at higher levels of learning.

The stimulus sampling theory of Estes has been the dominant approach within mathematical learning theories. The theory treats learning and performance as stochastic processes. The asymptotic properties of such processes serve in an important interpretative role in the analytical models of these processes. In the descriptive approach described earlier, learning models are suggested to explain the behavior of a subject responding to stimulii in a series of trials. For example, in the classic T–maze problem, a hungry rat is placed at the lower end of the middle limb of a T–maze (Figure 1.1). The rat can move along the limb and turn to the right or to the left. Food is sometimes kept at the end of the right arm and sometimes at the end of the left, according to a schedule prepared in advance by the experimenter. The interest here is in finding mathematical models of the behavior of the rat in choosing the arms during successive trials, for different schedules. The basic paradigm therefore consists of a subject, presented with a stimulus config-

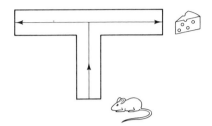

Figure 1.1: The T-maze problem.

uration, making a response and perceiving an outcome. Reinforcement of
the association between stimulus and response occurs if the outcome raises
the probability of the response in the presence of the stimulus. The experimenter prescribes the outcome probabilities and the task of the subject is
to learn these probabilities as in the simple example given above. Both simple learning based on only one stimulus configuration and complex learning
based on multiple configurations have been studied extensively.

In contrast to the experiments above, mathematical learning theory in
its prescriptive aspect attempts to formulate and develop principles for the
synthesis of learning systems. It is obvious that if the characteristics of
the environment of a machine are assumed to be similar to those in the
experiments described above, the learning algorithms used for descriptive
purposes may be used prescriptively also. In both cases the models used
to represent the learning process are iterative algorithms. Learning and
performance are related by feedback paths in which the process of response
selection is continuously modified by anticipation of reward or punishment.
The sequence of responses of the machine or the subject is conceived to be a
realization of a discrete parameter stochastic process. Learning models show
their descriptive power primarily by fitting data in multitrial experiments;
in their prescriptive role, such models provide the principles on which the
rational design of learning systems can be based.

1.2.2   Deterministic, Stochastic, and Adaptive Processes

In his book Adaptive Control Processes – A Guided Tour, Bellman (1961)
classified control problems that arise in systems theory into three categories
on the basis of the prior information available regarding the process to be
controlled. These categories, described as deterministic, stochastic, and
adaptive, according to Bellman, denote the three stages in the evolution
of control systems. Adaptive controllers, which belong to the third stage,

generally have to operate with the least information about their environments. The classification above may be extended to general information processing systems as well. The term "adaptive" is used here in a generic sense and subsumes all systems where some type of uncertainty exists, and includes the class of learning systems described in this book.

(i) *Deterministic Processes:* In any control system the controller is designed, using all available information regarding the process to be controlled, to satisfy either a set of performance criteria or to optimize a given index of performance. In most practical situations such a design must be carried out under various analytical, computational, and physical constraints. In systems that belong to the deterministic class, complete knowledge of the controlled process and external disturbances is assumed. Despite these simplifying assumptions, the design of practical estimators and controllers may be difficult due to analytical and computational reasons. For example, a general theory of synthesizing practical controllers is available only for linear dynamic systems. Although powerful results have also been derived using the dynamic programming approach of Bellman (1957) and the maximum principle of Pontryagin and his co–workers (1962) for the optimization of nonlinear systems subject to constraints, the realization of optimal controllers is far from easy even for relatively simple systems. Even from the earliest days of the development of optimal control theory, the practical design of such controllers has relied entirely on the numerical solution of the relevant equations using a digital computer.

In recent times many interesting problems related to deterministic processes have arisen in areas related to computer science and systems engineering which are difficult to solve because they are NP-complete (i.e. an exact solution requires a number of computational steps that grows faster than any finite power of the size of the problem). A classic example is the "Traveling Salesman Problem" which consists of finding the shortest tour between N cities visiting each one only once and ending at the starting point. In such problems, even though the problem is entirely deterministic, an exhaustive search becomes rapidly impractical. Many techniques such as simulated annealing (Kirkpatrick, Gelatt, and Vecchi, 1983), optimization by networks of artificial neurons (Hopfield and Tank, 1985), and genetic algorithms (Holland, 1975) have been suggested to obtain good (rather than optimal) solutions rapidly.

(ii) *Stochastic Control Processes:* In the second stage in the evolution of information processing systems, the process as well as the disturbances are assumed to be stochastic. The probabilistic characteristics of both are assumed to be given in terms of the relevant distributions. It is assumed that such distributions can be obtained independently using experimental techniques. Once again, the performance criterion as well as the constraint equations can be theoretically set up and the problem can be reduced to an optimization problem as in the deterministic case. The optimization of linear systems with quadratic performance indices and Gaussian disturbances is perhaps the most noteworthy achievement during this stage, and the general procedure used in such cases has become a major tool in the repertoire of the systems engineer. Despite the basic differences between deterministic and stochastic processes, the optimization problems as well as the numerical procedures used to solve them are found to be similar in the two cases.

(iii) *Adaptive Processes:* Many systems, including the class of learning systems considered in this book, belong to the third stage where the level of prior information is considerably less. In these systems very little may be known either about the environment or the disturbances. Such systems are ubiquitous in widely different fields such as economics, biology, engineering, psychology, operations research, and AI. While in theory the information needed for their estimation or control may be obtained by off–line experimentation as in the stochastic stage, the time it would take to obtain such information (e.g. the statistics of the process or the disturbance) would be prohibitively large to allow such a procedure to be adopted. By making observations on the process as it unfolds, further knowledge must be gained for optimization purposes. According to Bellman, such processes are to be regarded as learning or adaptive systems.

1.2.3   Hill Climbing

A great number of problems in science and engineering, including those of adaptation and learning, can be formulated as optimization problems in which a cost function has to be minimized. In static systems such a cost function $J(\alpha)$ is expressed in terms of a parameter vector α and the objective is to determine the optimal parameter vector α^* such that $J(\alpha^*) < J(\alpha)$ for all $\alpha \neq \alpha^*$. In dynamical systems the cost function also depends on an input function $u : [0, T] \rightarrow \mathcal{R}$ and the cost function is expressed as $J(u, \alpha)$. The optimization of such a system involves the determination of both the optimal control function u^* as well as the optimal parameter vector α^*. Numerous standard techniques exist in the systems literature for determining u^* and α^* when $J(u, \alpha)$ is known analytically. Even in cases where the latter is not known explicitly but $J(u, \alpha)$ can be measured for specific choices of u and α, recursive methods, generally referred to as hill climbing methods, exist for obtaining the optimal values. For example, in a static system, to determine α^*, an initial value α_0 of the parameter α is chosen and an estimate of the gradient $\nabla_\alpha J(\alpha)$ of $J(\alpha)$ at α_0 can be computed by perturbing α around its nominal value α_0. On the basis of this information, the parameter vector is altered from α_0 to the new value $\alpha_0 - \beta \nabla_\alpha J(\alpha_0)$ ($\beta > 0$), and the process is repeated. In case an analytic expression is known for $J(\alpha)$, which is also differentiable with respect to α, the maxima and minima of $J(\alpha)$ can also be computed by solving the nonlinear equations $\nabla_\alpha J(\alpha) = 0$.

The same ideas can also be extended directly to stochastic systems when the relevant distributions of the random processes are known. For example, if Q is a function which depends on a parameter vector α and a random process $x(t)$, the optimization problem may be expressed as the problem of determining the parameter α^*, which minimizes the expected value of Q defined by

$$J(\alpha) = E[Q(x, \alpha)] = \int_x Q(x, \alpha) p(x) dx \qquad (1.1)$$

where $p(x)$ is the probability density function of x. If $p(x)$ is known, $J(\alpha)$ can in theory be determined and hence the deterministic methods described earlier are found to be applicable. When $p(x)$ is unknown, optimization involves using observed data to estimate the statistics of the process x, determining $J(\alpha)$ and solving the nonlinear equations

$$\nabla_\alpha J(\alpha) = 0. \qquad (1.2)$$

The stochastic approximation method, originally developed by Robbins and Munro (1951) and Kiefer and Wolfowitz (1952) and later generalized by Dvoretzky (1956), Blum (1954), and others, can be considered to be a stochastic analog of the deterministic hill climbing methods. In contrast to the approach described above for stochastic systems, the stochastic approximation method combines into a single algorithm the two separate algorithms of estimating the unknown statistics and solving Eq.(1.2). Second, it can be employed in the absence of a priori knowledge of the process statistics and in the absence of detailed knowledge of the relationship between the parameter vector α and the observed data. This latter fact makes the approach very attractive in problems in learning and adaptation. Specifically, all that is required is that the regression function $J(\alpha)$ in Eq.(1.1) satisfy certain regularity conditions and that the regression problem have a unique solution.

In 1971, Tsypkin suggested that probabilistic methods in general and the stochastic approximation method in particular were ideal mathematical techniques for use in adaptive and learning systems (Tsypkin, 1971). In Tsypkin's book, he systematically applied the technique to a wide spectrum of problems including pattern recognition, identification, filtering, and control. If $\alpha(n)$ is the value of the parameter vector at stage n, its value at stage $n + 1$ is based directly on the realization $Q(x(n), \alpha(n))$ rather than on the regression function. The adjustment of α is accomplished by the rule

$$\alpha(n + 1) = \alpha(n) - \Gamma(n) \nabla_\alpha [Q(x(n), \alpha(n))] \qquad (1.3)$$

where $\nabla_\alpha Q$ is an estimate of the gradient measured at stage n. Specific constraints are imposed on the choice of the matrix $\Gamma(n)$ in Eq.(1.3) to ensure convergence of $\alpha(n)$ to the optimal value α^*. Since the processes $x(n)$ and hence $\alpha(n)$ are random, one of the many concepts of stochastic convergence must be used to describe the asymptotic behavior of $\alpha(n)$ (refer to Chapter 5).

1.2.4   Deductive and Inductive Inference

Inferential reasoning can be classified as either deductive or inductive. In the deductive process we start with a set of propositions that we accept for some reason and then come up with new propositions that we must also accept as they are contained in what was assumed. In short, from a hypothesis H and an auxiliary condition X, a conclusion C is drawn (Watanabe, 1962, 1975). All nonadaptive decision making may be considered to be based on deductive inference. For example, in pattern recognition, based on the classification rule that the elements in an n–space that lie on one side of a hyperplane belong to set A while those on the other side belong to set B, an inference regarding a specific pattern is made based on its location with respect to the hyperplane. In the example above the classification rule corresponds to H, the location of the specific element to condition X and the decision regarding its classification to conclusion C. Hence deduction leads to conclusions of a generality either equal to or less than that of its premises. Also, once the original propositions are assumed to be valid (for example, the classification rule above), deductive inference is safe and beyond controversy.

In contrast to deductive inference, the operation of discovering and proving general propositions based on observations involves inductive inference. Aristotle called induction "a passage from individuals to universals" and in his treatise <u>Systems of Logic</u>, John Stuart Mill defined induction as "...that operation of the mind by which we infer that what we know to be true in a particular case will also be true in all cases which resemble the former in certain assignable respects." In other words, in the inductive process we proceed from a finite set of observations under the condition X to the development of a hypothesis H. In the example considered earlier, from the observation that every observed element that lies on one side of the hyperplane belongs to set A, we attempt to draw the conclusion H that all elements on that side of the hyperplane correspond to set A. However, the conclusion H is not logical since it is a statement about an infinity of situations drawn from a finite number of observations. Hence induction leads from less general to more general propositions. The epistemological problems that originate from this inconclusive character of inductive reasoning have been the subjects of discourse of philosophers since the time of Hume. According to Watanabe, this extralogical conclusion is responsible for the creation of new information in the universe and partially answers the somewhat vaguely posed question as to why, if humans are merely information transducers, the information in the world does not entirely get lost with time.

Since all decisions in the real world and hence all learning is based on limited experience, we can say that our knowledge of the external world consists only of conjectures where some conjectures have a higher degree of credibility than others. For example, while many of the laws in the physical and natural sciences have proved to be very reliable conjectures, quite often they themselves tend to be superceded by new laws. Induction is the best way we know of accounting for observed data and for making conjectures about the unobserved. However, it is clear that inductive inference is provisional, controversial, and at times even hazardous.

Inductive and deductive inference do not contradict but merely complement each other and both are found to be essential for the learning process. The only case where arbitration is entirely dependent on deductive logic is when a counterexample is produced. If A implies B and B is shown to be false then A is exploded. However, if B is shown to be true, then the credibility of the hypothesis A is merely increased. In complex learning machines, the inductive and deductive processes may be interwoven at different levels. The machine may try to describe in complete generality what it observed, by proceeding from observations to the development of a hypothesis in the training or inductive stage. Having selected a hypothesis it predicts what it expects to observe in the future. This is the deductive stage where the logical consequences of the hypothesis are verified. If the observations violate the hypothesis the latter is modified in successive stages until a hypothesis is finally arrived at which is supported by all the available evidence (Polya, 1954).

Credibility and Induction: From our daily experience it is clear that some inductive arguments are stronger than others, but in general we do not have methods for quantifying them. It has been suggested that inductive probability or "credibility" be used as a measure of confidence we place in a hypothesis on the basis of observed data. If $q(H_i)$ is the inductive probability of H_i, where H_i is one of N competing hypothesis $H_1, H_2, \ldots, H_N$ we define

$$q(H_i) \geq 0, \quad \sum_{i=1}^{N} q(H_i) = 1$$

and agree on the convention that the value of q of unity would imply a law while a value of zero would imply a logically refuted hypothesis. We shall further assume that $q(H)$ satisfies the usual laws of probability. By the application of Bayes' rule many of our intuitive feelings about inductive inference can be expressed quantitatively in terms of credibility. For example, if $q(H_2|H_1) = 1$, then $q(H_1|H_2) \geq q(H_1)$. If H_1 implies H_2, the verification of H_2 renders H_1 more credible. Further details can be found in Watanabe (1960).

Inverse H–Theorem: Based on the verification of consequences, if a hypothesis is not exploded, its credibility is merely modified. In fact, if there are N competing hypotheses H_j $(j = 1, 2, \ldots, N)$, induction must be a process by which the credibility of one of the hypotheses increases while those of all the others decrease, resulting in a decrease of inductive entropy. This tendency of the inductive entropy to decrease with the number of experiments carried out is described as the inverse H–theorem of inductive learning by Watanabe (1975).

Let D_i $(i = 1, 2, \ldots, \ell)$ be ℓ possible experimental outcomes and H_j $(j = 1, 2, \ldots, N)$ the N hypotheses that have to be compared. Let $p(D_i|H_j)$ be the probability of occurrence of D_i based on the hypothesis H_j. If the experiment is repeated n times let the outcome D_i occur n_i times so that $\sum_{i=1}^{\ell} n_i = n$. The relative frequency of D_i is $\frac{n_i}{n} = \alpha_i$. Defining the credibility of the hypothesis H_j based on the n observations as

$$p^{(n)}(H_j|n_1, n_2, \ldots, n_\ell),$$

we will naturally be interested in the value of j for which this is a maximum. If one of the hypotheses (say H_j) is such that the experimental frequency of occurrence α_i of D_i for $i = 1, 2, \ldots, \ell$, is the same as $p(D_i|H_j)$, its credibility will be larger than that of any other hypothesis as n becomes large and in the limit

$$\lim_{n \to \infty} p^{(n)}(H_j|\alpha_1, \alpha_2, \ldots, \alpha_\ell) = 1 \quad \lim_{n \to \infty} p^{(n)}(H_k|\alpha_1, \alpha_2, \ldots, \alpha_\ell) = 0 \quad j \neq k.$$

Defining the inductive entropy at stage n as

$$S^{(n)} = -\sum_{j=1}^{N} p^{(n)}(H_j|\alpha_1, \alpha_2, \ldots, \alpha_\ell) \, \log \, p^{(n)}(H_j|\alpha_1, \alpha_2, \ldots, \alpha_\ell)$$

$S^{(n)}$ will decrease for sufficiently large n and

$$\lim_{n \to \infty} S^{(n)} = 0. \tag{1.4}$$

This is the inverse H–theorem of Watanabe (1975), which describes the most salient feature of inductive learning. The theorem implies that as the process of learning advances, the probability weights distributed over many alternatives become concentrated on fewer alternatives. Watanabe has used the theorem successfully in many learning contexts and regards the inverse H–theorem as a fundamental law of learning. Based on the ideas described thus far, he also described a propensity automaton in which the probabilities associated with an object are updated on the basis of possible outcomes. Similar ideas had already been suggested in the Soviet Union a decade earlier by Varshavskii and Vorontsova (1963). The principal algorithms of learning described in Chapters 4–7 of this book are concerned with the developments and refinements that have taken place in the last two decades. The objective in all cases is to determine the best of a finite set of actions based on the random responses of an environment. This is discussed further in Section 1.3.

1.2.5 Identification and Control

A problem of daily occurrence in our lives is the choice between identification and control. A homemaker preparing an apple pie has to decide between a well tested recipe or a variation of it, which she has heard tastes better; a tennis player can choose the best among his current repertoire of shots or attempt an untested one which may prove superior; and a surgeon has to choose between performing surgery on a patient or conducting more tests on the patient. Similar decisions are made countless times every day in almost all areas of human activity. In each case the decision maker must decide between probing further to improve his or her knowledge of the system – thus enabling him or her to take better actions in the future, or taking the best action on the basis of past experience. The former invariably involves additional cost and may result in very little return. However, the consequence of increased knowledge may be improved performance. This is the basic conflict between identification and control, which also arises in every aspect of systems theory (Witten, 1976).

From the earliest days of automatic control, a basic requirement has been a knowledge of the dynamic behavior of the plant or process to be controlled. Even in a device like Watt's fly–ball governor, which can be built with intuitive notions of engine behavior, its proper operation depends on the choice of parameters suited to the characteristics of the individual plant. If sophisticated controllers, resulting in more accurate control are to be built, more extensive information regarding the process is needed. Ever since feedback system design became a quantitative art, a mathematical model of the process has become a basis for the synthesis of a workable system.

The creation of a mathematical model is an inductive process. A system may be defined as a transformation f which maps an input set $\mathcal{U}$ to an output set $\mathcal{Y}$. The objective of modeling is to obtain an approximation $\hat{f}$ of f so that the error $f(u) - \hat{f}(u)$ is small in some sense for all inputs $u \in \mathcal{U}$. Identification is defined as the determination of $\hat{f}$ from a specified class of models $\mathcal{F}$, on the basis of a set of input–output measurements and an error criterion. In particular, using elements of a subset $\mathcal{U}_T$ of $\mathcal{U}$ called the training set, $\hat{f} \in \mathcal{F}$ is chosen so that the error criterion is satisfied for all $u \in \mathcal{U}_T$. Since in practice $\mathcal{U}_T$ is finite while the set $\mathcal{U}$ may have an infinity of elements, the acceptance of $\hat{f}$ as a model has to be based on inductive reasoning. The crucial test of a good model $\hat{f}$ however is its predictive ability. This corresponds to the deductive part of model making. Given any input $u \in \mathcal{U}_T^c$ where $\mathcal{U}_T^c$ is the complement of $\mathcal{U}_T$ in $\mathcal{U}$, the output is predicted using the model $\hat{f}$. A good model then corresponds to one that also satisfies the error criterion for inputs not contained in the training set. In general, the larger the training set $\mathcal{U}_T$ (and hence more representative of all the inputs in $\mathcal{U}$) the more accurate is the identification model $\hat{f}$ and hence the more likely it is to predict the response to a new input.

In systems theory, models may be used both for prediction and control. Let $\hat{f}(n)$ denote the identified model at stage n of a plant to be controlled. In the deterministic processes described in the previous section, it is assumed that identification has been in progress for a sufficiently long time so that a very accurate model of the plant is available i.e., $\lim_{n \to \infty} \hat{f}(n) \approx f$. The control input to the plant can therefore be computed accurately to optimize a given index of performance. However, if the identification process is not complete and $\hat{f}(n)$ is not a sufficiently accurate description of f, the control based on $\hat{f}(n)$ may also not be accurate. This corresponds to the adaptive situation described in Section 1.2.2 and the designer faces the identification and control conflict discussed earlier. One alternative is to continue the identification process until the plant is identified sufficiently and accurately as in the deterministic case. This procedure is generally very inefficient since, in most situations, the inputs needed to identify the system accurately are different from those needed to control it optimally. In the example of the surgeon given earlier, the former corresponds to additional tests on the patient and the latter to the decision regarding surgery. If, on the other hand, the designer decides to compute the optimal input based on the approximate model $\hat{f}(n)$, the response of the system may be poor and at times even lethal. In our simple example, this may correspond to a decision on the part of the surgeon not to operate on a patient whose true state warrants such action. In general dynamical systems the computation of optimal feedback control based on $\hat{f}(n)$ may result in instability. The fundamental nature of the conflict between identification and control in adaptive systems has been stressed by Feldbaum (1965) who calls it the "dual control problem." According to Feldbaum, in a general control problem where uncertainty is present, the controller has to solve two problems that are closely related but different in character. First, on the basis of new inputs it has to improve its knowledge of the characteristics of the system. Second, on the basis of the new knowledge it has to determine what actions are necessary for successful control. Hence, as suggested by Feldbaum, the input to the system must be chosen judiciously at every stage so that the identification model $\hat{f}(n)$ as well as the performance of the system are successively refined in a stable fashion, with the control input $u(n)$ evolving asymptotically to its optimal value. Much of the work that is currently in progress in the adaptive control area is related to this fundamental problem. One of the crucial realizations that has evolved out of these investigations is that identification followed by optimization at every stage need not result in an asymptotically optimal or even stable system.

1.2.6 Pattern Recognition

Pattern recognition is a field that has been investigated extensively in the past by philosophers, psychologists, and neurobiologists and more recently by systems theorists, engineers, and research workers in the area of AI. It deals with the issue of building a machine or a program that will display some capability of living organisms for classifying or discriminating sensory signals. In living organisms perception is the total process involving cognitive transformations of sensory input stimulii, interaction of these with information stored in the memory, and consequent changes in behavior and internal structure. Pattern recognition may be considered the last stage of the process involving the choice of appropriate responses to input signals.

The study of patterns has been described (Uhr, 1966) as the study of complexes – of structures, interactions, grammars, and syndromes. The object of pattern recognition is to sort patterns into different classes so that those patterns which belong to a class share some common properties. Mathematically, this implies a many–to–one mapping, so that the pattern space is divided into disjoint equivalent classes. Medical diagnosis, speech recognition, and scene analysis are typical examples of pattern recognition problems where considerable research is currently in progress.

The statement of the pattern recognition problem and the method used for its resolution are dependent on the available measurements, the prior information assumed, and the speed and accuracy with which the task is to be performed. In each of the examples mentioned earlier, a finite set of patterns is given and the proper classification of the patterns is provided. These may include case histories for medical diagnosis, signals for speech recognition, and pixel intensities for scene analysis. The input set in each case is referred to as a training set. The objective then is to locate from among all known candidates the one that best matches a new pattern and to match it rapidly in the presence of noise and distortions of the input. Assuming that various patterns typical of their classes are stored in some suitably defined space using training data, classifying the new pattern (referred to as a test pattern) amounts to determining the proximity of the given pattern to the various prototypes according to some distance function, and choosing the one corresponding to the minimum distance. Obviously, the success of the method critically depends on the prototypes used, the distance function chosen, and consequently on the space in which typical patterns are stored.

A general pattern recognition system may be considered to consist of three parts. Following the first part in which patterns are collected, in the second part the raw data of the patterns is converted into $\bar{n}$–dimensional feature vectors. The elements of the feature vectors, called *features*, are assumed to contain the essential attributes of the given patterns. The terms preprocessing, filtering, feature extraction, and dimensionality reduction have been applied to this phase of the problem, which is dictated by practical considerations. Much of the difficulty associated with pattern recognition may be attributed to the difficulty encountered in choosing good features, which is well recognized to be more an art than a science. Once this has been accomplished, in the third part methods for classification must be selected.

The relevance of pattern recognition concepts to a wide spectrum of areas in science and engineering is underscored by the fact that contributions to this field can be found in statistical decision theory, automata theory, switching theory, control theory, linguistics, neurobiology, psychology, mathematical programming, and recently neural network studies. Many of the developments of the last twenty years have dealt with decision theoretic approaches based on deterministic and stochastic methods for classifications. For example, if two classes ω^1 and ω^2 are equally likely and the class–conditional densities $p(x|\omega^1)$ and $p(x|\omega^2)$ are known, the decision process is relatively simple and patterns are classified according to the rule

$$p(x|w^1) > p(x|w^2) \Rightarrow x \in w^1 \qquad (1.5)$$

where x is the pattern. If the prior distributions are not known but the form of the density functions is assumed, the unknown parameters are estimated using the training set. The estimated density functions, in turn, are used to determine the decision surfaces for classification.

In many real–world problems where the assumptions above do not hold, nonstatistical parametric learning can be applied. In this case a functional form is assumed for the decision surface which depends on a parameter vector W. Unlike the statistical methods described above there is little probabilistic interpretation of the unknown parameters. Instead, the parameter vector is chosen to minimize a cost function such as the mean squared error based on the training data. Hill climbing methods are generally used for this purpose, which involves the determination of the gradient of the cost function at the nominal value of the parameter. The case where the patterns are linearly separable in the feature space has been extensively studied since the introduction of the perceptron by Rosenblatt (1958). Related work by Widrow and Hoff (1960) on adaptive networks led to the LMS algorithm in which the weight vector is chosen to minimize a mean squared error. These publications sparked considerable research in building intelligent machines from perceptrons. Minsky and Papert (1969), in their book <u>Perceptrons</u>, attempted to quiet this speculation by discussing the limitations of perceptron–type algorithms for cases where the classes are not linearly separable. The current interest in the AI community studying neural networks (discussed briefly in Section 1.1) was influenced by the realization that the weight vector in multiple layer networks could be adjusted using gradient methods for solving complex pattern recognition problems in which the classes are not linearly separable.

Since 1960, many investigators have recognized that the decision theoretic approaches discussed earlier, which are very successful in certain simple problems, have serious limitations. This is particularly applicable when the patterns are quite complex as in image analysis, handwriting recognition, and speech analysis. In such cases it is suggested that structural information should be used to simplify pattern representation. Drawing an analogy with the syntax of languages, this method is generally referred to as syntactic pattern recognition. Using this approach, a complex pattern is described in terms of simpler patterns. After each primitive within a pattern is identified, the recognition process is accomplished by performing a syntax analysis to determine whether the sentence describing the given pattern is syntactically correct (Glorioso and Colón Osorio, 1980).

Much of the present interest in pattern recognition is connected with real–time applications. Fast recognition is one of the goals of connectionist networks described earlier. The use of multiple layers of hidden units were suggested to combine raw observations into higher order features which will be more useful for pattern recognition purposes. The field appears to be on the threshold of some interesting developments.

1.2.7 Bayesian Learning

A well established tradition in statistics is to consider the problem of learning as the problem of estimating a functional that represents the process under study. Both parametric and nonparametric methods of estimation have been used for this purpose and are generally expressed as successive approximations of unknown quantities. In most cases of interest, these quantities can be reduced to parameters and are estimated using observation and experimentation. Identification of the parameters of the transfer function of a dynamical system or the decision surface in pattern recognition are typical examples.

In the Bayesian approach it is assumed that the unknown parameter θ

has a prior density function $p_0(\theta)$ which reflects our knowledge about it as a random variable. This is the point over which "Bayesians" and "Non–Bayesians" have differed from the very beginning. While the objectivistic view of probability of the latter group is restricted to situations in which the event can be repeated again and again, the subjectivist Bayesians hold that probability is an indication of personal belief in a particular proposition. Hence, the assumption concerning the prior distribution $p_0(\theta)$ is eminently in agreement with the Bayesian point of view.

The principal idea of the Bayesian approach is to extract information regarding the unknown parameter θ from observations $x_1, x_2, \ldots, x_N$ on the system. This is achieved by the successive application of the recursive Bayes' formula:

$$p(\theta|x_i) = \frac{p(x_i|\theta)p(\theta)}{p(x_i)} \tag{1.6}$$

where $p(x_i)$ is a constant of proportionality. If θ is supposed to be the cause and x_i the effect, by Eq.(1.6) the probability of the cause can be determined on the basis of the observation. The successive application of Eq.(1.6) results in the a posteriori density function $p(\theta|x_i)$ becoming more concentrated around its true value as the number of observations tends to infinity.

To facilitate the process above using a fixed algorithm, a prior density $p_0(\theta)$ is chosen for the parameter so that the a posteriori densities are members of the same family. This results in the learning process being reduced to the successive estimation of parameter values. This procedure has been used to determine both the mean μ and the covariance Σ of a random vector from observations.

1.2.8 Analytical Solutions, Algorithms, and Heuristics

As mentioned in the Introduction (Section 1.1), a major change in the thinking of systems theorists occurred in the 1960s when it was realized that practically implementable solutions to well posed problems could be developed without solving them in closed form. This resulted in the "algorithm" which is a sequence of well defined steps leading to the solution. From this point on, the emphasis gradually shifted to the development of algorithms and proving that they are stable and converge asymptotically to the correct solutions. As a result, in every field of science and engineering, countless numbers of algorithms have been developed for a wide variety of applications. In all cases, under the conditions stated, the solution to the problem is assured.

In contrast to the algorithm, a heuristic is a rule of thumb that aids in the solution of a specific problem. As the scope and complexity of problems increased, designers resorted more and more often to such strategies. This is because the number of alternatives from among which the solution has to be chosen becomes too large to be practical. Game–playing and theorem–proving machines are typical examples of systems where the need for heuristics becomes obvious.

For example, it is estimated (Cohen and Feigenbaum, 1981) that a full exploration of all possible moves in checkers would require an examination of roughly 10^{40} moves, which is practically impossible. Similar situations arise so frequently that approaches based on heuristics have taken a deep root in the AI community. It is not surprising that such approaches are currently being used both in simple and complex problems alike. Once a heuristic is used in a given problem, the result in turn is generally used to develop new heuristics to further improve the solution. However, it is well recognized that there is no guarantee that the entire procedure will converge to a stable solution or even provide an answer as to the existence of such a solution.

Undoubtedly algorithms are preferred to heuristics wherever they can be generated since they place the results on a firm theoretical foundation. However, in many problems adequate information regarding the system under consideration may not be available to develop algorithms. Hence heuristics are here to stay and cannot be avoided entirely, even in reasonably complex problems. A redeeming feature, as far as the analyst is concerned, is that a successful heuristic may provide strong motivation for the generation of a new theory and hence a new algorithm. As interest shifts to massively parallel systems and heuristics proliferate, there is a distinct sense that the research community would welcome more theoretical approaches to understand the phenomena better. In fact, in many cases, heuristics themselves are guided by the available theoretical results. Scientific research may be considered to proceed by means of an intimate interplay between heuristics and algorithms, where the former is represented by the appropriate pretheoretical conceptualizations and the latter by established laws.

1.3   Learning Automata

The intuitive yet analytically tractable concept of a learning automaton grew out of a fusion of the work of psychologists in modeling observed behavior, the efforts of statisticians to model the choice of experiments based on past observations, the attempts of operations researchers to implement optimal strategies in the context of the two–armed bandit problem (Robbins, 1952), and the endeavors of systems theorists to make rational decisions in random environments. We describe in this section how the various concepts of learning outlined earlier are to be found in such a device.

Interest in learning automata began with the outstanding work of Tsetlin in the early 1960s in the Soviet Union. As pointed out by Eden in a foreword (Tsetlin, 1973), the term "automaton theory" as used by Tsetlin, has little to do with the line of research followed by American and Western European automaton theorists. According to Eden it is much closer in spirit to learning theory and learning machines such as the perceptron. During the last two decades, researchers in different countries have consistently used the term "learning automaton" to describe both deterministic and stochastic schemes used in discrete systems that improve their performance in random environments. Several books (El–Fattah and Foulard, 1978, Lakshmivarahan, 1981, Baba, 1984) have appeared in recent years that also use the term. More recently, researchers in the area of artificial neural networks have begun to incorporate the learning automaton paradigm into their models. As a consequence "learning automaton" has become a standard term used by many sections of the learning community.

Although a detailed mathematical description of a learning automaton is undertaken in Chapter 2, the learning paradigm it represents, which was referred to in Section 1.1, may be qualitatively stated as follows: A finite number of actions can be performed in a random environment. When a specific action is performed the environment provides a random response which is either favorable or unfavorable. The objective in the design of the automaton is to determine how the choice of the action at any stage should be guided by past actions and responses. The important point to note here is that the decisions must be made with very little knowledge concerning the nature of the environment. The latter may have time–varying characteristics, or the decision maker may be a part of a hierarchical decision structure but unaware of his or her precise role in the hierarchy. Alternately, the uncertainty may be due to the fact that the output of the environment is influenced by the actions of other agents unknown to the decision maker. In all cases the automaton must be designed to improve some overall performance function. Both deterministic and stochastic rules for choosing the action at any stage are of interest. In the latter case the automaton updates the probabilities of the various actions on the basis of the information received. With the increasing interest of systems engineers and computer scientists in the modeling and control of large complex systems under great uncertainty, the ubiquitous nature of this paradigm, represented by the learning automaton, is becoming clear from the wide spectrum of seemingly unrelated decision problems in which it arises.

The aim of this book is to treat analytically the consequences of different strategies for updating at any stage the choice of an input to the environment. Starting with a single automaton that acts in a simple stationary random environment, the scope of the model is increased to include time-varying environments, multiple environments, hierarchies of automata, and distributed automata interacting in a complex environment. In each case, a precise mathematical model based on the theory of stochastic processes is developed and its asymptotic behavior is analyzed.

1.3.1   Learning Automata and Psychology

It was observed in Section 1.2.1 that behavior modification of living organisms adjusting to their environments may, in many cases, be attributed to learning. Positive reinforcement facilitates learning, and reinforcement stimulii which are congruent with prevailing motives in the organism change behavior in new directions. Much of the work done in mathematical learning theory can be traced back to this model based on stimulus–response theory of Estes.

In the extensive literature that exists in the area of mathematical learning theory, Norman's book (Norman, 1972) occupies a central place. In it, the learning automaton is used descriptively to explain learning processes in organisms. If a simple environment in which the organism operates is imposed by the designer, the basic problem is to determine a learning mechanism that can explain observed behavior. This is accomplished by the proper choice of the learning algorithm as well as the parameters it contains. In (Norman, 1972), finite state models are studied via Markov chain theory and "distance diminishing models" via Markov processes in a compact metric space. In particular, emphasis is placed on slow learning models in which the probability of a change in the state of the organism in any single trial is considered to be small. The monograph on learning algorithms by Lakshmivarahan (1981) gives a detailed account of stochastic algorithms based on slow learning.

In its prescriptive aspect, the learning automaton is intended to formulate and develop principles for the synthesis of learning systems. In engineering systems, as in living organisms, learning can be defined as the process by which the system improves its behavior on the basis of past experience. In many cases, this may involve the selection of a specific action out of a set of actions, so as to optimize a performance index. The learning mechanism in such a system performs one of the actions, classifies the output as either desirable or undesirable and uses it as a positive or negative reinforcement in making the next choice of the input. In this context the complexity of the overall system is determined by the complexity of the environment. For example, if a single automaton operates in a large data communication network, the latter corresponds to the environment. Different applications require different environmental models and it is important that the performance of the automata remain attractive over as wide a range of environments as possible.

The analysis used in this book relies heavily on the methods introduced by Norman, particularly the concept of slow learning. However, unlike Norman's book, our interest is primarily in the collective behavior of automata used prescriptively in the control of complex systems. The models and algorithms presented in Chapters 2–7 can be viewed as the essential building blocks for constructing such systems. Some preliminary work has been reported by Wheeler and Narendra (1985) for the generation of different models by suitably interconnecting different automata and the behavior of such models can be analyzed using game theory as shown in Chapter 8. However, much work remains to be done in this fertile area of research. Several applications of interconnected automata are given in Chapter 9.

1.3.2 Learning Automata in Deterministic and Random Environments

Consider the case where the output corresponding to each action is unique and lies in a bounded interval and the problem is to determine the action which corresponds to the minimum output. This can be achieved readily by the automaton merely trying all the actions once and selecting the one corresponding to the optimum. Such an exhaustive search of the action space is feasible only when the number of possibilities is not too large. As mentioned in Section 1.2.2, considerable research is currently in progress in noise–free optimization problems that involve numbers of computational steps that are too large from a practical standpoint. Although the learning automaton described in the chapters following can be also used for such problems, it is particularly effective in those cases where repeated experiments are needed for optimization in the face of underlying randomness.

An obvious approach that can be used when the output corresponding to a specific input is random, is to try each action a finite number of times, determine the average reward and choose the action corresponding to the maximum reward or minimum penalty. Such a procedure suffers from the drawback that a large number of experiments will be wasted using undesirable actions. Hence any learning scheme should be such that probability weights distributed over many alternatives become concentrated on fewer alternatives, as given by the inverse–H theorem, even as the process evolves.

The full potential of learning automata in stochastic optimization problems is realized when the latter can be posed as cooperative games of learning automata. The routing problems in communication networks, as well as the relaxation labeling problem and the problem of determining optimal discriminant functions for pattern recognition, discussed in Chapter 9, are cases in point.

1.3.3 Learning Automata and Stochastic Hill Climbing

In Section 1.2.3 it was stated that many adaptation and learning problems can be posed as hill climbing problems in an appropriate decision space. The search methods then involve moving from one point in the decision space to another at which the performance criterion is improved. If gradient methods are used, the performance criterion is assumed to be an analytic function of the parameters involved, and given a nominal value of the parameter, the search method results in a new value which results in the maximal increases in the performance index. As mentioned in Section 1.2.3, stochastic approximation schemes for climbing noisy hills are very well developed and are applicable to a large class of problems. The procedure, however, has a serious drawback in that it often ends up in local optima in multimodal search spaces.

In the learning automaton approach, where one of the actions is known to be the optimum, the concept of a neighborhood is not defined in the action space and hence a hill–climbing approach cannot be used directly. However, if a learning automaton is used and the probabilities of the different actions are updated, the procedure can be considered as hill climbing in probability space. At every stage the changes in probabilities are such that a performance criterion is improved monotonically in an expected sense. Under certain conditions this is shown to result in convergence to the optimal action with a probability arbitrarily close to one.

1.3.4 Learning Automata and Inductive Inference

The role of inductive inference in the learning automaton can be explained as follows: A prior probability distribution over the action set is given. This gives an assessment of the effectiveness of each action at this stage. The automaton uses the distribution to choose an action and the observation of the output leads to a change in the distribution over the action set. The latter can be called the inductive part while the former (in which the automaton deduces which action to choose) can be considered as the deductive part. Hence induction and deduction are alternately used in the learning process.

As mentioned in Section 1.2.4, since no hypothesis can be declared a law on the basis of a finite number of experiments, the best we can hope for is that as the body of evidence accumulates and the number of trials tends to infinity, the automaton converges to the optimal action. At any finite stage, the action corresponding to the highest probability has to be chosen tentatively as the best.

In many practical situations all conceivable alternative actions may not be included in the action set when the automaton is initiated. Provision must therefore be made so that new actions are added at any stage of the process. Similarly, provision can be made to remove certain actions from consideration when the corresponding probabilities fall below a preselected threshold, particularly in those cases where the total number of actions must be limited.

1.3.5 Learning Automata and Dual Control

The evolution of the learning automaton operating in a random environment also underscores the fundamental nature of the conflict between data acquisition for system identification and optimal system control as discussed in Section 1.2.5. Consider an automaton that chooses at every stage all the actions with a uniform probability distribution and updates the estimates of the environmental parameters on the basis of the responses. Such an automaton would obtain perfect information regarding the environment but would be very ineffective from the control point of view. The same also applies to an automaton that changes its action probabilities very slowly. However, if the automaton were to change them rapidly on the basis of the response to a specific action, convergence to the wrong action might result. Hence one of the principal difficulties in resolving the identification/control dilemma is closely connected with the choice of the learning algorithm that assures rapid convergence to the optimal action.

Although the description of the automaton as given above contains no explicit estimation of the parameters of the environment, as is done in indirect control, it has nevertheless been shown that such estimation leads to faster convergence (Thathachar and Sastry, 1985).

1.3.6   Learning Automata and Pattern Recognition

The ability of a system to classify new patterns on the basis of stored information, as described in Section 1.2.6, can also be used as an alternative paradigm for learning and it is not surprising that such machines have been referred to as learning machines. Close connections exist between learning automata and machines that recognize patterns and, by suitably redefining the former, the equivalence of the two in many contexts can be established. One possible approach is to consider a pattern recognizer as a learning machine whose actions are the various classes to which a given pattern can be assigned. Given a number of training patterns whose classifications are known, the machine learns to assign a new pattern to the most appropriate class, which corresponds to the optimal action. Situations in which the information concerning the training patterns is stochastic rather than deterministic have been considered (Barto and Anandan, 1985).

An alternative and perhaps more effective approach is to regard the actions of learning automata as the discrete values of discriminant function parameters in a pattern recognition context (Thathachar and Sastry, 1987). In this view, a team of cooperating learning automata essentially constitutes a pattern recognizer. An example of such a system is given in Chapter 9.

1.3.7   Learning Automata and Bayesian Learning

The emphasis of this book is on learning schemes in which the action probabilities of an automaton are updated on the basis of the responses of an environment. This process is naturally closely related to Bayesian learning discussed in Section 1.2.7 in which the distribution (or density) function of a parameter is updated at each instant on the basis of new information. However, the updating takes place according to Bayes' rule, while it is more general in a learning automaton. In fact, in the latter, no unique procedure exists and the specific scheme used depends on a number of factors such as accuracy, stability, and speed of convergence. Further, in Bayesian learning, there is no concept corresponding to choosing an action at each instant and information is used as it naturally becomes available.

1.3.8 Learning Automata: Algorithms and Heuristics

In the chapters following, a number of deterministic and stochastic algorithms are described by which the output set of the environment is mapped into the action set of the automaton. In fact, the algorithms together with the input and action sets, as described in the next chapter, constitute the automaton. Hence each algorithm, whether deterministic or stochastic, corresponds to a different automaton and once the choice of such an algorithm is made the designer no longer has control over the learning process. The algorithms describe the changes in the internal state or structure of the automaton at every stage based on the action chosen and the corresponding response of the environment.

In Chapters 3 and 4, heuristics are found to play an important role in the choice of the learning algorithms. However, the emphasis in both chapters is on the analytical behavior of the automaton–environment combination. In every case the asymptotic behavior is discussed and the improvement in performance is quantified. The heuristic nature of the choice of the algorithms in the initial stages also provides the motivation to search for more rigorous methods and lead to the derivation in some cases of both necessary and sufficient conditions to achieve desired behavior. The same pattern is also found to repeat in Chapters 6–8 where the performance of automata in nonstationary environments, environments with multiple outputs, and multi-automata situations are considered. As stated in Section 1.2.8, in all cases successful heuristics provide a convenient starting point for the generation of new algorithms.

1.3.9 Summary

The learning automaton described in this book is an inductive inference machine that uses a direct control approach to determine the effectiveness of its actions in a random environment. It uses a stochastic hill climbing procedure to update the probabilities of its various actions in order to improve a performance index. It can be used either descriptively or prescriptively in the context of complex systems containing a substantial degree of randomness.

1.4   Plan of This Book

Chapters 2–8 are arranged in increasing order of complexity based on the nature of the automaton and the environment in which it operates. A mathematical description of the input and output sets of the automaton and the simple P–model environment with binary response is introduced in Chapter 2. Measures of performance including expediency, optimality, ϵ–optimality, and absolute expediency are also defined. Chapter 3 is devoted to fixed-structure learning automata, which give rise to finite state Markov chains. Various schemes proposed by workers in the Soviet Union in the 1960s are included here. The treatment is not intended to be exhaustive but is merely meant to introduce the reader to the basic concepts involved. In Chapter 4 variable-structure automata are introduced wherein the transition probabilities of the automaton are themselves functions of time. Equivalently it is shown that the automaton can be considered as a probability distribution generator over the action set. Several linear, nonlinear, and hybrid algorithms are described in detail with emphasis on linear schemes with reward–penalty and reward–inaction updating. Synthesis procedures for generating absolutely expedient schemes are presented toward the end of the chapter.

Chapter 5 contains the theoretical base of the results derived in Chapter 4 and used subsequently throughout the book. Following some introductory statements concerning stochastic convergence, the behavior of L_{R-P} (linear reward–penalty) and L_{R-I} (linear reward–inaction) schemes are analyzed in detail. Using the approach proposed by Norman (1975) we show that the probability of converging to the optimum can be made as close to unity as desired by the proper choice of the adaptive step size in absolutely expedient schemes.

In Chapter 6 the P–model environment of Chapters 2–5 is generalized to Q– and S– models. In the former the response to an action can assume a finite number of values while in the latter it can assume continuous values over a finite interval. The algorithms presented in this chapter are the most general ones known at the present time and can be readily adapted to most applications.

One of the principal reasons for using learning is to cope with environments whose characteristics vary with time. This problem is treated in Chapter 7. Although complete mathematical analysis is no longer possible, it is shown that at least in four specific situations adequate analysis may be feasible. One of these situations corresponds to the case where the automata are connected in a hierarchical structure so that automata at the higher levels can be considered to operate into time–varying environments created by the lower level automata.

Interconnected automata are treated in Chapter 8, which provides a focus for the book as a whole. Using results of game theory and Markov processes, it is shown that decentralized or distributed automata can be used to model or control a large system effectively. The most important point is that automata operating in total ignorance of other automata or their strategies can evolve to their optimal actions asymptotically based entirely on their own action and the output of the environment.

Finally, in Chapter 9 numerous applications of learning automata are described. The most successful application thus far is the routing problem in circuit–switched and packet–switched networks. Flow control in packet–switched networks and applications to queueing systems are also considered. New applications include image data compression, relaxation labeling, and the generation of discriminant functions for pattern recognition. The last two are based on cooperative games of learning automata.

This book provides a rigorous introduction to the theory of learning automata which has been developed over the past two decades. The theory is intuitively appealing and the various fixed-structure and variable-structure algorithms are easy to implement. The authors believe that the greatest potential for the theory is in hierarchical and decentralized control of stochastic systems where a large number of learning automata are interconnected to accomplish a specific task in a complex random environment. We have already referred to the resurgence of interest in adaptation and learning in AI and cognitive science, where massively parallel approaches to computation are being studied (refer to Section 1.1). Some of the most interesting approaches to this work concern stochastic computational methods. Although the authors are confident that the learning methods described in this book will find application in many widely different areas of learning and adaptation, it is in the context of connectionist systems that they may prove relevant in the immediate future.

Chapter 2

The Learning Automaton

2.1 Introduction

As mentioned in Chapter 1, the automaton approach to learning involves the determination of an optimal action out of a set of allowable actions. In all the cases we will consider, these actions are assumed to be performed on an abstract random environment. The environment responds to the input action by producing an output, belonging to a set of allowable outputs, which is probabilistically related to the input action. The theory of learning automata is concerned with the analysis and synthesis of automata which operate in such random environments. In this chapter we consider in detail the nature of the random environments, the structure and characteristics of the automata, the norms for judging the behavior of automata operating in random environments, and the mathematical tools that are applicable to the analysis of such systems. This in turn will set the stage, in the succeeding chapters, for the consideration of different automata schemes and a comparison of their relative performance in a variety of environments.

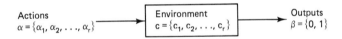

Figure 2.1: The environment.

2.2   The Environment

The term *environment* as commonly defined refers to the aggregate of all
the external conditions and influences affecting the life and development of
an organism. However, as used in the context of learning automata (or
elsewhere in systems theory), it is not always an easy matter to specify
what constitutes the environment. The definition encompasses a large class
of general unknown random media in which an automaton or a group of
automata can operate. We define an environment (Fig. 2.1) mathematically
by a triple $\{\underline{\alpha}, \underline{c}, \underline{\beta}\}$ where $\underline{\alpha} = \{\alpha_1, \alpha_2, \ldots, \alpha_r\}$ represents a finite input set,
$\underline{\beta} = \{\beta_1, \beta_2\}$ represents a binary output set, and $\underline{c} = \{c_1, c_2, \ldots, c_r\}$ a set of
penalty probabilities, where each element c_i of $\underline{c}$ corresponds to one input
action α_i.

The input $\alpha(n)$ to the environment belongs to $\underline{\alpha}$ and may be considered
to be applied to the environment at discrete time $t = n$ ($n = 0, 1, 2, \ldots$).
The output $\beta(n)$ of the environment belongs to $\underline{\beta}$ and can take on one of
two values β_1 and β_2. For mathematical convenience β_1 and β_2 are chosen to
be 0 and 1 respectively. An output $\beta(n) = 1$ is identified with a failure or an
unfavorable response and $\beta(n) = 0$ with a success or favorable response of
the environment. [1] The element c_i of $\underline{c}$ which characterizes the environment
may then be defined by[2]

$$Pr(\beta(n) = 1 | \alpha(n) = \alpha_i) = c_i \quad (i = 1, 2, \ldots, r) \qquad (2.1)$$

Consequently, c_i represents the probability that the application of an action
α_i to the environment will result in a penalty output.

It is seen from the definition above that the environment is implicitly
defined in terms of the input set $\underline{\alpha}$ and the output set $\underline{\beta}$. As in all practical

---

[1]Tsetlin (1961) introduced the binary environment model in the context of fixed-
structure automata and used the terms penalty and nonpenalty to describe unfavorable
and favorable environment responses (see Chapter 3). When variable-structure learning
schemes were introduced, the terms reward and penalty were used to denote changes in
the updating algorithm due to favorable and unfavorable responses (see Chapter 4). To
be precise, the terms penalty and reward refer to the automaton updating, while failure
(unfavorable response) and success (favorable response) refer to the environment response.
However, since the original usage of penalty and reward (nonpenalty is rarely used now)
is still quite widespread, we use the terms failure, unfavorable response, and penalty interchangeably to denote a "bad" environment response and success, favorable response,
and reward to denote a "good" response. Also, the use of 0 and 1 for success and failure
(again due to Tsetlin) is a matter of convention. Sometimes it is more convenient to use
1 and 0 or +1 and −1 (see Chapter 8).

[2]$Pr(\cdot)$ represents the probability of the event in the parentheses.

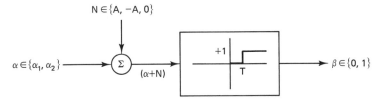

Figure 2.2: A simple measurement system.

applications of systems theory, defining a meaningful mathematical model of the environment in terms of the parameters described above constitutes one of the most difficult steps when setting up a real problem. This becomes particularly evident while considering applications in such areas as image processing and image understanding. The complexity of the allowed actions and the corresponding favorable and unfavorable responses determine the nature of the environment. The large class of media that fall within the scope of our definition becomes evident by considering a few simple examples.

First we consider the case where one has to choose from a finite set of specific actions. For example, a person may be interested in determining the better of two alternate routes to the office, choosing between air travel and car travel to a neighboring city, selecting one of two restaurants, or choosing between two candidates for a specific position. In each of the cases above, the action set consists of two elements (two routes, two restaurants, etc.). The medium in every case is assumed to be stochastic i.e., the outcome of every experiment or trial is random. For instance, in the first two examples, the time to reach the destination using one route or one mode of travel is assumed to be a random variable depending on traffic conditions. Similarly, in the last two examples, the quality of food and service in a restaurant and the performance of a candidate on any given occasion are assumed to be random variables. In all four cases the output can be made binary (with, say, 1 corresponding to "unfavorable" and 0 corresponding to a "favorable" response) by defining a suitable threshold. Such a threshold, in the first two cases, may be a prespecified time interval but in the last two cases would be entirely subjective depending on the individual who is making the decision. To complete the models, it is also assumed that the environments are stationary so that corresponding to each action in all four examples the probability of obtaining a favorable response is independent of time.

A simple though contrived example, in which a quantitative expression for the penalty probabilities may be obtained, is given below:

Example 2.1: Figure 2.2 illustrates a simple measurement system in which the input can take one of two values $\alpha_1, \alpha_2 \in \mathcal{R}$. The output is corrupted by additive noise N which can take one of three values $+A, -A$, and 0, with probabilities p_1, p_2, and p_3 respectively ($p_1 + p_2 + p_3 = 1$). The overall output of the system can assume two values $\{0, 1\}$ depending on whether the value $\alpha + N$ is less than or greater than some threshold T. The entire setup can be regarded as an environment with input α and response β. If the threshold T satisfies

$$\alpha_1 < T < \alpha_2$$
$$\alpha_2 - A < T < \alpha_1 + A,$$

and if 1 is regarded as an unfavorable response, the penalty probabilities are computed as:

$$
\begin{aligned}
c_1 &\triangleq Pr\{\beta = 1 | \alpha = \alpha_1\} = Pr\{\alpha + N > T | \alpha = \alpha_1\} = p_1 \\
c_2 &\triangleq Pr\{\beta = 1 | \alpha = \alpha_2\} = Pr\{\alpha + N > T | \alpha = \alpha_2\} = p_1 + p_3.
\end{aligned}
\tag{2.2}
$$

In all the examples considered thus far, the action set is finite and each element of the set can be represented by a scalar. However, in more complex situations, each action might itself be a finite set or a vector. For example, in the application to the telephone traffic routing problem we will consider in Chapter 9, the action set consists of finite sequences. A call arriving at a node can choose one of a finite set of paths to reach its destination and the problem is to determine the order in which the routes between intervening nodes are to be chosen. Hence, the action set in this case consists of all finite sequences generated by a permutation of the allowable routes. This example indicates that, in general, the action set to the environment is a finite set whose elements themselves can be finite sets. In more recent times, where learning automata methods have been applied in hierarchical systems, the actions of the automaton may correspond to sets of computer instructions.

If a dynamical system operating in continuous time is to be regarded as an environment, the action set could be a finite set of system inputs whose elements are defined over a finite interval of time. This interval corresponds to the period of observation of the environment. A functional of the output of the system, defined over the same period, representing a performance index, together with a suitable threshold may be used to define the binary output set of the environment. The input action $\alpha(n)$ in this case corresponds to the input function defined over the interval $(n - 1, n)$ and the output $\beta(n)$ to the binary performance index at the instant n.

As seen from the discussion above, the input set of the environment can assume a variety of forms. This flexibility makes the automaton approach applicable to many seemingly different problems.

The output set of the environment has thus far been assumed to be binary. Models in which the output can take only one of two values, 0 or 1 for example, are referred to as *P*–models. It was seen in the examples that an arbitrary threshold may be necessary to convert the actual outputs of the system into binary outputs, thereby distinguishing between favorable and unfavorable responses of the environment to a given action. A further generalization of the environment allows finite output sets with more than two elements that take values in the interval $[0, 1]$. This is achieved by the normalization and quantization of the performance index and such models are referred to as *Q*–models. When the output of the environment (i.e., the performance index) is a continuous random variable which assumes values in the interval $[0, 1]$, it is referred to as an *S*–model. *Q*– and *S*–models provide improved discrimination of the nature of the response of the environment to a given action and hence are of greater practical utility. However, many of the fundamental questions we will be interested in may be discussed in the context of *P*–models. The three chapters that follow deal exclusively with them. The concepts developed in these chapters are extended to *Q*– and *S*–models in Chapter 6.

In the preceding discussions, we assumed that the penalty probabilities c_i, which describe the environment, are constants. Such an environment is called a stationary environment. However, from both theoretical as well as practical viewpoints, learning is primarily of interest in environments whose characteristics vary with time i.e., one or more $c_i(i = 1, 2, \ldots, r)$ are not constant. In Chapter 7 different types of nonstationary environments are discussed including those in which $c_i(n)$ are (i) periodic, (ii) slowly varying, and (iii) random variables that depend on the actions of the automaton. In Chapter 8 the interaction of many automata is discussed. In such cases the nonstationarity of the environment as observed by an automaton stems from changes in the actions chosen by the other automata.

"Learning" in an environment similar to the type we have discussed in this section means the ability to determine, from the input–output operating record of the medium, the effectiveness of each action in producing a favorable response. If all the penalty probabilities c_i are known, ordering them would automatically introduce a corresponding ordering of the input actions. No learning is needed in this case and the action α_ℓ corresponding to the smallest penalty probability $c_\ell(= \min_i c_i)$ could be directly chosen as the best action. Hence, to define a meaningful problem, the penalty probabilities are always assumed to be unknown. Learning then involves the performance of experiments on the environment by choosing input actions and using the output data to update the strategy for picking a new action. A systematic way of choosing the input actions from the outputs of the environment to increase the occurrence of favorable responses may be accomplished by an object called an *automaton.*

2.3   The Automaton

The concept of an automaton as understood in automata theory is a very general one encompassing a wide variety of abstract systems. If $\underline{\Phi}$ is a set of internal states, $\underline{\beta}$ a set of input actions, $\underline{\alpha}$ a set of outputs, $\mathcal{F}(\cdot,\cdot) : \underline{\Phi} \times \underline{\beta} \to \underline{\Phi}$ a function that maps the current state and current input into the next state, and $\mathcal{H}(\cdot,\cdot) : \underline{\Phi} \times \underline{\beta} \to \underline{\alpha}$ a function that maps the current state and input into the current output, the automaton is defined by the quintuple $\{\underline{\Phi}, \underline{\alpha}, \underline{\beta}, \mathcal{F}(\cdot,\cdot), \mathcal{H}(\cdot,\cdot)\}$. In such an automaton the input and the current state together determine the next state as well as the current output. However, if the current output depends on only the current state, the automaton is referred to as a state–output automaton. In such a case the function $\mathcal{H}(\cdot,\cdot)$ in the definition above is replaced by an output function $\mathcal{G}(\cdot) : \underline{\Phi} \to \underline{\alpha}$. Both types of automata are said to be finite if the sets $\underline{\Phi}, \underline{\beta}$, and $\underline{\alpha}$ are finite.

In Chapter 3 we focus our attention on finite, state–output automata. Such automata are also called stochastic sequential machines and can be described precisely in terms of the following entities (Paz, 1971):

(i)   *The state* of the automaton at any instant n, denoted by $\phi(n)$, is an element of the finite set

$$\underline{\Phi} = \{\phi_1, \phi_2, \ldots, \phi_s\}. \tag{2.3}$$

(ii)   *The output or action* of an automaton at the instant n, denoted by $\alpha(n)$, is an element of the finite set

$$\underline{\alpha} = \{\alpha_1, \alpha_2, \ldots, \alpha_r\}. \tag{2.4}$$

(iii)   *The input* of an automaton at the instant n, denoted by $\beta(n)$, is an element of a set $\underline{\beta}$. This set could be either a finite set or an infinite set, such as an interval on the real line. Thus

$$\underline{\beta} = \{\beta_1, \beta_2, \ldots, \beta_m\} \text{ or } \underline{\beta} = \{(a, b)\} \tag{2.5}$$

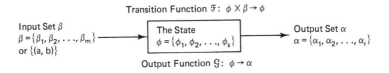

Figure 2.3: The automaton.

where a, b are real numbers.

(iv) *The transition function* $\mathcal{F}(\cdot, \cdot)$ determines the state at the instant $(n + 1)$ in terms of the state and input at the instant n

$$\phi(n + 1) = \mathcal{F}[\phi(n), \beta(n)], \tag{2.6}$$

or $\mathcal{F}$ is a mapping from $\underline{\Phi} \times \underline{\beta} \to \underline{\Phi}$ and could be either deterministic or stochastic.

(v) *The output function* $\mathcal{G}(\cdot)$ determines the output of the automaton at any instant n in terms of the state at that instant

$$\alpha(n) = \mathcal{G}[\phi(n)], \tag{2.7}$$

or $\mathcal{G}(\cdot)$ is a mapping $\underline{\Phi} \to \underline{\alpha}$ and is again either deterministic or stochastic.

Thus the automaton can be defined by the quintuple $\{\underline{\Phi}, \underline{\alpha}, \underline{\beta}, \mathcal{F}(\cdot, \cdot), \mathcal{G}(\cdot)\}$ and is shown in Fig. 2.3.

Basically, the automaton takes in a sequence of inputs and puts out a sequence of actions. The working of the automaton as the observation time n successively takes values over the set of nonnegative integers $0, 1, 2, \ldots$ can be conceived as follows. Given the initial state $\phi(0)$, the action $\alpha(0)$ is defined by $\mathcal{G}(\cdot)$. With the knowledge $\beta(0)$ of the input and the transition function $\mathcal{F}(\cdot, \cdot)$ the next state $\phi(1)$ is determined. When these operations are performed recursively, the state sequence and the action sequence are obtained for any given input sequence. Note that the state and the action at any instant n depend on only the state and input at the previous instant $n - 1$ and not on other past states or inputs.

The automaton is called a deterministic automaton if $\mathcal{F}$ and $\mathcal{G}$ are both deterministic mappings. In such a case, for a given initial state and input the succeeding state and action are uniquely specified. If $\mathcal{F}$ or $\mathcal{G}$ is stochastic, the automaton is called a stochastic automaton. In this case there is, in general,

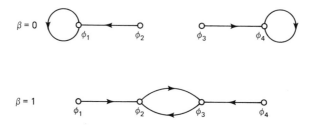

Figure 2.4: The transition graphs.

no certainty concerning the states and actions that follow a given initial state and input sequence; one can only consider probabilities associated with successive states and actions.

2.3.1   Deterministic Automaton

The mappings $\mathcal{F}$ and $\mathcal{G}$ for a deterministic automaton can be conveniently represented either in the form of matrices or graphs when the input set is finite. Corresponding to each input, there exists a matrix and a graph that indicate how any initial state is transferred to a new state as shown in the following example.

Example 2.2: Consider an automaton for which $\underline{\beta} = \{0,1\}$, $\underline{\alpha} = \{\alpha_1, \alpha_2\}$, and $\underline{\Phi} = \{\phi_1, \phi_2, \phi_3, \phi_4\}$.

The transition function is given by two graphs, each of which corresponds to an input symbol (Fig. 2.4). The graphs in Fig. 2.4 are self explanatory. Each node in the graph represents a state. A link in the graph represents a state transition in the direction of the arrow under the particular input. For example, if the initial state is ϕ_1, then under an input 0 the next state is again ϕ_1. Similarly, ϕ_2 changes to ϕ_3 following an input 1.

The same transition function can also be represented in terms of two matrices $F(0)$ and $F(1)$ where the entries f_{ij}^0 and f_{ij}^1 are defined as follows:

$$
\begin{aligned}
f_{ij}^{\beta} &= 1 \text{ if } \phi_i \rightarrow \phi_j \text{ for an input } \beta \\
&= 0 \text{ otherwise.}
\end{aligned}
$$

Figure 2.5: The output graph.

Thus the given transition function takes the form

$$F(0) = \begin{array}{c} \\ \phi_1 \\ \phi_2 \\ \phi_3 \\ \phi_4 \end{array} \begin{array}{cccc} \phi_1 & \phi_2 & \phi_3 & \phi_4 \\ \left[\begin{array}{cccc} 1 & 0 & 0 & 0 \\ 1 & 0 & 0 & 0 \\ 0 & 0 & 0 & 1 \\ 0 & 0 & 0 & 1 \end{array} \right] \end{array} \qquad F(1) = \begin{array}{c} \\ \phi_1 \\ \phi_2 \\ \phi_3 \\ \phi_4 \end{array} \begin{array}{cccc} \phi_1 & \phi_2 & \phi_3 & \phi_4 \\ \left[\begin{array}{cccc} 0 & 1 & 0 & 0 \\ 0 & 0 & 1 & 0 \\ 0 & 1 & 0 & 0 \\ 0 & 0 & 1 & 0 \end{array} \right] \end{array}.$$

The output function $\mathcal{G}$ can also be given a similar representation. Let us suppose ϕ_1 and ϕ_2 correspond to action α_1 and ϕ_3, ϕ_4 to α_2. The graph shown in Fig. 2.5 can be used in such a case. Alternatively, a matrix G with entries g_{ij} where

$$\begin{aligned} g_{ij} &= 1 & \text{if } G(\phi_i) = \alpha_j \\ &= 0 & \text{otherwise} \end{aligned}$$

can be used to represent the output transformation. In the present example we have:

$$G = \begin{array}{c} \\ \phi_1 \\ \phi_2 \\ \phi_3 \\ \phi_4 \end{array} \begin{array}{cc} \alpha_1 & \alpha_2 \\ \left[\begin{array}{cc} 1 & 0 \\ 1 & 0 \\ 0 & 1 \\ 0 & 1 \end{array} \right] \end{array}.$$

From the example above it is seen that, in general, the transition function $\mathcal{F}$ for a deterministic automaton can be represented by m matrices of dimension $s \times s$, where m is the number of inputs and s is the number of states. Similarly, the output function $\mathcal{G}$ can be represented by an $s \times r$ matrix, where r is the number of actions. Each of the elements of these matrices is either 0 or 1 and the sum of elements of any one row is unity.

2.3.2   The Stochastic Automaton

We now consider the stochastic automaton in which at least one of the two mappings $\mathcal{F}$ and $\mathcal{G}$ is stochastic. If the transition function $\mathcal{F}$ is stochastic, given the present state and input, the next state is random and $\mathcal{F}$ gives the probabilities of reaching the various states. Thus $\mathcal{F}$ can be specified in terms of the conditional probability matrices $F(\beta_1), F(\beta_2), \ldots, F(\beta_m)$ where each $F(\beta)$ for $\beta \in \underline{\beta}$ is an $s \times s$ matrix associated with an input symbol β and whose entries are given by

$$f_{ij}^{\beta} = Pr\{\phi(n+1) = \phi_j | \phi(n) = \phi_i, \beta(n) = \beta\}. \qquad \begin{aligned} i &= 1, 2, \ldots, s \\ j &= 1, 2, \ldots, s \\ \beta &= \beta_1, \beta_2, \ldots, \beta_m \end{aligned}$$

$$(2.8)$$

Thus f_{ij}^{β} represents the probability that the automaton moves from state ϕ_i to state ϕ_j following an input β.

The stochastic mapping $\mathcal{G}$ can be similarly represented by a conditional probability matrix G of dimension $s \times r$ whose entries are given by

$$g_{ij} = Pr\{\alpha(n) = \alpha_j | \phi(n) = \phi_i\}. \qquad \begin{aligned} i &= 1, 2, \ldots, s \\ j &= 1, 2, \ldots, r \end{aligned}$$

$$(2.9)$$

Hence, g_{ij} denotes the probability that the state ϕ_i corresponds to action α_j.

Since f_{ij}^{β} and g_{ij} are probabilities, they lie in the closed interval $[0, 1]$. Further, starting from an initial state ϕ_i, the automaton necessarily has to go to one of the s states at the next instant. Hence, to conserve probability measure we have

$$\sum_{j=1}^{s} f_{ij}^{\beta} = 1 \text{ for each } \beta \in \underline{\beta} \text{ and } i.$$

Similarly,

$$\sum_{j=1}^{r} g_{ij} = 1 \text{ for each } i. \qquad (2.10)$$

The equations above imply that the sum of row entries in each of the matrices is unity or the matrices F and G are stochastic.

The preceding discussion can be better understood with the aid of the following example, which is a modification of Example 2.2.

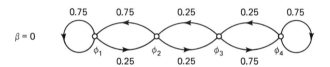

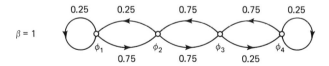

Figure 2.6: Stochastic state transition graphs.

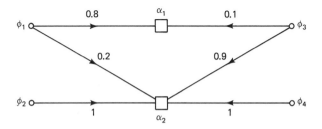

Figure 2.7: The stochastic output graph.

Example 2.3: Consider an automaton with the same sets $\underline{\beta}, \underline{\alpha}$, and $\underline{\Phi}$ as in Example 2.2. $\mathcal{F}$ and $\mathcal{G}$ are, however, stochastic as given in the graphs shown in Figs. 2.6 and 2.7.

In Figs. 2.6 and 2.7 the number shown by the side of each directed link is the probability of the transition represented by the link. For example,

$$f_{34}^0 = Pr\{\phi(n+1) = \phi_4 | \phi(n) = \phi_3, \beta(n) = 0\} = .75$$

and

$$f_{44}^1 = Pr\{\phi(n+1) = \phi_4 | \phi(n) = \phi_4, \beta(n) = 1\} = .25.$$

In the output graph, the square nodes represent the actions and each number denotes the probability with which a state corresponds to a particular action. For example,

$$g_{31} = Pr\{\alpha(n) = \alpha_1 | \phi(n) = \phi_3\} = 0.1.$$

The corresponding matrices can be identified as follows:

$$F(0) = \begin{bmatrix} .75 & .25 & 0 & 0 \\ .75 & 0 & .25 & 0 \\ 0 & .25 & 0 & .75 \\ 0 & 0 & .25 & .75 \end{bmatrix} \quad F(1) = \begin{bmatrix} .25 & .75 & 0 & 0 \\ .25 & 0 & .75 & 0 \\ 0 & .75 & 0 & .25 \\ 0 & 0 & .75 & .25 \end{bmatrix}$$

and

$$G = \begin{bmatrix} .8 & 0.2 \\ 0 & 1.0 \\ .1 & 0.9 \\ 0 & 1.0 \end{bmatrix}.$$

2.3.3   Fixed Structure and Variable Structure Automata

In Examples 2.2 and 2.3, the various conditional probabilities f_{ij} and g_{ij} were assumed to be constant i.e., independent of n and the input sequence. Such a stochastic automaton is referred to as a *fixed-structure stochastic automaton*. As will be seen later, it is useful to update the transition probabilities f_{ij} at each n on the basis of the input at that instant. In this case, the automaton is called a *variable-structure stochastic automaton*.

The main characteristics of the different automata we have considered thus far may be summarized as follows: For a deterministic automaton, the transition matrices $F(\beta)$ consist of elements that are only either 0 or 1. For a fixed-structure stochastic automaton, the elements of $F(\beta)$ are constants taking values in the interval $[0, 1]$ and each $F(\beta)$ is a stochastic matrix. In the case of a variable–structure stochastic automaton, the elements of $F(\beta)$ are in $[0, 1]$ but are no longer constants as they are updated with n. In the chapters following we consider all three types of automata.

Example 2.4: Consider the case where you have to choose between two restaurants – Simeone's and Delmonaco's. Let us assume that at stage $(n-1)$ you chose to go to Simeone's. If your decision, the next time you go out to eat at stage n, is to return to Simeone's if the food was good at stage $(n-1)$, and to switch to Delmonaco's if it was poor, then your decision corresponds to that of a deterministic automaton. If your decision is to go to the same restaurant if the food was good on the previous visit but to toss a coin to choose which of the two restaurants to visit if it was not, then you are acting like a fixed-structure stochastic automaton. Finally, if you update the probabilities of going to the two restaurants at every stage based on the outcome of the previous visit, your decision rule corresponds to that of a variable-structure stochastic automaton.

2.3.4 Stochastic Automata with Deterministic Output Mapping

In Example 2.3, the transition function $\mathcal{F}$ as well as the output function $\mathcal{G}$ were stochastic. However, it can be shown that generally, by a proper redefinition of states the output function of any stochastic automaton can be made deterministic by increasing the number of states of the system. This is achieved by considering the pairs (ϕ_i, α_j) as the new states of the system. Every state (ϕ_i, α_j) is mapped into α_j for all ϕ_i so that the new output function $\hat{\mathcal{G}}$ becomes deterministic (Paz, 1971).

Denoting the new states by $\hat{\phi}_{ij} = (\phi_i, \alpha_j)$, the new system has sr states. Let the conditional probability of the transition from $\hat{\phi}_{ij}$ to $\hat{\phi}_{k\ell}$ for an input β be $\hat{f}^{\beta}_{(ij)(k\ell)}$ and let the corresponding transition and output matrices be $\hat{F}(\beta)$ and $\hat{G}$ respectively.

$$\hat{f}^{\beta}_{(ij)(k\ell)} = Pr\{\phi(n+1) = \phi_k, \alpha(n+1) = \alpha_\ell | \phi(n) = \phi_i, \alpha(n) = \alpha_j, \beta(n) = \beta\}$$
(2.11)

and applying the chain rule

$$
\begin{aligned}
= \quad & Pr\{\alpha(n+1) = \alpha_\ell | \phi(n+1) = \phi_k, \phi(n) = \phi_i, \alpha(n) = \alpha_j, \beta(n) = \beta\} \\
& Pr\{\phi(n+1) = \phi_k | \phi(n) = \phi_i, \alpha(n) = \alpha_j, \beta(n) = \beta\}.
\end{aligned}
$$
(2.12)

Since $\alpha(n+1)$ only depends on $\phi(n+1)$ and $\phi(n+1)$ does not depend on $\alpha(n)$,

$$
\begin{aligned}
\hat{f}^{\beta}_{(ij)(k\ell)} = \quad & Pr\{\alpha(n+1) = \alpha_\ell | \phi(n+1) = \phi_k\} \\
& Pr\{\phi(n+1) = \phi_k | \phi(n) = \phi_i, \beta(n) = \beta\} \\
= \quad & g_{k\ell} f^{\beta}_{ik}.
\end{aligned}
$$
(2.13)

It is obvious that these transition probabilities do not depend on the initial action α_j. The output matrix $\hat{G}$ of the new system can be obtained as

$$\hat{g}_{(ij)(\ell)} = \begin{array}{l} 1 \text{ if } j = \ell \\ 0 \text{ if } j \neq \ell \end{array}$$
(2.14)

where

$$\hat{g}_{(ij)(\ell)} = Pr\{\alpha(n+1) = \alpha_\ell | \hat{\phi}(n+1) = \hat{\phi}_{ij}\}.$$

Thus, given any stochastic automaton, one can retain the same input–output behavior but redefine the states to make the output function deterministic.

Example 2.5: Consider the stochastic automaton of Example 2.3, which has four states and two outputs with both F and G matrices stochastic. To determine an equivalent system with a deterministic output mapping, we redefine the states. The new system has 8 states $\hat{\phi}_{ij}$ with $i = 1, 2, 3, 4$ and $j = 1, 2$ and is completely defined by two (8×8) transition matrices $\hat{F}(0)$ and $\hat{F}(1)$, obtained by using Eq.(2.13), and a new output matrix $\hat{G}$ defined by

$$\hat{G} = \begin{array}{c} \\ \hat{\phi}_{11} \\ \hat{\phi}_{12} \\ \hat{\phi}_{21} \\ \hat{\phi}_{22} \\ \hat{\phi}_{31} \\ \hat{\phi}_{32} \\ \hat{\phi}_{41} \\ \hat{\phi}_{42} \end{array} \begin{array}{cc} \alpha_1 & \alpha_2 \\ \begin{bmatrix} 1 & 0 \\ 0 & 1 \\ 1 & 0 \\ 0 & 1 \\ 1 & 0 \\ 0 & 1 \\ 1 & 0 \\ 0 & 1 \end{bmatrix} \end{array}$$

2.3.5   State and Action Probabilities

The output behavior of a stochastic automaton for a given input sequence can be obtained if the transition probabilities are known. However, it may frequently be important to know the probability with which the automaton is in a particular state at a given instant. These probabilities are known as (total) state probabilities and an alternative description of the operation of the automaton can be given in terms of these probabilities.

Let

$$\pi(n) = [\pi_1(n), \pi_2(n), \ldots, \pi_s(n)]^T \tag{2.15}$$

where $[\ ]^T$ denotes the transpose and

$$\pi_j(0) = Pr\{\phi(0) = \phi_j\}$$
$$\pi_j(n) = Pr\{\phi(n) = \phi_j | \beta(0), \ldots, \beta(n-1)\}.$$

Given the input and the initial state probability vector $\pi(0)$, the state probability vector at $n = 1$ can be obtained as follows:

$$
\begin{aligned}
\pi_j(1) &= Pr\{\phi(1) = \phi_j | \beta(0)\} \\
&= \sum_{i=1}^{s} Pr\{\phi(1) = \phi_j | \phi(0) = \phi_i, \beta(0)\} Pr\{\phi(0) = \phi_i\} \qquad (2.16) \\
&= \sum_{i=1}^{s} f_{ij}^{\beta(0)} \pi_i(0).
\end{aligned}
$$

Or, in the vector form Eq.(2.16) may be written as

$$\pi(1) = F^T(\beta(0))\pi(0). \qquad (2.17)$$

Applying the Eq.(2.16) recursively, one can get

$$\pi(n) = F^T(\beta(n-1))F^T(\beta(n-2))\ldots F^T(\beta(0))\pi(0). \qquad (2.18)$$

Thus, the state probability vector at any instant can be obtained in terms of the initial probability vector, the transition matrices, and the input sequence.

One can also consider the (total) action probability vector $p(n)$ whose i^{th} component $p_i(n)$ is given by

$$p_i(n) = Pr\{\alpha(n) = \alpha_i | \beta(0), \ldots, \beta(n-1)\} \qquad (i = 1, \ldots, r)$$

Since

$$
\begin{aligned}
p_i(n) &= \sum_{j=1}^{s} Pr\{\alpha(n) = \alpha_i | \phi(n) = \phi_j\} Pr\{\phi(n) = \phi_j | \beta(0), \beta(1), \ldots, \beta(n-1)\} \\
&= \sum_{j=1}^{s} g_{ji} \pi_j(n), \qquad \text{(using Eq.2.9)}
\end{aligned}
$$

it follows that

$$p(n) = G^T \pi(n). \qquad (2.19)$$

Thus, one can deal with either the state probability $\pi(n)$ or the action probability $p(n)$.

2.3.6 Random Inputs

The analysis carried out thus far enables one to compute either the state and action sequences or the probabilities associated with them, for a given deterministic input sequence. In the problems encountered in this book, the input sequences are random and our interest will be centered primarily around the behavior of automata subject to such sequences.

We first consider a deterministic automaton with an input sequence of zeros and ones. Let the input 1 occur with probability c and 0 with probability $1 - c$.

$$Pr\{\beta(n) = 1\} = c$$
$$Pr\{\beta(n) = 0\} = 1 - c \qquad \text{for all } n. \qquad (2.20)$$

We are considering here a sequence of independent identically distributed binary random variables which constitute a stationary random sequence. The random nature of the input now makes the state transitions, even in a deterministic automaton, random. Hence, one can consider the probability of such transitions.

Let

$$\tilde{f}_{ij} = Pr\{\phi(n+1) = \phi_j | \phi(n) = \phi_i\}. \qquad (2.21)$$

Since $\beta(n)$ can take only two values 0 and 1 and c is independent of the state, $\tilde{f}_{ij}$ can be computed as follows:

$$
\begin{aligned}
\tilde{f}_{ij} &= Pr\{\phi(n+1) = \phi_j | \phi(n) = \phi_i, \beta(n) = 0\} \, Pr\{\beta(n) = 0 | \phi(n) = \phi_i\} \\
&\quad + Pr\{\phi(n+1) = \phi_j | \phi(n) = \phi_i, \beta(n) = 1\} \, Pr\{\beta(n) = 1 | \phi(n) = \phi_i\} \\
&= f_{ij}^0(1 - c) + f_{ij}^1 c, \qquad (2.22)
\end{aligned}
$$

where f_{ij}^0 and f_{ij}^1 are the elements of the transition matrices $F(0)$ and $F(1)$, respectively, of the deterministic automaton and consequently have values 0 or 1. The operation of the automaton with the stationary random sequence can now be described by a single conditional probability matrix $\tilde{F}$ of transitions, whose elements $\tilde{f}_{ij}$ are constants belonging to the interval $[0, 1]$. It can also be easily verified from Eq.(2.22) that $\tilde{F}$ is a stochastic matrix. Thus, a deterministic automaton under the random input considered exhibits a behavior equivalent to that of a stochastic automaton with constant input.

We now consider the case where a fixed-structure automaton is subject to the same random input. The transition probability $\tilde{f}_{ij}$, as defined in Eq.(2.21), can once again be expressed as in Eq.(2.22). The only difference in this case is that f_{ij}^0 and f_{ij}^1 are constants in the interval $[0, 1]$. Thus, a fixed-structure stochastic automaton under the stationary random binary input can be regarded as equivalent to another fixed-structure stochastic automaton with constant input. The synthesis of stochastic automata using deterministic automata with random inputs has been suggested by Cleave (1962), Murray (1955), and Tsertsvadze (1963). The conclusions for deterministic as well as stochastic automata remain valid even when the input parameter c depends on the action of the automaton as will be shown in Chapter 3.

If, in the previous discussion, the fixed-structure stochastic automaton is replaced by a variable-structure automaton, the expressions of Eqs.(2.21) and (2.22) are valid provided $\tilde{f}_{ij}, f^0_{ij}$, and f^1_{ij} are understood to depend on n. Thus

$$
\begin{aligned}
\tilde{f}_{ij}(n) &= Pr\{\phi(n+1) = \phi_j | \phi(n) = \phi_i\}, \\
&= f^0_{ij}(n)(1-c) + f^1_{ij}(n)c.
\end{aligned}
\tag{2.23}
$$

Since $f^\beta_{ij}(n)$ is updated at every stage on the basis of the particular input sequence to the automaton, and each input sequence occurs with a certain probability, $f^\beta_{ij}(n)$ is a random variable. Similarly, using Eq.(2.23), $\tilde{f}_{ij}(n)$ is seen to be a random variable and this in turn implies that the state probability vector $\pi(n)$ is a random vector.

The analysis becomes considerably more complicated when the input parameter c itself varies in a random fashion. From Eq.(2.22) it is evident that even deterministic and fixed-structure stochastic automata subject to such an input will have transition probabilities that are random variables. Naturally, the analysis of variable–structure stochastic automata with such an input is significantly more difficult. However, it will be seen later that this kind of situation exists in some of the problems encountered in this book.

The theory of Markov chains and Markov processes (Isaacson and Madsen, 1976 and Cinlar, 1975), which has been developed extensively during the past few decades, forms the natural vehicle for the study of the behavior of automata under random inputs. From the previous description, it follows that the state sequence of either a deterministic automaton or a fixed-structure stochastic automaton having a stationary random binary input is a Markov chain, for the state transitions can be represented by a stochastic matrix $\tilde{F}$. The states of the Markov chain correspond to the states of the automaton. As the transition probabilities $\tilde{f}_{ij}$ are constants, the state sequence forms a homogeneous Markov chain.

In the case of a variable-structure stochastic automaton, two different points of view can be taken. If the automaton is considered as a process defined on the finite number of states, it corresponds to a nonhomogeneous Markov chain because the transition matrices are updated continuously. On the other hand, if the automaton is assumed to be described by the state or action probability vectors, it corresponds to a continuous–state, discrete–time stationary Markov process. The latter is used in Chapters 4 and 5 to describe variable-structure automata operating in stationary environments.

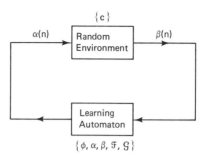

Figure 2.8: Feedback connection of automaton and environment.

The state space is defined as the r–dimensional simplex

$$\mathcal{S}_r = \{p| \sum_{i=1}^{r} p_i = 1; \ \ 0 \le p_i \le 1 \ ; \ i = 1, 2, \ldots, r\}$$

if the action probability vector is used to describe the system. If $p(n + 1)$ depends on the vector $p(n)$ at stage n but not explicitly on n, the sequence $\{p(n)\}_{n \ge 0}$ is a homogeneous Markov process defined on the state space $\mathcal{S}_r$.

2.4   Feedback Connection of Automaton and Environment

Thus far in this chapter we have considered the structure and properties of the environment and the automaton in isolation. We now consider the two connected in a feedback arrangement as shown in Fig. 2.8 so that the output of the environment $\beta(n)$ forms the input to the automaton and the action of the automaton $\alpha(n)$ provides the input to the environment. Starting from an initial state $\phi(0)$, the automaton generates the corresponding action $\alpha(0)$. The response of the environment to this input is $\beta(0)$, which, in turn, changes the state of the automaton to $\phi(1)$. This sequence of operations is then repeated to result in a sequence of states, actions, and responses of the environment. In the case of variable–structure stochastic automata, the probability vector $p(n)$ or the state transition matrix $F(\beta)$ also gets updated at each stage n. An automaton acting in an unknown random environment in this manner, so as to improve its performance in some specified sense, is referred to as a *Learning Automaton.*

The automaton approach to learning can be better understood in terms of the following example of a student with a probabilistic teacher. Let us suppose that a question is posed to the student and a finite set of alternative answers is provided. The student can select one of the alternatives, the teacher then responds in a binary manner indicating whether the chosen answer is right or wrong. The teacher, is however, probabilistic – there is a non–zero probability of eliciting either of the two responses for any of the answers selected by the student. The saving feature of this seemingly desperate situation is that the probability of the teacher giving a negative response is the least for the correct answer. Under these circumstances, the interest is in finding the manner in which the student should process the information obtained from the teacher so that the correct answer is learned.

In terms of the learning automaton model, the automaton corresponds to the student and the random environment in which it operates represents the probabilistic teacher. The actions of the automaton are the various alternatives provided. The responses of the environment for a particular action of the automaton are the teacher's probabilistic responses. The objective here is to obtain the optimal action that corresponds to the correct answer. The probabilistic teacher plays the role of a critic, and learning in this context is described as learning with a critic. In the recent literature on connectionist networks (Barto, Sutton, and Brouwer, 1981; Williams, 1986) this is also referred to as reinforcement learning.

Although the example above may appear to be somewhat contrived, it is worth mentioning that the situation described arises under different guises in a wide variety of learning problems.

One problem that has been extensively investigated is the two–armed bandit problem (Robbins, 1952), referred to in Chapter 1. A machine, called the two–armed bandit has, as the name implies, two arms. At the sound of a signal, signifying the start of the experiment, a human test subject operates the machine and chooses one of the two arms. The subject is rewarded or penalized according to a previously determined schedule that yields a fixed probability of reward for the two choices. The problem is to determine the choice the subject should make to optimize the performance and is very similar to the T–maze problem described in Chapter 1, as well as the problem of the stochastic teacher described earlier. All of these problems lead to the characteristic dilemma encountered between identification and control described in Section 1.2.5. In the present case the subject must decide which of the two arms should be chosen based on the past performance i.e., whether it is better to choose the arm believed to be the best in terms of performance or the arm about which the least is known so that the knowledge of the relative effectiveness of the two arms is increased.

2.5   Norms of Behavior

As defined in the previous section, a learning automaton generates a sequence of actions on the basis of its interaction with the environment. If the automaton is said to "learn" in the process, its performance must be compatible with intuitive notions of learning described in Chapter 1. To judge the learning process objectively, it is necessary to set up quantitative norms of behavior.

Even in the specific context of our model, a quantitative basis for assessing the learning behavior turns out to be quite complex and several different criteria can be distinguished. To keep the discussion simple, we shall confine our discussion to the P–model and stationary random environments in this section. Further, we shall also state our definitions in terms of the (total) action probabilities of variable–structure stochastic automata. The corresponding definitions for other automata may be obtained as special cases.

One gross manner in which learning can be established is by comparison with a pure chance situation. If no prior information is available, there is no basis on which the different actions $\alpha_i (i = 1, 2, \ldots, r)$ can be distinguished. In such a case, one would choose each action with equal probability i.e., by pure chance. The action probability vector $p(n)$ is then given by

$$p_i(n) = \frac{1}{r} \qquad i = 1, 2, \ldots, r.$$

We shall call such an automaton a "pure-chance automaton" and use it as the standard for comparison. Any automaton that is said to learn must then do at least better than such a pure-chance automaton.

To make this comparison we consider a stationary random environment with penalty probabilities $\{c_1, c_2, \ldots, c_r\}$. If two automata operate in this environment, the one that results in the environment emitting favorable responses more often is to be considered better. We define a quantity $M(n)$, which is the average penalty for a given action probability vector and which plays a useful role in the comparison of various automata.

$$
\begin{aligned}
M(n) \; &= \; E[\beta(n)|p(n)] = Pr[\beta(n) = 1|p(n)] \\
&= \; \textstyle\sum_{i=1}^{r} Pr[\beta(n) = 1|\alpha(n) = \alpha_i] Pr[\alpha(n) = \alpha_i] \qquad (2.24) \\
&= \; \textstyle\sum_{i=1}^{r} c_i p_i(n).
\end{aligned}
$$

For the pure–chance automaton, $M(n)$ is a constant denoted by M_0 and is given by

$$M_0 = \frac{1}{r} \sum_{i=1}^{r} c_i. \tag{2.25}$$

For an automaton to do better than pure chance, its average penalty must be less than M_0 at least asymptotically as $n \to \infty$. As $p(n), \lim_{n \to \infty} p(n)$, and consequently $M(n)$ and $\lim_{n \to \infty} M(n)$ are random variables in general, one has to compare $E[M(n)]$ with M_0. It may be noted that

$$\begin{aligned} E[M(n)] &= E\{E[\beta(n)|p(n)]\} \\ &= E[\beta(n)], \end{aligned} \tag{2.26}$$

or $E[M(n)]$ is merely the average input to the automaton. An automaton that performs better than the pure–chance automaton is said to be expedient.

Definition 2.1: A learning automaton is said to be *expedient*[3] if

$$\lim_{n \to \infty} E[M(n)] < M_0. \tag{2.27}$$

As stated earlier, expediency represents desirable behavior only in a rather gross sense. We would be more interested in determining an updating procedure which would result in $E[M(n)]$ attaining its minimum value. From Eq.(2.24) it can be seen that since $\sum_{i=1}^{r} p_i(n) = 1$,

$$\begin{aligned} \inf M(n) &= \inf_{p(n)}\{\sum_{i=1}^{r} c_i p_i(n)\} \\ &= \min_i\{c_i\} \stackrel{\triangle}{=} c_\ell. \end{aligned} \tag{2.28}$$

In such a case the automaton is said to be optimal.

Definition 2.2: A learning automaton is said to be *optimal* if

$$\lim_{n \to \infty} E[M(n)] = c_\ell$$

where

$$c_\ell = \min_i\{c_i\}. \tag{2.29}$$

---

[3]The concept of expediency was first introduced by Tsetlin (1961) for fixed-structure automata. The definition was similar to that given in Eq.(2.27) except that the expectation operator was not needed. The direct extension of this definition to variable-structure automata led to many erroneous conclusions in the literature and is discussed in Chapter 5. The definition given here, which can be applied to both fixed-structure and variable-structure automata was first suggested by Lakshmivarahan and Thathachar (1972).

From Eq.(2.29) it is evident that optimality implies that action α_ℓ associated with the minimum penalty probability c_ℓ is chosen asymptotically with probability one. While optimality appears very desirable in stationary environments, it may not be possible to achieve it in a given situation. In this case one might aim at a suboptimal performance. ϵ–optimality (Viswanathan and Narendra, 1973), as defined below, represents one such suboptimal behavior.

Definition 2.3: A learning automaton is said to be ϵ–*optimal* if

$$\lim_{n \to \infty} E[M(n)] < c_\ell + \epsilon \qquad (2.30)$$

can be obtained for any arbitrary $\epsilon > 0$ by a proper choice of the parameters of the automaton.

There are two factors that affect the performance of the automaton, but these are not mentioned explicitly in the previous definitions. The first one is the initial condition of the automaton and the second is the set of penalty probabilities of the environment. The initial condition of the automaton could be either the initial action probability vector or a more detailed specification such as the initial state. The penalty probabilities of the environment are generally assumed to be unknown, but in practical applications partial information may be available regarding them.

It is conceivable that some automata satisfy the conditions stated in the definitions for specified initial conditions and for certain sets of penalty probabilities. However, we are be interested in automata that exhibit desired behavior in arbitrary environments and for arbitrary initial conditions. These requirements are partially met by an absolutely expedient automaton (Lakshmivarahan and Thathachar, 1973), which is defined below:

Definition 2.4: A learning automaton is said to be *absolutely expedient* if

$$E[M(n+1)|p(n)] < M(n) \qquad (2.31)$$

for all n, all $p_i(n) \in (0,1)$ and for all possible sets $\{c_i\}(i = 1, 2, \ldots, r)$. [4]

Thus absolute expediency imposes an inequality on the conditional expectation of $M(n)$ at each instant. Since a specified $p(n)$ fixes the value of $M(n)$ in a given environment, (2.31) implies that $M(n)$ is a supermartingale (Appendix B). Taking expectations again in (2.31), it is seen further that

$$E[M(n+1)] < E[M(n)], \qquad (2.32)$$

---

[4]Here and in the following discussions it is tacitly assumed that random environments with all penalty probabilities equal are excluded.

and thus $E[M(n)]$ is strictly monotonically decreasing with n in all stationary random environments. If the initial conditions are such that for some n, $E[M(n)] < M_0$ (e.g. $n = 0$), this in turn implies expediency. Thus for such a set of initial conditions, absolute expediency implies expediency and is a stronger condition on the automaton. It will be shown in Chapter 5 that absolute expediency also implies ϵ–optimality in all stationary random environments.

2.6 Conclusion

In this chapter, a learning automaton was defined as an automaton that improves its performance while operating in a random environment. Both fixed- and variable-structure automata were defined and some norms of behavior were set up to evaluate their performance. In the following two chapters, we consider specific fixed- and variable-structure automata and their performance in stationary random environments.

Chapter 3

Fixed Structure Automata

3.1 Introduction

In a pioneering paper, Tsetlin (1961) first studied the behavior of deterministic automata functioning in random environments. A great deal of the work carried out since that time by Soviet research workers has followed the trend set by this outstanding paper. Although an extensive body of literature exists in this area, we attempt in this chapter merely to summarize some of the better known ideas presented in the 1960s, which are representative of the work. In the first part of the chapter, we consider in detail the deterministic schemes suggested by Tsetlin and examine the insights they provide for the design of general fixed-structure learning automata.

3.2 The Two–State Automaton $L_{2,2}$

An automaton has two states, ϕ_1 and ϕ_2, and two outputs, α_1 and α_2 (Fig. 3.1). The automaton accepts inputs from a set $\{0, 1\}$ and switches its states

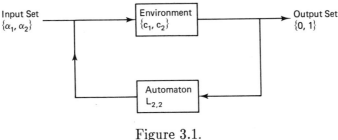

Figure 3.1.

59

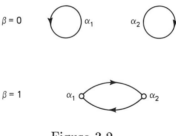

Figure 3.2.

upon encountering an input 1 (corresponding to an unfavorable response) and remains in the same state on receiving an input 0 (a favorable response). Consequently the transition matrices of the automaton can be expressed as

$$F(0) = \begin{bmatrix} 1 & 0 \\ 0 & 1 \end{bmatrix} \qquad F(1) = \begin{bmatrix} 0 & 1 \\ 1 & 0 \end{bmatrix} \qquad (3.1)$$

respectively and the corresponding graphs are shown in Fig. 3.2. An automaton that uses the strategy above is referred to as $L_{2,2}$ where the first subscript refers to the number of states and the second subscript to the number of actions. The environment is characterized by the set of penalty probabilities $\{c_1, c_2\}$ where $c_i (i = 1, 2)$ corresponds to the probability of getting a response $\beta = 1$ from the environment when the input is α_i. As mentioned in the previous chapter, the environment and automaton are connected in a feedback configuration, so that the responses of the environment form the inputs to the automaton and vice versa.

Qualitatively, the simple strategy used by the automaton implies that it continues to perform whatever action it was using earlier as long as the response is good but changes to the other action as soon as the response is bad. In view of the obvious intuitive appeal of this strategy, it has found application in many learning models of both natural and artificial systems. Selfridge (1978), for example, in a discussion of adaptation and movement strategies refers to it as "run and twiddle."

A pure–chance automaton operating in the same random environment would choose the input actions α_1 and α_2 with equal probability so that

$$M_0 = \frac{1}{2}(c_1 + c_2). \qquad (3.2)$$

To compare the performance of the two automata schemes, we proceed to determine the limiting probabilities of the two actions of $L_{2,2}$. Assuming that at stage n the automaton is in state ϕ_i, the probability $\tilde{f}_{ij}$ that the automaton will make a transition from state ϕ_i to ϕ_j is determined from the formula

$$\tilde{f}_{ij} = P_{ij} = c_i f_{ij}^1 + d_i f_{ij}^0, \qquad (3.3)$$

where $d_i = 1 - c_i$ is the probability of obtaining a favorable response of the environment to an action α_i. Hence, the matrix of transition probabilities can be represented by

$$P = \begin{bmatrix} d_1 & c_1 \\ c_2 & d_2 \end{bmatrix},$$

and is seen to be stochastic. Thus, the functioning of the automaton in the stationary random medium is seen to be described by a finite Markov chain. Since the chain is ergodic, the final probabilities of the two states $\phi_i (i = 1, 2)$ [and hence, the two actions $\alpha_i (i = 1, 2)$] can be obtained as $\pi_i (i = 1, 2)$,[1] where π_i are the elements of the vector π satisfying the equation

$$P^T \pi = \pi. \qquad (3.4)$$

From Eq.(3.4) we have

$$d_1 \pi_1 + c_2 \pi_2 = \pi_1, \quad c_1 \pi_1 + d_2 \pi_2 = \pi_2, \text{ and } \pi_1 + \pi_2 = 1$$

which yields

$$\pi_1 = \frac{c_2}{c_1 + c_2} \quad, \quad \pi_2 = \frac{c_1}{c_1 + c_2} \ . \qquad (3.5)$$

Hence[2]

$$\lim_{n \to \infty} M(n) = \sum_{i=1}^{2} c_i \pi_i = \frac{2 c_1 c_2}{c_1 + c_2} = M(L_{2,2}). \qquad (3.6)$$

If $c_1 \neq c_2$,

$$\frac{2 c_1 c_2}{c_1 + c_2} < \frac{1}{2}(c_1 + c_2) \qquad (3.7)$$

so that $M(L_{2,2}) < M_0$, or the automaton is expedient. From Eq.(3.5) it follows that in the limit the automaton chooses the two actions with probabilities π_i, which are inversely proportional to the penalty probabilities.

It is useful to list the various steps in the analysis of this simple example, since they are common to many of the general fixed-structure schemes discussed later in this chapter.

---

[1] π_i corresponds to $\lim_{n \to \infty} \pi_i(n)$ in Chapter 2.

[2] Throughout this chapter $M(n)$ and $\pi(n)$ are deterministic for a specified $\pi(0)$. Hence in the definitions of norms of behavior given in Section 2.5, $E[M(n)]$ can be replaced by $M(n)$. By ergodicity, $\lim_{n \to \infty} M(n)$ is independent of the initial probability vector $\pi(0)$.

(i)   Using heuristic arguments, the transition probability matrices for favorable and unfavorable inputs are first chosen.

(ii) The behavior of such an automaton, operating in a stationary random environment, is next shown to be described by a homogeneous Markov chain.

(iii) Using the ergodic property of the chain, the stationary state and action probabilities are determined next.

(iv) The expected penalty of the learning automaton is computed and the performance of the automaton is shown to be expedient.

It may be argued that since the transition probability matrices must be chosen heuristically, the analytical method described here is needed merely to justify that the approach will result in expedient behavior. Although this criticism may be partly valid, the rationale for the approach lies in the fact that it yields a quantitative measure of performance. As seen in the sections following, this enables the designer to choose the algorithms on the basis of the tradeoffs involved.

The behavior of fixed-structure schemes, operating in stationary environments, can be described by homogeneous Markov chains that are ergodic and, hence, possess unique final state probability vectors that depend only on the penalty probabilities of the environment. Ergodicity, and hence the existence of a stationary distribution, is the one central idea on which the analysis of fixed-structure automata is based. Appendix A provides a brief review of the properties of Markov chains used in this chapter.

3.3   Extensions of the $L_{2,2}$ Automaton

The transition matrices of Eq.(3.1) in the previous case were deterministic so that all rows of $F(i)$ $(i = 1, 2)$ contained only either zeros or ones and each row contained a single unit element. The question arises whether the expediency of the automaton could be improved by making the transition matrices stochastic so that

$$F(0) = \begin{bmatrix} 1 - \gamma_1 & \gamma_1 \\ \gamma_1 & 1 - \gamma_1 \end{bmatrix} \qquad F(1) = \begin{bmatrix} \gamma_2 & 1 - \gamma_2 \\ 1 - \gamma_2 & \gamma_2 \end{bmatrix}$$

$$ \tag{3.8}$$

$$0 < \gamma_i < 1 \; (i = 1, 2).$$

In such a case, when an action results in a favorable response, the automaton uses the same action with probability $1 - \gamma_1$ and switches to the other action with probability γ_1, and reverses this procedure using probabilities γ_2 and $(1 - \gamma_2)$ when the output of the environment is unfavorable. Proceeding as in the previous case, the matrix of transition probabilities of the automaton operating in the environment is seen to be

$$P = \begin{bmatrix} d_1(1 - \gamma_1) + c_1\gamma_2 & c_1(1 - \gamma_2) + d_1\gamma_1 \\ c_2(1 - \gamma_2) + d_2\gamma_1 & d_2(1 - \gamma_1) + c_2\gamma_2 \end{bmatrix}. \tag{3.9}$$

The final probabilities π_1 and π_2 of the two actions may be computed as:

$$\pi_1 = \frac{c_2(1 - \gamma_2) + d_2\gamma_1}{(c_1 + c_2)(1 - \gamma_2) + (d_1 + d_2)\gamma_1}, \qquad \pi_2 = \frac{c_1(1 - \gamma_2) + d_1\gamma_1}{(c_1 + c_2)(1 - \gamma_2) + (d_1 + d_2)\gamma_1} \tag{3.10}$$

Hence,

$$\lim_{n \to \infty} M(n) = M = \sum_{i=1}^{2} c_i \pi_i$$

$$= \frac{2c_1c_2(1 - \gamma_2) + (c_1d_2 + c_2d_1)\gamma_1}{(c_1 + c_2)(1 - \gamma_2) + (d_1 + d_2)\gamma_1}. \tag{3.11}$$

If $\gamma_1 = \gamma_2 = 0$, the matrices in Eq.(3.8) reduce to those in Eq.(3.1), and the automaton is deterministic. The limiting value of the expected penalty, as given by Eq.(3.11) coincides with Eq.(3.6) and the automaton is expedient. If $\gamma_1 = 0$ and $\gamma_2 \in [0, 1)$, the expected penalty as given by the expression of Eq.(3.11) is seen to be equal to $2c_1c_2/(c_1 + c_2)$ and independent of γ_2. If on the other hand $\gamma_1 \in [0, 1)$ and $\gamma_2 = 0$, the expression Eq.(3.11) reduces to

$$\frac{2c_1c_2 + (c_1d_2 + c_2d_1)\gamma_1}{c_1 + c_2 + (d_1 + d_2)\gamma_1},$$

which increases monotonically from $2c_1c_2/(c_1 + c_2)$ to $(c_1 + c_2)/2$ as γ_1 increases from 0 to 1. If $\gamma_1 = \gamma_2 = \gamma$, the automaton is seen to be expedient for $0 \leq \gamma < \frac{1}{2}$ and inexpedient when $\gamma = \frac{1}{2}$. For higher values of γ, the automaton is even more inexpedient, and the worst condition exists when $\gamma = 1$ and

$$M = \frac{c_1 + c_2 - 2c_1c_2}{2 - c_1 - c_2}.$$

The results above are generally in conformity with our intuition. However, this simple example also reveals the lack of symmetry that exists between the parameters γ_1 and γ_2 and the asymptotic behavior of the automaton. This asymmetry is discussed in greater detail in the context of variable-structure automata in Chapter 4, where it is found that rewarding a favorable response more than penalizing an unfavorable one may be preferable in some situations.

The case when $\gamma_1 = 0$ and $\gamma_2 \in [0, 1)$ deserves further attention. In this case,

$$F(0) = \begin{bmatrix} 1 & 0 \\ 0 & 1 \end{bmatrix} , \quad F(1) = \begin{bmatrix} \gamma_2 & 1 - \gamma_2 \\ 1 - \gamma_2 & \gamma_2 \end{bmatrix}. \qquad (3.12)$$
$$0 \le \gamma_2 < 1$$

The matrix P, the vector π, and the expected penalty are given in this case by

$$P = \begin{bmatrix} d_1 + c_1\gamma_2 & c_1(1 - \gamma_2) \\ c_2(1 - \gamma_2) & d_2 + c_2\gamma_2 \end{bmatrix}, \quad \pi = \begin{bmatrix} \dfrac{c_2}{c_1 + c_2} \\ \dfrac{c_1}{c_1 + c_2} \end{bmatrix} \quad M = \dfrac{2c_1 c_2}{c_1 + c_2}. \quad (3.13)$$

Hence, the automaton is expedient for all values of γ_2 in the interval $[0, 1)$. While the value of the parameter γ_2 is not found to affect the expediency of the automaton, it influences the speed of response, as is discussed in Section 3.7.

3.3.1   The Two Action Automaton with Memory: $L_{2N,2}$

The $L_{2,2}$ automaton is generally expedient but not optimal, since $M = 2c_1 c_2/(c_1 + c_2) > c_\ell = \min\{c_1, c_2\}$ for all $c_1, c_2 \in (0, 1]$. Naturally, the question may be asked whether it is possible to design an automaton for which M could be made to approach arbitrarily close to c_ℓ. Tsetlin suggested a modification of $L_{2,2}$ which can achieve this, provided the environmental penalty probabilities satisfy certain constraints. Such an automaton, denoted by $L_{2N,2}$, has $2N$ states and 2 actions and attempts to incorporate the past behavior of the system in its decision rule for choosing the sequence of actions. While the automaton $L_{2,2}$ switches from one action to another on receiving a failure response from the environment, $L_{2N,2}$ keeps an account of the number of successes and failures received for each action. It is only when the number of failures exceeds the number of successes (or some maximum value N) by one that the automaton switches from one action to another.

This is accomplished by enlarging the state space to $2N$ and specifying the rules of transition from one state to another.

As mentioned earlier, many fixed-structure learning schemes have been reported in the literature and all of them use the states of the automaton to keep track of past behavior. Invariably, all such automata schemes can be analyzed using Markov chain theory. Since the procedure in all cases is very similar we present in detail an analysis of the $L_{2N,2}$ automaton in this section. In the sections following only the expressions for the asymptotic behavior of the learning schemes are given without any analytical details.

The $L_{2N,2}$ automaton has $2N$ states, $\phi_1, \phi_2, \ldots, \phi_{2N}$ and two actions, α_1 and α_2. The states $\phi_1, \ldots, \phi_N$ correspond to action α_1 while states $\phi_{N+1}, \ldots, \phi_{2N}$ correspond to action α_2. Hence,

$$
\begin{aligned}
G[\phi_i] &= \alpha_1 && i = 1, 2, \ldots, N \\
&= \alpha_2 && i = N + 1, \ldots, 2N.
\end{aligned}
\tag{3.14}
$$

If the automaton is in a state $\phi_i (1 \le i \le N)$, it performs the action α_1. If this results in an unfavorable response, the state changes as follows:

$$\phi_i \to \phi_{i+1} \qquad (i = 1, 2, \ldots, N - 1)$$

and $\qquad \phi_N \to \phi_{2N}$.

Similarly, if the action results in a favorable response, the state transitions are as follows:

$$\phi_i \to \phi_{i-1} \qquad (i = 2, 3, \ldots, N)$$

and $\qquad \phi_1 \to \phi_1.$

In an entirely analogous way, we may express the state transitions of states ϕ_i, when $N + 1 \le i \le 2N$ and the corresponding action α_2 is performed, as follows:

$$
\left.
\begin{aligned}
&\phi_i \to \phi_{i+1} \ (i = N + 1, \ldots, 2N - 1) \\
&\phi_{2N} \to \phi_N
\end{aligned}
\right\} \alpha_2 \text{ results in an unfavorable response,}
$$

$$
\left.
\begin{aligned}
&\phi_i \to \phi_{i-1} \ (i = N + 2, \ldots, 2N) \\
&\phi_{N+1} \to \phi_{N+1}
\end{aligned}
\right\} \alpha_2 \text{ results in a favorable response.}
$$

$$\tag{3.15}$$

The state transition graphs are shown in Fig. 3.3; the corresponding state transition matrices are $F(0)$ and $F(1)$.

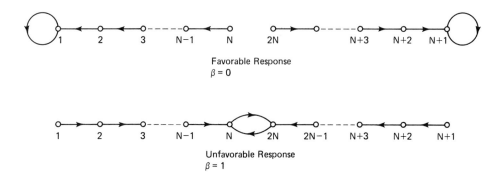

Figure 3.3: State transition graphs for $L_{2N,2}$ (*Courtesy Academic Press*).

The procedure described above is one convenient method of keeping track of the performances of the actions α_1 and α_2. As such, N is called the memory associated with each action, and the automaton is said to have a total memory of $2N$. For every favorable response, the state of the automaton moves deeper into the memory of the corresponding action, and for an unfavorable response, moves out of it. The depth of a state ϕ_α corresponding to an action α may therefore be conveniently defined as the minimum length of a sequence of input signals which brings ϕ_α out of the set of states $\Phi_\alpha = \{\phi_\alpha\}$ corresponding to the given action α. The depth of an automaton can then be defined as the greatest of the depths of its states (N in our example).

$$
\begin{bmatrix}
1 & 0 & 0 & . & . & . & . & . & . & . \\
1 & 0 & 0 & . & . & . & . & . & . & . \\
0 & 1 & 0 & . & . & . & . & . & . & . \\
. & . & . & . & . & . & . & . & . & . \\
0 & 0 & 0 & 1 & 0 & 0 & 0 & . & . & . \\
. & . & . & . & . & 1 & 0 & 0 & . & . \\
. & . & . & . & . & 1 & 0 & 0 & . & . \\
. & . & . & . & . & 0 & 1 & 0 & . & . \\
. & . & . & . & . & . & . & . & . & . \\
. & . & . & . & . & 0 & . & . & 1 & 0
\end{bmatrix}
$$

$$
\begin{bmatrix}
0 & 1 & 0 & . & . & . & . & . & . & . \\
0 & 0 & 1 & . & . & . & . & . & . & . \\
. & . & . & . & . & . & . & . & . & . \\
0 & 0 & 0 & . & 1 & . & . & . & . & . \\
0 & 0 & 0 & . & 0 & . & . & . & . & 1 \\
. & . & . & . & . & 0 & 1 & 0 & . & . \\
. & . & . & . & . & 0 & 0 & 1 & . & . \\
. & . & . & . & . & . & . & . & . & . \\
. & . & . & . & . & 0 & 0 & 0 & . & 1 \\
. & . & . & . & 1 & 0 & 0 & 0 & . & 0
\end{bmatrix}
$$

$$F(0)$$
$$(2N \times 2N)$$

$$F(1)$$
$$(2N \times 2N)$$

Using the matrices $F(0)$ and $F(1)$ and Eq.(3.3) for computing the probability of transition from state ϕ_i to ϕ_j, the overall state transition matrix may be expressed as:

$$
P = \left[\begin{array}{cccccc|cccccc}
d_1 & c_1 & 0 & . & . & . & . & . & . & . & . & . \\
d_1 & 0 & c_1 & . & . & . & . & . & . & . & . & . \\
0 & d_1 & 0 & c_1 & . & . & . & . & . & . & . & . \\
. & . & . & . & . & . & . & . & . & . & . & . \\
0 & 0 & 0 & d_1 & . & c_1 & . & . & . & . & . & . \\
. & . & . & . & d_1 & 0 & . & . & . & . & . & c_1 \\ \hline
. & . & . & . & . & . & d_2 & c_2 & . & . & . & . \\
. & . & . & . & . & . & d_2 & 0 & c_2 & . & . & . \\
. & . & . & . & . & . & 0 & d_2 & 0 & c_2 & . & . \\
. & . & . & . & . & . & . & . & . & . & . & . \\
. & . & . & . & . & . & 0 & 0 & . & d_2 & 0 & c_2 \\
. & . & . & . & . & c_2 & 0 & . & . & . & d_2 & 0
\end{array}\right] , \qquad (3.16)
$$

and the corresponding final state probabilities $\pi_i (i = 1, 2, \ldots, 2N)$ can be computed by solving Eq.(3.4), $P^T \pi = \pi$ for the vector π. This in turn can be written in expanded form as:

$$
\begin{array}{ll}
d_1 \pi_1 + d_1 \pi_2 = \pi_1 & d_2 \pi_{N+1} + d_2 \pi_{N+2} = \pi_{N+1} \\
c_1 \pi_1 + d_1 \pi_3 = \pi_2 & c_2 \pi_{N+1} + d_2 \pi_{N+3} = \pi_{N+2} \\
\cdots & \cdots \\
c_1 \pi_{K-1} + d_1 \pi_{K+1} = \pi_K & c_2 \pi_{N+K-1} + d_2 \pi_{N+K+1} = \pi_{N+K} \\
\cdots & \cdots \\
c_1 \pi_{N-1} + c_2 \pi_{2N} = \pi_N & c_2 \pi_{2N-1} + c_1 \pi_N = \pi_{2N} \quad .
\end{array} \qquad (3.17)
$$

In addition to the set of equations above, we also have the normalization condition

$$
\pi_1 + \pi_2 + \ldots + \pi_{2N} = 1 . \qquad (3.18)
$$

The typical equations in Eq.(3.17) are of the form $c_1 \pi_{K-1} + d_1 \pi_{K+1} = \pi_K$, $c_2 \pi_{N+K-1} + d_2 \pi_{N+K+1} = \pi_{N+K}$, which are second-order difference equations. The first, $N^{th}, N+1^{th}$, and $2N^{th}$ equations provide the boundary conditions needed to obtain the complete solution.

To solve Eqs.(3.17) and (3.18), we assume the solutions to be of the form $\pi_K = a_1 \lambda_1^{K-1}, \pi_{N+K} = a_2 \lambda_2^{K-1}$ and obtain the characteristic equation

$$d_i \lambda_i^2 - \lambda_i + c_i = 0 \qquad (i = 1, 2). \qquad (3.19)$$

The eigenvalues are $\lambda_1^{(1)} = 1, \lambda_1^{(2)} = \frac{c_1}{d_1} = e_1$ and $\lambda_2^{(1)} = 1, \lambda_2^{(2)} = \frac{c_2}{d_2} = e_2$ respectively. We now seek solutions of the form

$$\pi_K = A_1 e_1^{K-1} + B_1 \;\; ; \;\; \pi_{N+K} = A_2 e_2^{K-1} + B_2 \;. \qquad (3.20)$$

Using the first and $(N+1)^{th}$ equations for π_1 and π_{N+1} in Eq.(3.17) directly yields $B_1 = B_2 = 0$. Using the Nth and $2N^{th}$ equations in Eq.(3.17), we obtain

$$\frac{A_1 e_1^N}{1 + e_1} = \frac{A_2 e_2^N}{1 + e_2} \;. \qquad (3.21)$$

The stationary action probabilities p_1 and p_2 of the actions α_1 and α_2 are given by the sum of the probabilities of all the states corresponding to each action. Hence,

$$p_1 = \sum_{K=1}^N \pi_K = \frac{A_1(e_1^N - 1)}{(e_1 - 1)} \;\; ; \;\; p_2 = \sum_{K=1}^N \pi_{N+K} = \frac{A_2(e_2^N - 1)}{(e_2 - 1)} \;. \qquad (3.22)$$

Since $p_1 + p_2 = 1$, we can compute the expected penalty as

$$M(L_{2N,2}) = \frac{\frac{1}{c_1^{N-1}} \frac{c_1^N - d_1^N}{c_1 - d_1} + \frac{1}{c_2^{N-1}} \frac{c_2^N - d_2^N}{c_2 - d_2}}{\frac{1}{c_1^N} \frac{c_1^N - d_1^N}{c_1 - d_1} + \frac{1}{c_2^N} \frac{c_2^N - d_2^N}{c_2 - d_2}} \qquad (3.23)$$

For $N = 1$, $M(L_{2,2}) = 2c_1 c_2 / (c_1 + c_2)$ and the automaton degenerates to the simple $L_{2,2}$ automaton considered earlier. Further, the expression Eq.(3.23) is a decreasing function of the memory capacity, and if $\min_i \{c_i\} \leq \frac{1}{2}$,

$$\lim_{N \to \infty} M(L_{2N,2}) = \min(c_1, c_2). \qquad (3.24)$$

We demonstrate this by considering the three cases (i) $c_1 < c_2 < \frac{1}{2}$, (ii) $c_1 < \frac{1}{2} < c_2$, (iii) $\frac{1}{2} < c_1 < c_2$. In case (i) both $\frac{c_1}{d_1}$ and $\frac{c_2}{d_2}$ are less than 1 and $\left(\frac{c_1}{d_1}\right)^N$, $\left(\frac{c_2}{d_2}\right)^N$ as well as $\left[\frac{(c_1/d_1)}{(c_2/d_2)}\right]^N$ tend to zero as N tends to infinity. In case (ii) the second terms in both numerator and denominator of Eq.(3.23) are bounded as N grows without bound. Hence in both cases the expression of Eq.(3.23) tends to c_1 asymptotically with N. In case (iii) when both c_1 and c_2 are greater than $\frac{1}{2}$, $M(L_{2N,2})$ converges to the value $\frac{4c_1c_2-c_1-c_2}{2c_1+2c_2-2}$.

Eq.(3.24) implies that the automaton $L_{2N,2}$, for a sufficiently large memory capacity N (of each action), performs almost exclusively that action for which the probability of a penalty is a minimum.

The condition

$$\min\{c_1, c_2\} \leq \frac{1}{2} \qquad (3.25)$$

is called the ϵ–optimality condition for the $L_{2N,2}$ automaton. For systems with r actions ($r > 2$) a similar condition, $\min\{c_1, c_2, \ldots, c_r\} = c_\ell \leq \frac{1}{2}$, is found to be necessary for ϵ–optimality. This condition assumes prior information about the penalty probabilities of the environment and represents a significant restriction. A further discussion of this condition is included in Section 3.4.

Although from a theoretical standpoint the memory depth has to be infinite for the $L_{2N,2}$ automaton to be optimal, values of M close to the optimal value can be realized with relatively small memory depths.

For example if $c_1 = 0.2$ and $c_2 = 0.8$ in Eq.(3.23), the expected penalties for four different values of the memory depth N can be tabulated as shown below in Table 3.1.

N	$M(L_{2N,2})$
1	0.32
2	0.235
3	0.209
∞	0.200

Table 3.1

This fact has obvious implications in the design of practically efficient automata.

Results of simulation studies carried out on the two-state and multiple-state Tsetlin automata are shown in Figs. 3.4–3.7 (Nedzelnitsky and Narendra, 1979).

Simulation 3.1: Figure 3.4 shows the evolution of the probability of action 1 in a two-state automaton as a function of the trial number, for different environments (i.e., c_1, c_2 pairs). The initial probabilities of the two actions are assumed to be 0.5. The final stationary probabilities given by Eq.(3.5)

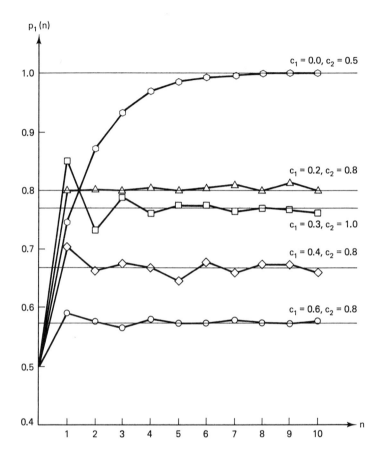

Figure 3.4: Probability of action 1 as a function of the trial number for a two–action, deterministic automaton.

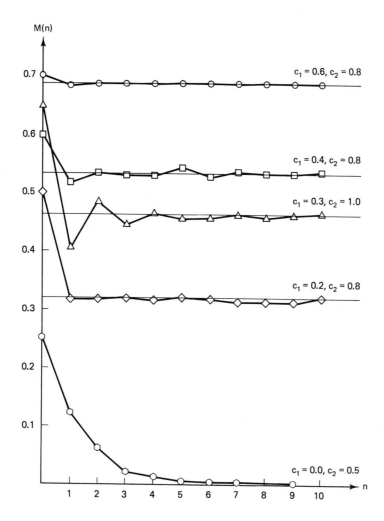

Figure 3.5: Average penalty as a function of the trial number for a two-action, deterministic automaton.

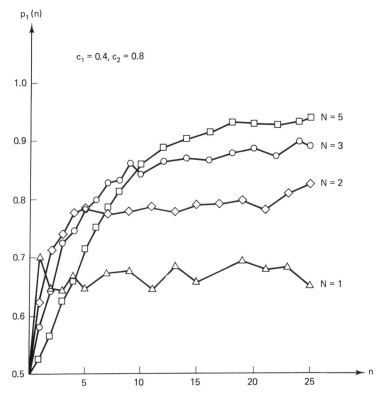

Figure 3.6: Action probability p_1 of two–action Tsetlin automaton.

are seen to be achieved in a relatively small number of steps. Figure 3.5 shows the corresponding average penalty as a function of the trial number.

Simulation 3.2: The behavior of a two action Tsetlin automaton with different memory depths for the two actions is considered in Figs. 3.6 and 3.7. In Fig. 3.6, the penalty probabilities of the environment were kept fixed at $c_1 = 0.4$ and $c_2 = 0.8$, and the system was simulated with the different memory depths $N = 1, 2, 3$, and 5. While the stationary probability of action 1 with a memory depth of 1 is approximately 0.65, it is seen to approach 1 rapidly as N is increased. For $N = 5$, the action probability is seen to be $\approx .94$ at the end of the twenty–fifth trial. Similar experiments performed on an environment with $c_1 = 0.6$ and $c_2 = 0.8$ [which do not satisfy the ϵ–optimality condition Eq.(3.25)], are shown in Fig. 3.7. The action probability $p_1(n)$ is seen to be less than 0.75, even when the memory depth is large.

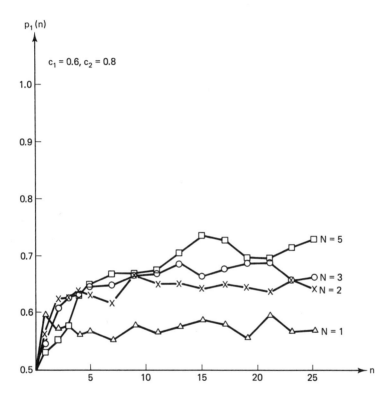

Figure 3.7: Action probability p_1 of two–action Tsetlin automaton.

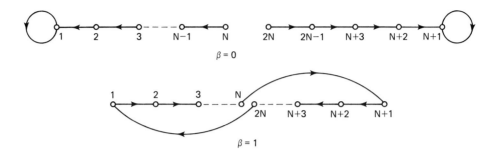

Figure 3.8: The state transition graphs of $G_{2N,2}$.

3.3.2   An Alternative Automaton Scheme with Memory: $G_{2N,2}$

The $L_{2N,2}$ automaton switches from state ϕ_N to state ϕ_{2N} when it encounters an unfavorable response from the environment. Since ϕ_{2N} corresponds to action α_2, this action is now performed. If this again results in an unfavorable response, the automaton switches back to state ϕ_N and the corresponding action α_1.

An alternative scheme, called the $G_{2N,2}$ automaton, was also proposed by Tsetlin (1961), in which the automaton switches from state ϕ_N to ϕ_{N+1} upon encountering an unfavorable response. Unlike the $L_{2N,2}$ automaton, this automaton performs the action α_2 at least N times (resulting in N consecutive penalties) before choosing action α_1 again. The state transition graphs of $G_{2N,2}$ are shown in Fig. 3.8 for both favorable and unfavorable responses. Proceeding as in the previous case, the expected penalty may be computed as

$$M(G_{2N,2}) = \frac{\theta}{1+\theta} \frac{(\theta^N - 1)^2 + N\theta^{N-1}(\theta - 1)^2}{(\theta^N - 1)(\theta^{N+1} - 1)} , \qquad (3.26)$$

where the penalty probabilities of the environment are c_1 and $1 - c_1$ respectively, and $\theta = c_1/(1 - c_1)$. It is found that $G_{2N,2}$, like $L_{2N,2}$, is asymptotically optimal provided $\min(c_1, c_2) \leq \frac{1}{2}$. However, the conservative approach used by the automaton results in a less expedient performance, since

$$M(G_{2N,2}) \geq M(L_{2N,2}). \qquad (3.27)$$

This is observed in the simulation studies shown in Fig. 3.9.

Comment 3.1: The automata described thus far were originally suggested by Tsetlin and are merely a few of a large number of feasible deterministic

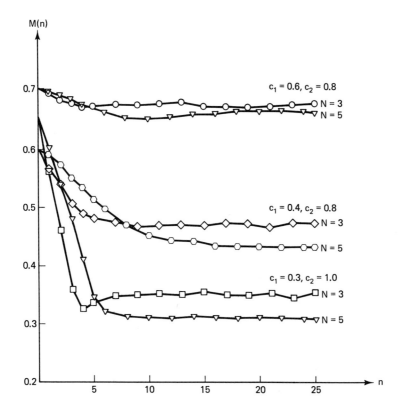

Figure 3.9: Average penalty of two–action $G_{2N,2}$ automaton.

schemes that one could generate. Some general comments can be made about all such schemes.

(i)   A set of states of the automaton is associated with each of its actions.

(ii) Using heuristic arguments, a procedure is set up for the transition from one state to another and, hence, for the transition from one action to another.

(iii) The state transition matrices can be constructed when the information in (ii) is available.

(iv) The total state transition matrix of the automaton working in the environment can be computed from the penalty probabilities of the environment and the state transition matrices corresponding to each input of the automaton.

(v)   If the Markov chain is ergodic, the final probabilities of the states, and hence the actions, can be obtained by solving Eq.(3.4). This in turn can be used to compute the expected penalty when the automaton operates in the random environment.

(vi) Realizing an expedient scheme is a relatively simple matter and depends primarily on step number (ii). However, schemes that are ϵ–optimal (with respect to a parameter such as memory) are more difficult to come by.

(vii) Automata that are ϵ–optimal in any stationary random environment are of theoretical interest. The $L_{2N,2}$ and the $G_{2N,2}$ automata are seen to be unconditionally expedient but only conditionally optimal, since ϵ–optimality is assured only when the condition of Eq.(3.25) is satisfied. The ϵ–optimal schemes discussed in the following section represent some of the attempts made to overcome precisely this restriction on the penalty probabilities of the environment.

The following example indicates how the concepts discussed in this section can be used in a simple game between a human player and an automaton. Refinements of this game, which are typical of many learning situations, are described in subsequent examples in this as well as following chapters.

Example 3.1a: The basic structure of a game between a human player and an automaton consists of a series of light sources $x_0, x_1, \ldots, x_N$ arranged in a linear fashion as shown in Fig. 3.10.

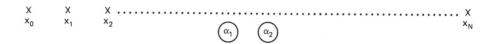

Figure 3.10: Game between a human player and an automaton.

At any instant the system is assumed to be in one of the states $x_i(i = 0, 1, 2, \ldots, N)$. x_0 corresponds to the state where the human player wins the game while x_N corresponds to the state where the automaton wins. The game starts in the state $x_{N/2}$ and each player alternately presses an action button α_1 or α_2. Pressing α_1 moves the state from x_i to x_{i+1} with probability d_1 and to state x_{i-1} with probability $1 - d_1$. Similarly, pressing button α_2 moves the state x_i to x_{i+1} with probability $(1 - d_1)$ and to state x_{i-1} with probability d_1 so the game is fair and neither player has an advantage. If $d_1 > .5$, it is clear that the action α_2 is the optimal action for the human player. The aim of the participants is to learn this fact from observing the response, as the game progresses so as to improve their chances of winning.

The strategy used by the two players will naturally depend on the prior information that is available, such as whether the transition probabilities are constant (as given earlier) or vary with state and/or time, whether each can observe the action chosen by the other player, etc. In this example we assume that both are aware at every instant of the state of the system as well as the fact that d_1 is a constant and identical for all states. The automaton uses the learning scheme of Tsetlin with a memory depth of 2, while the human uses whatever strategy is deemed necessary to win the game.

When d_1 is close to 1 both the player and the automaton tend to converge to their optimal actions in a relatively short time. The game then tends to oscillate between two adjacent states x_i and x_{i-1}. When d_1 is close to .5 the game tends to be of shorter duration. Both players have difficulty in determining the optimal action with the automaton having an advantage in the long run. It is only when d_1 assumes intermediate values that the resulting game becomes interesting. The automaton generally converges more rapidly to the optimal action, but in the long run both players play their optimal strategies.

Example 3.1b: Even slight modifications of the game described in Example 3.1a lead to more complex situations where the automaton is found to be distinctly superior. One such simple case is where the transition probabilities

depend on the states of the system. In this case the action to be used by
the automaton is determined by allocating a separate learning scheme (or
second-level automaton) to each of the states in which the automaton has to
act. Since the optimal actions are state dependent, the automaton is found
to perform significantly better than the human player.

Example 3.1c: A more complex game would result if the outcome at each
state depends on the actions of both the human player and the automaton.
This case belongs more appropriately in Chapter 8 where games of automata
are discussed.

3.4 ϵ–optimal Schemes[3]

The optimal action of an automaton is the one that results in the minimum
probability of an unfavorable response of the environment.   Hence, an
optimal scheme must be one that either implicitly or explicitly computes
the estimates of the penalty probabilities and chooses, more often, the action
corresponding to the minimum penalty probability. For ϵ–optimality, it is
obvious that each of the actions must be performed an infinite number of
times since the optimal action can be determined only when the estimates
of the penalty probabilities $c_i(i = 1, 2, \ldots, r)$ converge to their true values.

Although several simple schemes are available for estimating the penalty
probabilities c_i, most of them are impractical for use in an ϵ–optimal automaton; the estimation procedure takes an infinite time and there is no
provision to use the results of the estimation procedure in the choice of new
actions. A practically feasible ϵ–optimal scheme must therefore combine the
estimation procedure with the process of selecting new actions, so that all
the actions are chosen an infinite number of times though the probability of
performing the optimal action tends to 1 as time $n \to \infty$. Qualitatively, this
implies that more effort is spent trying better actions, until, in the limit, the
best action is tried almost exclusively.

In the case of deterministic schemes we are interested in asymptotic ϵ–
optimality as the memory depth tends to ∞. If, in an automaton with two
actions, the expected penalty is expressed as $M(c_1, c_2, N)$, the automaton
would be ϵ–optimal (asymptotically with respect to the memory N) if

$$\lim_{N \to \infty} M(c_1, c_2, N) = \min(c_1, c_2). \tag{3.28}$$

---

[3]These have been referred to as asymptotically optimal schemes in the earlier literature.

In Chapter 2, ε–optimality was defined in the context of general automata; the behavior of the automaton could be made as close to optimal as desired by suitably adjusting a parameter in the updating scheme. In the specific case of deterministic schemes we are considering here, the memory depth is chosen as the parameter, and we have the following definition of ε–optimality:

Definition 3.1: A deterministic automaton is said to be ε–optimal if, for every $\epsilon > 0$, there exists an N_1 such that for $N > N_1$

$$M \leq \min_i\{c_i\} + \epsilon, \tag{3.29}$$

where N is the memory depth of the automaton and $c_i(i = 1, 2, \ldots, r)$ lies in the closed interval $[0, 1]$.

In the rest of this section, we present some asymptotically ε–optimal schemes suggested in the literature by Krinsky (1964), Krylov (1964) and Ponomarev (1964). In all the cases, for ease of explanation, we shall consider only schemes with two actions. However, all of them can be extended to the multi–action case as shown in Section 3.6. Since the procedure for determining the expected penalty in each case is the same as that outlined in the previous section, we shall, for the most part, refrain from going into the details of the derivations and confine our attention to the qualitative features which make them ε–optimal.

The Krinsky Automaton (K_1): The state transition graphs in Fig. 3.11 show clearly that this automaton behaves exactly like the $L_{2N,2}$ automaton when the response of the environment is unfavorable. However, for a favorable response, any state $\phi_i(i = 1, 2, \ldots, N)$ passes to the state ϕ_1 and any state $\phi_i(i = N + 1, N + 2, \ldots, 2N)$ passes to the state ϕ_{N+1}. This, in turn, implies that a string of N consecutive unfavorable responses are needed, in general, to change from one action to another. The transition matrix $F(1)$ for an unfavorable response is the same as that for the Tsetlin automaton, while the elements of the transition matrix $F(0)$ are given by

$$f_{ij}^0 \quad = \quad 1 \quad \text{if } i = 1, 2, \ldots, N \qquad j = 1$$
$$0 \qquad\qquad\qquad\qquad\qquad j \neq 1$$

and
$$= \quad 1 \quad \text{if } i = N + 1, N + 2, \ldots, 2N \qquad j = N + 1$$
$$0 \qquad\qquad\qquad\qquad\qquad\qquad j \neq N + 1. \tag{3.30}$$

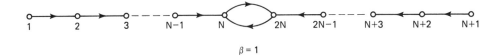

$\beta = 1$

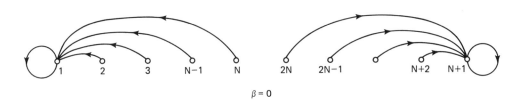

$\beta = 0$

Figure 3.11: State transition graphs of the Krinsky automaton.

The overall transition matrix of the system is given by

$$
P = \left[
\begin{array}{ccccc|ccccc}
d_1 & c_1 & & & & & & & & \\
d_1 & 0 & c_1 & & & & & & & \\
\cdot & & & c_1 & & & & \bigcirc & & \\
\cdot & & & & & & & & & \\
d_1 & 0 & \cdot & \cdot & 0 & & & & & c_1 \\
\hline
0 & & & & & d_2 & c_2 & & & \\
0 & & & & & d_2 & 0 & c_2 & & \\
\cdot & & \bigcirc & & & & & & & \\
\cdot & & & & & \cdot & \cdot & \cdot & \cdot & c_2 \\
0 & & & & c_2 & d_2 & 0 & \cdot & \cdot & 0
\end{array}
\right].
\qquad (3.31)
$$

The stationary probabilities $\pi_i (i = 1, 2, \ldots, 2N)$, as well as the corresponding action probabilities, can be computed as before and yield an expected penalty

$$
M(K_1) = \frac{c_1 c_2^N + c_2 c_1^N}{c_1^N + c_2^N} = \frac{\dfrac{1}{c_1^{N-1}} + \dfrac{1}{c_2^{N-1}}}{\dfrac{1}{c_1^N} + \dfrac{1}{c_2^N}}.
\qquad (3.32)
$$

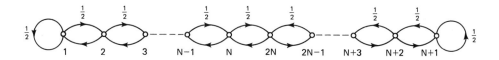

Figure 3.12: State transitions of Krylov automaton for unfavorable response of environment.

As the memory depth N tends to infinity, it is seen that

$$\lim_{N \to \infty} M(K_1) = \min(c_1, c_2).$$

Hence, the Krinsky automaton is ε-optimal in all stationary random environments.

The Krylov Automaton (K_2): This automaton has state transitions that are identical to the $L_{2N,2}$ automaton when the output of the environment is favorable. However, when the response of the environment is unfavorable, a state $\phi_i(i \neq 1, N, N+1, 2N)$ passes to a state ϕ_{i+1} with probability $\frac{1}{2}$ and to a state ϕ_{i-1} with a probability $\frac{1}{2}$, as shown in Fig. 3.12. When $i = 1$ or $N+1$, ϕ_i stays in the same state with probability $\frac{1}{2}$ and moves to ϕ_{i+1} with the same probability. When $i = N$, ϕ_N moves to ϕ_{N-1} and ϕ_{2N} each with probability $\frac{1}{2}$ and similarly, when $i = 2N$, ϕ_{2N} moves to ϕ_{2N-1} and ϕ_N each with probability $\frac{1}{2}$. The matrix $F(1) = \{f_{ij}^1\}$ is given by

$$f_{i,i-1}^1 = f_{i,i+1}^1 = \frac{1}{2} \quad i \neq 1, N, N+1 \text{ and } 2N$$
$$f_{11}^1 = f_{12}^1 = \frac{1}{2} \,; \, f_{N,N-1}^1 = f_{N,2N}^1 = \frac{1}{2}$$
$$f_{N+1,N+1}^1 = f_{N+1,N+2}^1 = \frac{1}{2} \,; \, f_{2N,2N-1}^1 = f_{2N,N}^1 = \frac{1}{2}.$$

If the same operations as before are carried out for the total transition matrix, the equations for the final probabilities may be written as:

$$\pi_1 = \tfrac{1}{2}c_1(\pi_1 + \pi_2) + \tfrac{1}{2}d_1(\pi_1 + \pi_2) \qquad \pi_{N+1} = \tfrac{1}{2}c_2(\pi_{N+1} + \pi_{N+2})$$
$$+ \tfrac{1}{2}d_2(\pi_{N+1} + \pi_{N+2})$$
$$\pi_2 = \tfrac{1}{2}c_1(\pi_1 + \pi_3) + \tfrac{1}{2}d_1\pi_3 \qquad \pi_{N+2} = \tfrac{1}{2}c_2(\pi_{N+1} + \pi_{N+3})$$
$$+ d_2\pi_{N+3}$$
$$\pi_K = \tfrac{1}{2}c_1(\pi_{K-1} + \pi_{K+1}) + \tfrac{1}{2}d_1\pi_{K+1} \qquad \pi_{N+K} = \tfrac{1}{2}c_2(\pi_{N+K-1} + \pi_{N+K+1})$$
$$+ d_2\pi_{N+K+1}$$
$$\pi_N = \tfrac{1}{2}c_1\pi_{N-1} + \tfrac{1}{2}c_2\pi_{2N} \qquad \pi_{2N} = \tfrac{1}{2}c_2\pi_{2N-1} + \tfrac{1}{2}c_1\pi_N .$$

$$(3.33)$$

If $\lambda_\alpha = \frac{c_\alpha}{1+d_\alpha}$ $(\alpha = 1, 2)$,
the expected penalty of the Krylov automaton can be expressed as

$$M(K_2) = \frac{\dfrac{1}{\lambda_1^{N-1}}\dfrac{\lambda_1^N - 1}{\lambda_1 - 1} + \dfrac{1}{\lambda_2^{N-1}}\dfrac{\lambda_2^N - 1}{\lambda_2 - 1}}{\dfrac{1}{c_1}\dfrac{1}{\lambda_1^{N-1}}\dfrac{\lambda_1^N - 1}{\lambda_1 - 1} + \dfrac{1}{c_2}\dfrac{1}{\lambda_2^{N-1}}\dfrac{\lambda_2^N - 1}{\lambda_2 - 1}} \qquad (3.34)$$

Again, $\lim_{N\to\infty} M(K_2) = \min(c_1, c_2)$.

In the Krylov automaton, we once again meet the asymmetric updating for favorable and unfavorable responses that we discussed in Section 3.3. In this case, however, making the scheme partly stochastic has the distinct advantage of making the automaton ϵ-optimal in all stationary random environments. V. I. Ponomarev constructed a finite automaton with similar properties. Ponomarev's scheme, which is given below, is considerably more complex than that of Krylov described here. However, unlike the latter automaton, it is entirely deterministic.

The Ponomarev Automaton: The fact that the automaton $L_{2N,2}$ is only conditionally ϵ-optimal can be partially explained qualitatively by the fact that, when $\min(c_1, c_2) > \tfrac{1}{2}$, the scheme does not permit repeated performance of the optimal action without switching to the other action. Hence, any modification of the Tsetlin automaton that attempts to achieve ϵ-optimality must take this fact into account. The automaton suggested by Ponomarev (1964) is an attempt in this direction. Figure 3.13 indicates the Ponomarev automaton with two actions. Open circles correspond to states in which action α_1 is performed and filled circles to states in which action α_2 is performed. The state transitions from each state for both favorable (de-

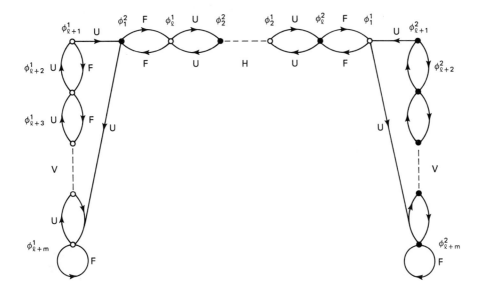

Figure 3.13: The Ponomarev automaton.

noted by F) and unfavorable (denoted by U) responses of the environment are indicated in the figure.

Figure 3.13 is seen to have two vertical parts denoted by V and a horizontal part H. The left vertical part V with m states corresponds entirely to action α_1, and the right vertical part with m states corresponds to action α_2. The behavior of the automaton in these states is identical to the Tsetlin automaton $L_{2m,2}$.

The 2ℓ states on the horizontal portion H correspond alternately to actions α_1 and α_2, with the first state corresponding to action α_2. The numbering of the states that correspond to action α_1 is from right to left (denoted by ϕ_i^1) and corresponding to action α_2 is from left to right (denoted by ϕ_j^2).

When the system is in a state in H, either a reward or a penalty results in a change of the action. However, there is a mean drift toward the better action corresponding to the minimum probability. In this region, the state transitions can be described by a random walk whose transition matrix P_1 is of the form

$$
P_1 =
\begin{bmatrix}
c_1 & 0 & d_1 & 0 & 0 & . & . & . \\
0 & d_2 & 0 & c_2 & 0 & . & . & . \\
0 & 0 & c_1 & 0 & d_1 & . & . & . \\
. & . & . & . & . & . & . & . \\
0 & 0 & . & . & c_1 & 0 & d_1 & 0 \\
0 & 0 & . & . & . & d_2 & 0 & c_2
\end{bmatrix}.
$$

In the vertical sections of Fig. 3.13, the automaton behaves exactly like the $L_{2m,2}$ automaton. However, a penalty in state $\phi_{\ell+1}^1$ moves the state to ϕ_1^2, while a penalty in state $\phi_{\ell+1}^2$ moves the state to ϕ_1^1. $\phi_{\ell+m}^1$ and $\phi_{\ell+m}^2$ are at the very bottom of the vertical sections (as in the Krinsky automaton), so that a multiple repetition of the corresponding action would be necessary before a change in action can take place. It is clear from the discussion above that the Ponomarev automaton incorporates the features of the Tsetlin automaton, as well as the Krinsky automaton. Qualitatively, the horizontal part in Fig. 3.13 can be considered to correspond to the training period of the automaton while the vertical parts correspond to states in which the automaton decides to attempt repeatedly the action learned from the training. In the horizontal part, irrespective of which action is chosen and what the response is, the automaton chooses the two actions alternately. Only the mean drift of the automaton is affected by the responses, which in turn determines the vertical states toward which the automaton moves.

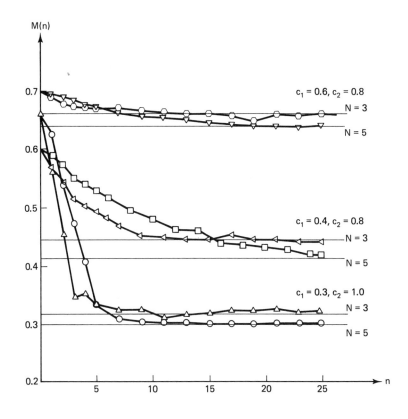

Figure 3.14: Average penalty of two–action Krinsky automaton.

Simulations of two-action Krinsky and Krylov automata with memory depths of 3 and 5 are shown in Figs. 3.14 and 3.15. Although these automata are theoretically ϵ–optimal as the memory depth N tends to infinity, their speed of response is found to be significantly less than that of the Tsetlin automaton (Figs. 3.6 and 3.7).

3.5 The Cover–Hellman Automaton

Perhaps the most successful of the fixed-structure learning schemes can be attributed to Cover and Hellman (1970). Much of the work in the 1970s was influenced by this paper, which effectively originated finite memory decision theory. In view of its importance, in this section we briefly discuss the principal results of this paper. For convenience of exposition, the automaton

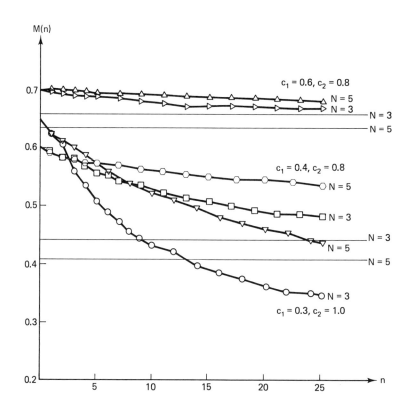

Figure 3.15: Average penalty for two–action Krylov automaton.

and environment are described using notation developed in Chapter 2.

Statement of the Problem: The general problem considered may be stated as follows: An environment is described by an input set $\underline{\alpha} = \{\alpha_1, \alpha_2\}$ and an output set $\mathcal{Y}$. Two probability measures $\mathcal{P}_0$ and $\mathcal{P}_1$, defined on a probability space $(\mathcal{Y}, \mathcal{B})$ are specified, where $\mathcal{B}$ is a σ–field of subsets over $\mathcal{Y}$. However, it is not known which of the two probability measures is associated with the actions α_1 and α_2. A success is said to occur if the action corresponding to the probability measure $\mathcal{P}_0$ is performed. The objective is to sequentially choose an action on the basis of past observations so as to maximize the proportion of the actions associated with $\mathcal{P}_0$, among all the actions chosen.

We shall confine our attention to a particular case of the general problem stated above, in which the output space is binary as in all the schemes described thus far. In terms of such a P–model, the environment is defined by the input set $\underline{\alpha} = \{\alpha_1, \alpha_2\}$, the output set $\underline{\beta} = \{0, 1\}$, and a set of penalty probabilities $\underline{c} = \{c_1, c_2\}$. However, unlike previous cases, c_1 and c_2 are specified, but it is not known a priori which of these are to be associated with the two actions. The automaton is defined by the input set $\underline{\beta}$, the output set $\underline{\alpha}$, and a finite state set $\underline{\Phi} = \{\phi_1, \phi_2 \ldots, \phi_m\}$, where the number of elements m is given. If $c_1 < c_2$, the objective in this case is to maximize the proportion of the actions α_i corresponding to c_1 among all the actions chosen.

If an action–output pair is denoted by $x(n) = (\alpha(n), \beta(n))$, attention is restricted to the algorithm [4]

$$\begin{aligned}
\phi(n) &= \mathcal{F}[\phi(n-1), x(n)] \\
\alpha(n) &= \mathcal{G}[\phi(n-1)] \qquad\qquad n = 1, 2, \ldots \; .
\end{aligned} \tag{3.35}$$

Both the state transition function $\mathcal{F}$ and the output function $\mathcal{G}$ are assumed to be stochastic, and the objective is to choose them in such a manner that the expected penalty $\lim_{n\to\infty} E[M(n)]$ is minimized.

Outline of Approach: Two possible hypotheses H_0 and H_1 can be made, relating the actions α_1 and α_2 to the given penalty probabilities c_1 and c_2.

H_0: Action α_1 corresponds to c_1 and action α_2 corresponds to c_2.

H_1: Action α_2 corresponds to c_1 and action α_1 corresponds to c_2.

Let P^0 and P^1 be the transition matrices of the overall system corresponding

---

[4]The state and output equations as defined here are somewhat different from those in Chapter 2 and conform to the notation used in Cover and Hellman (1970).

to the two hypotheses, and let π^0 and π^1 be the corresponding stationary state probabilities.

If G is the $(m \times 2)$ output matrix, then

$$g_{il} = Pr[\alpha(n+1) = \alpha_l | \phi(n) = \phi_i].$$

Let

$$\sum_{i=1}^{m} \pi_i^0 g_{il} \stackrel{\triangle}{=} r_0 \quad \text{and} \quad \sum_{i=1}^{m} \pi_i^1 (1 - g_{il}) \stackrel{\triangle}{=} r_1.$$

Then r_0 and r_1 are the asymptotic proportions of successes under the two hypotheses.

If the a priori probabilities of H_0 and H_1 are equal, the aim of the design is to maximize $(r_0 + r_1)/2$ over P^0 and P^1.

To achieve this, the following likelihood ratios are defined:

If β_i is an experimental outcome and

$$\ell_1(\beta_i) \stackrel{\triangle}{=} \frac{Pr[\beta(n) = \beta_i | H_0]}{Pr[\beta(n) = \beta_i | H_1]}, \qquad \ell_2(\beta_i) \stackrel{\triangle}{=} \frac{Pr[\beta(n) = \beta_i | H_1]}{Pr[\beta(n) = \beta_i | H_0]}, \qquad (3.36)$$

then ℓ_1 and ℓ_2 are the likelihood ratios of an experimental outcome β_i that results from actions α_1 and α_2 respectively. Let $\overline{\overline{\ell}}_1, \overline{\overline{\ell}}_2$ represent the maximum likelihood ratios and $\overline{\ell}_1, \overline{\ell}_2$ represent the minimum likelihood ratios for the actions α_1 and α_2 respectively. Let $\overline{\overline{\ell}} = \max(\overline{\overline{\ell}}_1, \overline{\overline{\ell}}_2)$ and $\overline{\ell} = \min(\overline{\ell}_1, \overline{\ell}_2)$. The likelihood ratio $\ell_\alpha(\beta)$ for any observation β due to any action α then satisfies the inequality

$$\overline{\ell} \leq \ell_\alpha(\beta) \leq \overline{\overline{\ell}}. \qquad (3.37)$$

Since c_1 and c_2 are given,

$$\overline{\overline{\ell}}_1 = \max\left(\frac{d_1}{d_2}, \frac{c_1}{c_2}\right) \quad \overline{\overline{\ell}}_2 = \max\left(\frac{d_2}{d_1}, \frac{c_2}{c_1}\right)$$
$$\text{and} \quad \overline{\overline{\ell}} = \max\left(\frac{d_1}{d_2}, \frac{c_1}{c_2}, \frac{d_2}{d_1}, \frac{c_2}{c_1}\right) \qquad (3.38)$$
$$\overline{\ell} = \min\left(\frac{d_1}{d_2}, \frac{c_1}{c_2}, \frac{d_2}{d_1}, \frac{c_2}{c_1}\right).$$

For example if $c_1 = .3$ and $c_2 = .2$ we have

$$\overline{\overline{\ell}} = \max\left(\frac{.7}{.8}, \frac{.3}{.2}, \frac{.8}{.7}, \frac{.2}{.3}\right) = \frac{3}{2}$$
$$\overline{\ell} = \min\left(\frac{.7}{.8}, \frac{.3}{.2}, \frac{.8}{.7}, \frac{.2}{.3}\right) = \frac{2}{3},$$

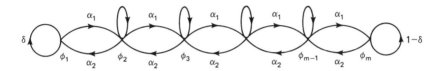

Figure 3.16: The Cover–Hellman Automaton.

or maximum and minimum likelihood ratio events are given by penalty with action α_1 and penalty with α_2 respectively.

In Cover and Hellman (1970) it is shown that, for an m–state automaton, the expected penalty is bounded by

$$1 - \frac{\overline{\overline{\ell}}^{m-1}}{\overline{\overline{\ell}}^{m-1} + 1} = \frac{1}{\overline{\overline{\ell}}^{m-1} + 1},$$

or

$$\lim_{n \to \infty} E[M(n)] \geq \frac{1}{\overline{\overline{\ell}}^{m-1} + 1}. \tag{3.39}$$

Structure of an ϵ-optimal Automaton: Having established an upper bound on the performance of the learning scheme, it is next shown that this bound can be reached arbitrarily closely by a class of ϵ–optimal automata.

Let $\ell_1(\beta_1) = \overline{\overline{\ell}}$. This implies that the observation (α_1, β_1) yields the maximum information favoring H_0 and, further, that $\ell_2(\beta_1) = \overline{\ell}$, so that (α_2, β_1) yields the maximum information favoring H_1. In other words, the experimental outcome β_1 yields the maximum information for testing H_0 versus H_1 regardless of the action chosen. An ϵ-optimal automata scheme designed using this fact is shown in Fig. 3.16. In states $\phi_2, \phi_3, \ldots, \phi_{m-1}$, the actions α_1 and α_2 are chosen with equal probability. In state ϕ_1, action α_1 is chosen with probability δ and, in state ϕ_m, with probability $1 - \delta$. If action α_1 results in output β_1 (the maximum likelihood event) hypothesis H_0 is supported and the state changes from ϕ_i to $\phi_{i+1}(i = 1, 2, \ldots, m-1)$. Similarly, if action α_2 results in β_1, the state changes from ϕ_i to $\phi_{i-1}(i = 2, 3, \ldots, m)$. For a response $\beta \neq \beta_1$, the state of the system remains unchanged.

From the transition matrix of the system above, the stationary probabilities and the expected penalty can be computed. In Cover and Hellman (1970) it is shown that the expected penalty may be made arbitrarily close to the theoretical lower bound by the proper choice of δ. Hence, the scheme is ϵ–optimal.

Comment 3.2:

(i)   The Cover–Hellman automaton differs from all the other automata
      schemes considered in this chapter in that both the state transition
      function $\mathcal{F}$ and the output map $\mathcal{G}$ are stochastic.

(ii) The scheme has characteristics similar to those of the Ponomarev
      scheme and other related two–armed bandit (TAB) schemes. The
      interior states can be considered to be allotted to hypothesis testing
      and the terminal states to utilizing this information to maximize the
      probability of success.

(iii) Transitions from one state to another are made only on maximal in-
      formation events.

(iv) The paper solves the classical TAB problem under the finite memory
      constraint. Variations of this problem include those in which the transi-
      tion and decision rules are deterministic or randomized, time–invariant,
      or time–varying, and in which the memory is finite or infinite and op-
      timality is achieved for finite or infinite numbers of observations. For
      further work in these areas, the reader is referred to Cover and Hellman
      (1970).

(v)   The Cover and Hellman paper discusses the case with two actions.
      Unfortunately, the design of optimal finite memory procedures for a
      general k–action problem has resisted solution since 1970. This may
      very well be its greatest limitation. For the interested reader, the paper
      by Chandrasekaran and Lakshmanan (1977) deals with some questions
      related to the multi-action case.

3.6   Automata with Multiple Actions

Thus far, all the automata we have discussed had only two actions. The same
concepts may be extended to cases where the automata can perform r actions
$\alpha_1, \alpha_2, \ldots, \alpha_r$. The principal difference between automata with many actions
and automata with two actions occurs in those states where the automaton
switches from one action to the next. This is best illustrated using a specific
automaton such as the $L_{KN,K}$ automaton, which is a generalization of the
Tsetlin automaton $L_{2N,2}$ to the K action case. Similar generalizations carry
over to other automata as well.

The state transition graphs for a favorable response ($\beta = 0$) and for an unfavorable response ($\beta = 1$) from the environment are shown in Fig. 3.17 for the case $K = 4$.

In this example, there are four actions $\alpha_j(j = 1, 2, 3,$ and 4). The N states $\phi_{jN+1}, \phi_{jN+2}, \ldots, \phi_{(j+1)N}$ correspond to the action $\alpha_{j+1}(j = 0, 1, 2, 3)$. For all values of $i \neq 1, N, N + 1, 2N, 2N + 1, 3N, 3N + 1,$ and $4N$, the automaton performs exactly as in the two-action case. Any state ϕ_i passes to ϕ_{i+1} with an unfavorable response, and to ϕ_{i-1} with a favorable response. For $i = 1, N + 1, 2N + 1,$ and $3N + 1$, the automaton remains in the same state for a favorable response. The manner in which the state transition takes place under an unfavorable response when $i = N, 2N, 3N,$ and $4N$ then completely determines the structure of the automaton.

In the generalization of the $L_{2N,2}$ automaton to the K action case (i.e., $L_{KN,K}$), Tsetlin assumed a fixed sequence in which the automaton would switch. For example, with an unfavorable response, the state transitions are $\phi_N \rightarrow \phi_{2N} \quad \phi_{2N} \rightarrow \phi_{3N} \quad \phi_{3N} \rightarrow \phi_{4N} \quad \phi_{4N} \rightarrow \phi_N$ as shown in Fig. 3.17. As an alternative to the procedure above, we may adopt a policy where the automaton in the state $\phi_j(j = N, 2N, 3N, 4N)$ may, under an unfavorable response, switch to any four of these states with a certain probability. This, in turn, makes this part of the automaton stochastic. The generalization of the $L_{KN,K}$ automaton to include this feature was called a beta automaton by Tsetlin. Simulation results of Tsetlin and Krinsky automata with four actions are shown in Figs. 3.18 and 3.19.

A logical extension of the scheme above is to vary the probabilities of transfer from $\phi_{jN}(j = 1, 2, 3, 4)$ to any one of the same four states on the basis of the performance of the automaton. This leads, naturally, to the concept of a two-level automaton, where the first-level automaton behaves like the automata described earlier and the second-level automaton merely determines the probabilities with which the first automaton should switch to a new action.

A Synthesis Approach: All the schemes considered thus far were developed more or less on a heuristic basis; the transition matrices for a favorable or unfavorable response from the environment are chosen first, and it is later shown that the corresponding schemes are either expedient or ϵ–optimal. The question can be raised as to what kind of logical structures would lead to expedient automata and hence learning. Some preliminary answers to this interesting question were provided by Aso and Kimura (1976). A P–model scheme with a transition matrix which is an identity matrix for a reward and

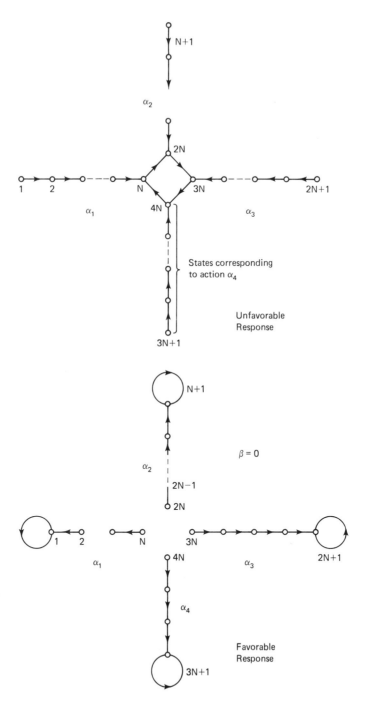

Figure 3.17: The $L_{KN,K}$ automaton $(K = 4)$ (*Courtesy Academic Press*).

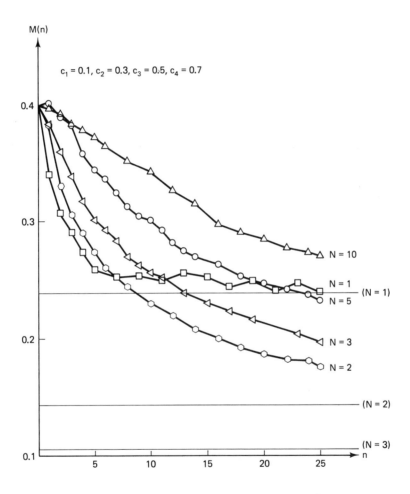

Figure 3.18: Average penalty for four–action Tsetlin automaton.

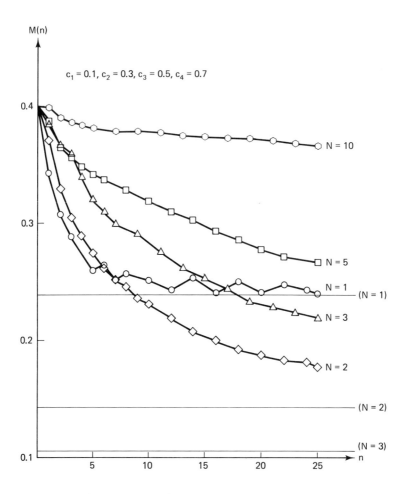

Figure 3.19: Average penalty for four–action Krinsky automaton.

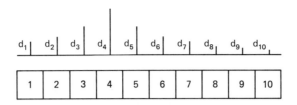

Figure 3.20: Detection of an object in a noisy background.

doubly stochastic (other than the unit matrix)[5] for a penalty was shown by them to be expedient [The simple example considered in Section 3.3 which satisfies this condition was shown to be expedient for all values of γ in the interval $[0, 1)$]. Further, these sufficient conditions for expediency also carry over to Q–models (Ref. Chapter 6) with multiple actions. However, sufficient conditions for ϵ–optimality or necessary conditions for expediency are currently not available.

Example 3.2: Figure 3.20 illustrates an example where an automaton A is used to detect an object which is in one of ten locations $1, 2, 3, \ldots, 10$. The detection is assumed to be carried out in a noisy background. If the object is in location i, the response to the query whether the object is in location $j, j \neq i$, also elicits a positive response with a probability d_j. It is assumed that $\max_j d_j = d_i$ and that d_j decreases monotonically with $|i - j|$. The aim is to use a learning scheme that accurately detects the location i of the object.

The problem above can be seen as one in which an automaton A with ten actions $\alpha_1, \alpha_2, \ldots, \alpha_{10}$ acts in a random environment. The action α_1 corresponds to the query whether the object is in location 1. Hence, $d_j (j = 1, 2, \ldots, 10)$ corresponds to the reward probability of action α_j.

If a fixed-structure learning scheme is used, a fixed memory depth N is associated with each of the actions i.e., N states, $i_1, i_2, \ldots, i_N$ are associated with action α_i. If the Tsetlin automaton is used, the automaton in state i_k moves to i_{k+1} for a favorable response and to i_{k-1} for an unfavorable response as described earlier. If the automaton is in state i_1 and gets a negative response, it moves to state $(i + 1)_1$ so that action α_{i+1} is chosen

---

[5]A stochastic matrix with the elements of all rows and columns summing to unity. This implies that P and P^T are stochastic.

(for $i = 1, 2, \ldots, 9$). The action following α_{10} is, however, α_1.

The scheme above is known to converge to the action α_i (for $d_i > 0.5$) as $N \to \infty$. In extensive simulation studies a memory depth of $N = 2$ was found to yield satisfactory results.

In many problems (e.g. Example 3.1b) multiple automata may have to be used to achieve satisfactory performance. In fact one automaton is needed in each state in which a decision must be made. Since the convergence of each automaton depends on the number of times the corresponding state is visited, this generally involves inefficient use of the various automata. When prior information regarding the relation between penalty probabilities in various states is available, a satisfactory solution that is practically attractive may be achieved using a finite number of automata. Although this is discussed further in Chapter 7 we illustrate it here with the following example.

Example 3.3: A bug B lives in a two-dimensional world and has two actions α_1 and α_2. A continuous curve Γ passing through the origin as shown in Fig. 3.21 divides the plane into two regions D_1 and D_2. In D_2 $Pr[\beta = 0|\alpha = \alpha_2] > Pr[\beta = 0|\alpha = \alpha_1]$ while the opposite is true in D_1. Equivalently the action α_1 is optimal in D_1 while action α_2 is optimal in D_2. The bug must determine this from the response of the environment.

For simplicity we shall assume that the curve Γ is composed of two straight lines. The entire plane is divided into d–sectors and it is assumed that one automaton is assigned to each of the sectors. When the bug, which executes a random walk in $\mathcal{R}^2$ enters a particular sector, the corresponding automaton is activated. As the bug performs actions and receives responses from the environment, the automaton updates its actions. In the limit it is found that the optimal action in all but two sectors can be determined. The automata, corresponding to the sectors in which the curve Γ lies, do not converge to any one action. From the actions chosen in each of the sectors as the bug wanders in $\mathcal{R}^2$, the approximate location of Γ (which is also the switching curve) can be estimated.

3.7   Rate of Convergence

The discussion thus far has been confined mostly to the behavior of various automata as a function of the memory depth. In particular, a rapid decrease in $M(n)$ with N has been the most sought–after property. An equally important consideration is the behavior of the automata with stage

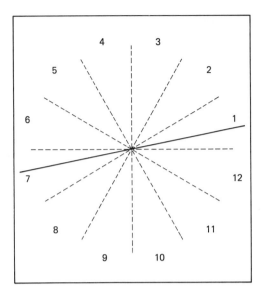

Figure 3.21: Use of multiple automata.

number n. Since all the automata referred to earlier can be represented by ergodic Markov chains, the rate of convergence of the state probabilities toward their final values is a characteristic quantity that describes the time behavior of the automata. As is well known in the theory of Markov chains, the rate of convergence is dependent solely on the eigenvalues of the transition probability matrix P. In particular, the eigenvalue closest to the unit circle and different from unity is the one whose effect is dominant. One could therefore choose the magnitude of this eigenvalue as a measure of the rate of convergence of an automaton. A formal development can be made as follows.

The state probability vector $\pi(n)$ at any instant n is given by

$$\pi(n) = (P^T)^n \pi(0). \tag{3.40}$$

Let the eigenvalues of P be $\lambda_1, \lambda_2, \ldots, \lambda_s$, and let these be ordered in decreasing magnitude:

$$|\lambda_1| \geq |\lambda_2| \geq \ldots \geq |\lambda_s|.$$

Assuming the chain to be ergodic, we have one eigenvalue as unity, i.e.,

$$\lambda_1 = 1. \tag{3.41}$$

For convenience, we assume that the eigenvalues are distinct and that the set of eigenvectors is $\{\underline{v}_i\}$ where $\underline{v}_i$ corresponds to the eigenvalue λ_i. Expressing P^T and $\pi(0)$ in terms of the eigenvectors, Eq. (3.40) takes the form

$$\pi(n) = k_1\lambda_1^n\underline{v}_1 + k_2\lambda_2^n\underline{v}_2 + \ldots + k_s\lambda_s^n\underline{v}_s, \qquad (3.42)$$

where k_i are constants depending upon $\pi(0)$. From Eqs. (3.41) and (3.42),

$$\lim_{n\to\infty} \pi(n) = k_1\underline{v}_1 = \pi^* \text{ (say)}.$$

Now $\|\pi(n+1)-\pi^*\|/\|\pi(n)-\pi^*\|$ [6] can be regarded as a measure of the rate of decrease of $\|\pi(n)-\pi^*\|$ to zero. Since $|\lambda_i| < |\lambda_2|$ for $i = 3, 4, \ldots, s$, and

$$\frac{\|\pi(n+1)-\pi^*\|}{\|\pi(n)-\pi^*\|} = \frac{\|k_2\lambda_2^{n+1}\underline{v}_2 + k_3\lambda_3^{n+1}\underline{v}_3 + \ldots + k_s\lambda_s^{n+1}\underline{v}_s\|}{\|k_2\lambda_2^n\underline{v}_2 + k_3\lambda_3^n\underline{v}_3 + \ldots + k_s\lambda_s^n(v)_s\|},$$

$$\lim_{n\to\infty} \frac{\|\pi(n+1)-\pi^*\|}{\|\pi(n)-\pi^*\|} = |\lambda_2|.$$

Thus, $|\lambda_2|$ is a suitable index of the rate of convergence, and faster convergence results from smaller values of $|\lambda_2|$.

For simple automata such as the Tsetlin automaton considered in Section 3.2, the value of $|\lambda_2|$ can be easily computed. In this case, $\lambda_1 = 1$ and $\lambda_2 = 1-c_1-c_2$, so that the rate of convergence is improved as $|1-c_1-c_2|$ decreases. In other words, convergence is rapid when $(c_1 + c_2)$ is approximately unity, and when $c_1 + c_2 = 1$ the stationary probability vector $[d_1, d_2]^T$ is achieved in one step.

It was shown in Section 3.3 that, when the transition matrix for the Tsetlin automaton is stochastic for unfavorable outputs, the expected penalty is independent of the parameter γ_2. The overall transition matrix P in this case is given by

$$P = \left[\begin{array}{cc} d_1 + c_1\gamma_2 & c_1(1 - \gamma_2) \\ c_2(1 - \gamma_2) & d_2 + c_2\gamma_2 \end{array} \right],$$

so that the eigenvalue λ_2 is given by

$$\lambda_2 = 1 - (1 - \gamma_2)(c_1 + c_2).$$

Hence, in this case, it is possible to control the rate of convergence by varying γ_2. If $c_1 + c_2 < 1$, $|\lambda_2|$ is a minimum when $\gamma_2 = 0$; if $c_1 + c_2 \geq 1$, the best

---

[6] $\| : \|$ represents the Euclidean norm.

result is obtained by setting $\lambda_2 = 0$ by choosing $\gamma_2 = 1-1/(c_1+c_2)$. However, in general, the values of c_1 and c_2 are unknown, and hence the value of γ_2 can be chosen using only prior estimates of the penalty probabilities. If it is assumed that $(c_1 + c_2)$ is uniformly distributed over the interval $[0,2]$, the best average value of γ_2 is given by

$$\gamma_2 = \gamma_{av} = \int_1^2 \left(1 - \frac{1}{x}\right) \frac{1}{2} dx \approx .153.$$

It is useful to know that the low value of γ_{av} implies that only a small departure is required from the Tsetlin automaton $L_{2,2}$ for best results and that if $c_1 + c_2 < 1$, the stochastic automaton cannot give a better rate of convergence than the deterministic automaton.

Similar comments may also be made for multi-state and multi-action automata such as $L_{2N,2}$ and $L_{KN,K}$. However, the computation of the eigenvalue λ_2 is significantly more tedious in these cases.

Speed and Accuracy: Two significant quantities associated with the operation of an automaton have been considered in the analysis made thus far. These are the average penalty M and the rate of convergence represented by the magnitude of the eigenvalue $|\lambda_2|$. The average penalty M could be regarded as a measure of the accuracy of the automaton, for it gives an idea of the probability with which the desired action is selected. The closer M is to the minimum penalty probability c_ℓ, the more accurate is the automaton. The rate of convergence, on the other hand, is a measure of the speed of the automaton. It gives an indication of the time taken by the automaton to reach the stationary state.

In practice, both these quantities are important. One would like to have maximum accuracy with the best possible speed. However, as is well known in systems theory, the two requirements frequently conflict and it is necessary to compromise. For example, the Krinsky automaton is ϵ–optimal in any environment. This implies that by choosing a sufficiently large memory depth N its performance can be made as close to optimal as desired. However, the choice of a large N significantly reduces its speed of convergence as is seen from the simulation studies in Fig. 3.19. The Tsetlin automaton, on the other hand, has fast convergence rate, but cannot be made ϵ–optimal if the condition of Eq. (3.25) is not satisfied.

3.8   Significance of Fixed Structure Automata

In the preceding sections we discussed different deterministic and stochastic automata of fixed structure that learn to choose asymptotically better actions with higher probability, while operating in a stationary random environment. As mentioned in Chapter 1, our interest in this book is in general learning methods that can be applied to the modeling and/or control of complex systems in the presence of uncertainty. The learning automata developed in this chapter can be conceived of as building blocks for such descriptive and prescriptive efforts. However, many generalizations and extensions are needed before any simple scheme qualifies as a candidate for a building block. First, the scheme must be able to perform adequately in nonstationary environments. After all, nonstationary environments provide much of the motivation to study adaptive or learning systems in the first place. Second, the scheme must be amenable to easy modification for dealing with inputs from several environments simultaneously as well as with environments having multiple outputs (i.e., Q- and S-models). Finally, and perhaps most important, in the study of complex systems, a methodology must exist for interconnecting building blocks to solve tasks that are inappropriate for a single automaton. These are some of the questions addressed in Chapters 6, 7, and 8.

Although fixed-structure schemes in principle meet these concerns, practical limitations are soon encountered. Even in the case of the simple Tsetlin automaton, $L_{2N,2}$, which has $2N$ states and 2 actions, the problem of determining the stationary probabilities of the states and actions involves the solution of the linear equation (3.4) of dimension $2N$. As the number of automata involved and the number of states and actions of each increase, the solution of the problem, while conceptually straightforward, becomes algebraically more unwieldy. Hence we shall concentrate, in the following three chapters, on variable-structure stochastic automata, in which some of these difficulties are circumvented by updating transition probabilities. Since the mathematical tools used to describe such automata are different from the finite state Markov chain theory used in this chapter, many of the algebraic difficulties encountered here are avoided. However, note that the variable-structure automata, described in detail in Chapter 4, had their origins in the fixed-structure schemes discussed here and are conceptually closely related. Since the extensions and generalizations that were mentioned earlier are common to both types of automata, we shall consider them jointly in Chapters 7 and 8. In particular, the Markovian switching environment of

Tsetlin described in Chapter 7 and the games of fixed-structure automata considered in Chapter 8 use the learning schemes discussed in Sections 3.3–3.6.

Although the emphasis in the rest of the book is on variable-structure stochastic automata, it should be kept in mind that the fixed-structure automata of Tsetlin, Krinsky, and Krylov can be used in their place in many of the applications discussed in Chapter 9. This may be desirable since these schemes, though difficult to analyze, are simple to implement.

3.9 Related Historical Developments

The learning automata schemes described in the previous sections can be considered as different schemes for the sequential choice of actions out of a prescribed set to optimize responses from a random environment. Such schemes have also been investigated extensively in many other fields, such as statistics and operations research. These parallel developments underscore the ubiquitous nature of the problem. The common statistical basis of these efforts has been masked to some extent by different terminologies: "sequential design of experiments" and "hypotheses testing" in statistics and the "two-armed bandit problem" (TABP) in operations research.

The results reported in Sections 3.2–3.6 are some of the highlights of the vast amount of work reported from the Soviet Union following the pioneering paper of Tsetlin. Quite independently, fairly extensive research was carried out in the United States since the early 1950s on the two-armed bandit problem. Although there was very little direct interaction between the two groups, the questions raised and the solutions suggested in the two countries have proceeded along remarkably parallel lines.

The TABP was formulated and solved by Robbins in 1952. He suggested an algorithm for choosing asymptotically the action $\alpha_i (i = 1, 2)$ which corresponds to the smaller of the penalty probabilities c_1 and c_2. This solution was the precursor of the Tsetlin automaton, which appeared in 1961. Robbins also suggested a modification of his rule in 1956, which, in turn, is related to the Krinsky automaton. Following this Isbell (1959) and, later, Smith and Pyke (1965) and Samuels (1968) improved on Robbins' scheme. The first two are similar to Ponomarev's scheme and involve the two distinct stages discussed in Section 3.4. Samuels considered randomized schemes and demonstrated them to be uniformly better than the earlier deterministic schemes. It is safe to say that every solution suggested for the TABP can also be modified for use in learning automata schemes.

Chapter 4

Variable Structure Stochastic Automata

4.1 Introduction

In Chapter 3, we considered the behavior of fixed-structure automata operating in stationary random environments. Such automata are characterized by state transition probabilities that are fixed. The theory of homogeneous Markov chains was the principal mathematical tool used in their analysis and in most of the cases considered, expedient behavior was achieved by the proper choice of the state transition probabilities of the automaton in response to the output of the environment. The latter, which is based on simple heuristics, directly determines the state transition matrix of the Markov chain describing the overall system and hence its asymptotic behavior.

Greater flexibility can be built into the models by considering more general stochastic systems in which the state transitions or action probabilities themselves are updated at every stage using a reinforcement scheme. Such automata, termed variable-structure stochastic automata, are introduced in this chapter. We first consider, in some detail, linear schemes that possess characteristics typical of all the schemes discussed throughout the book. To make the principal ideas transparent, the schemes are first discussed in the context of automata with two actions before extending the results to the multiple–action case. Following this, several nonlinear updating schemes, which have been proposed in the literature, are also discussed.

The theory of Markov processes forms the principal vehicle for the study of variable-structure automata. The learning schemes, when used in automata operating in stationary random environments, result in Markov processes that either are ergodic or contain absorbing states. In this chapter we merely introduce some of the principal definitions and concepts used for the description of such processes. A more detailed analysis of their behavior is postponed to Chapter 5, which together with this chapter, provides the mathematical basis for most of the results presented in Chapters 6 to 9.

The learning schemes used in variable-structure automata, as in the case of fixed-structure automata, evolved at first using heuristic arguments. Efforts to synthesize learning schemes, to achieve specific overall objectives, led eventually to the concept of absolutely expedient schemes introduced in Section 4.9. Necessary and sufficient conditions, which the reinforcement schemes have to satisfy to achieve absolute expediency, are discussed in this section. Simulation results of selected examples of variable-structure learning automata schemes are presented in Section 4.10.

4.2   Variable Structure Stochastic Automata

Variable-structure stochastic automata, as mentioned in the previous section, update either the transition probabilities or the action probabilities on the basis of the input. Varshavskii and Vorontsova (1963) were the first to suggest automata that update transition probabilities. Later developments by Fu and his associates (1965,1966,1970) made extensive use of action probabilities as these were found to be mathematically more tractable. The automata are now represented by the quintuple

$$\{\underline{\Phi}, \underline{\alpha}, \underline{\beta}, A, G\}, \tag{4.1}$$

where A is the updating algorithm (also known as the reinforcement scheme) and the remaining symbols correspond to the definitions given in Chapter 2, Section 2.3.

In Section 4.3, updating of both state probabilities and action probabilities is discussed. However, the emphasis throughout this book is on schemes for updating action probabilities. In such cases, for mathematical simplicity, it is assumed that each state corresponds to one distinct action. Thus $r = s < \infty$ and G is an identity mapping. Hence, we can speak interchangeably of states or actions and represent the automaton by the triple

$$\{\underline{\alpha}, \underline{\beta}, A\}. \tag{4.2}$$

For variable-structure automata, a mathematical description different from that given in Chapter 2 is found to be more convenient for purposes of analysis. According to this description the automaton is represented by the action probability sequence $\{p(n)\}_{n \geq 0}$ which is a discrete–time Markov process defined on a suitable state space (refer to Section 4.5).

4.3 Reinforcement Schemes

In general terms a reinforcement scheme can be represented either by

$$p(n+1) = T[p(n), \alpha(n), \beta(n)] \tag{4.3}$$

or by

$$f_{ij}^{\beta}(n+1) = T'[f_{ij}^{\beta}(n), \phi(n), \phi(n+1), \beta(n)], \tag{4.4}$$

where T and T' are mappings. In Eq.(4.3), the action probability at stage $(n+1)$ is updated on the basis of its previous value, the action $\alpha(n)$ at the instant n and the input $\beta(n)$. In Eq.(4.4), the transition probability $f_{ij}^{\beta}(n+1)$ relating a transition $\phi_i \rightarrow \phi_j$ at the instant $(n+1)$ for an input β depends on the value of this transition probability at the instant n, the states of the automaton at n and $n+1$ and the actual input $\beta(n)$ at n. When an automaton using either of these learning schemes operates in a stationary random environment, $\beta(n)$ corresponds to the output of the environment at stage n. Reinforcement schemes are generally classified on the basis of:

(i)   the asymptotic behavior of a learning automaton using the scheme e.g., expedient, ϵ–optimal or optimal, or

(ii)   the nature of the mapping T or T' in Eq.(4.3) or (4.4) e.g., linear, nonlinear or hybrid, or

(iii)   the properties of the Markov process describing the learning automaton e.g., ergodic or nonergodic.

If $p(n+1)$ is a linear function of $p(n)$, the reinforcement scheme is said to be linear; otherwise it is termed nonlinear. Sometimes, two or more schemes are combined to form a hybrid scheme. The aim of such a scheme is to realize the advantages (in a practical sense) of the constituent schemes, for example, speed of convergence or variance. The particular constituent scheme to be used at any moment could then be determined by the value of $p(n)$. Similar remarks also hold for transition probabilities as given by Eq.(4.4).

The basic idea behind a reinforcement scheme (as in the updating schemes for deterministic automata in Chapter 3) is a rather simple one. If the automaton selects an action α_i at instant n and a favorable input [1] $(\beta(n) = 0)$ results, the action probability $p_i(n)$ is increased and all the other components of $p(n)$ are decreased. For an unfavorable input i.e., $\beta(n) = 1, p_i(n)$ is decreased and all the other components are increased. These changes in $p_i(n)$ are known as *reward*[2] and *penalty* respectively. Occasionally, the action probabilities may be retained at their previous values and in such a case the status quo is known as "inaction."

The same idea can also be used for the updating of transition probabilities. If $\phi(n) = \phi_i, \phi(n + 1) = \phi_j$ and $\beta(n) = \beta, f_{ij}^{\beta}(n)$ is increased when $\beta = 0$ and decreased when $\beta = 1$. To preserve the stochastic nature of the transition matrix, the other elements of the ith row must be changed in the opposite fashion. The rest of the transition probabilities are maintained at their original values.

The precise manner in which $p(n)$ is changed depending on the action α_i performed at stage n and the response $\beta(n)$ of the environment, completely defines the reinforcement scheme. This, in turn, determines the resulting Markov process and hence the behavior of the overall system. In the sections following we shall for the most part consider the manner in which the action probabilities are updated. Wherever it is relevant, attention will be drawn to schemes based on transition probabilities.

4.4   General Reinforcement Scheme

4.4.1   Action Probabilities

Let a variable-structure automaton with r actions operate in a stationary environment with $\beta = \{0, 1\}$. Let $n \in N$ be the set of nonnegative integers. A general scheme for updating action probabilities can be represented as follows:

If

$$\alpha(n) = \alpha_i \qquad (i = 1, 2, \ldots, r)$$

$$p_j(n + 1) = p_j(n) - g_j[p(n)] \text{ when } \beta(n) = 0 \qquad (4.5)$$

$$p_j(n + 1) = p_j(n) + h_j[p(n)] \text{ when } \beta(n) = 1$$

for all $j \neq i$.

---

[1] Defined as output of the environment.
[2] A term derived from psychology.

For preserving probability measure we have $\sum_{j=1}^{r} p_j(n) = 1$ so that

$$p_i(n+1) = p_i(n) + \sum_{\substack{j=1 \\ j \neq i}}^{r} g_j(p(n)) \qquad \text{when } \beta(n) = 0$$

$$p_i(n+1) = p_i(n) - \sum_{\substack{j=1 \\ j \neq i}}^{r} h_j(p(n)) \qquad \text{when } \beta(n) = 1. \qquad (4.6)$$

The following assumptions are made regarding the functions g_j and $h_j(j = 1, 2, \ldots, r)$.

$\quad Assumption\ 1:\quad g_j$ and h_j are continuous functions

$\quad Assumption\ 2:\quad g_j$ and h_j are nonnegative functions

$\quad Assumption\ 3:\quad 0 < g_j(p) < p_j \qquad\qquad\qquad\qquad (4.7)$

$$0 < \sum_{\substack{j=1 \\ j \neq i}}^{r} [p_j + h_j(p)] < 1$$

for all $i = 1, 2, \ldots, r$ and all p whose elements are all in the open interval $(0, 1)$.

Comment 4.1: The updating scheme is given at every instant separately for that action which is attempted at stage n (i.e., action α_i) in Eq.(4.6), and separately for all those actions that are not attempted (i.e., actions $\alpha_j, j \neq i$) in Eq.(4.5). There is good reason to express the updatings in the particular form given in Eqs.(4.5) and (4.6). While the action that is performed is either rewarded or penalized on the basis of the environment's response, it is not clear how the probabilities of the other actions are to be changed. Hence, in the form stated, the question of determining the updating scheme becomes one of determining the functions g_j and h_j. It is further implied in Eq.(4.5) that as long as $j \neq i$, the functions g_j, h_j are independent of the particular α_i chosen.

The continuity assumption on g_j and h_j is one of mathematical convenience. The fact that both g_j and h_j are nonnegative maintains the reward and penalty nature of the updatings. Assumption 3 ensures that all the components of $p(n+1)$ remain in $(0, 1)$ when those of $p(n)$ are in the same open interval. Strict inequality is imposed in Eq.(4.7) so that

$$p(n+1) \neq p(n)$$

when all the components of $p(n)$ are in the open interval $(0, 1)$.

The effect of relaxing some of these assumptions will be discussed later in Section 4.9.

4.4.2   Transition Probabilities

A general reinforcement scheme, in which the transition probabilities rather than action probabilities are updated, takes the following form:
    If

$$\phi(n) = \phi_i, \phi(n+1) = \phi_j$$

$$f_{ik}^0(n+1) = f_{ik}^0(n) - g_{ik}[F^0(n)] \qquad \text{when } \beta(n) = 0 \qquad (4.8)$$

$$f_{ik}^1(n+1) = f_{ik}^1(n) + h_{ik}[F^1(n)] \qquad \text{when } \beta(n) = 1$$

for all $k = 1, 2, \ldots, s, \quad k \neq j$.
Further,

$$f_{ij}^0(n+1) = f_{ij}^0(n) + \sum_{\substack{k=1 \\ k \neq j}}^{s} g_{ik}[F^0(n)] \qquad \text{when } \beta(n) = 0$$

$$f_{ij}^1(n+1) = f_{ij}^1(n) - \sum_{\substack{k=1 \\ k \neq j}}^{s} h_{ik}[F^1(n)] \qquad \text{when } \beta(n) = 1 \qquad (4.9)$$

and for all $u \neq i$ and/or $\beta(n) \neq \beta$

$$f_{uv}^\beta(n+1) = f_{uv}^\beta(n). \qquad (4.10)$$

In this algorithm, $g_{ik}(\cdot)$ and $h_{ik}(\cdot)$ are nonnegative continuous functions mapping $s \times s$ stochastic matrices into $\mathcal{R}[0,1]$. It is also clear that the algorithm updates only the ith row elements of the state transition matrix associated with $\beta(n)$ and that the remaining transition probabilities are maintained at their previous values. As in the case of action probabilities discussed earlier, the functions $g_{ik}(\cdot)$ and $h_{ik}(\cdot)$ satisfy subsidiary conditions to assure that all transition probabilities remain in the interval $(0,1)$.

4.5   Variable Structure Learning Automaton as a Markov Process

The vector $p(n)$ as defined by Eqs.(4.5) and (4.6) is a random vector; similarly the matrices $[f_{ij}^0(n)]$ and $[f_{ij}^1(n)]$ defined by Eqs.(4.8) and (4.9) are random matrices. If the penalty probabilities $c_i(i = 1, 2, \ldots, r)$ of the environment are constant and the functions g and h in Eqs.(4.5) to (4.9) are independent of the stage number n, the probability $p(n+1)$ is determined completely by $p(n)$ and hence $\{p(n)\}_{n \geq 0}$ is also a discrete–time homogeneous

Markov process. Since the learning schemes treated in this book pertain mainly to action probabilities, we shall confine our attention in this section to the discrete process $\{p(n)\}_{n\geq 0}$ and define concepts that are found to be relevant for its description.

At every stage n, the elements of the vector $p(n)$ lie in the interval $[0,1]$ and $\sum_{i=1}^{r} p_i(n) = 1$. Hence the unit simplex

$$S_r \triangleq \{p|p^T = [p_1, p_2, \ldots, p_r], 0 \leq p_i \leq 1, \sum_{i=1}^{r} p_i = 1\} \qquad (4.11)$$

represents the state space of the process $\{p(n)\}_{n\geq 0}$. The interior of S_r where all p_i are in the open interval $(0,1)$ is denoted by S_r^0. Let e_i be the r dimensional unit vector $e_i^T \triangleq [0,0,\ldots,1,0,0,0]$ where the ith element is unity. e_i is a vertex of the simplex S_r. Let V_r denote the set of all vertices of S_r i.e.,

$$V_r \triangleq \{e_1, e_2, \ldots, e_r\}. \qquad (4.12)$$

A state $p^* \in S_r$ is said to be an "absorbing state" if $p(n) = p^*$ implies $p(k) = p^*$ with probability one for all $k \geq n$. A state that does not satisfy the condition above is called a nonabsorbing state.

The learning algorithm of Eq.(4.5) represents a mapping $T : S_r \to S_r$ and hence $\{p(n)\}_{n\geq 0}$ is a discrete–time Markov process defined on the state space S_r and having a stationary transition function. The functions g_j and h_j in Eq.(4.5) can be so chosen that the process above has one or more absorbing states. Such an algorithm is referred to as an "absorbing algorithm." Similarly "nonabsorbing algorithms" result in Markov processes that have no absorbing states. As might be expected, the asymptotic behavior of the two types of schemes is quite different and is treated in some detail in Chapter 5.

The design of variable-structure stochastic learning automata involves the choice of the learning algorithm T or more specifically the choice of the functions g_j and $h_j(j = 1, 2, \ldots, r)$ such that the overall system satisfies one of the measures of performance, for example, expediency, ϵ–optimality, etc., defined in Chapter 2.

4.6 Learning Automata with Two Actions

A variety of linear, nonlinear and hybrid schemes have been reported in the literature. Considerable attention has been paid to linear schemes on account of their analytical tractability. Three such linear schemes are the linear reward–penalty scheme (L_{R-P}), the linear reward–ϵ–penalty scheme ($L_{R-\epsilon P}$) and the linear reward–inaction scheme (L_{R-I}). These schemes exhibit interesting and significantly different characteristics and at present are prototypes for distinct types of behavior observed in all learning automata. We consider, in this section, these three linear schemes for the simple case when the automaton has only two actions.

4.6.1   Linear Reward–Penalty (L_{R-P}) Scheme

The linear reward–penalty scheme is perhaps the earliest scheme considered in mathematical psychology (Bush and Mosteller, 1958). The properties of this scheme have been studied in detail by a number of research workers in this field (Fu and McLaren, 1965; Fu and McMurtry, 1966; Chandrasekaran and Shen, 1968; Viswanathan and Narendra, 1972; Norman, 1972; Lakshmivarahan and Thathachar, 1973). Considering a learning automaton with two actions, let

$$g_j(p(n)) = ap_j(n)$$

and   (4.13)

$$h_j(p(n)) = b(1 - p_j(n))$$

in Eqs.(4.5) and (4.6) where a and b are reward and penalty parameters and $0 < a < 1$, $0 \leq < b < 1$. Substituting Eq.(4.13) in Eqs.(4.5) and (4.6) the updating algorithm can be written as follows:

$$\left. \begin{array}{l} p_1(n+1) = p_1(n) + a(1 - p_1(n)) \\ p_2(n+1) = (1-a)p_2(n) \end{array} \right\} \quad \alpha(n) = \alpha_1, \beta(n) = 0$$

$$\left. \begin{array}{l} p_1(n+1) = (1-b)p_1(n) \\ p_2(n+1) = p_2(n) + b(1 - p_2(n)) \end{array} \right\} \quad \alpha(n) = \alpha_1, \beta(n) = 1. \quad (4.14)$$

Equivalently this can also be written in terms of $p_1(n+1)$ alone as

$$
\begin{array}{lll}
p_1(n+1) = p_1(n) + a(1 - p_1(n)) & \alpha(n) = \alpha_1 & \beta(n) = 0 \\
p_1(n+1) = (1-b)p_1(n) & \alpha(n) = \alpha_1 & \beta(n) = 1 \\
p_1(n+1) = (1-a)p_1(n) & \alpha(n) = \alpha_2 & \beta(n) = 0 \\
p_1(n+1) = p_1(n) + b(1 - p_1(n)) & \alpha(n) = \alpha_2 & \beta(n) = 1.
\end{array}
$$

(4.15)

Equations (4.14) and (4.15) will be referred to as the general L_{R-P} updating algorithm. From these equations it follows that if action α_i is attempted at stage n, the probability $p_j(n)(j \neq i)$ is decreased at stage $n+1$ by an amount proportional to its value at stage n for a favorable response and increased by an amount proportional to $[1 - p_j(n)]$ for an unfavorable response.

The specific case when $a = b$ is called the linear reward–penalty scheme (L_{R-P}) and results in symmetric equations. From Eq.(4.15) it is seen that the effect on the probability of action α_1 is the same whether α_1 is performed and results in a favorable (unfavorable) response or α_2 is performed and results in unfavorable (favorable) response.

From Eq.(4.14) it follows that $\{p(n)\}_{n \geq 0}$ is a discrete–time Markov process defined on the state space which is the unit simplex $S_2 : \{p : p_1 + p_2 = 1, p_1, p_2 \geq 0\}$ with stationary state transition function. Equivalently, from Eq.(4.15), $\{p_1(n)\}_{n \geq 0}$ can also be described by a Markov process whose state space is the unit interval $[0, 1]$. Hence the asymptotic behavior of the action probabilities, which is of paramount importance, can be computed from Eq.(4.15), when the automaton operates in an environment with penalty probabilities $\{c_1, c_2\}$. A common method used in such studies is to compute the conditional expectation of $p_1(n + 1)$ given $p_1(n)$. For the L_{R-P} scheme

$$
\begin{aligned}
E[p_1(n+1)|p_1(n)] &= [p_1(n) + a(1 - p_1(n))][p_1(n)(1 - c_1) + (1 - p_1(n))c_2] \\
&\quad + (1 - a)p_1(n)[p_1(n)c_1 + (1 - p_1(n))(1 - c_2)] \\
&= [1 - a(c_1 + c_2)]p_1(n) + ac_2.
\end{aligned}
$$

Taking expectations on both sides, we have

$$
E[p_1(n + 1)] = [1 - a(c_1 + c_2)]E[p_1(n)] + ac_2, \tag{4.16}
$$

which is a linear difference equation in $E[p_1(n)]$. The solution of Eq.(4.16) yields

$$
E[p_1(n)] = [1 - a(c_1 + c_2)]^n p_1(0) + \frac{[1 - \{1 - a(c_1 + c_2)\}^n]}{a(c_1 + c_2)} ac_2 \tag{4.17}
$$

or

$$
\lim_{n \to \infty} E[p_1(n)] = \frac{c_2}{c_1 + c_2} \text{ if } |1 - a(c_1 + c_2)| < 1. \tag{4.18}
$$

Hence

$$
\lim_{n \to \infty} E[p_2(n)] = \frac{c_1}{c_1 + c_2}. \tag{4.19}
$$

Thus if $c_2 < c_1 \lim_{n \to \infty} E[p_1(n)] < \lim_{n \to \infty} E[p_2(n)]$ or, on the average, action α_2 is chosen asymptotically with a higher probability than action α_1. The asymptotic value of the average penalty is given by

$$
\begin{aligned}
\lim_{n \to \infty} E[M(n)] &= c_1 \lim_{n \to \infty} E[p_1(n)] + c_2 \lim_{n \to \infty} E[p_2(n)] \\
&= 2c_1 c_2/c_1 + c_2 < c_1 + c_2/2 = M_0.
\end{aligned}
\tag{4.20}
$$

The reader is referred to Eqs.(3.5)–(3.7) which pertain to the action probabilities and the corresponding expected penalty of the two state Tsetlin automaton and the corresponding results in Eqs.(4.18)–(4.20) for the variable-structure case.

As seen from Eq.(4.17), the inequality of Eq.(4.20) is true irrespective of the relative values of c_1 and c_2 and the value of the initial probability $p_1(0)$. Hence the L_{R-P} scheme is expedient for all initial conditions and all stationary environments (with $c_1 \neq c_2$).

4.6.2 Linear Reward–Inaction (L_{R-I}) Scheme

This is another simple linear scheme that can be derived by a modification of the general L_{R-P} scheme given in Eqs.(4.14) and (4.15). However, it exhibits an asymptotic behavior which is entirely different from that of the L_{R-P} scheme. The basic idea of the scheme is not to change probabilities whenever an unfavorable response results from the environment. Following a favorable response, however, the probability of the action is increased as in the L_{R-P} scheme. The L_{R-I} scheme was considered first in mathematical psychology by Norman (1968) but was later independently conceived and introduced into the engineering literature by Shapiro and Narendra (1969).

The L_{R-I} scheme can be derived from Eq.(4.14) or (4.15) by making the parameter b equal to zero. In such a case Eq.(4.15) may be written as

$$
\begin{aligned}
p_1(n+1) &= p_1(n) + a(1 - p_1(n)) & \alpha(n) &= \alpha_1 & \beta(n) &= 0 \\
p_1(n+1) &= p_1(n) & \alpha(n) &= \alpha_1 & \beta(n) &= 1 \\
p_1(n+1) &= (1-a)p_1(n) & \alpha(n) &= \alpha_2 & \beta(n) &= 0 \\
p_1(n+1) &= p_1(n) & \alpha(n) &= \alpha_2 & \beta(n) &= 1.
\end{aligned}
\tag{4.21}
$$

From Eq.(4.21) it follows that the probability $p_1(n)$ is increased if action α_1 is performed and results in a favorable response, is unchanged if an unfavorable response results when α_1 or α_2 is performed and is decreased only when the other action α_2 is performed and results in a favorable response.

From Eq.(4.14) it is seen that the L_{R-P} scheme has no absorbing states. In contrast to this the L_{R-I} scheme has absorbing states e_1 and e_2 where $e_1^T = [1,0]$ and $e_2^T = [0,1]$. Since $p_1(n)$ (or $p_2(n)$) can decrease only when α_2 (or α_1) is chosen and results in a favorable response, $p(k) = e_i$ if $p(n) = e_i$ for $i \in \{1,2\}$ and all $k \geq n$. Hence $V_2 \overset{\triangle}{=} \{e_1, e_2\}$ represents the set of all absorbing states and the Markov process $\{p(n)\}_{n\geq 0}$ generated by an L_{R-I} scheme converges to the set V_2 with probability one. We shall consider this aspect in greater detail in Chapter 5.

To study the asymptotic behavior of the process $\{p_1(n)\}_{n\geq 0}$ we consider the conditional expectation of $p_1(n+1)$. Let

$$\Delta p_1(n) \overset{\triangle}{=} E[p_1(n+1)|p_1(n)] - p_1(n). \qquad (4.22)$$

Then from Eq.(4.21)

$$\Delta p_1(n) = ap_1(n) \ (1 - p_1(n))(c_2 - c_1)$$

or

$$\begin{aligned} \Delta p_1(n) &\geq 0 && \text{if } c_2 > c_1 \\ &\leq 0 && \text{if } c_2 < c_1. \end{aligned} \qquad (4.23)$$

Further $\Delta p_1(n) = 0$ if and only if $p_1(n) \in \{0,1\}$.
Taking expectations on both sides

$$E[p_1(n+1)] \overset{>}{\underset{<}{}} E[p_1(n)] \qquad (4.24)$$

according as $c_2 \overset{>}{\underset{<}{}} c_1$ when $p_1(n) \in (0,1)$. Hence the expected value of $p_1(n)$ increases or decreases monotonically with n depending on whether c_2 is greater than or less than c_1. In the two–action case under consideration, this implies that the probability of the action corresponding to the minimum penalty probability increases monotonically with n. These results hold in arbitrary random environments and for arbitrary initial conditions provided the initial probabilities are not 0 or 1. As mentioned earlier $p_1(n)$ converges to either 0 or 1 $w.p.1$, from any initial state $p_1(0)$ and the probability of convergence to either of these values is also determined by $p_1(0)$. It is shown in Chapter 5 that $p_1(n)$ converges to 0 with a higher probability when $c_1 > c_2$ and to 1 with a higher probability when $c_2 > c_1$ if the initial probability is $p(0)^T = [\frac{1}{2}, \frac{1}{2}]$. Determining the probability of convergence to the optimal action is an important question and is considered further in Chapter 5.

4.6.3   Linear Reward–ϵ–Penalty ($L_{R-\epsilon P}$) Scheme

In the preceding subsections it was seen that the choice of the parameter b in the general L_{R-P} scheme of Eq.(4.15) determines whether the learning scheme will be of the L_{R-P} or the L_{R-I} type; $b = a$ resulting in the L_{R-P} scheme and $b = 0$ in the L_{R-I} scheme. The asymptotic behavior of the two schemes is also quite different. Qualitatively, with the L_{R-P} scheme, the distribution functions of the sequence of action probabilities converge to a distribution function at all points of continuity of the latter function. In the case of the L_{R-I} scheme the sequence $\{p(n)\}_{n \geq 0}$ converges to the set of absorbing states V_2 with probability one. More generally, the scheme of Eq.(4.15) can be shown to have no absorbing states for $b \in (0,1]$ and the nature of the convergence of $\{p(n)\}_{n \geq 0}$ is similar to that of the L_{R-P} scheme. However, the performance criterion {i.e., $E[M(n)]$} can be shown to be a continuous function of the parameter b for a specified value of a. Hence two schemes realized using $b = 0$ and $b > 0$ but sufficiently small would have approximately the same value of the performance criterion while exhibiting very different asymptotic behavior (Section 4.6.4).

It is shown in Chapter 5 that the L_{R-I} scheme is ϵ–optimal with respect to the parameter a. Hence, by the previous arguments, it must be possible to generate ergodic schemes with $b \neq 0$ which are also ϵ–optimal. It is this latter fact that led to a detailed study of $L_{R-\epsilon P}$ scheme with small values of the parameter b (relative to a) (Lakshmivarahan, 1979).

Proceeding as in the L_{R-P} case of Eq.(4.16) but with $b \neq a$, the conditional expectation of $p_1(n+1)$ can be expressed as

$$E[p_1(n+1)|p_1(n)] = p_1 + b[(1 - p_1)^2 c_2 - p_1^2 c_1] + a p_1(1 - p_1)(c_2 - c_1)$$

or

$$\Delta p_1(n) = b[(1 - p_1)^2 c_2 - p_1^2 c_1] + a p_1(1 - p_1)(c_2 - c_1)$$

$$(4.25)$$

which is nonlinear in p_1. For convenience $p_1(n)$ is replaced by p_1 in the right-hand side above.

The second term in the right-hand side of Eq.(4.25) corresponds to the case when $b = 0$ i.e., L_{R-I}. When $b = a$ the right–hand side reduces to $-a(c_1 + c_2)p_1 + ac_2$ given in Eq.(4.16) for the L_{R-P} case. For $0 < b << a$, $\Delta p_1(n)$ is a continuous function, positive for $p_1 = 0$, negative for $p_1 = 1$, and hence assuming the value zero for some value $\bar{p}_1$ of p_1 in the interval $[0, 1]$. By choosing b arbitrarily small, $\bar{p}_1$ can be made to be as close to 1 as desired when $c_2 > c_1$ and arbitrarily close to zero when $c_2 < c_1$.

In summary, considering the Markov process $\{p(n)\}_{n \geq 0}$ we have for the three cases of L_{R-P}, $L_{R-\epsilon P}$ and L_{R-I}

$$\Delta p_1(n) \triangleq E[p_1(n+1)|p_1(n)] - p_1(n)$$

$$\Delta p_1(n) = ac_2[1 - p_1] - ac_1p_1 \qquad [L_{R-P}]$$

$$\Delta p_1(n) = b[(1 - p_1)^2 c_2 - p_1^2 c_1] + ap_1(1 - p_1)(c_2 - c_1) \quad [L_{R-\epsilon P}]$$

and

$$\Delta p_1(n) = ap_1(1 - p_1)(c_2 - c_1). \qquad [L_{R-I}]$$

$$(4.26)$$

Variance: When the parameters a and b are small, the theory of Markov processes that evolve by small steps due to Norman (1972) can be used to characterize the process $\{p(n)\}_{n \geq 0}$. If $\delta p(n) \triangleq p(n+1) - p(n)$, this approach attempts to characterize the sample path behavior of the process from the values of parameters a and b and the mean and variance of $\delta p(n)$ conditioned on $p(n) = p$. As defined in the previous subsection we have

$$\Delta p_1(n) = E[\delta p_1(n)|p_1(n)]. \qquad (4.27)$$

The conditional variance of $\delta p_1(n)$ defined as $S(p_1)$ where

$$S(p_1) = E[(\delta p_1(n) - \Delta p_1(n))^2 | p_1(n)]$$

for the three cases described above can be computed as follows:

$$S(p_1) = a^2[c_1 p_1^2 + c_2(1 - p_1)^2 + (1 - c_1 - c_2)p_1(1 - p_1)] \quad (L_{R-P})$$

$$S(p_1) = a^2 p_1(1 - p_1)[1 - c_1(1 - p_1) - c_2 p_1] + b^2[p_1^3 c_1 + (1 - p_1)^3 c_2] \quad (L_{R-\epsilon P})$$

and

$$S(p_1) = a^2 p_1(1 - p_1)[1 - c_1(1 - p_1) - c_2 p_1] \qquad (L_{R-I}).$$

$$(4.28)$$

4.6.4 Qualitative Description of the Sample Path Behavior of $\{p(n)\}_{n \geq 0}$

In Chapter 5 the behavior of ergodic processes (the general L_{R-P} with $b \in (0, 1]$) and processes with absorbing states is analyzed in detail. In this section we briefly outline the differences in the sample path behavior of such automata.

As stated in earlier sections, the L_{R-I} scheme is nonergodic and the Markov process $\{p(n)\}_{n\geq 0}$ converges to the absorbing set with probability one. The absorbing set V_2 in the two–action case contains the two elements e_1 and e_2. Hence any sample path is such that asymptotically $p(n) = e_i$ w.p.1 or only one action is chosen with probability 1. The probability with which the process converges to e_1 or e_2 depends on the initial state $p(0)$ and the penalty probabilities c_1 and c_2. To make the scheme ϵ–optimal the parameter a is chosen sufficiently small so that the probability of converging to the optimal action is as close to 1 as desired. Hence in an ϵ–optimal L_{R-I} scheme we can say that starting from an initial state $p(0)$ the process will asymptotically evolve to a single action along any sample path and the probability that this is the optimal action can be made arbitrarily close to one.

In contrast to the above discussion, the general L_{R-P} scheme with $b \neq 0$ has no absorbing states and is ergodic. The action probability vector $p(n)$ converges in distribution to a random variable p^* which is independent of the initial state $p(0)$. The mean and variance of p^* depend on a, b and the penalty probabilities. In the case of the $L_{R-\epsilon P}$ scheme which is ϵ–optimal, the mean value of p^* can be made as close as desired to the optimal unit vector by choosing a and b sufficiently small.

Due to the ergodic nature of the process $p(n)$, every sample path is typical of the process. Hence the use of the $L_{R-\epsilon P}$ scheme implies that the probability of choosing the optimal action asymptotically along any sample path can be made arbitrarily close to unity. This fact has major implications in nonstationary environments discussed in Chapters 7–9.

4.7   Multi–Action Learning Automata

The results derived in Section 4.6 for the linear schemes with two actions carry over to multi–action automata also. The general scheme corresponding to Eq.(4.14) is obtained by substituting

$$
\begin{aligned}
g_j[p(n)] &= ap_j(n) & 0 < a < 1 \\
h_j[p(n)] &= \tfrac{b}{r-1} - bp_j(n) & 0 < b < 1.
\end{aligned}
\tag{4.29}
$$

This yields the following scheme corresponding to the general L_{R-P} case:

If

$$\alpha(n) = \alpha_i$$

$$p_i(n+1) = p_i(n) + a[1 - p_i(n)] \qquad \beta(n) = 0$$

$$p_j(n+1) = (1 - a)p_j(n), \; j \neq i \qquad\qquad\qquad (4.30)$$

$$p_i(n+1) = (1 - b)p_i(n) \qquad \beta(n) = 1$$

$$p_j(n+1) = \tfrac{b}{r-1} + (1 - b)p_j(n), \; j \neq i.$$

The updating equations for the L_{R-P} and L_{R-I} scheme are obtained by substituting $b = a$ and $b = 0$ respectively in Eq.(4.30).

4.7.1 L_{R-P} Scheme

If an L_{R-P} automaton using the scheme of Eq.(4.30) with $b = a$ operates in a stationary random environment, the difference equation for the evolution of the expected value of $p(n)$ may be derived as in the two–action case. This has the form

$$E[p_i(n+1)] = (1 - ac_i)E[p_i(n)] + \sum_{j \neq i} \frac{ac_j}{(r-1)} E[p_j(n)]. \qquad (4.31)$$

Combining equations of the form in Eq.(4.31) for all i in a matrix form, we have

$$E[p(n+1)] = A^T E[p(n)] \qquad\qquad (4.32)$$

where A is an $(r \times r)$ matrix with elements

$$a_{ii} = (1 - ac_i) \; ; \; a_{ij} = ac_i/(r-1) \qquad \begin{array}{l} j = 1, 2, \ldots, r \\ j \neq i. \end{array} \qquad (4.33)$$

Since each $a_{ij} \geq 0$ for all i, j and $\sum_{j=1}^{r} a_{ij} = 1$, A is a stochastic matrix. The eigenvalues of A are on or inside the unit circle. Further, it can be shown that there is only one eigenvalue on the unit circle and this corresponds to unity. The asymptotic solution of the set of difference equations (4.32) is the eigenvector of A corresponding to the unity eigenvalue and is given by

$$\lim_{n \to \infty} E[p_i(n)] = \frac{1/c_i}{\sum_{j=1}^{r} 1/c_j} \qquad (i = 1, \ldots, r). \qquad (4.34)$$

It immediately follows that

$$\lim_{n \to \infty} E[p_i(n)] \; \begin{array}{c} > \\ < \end{array} \; \lim_{n \to \infty} E[p_j(n)] \qquad\qquad (4.35)$$

according as $c_i \begin{smallmatrix} < \\ > \end{smallmatrix} c_j$, or the expected probability of the ith action is greater than that of the jth action, if the penalty probability c_i is less than c_j and vice versa. In short, actions corresponding to lower penalty probabilities are chosen with higher expected probabilities and the odering of $\lim_{n \to \infty} E[p_i(n)]$ is the reverse of the corresponding penalty probabilities c_i.

It also follows from Eq.(4.34) that

$$\lim_{n \to \infty} E[M(n)] = \frac{r}{\sum_{j=1}^{r} 1/c_j} < \frac{\sum_{j=1}^{r} c_j}{r} = M_0 \qquad (4.36)$$

and, hence, an automaton using the L_{R-P} scheme is expedient for all initial action probabilities and in all stationary random environments.

4.7.2 L_{R-I} Scheme

With $b = 0$ in Eq.(4.30) the multi–action L_{R-I} scheme can be expressed as follows:

If

$$\alpha(n) = \alpha_i$$
$$p_i(n + 1) = p_i(n) + a[1 - p_i(n)] \qquad\qquad \beta(n) = 0$$
$$p_j(n + 1) = (1 - a)p_j(n), \ j \neq i \qquad\qquad\qquad (4.37)$$

and

$$p_i(n + 1) = p_i(n) \qquad \text{for all } i \text{ if} \qquad \beta(n) = 1.$$

Proceeding as in the two–action case

$$\begin{aligned} \Delta p_i(n) &= E[p_i(n + 1)|p(n)] - p_i(n) \\ &= ap_i(n) \sum_{j \neq i}^{r} p_j(n)(c_j - c_i). \end{aligned} \qquad (4.38)$$

If $c_\ell = \min_i\{c_i\}$ and $c_h = \max_i\{c_i\}$ are unique, $(c_j - c_\ell) > 0$ $j \neq \ell$, and $(c_j - c_h) < 0$ $j \neq h$. Hence it follows that

$$\Delta p_\ell(n) > 0$$

and $\qquad\qquad\qquad\qquad\qquad\qquad\qquad\qquad\qquad\qquad (4.39)$

$$\Delta p_h(n) < 0 \qquad\qquad \text{for } p_\ell(n), p_h(n) \in (0, 1).$$

Furthermore $E[p_\ell(n)]$ is monotonically increasing and $E[p_h(n)]$ is monotonically decreasing with n whenever $p_\ell(n), p_h(n) \in (0, 1)$. The states

$e_1, e_2, \ldots, e_r$ are the absorbing states of the Markov process and in Chapter 5 it is shown that $\{p(n)\}_{n \geq 0}$ converges to the set V_r w.p.1. Further by making the parameter a arbitrarily small one can make

$$Pr\{\lim_{n \to \infty} p_\ell(n) = 1\} \qquad (4.40)$$

as close to unity as desired i.e., make the learning automata ϵ–optimal.

Examples 3.1–3.3 described in Chapter 3 in the context of fixed-structure automata can also be used to illustrate how variable-structure automata may find application in simple situations.

Example 4.1: In the game described in Example 3.1a the automaton operates in $(N - 2)/2$ of the states. Since the reward probability is known to be the same for all states, a single variable-structure automaton will suffice in this case. When the reward probability varies from state to state, a set of $(N - 2)/2$ lower level automata need to be used, with each automaton corresponding to one of the states. In this case the convergence time is considerably longer, since each of the automata updates its probabilities only when the corresponding state is visited.

Example 4.2: Let an automaton be used as a sensor in a situation described in Example 3.2. If the automaton is of the variable-structure type, it can be considered as one having ten actions. The probabilities $d_j(j = 1, 2, \ldots, 10)$ correspond to the reward probabilities of the environment and hence if the automaton is of the L_{R-I} type, it will converge to the optimal action (action state 4) with a probability arbitrarily close to 1. The rate of convergence depends both on the learning parameter a as well as the magnitude of the probability d_4 relative to $d_i(i \neq 4)$.

Example 4.3: In Example 3.3 the bug B has to determine the regions $D_i(i = 1, 2)$ in which the actions α_i are optimal. The reward probabilities corresponding to each action α_i is assumed to vary from point to point in $\mathcal{R}^2$. If variable-structure automata are used in the place of the fixed-structure automata described in Example 3.3, the probabilities of the automaton A_i are updated as long as B is in the ith sector. Simulation studies on a bug that executes a random walk with a deterministic angular component yielded the following probabilities for action α_1 in the twelve sectors after 600 steps.

$$p^1 = .036, p^2 = .965, p^3 = .741, p^4 = .953, p^5 = .914, p^6 = .886,$$
$$p^7 = .274, p^8 = .112, p^9 = .003, p^{10} = .013, p^{11} = .014, p^{12} = .008$$

This indicates that sectors 2, 3, 4, 5, and 6 may lie in D_1 while sectors 8, 9, 10, 11, and 12 lie in D_2 with the curve Γ lying in sectors 1 and 7.

4.8   Some Nonlinear Learning Schemes

Early studies of reinforcement schemes were centered mostly around linear schemes, and, in particular, the L_{R-P} scheme, for reasons of analytical simplicity. A few attempts were, however, made to study nonlinear schemes. These were mostly confined to the case of two actions, as it was not clear how the nonlinear increments were to be distributed among the various actions not selected by the automaton. Below we give some of the early nonlinear schemes put forward on a heuristic basis.

Nonlinear Scheme 1 (Shapiro and Narendra, 1969):

This is a modification of the first nonlinear scheme proposed by Varshavski and Vorontsova for the two–action automaton in terms of transition probabilities. Shapiro and Narendra extended it to the r–action automaton and gave a modified form using action probabilities. In terms of the general reinforcement scheme of Eq.(4.5), this scheme corresponds to the choice[3]

$$g_j(p(n)) = \frac{a}{r-1}p_i(n)(1 - p_i(n)) = h_j(p(n)) \tag{4.41}$$

where $0 < a \leq 1$.

Thus, the scheme distributes the nonlinear increment $ap_i(n)(1 - p_i(n))$ equally among all the actions not selected by the automaton at the instant n. It may also be noted that $g_j(p)$ depends on α_i, the action chosen and is not strictly in the class of schemes in Eq.(4.5).

Consider the two–action case for a simple understanding of the scheme. Proceeding along familiar lines,

$$\Delta p_1(n) = ap_1(1 - p_1)[(2c_2 - 1) + 2(1 - c_1 - c_2)p_1], \tag{4.42}$$

where the argument n is omitted on the r.h.s. Since $\Delta p_1(n) + \Delta p_2(n) = 0$ for all n, one can conclude from Eq.(4.42) that

$$\text{if } c_1 < \frac{1}{2} < c_2 \tag{4.43}$$

$$\Delta p_1(n) > 0 \qquad \text{and} \qquad \Delta p_2(n) < 0 \tag{4.44}$$

whenever $p_1 \in (0, 1)$.

Similarly, if

$$c_2 < \frac{1}{2} < c_1 \tag{4.45}$$

---

[3]As in Eq.(4.5), $\alpha(n) = \alpha_i$ is assumed in the description of the various schemes that follow.

$$\Delta p_1(n) < 0 \qquad \text{and} \qquad \Delta p_2(n) > 0. \qquad (4.46)$$

Thus, a proper sign definiteness of $\Delta p_i(n)$ is assured, provided the additional restrictions of Eqs.(4.43) or (4.45) are imposed on the environment. It can also be seen that

$$\Delta M(n) = \Delta p_1(n)(c_1 - c_2) < 0$$

whenever Eq.(4.43) or (4.45) is satisfied. Hence, the scheme is absolutely expedient for restricted initial conditions and for restricted environments.

A further generalization of the scheme can be obtained by making the reward and penalty increments unequal. One could choose

$$g_j(p) = ap_i(1 - p_i)$$

and $\qquad\qquad\qquad\qquad\qquad\qquad\qquad\qquad\qquad$ (4.47)

$$h_j(p) = bp_i(1 - p_i)$$

where a and b are unequal. The conditions on c_1 and c_2 to make $\Delta M(n) < 0$ must now be changed to:

$$c_1 < \frac{a}{a + b} < c_2 \qquad \text{or} \qquad c_2 < \frac{a}{a + b} < c_1 \qquad (4.48)$$

Nonlinear Scheme 2 (Chandrasekharan and Shen, 1968):

Another direction in which the scheme can be generalized was shown by Chandrasekharan and Shen. Their scheme is described by

$$g_j(p) = p_j - \phi(p_j)$$

$$h_j(p) = \frac{p_i - \phi(p_i)}{(r-1)} \qquad \begin{cases} j = 1, 2, \ldots, r \\ j \neq i \end{cases} \qquad (4.49)$$

where $0 \leq \phi(p_j) \leq p_j$.

The authors of this scheme investigated nonlinearities of the type

$$\phi(x) = ax^m \qquad \begin{matrix} (0 < a \leq 1) \\ (m = 2, 3, \ldots). \end{matrix} \qquad (4.50)$$

As expected, stringent conditions on the penalty probabilities are needed, if sign definiteness of $\Delta p_\ell(n)$ is to be assured. These take the form

$$c_\ell < \frac{1}{m}, \ c_j > \frac{1}{m} \ (j \neq \ell). \qquad (4.51)$$

Beta Model (Luce, 1959):

This scheme was originally proposed by Luce in mathematical psychology as an alternative to Bush and Mosteller's L_{R-P} scheme, referred to as the α–model. The scheme, as originally proposed, applies to the two–action case and is given by

$$g_j(p) = (b-1)p_j(1-p_j)/[b(1-p_j) + p_j]$$
$$h_j(p) = (b-1)p_j(1-p_j)/[(1-p_j) + bp_j] \qquad (j=1,2)$$
(4.52)

where[4] $b > 1$.

The expression for $\Delta p_1(n)$ is

$$\Delta p_1(n) = \frac{(b-1)p_1(1-p_1)}{[b(1-p_1) + p_1][(1-p_1) + bp_1]} \; [bc_2 - (1-c_2) + p_1(2-(b+1)(c_1+c_2))]$$
(4.53)

If we demand sign definiteness of $\Delta p_1(n)$ for all $p_1 \in (0,1)$, c_1 and c_2 have to be restricted in a suitable way which can be found from Eq.(4.53). In this respect, the Beta model follows the earlier nonlinear schemes 1 and 2.

Actually, the Beta model can be regarded as a particular case of Eq.(4.49), the nonlinear scheme of Chandrasekaran and Shen, with the choice,

$$\phi(x) = \frac{x}{b(1-x) + x}$$

and can therefore be generalized to the r–action case. It has been observed in Chandrasekaran and Shen (1968) that the performance of the Beta model in terms of the final expected values of action probabilities is very similar to the nonlinear scheme of Eq.(4.49) with $\phi(x)$ as in Eq.(4.50). Given a value of m in Eq.(4.50), one can find a, b such that the performance of the two schemes is similar.

Nonlinear Scheme 3 (Vorontsova, 1965):

The scheme proposed by Vorontsova applies only to a two–action automaton. The scheme has the form

$$g_j(p) = a\phi(p_1, 1-p_1)p_j^{\theta+1}(1-p_j)^\theta$$
$$h_j(p) = b\phi(p_1, 1-p_1)p_j^{\theta+1}(1-p_j)^\theta \qquad (j=1,2),$$
(4.54)

where

$$\phi(p_1, 1-p_1) = \phi(1-p_1, p_1)$$
(4.55)

---

[4]The parameter b was originally called β and hence the name Beta model.

is a nonlinear function which can be suitably selected and $\theta \geq 1$. The positive constants a and b must be chosen properly to satisfy the bounds in Eq.(4.7). This scheme has the distinction that the limiting case of a continuous–time automaton using the scheme is optimal. In fact, Vorontsova has developed sufficient conditions for ensuring optimality of the continuous–time automaton. The schemes described by Eq.(4.54) represent a general class that satisfies the above optimality conditions.

Nonlinear Scheme 4 (Viswanathan and Narendra, 1972):

This scheme combines the L_{R-I} scheme and Vorontsova's scheme. It is, however, again limited to the two–action case. The functions of interest are

$$g_j(p) = p_j[a_1 + a_2 p_j^\theta (1 - p_j)^\theta]$$
$$h_j(p) = b p_j^{\theta+1}(1 - p_j)^\theta \qquad (j = 1, 2) \qquad (4.56)$$

where the positive constants a_1, a_2, b are to be chosen properly to satisfy Eq.(4.7). As before, $\theta \geq 1$.

On comparison with Vorontsova's scheme of Eq.(4.54), it can be seen that

$$\phi(p_1, 1 - p_1) \equiv 1 \qquad (4.57)$$

in the present case. The scheme combines the fast speed of operation of the L_{R-I} scheme and the optimality property of the Vorontsova scheme.

Hybrid Scheme $H(L_{R-I}, \hat{L}_{R-P})$ (Viswanathan and Narendra, 1972):

This hybrid scheme is obtained by a combination of the L_{R-I} and a linear reward–penalty scheme designated as $\hat{L}_{R-P}$ scheme. The action probabilities are updated according to one of these schemes depending on the intervals in which the values of the action probabilities lie. The scheme can be described as follows:

$$g_j(p) = A_1 p_j$$
$$h_j(p) = A_2 p_j \qquad (4.58)$$

where

$$A_1 = a$$
$$A_2 = \begin{cases} a \text{ if } p_i \in [\frac{a}{1+a}, \frac{1}{1+a}] \\ 0 \text{ otherwise} \end{cases} \qquad (4.59)$$
$$0 < a < 1.$$

Thus when $\alpha(n) = \alpha_i$, the updating is done with a symmetric linear reward and penalty if,

$$\frac{a}{1+a} \leq p_i(n) \leq \frac{1}{1+a} \tag{4.60}$$

and according to the L_{R-I} scheme otherwise. The updating with $A_1 = A_2 = a$ is called the $\hat{L}_{R-P}$ scheme. It is seen that this is quite different from the L_{R-P} scheme discussed in Sections 4.6 and 4.7. It can be verified that if bounds are not put on the action probabilities, they can go outside $[0, 1]$ when updating is done in accordance with $\hat{L}_{R-P}$ scheme. However, the scheme has the merit of a fast speed of response and this is made use of in the hybrid scheme when an action probability is not near zero or one. In the vicinity of these extreme values, the properties of the L_{R-I} scheme are exploited.

Although the constituent schemes of this hybrid scheme are linear, the scheme itself is in fact nonlinear as h_j is not a linear function of p. At best, the scheme could be described as piecewise linear. One departure from the general scheme of Eq.(4.5) is that now the function h_j has a discontinuity.

Hybrid schemes using combinations of nonlinear schemes can also be generated. Some of these are described by Viswanathan and Narendra (1972). Although many of these schemes (including L_{R-I} and $\hat{L}_{R-P}$) exhibit a superior speed of operation, and hence are of interest in practical application, the main problem with them is that it is difficult to get analytical results concerning aspects of their convergence. In the section following we shall confine our attention to linear and nonlinear schemes that are analytically tractable and that can provide the basis for the precise design of learning automata.

4.9   Absolutely Expedient Schemes

The discussions in the earlier sections show clearly that evolution of early reinforcement schemes occurred mostly in a heuristic manner. Simple functions based on the concepts of reward and penalty were tried in the schemes and only the fittest of these schemes survived. Intuition was very helpful in designing schemes for the two–action case as, in effect, only one probability was being updated. Generalization of such schemes to the multi–action case was not straightforward.

Dissatisfaction with this situation led to a synthesis approach toward reinforcement schemes. The question posed was the following: What are the conditions on the functions appearing in the reinforcement scheme of an automaton that ensure a desired behavior? The problem viewed in this manner led to the concept of absolute expediency (Lakshmivarahan and Thathachar, 1973).

The importance of absolutely expedient schemes arises partly from the fact that at the present time they represent the only class of schemes for which necessary and sufficient conditions of design are available. This class of schemes can be considered as the generalization of the L_{R-I} scheme studied in Sections 4.6 and 4.7. An attractive feature of such schemes is that they are ϵ–optimal in all stationary environments.

Consider the general reinforcement scheme of Eqs.(4.5) and (4.6) which can be rewritten as follows. For any i $(i = 1, 2, \ldots, r)$,

$$
\begin{aligned}
p_i(n + 1) \ &= p_i(n) - g_i(p(n)) \text{ if } \alpha(n) \neq \alpha_i, \ \beta(n) = 0 \\
&= p_i(n) + h_i(p(n)) \text{ if } \alpha(n) \neq \alpha_i, \ \beta(n) = 1 \\
&= p_i(n) + \sum^r_{\substack{j = 1 \\ j \neq i}} g_j(p(n)) \text{ if } \alpha(n) = \alpha_i, \ \beta(n) = 0 \\
&= p_i(n) - \sum^r_{\substack{j = 1 \\ j \neq i}} h_j(p(n)) \text{ if } \alpha(n) = \alpha_i, \ \beta(n) = 1.
\end{aligned}
\tag{4.61}
$$

The functions g_j, h_j $(j = 1, \ldots, r)$ satisfy the assumptions 1, 2, and 3 of Eq.(4.7).

Defining $\Delta p_i(n)$ as in Section 4.6

$$
\begin{aligned}
\Delta p_i(n) \ &= E[p_i(n + 1) - p_i(n)|p(n)] \\
&= p_i(n) \sum^r_{\substack{j = 1 \\ j \neq i}} g_j(p(n)) - g_i(p(n)) \sum^r_{\substack{j = 1 \\ j \neq i}} p_j(n) \\
&\quad -c_i p_i(n) \sum^r_{\substack{j = 1 \\ j \neq i}} [g_j(p(n)) + h_j(p(n))] \\
&\quad +[g_i(p(n)) + h_i(p(n))] \sum^r_{\substack{j = 1 \\ j \neq i}} c_j p_j(n).
\end{aligned}
\tag{4.62}
$$

The right–hand side of Eq.(4.62) contains linear terms in c_i. Using this expression for Δp_i, the conditional expectation of the increment in $M(n)$ can be computed using the relation

$$
\begin{aligned}
\Delta M(n) \ &= E[M(n + 1) - M(n)|p(n)] \\
&= \sum^r_{i=1} c_i \Delta p_i(n).
\end{aligned}
$$

Hence $\Delta M(n)$ is a quadratic plus linear form in the variables $c_i (i = 1, 2, \ldots, r)$.

The exact form of $\Delta M(n)$ can be shown to be

$$
\begin{aligned}
\Delta M(n) \quad &= \sum_{i=1}^{r} \sum_{j\neq i}^{r} c_i c_j p_j(n)[g_i(p(n)) + h_i(p(n))] \\
&\quad - \sum_{i=1}^{r} \sum_{j\neq i}^{r} c_i^2 p_i(n)[g_j(p(n)) + h_j(p(n))] \qquad (4.63) \\
&\quad + \sum_{i=1}^{r} \sum_{j=1}^{r} c_i p_i(n) g_j(p(n)) - \sum_{i=1}^{r} c_i g_i(p(n)).
\end{aligned}
$$

or

$$
\Delta M(n) = c^T J c + c^T b \qquad (4.64)
$$

where

$$
c^T = [c_1, c_2, \ldots, c_r]
$$

$$
J \text{ is an } r \times r \text{ matrix}
$$

and

$$
b \text{ is an } r \times 1 \text{ vector with}
$$

$$
J_{ij} = p_j(g_i + h_i)
$$

$$
J_{ii} = -p_i \sum_{j\neq i}(g_j + h_j)
$$

and

$$
b_i = p_i \sum_{j=1}^{r} g_j - g_i. \qquad (4.65)
$$

When all the elements c_i are equal to c_0, $\Delta M(n) = c_0 \sum_{i=1}^{r} \Delta p_i(n) = 0$ [by the definition of $\Delta p_i(n)$], so that in a trivial random environment the conditional expectation of the change in $M(n)$ is zero. For absolute expediency the functions g_i and h_i must be so chosen that $\Delta M(n) < 0$ in all nontrivial environments. We naturally attempt to achieve this by minimizing the expression of Eq.(4.63) for $\Delta M(n)$. In the section following necessary and sufficient conditions for absolute expediency are given. These conditions make $\Delta M(n)$ quadratic in both c as well as p.

Theorem 4.1: A learning automaton using the general reinforcement scheme of Eq.(4.5) is absolutely expedient, if and only if, the $g_i(p)$ and $h_i(p)$ satisfy the following symmetry conditions:

$$
\frac{g_1(p)}{p_1} = \frac{g_2(p)}{p_2} = \cdots = \frac{g_r(p)}{p_r} \qquad (4.66)
$$

and

$$
\frac{h_1(p)}{p_1} = \frac{h_2(p)}{p_2} = \cdots = \frac{h_r(p)}{p_r}. \qquad (4.67)
$$

Proof:

Sufficiency: We first consider the sufficiency of the conditions of Eqs.(4.66) and (4.67) for absolute expediency. Let

$$g_i(p)/p_i = \lambda(p)$$

and
$$\tag{4.68}$$

$$h_i(p)/p_i = \mu(p) \qquad (i = 1, 2, \ldots, r)$$

Substituting Eq.(4.68) in Eq.(4.63) we obtain

$$\Delta M = [\lambda(p) + \mu(p)][\textstyle\sum_i \sum_{j \neq i} c_i c_j p_i p_j - \sum_i \sum_{j \neq i} c_i^2 p_i p_j]$$
$$+ \lambda(p)[\textstyle\sum_i \sum_j c_i p_i p_j - \sum_i c_i p_i]. \tag{4.69}$$

The last term in Eq.(4.69) is zero since $\sum_{j=1}^r p_j = 1$. Hence, we have

$$\Delta M = [\lambda(p) + \mu(p)][\sum_i \sum_{j \neq i} (c_i c_j - c_i^2) p_i p_j]. \tag{4.70}$$

The latter part of the expression of Eq.(4.70) is a quadratic form in p. Taking the symmetric part of the matrix defining the quadratic form,

$$\Delta M = [\lambda(p) + \mu(p)]p^T C p \tag{4.71}$$

where C is a symmetric $r \times r$ matrix with elements

$$C_{ij} = [(c_i c_j - c_i^2) + (c_j c_i - c_j^2)]/2 = -\tfrac{1}{2}(c_i - c_j)^2$$
$$C_{ii} = 0. \tag{4.72}$$

Thus, C consists only of negative or zero elements and hence $p^T C p \leq 0$ for all p. Further, whenever all the penalty probabilities c_i are not equal, there are at least some nonzero elements of C. Thus, when all the $p_i \in (0,1)$,

$$p^T C p < 0 \tag{4.73}$$

from Eq.(4.70). Also from Eqs.(4.7) and (4.68) $\lambda(p) + \mu(p) > 0$ and Eq.(4.71) leads to

$$\Delta M(n) < 0 \tag{4.74}$$

for all n. This by definition corresponds to absolute expediency.

Necessity: We now consider the necessity of the conditions Eqs.(4.66)–(4.67). For a proof of this part, we start from the given condition that $\Delta M(n) < 0$

for all c except those which have all their components c_i equal and show that Eqs.(4.66)–(4.67) follow.

The given conditions imply that $\Delta M(n)$ of Eq.(4.64), over the region

$$\{0 \leq c_i \leq 1; \ i = 1, 2, \ldots, r\}, \tag{4.75}$$

is negative–semidefinite and has maxima (corresponding to value zero) only at those c which satisfy

$$c_1 = c_2 = c_3 = \ldots = c_r = c_0 \tag{4.76}$$

for arbitrary c_0. $(0 \leq c_0 \leq 1)$.

A necessary condition for such a result is that Eq.(4.76) must be the only solutions of the set of equations

$$\frac{\partial \Delta M(n)}{\partial c_k} = 0 \qquad (k = 1, \ldots, r). \tag{4.77}$$

Using Eq.(4.64), Eq.(4.77) takes the form,

$$(J + J^T)c + b = 0. \tag{4.78}$$

Using Eqs.(4.76) and (4.65) it can be seen that Eq.(4.78) takes the form

$$c_0[g_k + h_k - p_k \sum_{j=1}^{r}(g_j + h_j)] + p_k \sum_{j=1}^{r} g_j - g_k = 0. \tag{4.79}$$

Equation (4.79) holds good for every c_0 satisfying

$$0 \leq c_0 \leq 1.$$

This is possible, if and only if,

$$g_k + h_k - p_k \sum_{j=1}^{r}(g_j + h_j) = 0 \tag{4.80}$$

and

$$p_k \sum_{j=1}^{r} g_j - g_k = 0 \qquad (k = 1, 2, \ldots, r). \tag{4.81}$$

This in turn means that

$$\frac{g_k}{p_k} = \sum_{j=1}^{r} g_j \qquad (k = 1, 2, \ldots, r) \tag{4.82}$$

or the condition of Eq.(4.66) is satisfied. Substituting this in Eq.(4.80) gives

$$\frac{h_k}{p_k} = \sum_{j=1}^{r} h_j \qquad (k = 1, 2, \ldots, r) \qquad (4.83)$$

which shows that the condition of Eq.(4.67) must be satisfied.

Comment 4.2: An important consequence of Theorem 4.1 is that even though apparently there are 2r arbitrary functions $g_i(p), h_i(p)$ in the re-inforcement scheme of Eq.(4.5), the number is reduced to only two functions $\lambda(p)$ and $\mu(p)$ when we demand absolute expediency. Once $\lambda(p)$ and $\mu(p)$ are specified, $g_i(p)$ and $h_i(p)$ $(i = 1, 2, \ldots, r)$ can be obtained from Eq.(4.68). Equations (4.68), (4.82), and (4.83) further give the relations $\lambda(p) = \sum_{j=1}^{r} g_j(p)$, $\mu(p) = \sum_{j=1}^{r} h_j(p)$. In terms of these functions the most general absolutely expedient scheme can be written as follows.

For any i $(i = 1, 2, \ldots, r)$,

$$\left.\begin{aligned}
p_i(n+1) &= p_i(n)[1 - \lambda(p(n))] \text{ if } \alpha(n) \neq \alpha_i, \ \beta(n) = 0 \\
&= p_i(n)[1 + \mu(p(n))] \text{ if } \alpha(n) \neq \alpha_i, \ \beta(n) = 1 \\
&= p_i(n) + \lambda(p(n))(1 - p_i(n)) \text{ if } \alpha(n) = \alpha_i, \ \beta(n) = 0 \\
&= p_i(n) - \mu(p(n))(1 - p_i(n)) \text{ if } \alpha(n) = \alpha_i, \ \beta(n) = 1.
\end{aligned}\right\}$$

$$(4.84)$$

The assumptions 1 to 3 made on g_j and h_j can be translated to λ and μ as

follows:

$\lambda(p)$ and $\mu(p)$ are continuous functions mapping S_r into $\mathcal{R}[0, 1]$.

Further

$$\left.\begin{aligned}
&0 < \lambda(p) < 1 \\
\text{and} \qquad &0 \leq \mu(p) < \min_i \{p_i/1 - p_i\}
\end{aligned}\right\} \qquad (4.85)$$

whenever all the components of p are in $(0, 1)$.

Comment 4.3: Reward–inaction schemes can be obtained by setting $\mu(p) \equiv 0$. In particular, the L_{R-I} scheme corresponds to the choice,

$$\lambda(p) \equiv a, \quad \mu(p) \equiv 0. \qquad (4.86)$$

In a similar way, inaction–penalty schemes can be obtained by setting $\lambda(p) \equiv 0$. This choice is apparently not permissible in Eq.(4.85). However, by going back to Eq.(4.7), replacing the condition on $g_j(p)$ by

$$0 \leq g_j(p) < p_j \tag{4.87}$$

and proceeding as before, one can permit $\lambda(p) \equiv 0$. This must be accompanied by

$$0 < \mu(p) < \min_i \frac{p_i}{1 - p_i} \tag{4.88}$$

so that

$$p(n+1) \neq p(n)$$

whenever all the components of $p(n)$ are in $(0,1)$.

Comment 4.4: The conditions of Eq.(4.85) show that there is once again an asymmetry with regard to the functions λ and μ associated with reward and penalty. The conditions on μ are much more stringent than those on λ. Qualitatively, one could say that the functions appearing in the "penalty" part of a reinforcement scheme should be chosen much more carefully than the functions appearing in the "reward" part. Equation (4.85) further implies that

$$\mu(p) = 0$$

whenever any component p_i of p is zero. Thus a typical choice of $\mu(p)$ would be

$$\mu(p) = bp_1 p_2 \ldots p_r \tag{4.89}$$

where the positive constant b is suitably chosen. It also follows that μ cannot be chosen as a nonzero constant unlike λ. This explains why, among linear reward–penalty schemes, the limiting case of L_{R-I} scheme is the only one which is absolutely expedient.

Comment 4.5: Generalizing the idea in Eq.(4.89), Lakshmivarahan and Thathachar (1973) proposed the following absolutely expedient algorithm.

$$\lambda(p) = ap_1^{\theta_1} p_2^{\theta_2} \ldots p_r^{\theta_r}$$
$$\mu(p) = bp_1^{\theta} p_2^{\theta} \ldots p_r^{\theta}$$

where $\theta_i \geq 0$, $\theta \geq 0$.

The nonnegative constants a, b are to be chosen properly depending on $\{\theta_i\}$, θ and r so as to satisfy Eq.(4.7). One could also use linear combinations of the terms given provided Eq.(4.7) is not violated.

Other schemes given in the previous section, such as the hybrid scheme and nonlinear schemes 3 and 4, can also be seen to be absolutely expedient.

Comment 4.6: The nonnegativity condition on λ and μ is required only for maintaining the reward–penalty character of the two functions. One could relax this condition without affecting absolute expediency. Thus, one could consider reward–reward schemes where $\lambda \geq 0$, $\mu \leq 0$ and penalty–penalty schemes where $\lambda \leq 0$, $\mu \geq 0$. Only the lower limits in Eq.(4.85) are modified in such cases, as follows:

$$- \min_j \left(\frac{p_j}{1-p_j} \right) < \lambda(p) < 1.$$
$$-1 < \mu(p) < \min_j \left(\frac{p_j}{1-p_j} \right).$$

In addition one must ensure that $\lambda(p) + \mu(p) > 0$ for every p whose components are all in $(0,1)$. Thus $\mu(p)$ can be a negative constant and hence linear reward–reward schemes are absolutely expedient.

Comment 4.7: It is useful to explore the effect of the symmetry conditions of Eqs.(4.66)–(4.67) on the form of ΔM in Eq.(4.63). One can immediately see from Eq.(4.65) that

$$b_i = 0 \ (i = 1, \ldots, r)$$

and

$$J_{ij} = [\lambda(p) + \mu(p)]p_i p_j \qquad (i \neq j)$$
$$J_{ii} = -[\lambda(p) + \mu(p)]p_i(1 - p_i). \tag{4.90}$$

The quantities in Eq.(4.90) can be checked to form a negative–semidefinite matrix J. Thus symmetry conditions reduce ΔM to the negative–semidefinite quadratic form

$$\Delta M = c^T J c. \tag{4.91}$$

Referring to Eqs.(4.71) and (4.73), ΔM can also be alternatively expressed in terms of a negative–semidefinite quadratic form in p as

$$\Delta M = [\lambda(p) + \mu(p)]p^T C p. \tag{4.92}$$

Either of the two forms can be used depending on the demands of the situation.

Comment 4.8: It may be observed from the updating schemes of Eq.(4.84) that the symmetry conditions force the reinforcement scheme to update the probability of the action selected by the automaton at an instant n in one manner and all the other action probabilities in another manner. No distinction is made between the actions not selected by the automaton in the sense that, if $\alpha(n) = \alpha_j$, $p_i(n+1)/p_i(n)$ is the same for all $i \neq j$.

Comment 4.9: It has been observed (Eq. 4.39) that a useful property of the L_{R-I} scheme is that $\Delta p_\ell(n) > 0$ in all stationary environments with a unique c_ℓ. It is worth investigating whether this desirable property is shared by all absolutely expedient schemes. We will deal with this problem in Theorem 4.2. However, to simplify further analysis, we make the following assumption regarding the environment. The penalty probability c_ℓ defined by:

$$c_\ell = \min_i \{c_i\} \tag{4.93}$$

is unique. With this restriction we explore the sign definiteness of $\Delta p_\ell(n)$ in the following theorem.

Theorem 4.2: Consider a learning automaton with a general reinforcement scheme of Eq.(4.5) and operating in any stationary random environment with unique c_ℓ as in Eq.(4.93). The condition

$$\Delta p_\ell(n) > 0 \tag{4.94}$$

holds for all n, all $p(n) \in S_r^0$ and all environments considered above, if and only if,

$$\frac{g_1(p)}{p_1} = \frac{g_2(p)}{p_2} = \cdots = \frac{g_r(p)}{p_r} \tag{4.95}$$

and

$$\frac{h_1(p)}{p_1} = \frac{h_2(p)}{p_2} = \cdots = \frac{h_r(p)}{p_r}. \tag{4.96}$$

Proof:

Sufficiency: Using the symmetry conditions of Eqs.(4.95) and (4.96) in Eq.(4.62) and simplifying,

$$\Delta p_i(n) = [g_i(p(n)) + h_i(p(n))] \sum_{j=1}^{r} p_j(n)(c_j - c_i). \tag{4.97}$$

Noting that

$$c_j - c_\ell > 0 \qquad \forall j \neq \ell$$

and that

$$g_i(p(n)) + h_i(p(n)) > 0$$

when $p(n) \in S_r^0$, it follows that Eq.(4.94) holds.

Necessity: The necessity proof is based on the fact that the automaton operates with the same reinforcement scheme in any environment in which it is placed. Hence if a condition on the functions in the reinforcement scheme is needed in a specific environment it is also needed in general.

Rewriting the expression for $\Delta p_\ell(n)$ from Eq.(4.62)

$$\Delta p_\ell(n) = p_\ell \sum_{j=1}^{r} g_j - g_\ell - c_\ell p_\ell \sum_{j=1}^{r}(g_j + h_j) + (g_\ell + h_\ell) \sum_{j=1}^{r} c_j p_j \qquad (4.98)$$

where the arguments of the r.h.s. are suppressed as in the proof of Theorem 4.1. Thus p_ℓ denotes $p_\ell(n)$ etc. In writing Eq.(4.98) i is set equal to ℓ in Eq.(4.62) and also terms corresponding to $j = i$ are added. All such terms however, cancel.

Let

$$c_j = c_\ell + \delta_j \qquad (4.99)$$

where $\delta_j > 0$ from Eq.(4.93) for all $j \neq \ell$. Now Eq.(4.98) can be rewritten as

$$\Delta p_\ell(n) = \; [p_\ell(n) \textstyle\sum_{j=1}^{r} g_j - g_\ell] + c_\ell[h_\ell - p_\ell \sum_{j=1}^{r} h_j + g_\ell - p_\ell \sum_{j=1}^{r} g_j]$$
$$+(g_\ell + h_\ell) \textstyle\sum_{j=1}^{r} \delta_j p_j.$$
$$(4.100)$$

The δ_j can be arbitrarily small. Also c_ℓ can take any value in $[0, 1)$. Hence if $\Delta p_\ell(n) > 0$ in all environments, it is necessary that

$$p_\ell \sum_{j=1}^{r} g_j - g_\ell \geq 0. \qquad (4.101)$$

The subscript ℓ can take any value from 1 to r. For Eq.(4.101) to hold in each such case,

$$p_i \sum_{j=1}^{r} g_j - g_i \geq 0 \qquad (i = 1, \ldots, r). \qquad (4.102)$$

It will next be shown by contradiction that Eq.(4.102) is an equality.

Suppose Eq.(4.102) is a strict inequality. Summing the l.h.s. over all i and noting $\sum_{i=1}^{r} p_i = 1$,

$$\sum_{j=1}^{r} g_j - \sum_{i=1}^{r} g_i > 0, \qquad (4.103)$$

which is a contradiction. Hence, for all n,

$$p_i \sum_{j=1}^{r} g_j - g_i = 0 \qquad (i = 1, \ldots, r). \qquad (4.104)$$

Rewriting Eq.(4.104),

$$\frac{g_i}{p_i} = \sum_{j=1}^{r} g_j \qquad (i = 1, \ldots, r) \qquad (4.105)$$

thus resulting in Eq.(4.95).

Substituting Eq.(4.105) in Eq.(4.100) and following the same arguments as for g_j, the condition Eq.(4.96) can be derived.

Comment 4.10: The property of positivity exhibited by $\Delta p_\ell(n)$ and its equivalence with symmetry conditions can be extended to another action probability as well. Suppose

$$c_h = \max_i\{c_i\} \qquad (4.106)$$

and is unique. It can then be shown that

$$\Delta p_h(n) < 0 \qquad (4.107)$$

for all $p(n) \in S_r^0$, all n and all stationary random environments is again equivalent to the symmetry conditions.

Comment 4.11: The role of uniqueness of c_ℓ in Theorem 4.2 can be probed further. If more than one penalty probability has the minimum value c_ℓ, it can be seen from Eq.(4.97) that

$$\Delta p_\ell(n) = 0$$

even for some points $p(n) \in S_r^0$. Thus the strict inequality $\Delta p_\ell(n) > 0$ is not valid over S_r^0. However $\Delta p_\ell(n) \geq 0$ continues to hold and so does $\Delta p_h(n) \leq 0$.

Comment 4.12: Theorem 4.1 established the equivalence of absolute expediency and the symmetry conditions. Theorem 4.2, in turn, proved that the symmetry conditions are equivalent to the sign definiteness of $\Delta p_\ell(n)$. Hence the latter condition is an alternative necessary and sufficient condition for absolute expediency when c_ℓ is unique. From comment 4.9 it follows that $\Delta p_h(n) < 0$ is also an equivalent condition when c_h is unique.

Comment 4.13: The sign definiteness of $\Delta p_\ell(n)$ implies, as observed earlier, that $E[p_\ell(n)]$ is monotonically increasing *w.r.t* n. Theorem 4.2 leads us to the comforting thought that by using absolutely expedient schemes we are making $p_\ell(n)$ move in the right direction at least in an expected value sense. Similar remarks hold for $p_h(n)$.

Comment 4.14: Although symmetry conditions identify a fairly wide class of absolutely expedient schemes, they do not exhaust such schemes. The key to the recognition of other classes of absolutely expedient schemes is the modification of the basic reinforcement scheme of Eq.(4.5) or (4.61). One such example follows:

If $\alpha(n) = \alpha_i$,

$$
\left.
\begin{aligned}
p_i(n+1) &= p_i(n) + g_i(p(n)), \\
p_j(n+1) &= p_j(n) - g_i(p(n))/(r-1), \quad (j \neq i)
\end{aligned}
\right\} \quad \text{if } \beta(n) = 0
$$

$$
\left.
\begin{aligned}
p_i(n+1) &= p_i(n) - h_i(p(n)), \\
p_j(n+1) &= p_j(n) + h_i(p(n))/(r-1), \quad (j \neq i)
\end{aligned}
\right\} \text{if } \beta(n) = 1. \quad (4.108)
$$

In the updating scheme above, the increments depend on the action chosen and the functions g_i, h_i associated with this action. The increments of the probabilities of actions not selected are all equal. As before, some conditions are needed on g_i, h_i for keeping the probabilities in $[0,1]$.

Going through arguments similar to those in Theorem 4.1 it can be shown that necessary and sufficient conditions for a learning automaton using Eq.(4.108) to be absolutely expedient are

$$
\left.
\begin{aligned}
&\text{(a) } g_1(p)p_1 = g_2(p)p_2 = \cdots = g_r(p)p_r \\
&\text{(b) } h_1(p)p_1 = h_2(p)p_2 = \cdots = h_r(p)p_r
\end{aligned}
\right\} . \quad (4.109)
$$

Consequently, as in the earlier class of absolutely expedient schemes, only two functions control the updating of all action probabilities. The distinction between the two classes of schemes is that in the former case the increments g_j, h_j of the probabilities of actions not selected are proportional to p_j whereas such increments are all equal in the latter case.

Comment 4.15: The most general absolutely expedient scheme known thus far has been given by Aso and Kimura (1979). The updating functions in this scheme depend on both the action chosen and the action probability being updated. Any reinforcement scheme of this type can be represented as follows:

If $\alpha(n) = \alpha_i$,

$$
\begin{aligned}
p_j(n+1) &= p_j(n) - g_{ij}(p(n)) && \text{if } \beta(n) = 0 \\
p_j(n+1) &= p_j(n) + h_{ij}(p(n)) && \text{if } \beta(n) = 1.
\end{aligned}
\tag{4.110}
$$

Correspondingly,

$$
\begin{aligned}
p_i(n+1) &= p_i(n) + \sum_{j \neq i} g_{ij}(p(n)) && \text{if } \beta(n) = 0 \\
p_i(n+1) &= p_i(n) - \sum_{j \neq i} h_{ij}(p(n)) && \text{if } \beta(n) = 1.
\end{aligned}
$$

In the scheme above, g_{ij} and h_{ij} are continuous functions that map the open simplex S_r^o into the interval $(0, 1)$ and further satisfy the probability preserving conditions

$$
\begin{aligned}
&\text{i)} && g_{ij}(p(n)) < p_j(n) \\
&\text{ii)} \sum_{j \neq i} && h_{ij}(p(n)) < p_i(n)
\end{aligned}
\tag{4.111}
$$

for all i and j and for all $p(n) \in S_r^o$.

It can be checked that Eq.(4.110) includes Eqs.(4.5)–(4.6) and Eq.(4.108) as particular cases.

Let $G(p)$ and $H(p)$ be $r \times r$ matrices whose $(i, j)^{th}$ elements are $g_{ij}(p)$ and $h_{ij}(p)$ respectively. Let the $(i, i)^{th}$ diagonal elements of the two matrices be defined by

$$
\begin{aligned}
g_{ii}(p) &= - \sum_{j \neq i} g_{ij}(p) \\
h_{ii}(p) &= - \sum_{j \neq i} h_{ij}(p).
\end{aligned}
\tag{4.112}
$$

In terms of the notation above, necessary and sufficient conditions for a learning automaton using Eq.(4.110) to be absolutely expedient can be stated as follows:

$$
\begin{aligned}
&\text{(i)} && p^T G(p) = 0 \\
&\text{(ii)} && p^T H(p) = 0
\end{aligned}
\tag{4.113}
$$

for all $p \in S_r^o$.

It is easy to show that the conditions of Eq.(4.113) reduce to Eqs.(4.95)–(4.96) or Eq.(4.109) as special cases.

Meybodi and Lakshmivarahan (1982) have shown the ϵ–optimality of the algorithm in stationary random environments.

4.10 Simulation Results

The various learning schemes discussed in Sections 4.6 to 4.9 have been simulated extensively on the digital computer and we discuss briefly in this section some of the major conclusions that have been drawn from them. The applicability of an automaton in a practical situation depends to a large extent on its speed of convergence as well as how closely it approaches optimal behavior (refer to Chapter 9). In fact, speed and accuracy generally serve as a basis of comparison of various schemes. The number of actions r of the automaton, the penalty probabilities $c_i (i = 1, 2, \ldots, r)$ of the environment and the reward and penalty parameters a and b of the algorithms are some of the factors that influence these characteristics and their separate effects are considered here. Three typical examples, corresponding to environments with two, five, and ten actions respectively, have been chosen for presenting the results of the simulation studies (Viswanathan and Narendra, 1971).

Problem I : $r = 2$ (two actions)

Penalty probabilities : $c_1 = 0.4, \ c_2 = 0.8$

Problem II : $r = 5$ (five actions)

$c_1 = 0.65, c_2 = 0.2, c_3 = 0.5, c_4 = 0.4, c_5 = 0.85$

Problem III : $r = 10$ (ten actions)

$c_1 = 0.9, c_2 = 0.55, c_3 = 0.16, c_4 = 0.24, c_5 = 0.80$

$c_6 = 0.6, c_7 = 0.40, c_8 = 0.30, c_9 = 0.50, c_{10} = 0.70$

In all the experiments, we are interested in the evolution of the action probabilities $p_i(n)$ as well as the overall performance of the automaton, as indicated by $M(n)$. At each instant n, the average values of $p_i(n)$ and $M(n)$, denoted by $\tilde{p}_i(n)$ and $\tilde{M}(n)$, are computed by taking the average over several sample runs.

We first consider linear schemes applied to problems I to III.

Linear Schemes:

L_{R-P} schemes with different values of the reward parameter a and the penalty parameter b are considered. A useful quantity here is the reward–to–penalty ratio

$$\gamma = a/b.$$

The L_{R-I} scheme corresponds to the limiting case of infinite γ. The simulation results are given in Figs. 4.1 to 4.3.

From Fig. 4.1, it can be seen that, in problem I, $\tilde{p}_1$ increases at a faster rate *w.r.t.* n as γ is increased and has the maximum rate for the L_{R-I} scheme. The final value of $\tilde{p}_1$ is also the highest for the L_{R-I} scheme. Similar remarks hold for problems II and III as illustrated in Fig. 4.2(a) and Fig. 4.3(a). The decrease of $\tilde{M}$ with n is given in Figs. 4.2(b) and 4.3(b) and again the L_{R-I} scheme is seen to give the best results.

ε-optimality:

In problem I, optimality implies that $p_1 \to 1$ as $n \to \infty$. However, the L_{R-I} scheme is only ϵ–optimal and we should expect a convergence of p_1 to the wrong value, namely zero, if the parameter a is too close to 1. This is illustrated in Table 4.1 which gives the percentage of runs over which $p_1 \to 0$ as a function of a.

a	% of Wrong Convergence
0.9	22
0.5	12
0.3	5
0.1	0
0.01	0
0.001	0

Table 4.1

From Table 4.1 it is clear that if one were to tolerate a 5% error, a value of 0.3 can be chosen for the step size a, thereby substantially increasing the speed of response.

Time for Convergence:

It is evident from Figs. 4.1 to 4.3 that the time for convergence depends on the number of actions r as well as the step size a. The nature of this dependence is of interest. The L_{R-I} scheme was tried on all the problems with different values of a and the initial probabilities set equal. The time taken for $\tilde{p}_{\text{opt}}$ to reach the values 0.8 and 0.95[5] for $a = 0.015$ are shown in Table 4.2.

---

[5] p_{opt} is the probability of the action associated with minimum penalty probability, e.g. p_1 in problem I.

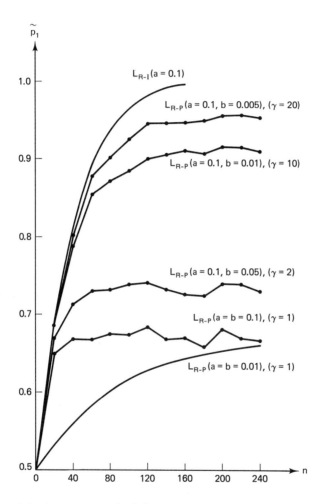

Figure 4.1: Average probability versus trial number, problem I.

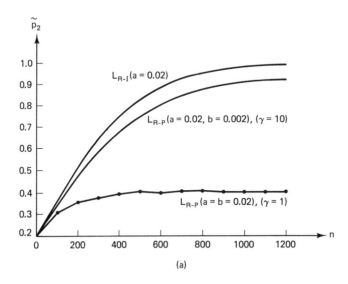

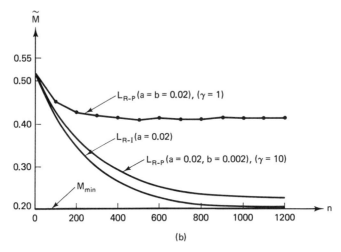

Figure 4.2: Plots for problem II (a) average probability versus trial number (b) average performance versus trial number.

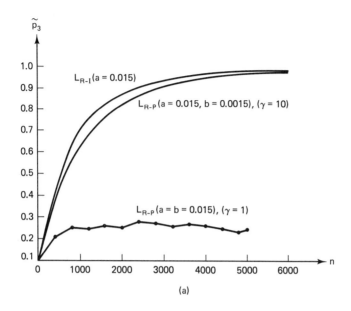

(a)

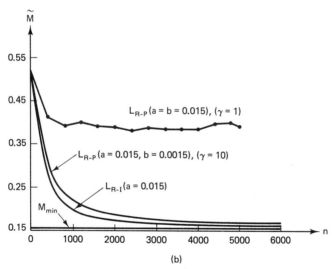

(b)

Figure 4.3: Plots for problem III (a) average probability versus trial number (b) average performance versus trial number.

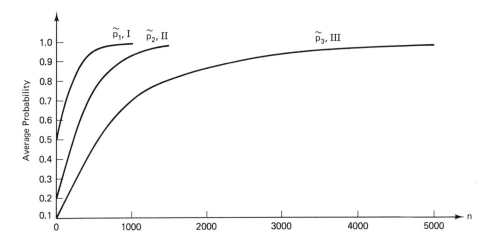

Figure 4.4: Average probability versus trial number, $L_{R-I}(a = 0.015)$.

Problem	Number of Actions	Time for $\tilde{p}_{\text{opt}}$ to to Reach 0.8	Time for $\tilde{p}_{\text{opt}}$ to to Reach 0.95
1	2	50	480
2	5	480	1150
3	10	1300	3500

Table 4.2

The actual evolution of $\tilde{p}_{\text{opt}}$ with n when $a = 0.015$ is given in Fig. 4.4.

Nonlinear Schemes:

For purposes of comparison, the schemes described in Section 4.8 can be divided into two categories. The nonlinear schemes 1 and 2 as well as the Beta model form one category as these are expedient only for restricted environments. The rest of the schemes are absolutely expedient and they form a second category together with the L_{R-I} scheme.

Figure 4.5 shows the performance of nonlinear scheme 1 and the Beta model in problem I. It may be observed that the environment in this problem satisfies the conditions for sign definiteness of $\Delta p_\ell(n)$ and the schemes are ϵ-optimal. The results of simulation show the better performance of nonlinear scheme 1. Similar results appear for problem II in Fig. 4.6.

Some absolutely expedient schemes are compared in Fig. 4.7. Nonlinear

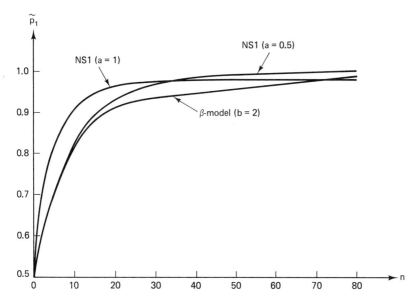

Figure 4.5: Average probability versus trial number, problem I.

scheme 4 and the hybrid scheme $H(L_{R-I}, \hat{L}_{R-P})$ appear to give the best results in problem I. As many of these nonlinear schemes apply only to the case of two actions, only the L_{R-I} and the $H(L_{R-I}, \hat{L}_{R-P})$ schemes were used in problems II and III. The results given in Figs. 4.7 and 4.8 show the superiority of the hybrid scheme.

The nature of evolution of action probabilities when the minimum penalty probability is not unique is considered next. Let the penalty probabilities of an environment with five actions be:

$$c_1 = 0.3, c_2 = 0.5, c_3 = 0.7, c_4 = 0.3 \text{ and } c_5 = 0.8. \tag{4.114}$$

Since c_1 and c_4 are both equal and have the minimum value, the corresponding actions α_1 and α_4 are both optimal. The performance of the L_{R-I} scheme in this problem showed that both $\tilde{p}_1$ and $\tilde{p}_4$ increase from the initial values. The average penalty M decreased to its minimum value. Of the 50 experiments performed, 10 yielded convergence to α_1 [i.e., $p_1(n) \to 1$], 8 to α_4 [i.e., $p_4(n) \to 1$], and the rest resulted in $p_1(n) + p_4(n) \to 1$.

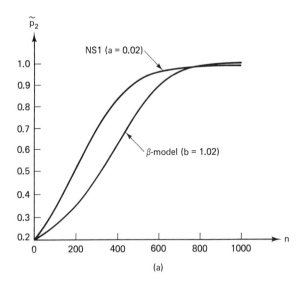

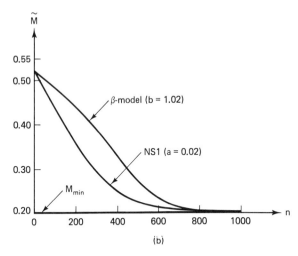

Figure 4.6: Plots for problem II (a) average probability versus trial number (b) average performance versus trial number.

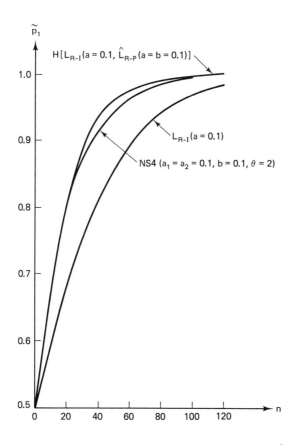

Figure 4.7: Comparison of the schemes $L_{R-I}, H[L_{R-I}, \hat{L}_{R-P}]$ and $NS4$, problem I.

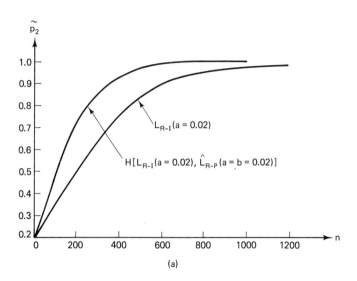

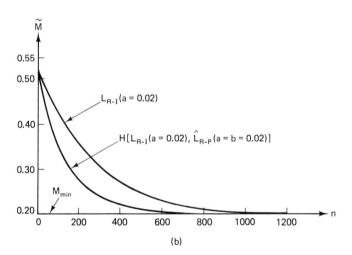

Figure 4.8: Plots for problem II (a) average probability versus trial number (b) average performance versus trial number.

4.11 Related Developments

There are a number of other updating schemes proposed for variable-structure stochastic automata. For instance one could refer to the "Special Issue on Learning Automata of the Journal of Cybernetics and Information Science" (1977) as well as Mars and Poppelbaum (1981). In the former, Tsypkin and Poznyak (1977) attempt to unify the various learning algorithms within the general framework of stochastic approximation. Thathachar and Sastry (1985) incorporate estimates of the reward probabilities in the updating scheme and prove its ϵ–optimality. Such schemes have been called estimator algorithms and have a high rate of convergence in stationary random environments in comparison with L_{R-I} and other schemes. One version of the estimator algorithm called the *pursuit algorithm* (Thathachar and Sastry 1986) computes the optimal unit vector for the action probability based on the current estimates of the reward probabilities and moves the action probability vector by a small distance towards the optimal unit vector.

There are updating schemes suitable for the discretized probability space. By a proper choice of parameters the automata using such schemes can be made to have desirable properties of speed and accuracy. (Thathachar and Oommen 1979, Oommen 1986). Learning automata with changing number of actions have been studied by Thathachar and Harita (1987) who use a modified form of the L_{R-I} algorithm to assure absolute expediency and ϵ–optimality even with changing action sets.

Chapter 5

Convergence

5.1 Introduction

The variable-structure stochastic automaton that updates its action probabilities on the basis of the responses of its environment was described in Chapter 4. Several linear and nonlinear updating schemes, as well as definitions and concepts that are pertinent for describing the resulting Markov processes $\{p(n)\}_{n\geq0}$, were also introduced. In all cases the nature of convergence of the vector $p(n)$ was shown to be a problem of fundamental importance. In this chapter we discuss convergence–related issues in learning automata in greater detail. As mentioned earlier, the results presented in Chapters 4 and 5 provide the mathematical basis for all the results discussed in the chapters that follow. The reader interested primarily in basic concepts rather than mathematical proofs may skip the latter without any significant loss of continuity.

The concepts associated with the convergence problems of learning automata are rather intricate and require sophisticated mathematical tools. It was shown in Chapter 4 that the nature of convergence depends on the kind of reinforcement scheme employed. For example, the linear reward–penalty (L_{R-P}) and the linear reward–ϵ penalty $(L_{R-\epsilon P})$ schemes illustrate one typical mode of convergence, while the linear reward–inaction (L_{R-I}) and other absolutely expedient schemes depict another. The martingale convergence theorem (Appendix B) and the concept of distance diminishing operators (Appendix C) are two of the principal analytical tools that can be used for their analysis. The results derived in this chapter form the basis for most of the discussions in later chapters where the behavior of automata operating in more complex situations is discussed.

In Section 5.2, different definitions of convergence of random variables are introduced. The nature of convergence of ergodic schemes such as L_{R-P} and $L_{R-\epsilon P}$ is discussed first in Section 5.3 and it is shown that the convergence problem essentially reduces to the study of the stability properties of the equilibrium state of an associated ordinary differential equation. Based on this study it is shown that the ϵ–optimality of some ergodic schemes can be demonstrated.

Another important question addressed in the chapter is the relation between absolute expediency and ϵ–optimality. In Section 5.4 it is first shown that when an absolutely expedient algorithm is used, the resulting Markov process converges $w.p.1$ to the set of all unit vectors. The more important question of determining a bound on the probability of convergence to the absorbing state corresponding to the optimal action is addressed next. This is then used to prove that every absolutely expedient scheme (satisfying a minor constraint) is ϵ–optimal in all stationary random environments. This, in turn, enables any one of them to be used in practical applications to achieve ϵ–optimal performance.

For the practical utilization of the automaton, a quantitative estimate of the rate of convergence is needed. Expressions for the rate of convergence are derived for absolutely expedient schemes and the L_{R-P} scheme. The parameters that affect the rate of convergence are identified and the consequences of the present analysis are compared with those obtained in simulation studies. The discussion of the rate of convergence in turn leads to the problem of speed versus accuracy mentioned earlier. Considerations that lead to a satisfactory performance of variable-structure stochastic automata are explored toward the end of the chapter.

5.2   Concepts of Convergence

It was indicated in Section 4.5 that each of the variable-structure learning algorithms discussed in Chapter 4 represents a mapping $T : S_r \to S_r$ and that $\{p(n)\}_{n \geq 0}$, where $p(n)$ is the action probability vector, is a discrete–time Markov process defined on the state space S_r. In this chapter, we are interested in the convergence behavior of the various schemes. Since there are several notions of convergence of a sequence of random variables $\{X_n\}_{n \geq 0}$ that are of interest (Heathcote 1971, Loève 1955) we shall first define them and indicate briefly where they are pertinent in the analysis of learning schemes.

The convergence of a sequence of real numbers forms a convenient starting point for the study of stochastic convergence of a sequence of random variables. The former is said to be convergent if there exists a real number x such that, for large values of the index of the sequence, the terms of the sequence are arbitrarily close to it. This is formally stated as follows:

Definition 5.1: A sequence of real numbers $\{x_n\}$ is called convergent (with a limit x), if for every $\epsilon > 0$ there exists $N = N(\epsilon)$ such that $|x_n - x| < \epsilon$, for all $n \geq N$. We write

$$\lim_{n \to \infty} x_n = x. \tag{5.1}$$

The concept above can be extended to any metric space (X, d) where X is a nonempty set and d is a metric function $d : X \times X \to \mathcal{R}^+$. In such a case a sequence $\{x_n\}$ in (X, d) is said to be convergent (to x), if and only if, there exists $x \in X$ such that $d(x_n, x) \to 0$ as $n \to \infty$. Hence convergence in $\mathcal{R}^n$, **c** the space of convergent sequences, **c**$_0$ the space of sequences that converge to zero and $C[0, 1]$ the metric space of continuous real functions on the closed interval $[0, 1]$ can be defined (Maddox, 1970).

As mentioned earlier, the concept of convergence of a sequence of random variables can be defined in a number of ways depending on the viewpoint we adopt. Prominent among such concepts are four which we will discuss briefly in this section. These are: (i) convergence with probability 1, (ii) mean square convergence, (iii) convergence in probability, and (iv) convergence in distribution.

Convergence *w.p.*1: This type of convergence is also known as almost sure convergence and the emphasis here is on the sample space behavior of the concerned random variables.

Since a random variable is a real valued function defined over the sample space, it assumes real values corresponding to different sample points. Hence a sequence of random variables is represented by a collection of real number sequences with each sequence corresponding to one sample point. One method of extending the concept of convergence given in Definition 5.1 is to require that the real number sequences represented by each sample point be convergent. However, this definition is found to be too restrictive and is seldom satisfied in practice. A slight modification of the above idea is to demand the convergence of real number sequences associated with a subset of the sample points whose probabilities sum to unity. Thus sample points with probability zero can be omitted for considerations of convergence. This type of convergence is known as convergence *w.p.*1 or almost sure convergence.

Definition 5.2: A sequence of random variables $\{X_n\}$ is said to converge to a random variable X $w.p.1$ if for any $\delta > 0$, $\epsilon > 0$

$$Pr\{\omega : |X_n(\omega) - X(\omega)| < \epsilon\} > 1 - \delta \qquad (5.2)$$

is satisfied for all $n \geq N$ where N may depend on both δ and ϵ.
Alternately

$$Pr\{\omega : \lim_{n \to \infty} X_n(\omega) = X(\omega)\} = 1. \qquad (5.3)$$

As illustrations of convergence $w.p.1$ consider the following examples.

Example 5.1: Let the sample space be the unit interval $[0, 1]$. The probability of an event corresponding to an interval $[a, b]$ is the length of the interval, $b - a$. If X_n is a sequence of random variables such that the values taken by them are

$$X_n(\omega) = \quad 1 \qquad \omega \in [0, \tfrac{1}{n})$$
$$0 \qquad \text{otherwise.}$$

Then

$$\lim_{n \to \infty} X_n(\omega) = \quad 1 \qquad \omega = 0$$
$$0 \qquad \omega \in (0, 1].$$

Hence the sequences associated with all the sample points except $\omega = 0$ converge to zero. Since the probability associated with any isolated point is zero, X_n converges to 0 $w.p.1$.

Example 5.2: Let $\{X_n\}$ be a sequence of random variables on a sample space with zero means and variances Var X_n satisfying the condition $\sum_{n=1}^{\infty}$ Var $X_n < \infty$. Since by Chebychev's inequality

$$Pr(|X_n| > \frac{1}{\mu}) \leq \mu^2 \text{ Var } X_n$$

for every $n \geq 1$ and any $\mu > 0$, it follows that

$$\sum_{n=1}^{\infty} Pr(|X_n| > \frac{1}{\mu}) < \infty.$$

This in turn assures the almost sure convergence of X_n to the degenerate random variable $X(\omega) = 0$ for all $\omega \in \Omega$.

Mean–Square Convergence: In this mode of convergence the distance between X_n and X is measured by the expectation of the square of the distance between them. The sequence of random variables is said to converge if this tends to zero as n becomes large.

Definition 5.3: A sequence $\{X_n\}$ of random variables is said to converge to a random variable X in the mean–square sense if

$$E|X_n - X|^2 \to 0 \text{ as } n \to \infty$$

or

$$\lim_{n \to \infty} E|X_n - X|^2 = 0. \tag{5.4}$$

In the definition above, the modulus is used to take care of cases where the random variables are complex valued.

Example 5.3: Consider the sequence $\{X_n\}$ in Example 5.1. $E[(X_n - 0)^2] = 1 \cdot \frac{1}{n} + 0 = \frac{1}{n} \to 0$ as $n \to \infty$. Hence $\{X_n\}$ converges to 0 in the mean–square sense as well.

Convergence in Probability: If $X_1, X_2, \ldots, X_n$ are identically distributed random variables with expectation μ, then for a large n the sample average given by

$$\frac{1}{n} S_n = \frac{1}{n} \sum_{i=1}^{n} X_i$$

takes values close to μ. The formal statement of the classical form of the weak law of large numbers states that for every $\epsilon > 0$

$$\lim_{n \to \infty} Pr[|\frac{1}{n} S_n - \mu| \geq \epsilon] = 0.$$

If $E[X_j] = \mu_j$ and $\text{Var}[X_j] = \sigma_j^2$ and the random variables are not independent, it can still be shown that provided the variances and covariances of X_j are such that $\lim_{n \to \infty} \frac{1}{n^2} \text{Var } S_n = 0$ we have

$$\lim_{n \to \infty} Pr[|\frac{1}{n} S_n - \frac{1}{n} \sum_{j=1}^{n} \mu_j| \geq \epsilon] = 0.$$

From the equation above, it is apparent that the mode of convergence prescribed by the weak law may apply to random variables other than averages. This in turn leads to the introduction of a new term, "convergence in probability."

Definition 5.4: The sequence $\{X_n\}$ of random variables converges in probability to the random variable X if for every $\epsilon > 0$

$$\lim_{n \to \infty} Pr\{|X_n - X| \geq \epsilon\} = 0. \tag{5.5}$$

In contrast to Definition 5.2, the limit is determined here after the probability is computed. Thus convergence in probability involves the limit of a sequence of probabilities, which is a sequence of real numbers.

Example 5.4: Let X_n be a random variable taking value 0 with probability $(1 - \frac{1}{n})$ and 1 with probability $\frac{1}{n}$. Then for any ϵ such that $0 < \epsilon < 1$

$$Pr(|X_n - 0| \geq \epsilon) = \frac{1}{n} \to 0 \text{ as } n \to \infty.$$

Hence $\{X_n\}$ converges to 0 in probability.

Convergence in Distribution: Instead of using a measure of the distance between X_n and X one could consider the distribution functions F_n of X_n and F of X. If the sequence of distribution functions $\{F_n(x)\}$ converges to $F(x)$ then $\{X_n\}$ is said to converge to X in distribution. This mode of convergence is also called convergence in law. By the weak convergence of a sequence of functions is meant their convergence to a limit function at all points of continuity of the latter. The mode of convergence described above is concerned with sequences of distribution functions convergent in this sense. The importance of this form of convergence lies in the fact that it enables one to approximate for large n the distribution function of the nth member of the sequence of random variables.

Definition 5.5: The sequence of random variables $\{X_n\}$ is said to converge to a random variable X in distribution if the distribution functions $F_n(x)$ of X_n converge to the distribution function $F(x)$ of X at all points of continuity of $F(\cdot)$ i.e.,

$$\lim_{n \to \infty} F_n(x) = F(x) \tag{5.6}$$

for all x at which $F(x)$ is continuous.

General results on convergence in distribution were first formulated in the eighteenth century for sequences of binomially distributed random variables. Following is a typical example.

Example 5.5: Let X_n be a binomial random variable. X_n denotes the number of successes in n trials of an experiment with binary outcome. Let

p_n be the success probability in the nth trial.

$$Pr\{X_n = k\} = \binom{n}{k} p_n^k (1 - p_n)^{n-k} \quad k = 0, 1, 2 \ldots$$

As shown in elementary texts on probability, if $np_n \to \lambda > 0$ as $n \to \infty$ then

$$\lim_{n \to \infty} \binom{n}{k} p_n^k (1 - p_n)^{n-k} = \frac{e^{-\lambda} \lambda^k}{k!}.$$

The r.h.s. is the probability mass function of a Poisson random variable X.

$$Pr\{X = k\} = \frac{e^{-\lambda} \lambda^k}{k!}.$$

Thus under the conditions mentioned, a sequence of binomial random variables converges in distribution to a Poisson random variable X.

Example 5.6: In the previous example p_n, the probability of success at the nth trial tended to zero. If instead $p_n = p$ is a constant at every trial, the mean and variance of X_n are given by

$$E[X_n] = np$$
$$\text{Var}[X_n] = np(1 - p)$$

and increase with n. Defining a standardized random variable

$$z_n = \frac{X_n - np}{\sqrt{np(1-p)}}$$

it follows that $E[z_n] = 0$ and $\text{Var}[z_n] = 1$. It can be shown through the classical DeMoivre–Laplace theorem, that as $n \to \infty$, z_n converges in distribution to a normal random variable with mean zero and unit variance.

There is considerable interrelationship between the different modes of convergence. Figure 5.1 shows this relationship in the form of an implication diagram.

From Fig. 5.1 it is clear that all the modes of convergence we have considered imply convergence in distribution. Hence this is the weakest type of convergence. Defining a degenerate random variable as one whose probability mass is concentrated at a single point [i.e., $Pr(X = c) = 1$, $Pr(X \neq c) = 0$], convergence in distribution also implies convergence in probability if the limit variable is degenerate. However, that this is not true in general is

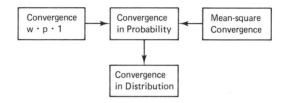

Figure 5.1: Concepts of stochastic convergence.

evident by considering a sequence $\{X_n\}$ of identically distributed and independent random variables. The latter converges in distribution but not in probability.

Almost–sure convergence and mean–square convergence are the strongest types of convergence. However neither one implies the other. At the same time it is also known that the two are not mutually exclusive i.e., there are sequences which converge in both modes as evident from Examples 5.1 and 5.3.

Convergence in learning automata: In the sections following, the convergence concepts introduced thus far are applied to characterize the asymptotic behavior of learning schemes. While our main concern will be with the convergence of the action probability vector $p(n)$, the asymptotic behavior of related quantities such as the average penalty $M(n)$ is also of interest. The nature of convergence of the various quantities is inseparably linked with the specific learning scheme used. In particular the concepts of convergence in distribution and convergence $w.p.1$ are found to be relevant in the analysis in the following sections. In Section 5.3 ergodic schemes are considered and it is seen that both L_{R-P} and $L_{R-\epsilon P}$ schemes converge in distribution. It is further shown that the nature of the distribution may be more precisely characterized for the case of "slow learning" when the learning parameters are chosen to be sufficiently small. In Section 5.4 the convergence of absolutely expedient schemes is discussed and it is shown that such schemes converge with probability 1 to the set of unit vectors in S_r.

5.3 Ergodic Schemes

An ergodic scheme is characterized by the property that the Markov process $\{p(n)\}_{n \geq 0}$ generated by the scheme is an ergodic process. In such schemes the vector $p(n)$ converges to a random vector p^* whose distribution function is independent of the initial value $p(0)$ (Norman, 1968, Iosifescu and Theodorescu, 1969). A rigorous proof of the convergence of $p(n)$ to p^*, depends on a uniform ergodic theorem of Ionescu Tulcea and Marinescu (1950) and is beyond the scope of this book. However, the comments that follow may prove helpful to the reader in understanding how the result is qualitatively related to those discussed earlier in Chapter 3 for fixed-structure learning automata. Norman (1968) studies "distance diminishing" models (refer to Appendix C) via Markov processes in a compact metric space. Since the process, $\{p(n)\}_{n \geq 0}$, of interest to us is defined on the state space S_r, it is a compact Markov process. Norman's theory of such processes is completely analogous to that of Markov chains. In an an ergodic finite Markov chain $\{X(n)\}_{n \geq 0}$, it is known (refer to Appendix A) that the distribution of $X(n)$ converges as $n \to \infty$ to a limiting distribution, independent of the initial distribution. The convergence of $p(n)$ to p^* is the generalization of the same result to a compact Markov process.

Effect of Small Parameter a: For saying more about the asymptotic behavior of ergodic schemes, additional assumptions need to be made. An assumption that is generally made, based on practical considerations as well as mathematical tractability, is that the learning parameter a is small. Let the ergodic scheme be denoted by

$$p(n + 1) = p(n) + aF[p(n), \alpha(n), \beta(n)]$$

where a is the learning parameter. The following averages are computed for the scheme.

Let

$$E[p(n + 1) - p(n)|p(n) = p] = aW(p) + O(a^2) \tag{5.7}$$

$$\text{Cov}[p(n + 1) - p(n)|p(n) = p] = a^2 S(p) + o(a^2) \tag{5.8}$$

$$E[\|p(n + 1) - p(n)\|^3|p(n) = p] = O(a^3) \tag{5.9}$$

uniformly over $p \in S_r$. The error terms above satisfy

$$\sup_{\substack{0 < a < 1 \\ p \in S_r}} \frac{\|O(a^2)\|}{a^2} < \infty \tag{5.10}$$

and

$$\sup_{p \in S_r} \frac{\|o(a^2)\|}{a^2} \to 0 \text{ as } a \to 0. \tag{5.11}$$

When the parameter a is small it is evident that the step size in updating $p(n)$ is small and the Markov process $\{p(n)\}$ evolves by small steps. Learning that results from such schemes is referred to as "slow learning." In slow learning schemes, $p(n)$ can be approximated by the solution of an associated differential equation, which can be readily derived from the learning algorithm chosen. Further, it can be shown that the limiting distribution of $p(n)$ is normal. To make the principal ideas involved readily apparent we first consider a two–action learning automaton and later generalize the results to the case when the automaton has $r(> 2)$ actions. The obvious advantage of the two–action case is that we can confine our attention to the convergence of one of the components [say $p_1(n)$] on the unit interval $[0,1]$. Since L_{R-P} and $L_{R-\epsilon P}$ schemes are ergodic schemes, they are discussed toward the end of this section to illustrate the theory through examples.

In a two–action automaton, the following scalar equations are found to be important in setting up the associated differential equations. Let

$$E[p_1(n+1) - p_1(n)|p_1(n) = p_1] = a\tilde{W}(p_1) + O(a^2) \tag{5.12}$$

$$\text{Var}[p_1(n+1) - p_1(n)|p_1(n) = p_1] = a^2\tilde{S}(p_1) + o(a^2) \tag{5.13}$$

$$E[|p_1(n+1) - p_1(n)|^3|p_1(n) = p_1] = O(a^3). \tag{5.14}$$

Equation (5.12) refers to the mean increments in $p_1(n)$ and leads to a differential equation whose solution approximates the mean value of $p_1(n)$. Equation (5.13) leads to a second differential equation whose solution approximates the variance. Equation (5.14) mainly assures us that the higher moments are negligible when the parameter a is small. The tilde $(\sim)$ superscript notation will be made clear shortly.

For small values of the parameter a, the solutions of the difference equations (5.12) and (5.13) can be approximated by those of the differential equations

$$\frac{d\tilde{f}}{dt} = \tilde{W}[\tilde{f}(t)] \tag{5.15}$$

$$\frac{d\tilde{g}}{dt} = 2\left[\frac{d\tilde{W}}{d\tilde{f}}\right]\tilde{g} + \tilde{S}[\tilde{f}(t)] \tag{5.16}$$

The function $\tilde{W}(\cdot)$ in Eq.(5.15) is the same as that in Eq.(5.12) and $\tilde{f}(t)$ approximates $p_1(n)$ where the time $t = na$. Similarly $\tilde{S}(\cdot)$ is the same in Eqs.(5.13) and (5.16) and a $\tilde{g}(t)$ is an approximation of the variance of $p_1(n)$.

Let

$$\tilde{W}(p_1) = 0$$

have a unique root at $p_1 = \overline{p}_1$ and further let

$$\tilde{W}'(\overline{p}_1) \triangleq \left. \frac{d\tilde{W}(p_1)}{dp_1} \right|_{p_1 = \overline{p}_1} < 0.$$

This implies that $\overline{p}_1$ is the unique equilibrium state of the differential equation (5.15) and $\tilde{W}(p_1) > 0$ for $p_1 < \overline{p}_1$ and $\tilde{W}(p_1) < 0$ for $p_1 > \overline{p}_1$. Hence the equilibrium state of the differential equation (5.15) is globally asymptotically stable so that $\lim_{t \to \infty} \tilde{f}(t) = \overline{p}_1$ for any initial condition $\tilde{f}(0) = p_1(0) \in [0,1]$.

To relate the solution $p_1(n)$ of Eq.(5.12) to $\tilde{f}(t)$ we define the quantity $z(n)$ as

$$z(n) \triangleq \frac{p_1(n) - \tilde{f}(na)}{\sqrt{a}}. \tag{5.17}$$

It can then be shown that as $a \to 0$ such that $na \to \infty$, $z(n)$ converges in distribution to a normal random variable with zero mean and variance $\tilde{g}(\infty)$. Setting the r.h.s. in Eq.(5.16) to zero we obtain

$$\tilde{g}(\infty) = \frac{-\tilde{S}(\overline{p}_1)}{2\tilde{W}'(\overline{p}_1)}. \tag{5.18}$$

Since $\tilde{f}(t) \to \overline{p}_1$ as $t \to \infty$ it follows that asymptotically $p_1(n)$ has a normal distribution with mean $\overline{p}_1$ and variance $a\,\tilde{g}(\infty)$.

Multiple–Action Case: The results of the previous section for a learning automaton with two actions can be extended directly to the multiple–action case, where the automaton has $r(> 2)$ actions. The following notation is found to be convenient for obtaining corresponding differential equations and the limiting distribution of $p(n)$.

Let $f(t) \in S_r$ and let the elements of f be denoted by $f_i(t)$ ($i = 1, 2, \ldots, r$). Let $g(t)$ be an $r \times r$ matrix. The differential equations corresponding to the difference equations (5.7) and (5.8) can be expressed as

$$\frac{df}{dt} = W(f(t)) \tag{5.19}$$

$$\frac{dg}{dt} = \left(\frac{dW}{df}\right) g + g \left(\frac{dW}{df}\right)^T + S(f(t)) \tag{5.20}$$

where

$$W : S_r \to \mathcal{R}^r \text{ and } S : S_r \to \mathcal{R}^{r \times r}.$$

Let S be Lipschitz and let W have a bounded Lipschitz derivative. Under these assumptions the differential equations (5.19) and (5.20) have unique solutions. Since f belongs to S_r one of the equations in Eq.(5.19) is redundant and can be derived from the other $(r-1)$ equations. Similarly, one row (or one column) in the matrix equation (5.20) is also linearly dependent on the other rows (columns). Since, for analytic purposes it is easier to deal with independent equations, we consider only $(r-1)$ of the variables. If $\tilde{f}$ denotes f with the rth variable f_r deleted and $\tilde{g}$ and $\tilde{S}$ are $(r-1) \times (r-1)$ matrices obtained by deleting the rth row and r^{th} column of g and S the approximating equations in $\mathcal{R}^{r-1}$ can be expressed in terms of $\tilde{f}, \tilde{W}, \tilde{g}$ and $\tilde{S}$ respectively. Equations (5.19) and (5.20) can now be written as

$$\frac{d\tilde{f}}{dt} = \tilde{W}(\tilde{f}) \tag{5.21}$$

$$\frac{d\tilde{g}}{dt} = \left(\frac{d\tilde{W}}{d\tilde{f}}\right) \tilde{g} + \tilde{g} \left(\frac{d\tilde{W}}{d\tilde{f}}\right)^T + \tilde{S}(\tilde{f}). \tag{5.22}$$

If $\tilde{p}(n) = [p_1(n), p_2(n), \ldots, p_{r-1}(n)]^T$, $\tilde{f}(t)$ approximates $\tilde{p}(n)$ for $t = na$. Using the notation

$$z(n) = \frac{\tilde{p}(n) - \tilde{f}(na)}{\sqrt{a}} \qquad \tilde{p}(0) = \tilde{p}_0 \tag{5.23}$$

the asymptotic behavior of $\tilde{p}(n)$ can also be expressed in terms of $z(n)$.

Let $\bar{\tilde{p}}$ be the unique equilibrium state of the differential equation (5.21) so that $\tilde{W}(\bar{\tilde{p}}) = 0$. Further, let this equilibrium state be globally asymptotically stable. Then for any initial condition $\tilde{f}(0)$, $\lim_{t \to \infty} \tilde{f}(t) = \bar{\tilde{p}}$. If $\mathcal{L}(z)$ denotes the distribution of the random variable z, and if $N(\mu, \Sigma)$ denotes a normal distribution with mean μ and covariance Σ, the following theorem (Norman, 1974) gives the asymptotic behavior of $z(n)$ [and consequently $\tilde{p}(n)$ and $p(n)$] for small values of the parameter a.

Theorem 5.1: Given the difference equations (5.7)–(5.9) and the differential equations (5.21) and (5.22) let the following conditions be satisfied:

(i) there exists a point $\bar{p} \in S_r$ such that $W(\bar{p}) = 0$

(ii) if $x \in \mathcal{R}^{r-1}$ and P is an $(r-1) \times (r-1)$ symmetric positive–definite matrix such that the inner product of $(x - \tilde{\bar{p}})$ and $\tilde{W}(x)$ satisfies the condition

$$[(x - \tilde{\bar{p}}), \tilde{W}(x)] < 0 \qquad \forall \, x \neq \tilde{\bar{p}} \tag{5.24}$$

where $[x, y] \triangleq x^T P y$ and

(iii)

$$[\eta, \tilde{A}\eta] < 0 \qquad \forall \, \eta \in \mathcal{R}^{r-1}, \, \eta \neq 0 \tag{5.25}$$

then

$$\mathcal{L}(z(n)) \to N[0, \tilde{g}(\infty)] \text{ as } a \to 0 \text{ and } na \to \infty, \tag{5.26}$$

where $z(n)$ is defined in Eq.(5.23).

Furthermore, $\tilde{g}(\infty)$ is the unique solution of the matrix equation

$$\tilde{A}\tilde{g}(\infty) + \tilde{g}(\infty)\tilde{A}^T + \tilde{S}(\tilde{\bar{p}}) = 0 \tag{5.27}$$

where

$$A = W'(\bar{p}) = \left. \frac{dW(f)}{df} \right|_{f=\bar{p}} \tag{5.28}$$

and $\tilde{A}$ is obtained from A by deleting the rth row and column.

Comment 5.1: The condition of Eq.(5.24) implies that $\bar{p}$ is the only zero of $W(p)$. Moreover, the condition ensures that a quadratic Lyapunov function with a negative–definite time derivative exists for the differential equation (5.21). Thus the condition of Eq.(5.24) is sufficient for the global asymptotic stability of the equilibrium state $\tilde{\bar{p}}$.

Comment 5.2: Condition (iii) implies that the differential equation (5.21) linearized around the equilibrium point $\tilde{\bar{p}}$ is asymptotically stable. The stability result follows once again from a quadratic Lyapunov function.

Comment 5.3: If the differential equation (5.21) is linear and has a unique equilibrium point $\tilde{\bar{p}}$ which is asymptotically stable, the conditions of Eqs.(5.24) and (5.25) coincide and are satisfied automatically.

The results presented thus far apply to any ergodic scheme. Since L_{R-P} and $L_{R-\epsilon P}$ schemes are ergodic schemes, the results can be specialized to these two cases.

5.3.1 The L_{R-P} Scheme

Consider an r–action automaton operating in a stationary random environment according to an L_{R-P} scheme. The updating equations can be concisely written as follows.

If $\alpha(n) = \alpha_i$

$$p(n+1) = p(n) \quad +a(1 - \beta(n))[e_i - p(n)]$$
$$+a\beta(n)\left[\{1/(r-1)\}(1_r - e_i) - p(n)\right] \tag{5.29}$$

where e_i is the unit $(r \times 1)$ vector with 1 as the ith element and the rest zero. 1_r is a $(r \times 1)$ vector all of whose elements are unity. Two properties of the scheme can be deduced from Eq.(5.29) as follows.

(i) There are no absorbing states for $\{p(n)\}$. This can be seen by setting $p(n) = p$ and checking whether for any value of p, $p(n+1) = p$ w.p.1.

From Eq.(5.29) $p(n+1) = p$ w.p.1 if and only if

$$ae_i - ap = 0 \qquad\qquad \text{corresponding to } \beta(n) = 0$$

and

$$\{a/(r-1)\}(1_r - e_i) - ap = 0 \quad \text{corresponding to } \beta(n) = 1$$

each of which occurs with a nonzero probability if $c_i \in (0, 1)$. There is no value of p that satisfies both the equations. Hence there are no absorbing states for the Markov process $\{p(n)\}$ unless some $c_i = 0$ or 1.

(ii) The L_{R-P} scheme is strictly distance diminishing (refer to Appendix C). To see this, consider two starting values of $p(n)$. Let us call these p and q and the corresponding values of $p(n+1)$ as p' and q'.

Now from

$$p' - p = a(1 - \beta(n))(e_i - p) + a\beta(n)\left[\{1/(r-1)\}(1_r - e_i) - p\right]$$
$$q' - q = a(1 - \beta(n))(e_i - q) + a\beta(n)\left[\{1/(r-1)\}(1_r - e_i) - q\right]$$

If $\beta(n) = 1$,
$$\|p' - q'\| = (1 - a)\|p - q\|.$$

Similarly if $\beta(n) = 0$,

$$\|p' - q'\| = (1 - a)\|p - q\|.$$

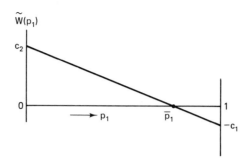

Figure 5.2: $\tilde{W}(p_1)$ versus p_1 for a two-action L_{R-P} automaton.

Since $0 < a < 1$, it follows that

$$\|p' - q'\| < \|p - q\|. \tag{5.30}$$

Thus the L_{R-P} scheme is strictly distance diminishing. It follows that if $p(n+m) = p^{(m)}$ when $p(n) = p$ and $p(n+m) = q^{(m)}$ when $p(n) = q$,

$$\|p^{(m)} - q^{(m)}\| = (1-a)^m \|p - q\| \tag{5.31}$$

and the r.h.s. $\to 0$ as $m \to \infty$. Hence $p^{(m)} \to q^{(m)}$ irrespective of the initial values p and q.

The properties above lead to the ergodic character of the L_{R-P} scheme. Hence by the comments made regarding general ergodic schemes, it follows that the sequence $\{p(n)\}_{n\geq 0}$ converges in distribution to a random variable p^*.

Two–Action Case: For the two–action L_{R-P} automaton $\tilde{W}(\tilde{p}) = \tilde{W}(p_1)$ in Eq.(5.12) can be computed as

$$\tilde{W}(p_1) = c_2(1 - p_1) - c_1 p_1 = c_2 - (c_1 + c_2)p_1. \tag{5.32}$$

A plot of $\tilde{W}(p_1)$ is shown in Fig. 5.2. At $p_1 = 0$, $\tilde{W}(0) = c_2$ while at $p_1 = 1$ $\tilde{W}(p_1) = -c_1$. $\tilde{W}(p_1)$ has a unique zero at $\overline{p}_1 = c_2/(c_1 + c_2)$ and $d\tilde{W}/dp_1 = -(c_1+c_2) < 0$. Hence $\tilde{W}(p_1)$ satisfies all the conditions given in Theorem 5.1, and $\lim_{t\to\infty} \tilde{f}(t) = c_2/(c_1 + c_2)$. With $a \to 0$ and $na \to \infty$, $p_1(n)$ converges in distribution to $N[(c_2/(c_1 + c_2), (ac_1c_2)/(2(c_1 + c_2)^3)]$. Alternately, for a small value of the parameter a we can say that the asymptotic distribution of $p_1(n)$ will be approximately normal and can be approximated by the mean value $c_2/(c_1 + c_2)$.

Multiple–Action Case: When the L_{R-P} automaton has r actions ($r > 2$), $\Delta p(n) = E[p(n+1) - p(n)|p(n)]$ can be computed as

$$\Delta p(n) = a B^T E[p(n)] \tag{5.33}$$

where the $(r \times r)$ matrix B is given by

$$B = \begin{bmatrix} -c_1 & c_1/(r-1) & \cdots & c_1/(r-1) \\ c_2/(r-1) & -c_2 & c_2/(r-1) & c_2/(r-1) \\ \vdots & & & \\ c_r/(r-1) & c_r/(r-1) & \cdots & -c_r \end{bmatrix} \tag{5.34}$$

The differential equation associated with Eq.(5.33) has the form

$$\frac{df}{dt} = B^T f(t). \tag{5.35}$$

The equilibrium points of the differential equation are given by the solutions of

$$B^T f = 0 \tag{5.36}$$

satisfying the constraint $\sum_{i=1}^{r} f_i = 1$ and $0 \leq f_i \leq 1$ ($i = 1, \ldots, r$). From the form of B in Eq.(5.34) it can be checked that Eq.(5.36) has a unique solution given by

$$f = \overline{p} = \left[\frac{1/c_1}{\sum_{i=1}^{r} 1/c_i}, \frac{1/c_2}{\sum_{i=1}^{r} 1/c_i}, \ldots, \frac{1/c_r}{\sum_{i=1}^{r} 1/c_i} \right]^T. \tag{5.37}$$

The stability properties of this equilibrium point are of interest in determining the asymptotic behavior of the solutions of Eq.(5.35).

We need to write the equation corresponding to Eq.(5.33) for independent action probabilities. For convenience, we omit the last component of p, namely p_r, and write the equation for the first $(r - 1)$ components. As per the notation discussed earlier, we denote the resulting $(r - 1) \times 1$ action probability vector as $\tilde{p}$ and the equation takes the form

$$\Delta \tilde{p}(n) = a \tilde{B}^T E[\tilde{p}(n)] \tag{5.38}$$

where the $(r - 1) \times (r - 1)$ matrix $\tilde{B}$ is obtained by deleting the rth row and r^{th} column from B.

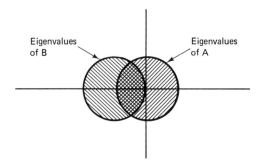

Figure 5.3: Location of eigenvalues.

The associated differential equation (5.35) now becomes

$$\frac{d\tilde{f}}{dt} = \tilde{B}^T \tilde{f}(t).$$ (5.39)

The asymptotic behavior of $p(n)$ depends on the stability properties of Eq.(5.39) which in turn are entirely determined by the eigenvalues of $\tilde{B}$.

Recalling the relation of Eq.(4.33) of Chapter 4 it is seen that

$$B = A - I$$ (5.40)

where A is a stochastic matrix [1] and I is the unit matrix. The eigenvalues of A are in the interior of the unit circle except for one eigenvalue at unity. Consequently the eigenvalues of B are in the interior of a circle with center at $(-1,0)$ and radius unity except for one eigenvalue at the origin. This is depicted in Fig. 5.3. The eigenvalue at the origin is removed when the rth row and column are removed from B while the rest of the eigenvalues remain in the open left-half plane. Hence the eigenvalues of $\tilde{B}$ are all in the open left-half plane and the system of differential equations (5.39) is asymptotically stable.

Thus in the case of the L_{R-P} scheme, the associated differential equation is linear and asymptotically stable. For this situation all the conditions of Theorem 5.1 are satisfied (see Comment 5.3 following the theorem) with

$$\tilde{\tilde{p}} = \left[\frac{1/c_1}{\sum_{i=1}^r 1/c_i}, \frac{1/c_2}{\sum_{i=1}^r 1/c_i}, \cdots, \frac{1/c_{r-1}}{\sum_{i=1}^r 1/c_i} \right]^T.$$ (5.41)

---

[1]The matrix A in Eq.(5.40) corresponds to A in Eq.(4.33) with $a = 1$.

5.3.2   The $L_{R-\epsilon P}$ Scheme

As noted in Chapter 4, the $L_{R-\epsilon P}$ scheme is obtained by adding a small penalty term to the L_{R-I} scheme. Alternatively one could regard it as derived from the L_{R-P} scheme where the penalty terms are made small in comparison with the reward terms.

The updating equations for the $L_{R-\epsilon P}$ scheme can be written as follows. If $\alpha(n) = \alpha_i$,

$$
\begin{aligned}
p(n+1) &= p(n) + a(1 - \beta(n))[e_i - p(n)] \\
&\quad + b\beta(n)[\tfrac{1}{r-1}(1_r - e_i) - p(n)]
\end{aligned}
\tag{5.42}
$$

where $0 < b << a < 1$ and 1_r, e_i are as defined in Eq.(5.29).

In Eq.(5.42), the penalty parameter b is regarded as small in comparison with the reward parameter a. One could write $b = \epsilon a$ where $0 < \epsilon << 1$.

The following points may be noted about the $L_{R-\epsilon P}$ scheme:

(i)   Setting $b = a$ modifies the scheme to the L_{R-P} scheme and $b = 0$ to the L_{R-I} scheme.

(ii)   The $L_{R-\epsilon P}$ scheme has no absorbing states. This fact can be checked as in the case of the L_{R-P} scheme.

(iii)   The $L_{R-\epsilon P}$ scheme is strictly distance diminishing. This property also follows from the arguments used for the L_{R-P} scheme.

(iv)   As a consequence of the above, the $L_{R-\epsilon P}$ scheme is also ergodic and $p(n)$ converges in distribution to a random variable p^* independent of the initial probability $p(0)$.

(v)   The effect of small values of parameter a (and consequently b) can be studied as in the L_{R-P} case.

From Eq.(5.42),

$$
\begin{aligned}
\Delta p(n) &= \sum_{i=1}^r a(1 - c_i)(e_i - p(n))p_i(n) \\
&\quad + \sum_{i=1}^r bc_i[\tfrac{1}{r-1}(1_r - e_i) - p(n)]p_i(n).
\end{aligned}
\tag{5.43}
$$

Setting $b = \epsilon a$ where $\epsilon > 0$, from Eq.(5.7)

$$
W(p) = \sum_{i=1}^r \left\{ (1 - c_i)(e_i - p) + \epsilon c_i[\frac{1}{r-1}(1_r - e_i) - p] \right\} p_i
\tag{5.44}
$$

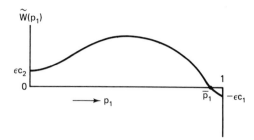

Figure 5.4: $\tilde{W}(p_1)$ versus p_1 for a two-action $L_{R-\epsilon P}$ automaton.

and there are no terms $O(a^2)$.

Two–Action Case: When the $L_{R-\epsilon P}$ automaton has only two actions the scalar function $\tilde{W}(\tilde{p}) = \tilde{W}(p_1)$ can be written as

$$\tilde{W}(\tilde{p}) = (c_2 - c_1)p_1(1 - p_1) + \epsilon[c_2(1 - p_1)^2 - c_1 p_1^2]. \qquad (5.45)$$

Assuming that $c_1 < c_2$ (so that the first action is the optimal one), $\tilde{p}$ at which $\tilde{W}(\tilde{p}) = 0$ can be computed as

$$\tilde{p} = \overline{p}_1 = 1 - \frac{\epsilon c_1}{c_2 - c_1}. \qquad (5.46)$$

For small values of ϵ it is obvious from Eq.(5.46) that $\overline{p}_1$ is close to unity (Fig. 5.4). Further the derivative of $\tilde{W}(\tilde{p})$ with respect to $\tilde{p}$ at $\tilde{p} = \overline{p}_1$ can be computed as

$$\frac{d\tilde{W}}{d\tilde{p}}\bigg|_{\tilde{p}=\overline{p}_1} = (c_2 - c_1)[1 - 2(1 - \epsilon)\overline{p}_1] - 2\epsilon c_2 < 0 \qquad (5.47)$$

when $\epsilon << 1$.

Hence, once again the conditions of Theorem 5.1 are satisfied and $p_1(n)$ converges in distribution and can be approximated by $\overline{p}_1$. This in turn implies that the $L_{R-\epsilon P}$ scheme is ϵ–optimal.

Multiple–Action Case: As in the L_{R-P} scheme the first step is to determine the zeros of $W(p)$, when the automaton has $r(> 2)$ actions. This depends on the values of the parameters a and b. As before, set $b = \epsilon a$. When $b = 0$, the scheme reduces to the L_{R-I} scheme and all the r unit vectors $e_i(i = 1, \dots, r)$ which are the vertices of the simplex S_r are the zeros of $W(p)$. Since the zeros of $W(p)$ are continuous functions of ϵ (or equivalently of b) they remain in the vicinity of the vertices of S_r for small values of ϵ. It can be shown that for sufficiently small values of ϵ, there will be only one zero near the vertex e_ℓ (associated with the lowest penalty probability c_ℓ) within S_r while the other zeros lie outside the simplex. In fact neglecting second–order terms, the zero $\overline{p}$ of $W(p)$ can be approximated by

$$\overline{p}_i = \epsilon c_\ell / \left[(r-1)(c_i - c_\ell)\right] \qquad \begin{array}{l} (i = 1, \ldots, r) \\ i \neq \ell \end{array} \qquad (5.48)$$

$$\overline{p}_\ell = 1 - \sum_{i \neq \ell} \overline{p}_i.$$

Thus $\overline{p}$ can be made as close to the optimal vector e_ℓ as desired by choosing ϵ sufficiently small (Thathachar and Ramachandran, 1984).

Theorem 5.1 can now be applied and satisfaction of its conditions essentially implies that as $a \to 0$ and $na \to \infty$, $p(n)$ converges in distribution to a normal process with mean $\overline{p}$. Since $\overline{p}$ can be made arbitrarily close to the optimal vector e_ℓ, the reasoning above concludes that the $L_{R-\epsilon P}$ scheme is ϵ–optimal. However, assuring that the conditions of Theorem 5.1 are satisfied is considerably more involved than in the case of the L_{R-P} scheme. This is due to the fact that $W(p)$ is a nonlinear function of p and it is hard to find a positive–definite matrix P which satisfies the conditions of Eqs.(5.24) and (5.25) of the theorem. Thus establishment of ϵ–optimality of the $L_{R-\epsilon P}$ scheme in the r–action case in general terms is incomplete. However, it is reasonable to assume that the arguments given for the two–action case carry over to the r–action case also.

5.4   Absolutely Expedient Schemes

The convergence properties of absolutely expedient schemes such as the L_{R-I} scheme are radically different from those of ergodic schemes such as the L_{R-P} scheme. As we shall see presently, absolutely expedient schemes have absorbing states and the action probability vector converges to one of these states with probability 1. Also, the powerful martingale convergence theorem can be applied here and can be used to prove convergence $w.p.1$. The state to which the action probability converges is very much dependent on the initial value $p(0)$ unlike the case of ergodic algorithms.

Let us consider a general class of absolutely expedient algorithms studied in Chapter 4. These have the general form given in Eq.(4.84) and are given below.

$$
\begin{aligned}
p_i(n+1) \quad &= p_i(n)(1 - \lambda(p(n))) && \text{if } \alpha(n) \neq \alpha_i,\ \beta(n) = 0 \\
&= p_i(n)(1 + \mu(p(n))) && \text{if } \alpha(n) \neq \alpha_i,\ \beta(n) = 1 \\
&= p_i(n) + \lambda(p(n))(1 - p_i(n)) && \text{if } \alpha(n) = \alpha_i,\ \beta(n) = 0 \\
&= p_i(n) - \mu(p(n))(1 - p_i(n)) && \text{if } \alpha(n) = \alpha_i,\ \beta(n) = 1
\end{aligned}
\tag{5.49}
$$

where $\lambda(p)$ and $\mu(p)$ are continuous functions satisfying

$$
\begin{aligned}
0 &< \lambda(p) < 1 \\
0 &\leq \mu(p) < \min_i \tfrac{p_i}{1 - p_i}
\end{aligned}
\tag{5.50}
$$

for all p belonging to the open simplex S_r^0. The conditions above apply to reward–inaction and reward–penalty schemes. We shall make two further assumptions that will be helpful in later developments.

Assumption A

$$
\lambda(p) = 0 \text{ only if } p \text{ is a unit vector} \tag{5.51}
$$

Assumption B

$$
\text{The penalty probabilities } c_1, c_2, \ldots, c_r \text{ are distinct.} \tag{5.52}
$$

Comment 5.4: Assumption A ensures that $\lambda(p)$ cannot be zero unless p is a unit vector. It does not exclude cases where $\lambda(p)$ is not zero for any value of p. An important consequence of this assumption is that the unit vectors (or the corners of the simplex S_r) are the only absorbing states of the process $\{p(n)\}$.

Comment 5.5: Assumption B is needed to simplify the convergence results developed in this chapter. It is fairly easy to see how the results should be modified when the assumption is not justified. Comments on this aspect will be made at appropriate points.

We consider next the asymptotic behavior of the Markov process $\{p(n)\}$ in the following theorems.

Theorem 5.2: Under Assumptions A and B, the set of unit r–vectors forms the set of all absorbing states of the Markov process $\{p(n); n \geq 0\}$.

Proof: Rewrite the absolutely expedient scheme of Eq.(5.49) in the vector form, as follows.

If $\alpha(n) = \alpha_i$,

$$
\begin{aligned}
p(n+1) = \ & p(n) + (e_i - p(n))\lambda(p(n))(1 - \beta(n)) \\
& -(e_i - p(n))\mu(p(n))\beta(n).
\end{aligned}
\tag{5.53}
$$

An absorbing state corresponds to the value of $p(n)$ for which

$$
p(n+1) = p(n) \ \ w.p.1.
\tag{5.54}
$$

Suppose $p(n) = e_i$. It can be seen from Eq.(5.53) that $p(n+1) = p(n)$ $w.p.1$. Thus all unit vectors are absorbing states of $\{p(n)\}$. To show that there are no other absorbing states, observe that,

$$
\begin{aligned}
p(n+1) - p(n) = \ & (e_i - p(n))\lambda(p(n)) \\
& \text{with probability } p_i(n)(1 - c_i)
\end{aligned}
\tag{5.55}
$$

$$
\begin{aligned}
p(n+1) - p(n) = \ & (e_i - p(n))\mu(p(n)) \\
& \text{with probability } p_i(n)c_i.
\end{aligned}
\tag{5.56}
$$

For Eq.(5.54) to be satisfied, at least one of the following two conditions should be true.

(i)   The expressions on the r.h.s. of Eqs.(5.55) and (5.56) are zero.

(ii)   The probabilities associated with the expressions are zero.

The r.h.s. of Eq.(5.55) can be zero only for a unit vector because of Eq.(5.51) (Assumption A). When $p_i(n) \neq 0$, the probability $p_i(n)(1 - c_i) \neq 0$ for at least $(r - 1)$ values of $i(i = 1, \dots, r)$ as all the c_i cannot be equal to unity in view of Eq.(5.52) (Assumption B). If $p_i(n) = 0$ for these $r - 1$ components of $p(n)$, then $p(n)$ becomes a unit vector. Thus no absorbing states other than unit vectors are possible.

Comment 5.6: The proof of Theorem 5.2 indicates that the full force of Assumption B is not needed. It is enough if it is assumed that not more than one penalty probability is equal to unity.

The next theorem probes the convergence of $\{p(n)\}$ further.

Theorem 5.3: Under Assumptions A and B, the Markov process $\{p(n)\}$ converges $w.p.1$ to the set of unit r–vectors.

Proof: It has been shown in Chapter 4 [Eq.(4.71)] that for the absolutely expedient scheme of Eq.(5.49),

$$\begin{aligned} \Delta M(n) &= E[M(n+1) - M(n)|p(n)] \\ &= [\lambda(p(n)) + \mu(p(n))]p^T(n)Cp(n) \end{aligned} \tag{5.57}$$

where C is an $(r \times r)$ matrix with elements

$$C_{ij} = -\frac{1}{2}(c_i - c_j)^2. \tag{5.58}$$

Further it has been shown that $\Delta M(n)$ is negative–semidefinite and thus the sequence $\{M(n)\}$ is a supermartingale. $M(n)$ is positive and is bounded above by the highest penalty probability c_h and hence by the martingale convergence theorem (Appendix B) $M(n)$ converges to a random variable $w.p.1$. It also follows from the corollary to the martingale convergence theorem that

$$\lim_{n \to \infty} \Delta M(n) = 0 \quad w.p.1. \tag{5.59}$$

Observe from Eq.(5.57) that Eq.(5.59) is possible only if either

$$\left. \begin{array}{l} \text{(i) } \lambda(p(n)) + \mu(p(n)) \to 0 \\ \text{or} \\ \text{(ii) } p^T(n)Cp(n) \to 0 \end{array} \right\} \quad w.p.1. \tag{5.60}$$

As seen earlier, Assumption A [Eq.(5.51)] and the continuity of $\lambda(\cdot)$ and $\mu(\cdot)$ require

$$\lim_{n \to \infty} p(n) \in \{e_i\} \quad (i = 1, 2, \ldots, r)$$

for (i) to be satisfied. Now consider (ii)

$$p^T(n)Cp(n) = -\frac{1}{2} \sum_{i=1}^{r} \sum_{j=1}^{r} (c_i - c_j)^2 p_i(n)p_j(n). \tag{5.61}$$

All the terms on the r.h.s. are of the same sign and further the coefficients $(c_i - c_j)^2$ are nonzero when $i \neq j$ because of Assumption B [Eq.(5.52)]. Hence (ii) is satisfied only when $p_i(n)p_j(n) \to 0$ for all $i \neq j$. This in turn means that $p(n)$ converges to a unit vector $w.p.1$. Thus when either (i) or (ii) is satisfied,

$$\lim_{n \to \infty} p(n) \in \{e_i\} \quad (i = 1, 2, \ldots, r). \tag{5.62}$$

Comment 5.7: The effect of Assumptions A [Eq.(5.51)] and B [Eq.(5.52)] not being satisfied on the conclusions of Theorem 5.3 can be argued as follows.

Suppose Assumption A is not satisfied. Then from (i) of Eq.(5.60), $p(n)$ can converge to a vector p for which

$$\lambda(p) + \mu(p) = 0 \tag{5.63}$$

and as we know this can happen even when p is not a unit vector and lies on the boundary of the simplex S_r. Hence the set of limiting vectors for $p(n)$ has to be enlarged beyond the set of unit r–vectors.

Now suppose Assumption B is not satisfied and the penalty probabilities are not all distinct. For the sake of argument let $c_2 = c_3$. From (ii) of Eqs.(5.60) and (5.61) it follows that since $c_2 - c_3 = 0$, $p^T C p$ can be zero even when $p_2 p_3 \neq 0$. As the other $c_i (i \neq 2,3)$ are distinct, the limiting values of $p_2(n)$ and $p_3(n)$ can be nonzero while all the other components of $p(n)$ tend to zero. Hence $p(n)$ can tend to a vector p w.p.1 such that $p_2 + p_3 = 1$. Thus again the limiting vector is not necessarily a unit vector.

Continuing the argument, if we now coalesce actions 2 and 3 into a single action whose probability is $p_2 + p_3$, the limiting vector remains a unit vector, but has $(r - 1)$ components. The argument can be extended to any number of coincidences in the penalty probability set.

5.4.1   Convergence Probabilities

Theorem 5.3 assures us that $p(n)$ converges to one of the unit vectors with probability 1. However, we do not know to which unit vector it converges.

In the two–action case, for example, we know that $p_1(n)$ converges to 0 or 1 w.p.1. This means that in a number of runs of the automaton, in some runs $p_1(n)$ converges to zero and in almost all the rest it converges to 1. If $c_1 < c_2$ the optimal value of $p_1(n)$ is 1 and we are interested in knowing more about the possible convergence of $p_1(n)$ to 1. Thus the next question is to find the probability of convergence of $p_1(n)$ to 1 as $n \to \infty$. This probability is called a *convergence probability*.

More generally, in the r–action case $p(n)$ is a Markov process with r absorbing states each corresponding to a unit vector. The probability with which $p(n)$ converges to each of the unit vectors is a convergence probability. From the theory of Markov processes with absorbing states, it is well known that these convergence probabilities depend very much on the initial action probability vector $p(0)$. Thus we can define the convergence probabilities as follows.

Let

$$\Gamma_i(p) = Pr[p_i(\infty) = 1|p(0) = p] \quad (i = 1, 2, \ldots, r). \tag{5.64}$$

In other words $\Gamma_i(p)$ is the probability with which $p(n)$ converges to e_i when the initial probability is p. Hence $\Gamma_i(p)$ can also be expressed as

$$\Gamma_i(p) = Pr[p(\infty) = e_i|p(0) = p] \quad (i = 1, 2, \ldots, r). \tag{5.65}$$

There are r such functions corresponding to the r values of i and we will refer to them as the convergence probabilities of the learning automaton operating according to an absolutely expedient reinforcement scheme.

If c_ℓ is the minimum penalty probability, α_ℓ is the optimal action. We are particularly interested in the probability with which the automaton asymptotically chooses action α_ℓ which may be called the desired action. In other words, the quantity of interest is the probability that $p(n)$ converges to the unit vector e_ℓ. Of all the r convergence probabilities, the convergence probability $\Gamma_\ell(p)$ is of major interest. It also follows that

$$1 - \Gamma_\ell(p) = Pr[p_\ell(\infty) = 0|p(0) = p] \tag{5.66}$$

denotes the probability of convergence of $p(n)$ to the undesired actions.

For judging the behavior of the automaton it would be good to have a knowledge of $\Gamma_\ell(p)$. In fact, we would like $\Gamma_\ell(p)$ to be as close to 1 as possible. However, it appears difficult to evaluate this function for any given reinforcement scheme. An alternative is to get bounds on $\Gamma_\ell(p)$. This will be attempted in the next subsection.

5.4.2 Bounds on $\Gamma_i(p)$

It will be shown in this subsection that $\Gamma_i(p)$ $(i = 1, 2, \ldots, r)$ satisfies a functional equation with appropriate boundary conditions (Norman, 1968). In view of the difficulty encountered in solving such equations, an attempt is made to determine bounds on $\Gamma_i(p)$ $(i = 1, 2, \ldots, r)$ which satisfy functional inequalities. In this context it becomes necessary to define classes of functions which are particularly suited for use in such functional inequalities and equations. Such functions are called superregular and subregular functions and are discussed in this section.

As before let S_r denote the simplex of r action probabilities and let S_r^0 denote the interior of the simplex where $p_i > 0$ for each i. Also let $C(S_r)$ denote the class of all continuous functions mapping $S_r \to \mathcal{R}$ where $\mathcal{R}$ is the real line. We define an operator U on such functions as follows.

Definition 5.6: If $\psi(\cdot) \in C(S_r)$, then

$$U\psi(p) = E[\psi(p(n+1))|p(n) = p] \tag{5.67}$$

Comment 5.8: Thus $U\psi(p)$ is the conditional expectation of $\psi(p(n+1))$, the conditioning being on the action probability vector at the previous instant. It is evident that $U\psi(p)$ depends on the manner of updating of $p(n)$ and hence varies with the reinforcement scheme and the environment. It is thus tied to the particular automaton model being considered. It may be noted that $U\psi(p)$ is independent of n which occurs on the r.h.s. of Eq.(5.67). This implies that we tacitly assume a reinforcement scheme which does not have parameters explicitly dependent on n. We have been considering only such schemes all along. Because of this property, one can replace n by any positive integer in Eq.(5.67) without affecting $U\psi(p)$.

Comment 5.9: Since the expectation operator is linear, U is a linear operator. Further, as the expectation of a nonnegative function remains nonnegative, U preserves nonnegative functions. In other words, if $\psi(p) \geq 0$ for all $p \in S_r$, then $U\psi(p) \geq 0$ for all $p \in S_r$.

Comment 5.10: The operator U can be applied repeatedly. It follows from the definition of U that the application of U repeatedly n times can be represented by U^n in the following manner.

$$U^n\psi(p) = E[\psi(p(n))|p(0) = p]. \tag{5.68}$$

Thus U^n for $n \geq 1$ gives the conditional expectation of $\psi(p(n))$ conditioned on the action probability vector n steps earlier.

Superregular and Subregular Functions: Based on the operator U, three classes of functions can be defined as follows.

Definition 5.7: A function $\psi \in C(S_r)$ is called *superregular* if

$$\psi(p) \geq U\psi(p) \tag{5.69}$$

for all $p \in S_r$.

Similarly, $\psi(\cdot)$ is called *regular*, if

$$\psi(p) = U\psi(p) \tag{5.70}$$

and *subregular*, if

$$\psi(p) \leq U\psi(p) \tag{5.71}$$

over $p \in S_r$.

It is evident from the definition that if $\psi(\cdot)$ is superregular then $-\psi(\cdot)$ is subregular and vice versa. Further, a regular function can be regarded as both super– and subregular. The function $\psi(p) \equiv k$, a constant, falls under the class of such regular functions. The three classes of functions will be collectively referred to as regular functions.

There is a close connection between regular functions and martingales. It can be seen from their definitions that similar conditional expectations and inequalities are involved. However, a major difference is that martingales are sequences whereas regularity mainly concerns properties of functions. Further, the expectation, in the case of martingales, is conditioned on all the previous elements of the sequence, while only one previous element is involved in regular functions.

Suppose we have a sequence $\{p(n)\}$, which has the Markov property i.e., conditioning on all the previous elements of the sequence is the same as conditioning on just the latest previous element. Then, if $\psi(p)$ is superregular,

$$\psi(p) \geq E[\psi(p(n+1)|p(n) = p] \tag{5.72}$$

that is,

$$\psi(p(n)) \geq E[\psi(p(n+1))|p(n), p(n-1), \ldots, p(0)]. \tag{5.73}$$

It follows from the definition (Appendix B) that the sequence $\{\psi(p(n))\}$ is a supermartingale. The situation is the same with regard to subregular functions and submartingales. Thus we can conclude that superregular functions induce supermartingales and subregular functions induce submartingales.

Some other properties of regular functions that immediately follow from their definition are given below.

Property 1. If $\psi(\cdot)$ is superregular, so is $k\psi(\cdot)$ for any $k \geq 0$.

Property 2. If $\psi_1(\cdot)$ and $\psi_2(\cdot)$ are superregular, so is $\psi_1(\cdot) + \psi_2(\cdot)$.

Similar properties hold for subregular functions.

Let us consider one example that uses the properties above in the sequel.

Example 5.7: Let $\psi_i(p) = e^{-x_i p_i}$ be superregular. x_i is a positive constant and p is a probability vector. Clearly, when p is a unit vector,

$$\psi_i(e_i) = e^{-x_i}$$
$$\psi_i(e_j) = 1 \text{ for } j \neq i.$$

Consider a related function,

$$\phi_i(p) = (\psi_i(e_j) - \psi_i(p))/(\psi_i(e_j) - \psi_i(e_i))$$
$$= (1 - e^{-x_i p_i})/(1 - e^{-x_i}) \tag{5.74}$$

Now $-e^{-x_i p_i}$ is subregular and $1 - e^{-x_i} > 0$. Hence by properties 1 and 2, $\phi_i(p)$ is subregular.

It is evident from the considerations above that if $\psi_i(p)$ is subregular, $\phi_i(p)$ will then be superregular.

The main results in obtaining bounds on the convergence probabilities can now be derived. The basic idea in obtaining bounds is stated in the form of the following proposition.

Proposition 5.1 Let $\psi_i(\cdot) \in C(S_r)$ be superregular with $\psi_i(e_i) = 1$ and $\psi_i(e_j) = 0$ (for $j \neq i$); then

$$\psi_i(p) \geq \Gamma_i(p) \tag{5.75}$$

for all $p \in S_r$.

If $\psi_i(\cdot) \in C(S_r)$ is subregular with the same boundary conditions, then

$$\psi_i(p) \leq \Gamma_i(p) \tag{5.76}$$

for all $p \in S_r$.

Proof: Let $\psi_i(\cdot)$ be superregular, that is,

$$\psi_i(p) - U\psi_i(p) \geq 0 \tag{5.77}$$

for all $p \in S_r$. Applying U again to the l.h.s. of Eq.(5.77) and recognizing the fact that U is linear and preserves nonnegative functions,

$$U\psi_i(p) - U^2\psi_i(p) \geq 0$$

or

$$U\psi_i(p) \geq U^2\psi_i(p).$$

A repeated application of the operation yields

$$U\psi_i(p) \geq U^2\psi_i(p). \geq \ldots \geq U^\infty\psi_i(p). \tag{5.78}$$

From Theorem 5.3, we know that $p(n)$ converges $w.p.1$. It follows that $U^\infty\psi_i(p)$ exists and is unique. Moreover,

$$U^\infty\psi_i(p) = E[\psi_i(p(\infty))|p(0) = p] \text{ by definition}$$
$$= \sum_{j=1}^r \psi_i(e_j)Pr[p(\infty) = e_j|p(0) = p] \text{ by Theorem 5.3} \tag{5.79}$$
$$= Pr[p(\infty) = e_i|p(0) = p]$$

since $\psi_i(e_j) = 0$ for $j \neq i$ and $\psi_i(e_i) = 1$.

Thus by inspection of the r.h.s. of Eq.(5.79)

$$U^\infty \psi_i(p) = \Gamma_i(p) \tag{5.80}$$

From Eqs.(5.77),(5.78), and (5.80) it follows that

$$\psi_i(p) \geq \Gamma_i(p).$$

The reverse inequality follows in a similar fashion when $\psi_i(\cdot)$ is subregular.

Comment 5.11: Proposition 5.1 reduces the problem of obtaining bounds on $\Gamma_i(p)$ to finding super– and subregular functions with appropriate boundary conditions.

The development above also leads to the functional equation to be satisfied by $\Gamma_i(p)$. From Eq.(5.80),

$$U^\infty \psi_i(p) = \Gamma_i(p).$$

Since $UU^\infty \psi_i(p) = U^\infty \psi_i(p)$, it follows that

$$U\Gamma_i(p) = \Gamma_i(p) \tag{5.81}$$

for all $p \in S_r$. Thus $\Gamma_i(p)$ is the solution of the functional equation (5.81) with boundary conditions, $\Gamma_i(e_i) = 1$, $\Gamma_i(e_j) = 0$ $(j \neq i)$.

5.4.3 Determination of $\psi_i(p)$

Proposition 5.1 has shown that we need to find superregular and subregular functions for computing bounds on convergence probabilities. To do this we need to satisfy the inequalities of Eqs.(5.69) and (5.71) involving the operator U. This operator is completely defined in terms of the reinforcement scheme and the environment. Thus satisfaction of Eqs.(5.69) and (5.71) is problem dependent.

No general method of identifying super– and subregular functions is presently known; one has to start with a promising functional form and evaluate the parameters of the function so that the required inequality is satisfied. In this context regular functions can be compared with Lyapunov functions of stability theory.

Let us start with a simple form of $\psi_i(p)$. Consider,

$$\psi_i(p) = e^{-x_i p_i} \tag{5.82}$$

where $x_i > 0$. The weakness of this function is that it depends on a single component of p namely p_i; it disregards the other components of the initial probability vector. However, it has the merit of leading to expressions that can be handled conveniently.

We shall now derive conditions on x_i so that $\psi_i(\cdot)$ is superregular or subregular (Lakshmivarahan and Thathachar, 1976).

From the reinforcement scheme of Eq.(5.49) and the definition of Eq.(5.67) of the operator U, it can be seen that [2]

$$
\begin{aligned}
U\psi_i(p) - \psi_i(p) \; &= E[\exp(-x_i p_i(n+1)|p(n) = p] - \exp(-x_i p_i) \\
&= \sum_{\substack{j=1 \\ j \neq i}}^{r} \exp[-x_i p_i(1 - \lambda(p))]p_j(1 - c_j) \\
&+ \sum_{\substack{j=1 \\ j \neq i}}^{r} \exp[-x_i p_i(1 + \mu(p))]p_j c_j \\
&+ \exp[-x_i p_i - x_i(1 - p_i)\lambda(p)]p_i(1 - c_i) \\
&+ \exp[-x_i p_i + x_i(1 - p_i)\mu(p)]p_i c_i \\
&- \exp[-x_i p_i].
\end{aligned}
\tag{5.83}
$$

This expression is somewhat unwieldy and hence the following abbreviation is useful.

Let a function $V(\cdot)$ mapping $\mathcal{R} \to \mathcal{R}$ be defined by,

$$
\begin{aligned}
V(u) \; &= (e^u - 1)/u \text{ for } u \neq 0 \\
&= 1 \text{ for } u = 0
\end{aligned}
\tag{5.84}
$$

The following properties of the function $V(\cdot)$ are worth noting for future use. It can be checked that

(i) $V(u) > 0$ for all u.

(ii) $V(u)$ is strictly monotonically increasing.

(iii) $V(u)$ is convex.

A related function is

$$H(u) = Ln \, V(u) \tag{5.85}$$

where Ln denotes logarithm to base e. The properties (ii) and (iii) listed above for $V(u)$ carry over to $H(u)$ also.

---

[2] $\exp(z)$ denotes e^z.

In terms of $V(\cdot)$, Eq.(5.83) can be written as

$$U\psi_i(p) - \psi_i(p) = -x_i G_i(x_i, p)\exp(-x_i p_i) \tag{5.86}$$

where

$$
\begin{aligned}
G_i(x_i, p) &= p_i(1 - p_i)(1 - c_i)\lambda(p)V[-x_i(1 - p_i)\lambda(p)] \\
&\quad - p_i(1 - p_i)c_i\mu(p)V[x_i(1 - p_i)\mu(p)] \\
&\quad - \left(\sum_{j\neq i} p_j(1 - c_j)\right) p_i\lambda(p)V[x_i p_i\lambda(p)] \\
&\quad + \left(\sum_{j\neq i} p_j c_j\right) p_i\mu(p)V[-x_i p_i\mu(p)].
\end{aligned} \tag{5.87}
$$

Now $\psi_i(p)$ is subregular if

$$G_i(x_i, p) \leq 0 \quad \text{for all } p \in S_r \tag{5.88}$$

and superregular if

$$G_i(x_i, p) \geq 0 \quad \text{for all } p \in S_r. \tag{5.89}$$

These are the governing inequalities for the most general absolutely expedient scheme. To obtain the best bounds one has to find the limiting values of x_i for which the inequalities hold good. For the purpose of illustrating the idea, a special but nontrivial case of the nonlinear reward–inaction (N_{R-I}) algorithm is considered first by setting $\mu(\cdot) \equiv 0$.

The Nonlinear Reward–Inaction (N_{R-I}) Scheme: Setting $\mu(\cdot) \equiv 0$ in Eq.(5.87) it follows that $\psi_i(p)$ is subregular if,

$$f(p, x_i) = \frac{V[-x_i(1 - p_i)\lambda(p)]}{V[x_i p_i\lambda(p)]} \leq \frac{\sum_{j\neq i} p_j(1 - c_j)}{(1 - p_i)(1 - c_i)} \tag{5.90}$$

and superregular if,

$$f(p, x_i) \geq \frac{\sum_{j\neq i} p_j(1 - c_j)}{(1 - p_i)(1 - c_i)} \tag{5.91}$$

The r.h.s. of Eqs.(5.90) and (5.91) consist only of nonnegative quantities. Thus substituting $d_j = 1 - c_j$, we can write

$$\left(\sum_{j\neq i} p_j\right) \min_{j\neq i}\left(\frac{d_j}{d_i}\right) \leq \sum_{j\neq i} p_j\frac{d_j}{d_i} \leq \left(\sum_{j\neq i} p_j\right) \max_{j\neq i}\left(\frac{d_j}{d_i}\right). \tag{5.92}$$

Recognizing

$$\sum_{j\neq i} p_j = 1 - p_i$$

the r.h.s. of Eq.(5.90) can now be bounded as

$$\min_{j\neq i}\left(\frac{d_j}{d_i}\right) \leq \frac{\sum_{j\neq i} p_j d_j/d_i}{\sum_{j\neq i} p_j} \leq \max_{j\neq i}\left(\frac{d_j}{d_i}\right). \qquad (5.93)$$

Thus according to Eqs.(5.90) and (5.91), $\psi_i(p)$ is

$$\left.\begin{array}{l} (i) \text{ superregular if } f(p, x_i) \geq \max_{j\neq i}(d_j/d_i) \text{ for all } p \in S_r \\ (ii) \text{ subregular if } f(p, x_i) \leq \min_{j\neq i}(d_j/d_i) \text{ for all } p \in S_r \end{array}\right\} \qquad (5.94)$$

For further simplification let us employ logarithms. Let

$$\Delta(p, x_i) = Ln \; f(p, x_i). \qquad (5.95)$$

From Eqs.(5.75) and (5.80)

$$\begin{aligned} \Delta(p, x_i) &= H[-x_i(1 - p_i)\lambda(p)] - H[x_i p_i \lambda(p)] \\ &= \int_{t_1}^{-t_2} H'(u)du \end{aligned} \qquad (5.96)$$

where

$$H'(u) = \frac{dH(u)}{du}, \; t_1 = x_i p_i \lambda(p), \; t_2 = x_i(1 - p_i)\lambda(p).$$

$H'(u)$ is nonnegative and monotonically increasing. Hence it can be easily checked that

$$\int_a^{-b} H'(u)du \leq \int_0^{-(a+b)} H'(u)du \qquad (5.97)$$

and

$$\int_a^{-b} H'(u)du \geq -\int_0^{a+b} H'(u)du \qquad (5.98)$$

for any $a, b > 0$.

Using the inequalities above, $\Delta(p, x_i)$ in Eq.(5.96) can be bounded as follows.

$$-\int_0^{x_i \lambda_{\max}} H'(u)du \leq \Delta(p, x_i) \leq \int_0^{-x_i \lambda_{\min}} H'(u)du \qquad (5.99)$$

where

$$\begin{aligned} \lambda_{\max} &= \sup_{S_r} \lambda(p) \\ \lambda_{\min} &= \inf_{S_r} \lambda(p). \end{aligned} \qquad (5.100)$$

Taking exponentials throughout Eq.(5.99), we get,

$$\frac{1}{V(x_i\lambda_{\max})} \leq f(p, x_i) \leq V(-x_i\lambda_{\min}) \tag{5.101}$$

Comparing with Eq.(5.94), let us set

$$V(x_i\lambda_{\max}) = \frac{1}{\max_{j\neq i}\left(\frac{d_j}{d_i}\right)} \tag{5.102}$$

and

$$V(-x_i\lambda_{\min}) = \min_{j\neq i}\left(\frac{d_j}{d_i}\right) \tag{5.103}$$

Let a_i and b_i be the values of $x_i > 0$ for which Eqs.(5.102) and (5.103) are satisfied respectively. It can be seen that such values can always be found when $\lambda_{\min} \neq 0$ and d_j/d_i is less than unity for all $j \neq i$. In fact the latter condition is automatically satisfied when $i = \ell$.

The inequality of Eq.(5.94) indicates that

$$\psi_i(p) = \exp(-x_ip_i)$$

is superregular when $x_i = a_i$ and subregular when $x_i = b_i$.

However, $\psi_i(p)$ cannot be directly used as a bound on $\Gamma_i(p)$ as it does not satisfy the boundary conditions stated in Proposition 5.1. Hence define, as in Eq.(5.74),

$$\phi_i(p) = \frac{1 - \exp(-x_ip_i)}{1 - \exp(-x_i)} \tag{5.104}$$

which satisfies $\phi_i(e_i) = 1$ and $\phi_i(e_j) = 0$. As seen in Example 5.7, $\phi_i(p)$ is subregular when $\psi_i(p)$ is superregular and is superregular when $\psi_i(p)$ is subregular. It follows that $\phi_i(p)$ provides the needed bounds on $\Gamma_i(p)$. Thus,

$$\frac{1 - \exp(-a_ip_i)}{1 - \exp(-a_i)} \leq \Gamma_i(p) \leq \frac{1 - \exp(-b_ip_i)}{1 - \exp(-b_i)}. \tag{5.105}$$

The procedure for finding the bounds can now be summarized as follows.

(i) For finding the bounds on $\Gamma_i(p)$, first evaluate $\max_{j\neq i}(d_j/d_i)$ and $\min_{j\neq i}(d_j/d_i)$.

(ii) Find $\lambda_{\max}$ and $\lambda_{\min}$ from the reinforcement scheme as per Eq.(5.100).

(iii) Evaluate $x_i = a_i$, the solution of Eq.(5.102), where V is defined in Eq.(5.84).

(iv) Evaluate $x_i = b_i$, the solution of Eq.(5.103).

(v) The bounds on $\Gamma_i(p)$ for the given initial action probability vector $p(0) = p$ are now given by Eq.(5.105).

With this background we are now ready to consider the general nonlinear reward–penalty scheme.

The Nonlinear Reward–Penalty (N_{R-P}) **Scheme:** This is the most general case and here it is not possible to give explicit equations for the determination of the parameters a_i and b_i as in the N_{R-I} scheme. The procedure for finding them is however conceptually straightforward as follows.

Find the *maximum* value of $x_i > 0$ for which

$$G_i(x_i, p) \geq 0 \text{ for all } p \in S_r. \tag{5.106}$$

Set this value of $x_i = a_i$. Similarly find the *minimum* value of $x_i > 0$ for which

$$G_i(x_i, p) \leq 0 \text{ for all } p \in S_r. \tag{5.107}$$

Set this value of $x_i = b_i$. It can be seen that such values a_i, b_i exist at least when $i = \ell$; for, from Eq.(5.87),

$$\begin{aligned}
G_\ell(0, p) &= p_\ell \lambda(p) \sum_{j \neq \ell} p_j(d_\ell - d_j) \\
&\quad + p_\ell \mu(p) \sum_{j \neq \ell} p_j(c_j - c_\ell) \\
&> 0
\end{aligned}$$

and $G_\ell(x_\ell, p) \to -\infty$ as $x_\ell \to \infty$.

As shown in the case of the N_{R-I} scheme, it follows that $\phi_i(p)$ is subregular when $x_i = a_i$ and is superregular when $x_i = b_i$. Thus Eq.(5.105) again provides bounds on $\Gamma_i(p)$.

The results above can be stated in the form of the following theorem.

Theorem 5.4: Let a learning automaton operate according to the absolutely expedient scheme of Eq.(5.49) satisfying Assumption A in a random environment which fulfills Assumption B. The convergence probabilities $\Gamma_i(p)$ $(i = 1, 2, \dots, r)$ can then be bounded as given in Eq.(5.105) as

$$\frac{1 - e^{-a_i p_i}}{1 - e^{-a_i}} \leq \Gamma_i(p) \leq \frac{1 - e^{-b_i p_i}}{1 - e^{-b_i}}$$

for all $p \in S_r$ where a_i, b_i are given by Eqs.(5.106) and (5.107).

Comment 5.12: Although a general subscript i has been used for $\Gamma_i(p)$ in getting the bounds, the form of the bounds chosen is most appropriate for the case $i = \ell$ i.e., convergence to the desired action α_ℓ. For other actions possibly only one of the bounds may be obtained from the indicated procedure.

5.4.4 Examples

The computation of bounds will be illustrated by the following four examples.

Example 5.8: Consider a ten–action automaton operating in a random environment whose penalty probability set is given by

$$\{0.1, 0.45, 0.5, 0.55, 0.60, 0.78, 0.87, 0.90, 0.93, 0.95\}.$$

The reinforcement scheme is L_{R-I} with

$$\lambda(p) \equiv 0.10, \ \mu(p) \equiv 0.$$

It is desired to compute bounds on $\Gamma_\ell(p)$.

From the data above, $c_\ell = 0.1$, but the value of ℓ is not known. Referring to Eq.(5.94),

$$\max_{j \neq \ell} \tfrac{d_j}{d_\ell} = \tfrac{1-0.45}{1-0.1} = 0.55/0.9 = 11/18$$

$$\min_{j \neq \ell} \tfrac{d_j}{d_\ell} = \tfrac{1-0.95}{1-0.1} = 0.05/0.9 = 1/18.$$

Substituting the above values in Eqs.(5.102) and (5.103) with $\lambda_{\max} = \lambda_{\min} = 0.1$ and solving for a_ℓ and b_ℓ we get

$$a_\ell = 9.2 \ , \ b_\ell = 180.$$

The upper and lower bounds can now be obtained as

$$\frac{1 - e^{-a_\ell p_\ell}}{1 - e^{-a_\ell}} \leq \Gamma_\ell(p) \leq \frac{1 - e^{-b_\ell p_\ell}}{1 - e^{-b_\ell}}$$

for different initial values $p_\ell(0) = p_\ell$ and are listed below.

p_ℓ	0.1	0.2	0.5
lower bound	0.60	0.84	0.99
upper bound	1.00	1.00	1.00

In practice only the first column is relevant as all the initial action probabilities are usually made equal.

Example 5.9: Consider now a two–action automaton operating in a random environment with the penalty probability set $\{0.4, 0.8\}$. The bounds on $\Gamma_\ell(p)$ for $p_1 = p_2 = \frac{1}{2}$ and a number of values of the parameter a can be computed. The following five steps yield the bounds on $\Gamma_\ell(p)$:

(i) $\max_{j \neq \ell} d_j/d_\ell = \min_{j \neq \ell} d_j/d_\ell = 0.2/0.6 = 1/3$

(ii) $\lambda_{\max} = \lambda_{\min} = a$
Let $a = 0.9$.

(iii) From Eq.(5.102)
$V(0.9a_\ell) = 3$
Solving, $a_\ell = 2.12$

(iv) From Eq.(5.103),
$V(0.9b_\ell) = 1/3$
Solving, $b_\ell = 3.13$

(v) Now using Eq.(5.105),
$1 - \exp(-2.12p_\ell)/[1 - \exp(-2.12)] \leq \Gamma_\ell(p) \leq 1 - \exp(-3.13p_\ell)/[1 - \exp(-3.13)]$.

For instance, if $p_\ell(0) = p_\ell = 1/2$,

$$0.743 \leq \Gamma_\ell(p) \leq 0.826.$$

The values of a_ℓ, b_ℓ and the bounds for $p_\ell = \frac{1}{2}$ are shown in Table 5.1 for various values of a.

a	a_ℓ	b_ℓ	Lower Bound on $\Gamma_\ell(p)$	Upper Bound on $\Gamma_\ell(p)$
0.01	191	282	$1 - 3.35 \times 10^{-42}$	$1 - 5.81 \times 10^{-62}$
0.1	19.1	28.2	$1 - 7.12 \times 10^{-5}$	$1 - 7.52 \times 10^{-7}$
0.3	6.37	9.4	0.960	0.991
0.4	4.78	7.05	0.916	0.971
0.9	2.12	3.13	0.743	0.826

Table 5.1

It can be seen from the table above that $\Gamma_\ell(p)$ is practically 1.0 for values of a below 0.1. Higher values of a can be used if a higher probability of wrong convergence can be tolerated.

Example 5.10: A nonlinear scheme is considered in this example. The penalty probability set of the environment is $\{0.6, 0.2\}$. The automaton operates according to the N_{R-I} scheme,

$$\lambda(p) = 0.06 + 0.12p_1p_2$$
$$\mu(0) \equiv 0.$$

Following the previous procedure, the bounds for $p_\ell(0) = p_\ell = 1/2$ are given by

$$(1 - 9.12 \times 10^{-4}) \le \Gamma_\ell(p) \le (1 - 1.59 \times 10^{-6}).$$

Suppose an L_{R-I} scheme with $a = 0.08$ is used in the same environment. As will be shown later this value of a is chosen as the scheme has the same rate of convergence as the N_{R-I} scheme. Following the previous procedure,

$$a_\ell = 15.75 \quad b_\ell = 20$$

and the bounds for $p_\ell(0) = p_\ell = \frac{1}{2}$ are

$$(1 - 3.78 \times 10^{-4}) \le \Gamma_\ell(p) \le (1 - 6.56 \times 10^{-5}).$$

Example 5.11: A nonlinear reward–penalty scheme is considered next. The penalty probability set continues to be $\{0.6, 0.2\}$. The reinforcement scheme is given by

$$\lambda(p) = 0.05 + 0.08p_1p_2$$
$$\mu(p) = 0.1p_1p_2.$$

The general procedure for N_{R-P} schemes must be used here for evaluating a_ℓ and b_ℓ. Using Eqs.(5.106) and (5.107),

$$a_\ell = 12.17 \quad b_\ell = 14.61.$$

The bounds on $\Gamma_\ell(p)$ for $p_\ell = \frac{1}{2}$ are then given by

$$(1 - 2.18 \times 10^{-3}) \le \Gamma_\ell(p) \le (1 - 6.75 \times 10^{-4}).$$

5.4.5   Absolute Expediency and ϵ–optimality

The bounds on convergence probabilities can be utilized to show the relationship between absolutely expedient schemes and ϵ–optimality. This topic is of particular interest following the counterexample of Kushner et al.

(Viswanathan and Narendra, 1972) which showed that the L_{R-I} and associated schemes are not optimal. In the absence of optimal schemes, attention was focused on ϵ–optimal schemes where the probability of choosing an undesired action can be made as small as required by a proper choice of the parameters of the scheme. It will be shown presently that every absolutely expedient scheme satisfying the additional Assumption A is ϵ–optimal in all stationary random environments. Thus a general form of absolutely expedient schemes can now be regarded as representing one class of ϵ–optimal schemes valid in all stationary random environments. It is interesting to note that the only optimal scheme reported in the literature (Vorontsova, 1965) refers to a continuous–time two–state automaton.

Consider Eq.(5.49) which represents one general form of absolutely expedient schemes. Let us introduce a parameter θ, such that

$$\left.\begin{array}{l} \lambda(p) = \theta\lambda_1(p) \\ \mu(p) = \theta\mu_1(p) \end{array}\right\} \tag{5.108}$$

where $0 \le \theta \le 1$ and $\lambda_1(\cdot), \mu_1(\cdot)$ are functions that satisfy the same conditions of Eq.(5.50) as $\lambda(\cdot)$ and $\mu(\cdot)$. Thus as $\theta \to 0$, $\lambda(\cdot)$ and $\mu(\cdot) \to 0$ for any value of p.

Suppose θ is very small i.e., $\theta \simeq 0$. Observing from Eq.(5.84) that for small values of u (taking the first three terms in the series for e^u)

$$V(u) \simeq 1 + \frac{u}{2}$$

and using Eqs.(5.87) to (5.89) it follows that $\psi_i(p)$ is super (sub) regular according to

$$x_i \begin{array}{c} \ge \\ (\le) \end{array} \frac{(\lambda_1(p) + \mu_1(p))(\sum_{j \ne i} p_j(c_j - c_i))}{\frac{1}{2}\theta D(p)} \tag{5.109}$$

for all $p \in S_r$, where

$$\begin{aligned} D(p) = \ & \lambda_1^2(p)[(1 - c_i)(1 - p_i)^2 + p_i \sum_{j \ne i} p_j(1 - c_j)] \\ & + \mu_1^2(p)[c_i(1 - p_i)^2 + p_i \sum_{j \ne i} p_j c_j] \end{aligned}$$

Setting $i = \ell$ and recognizing $(c_j - c_\ell) > 0$ for all $j \ne \ell$, the r.h.s. of Eq.(5.109) $\to +\infty$ as $\theta \to 0$. Hence a_ℓ in Eq.(5.105), which is the highest value of x_ℓ, satisfying the second inequality ($\le$) in Eq.(5.109) approaches $+\infty$ as $\theta \to 0$.

Substituting $i = \ell$ in Eq.(5.105) it is seen that (when $p_\ell \neq 0$)

$$\Gamma_\ell(p) \geq \frac{1 - e^{-a_\ell p_\ell}}{1 - e^{-a_\ell}} \to 1 \text{ as } \theta \to 0.$$

As $\Gamma_\ell(p)$ is a probability,

$$\Gamma_\ell(p) \to 1 \text{ as } \theta \to 0 \tag{5.110}$$

and this is true irrespective of the values of the penalty probabilities. Thus the probability of convergence to the desired action can be made arbitrarily close to unity by selecting a sufficiently small θ. Hence every absolutely expedient scheme satisfying Assumption A is ϵ–optimal in all stationary random environments. [3]

5.5 Rate of Convergence

An important aspect of convergence not considered thus far is the rate of convergence of learning automata. The previous analysis in this chapter focused on the mode of convergence and the convergence probabilities. These may be regarded as aspects of study of the accuracy of the automaton. Equally important is the speed of operation of the automaton. Often in applications, the speed of operation determines whether the learning automaton offers a successful solution or not. It is thus necessary to have a measure of the rate of convergence (Bhakthavathsalam, 1987).

We have seen that the automaton takes an infinite number of steps to converge to the desired action. If we wish to have an index of the rate of convergence, this would naturally be of the nature of a time constant, so commonly used in differential systems. Such an index would serve as a basis of comparison of the number of steps effectively needed by different reinforcement schemes to approach the final values of the action probability vector or other related quantities. We shall first consider absolutely expedient schemes.

5.5.1 Absolutely Expedient Schemes

In learning automata using absolutely expedient schemes, the action probability vector $p(n)$ converges *w.p.*1 to a member of the set of unit vectors.

---

[3]Following Comment 7 it can be seen that Assumption B is not needed for this conclusion.

Correspondingly, the average penalty $M(n)$ also converges to a random variable M^* w.p.1. Furthermore, $E[M(n)]$ converges to $E[M^*]$ and this convergence is monotonic. From the latter property, a natural measure of the instantaneous rate of convergence at stage n is

$$\hat{\rho}(n) = \frac{E[M(n+1)] - E[M^*]}{E[M(n)] - E[M^*]}. \tag{5.111}$$

This index $\hat{\rho}(n)$ indicates how close $E[M(n+1)]$ is to $E[M^*]$ in comparison with $E[M(n)]$. As $E[M(n)]$ is a monotonically decreasing function of n, $E[M(n+1)] \leq E[M(n)]$ and consequently, $\hat{\rho}(n) \leq 1$ for all n.

There is, however, a difficulty with the expression for $\hat{\rho}(n)$ in Eq.(5.111), i.e., $E[M^*]$ is unknown. Since $E[M^*] = c_\ell$ for an optimal scheme and $E[M^*] \geq c_\ell$ for an absolutely expedient scheme it follows that if in Eq.(5.111), $E[M^*]$ is replaced by c_ℓ then $\hat{\rho}(n)$ is approximated by

$$\hat{\rho}(n) \approx 1 - \frac{E[M(n) - M(n+1)]}{E[M(n)] - c_\ell}. \tag{5.112}$$

Using the expression of Eq.(5.57) for $\Delta M(n)$, Eq.(5.112) can be expressed as

$$\hat{\rho}(n) \approx 1 + \frac{E[\lambda(p(n)) + \mu(p(n))]p^T(n)Cp(n)}{E[p^T(n)c] - c_\ell}. \tag{5.113}$$

Once again, the right–hand side of Eq.(5.113) cannot be computed since the distribution of $p(n)$ is unknown. Hence, using the instantaneous value of $p(n)$, an instantaneous index of the rate of convergence can be defined as

$$\rho(n) = 1 + \frac{[\lambda(p(n)) + \mu(p(n))]p^T(n)Cp(n)}{p^T(n)c - c_\ell}. \tag{5.114}$$

Since from a practical standpoint, it is desirable to have an index of the rate of convergence that is a constant, an average rate of convergence ρ_{av} is derived using the values of $\rho(n)$ at $n = 0$ and $n = \infty$, which can be computed readily.

At $n = 0$ the action probability vector has all components equal so that $p_i(0) = \frac{1}{r}$ $(i = 1, 2, \ldots, r)$. Hence, using these values in Eq.(5.114), $\rho(0)$ can be determined. At $n = \infty$, $p_\ell(\infty) = 1 - \epsilon$ while $p_i(\infty)$ can be approximated by $\epsilon/(r-1)$ for $(i \neq \ell)$.

Expressing $\rho(n)$ in Eq.(5.114) as

$$\rho(n) = 1 - \frac{[\lambda(p(n)) + \mu(p(n))][\sum_{j=1}^{r}(\frac{1}{2})(c_i - c_j)^2 p_i(n)p_j(n)]}{\sum_{i=1}^{r} c_i p_i(n) - c_\ell} \tag{5.115}$$

and substituting for $p(\infty)$, we obtain as $\epsilon \to 0$

$$\rho(\infty) = 1 - \frac{[\lambda(p(\infty)) + \mu(p(\infty))][\sum_{i=1}^{r}(c_i - c_\ell)^2}{(\sum_{i=1}^{r}(c_i - c_\ell)}. \tag{5.116}$$

The average rate of convergence ρ_{av} is then defined as

$$\rho_{av} = \sqrt{\rho(0)\rho(\infty)}. \tag{5.117}$$

It is clear from the analysis above that a number of approximations must be made to obtain a practical measure ρ_{av} of the rate of convergence. The geometric mean of $\rho(0)$ and $\rho(\infty)$ chosen in Eq.(5.117) is also arbitrary. Hence ρ_{av} as defined above is not unique and other definitions for the rate of convergence can also be given. However, it is worth stating that despite the many approximations made, ρ_{av} as given by Eq.(5.117) has proved satisfactory while evaluating simulation results.

If ρ_{av} is used as an approximation of $\hat{\rho}(n)$ as defined in Eq.(5.111) it follows that

$$\rho_{av} \approx \frac{E[M(n+1) - M^*]}{E[M(n) - M^*]},$$

which implies that at every instant $E[M(n) - M^*]$ decreases by a factor of ρ_{av}. Hence, if $\tilde{T}$ is the time taken for $E[M(0) - M^*]$ to decrease to b times its value, it can be shown that

$$\tilde{T} = \log b / \log \rho_{av}. \tag{5.118}$$

In any application, the value of b can be specified so that $\tilde{T}$ represents the time of convergence to the desired value.

Comment 5.13: The expression of Eq.(5.114) for $\rho(n)$ indicates that the rate of convergence depends both on the reinforcement scheme as well as the environment.

Comment 5.14: The speed–accuracy conflict mentioned in Chapter 3 in connection with deterministic automata appears here also. It was shown in Section 5.4.5 that $\Gamma_\ell(p)$ approaches 1 as $[\lambda(p) + \mu(p)]$ tends to zero. Thus accuracy increases as $[\lambda(p) + \mu(p)]$ decreases. However, the latter implies that the rate of convergence will decrease. Hence the choice of the functions $\lambda(\cdot)$ and $\mu(\cdot)$ involves a tradeoff between speed and accuracy.

We shall consider a few numerical examples illustrating the computation of the rate of convergence and simulation results that appear to justify some of the assumptions made.

Example 5.12: Consider a learning automaton using L_{R-I} scheme operating in an environment with penalty probabilities $\{0.6, 0.2\}$. Let the parameter a be 0.08. For this problem $\rho(0)$, $\rho(\infty)$ are given by

$$\rho(0) = 0.984 \qquad \rho(\infty) = 0.968$$

and

$$\rho_{av} = \sqrt{(0.984)(0.968)} = 0.975.$$

Suppose we wish to find the time taken by $E[M(n) - M^*]$ to fall to 1% of its initial value. Setting $b = 0.01$, from Eq.(5.118)

$$\tilde{T} = \frac{\log 0.01}{\log 0.975} \simeq 195.$$

Thus about 195 time steps are needed for the automaton to converge in the sense indicated above.

Example 5.13: We now consider a nonlinear reward–inaction scheme operating in the same environment as in the previous example. The scheme is given by

$$\lambda(p) = 0.06 + 0.12 p_1 p_2$$

$$\mu(p) \equiv 0.$$

Making the same computations as before, we obtain

$$\rho(0) = 0.982 \quad \rho(\infty) = 0.976 \quad \rho_{av} = 0.979 \ \tilde{T} \simeq 200.$$

Thus the nonlinear scheme also has nearly the same speed of convergence as the L_{R-I} scheme in the previous example.

Example 5.14: As the third example we choose a nonlinear reward–penalty scheme. The parameters of the scheme are,

$$\lambda(p) = 0.05 + 0.08 p_1 p_2$$

$$\mu(p) = 0.1 p_1 p_2$$

and the environment remains the same. Following the previous procedure, we can compute the relevant parameters as

$$\rho(0) = 0.981 \quad \rho(\infty) = 0.980 \quad \rho_{av} = 0.9805 \ \tilde{T} \simeq 205.$$

It can be observed that the parameters of the schemes in Examples 5.12 to 5.14 have been so chosen that the rates of convergence are very nearly the

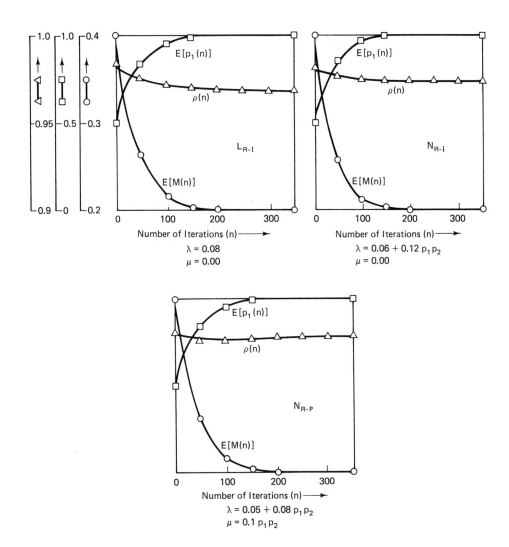

Figure 5.5: Convergence of $E[M(n)]$, $E[p_1(n)]$, and $\rho(n)$ in Example 5.14.

same. This is also confirmed by simulation results which are shown in Fig. 5.5.

In this figure the variation of $E[M(n)]$ and $\rho(n)$ are plotted *w.r.t.n* for all three examples. The expectations represent averages taken over 40 runs of the experiment. It may be seen that in all the examples $E[M(n)]$ converges in about 200 steps as predicted by the theory. Also $\rho(n)$ is nearly constant.

The three examples above were also discussed in connection with bounds on convergence probabilities as Examples 5.10 and 5.11. Note that although the three schemes have nearly the same rate of convergence, they differ with regard to bounds on $\Gamma_\ell(p)$. In Example 5.10 the nonlinear reward–inaction scheme can be seen to have a higher upper bound in comparison with the L_{R-I} scheme, and hence possesses an advantage. The lower bound is slightly worse than that for the L_{R-I} scheme. The N_{R-P} scheme of Example 5.11 is poorer than the N_{R-I} and L_{R-I} schemes of Example 5.10 from the viewpoint of bounds on convergence probabilities.

5.5.2   The Linear Reward–Penalty Scheme

We have seen in Section 5.3.1 that in a learning automaton using an L_{R-P} scheme, the action probability converges to a random variable p^* in distribution. Consequently, $M(n)$ also converges to M^* in distribution. Also p^* and M^* are independent of $p(0)$. Although the nature of the convergence of the L_{R-P} scheme is different from that of absolutely expedient schemes, many of the ideas used in connection with the study of the rate of convergence of the latter schemes carry over to the L_{R-P} scheme as well. As before we can define an index of rate of convergence as

$$\rho(n) = \frac{|E(M(n+1)) - E(M^*)|}{|E(M(n)) - E(M^*)|}. \tag{5.119}$$

In Eq.(5.119) moduli are used, as $E[M(n)]$ is not necessarily monotonically decreasing. The computation is easier here as we know from Eq.(4.36) that

$$E[M^*] = \frac{r}{\sum_{j=1}^{r}(1/c_j)}.$$

From Eq.(4.32) which connects $E[p(n+1)]$ with $E[p(n)]$ we can evaluate $\rho(n)$ from Eq.(5.119) as

$$\rho(n) = |1 - \frac{a}{r-1}\delta(n)| \tag{5.120}$$

where

$$\delta(n) = \frac{r \sum_{i=1}^{r} c_i^2 E[p_i(n)] - (\sum_{i=1}^{r} c_i) \sum_{i=1}^{r} c_i E[p_i(n)]}{\sum_{i=1}^{r} c_i E[p_i(n)] - r/\sum_{i=1}^{r}(1/c_i)}. \qquad (5.121)$$

For essentially the same reasons as in the case of absolutely expedient schemes, the average rate of convergence ρ_{av} is defined as

$$\rho_{av} = \sqrt{\rho(0)\rho(\infty)}$$

and involves the determination of $\rho(0)$ and $\rho(\infty)$. Since $p_i(0) = \frac{1}{r}$ ($i = 1, 2, \ldots, r$), $\delta(0)$ and hence $\rho(0)$ are readily evaluated. The computation of $\rho(\infty)$ cannot be carried out directly since $E[p_i(\infty)] = (1/c_i)/\sum_{j=1}^{r}(1/c_j)$ makes the r.h.s. of Eq.(5.121) indeterminate. Hence a procedure similar to that used for absolutely expedient schemes is once again followed and $\delta(\infty)$ is computed as

$$\delta(\infty) = \frac{r \sum_{i=1}^{r}(c_i^2 - c_\ell^2) - (\sum_{i=1}^{r} c_i) \sum_{i=1}^{r}(c_i - c_\ell)}{\sum_{i=1}^{r}(c_i - c_\ell)}. \qquad (5.122)$$

Having evaluated $\delta(0)$ and $\delta(\infty)$, ρ_{av} and $\tilde{T}$ can now be computed.

In the case of the two–action automaton with penalty probabilities c_ℓ and c_h, the values of $\delta(0)$ and $\delta(\infty)$ coincide and we have $\delta(0) = \delta(\infty) = c_\ell + c_h$. Hence $\rho_{av} = |1 - a(c_\ell + c_h)|$.

Comment 5.15: The rate of convergence is higher if $\rho(n)$ has a lower value. As the parameter a is generally chosen to be small, faster convergence is obtained for higher values of $\delta(n)$. In the two–action case this means that larger values of $(c_\ell + c_h)$ lead to higher speed of operation.

Comment 5.16: In a learning automaton using the L_{R-P} scheme the accuracy of operation is measured by the variance of the components of the limiting action probability p^*. The variance is higher for larger values of a. If an attempt is made to reduce a, this, in turn, lowers the rate of convergence. Thus the speed–accuracy conflict occurs here also and a compromise is needed for satisfactory design.

Problems I, II, and III discussed in Section 4.10 of Chapter 4 can be used to illustrate the results on rate of convergence of L_{R-P} schemes derived in this section. In the following examples, the significant parameters in the study are computed and compared with results obtained from simulations reported in Chapter 4.

Example 5.15: In problem I, the automaton has two actions and the penalty probabilities are $\{0.4, 0.8\}$. Parameter $a = 0.1$. Using the expressions derived earlier,

$$
\begin{aligned}
E[p_\ell^*] \quad &= 0.8/(0.4 + 0.8) = 0.667 \\
E[M^*] \quad &= (2(0.8)(0.4))/(0.8 + 0.4) = 0.534 \\
\rho_{av} = \rho(0) \quad &= |1 - (0.1)(0.8 + 0.4)| \\
&= 0.88.
\end{aligned}
$$

The number of steps needed for $|E[M(n)] - E[M^*]|$ to fall to 1% of the initial value is given by

$$
\begin{aligned}
\tilde{T} \quad &= \log 0.01/\log 0.88 \\
&\simeq 36.
\end{aligned}
$$

Figure 4.1 of Chapter 4 indicates the results of simulation. It can be seen that about forty iterations are needed for $\tilde{p}_1$ and consequently $E[M(n)]$ to reach the vicinity of the final value and this is well approximated by the computed value of $\tilde{T}$. In this and the following examples the values of $\tilde{T}$ are not very accurate but are to be taken as indicative of the order of magnitude of the number of steps for convergence.

Example 5.16: In problem II we consider a five–action automaton operating in the following environment.

$$
c_1 = 0.65, \; c_2 = 0.2, \; c_3 = 0.5, \; c_4 = 0.4, \; c_5 = 0.85
$$

The parameter $a = 0.02$. The optimal action is α_2 and the following quantities of interest can be computed:

$$
\delta(0) = 2.2 \; \delta(\infty) = 1.76 \; \delta_{av} = 1.97 \; \rho_{av} = 0.99 \; \tilde{T} = \frac{\log 0.01}{\log 0.99} \simeq 458.
$$

Graphs of $\tilde{p}_2$ and $\tilde{M}$ were shown in Fig. 4.2. These confirm the analytical results.

Example 5.17: In problem III we have a ten–action automaton operating in an environment whose penalty probabilities are given below.

$$
\begin{aligned}
&c_1 = 0.9, \; c_2 = 0.55, \; c_3 = 0.16, \; c_4 = 0.24, \; c_5 = 0.8 \\
&c_6 = 0.6, \; c_7 = 0.4, \; c_8 = 0.3, \; c_9 = 0.5, c_{10} = 0.7
\end{aligned}
$$

With the choice of $a = 0.015$ the relevant quantities are as follows.

$$\delta(0) = 4.34 \quad \delta(\infty) = 3.10 \quad \delta_{av} = 3.67 \quad \rho_{av} = 0.994 \quad \tilde{T} = \frac{\log 0.01}{\log 0.994} \simeq 765.$$

Graphs shown in Fig. 4.3 show concordance with the computations above.

5.6 Caution for Convergence Results

The problem of convergence of action probabilities was recognized to be important even in the early studies of learning automata. Several attempts were made to simplify the procedures involved in establishing convergence. Some intuitively attractive ideas were employed extensively in this context, but on closer scrutiny they have been found to be incorrect. The mechanism of convergence, as developed in this chapter, now seems to be more complex than what was thought earlier. Attention will be drawn to some of the fallacious arguments employed in earlier studies.

(i) In the case of a two–action automaton, operating in a random environment with $c_1 < c_2$, suppose $p_1(n)$ satisfies

$$\left. \begin{array}{rl} \Delta p_1(n) = & E[p_1(n+1) - p_1(n)|p_1(n)] > 0 \\ & \text{for all } 0 < p_1(n) < 1 \\ \text{and} & \\ \Delta p_1(n) = & 0 \quad \text{for } p_1(n) = 0 \text{ or } 1. \end{array} \right\} \tag{5.123}$$

It follows immediately from Theorem 5.3 that

$$\lim_{n \to \infty} p_1(n) \in \{0, 1\} \tag{5.124}$$

and that $E[p_1(n)]$ is strictly monotonically increasing when $0 < p_1(n) < 1$. It has further been contended that since $E[p_1(n)]$ is bounded above by unity, $E[p_1(n)] \to 1$ as $n \to \infty$. This in turn implies $p_1(n) \to 1$ w.p.1.

If the argument above were correct, every scheme satisfying Eq.(5.123) (e.g., absolutely expedient schemes) would be optimal. However, as we know, $p_1(n)$ can converge to 0 or 1 with nonzero probabilities and the conclusion that $E[p_1(n)] \to 1$ is false. The fallacy here lies in assuming that a strictly monotonically increasing sequence tends to the highest possible value.

(ii) A stability argument described below has been widely used (Varshavski and Vorontsova, 1963, Chandrasekaran and Shen, 1968) in gaining insight into the nature of convergence. Let $p_{1i}(i = 1, 2, \ldots)$ be the roots in the unit interval of the martingale equation

$$\Delta p_1(n) = E[p_1(n+1) - p_1(n)|p_1(n)] = 0.$$

The roots satisfying

$$\left. \frac{d\Delta p_1(n)}{dp_1} \right|_{p_1 = p_{1i}} < 0$$

are called stable roots and the rest unstable. It is then argued, on the basis of regarding $\Delta p_1(n)$ as an increment in $p_1(n)$, that $p_1(n)$ converges to the stable roots $w.p.1$. When $\Delta p_1(n)$ is sign–definite, the argument reduces to that in (i) above.

On making a deeper analysis, no justification of this argument has been found. It does not generally appear possible to prove convergence with probability one when there are roots of the martingale equation other than those corresponding to absorbing states. The only hope in such cases appears to be the weak convergence theory (Kushner, 1984), which is applicable when the parameters in the reinforcement scheme are small.

In view of the considerations above, some of the results mentioned in the earlier literature must be modified. The nonlinear schemes regarded as optimal in restricted environments by Varshavski and Vorontsova as well as by Chandrasekaran and Shen are now only seen to be ϵ–optimal. Similarly the L_{R-I} scheme of Shapiro and Narendra (1969) and the absolutely expedient nonlinear schemes given by Viswanathan and Narendra (1972) and Lakshmivarahan and Thathachar (1972) are only ϵ–optimal in all stationary environments. The nonlinear schemes in Chandrasekaran and Shen (1968), which have roots of the martingale equation other than those corresponding to the absorbing states, need further analysis for making definitive statements about their convergence.

Another source of error is in the concept of convergence associated with the L_{R-P} scheme. It is sometimes believed that here the action probability vector $p(n)$ itself converges in some sense to a fixed vector p^*. It is not recognized that p^* is a random variable and has its own distribution.

5.7   Conclusion

In this chapter different concepts of convergence of sequences of random variables were introduced and applied to the asymptotic behavior of $p(n)$, the action probability vector. In the case of ergodic schemes, such as L_{R-P}

and $L_{R-\epsilon P}$, $p(n)$ converges in distribution to a random variable. For small values of the step size, the asymptotic behavior can be described in terms of the equilibrium state of an associated differential equation and the limiting distribution is normal. In the case of absolutely expedient schemes, such as the L_{R-I} scheme, the process converges with probability one to the set of unit vectors and attention is focused on the probability of convergence to the optimal action. Bounds on the latter are computed and it is shown that by choosing the step size to be sufficiently small, the probability of convergence to the optimal action may be made as close to 1 as desired.

Toward the end of the chapter some useful measures of rates of convergence of absolutely expedient and ergodic schemes are given. Illustrative examples are included to demonstrate that these measures are useful in practical applications to estimate approximately the number of iterations needed for a desired level of accuracy.

All the results presented in the chapter pertain to a single environment. In Chapters 7 and 8 more complex situations are discussed where several automata interact in different ways. The results presented here provide the basis for the analysis of such problems also.

Chapter 6

Q and S Models

6.1 Introduction

The emphasis in the previous chapters has been on the P–model environment, which has only a binary valued response. As discussed in Chapter 2, situations arise in practice very often where a P–model makes too gross an evaluation of the output of the environment. In such cases, finer distinctions may have to be made in the outputs in response to specific inputs and these in turn create the need for Q– and S–models of learning automata.

In a Q–model, corresponding to an action α_i of the automaton, the environment has an output that has more than two but a finite number of possible values. In practice this can arise by a quantization of a continuous performance index. By normalizing the output values, every Q–model can therefore be characterized by a finite number of values of the environment outputs in the unit interval [0,1]. The actual number of these output values can also differ from action to action and is denoted by m_i for action $\alpha_i (i = 1, 2, \ldots, r)$.

A further step in this direction is the S–model whose responses can take continuous values over an interval. Again by normalization the responses can be made to assume values over the unit interval [0,1]. Such a model is very relevant in control systems with a continuous valued performance index. In this chapter, we extend the concepts developed in Chapters 4 and 5, in the context of P–models, to the more general Q– and S–models.

In Chapter 4 different methods of updating the action probabilities of P–models were discussed and in this chapter we show that these methods carry over to Q– and S–models, with only minor modifications. For P–models the algorithms were stated in terms of the functions g_i and h_i which are, respectively, the reward and penalty functions. Since in $Q-$ and $S-$models the outputs lie in the interval [0,1] and hence are neither totally favorable nor totally unfavorable the main problem is to determine how the probabilities of all the actions are to be updated. This is discussed in Section 6.3. In later sections it is shown that with such schemes all the principal results derived for the $P-$model carry over to the more realistic $Q-$ and $S-$models also.

6.1.1   Normalization

We shall first examine the general characteristics of $Q-$ and $S-$models and establish some norms of behavior of automata operating in them.

Let the response of the environment in a $Q-$model to an input α_i be given by $\overline{\beta}_1^i, \overline{\beta}_2^i, \ldots, \overline{\beta}_{m_i}^i$ where

$$\overline{\beta}_1^i < \overline{\beta}_2^i < \ldots < \overline{\beta}_{m_i}^i. \tag{6.1}$$

A normalized set of responses $\{\beta_j^i\}$ can then be defined as

$$\beta_j^i = \frac{\overline{\beta}_j^i - a}{b - a} \quad j = 1, 2, \ldots, m_i. \tag{6.2}$$

where $a = \min_i\{\overline{\beta}_1^i\}$ and $b = \max_i\{\overline{\beta}_{m_i}^i\}$

From Eq.(6.2) it is obvious that

$$0 \leq \beta_1^i < \beta_2^i < \ldots < \beta_{m_i}^i \leq 1 \tag{6.3}$$

or every normalized response β_j^i lies in the unit interval [0,1].

A similar normalization can be carried out for the $S-$model also. Let the response $\overline{\beta}^i$ of the environment to action α_i for all values of i, lie in the interval $[a, b]$. A normalized response is defined as

$$\beta^i = \frac{\overline{\beta}^i - a}{b - a} \tag{6.4}$$

and always lies in the interval [0,1]. In the section following it is shown that this normalization procedure does not affect the conclusions drawn regarding the performance of the system when different learning schemes are used.

It is clear from Eq.(6.4) that the normalization procedure requires knowledge of a and b. Although this may not be realistic in some practical situations it will be assumed in what follows that the normalization has been carried out so that the response of the environment belongs to the interval

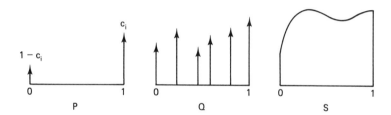

Figure 6.1: Probability density function of β^i for $\alpha = \alpha_i$.

[0,1]. With this assumption $P-$, $Q-$, and $S-$ models can be distinguished by the nature of the probability density functions of β^i for a given action α_i as shown in Fig. 6.1. The vertical lines with arrowheads denote delta functions.

The analysis in the sections following will be confined to normalized $Q-$ and $S-$models.

6.2 Performance Criteria

Let an $r-$action automaton with variable structure operate in a $Q-$ or $S-$ model environment. The average penalty $M(n)$ can be defined as earlier,

$$M(n) = E[\beta(n)|p(n)] \tag{6.5}$$

where $p(n)$ is the action probability vector. Further

$$\begin{aligned} M(n) &= \sum_{i=1}^{r} E[\beta(n)|p(n), \alpha(n) = \alpha_i] P_r[\alpha(n) = \alpha_i] \\ &= \sum_{i=1}^{r} s_i p_i \end{aligned} \tag{6.6}$$

where

$$s_i = E[\beta(n)|\alpha(n) = \alpha_i]. \tag{6.7}$$

The value of the output $\overline{\beta}$ of the system was shown to be related to the normalized output β by the relation Eq.(6.4). This implies that

$$E[\overline{\beta}(n)|\alpha(n) = \alpha_i] \overset{\triangle}{=} \overline{s}_i = (b - a)s_i + a.$$

Hence the normalization procedure does not affect the ordering of s_i or any of the conclusions arrived at in this section based on the values of $s_i (i = 1, 2, \ldots, r)$.

Each s_i in Eq.(6.6) can be obtained from the density function of $\beta(n)$ conditioned on $\alpha(n) = \alpha_i (i = 1, 2, \ldots, r)$ as shown in Fig. 6.1. In the case of the P–model notice that

$$s_i = E[\beta(n)|\alpha(n) = \alpha_i] = 1 \cdot c_i + 0 \cdot (1 - c_i) = c_i.$$

Thus in Q– and S–models $s_i (i = 1, 2, \ldots, r)$ play the same role as the penalty probabilities c_i in the P–model and are referred to as *penalty strengths*.

In a Q–model let

$$c_{ij} = Pr\{\beta(n) = \beta_j^i | \alpha(n) = \alpha_i\}$$

$$i = 1, 2, \ldots, r \qquad\qquad (6.8)$$

$$j = 1, 2, \ldots, m_i.$$

Then

$$\begin{aligned} s_i &= E[\beta(n)|\alpha(n) = \alpha_i] \\ &= \sum_{j=1}^{m_i} \beta_j^i c_{ij}. \end{aligned} \qquad (6.9)$$

Hence, knowing the outputs corresponding to an action α_i and their corresponding probabilities c_{ij}, the values of $s_i (i = 1, 2, \ldots, r)$ can be obtained. It is also worth noting that the average penalty $M(n)$ of our models depends only on the values s_i and not on details such as β_j^i and c_{ij}. For an S–model for which the probability density functions $f_i(\beta)$ of β are given, the s_i correspond to the expected values of the outputs.

A pure–chance automaton with all the action probabilities equal will have an average penalty M_0 given by

$$M_0 = \frac{1}{r} \sum_{i=1}^{r} s_i. \qquad (6.10)$$

As in the case of the P–model we can now proceed to define expediency on the basis of the limiting behavior of $E[M(n)]$.

Definition 6.1: A learning automaton operating in a Q– or S–model environment is said to be *expedient* if

$$\lim_{n\to\infty} E[M(n)] < \frac{1}{r} \sum_{i=1}^{r} s_i.$$

A comparison of the expression for the average penalty $M(n)$ in a Q– or S–model with that of a P–model reveals that the only difference between the two is that s_i replaces c_i in the former. The definitions of other norms of behavior can also be similarly stated for $Q-$ and $S-$models by making the necessary changes in the corresponding $P-$model. For example, optimality of the automaton can be defined as follows:

Definition 6.2: A learning automaton operating in a $Q-$ or $S-$model environment is said to be *optimal* if

$$\lim_{n\to\infty} E[M(n)] = s_\ell$$

where

$$s_\ell = \min_i\{s_i\}.$$

The related definitions of ϵ-optimality and absolute expediency take the following forms.

Definition 6.3: A learning automaton operating in a $Q-$ or $S-$model environment is said to be ϵ-*optimal* if

$$\lim_{n\to\infty} E[M(n)] < s_\ell + \epsilon$$

can be obtained for every $\epsilon > 0$ by a proper choice of the parameters of the automaton.

Definition 6.4: A learning automaton operating in a $Q-$ or $S-$model environment is said to be *absolutely expedient* if

$$E[M(n+1) - M(n)|p(n)] < 0$$

for all n, all $p_i(n) \in (0,1)$ for $i = 1, 2, \ldots, r$ and all possible sets $\{s_i\}$ excluding the trivial environments in which all the s_i are equal.

With the definitions above as a basis, we can now turn to a study of reinforcement schemes that result in the different types of behavior discussed in Chapter 2.

6.3   General Reinforcement Scheme

Consider a general nonlinear reinforcement scheme of the following form

$$p_i(n+1) = p_i(n) - (1 - \beta(n))g_i(p(n)) + \beta(n)h_i(p(n))$$
$$\text{if } \alpha(n) \neq \alpha_i$$

$$p_i(n+1) = p_i(n) + (1 - \beta(n))\sum_{j \neq i} g_j(p(n)) - \beta(n) \sum_{j \neq i} h_j(p(n))$$
$$\text{if } \alpha(n) = \alpha_i$$

(6.11)

Note that Eq.(6.11) is a direct generalization of Eq.(4.61) in Chapter 4 of the reinforcement scheme for a P–model. The earlier scheme of Eq.(4.61) can be obtained by substituting $\beta(n) = 0$ and 1 in Eq.(6.11). The modified scheme represented by Eq.(6.11) applies to both Q– and S–models.

The functions $g_j(\cdot)$ and $h_j(\cdot)$ can be associated with reward and penalty respectively as in Chapter 4. $(1 - \beta(n))$ is an indication of how far $\beta(n)$ is away from the maximum possible value of unity and is a maximum when $\beta(n) = 0$. In Eq.(6.11) $g_j(\cdot)$ contributes a term proportional to $[1 - \beta(n)]$ and $h_j(\cdot)$ contributes a term proportional to $\beta(n)$. For $\beta(n) = 0$ and 1 these terms correspond exactly to the terms in Eq.(4.61).

Obviously $g_j(\cdot)$ and $h_j(\cdot)$ have to satisfy some constraints if $p_i(n)$ ($i = 1, 2, \ldots, r$) are to remain within the interval [0,1] at each instant. If we retain the nonnegativity of these functions so as to maintain their reward–penalty character, the conditions stated in Chapter 4 will again suffice. These conditions are listed below for easy reference.

(i) $g_j(\cdot)$ and $h_j(\cdot)$ are continuous functions mapping $\mathcal{S}_r^0 \to (0, 1)$

(ii) $g_j(p) \geq 0 \;\; h_j(p) \geq 0$ for all probability vectors $p \in \mathcal{S}_r$

(iii)

$$0 < g_j(p) < p_j \tag{6.12}$$

$$0 < \sum_{j \neq i}(h_j(p) + p_j) < 1 \tag{6.13}$$

for all $p_j \in (0, 1)$ for all $i, j = 1, 2, \ldots, r$.

In case we do not wish to maintain the reward–penalty character of $g_j(\cdot)$ and $h_j(\cdot)$, the condition (ii) can be eliminated and (iii) can be replaced by the following condition (ii)'.

(ii)′ $\quad\quad\quad -(\min_i \frac{p_i}{1-p_i})p_j < g_j(p) < p_j$

$$0 < \sum_{j \neq i}[h_j(p) + p_j] < 1 \; ; \; h_j(p) > -p_j.$$
for all $p_j \in (0,1)$ and all $i, j = 1, 2, \ldots, r.$

One important feature of this general scheme is that it is linear in $\beta(n)$. More general schemes can be tried if this requirement is dropped. However, no systematic study of such schemes, nonlinear in $\beta(n)$, has been made thus far.

6.3.1 Extension of P–Model Schemes to Q– and S–models

The various schemes described in Chapter 4 for P–models carry over directly to Q– and S–models and possess similar properties as described later in this chapter. We describe in this section how P–model algorithms, when modified to apply to Q– and S–models assume the form given by Eq.(6.11), which consequently plays a central role in their design.

Let a P–model scheme be described as follows:

$$\begin{aligned}
p_i(n + 1) &= p_{i0}(n) & \alpha(n) \neq \alpha_i & \quad \beta(n) = 0 \\
&= p_{i1}(n) & \alpha(n) \neq \alpha_i & \quad \beta(n) = 1
\end{aligned} \tag{6.14}$$

where $p_{i0}(n)$ and $p_{i1}(n)$ represent functions of $p(n)$. In terms of the general reinforcement scheme of Eq.(4.5) of Chapter 4,

$$\begin{aligned}
p_{i0}(n) &= p_i(n) - g_i(p(n)) \\
p_{i1}(n) &= p_i(n) + h_i(p(n)).
\end{aligned} \tag{6.15}$$

For Q– and S–models, when the output $\beta(n) \in [0,1]$, $p_i(n+1)$ for $\alpha(n) \neq \alpha_i$ is expressed as a linear combination of $p_{i0}(n)$ and $p_{i1}(n)$ where the weighting coefficients are proportional to the distance of $\beta(n)$ from 0 and 1 respectively. Hence

$$p_i(n + 1) = (1 - \beta(n))p_{i0}(n) + \beta(n)p_{i1}(n) \quad\quad \alpha(n) \neq \alpha_i$$

and

$$\begin{aligned}
p_i(n + 1) = {}& 1 - (1 - \beta(n)) \sum_{j \neq i}^{r} p_{j0}(n) \\
& -\beta(n) \sum_{j \neq i}^{r} p_{j1}(n) \quad\quad\quad\quad \text{for } \alpha(n) = \alpha_i
\end{aligned}$$

$$\tag{6.16}$$

represents the general scheme in such cases. It is easily verified that this is identical to the general scheme given by Eq.(6.11).

Ergodic and absolutely expedient schemes described in Chapters 4 and 5 have their counterparts in $Q-$ and $S-$models. These are obtained by first determining g_i and h_i for the corresponding $P-$models and using them in Eq.(6.11) for the more general cases. Some of these schemes are described in the sections following.

6.4   Some Specific Reinforcement Schemes

The origin of $Q-$model schemes can be traced back to mathematical psychology. Bush and Mosteller (1958) described a $Q-$model version of the L_{R-P} scheme. The $S-$model schemes were introduced by Fu, McLaren, and Mc-Murtry (1965,1966), who suggested an $S-$model version of the L_{R-P} scheme. $Q-$ and $S-$model versions of the L_{R-I} scheme and the N_{R-P} scheme of Vorontsova were introduced by Narendra and Viswanathan (1972). $S-$model versions of other nonlinear schemes were also analyzed by Chandrasekaran and Shen (1968). In this section some of these specific schemes are considered. A prefix S (e.g., SL_{R-I}) is used to denote the $Q-$ and $S-$model versions derived from schemes described in earlier chapters.

Note that the $S-$model represents the most general version of the three models considered. Once an $S-$model scheme is derived, it can be specialized to $Q-$ and $P-$models as well.

(i) SL_{R-I} *Scheme:* This is obtained by setting

$$g_j(p) = ap_j$$
$$0 < a < 1 \tag{6.17}$$
$$h_j(p) = 0$$

in Eq.(6.11). Hence the reinforcement scheme can be expressed as

$$
\begin{aligned}
p_i(n+1) &= p_i(n) - a(1 - \beta(n))p_i(n) & \alpha(n) \neq \alpha_i \\
p_i(n+1) &= p_i(n) + a(1 - \beta(n))\sum_{j \neq i} p_j(n) & \alpha(n) = \alpha_i.
\end{aligned}
\tag{6.18}
$$

As shown in Section 6.5 this shares many of the properties of the corresponding $P-$model scheme. In particular it is absolutely expedient. The scheme has also been proved to be $\epsilon-$optimal when used in a $Q-$model environment (Baba, 1976).

(ii) SL_{R-P} *Scheme:* In Chapter 4 it was shown that by choosing

$$g_i(p) = ap_i(n)$$

and (6.19)

$$h_i(p) = a/(r-1) - ap_i(n)$$

an r–action L_{R-P} scheme can be obtained. Using the same functions g_i and h_i in Eq.(6.11), the following scheme for Q– and S–models can be generated.

$$p_i(n+1) = p_i(n) \quad +\beta(n)[a/(r-1) - ap_i(n)] - [1 - \beta(n)]ap_i(n)$$
$$\text{when } \alpha(n) \neq \alpha_i;$$
$$p_i(n+1) = p_i(n) \quad -\beta(n)ap_i(n) + (1 - \beta(n))a(1 - p_i(n))$$
$$\text{when } \alpha(n) = \alpha_i.$$

(6.20)

Taking expectations as in Chapter 4,

$$E[p(n+1)] = A^T E[p(n)] \tag{6.21}$$

where

$$a_{ii} = 1 - as_i$$
$$a_{ji} = [a/(r-1)] s_j. \tag{6.22}$$

The expressions in Eq.(6.22) are the same as those in Eq.(4.33) of Chapter 4 with s_i replacing c_i. Thus when all s_i are nonzero $E[p(n)]$ forms the total probability vector of an ergodic Markov chain and converges to a fixed vector irrespective of the initial value $p(0)$. Further, proceeding as before

$$\lim_{n \to \infty} E[p_i(n)] = \frac{1/s_i}{\sum_{i=1}^{r}(1/s_i)} \qquad i = 1, 2, \ldots, r \tag{6.23}$$

It also follows that

$$\lim_{n \to \infty} E[M(n)] = \frac{r}{\sum_{i=1}^{r}(1/s_i)}. \tag{6.24}$$

Thus the SL_{R-P} scheme has analogous properties to the L_{R-P} scheme. For example, it is expedient in all stationary random environments and the limiting expectations of action probabilities are inversely proportional to the corresponding s_i. The method adopted for the L_{R-P} scheme to determine the rate of convergence can also be used for the SL_{R-P} scheme by replacing c_i with $s_i(i = 1, 2, \ldots, r)$.

(iii)*A Nonlinear Scheme (SN)*: This scheme is a $Q-$ and $S-$model version of the two–action scheme originally suggested by Vorontsova (1965). As already noted, the corresponding $P-$model scheme is optimal while operating in continuous time. The scheme corresponds to the following choice in Eq.(6.11):

$$g_j(p) = a\phi(p_1, 1 - p_1)p_j^{\theta+1}(1 - p_j)^\theta$$

$$(j = 1, 2) \qquad (6.25)$$

$$h_j(p) = b\phi(p_1, 1 - p_1)p_j^{\theta+1}(1 - p_j)^\theta$$

where
$$\phi(p_1, 1 - p_1) = \phi(1 - p_1, p_1) \qquad (6.26)$$

is a nonlinear function to be selected and $\theta \geq 1$. The positive constants a and b must be suitably selected so as to satisfy the bounds in Eq.(6.13).

From the results stated in the section following it also follows that this scheme is absolutely expedient. ϵ–optimality appears to follow in all stationary environments but has not been proved. It is also not known whether the continuous–time version is optimal as in the $P-$model case.

6.5   Absolutely Expedient Schemes

The structure of general schemes that result in the property of absolute expediency can be determined for $Q-$ and $S-$models using the same procedure adopted for $P-$models. It is comforting that the same symmetry conditions on the nonlinear functions $g_j(\cdot)$ and $h_j(\cdot)$ arise in this case also. A formal statement of the result can be made as shown in the theorems following (Lakshmivarahan and Thathachar, 1976).

Theorem 6.1: A learning automaton operating in a $Q-$ or $S-$model environment according to a reinforcement scheme of the type in Eq.(6.11) is absolutely expedient, if and only if,

$$(g_1(p))/p_1 = (g_2(p))/p_2 = \ldots = (g_r(p))/p_r = \lambda(p)$$

and $\qquad\qquad\qquad\qquad\qquad\qquad\qquad\qquad\qquad (6.27)$

$$(h_1(p))/p_1 = (h_2(p))/p_2 = \ldots = (h_r(p))/p_r = \mu(p)$$

for all $p_i \in (0, 1)$; $i = 1, 2, \ldots, r$, where $\lambda(\cdot)$ and $\mu(\cdot)$ are arbitrary functions.

The proof of Theorem 6.1 follows along the same lines as that of Theorem 4.1 of Chapter 4 except that c_i are replaced by s_i. This is evident since the expressions for $\Delta p_i(n)$ and $\Delta M(n)$ in the present situation can be seen to be the same as the previous ones with s_i used in the place of c_i.

The related property of sign definiteness of $\Delta p_\ell(n)$ is also equivalent to the symmetry conditions when s_ℓ is unique in the set $\{s_i\}$. The result can be stated as follows:

Theorem 6.2: Let a learning automaton operate in any stationary $Q-$ or S-model environment having a unique s_ℓ, according to the general reinforcement scheme of Eq.(6.11). The condition

$$\Delta p_\ell(n) > 0$$

holds for all n, all $p_i(n) \in (0,1)$ and all environments being considered, if and only if, the symmetry conditions of Eq.(6.27) are satisfied.

The proof of Theorem 6.2 again follows that of Theorem 4.2 of Chapter 4 with s_i replacing the corresponding c_i.

Comment 6.1: If $s_h = \max_i\{s_i\}$ is unique, the symmetry conditions also ensure

$$\Delta p_h(n) < 0$$

for all n, all $p_i \in (0,1)$ and all environments of the type being considered.

Comment 6.2: Theorems 6.1 and 6.2 show that absolute expediency and sign definiteness of $\Delta p_\ell(n)$ are equivalent when s_ℓ is unique.

Comment 6.3: When symmetry conditions are imposed, the reinforcement scheme of Eq.(6.11) takes the following form:

$$
\begin{aligned}
p_i(n+1) &= p_i(n) - (1 - \beta(n))\lambda(p(n))p_i(n) + \beta(n)\mu(p(n))p_i(n) \\
&\qquad\qquad\qquad\qquad \text{if } \alpha(n) \neq \alpha_i \\
&= p_i(n) + (1 - \beta(n))\lambda(p(n))(1 - p_i(n)) \\
&\quad - \beta(n)\mu(p(n))(1 - p_i(n)) \quad \text{if } \alpha(n) = \alpha_i
\end{aligned}
$$

$$(6.28)$$

Comment 6.4: The convergence results derived for absolutely expedient schemes in P-model environments carry over to Q-models after replacing c_i by s_i. Although similar results appear to carry over to S-models as well, formal proofs are currently not available.

Comment 6.5: The expressions for rate of convergence of P–model absolutely expedient schemes can now be used with c_i replaced by s_i.

6.6 Specific Q Model

A Q–model environment that has been given particular attention in the literature has a response set $\{-1, 0, 1\}$ for all actions. One reason for this is the fact that such an environment arises in a game situation where a player may lose, draw, or win. These three payoffs to the player can be made to correspond to the three possible values of the response of the environment. The player then corresponds to the automaton and his or her strategies are the actions of the automaton. *In contrast to the models that have been analyzed thus far, an output 1 from the environment is seen to correspond to a success rather than a failure.* If the probabilities corresponding to the three outputs for the different actions are unknown, the problem is once again to find the action that gives rise to the maximum expected payoff.

The schemes described in Sections 6.1–6.5 can be applied to this problem, after the response set $\{-1, 0, 1\}$ has been normalized to correspond to the set $\{0, \frac{1}{2}, 1\}$. However, we shall discuss this problem in greater detail, attempting in the process to establish the natural way in which general schemes of the form of Eq.(6.11) arise. In particular we shall demonstrate that even if we start with a more general scheme, a scheme of the type of Eq.(6.11) will evolve along with the symmetry conditions of Eq.(6.27) if it is to be absolutely expedient.

Let the environment characteristics be described by the probability of the various responses for any action $\alpha(n) = \alpha_i$ as follows:

$$Pr\{\beta(n) = -1 | \alpha(n) = \alpha_i\} = u_i \; ; \; Pr\{\beta(n) = 0 | \alpha(n) = \alpha_i\} = v_i$$

and

$$Pr\{\beta(n) = +1 | \alpha(n) = \alpha_i\} = 1 - u_i - v_i$$

$$0 < u_i < 1$$
$$0 < v_i < 1$$
$$0 < u_i + v_i < 1.$$

$$(6.29)$$

An automaton operates in this environment and the objective is to select the action associated with the maximum value of $E[\beta(n)]$.

From Eq.(6.9) it follows that

$$s_i = E[\beta(n)|\alpha(n) = \alpha_i] = 1 - 2u_i - v_i$$

and   (6.30)

$$M(n) = \sum_{i=1}^{r} p_i(n)s_i.$$

We now consider a general class of reinforcement schemes defined by the following:

For $i = 1, 2, \ldots, r$

$$
\begin{aligned}
p_i(n+1) &= p_i(n) - g_i(p(n)) & \text{if } \alpha(n) \neq \alpha_i \quad \beta(n) = +1 \\
&= p_i(n) - f_i(p(n)) & \text{if } \alpha(n) \neq \alpha_i \quad \beta(n) = 0 \qquad (6.31) \\
&= p_i(n) + h_i(p(n)) & \text{if } \alpha(n) \neq \alpha_i \quad \beta(n) = -1
\end{aligned}
$$

$$
\begin{aligned}
p_i(n+1) &= p_i(n) + \sum_{j \neq i} g_j(p(n)) & \text{if } \alpha(n) = \alpha_i \quad \beta(n) = +1 \\
&= p_i(n) + \sum_{j \neq i} f_j(p(n)) & \text{if } \alpha(n) = \alpha_i \quad \beta(n) = 0 \\
&= p_i(n) - \sum_{j \neq i} h_j(p(n)) & \text{if } \alpha(n) = \alpha_i \quad \beta(n) = -1.
\end{aligned}
$$

(6.32)

The functions $g_j(\cdot), f_j(\cdot)$ and $h_j(\cdot)$ are real–valued continuous nonnegative functions satisfying

$$
\begin{aligned}
\text{(a)} &\quad 0 < g_j(p) < p_j \\
\text{(b)} &\quad 0 < f_j(p) < p_j \qquad\qquad\qquad\qquad (6.33) \\
\text{(c)} &\quad 0 < \sum_{j \neq i}[p_j + h_j(p)] < 1
\end{aligned}
$$

for all $p \in S_r^0$ and all $j = 1, 2, \ldots, r$.

Comment 6.6: The scheme described above is more general than Eq.(6.11) because it does not assume linearity with respect to $\beta(n)$. The two schemes become identical only when

$$f_i = \frac{g_i - h_i}{2} \qquad (i = 1, 2, \ldots, r) \qquad\qquad (6.34)$$

and $\beta(n)$ is normalized to the interval $[0, 1]$.

Comment 6.7: When $\alpha(n) = \alpha_i$ the algorithm above increases $p_i(n)$ if $\beta(n) = +1$ or zero and decreases $p_i(n)$ if $\beta(n) = -1$. Thus it could be called a nonlinear reward–reward–penalty algorithm (N_{R-R-P}). Other combinations of rewards and penalties can also be attempted provided proper constraints on the functions, similar to Eq.(6.33), can be included. In particular, a constraint of the form of part (c) of Eq.(6.33) must be imposed on "penalty" functions whereas the form (a) or (b) must be used with "reward" functions.

The consequences of requiring the automaton operating according to the scheme of Eqs.(6.31–6.32) to be absolutely expedient can now be examined. We note first that

$$
\begin{aligned}
\Delta p_i(n) &= E[p_i(n+1) - p_i(n)|p(n)] \\
&= p_i(n)[(1 - u_i - v_i)\sum_{j\neq i} g_j(p(n)) + v_i \sum_{j\neq i} f_j(p(n)) \\
&\quad - u_i \sum_{j\neq i} h_j(p(n))] - \sum_{j\neq i} p_j(n)[g_i(p(n))(1 - u_j - v_j) \\
&\quad + v_j f_i(p(n)) - u_j h_i(p(n))]
\end{aligned}
$$

$$(6.35)$$

and hence

$$
\Delta M(n) = \sum_{i=1}^{r} \Delta p_i(n) s_i \tag{6.36}
$$

becomes, after considerable simplification,

$$
\begin{aligned}
\Delta M(n) = \ &\sum_{i=1}^{r} g_i(p(n)) \sum_{j=1}^{r} (u_j + v_j - 1)(s_i - s_j) p_j(n) \\
&+ \sum_{i=1}^{r} h_i(p(n)) \sum_{j=1}^{r} u_j(s_i - s_j) p_j(n) \\
&- \sum_{i=1}^{r} f_i(p(n)) \sum_{j=1}^{r} v_j(s_i - s_j) p_j(n).
\end{aligned} \tag{6.37}
$$

Since $s_j = 1 - 2u_j - v_j$, Eq.(6.37) can be expressed in terms of only s_j and u_j as follows:

$$
\begin{aligned}
\Delta M(n) = \ &\sum_{i=1}^{r} g_i(p(n)) \sum_{j=1}^{r} (-u_j - s_j)(s_i - s_j) p_j(n) \\
&+ \sum_{i=1}^{r} h_i(p(n)) \sum_{j=1}^{r} u_j(s_i - s_j) p_j(n) \\
&- \sum_{i=1}^{r} f_i(p(n)) \sum_{j=1}^{r} (1 - 2u_j - s_j)(s_i - s_j) p_j(n).
\end{aligned} \tag{6.38}
$$

The conditions for absolute expediency can now be stated in the following theorem.

Theorem 6.3: Necessary and sufficient conditions for an automaton operating in the Q–model random environment of Eq.(6.29) according to a reinforcement scheme of the form of Eqs.(6.31) and (6.32) to be absolutely expedient are that

$$
\begin{aligned}
(g_1(p))/p_1 &= (g_2(p))/p_2 = \ldots = (g_r(p))/p_r \\
(h_1(p))/p_1 &= (h_2(p))/p_2 = \ldots = (h_r(p))/p_r
\end{aligned} \tag{6.39}
$$

and

$$f_i(p) = \frac{1}{2}[g_i(p) - h_i(p)] \qquad i = 1, 2, \ldots, r. \qquad (6.40)$$

Proof:
Sufficiency:

$$\text{Setting} \quad (g_i(p))/p_i = \lambda(p) \qquad (i = 1, 2, \ldots, r)$$
$$\text{and} \quad (h_i(p))/p_i = \mu(p) \qquad (i = 1, 2, \ldots, r) \qquad (6.41)$$

Eq.(6.40) becomes

$$f_i(p) = \frac{1}{2}p_i[\lambda(p) - \mu(p)]. \qquad (6.42)$$

Substituting in Eq.(6.38)

$$
\begin{aligned}
\Delta M(n) &= -\tfrac{1}{2}\lambda(p) \sum_{i=1}^{r} \sum_{j=1}^{r} p_i p_j (s_i - s_j) s_j \\
&\quad -\tfrac{1}{2}\mu(p) \sum_{i=1}^{r} \sum_{j=1}^{r} p_i p_j (s_i - s_j) s_j \\
&\quad -\tfrac{1}{2}[\lambda(p) - \mu(p)] \sum_{i=1}^{r} \sum_{j=1}^{r} p_i p_j (s_i - s_j)
\end{aligned} \qquad (6.43)
$$

where p_i denotes $p_i(n)$. Eq.(6.43) can also be expressed as

$$\Delta M(n) = \frac{1}{2}[\lambda(p) + \mu(p)]p^T S p \qquad (6.44)$$

where the element S_{ij} of the matrix S is given by

$$S_{ij} = \frac{1}{2}(s_i - s_j)^2. \qquad (6.45)$$

Hence $\Delta M(n) > 0$ whenever $p \in \mathcal{S}_r^0$.

We note that the inequality in Definition 6.4 is reversed here as we are maximizing $E[\beta(n)]$.

Necessity: For proving the necessity of the conditions of Eqs.(6.39) and (6.40) it is helpful to recognize that the P–model is a particular case of the Q–model described here, and hence the conditions for absolute expediency in the P–model are necessary conditions in the Q–model as well. Thus setting

$$u_i \equiv 0 \qquad (i = 1, 2, \ldots, r) \qquad (6.46)$$

we obtain a P–model with $f_i(\cdot)$ and $g_i(\cdot)$ as the functions in the nonlinear reinforcement scheme. Hence from Theorem 4.1

$$\frac{g_1(p)}{p_1} = \frac{g_2(p)}{p_2} = \cdots = \frac{g_r(p)}{p_r} = \lambda(p) \qquad (6.47)$$

$$\frac{f_1(p)}{p_1} = \frac{f_2(p)}{p_2} = \cdots = \frac{f_r(p)}{p_r} = \nu(p) \qquad (6.48)$$

Similarly setting $v_i = 0$ $(i = 1, 2, \ldots, r)$ we need

$$\frac{g_1(p)}{p_1} = \frac{g_2(p)}{p_2} = \cdots = \frac{g_r(p)}{p_r} = \lambda(p) \qquad (6.49)$$

and

$$\frac{h_1(p)}{p_1} = \frac{h_2(p)}{p_2} = \cdots = \frac{h_r(p)}{p_r} = \mu(p).$$

It only remains to show that $f_i(p) = \frac{1}{2}\left[g_i(p) - h_i(p)\right]$.

Since absolute expediency implies that $\Delta M(n)$ has an extremum at

$$s_1 = s_2 = \cdots = s_r = s \qquad (6.50)$$

where s can take values in $[-1,1]$,

$$\frac{\partial \Delta M(n)}{\partial s_k} = 0 \qquad (k = 1, 2, \ldots, r). \qquad (6.51)$$

Substituting Eq.(6.50) in Eq.(6.38)

$$\left. \frac{\partial \Delta M(n)}{\partial s_k} \right|_{s_i = s} = [u_k p_k - \sum_{j=1}^{r} u_j p_j][\lambda(p) - \mu(p) - 2\nu(p)]. \qquad (6.52)$$

The right–hand side of Eq.(6.52) can be zero for all k, u_k and all $p \in S_r^0$ only if

$$\lambda(p) - \mu(p) - 2\nu(p) = 0$$

or

$$\nu(p) = \frac{\lambda(p) - \mu(p)}{2}.$$

Comment 6.8: The condition of Eq.(6.40) implies that the reinforcement scheme has to be of the form shown in Eq.(6.11) if absolute expediency is desired. Or alternately, absolute expediency requires the linearity of the reinforcement scheme with respect to $\beta(n)$.

Comment 6.9: To minimize the response of the environment, it is only necessary to change the signs of the terms to the right of $p_i(n)$ in Eqs.(6.31) and (6.32). Correspondingly, the constraints on $g_i(\cdot)$, $f_i(\cdot)$ on the one hand and $h_i(\cdot)$ on the other must be interchanged in Eq.(6.33).

6.7 Simulation Results

A number of $Q-$ and $S-$models have been simulated (Viswanathan and Narendra, 1971) and some of them are described below.

$Q-$Model Examples

Example 6.1: Consider a $Q-$model with input set $\{-1, 0, 1\}$ as in Section 6.6.

Let the input set correspond to two actions and let the environment parameters be

$$u_1 = 0.2 \qquad u_2 = 0.4$$
$$v_1 = 0.5 \qquad v_2 = 0.3$$

The problem is to find the action corresponding to the maximum expected response of the environment.

From Eq.(6.30) we have

$$s_1 = 1 - 2u_1 - v_1 = 0.1$$
$$s_2 = 1 - 2u_2 - v_2 = -0.1.$$

α_1, which maximizes the expected value of the output, is the optimal action. Using Vorontsova's scheme Eqs.(6.25) and (6.26) with parameters $a = 2.5$, $b = 1.5$ and $\theta = 2$, average values of $p_1(n)$ and $M(n)$ ($\tilde{p}_1(n)$ and $\tilde{M}(n)$) were computed and these converged to neighborhoods of the optimum values in 1000 iterations (Fig. 6.2).

Example 6.2: A ten–action $Q-$model using the SL_{R-I} scheme is considered in this problem. The parameters of the environment are described in Table 6.1 and and clearly α_8 is seen to be the optimal action for the maximization problem. Figure 6.3 gives the plots of $\tilde{p}_8(n)$ and $\tilde{M}(n)$ for the SL_{R-I} scheme with $a = 0.01$.

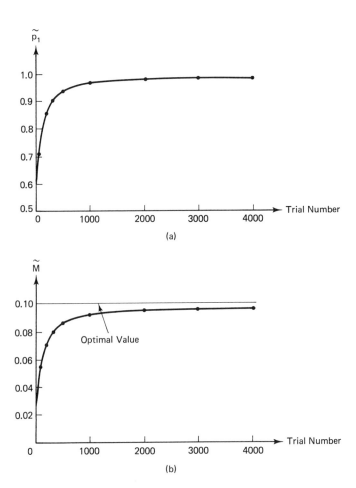

Figure 6.2: Example 6.1 (a)average probability versus trial number; (b) average performance versus trial number.

Action	Probability of Unit Loss u_i	Probability of a Draw v_i	Probability of Unit Gain $1 - u_i - v_i$	$s_i = 1 - 2u_i - v_i$
α_1	0.7	0.2	0.1	-0.6
α_2	0.2	0.4	0.4	0.2
α_3	0.2	0.6	0.2	0.0
α_4	0.1	0.4	0.5	0.4
α_5	0.6	0.4	0.0	-0.6
α_6	0.3	0.2	0.5	0.2
α_7	0.4	0.2	0.4	0
α_8	0.1	0.2	0.7	0.6
α_9	0.3	0.6	0.1	-0.2
α_{10}	0.15	0.5	0.35	0.2

Table 6.1

S–**Model Examples:** Two examples of *S*–model environments are described below. In each case the response of the environment is assumed to be uniformly distributed on the interval $[-0.2, 0.2]$ around the mean value of each action. In other words, for $\alpha(n) = \alpha_i$

$$\beta(n) = s_i + z(n)$$

where $z(n)$ is uniformly distributed over $[-0.2, 0.2]$.

Example 6.3: In a two–action *S*–model where $s_1 = 0.4$, $s_2 = 0.8$, four schemes with parameters as indicated below were tried.

$$SL_{R-I}: \quad a = 0.1$$

$$SN: \quad a = 5 \ b = 3, \ \theta = 2$$

$$SH(L_{R-I}, N): \quad a = 0.1 \quad \text{(for } L_{R-I})$$

$$a = 5, \ b = 3, \ \theta = 2 \quad \text{(for } N)$$

$$SH(L_{R-I}, \hat{L}_{R-P}): \quad a = 0.1$$

The last two are hybrid schemes that are combinations of the two schemes indicated. The combination is made as described in the *P*–model case in

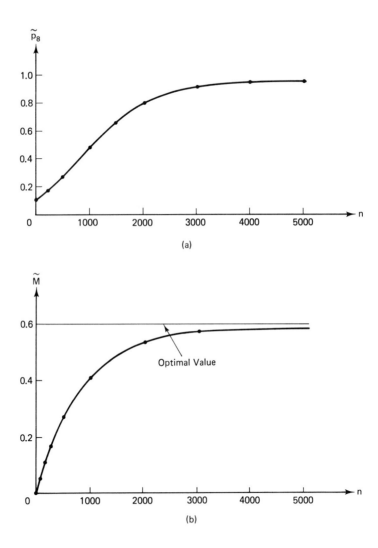

(a)

(b)

Figure 6.3: Example 6.2 (a) average probability versus trial number; (b) average performance versus trial number.

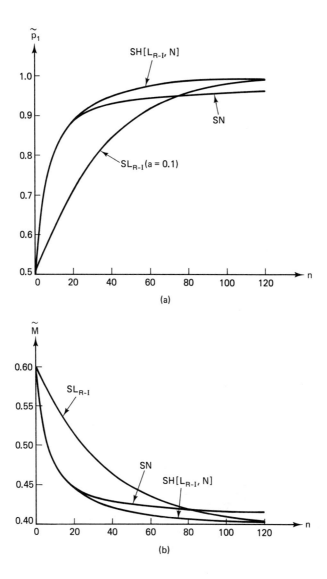

Figure 6.4: Example 6.3 (a) average probability versus trial number; (b) average performance versus trial number.

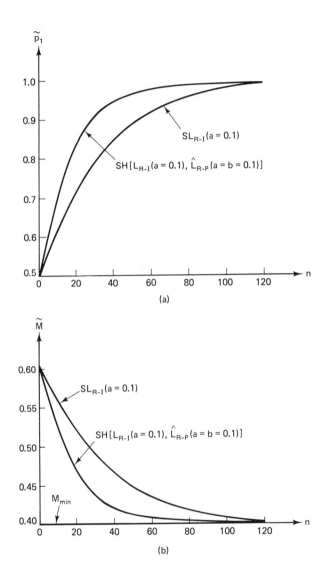

Figure 6.5: Example 6.3 (a) average probability versus trial number; (b) average performance versus trial number.

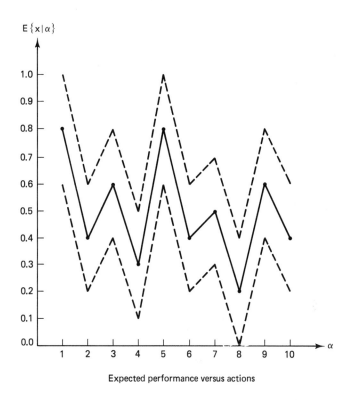

Figure 6.6: Example 6.4 – A multimodal performance index.

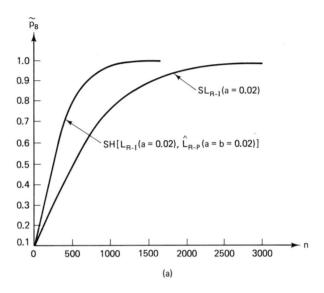

(a)

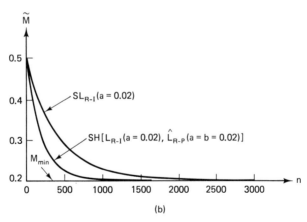

(b)

Figure 6.7: Plots for Example 6.4 (a) average probability versus trial number; (b) average performance versus trial number.

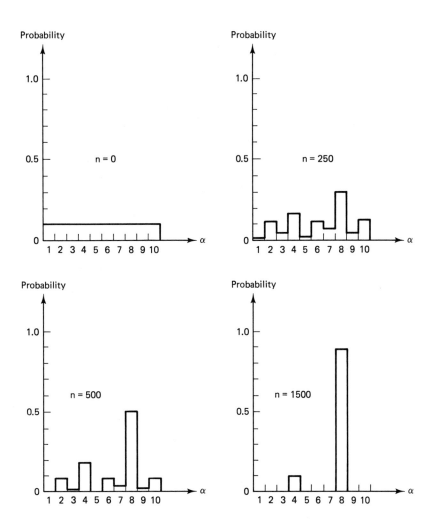

Figure 6.8: Average probability density $(SL_{R-I}$ scheme) for Example 6.4.

Chapter 4. Figures 6.4 and 6.5 give the variation of average values of $p_1(n)$ and $M(n)$ with n. As in the P–model case it is evident that the hybrid schemes have higher rates of convergence.

Example 6.4: A ten–action S–model example is now considered. The problem involves minimization of a multimodal stochastic performance index. Shown in Fig. 6.6 are the mean, upper, and lower bounds of the environment's response for each of the ten actions. Note that there are many local minima in the mean response, but action α_8 corresponds to the global minimum of 0.2. As mentioned earlier, the additive noise is distributed uniformly between –0.2 and +0.2. The points corresponding to the various actions are connected by straight lines merely for convenience in reading the graph.

Similar examples were first considered by Shapiro and Narendra (1969). The characteristic feature of such examples is that in addition to being multimodal, they are highly noisy. The noise components of the performance variable could well have magnitudes larger than the difference between two minima. Compare, for example, the global minimum at α_8 and the lower bound on the performance variable at α_4 in Fig. 6.6. Thus the example is a good testing ground for assessing the accuracy of the learning automaton.

The schemes tested were the following:

$$SL_{R-I}: \quad a = 0.02$$

$$SH(L_{R-I}, \hat{L}_{R-P}): \quad a = 0.02.$$

The plots of average values of $p_8(n)$ and $M(n)$ are shown in Fig. 6.7. Although both the schemes converge to the optimal action, again the hybrid scheme shows a higher rate of convergence. The evolution of action probabilities is shown in Fig. 6.8 for the SL_{R-I} scheme.

6.8   Conclusion

The principal aim of this chapter is to demonstrate that the results of Chapters 4 and 5 can be extended to Q– and S–models. In one view, such an effort can be regarded as straightforward. Yet, when one tries to write down the updating algorithms for Q– and S–models, there appear to be many possibilities and the extension from P–models needs some guidance. The chapter has also brought out the need for linearity of the reinforcement scheme with respect to $\beta(n)$ in absolutely expedient schemes. Examples of optimization with multimodal performance indices serve as illustrations of some realistic situations where the automaton approach is possibly effective.

A recent development is the use of the pursuit algorithm (Thathachar and Sastry, 1986) in S–models also. This ϵ–optimal algorithm depends only on the ordering of the estimates of penalty strengths s_i and not on their numerical values and hence $\beta(n)$ need not be in $[0, 1]$. This property results in a significant advantage in practical applications.

Chapter 7

Nonstationary Environments

7.1 Introduction

Thus far we have been concerned exclusively with learning schemes operating in the relatively elementary setting of stationary random environments. The analysis carried out in Chapters 2–6 has revealed the complexities of even these simple situations and has provided valuable insights. However, as is clear from the discussions in Chapter 2, the need for learning and adaptation in systems is principally due to the fact that the environment changes with time. It is precisely in such a context that the performance of a learning automaton should be judged.

As an environment changes, the ordering of the input actions with respect to the performance criterion ($E[M(n)]$) may vary. If a learning automaton with a fixed strategy is used in such an environment, it may become less expedient with time and even inexpedient. Hence, improved performance can be obtained only by using learning schemes that have sufficient flexibility to "track" the better actions. The aim in these cases is not to evolve to a single action which is optimal, but to choose the actions with a view toward minimizing the expected penalty. As in some areas of control theory (e.g., adaptive control) the practical justification for the detailed study of learning algorithms in stationary environments is based on the assumption that if a scheme converges sufficiently rapidly, then qualitatively it can be expected to perform satisfactorily even in slowly varying environments.

In this chapter we deal with the operation of automata in specific types of nonstationary environments. Although a complete mathematical analysis is no longer possible in all cases, there are four situations in which the analytical tools developed earlier are adequate to obtain fairly complete mathematical descriptions of the overall processes. The first of these was described by Tsetlin (1961) in the context of fixed-structure automata in Markovian environments. The analysis, which establishes quantitatively the nature of the relationship between memory and optimality of the Tsetlin automaton in a time–varying environment, is included here because of its general relevance to learning theory.

The second case deals with variable-structure automata and was first introduced by Narendra and Thathachar (1980). Here, the penalty probabilities vary with time and depend on the input action chosen. Later this model was extended by Srikantakumar and Narendra (1982) to cases where the penalty probabilities c_i ($i = 1, 2, \ldots, r$) are functions of the action probabilities. The theory of Markov processes developed in Chapters 4 and 5 can be directly used to determine the asymptotic behavior of these models.

The third situation refers to a hierarchy of automata where the automata at higher levels are connected to the environment through the lower level automata. Effectively, the automata at higher levels operate in a nonstationary environment because of the changing action probabilities of the other automata. However, an analytical study is possible here because of the specific structure of the system.

Last, we consider nonstationary environments where a single action continues to be optimal at all instants. Since the analysis here closely follows that of stationary environments, we merely point out the slightly stronger hypothesis needed to carry over the previous results.

In this chapter the four types of nonstationary environments mentioned above are considered first. Following this, it is shown that the theory developed in the previous chapters can also be extended to situations where a single automaton operates in multiple environments. If the automaton uses one of the schemes discussed in Chapter 4 and responds to the average output of the multiple environments, the overall performance can be shown to be absolutely expedient. The ideas contained in the earlier sections of this chapter are also found to be useful in analyzing specific cases where the environments are nonstationary. Later sections deal with other cases that are less precisely understood analytically but are nevertheless of great practical interest. The last section contains a brief description of attempts made in recent years to generalize the learning automaton model by including contextual information in the learning process.

7.2 Nonstationary Environments

An environment is nonstationary if the penalty probabilities c_i $(i = 1, 2, ., r)$ corresponding to the various actions vary with time. Typically $c_i(n)$ may vary from instant to instant by small increments or alternately $c_i(n)$ may be a constant over an interval $[n, n+T-1]$ and switch to a new value at time $n+T$. Strictly speaking, every new set of penalty probabilities corresponds to a new environment so that learning in a time–varying environment corresponds to learning in multiple random environments. To make the problem analytically tractable it becomes necessary to impose constraints on the nature of the time variations of $c_i(n)$. The success of the learning procedure will then depend both on the manner in which the environments evolve as well as the prior information the designer has about the environment.

From an analytic standpoint, the simplest situation is one in which the penalty probability vector $c(n)$ can assume a finite number of values. This implies that the automaton operates in one of a finite set of stationary environments E_i $(i = 1, 2, \ldots, d)$ at any instant and switches from E_i to any member of the set at the next instant according to a specific rule. If it is assumed that the automaton is aware of the specific environment E_i it is operating into at any instant, the methods outlined in the previous chapters can be used to determine ϵ–optimal strategies. In particular (assuming that the automaton consists of d subautomata), assigning an automaton A_i to the environment E_i and updating the probabilities of the actions of A_i only when E_i is the environment, the problem can be decoupled. If each automaton A_i uses an absolutely expedient scheme, then ϵ–optimality can be achieved asymptotically in each of the environments and hence for the overall system. However, it is tacitly assumed here that each of the environments E_i occurs an infinite number of times during the course of the operation of the composite automaton. This represents the simplest problem of learning automata operating in nonstationary environments that we will encounter. Examples 3.3 and 4.3, which describe a bug in a two–dimensional world, correspond to this case; it is assumed that the same automaton A_i can be used, when the bug is anywhere in the ith sector.

The method described above suffers from two principal weaknesses. Assigning a separate automaton A_i to an environment E_i is practically feasible only when the total number of environments d is not too large. In most problems of interest this is not the case however and quite often the number of environments is infinite. Further, since the automaton A_i is updated only when the environment is E_i, updating the strategies of A_i may happen only infrequently so that the corresponding action probabilities do not converge. Hence it is evident that some kind of generalization is needed whereby the same automaton can be used for several environments in some neighborhood of a suitably defined metric space. Toward the end of this chapter we shall briefly describe attempts that have been made recently to generalize the learning automaton model.

The second major weakness of the method described earlier is that at every instant it is assumed that the automaton is aware of the environment in which it operates. This is a requirement that is not satisfied in practice very often. Hence methods that perform effectively under more realistic assumptions concerning the time variations of the environment must be developed. Two classes of environments that have been investigated analytically are described below. In each case the automaton is assumed to operate in one of a finite number of environments $E_1, E_2, \ldots, E_d$.

(i) *Markovian Switching Environment:*   In this case it is assumed that E_i ($i = 1, \ldots, d$) are themselves states of a Markov chain. Such a composite environment is referred to as a Markov switching environment (MSE). If the chain is ergodic an automaton that is connected to such an environment will be in each of the component environments with a fixed probability corresponding to the asymptotic probability distribution of the ergodic chain. Although in general, a fixed-structure automaton in a nonstationary environment is described by a nonhomogeneous Markov chain, when the nonstationary environment is MSE, the overall system (as shown in Section 7.4.1) is equivalent to a homogeneous Markov chain.

(ii) *State Dependent Nonstationary Environments:* If $E = \{E_1, E_2, \ldots, E_d\}$ is the finite state space of the environment and the environment is nonstationary, the states will vary with the stage number n. Such variations may depend either explicitly or implicitly on n. For example, implicit dependence may arise if the state transitions are determined by the actions of the automaton. In Section 7.5 such environments are considered and are described by penalty probabilities c_i which depend on the action probability $p(n)$. We shall refer to such environments as state–dependent nonstationary environments.

If the transition probabilities depend explicitly only on the action probabilities of the automaton and not on stage number n, the overall system can be described by a homogeneous Markov process. In such a

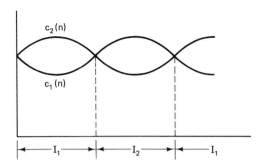

Figure 7.1: Time-varying penalty probabilities.

case, the results discussed in Chapter 5 can be applied directly to determine its behavior. Learning automata models of this type have wide application and the telephone network routing problem considered in Chapter 9 is an important case in point.

In this chapter we shall first consider types (i) and (ii) in detail before considering other special cases.

7.3 Expediency and Related Concepts

To study the behavior of automata in nonstationary environments we need to re–examine fundamental concepts such as expediency, optimality, and absolute expediency which were defined in the context of stationary environments in Chapter 2. Consider for example the case of a single automaton A with two actions α_1 and α_2 operating in an environment whose penalty probabilities $c_1(n)$ and $c_2(n)$ vary as shown in Fig. 7.1. For convenience, time (or equivalently stage number) is shown as a continuous variable. In the intervals in which $c_1(n) > c_2(n)$ (shown as I_2) α_2 is the optimal action, whereas in the intervals where $c_1(n) < c_2(n)$ (shown as I_1) α_1 is the optimal action. Thus the optimal action varies with time. If $c_i(n)$ $(i = 1, 2)$ were known, the optimal action would switch from α_1 when $n \in I_1$ to α_2 when $n \in I_2$. In the learning procedure, however, since $c_1(n)$ and $c_2(n)$ are not known the automaton must determine its actions on the basis of the responses of the environment. Precisely what learning algorithm to choose and how far the corresponding performance would deviate from the optimal would be of interest. In particular, the memory depth of fixed-structure automata and the magnitudes of the learning parameters a and b, when variable-structure automata (e.g., L_{R-P} scheme) are used, become critical parameters. It is in this context that the following definitions of expediency, optimality, and absolute expediency in nonstationary environments become important.

7.3.1   Expediency

The distinguishing feature of nonstationary environments is that the penalty probabilities vary with time. Let us first assume that this variation is deterministic. In such a case, confining our attention to the P–model,

$$
\begin{aligned}
c_i(n) &= Pr\{\beta(n) = 1 | \alpha(n) = \alpha_i\} \\
       &= E[\beta(n) | \alpha(n) = \alpha_i]
\end{aligned}
\tag{7.1}
$$

as in a stationary environment. The average penalty $M(n)$ becomes

$$
\begin{aligned}
M(n) &= E[\beta(n) | p(n)] \\
     &= Pr[\beta(n) = 1 | p(n)] \\
     &= \sum_{i=1}^{r} Pr[\beta(n) = 1 | p(n), \alpha(n) = \alpha_i] Pr[\alpha(n) = \alpha_i] \\
     &= \sum_{i=1}^{r} c_i(n) p_i(n).
\end{aligned}
\tag{7.2}
$$

The pure–chance automaton, with all the action probabilities equal, has an average penalty M_0 as a function of time where

$$
M_0(n) = \frac{1}{r} \sum_{i=1}^{r} c_i(n).
\tag{7.3}
$$

In defining expediency the dependence of M_0 on n has to be taken into account. Thus a learning automaton can be defined as *expedient* in a nonstationary environment if there exists a n_0 such that for all $n > n_0$,

$$
[E[M(n)] - M_0(n)] < 0.
\tag{7.4}
$$

7.3.2   Optimality and Absolute Expediency

In some specific nonstationary environments the earlier concept of optimality can be carried over. If, for example, for a fixed ℓ,

$$
c_\ell(n) < c_i(n) \qquad (i = 1, 2, \ldots, r \qquad , i \neq \ell)
\tag{7.5}
$$

for all n (or at least for all $n > n_1$, for some n_1) then α_ℓ is the optimal action and the original definitions of optimality and ϵ–optimality hold good.

In general nonstationary environments where there is no fixed optimal action, an automaton can be defined as *optimal* if it minimizes

$$\lim_{T \to \infty} \frac{1}{T} \sum_{n=1}^{T} E[\beta(n)].$$

The definition of absolute expediency can be retained as before, with time–varying penalty probabilities, and the new interpretation of $M(n)$ as in Eq.(7.2).

When the environment is periodic, it appears reasonable to regard one period (T) as a unit and use the average value of $M(n)$ over one period as a measure of the performance. Thus, one can define

$$\hat{M}(n) = \frac{1}{T} \sum_{i=1}^{r} \sum_{t=n}^{n+T-1} c_i(t) p_i(t). \tag{7.6}$$

It is usual to consider $\hat{M}(n)$ in the place of $M(n)$ in evaluating the performance of an automaton in periodic environments.

7.3.3 Expediency in Markovian Environments

Consider an MSE with state space $E = \{E_1, E_2, \ldots, E_d\}$. Let an automaton with r actions act in such an environment. If S is the state space of the automaton, the state space of the composite system is the product space $S \times E$. If $p_i(n)$ is the probability of choosing the ith action α_i at stage n, $q_j(n)$ is the probability that the MSE is in state E_j and c_i^j is the penalty probability corresponding to action α_i in environment E_j, the average penalty $M(n)$ is given by

$$M(n) = \sum_{i=1}^{r} p_i(n) \{ \sum_{j=1}^{d} q_j(n) c_i^j \}. \tag{7.7}$$

If

$$\lim_{n \to \infty} E[M(n)] < \frac{1}{r} \sum_{i=1}^{r} \sum_{j=1}^{d} q_j^* c_i^j \tag{7.8}$$

where q_j^* are the steady–state probabilities of the MSE, we say that the learning automaton is expedient.

7.4 Automata in MSE

7.4.1 Fixed Structure Automata

The behavior of a fixed-structure automaton in an MSE containing two states E_1 and E_2 was analyzed in detail by Tsetlin (1961). Although the mathematical details for determining the asymptotic behavior are similar to the case of a single environment described in Chapter 3, the conclusions drawn from the analysis are different and quite significant in the context of nonstationary environments. Our emphasis in this section will be on these qualitative aspects.

Let the penalty probabilities associated with the two environments E_1 and E_2 be $\{c_1^1, c_2^1, \ldots, c_r^1\}$ and $\{c_1^2, c_2^2, \ldots, c_r^2\}$ respectively, where c_i^j denotes the penalty probability due to action $i(= 1, 2, \ldots, r)$ in environment $j(= 1, 2)$. Let the Markovian environment E have a transition matrix

$$\begin{bmatrix} 1-\delta & \delta \\ \delta & 1-\delta \end{bmatrix} \tag{7.9}$$

so that δ represents the average frequency ($0 < \delta < 1$) with which the state of the environment switches. Equivalently, we can define $T \triangleq \frac{1}{\delta}$ as the average number of cycles during which the state of the medium remains constant ($\sum_{m=1}^{\infty} m(1-\delta)^{m-1}\delta = \frac{1}{\delta} = T$).

It is seen that while the stationary probabilities of the Markov chain are $(\frac{1}{2}, \frac{1}{2})$ for all values of $\delta \in (0, 1)$, the average length of the interval over which the environment remains in E_1 or E_2 is determined by δ. Hence if an automaton were to operate in such an environment, the overall performance would necessarily depend on δ. This is brought out clearly by the analysis which follows.

Let the automaton transition matrices corresponding to reward and penalty be the $\overline{N} \times \overline{N}$ matrices $F(0)$ and $F(1)$, where $\overline{N}$ denotes the number of states of the automaton.

If $f_{ij}(0)$ and $f_{ij}(1)$ are, respectively, the $(i, j)^{th}$ elements of $F(0)$ and $F(1)$, then

$$p_{ij}^k = f_{ij}(1)c_{\alpha(i)}^k + f_{ij}(0)d_{\alpha(i)}^k \tag{7.10}$$

is the probability that the automaton will make a transition in environment E_k from state ϕ_i to state ϕ_j. Here $\alpha(i)$ is the action corresponding to state ϕ_i.

We shall say that the automaton and environment are together in state $\phi_i^k(i = 1, 2, \ldots, \overline{N}, \ k = 1, 2)$ if the automaton is in state ϕ_i and the environment is in state E_k. Since the transition probability from any state ϕ_i^k to any other state $\phi_j^{k'}$ $(k, k' = 1, 2)$ and $(i, j = 1, 2, \ldots, \overline{N})$ is constant, the behavior of a fixed-structure automaton in an MSE is described by a homogeneous Markov chain in the state space $S \times E$. In this composite environment, a (2×2) element of the overall transition probability matrix representing transitions from $\phi_i^k \rightarrow \phi_j^{k'}$ $(k, k' = 1, 2)$ is given by

$$
\begin{array}{cc}
\phi_j^1 & \phi_j^2
\end{array}
$$
$$
\begin{array}{c}
\phi_i^1 \\
\phi_i^2
\end{array}
\left[
\begin{array}{cc}
p_{ij}^1(1 - \delta) & p_{ij}^1 \delta \\
p_{ij}^2 \delta & p_{ij}^2(1 - \delta)
\end{array}
\right]
\quad i, j = 1, \ldots, \overline{N}. \quad (7.11)
$$

If the overall transition probability matrix corresponds to that of an ergodic chain (this is true for example in the case of the Tsetlin automaton when $0 < c_{\alpha(i)}^k < 1$ for all i and k) the final state probabilities will not depend on the initial states. These final probabilities of states and actions can then be computed using standard techniques (refer to Chapter 3).

In his paper, Tsetlin considered the simple case of a two–action $2N$ state automaton operating in stationary environments E_1 and E_2 where

$$
c_1^1 = c = 1 - c_2^1 \quad \text{and} \quad c_1^2 = 1 - c = 1 - c_2^2
$$

(i.e., if $c < \frac{1}{2}$, α_1 is the better action in E_1 and α_2 is the better action in E_2).

The equivalent automaton has $4N$ states and four actions. The $4N \times 4N$ transition matrix P is made up of cell matrices of the form

$$
p_{ij} =
\left[
\begin{array}{cc}
\{cF_{ij}(1) + (1 - c)F_{ij}(0)\}(1 - \delta) & \{cF_{ij}(1) + (1 - c)F_{ij}(0)\}\delta \\
\{(1 - c)F_{ij}(1) + cF_{ij}(0)\}\delta & \{(1 - c)F_{ij}(1) + cF_{ij}(0)\}(1 - \delta)
\end{array}
\right].
$$

$$(7.12)$$

Considering the first element of the cell matrix p_{ij} i.e. $\{cF_{ij}(1) + (1 - c)F_{ij}(0)\}(1 - \delta)$, this represents the transition probability of the ith state of the automaton to the jth state while the first state of the environment remains unchanged. The other three elements of the cell matrix are similarly defined. Since $F(0)$ and $F(1)$ are matrices with elements that are either 0 or 1 and since $F_{ij}(0)$ and $F_{ij}(1)$ are not 1 simultaneously, p_{ij} has the form

$$
Q =
\left[
\begin{array}{cc}
c(1 - \delta) & c\delta \\
(1 - c)\delta & (1 - c)(1 - \delta)
\end{array}
\right]
\quad \text{or} \quad
S =
\left[
\begin{array}{cc}
(1 - c)(1 - \delta) & (1 - c)\delta \\
c\delta & c(1 - \delta)
\end{array}
\right].
$$

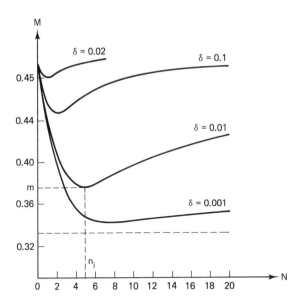

Figure 7.2: M versus N for different values of δ (*Courtesy Plenum Publishing Corp.*).

The equation $P^T \pi = \pi$ that must be solved to obtain the stationary probabilities can now be written in terms of the matrices Q and S as follows:

$$
\begin{array}{ll}
R_1 = QR_1 + QR_2 & R_{n+1} = SR_{n+1} + SR_{n+2} \\
R_2 = SR_1 + QR_3 & R_{n+2} = QR_{n+1} + SR_{n+3} \\
- - - - - - & - - - - - - - \\
R_k = SR_{k-1} + QR_{k+1} & R_{n+k} = QR_{n+k-1} + SR_{n+k+1} \\
- - - - - - & - - - - - - - \\
R_n = SR_{n-1} + QR_{2n} & R_{2n} = QR_{2n-1} + SR_n.
\end{array}
\tag{7.13}
$$

Equation (7.13) has the same form as Eq.(3.17) except that the scalar elements in the latter are replaced by matrices in the former. Further R_i in Eq.(7.13) represents a two dimensional vector

$$
R_i = \begin{bmatrix} \pi_{i1} \\ \pi_{i2} \end{bmatrix} \qquad i = 1, 2, \ldots, 2N.
$$

Although the procedure adopted for solving Eqs.(7.13) and (3.17) are similar, the latter is considerably more involved algebraically. This reveals

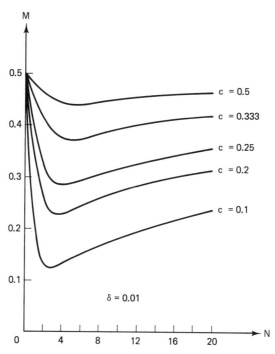

Figure 7.3: M versus N for different values of c. (*Courtesy Plenum Publishing Corp.*).

that the use of fixed-structure automata and the corresponding analysis using the Markov chain theory may become mathematically cumbersome even for relatively simple systems. In the present context, Tsetlin has analyzed the problem in detail and obtained expressions for R_i from which the expected penalty M can be calculated.

For the specific environment considered, the expression for $\lim_{n\to\infty} M(n)$ $= M$ is obtained in Tsetlin (1961) as a function of the penalty probability c, δ, and the memory depth N of the Tsetlin automaton. The general form of the curves is shown in Figs. 7.2 and 7.3. The following comments can be made regarding these curves: Even though the results apply to a very specific simple example, they carry over qualitatively to more complex situations and are found to be very valuable in the design of learning automata.

(i) In Fig. 7.2 M versus N is plotted for $c = .33$ and various values of δ. The curve has a minimum with respect to N. If the memory is increased beyond that value, the automaton tends to average out the statistical properties of the two media. This is found to be true for any constant value of c.

(ii)   As $\delta \to 0$ (i.e., the environment switching frequency decreases), $N_{opt} \to \infty$ (where N_{opt} is the optimal value of N).

(iii) As δ increases, the optimal memory depth decreases until a stage is reached when $N_{opt} = 1$. This implies that if the environment switches at a certain rate or higher, the optimal policy is to have a memory of unity or the automaton should act purely on the basis of the response to an action at that stage.

(iv)   It is also found (refer to Fig. 7.3) that if c increases (i.e., c and $d = 1 - c$ are closer to each other) it requires a larger memory to distinguish between the two media.

Table 7.1 shows the value of the optimal memory depth and the deviation $(M_0 - M)$ of the minimum expected penalty from M_0 $(= \frac{1}{2}$ for the problem under consideration) corresponding to specified values of c and δ.

	$\delta = .001$	$\delta = .010$	$\delta = .032$	$\delta = .100$	$\delta = .320$	$\delta = .450$
$c = .10$	3; 0.396	2; 0.372	2; 0.336	1; 0.256	1; 0.115	1; 0.032
.20	5; 0.294	3; 0.266	2; 0.223	2; 0.157	1; 0.065	1; 0.018
.25	6; 0.244	4; 0.212	3; 0.172	2; 0.116	1; 0.045	1; 0.012
.33	8; 0.158	5; 0.125	3; 0.091	2; 0.055	1; 0.020	1; 0.006
.40	11; 0.089	6; 0.056	4; 0.037	2; 0.020	1; 0.007	1; 0.002
.45	16; 0.036	7; 0.017	4; 0.010	2; 0.005	1; 0.002	1; 0.001

Table 7.1

From the analysis above the following general comments can be made: The main problem in a composite medium with many environments is that the optimal action is, in general, different in the different environments. Also, the initial state E_i of the environment is unknown. Hence, the automaton has to perceive the changes in the environment solely on the basis of its response and alter its action probabilities accordingly. Thus, if an automaton were to perform satisfactorily in such an environment, it must in general choose all the actions with a nonzero probability.

The main conclusion reached from the analysis of fixed-structure automata operating in environments with two states is that, depending on the penalty probabilities and the switching frequency, there is an optimum memory depth for obtaining the minimum average penalty. Even though an analysis of multiple–environment media has not been carried out, it is safe to conclude that these qualitative results would carry over to such cases also.

7.4.2 Variable Structure Automata

Variable-structure automata can also be used to give good performance in MSE. Obviously, absolutely expedient schemes such as the L_{R-I} scheme are not of much use here since the automaton tends to get trapped in absorbing states. Hence ergodic schemes such as the $L_{R-\epsilon P}$ or L_{R-P} are called for, so that the different actions are chosen with nonzero probabilities. However, an $L_{R-\epsilon P}$ with very small parameter b is found to be too slow in most practical situations and hence nonoptimal.

Varshavskii and Vorontsova (1963) first applied a variable-structure automaton for the choice of actions in an MSE. By choosing functions of the form

$$g_{ik} = a f_{ik}^0 (1 - f_{ik}^0) \left.\right\}$$
$$h_{ik} = a f_{ik}^1 (1 - f_{ik}^1) \left.\right\} \tag{7.14}$$

in the reinforcement scheme of Eq.(4.41), they showed through simulations, that the time–average of the penalty response

$$\hat{M}(n) = \frac{1}{n} \sum_{i=1}^{n} \beta(i) \tag{7.15}$$

converges close to the minimum possible value. For the problem considered in the previous section with a Markov switching environment and $c = .1$, $\delta = .01$, $\hat{M}(n)$ attained a value close to the minimum value of .128 attainable by a Tsetlin automaton in approximately 2^{16} iterations.

The asymptotic value of $\hat{M}(n)$ depends on the parameter a as well. If a is too small, the updating scheme is too slow and cannot cope with the changes in the environment. Hence $\hat{M}(n)$ will tend to a value much larger than the minimum. If a is too large, the increments in the transition probabilities are too high and the automaton's accuracy in perceiving the optimal action becomes low. Once again $\hat{M}(n)$ will tend to high values. Thus there is an optimum value of a for which $\hat{M}(n)$ tends to the minimum value.

Similar remarks hold for the choice of parameters a and b when L_{R-P} or $L_{R-\epsilon P}$ schemes are used in a Markov switching environment. It can be seen that the dependence here on the parameters of the reinforcement scheme is analogous to the dependence of the Tsetlin automaton on the memory depth.

7.5 State Dependent Nonstationary Environments

In recent years two new mathematical models of learning automata have been proposed that are state-dependent nonstationary according to the description in Section 7.2. In both of them the actions of the automaton affect the response characteristics of the environment. Both models were motivated by applications in telephone traffic routing (refer to Chapter 9) and have given rise to interesting theoretical questions in learning automata theory. Such models are also applicable to problems that arise in economics. Of the two models (referred to as Model A and Model B), the second is analytically tractable and is considered in much greater detail. An extension of this model to the case where the environment is also dynamic, referred to as Model C, is treated in Section 7.5.3.

7.5.1 Model A

In Model A introduced by Narendra and Thathachar (1980), when an action α_i is performed at any stage n the corresponding penalty probability c_i of the environment increases while c_j $(j \neq i)$ decreases. This implies that an action that is performed becomes worse for subsequent stages while one that is not performed improves with time. Mathematically the environment may be described as follows:

If $Pr[\beta(n) = 1 | \alpha(n) = \alpha_i] = c_i(n)$ $i = 1, 2, \ldots, r$ and $\alpha(n) = \alpha_i$

$$\left. \begin{array}{l} c_i(n+1) = c_i(n) + \theta_i(n) \\ c_j(n+1) = c_j(n) - \phi_j(n) \quad (j \neq i) \end{array} \right\} \tag{7.16}$$

where $\theta_i(n)$ and $\phi_j(n)$ $(i, j = 1, 2, \ldots, r)$ are nonnegative functions of the stage number n. In general θ_i and ϕ_i can be functions of $p(n)$ as well as $c_i(n)$ but to keep the model simple and tractable we make the assumption $\theta_i(n) = \theta_i$ a constant if $c_i(n) + \theta_i \leq 1$ and $\theta_i(n) = 1 - c_i(n)$ otherwise.

Similarly

$$\phi_i(n) = \phi_i \qquad \text{a positive constant}$$

if

$$c_i(n) - \phi_i \geq 0$$

and

$$\phi_i(n) = c_i(n) \qquad \text{otherwise.}$$

By the definitions above the increase in the penalty probabilities $\theta_i(n)$ or the decrease in penalty probabilities $\phi_i(n)$ are constants except when the new penalty probabilities lie outside the unit interval.

The updating procedure described thus far reflects qualitatively the type of behavior encountered in many practical systems. However, in view of the non–Markovian nature of the overall stochastic process the powerful methods of Norman used in Chapter 5 cannot be directly applied here. The importance of this model lies in the fact that it eventually led to Model B for which such methods are applicable. Some qualitative analysis of this model and simulation results are available in Narendra and Thathachar (1980).

7.5.2 Model B

Srikantakumar and Narendra (1982) suggested an alternative model in which the penalty probabilities are functions of the corresponding action probabilities (Fig. 7.4). The automaton–environment interaction in such a case can be described by a homogeneous Markov process and hence the methods of Chapter 5 can be used to analyze it in detail. After characterizing the environment, we first consider L_{R-P} and $L_{R-\epsilon P}$ learning automata with two actions and later extend the results to automata with multiple actions.

The Environment: The following assumptions are made regarding the penalty probabilities of the environment. If $p(n) = p$, the penalty probabilities are functions of p and denoted as $c_i(p)$.

(i) $c_i(p_1, p_2, \ldots, p_r)$ is continuous in p_j $(i, j = 1, 2, \ldots, r)$.

(ii) $\partial c_i(p)/\partial p_i > 0 \qquad \forall i$ and $p \in S_r$
  $\partial c_j/\partial p_i << \partial c_i/\partial p_i$ for $j \neq i$ [1]. $\qquad\qquad$ (7.17)

---

[1]Since $\sum_{i=1}^{r} p_i = 1$, the partial derivatives $\frac{\partial c_i}{\partial p_i}$ are meaningful only if each c_i is considered to be a function of $(r-1)$ of the variables $p_1, p_2, \ldots, p_r$. As a consequence, the second inequality in (ii) is irrelevant in the case of a two–action automaton.

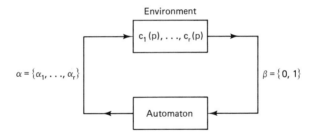

Figure 7.4: Model B.

(iii) $c_i(\cdot)$ is continuously differentiable in all its arguments.

(iv) $c_i(\cdot)$ and $(\partial c_i(\cdot))/(\partial p_i)$ are Lipschitzian functions of all their arguments.

Although assumption (i) is subsumed by (ii), (iii), and (iv) we state them separately since the stricter assumptions are not always required.

The principal assumption is that $c_i(p)$ is a monotonically increasing function of p_i. (In the telephone traffic routing example considered in Chapter 9 this implies that the blocking probability along a trunk group increases monotonically with the probability with which calls are routed along that trunk group.) The condition on the cross partial derivatives implies that a change in p_i affects primarily $c_i(p)$ and to a much lesser extent $c_j(p)$ $(j \neq i)$.

Learning Automata with Two Actions:

L_{R-P} *Scheme:* Let the automaton use an L_{R-P} scheme to update its action probabilities. The probability with which the automaton receives a penalty at time n from action α_i is given by

$$c_i(p(n))p_i(n) \stackrel{\triangle}{=} f_i(p(n)). \tag{7.18}$$

Proposition: In a two–action automaton assumptions (i) and (ii) assure the existence and uniqueness of a constant vector $\bar{p}$ such that

$$f_1(\bar{p}) = f_2(\bar{p}). \tag{7.19}$$

This follows from the fact that $f_2(p) - f_1(p)$ is continuous in p_1 and is equal to $c_2(0,1)$ for $p_1 = 0$ and $-c_1(1,0)$ for $p_1 = 1$. Hence by the intermediate value theorem a vector $\bar{p}$ exists such that $f_2(\bar{p}) - f_1(\bar{p}) = 0$. Uniqueness follows since the derivative *w.r.t.* p_1 is negative for all $p_1 \in [0,1]$.

As in Chapter 4, the conditional expectation $\Delta p_1(n)$ for the general L_{R-P} scheme can be written as follows.

$$
\begin{aligned}
\Delta p_1(n) &= E[p_1(n+1) - p_1(n)|p(n) = p] \\
&= p_1 d_1(p)[ap_2] + p_2 d_2(p)[-ap_1] \\
&\quad - p_1 c_1(p)[bp_1] + p_2 c_2(p)[bp_2]
\end{aligned}
\tag{7.20}
$$

with $d_i(p) \overset{\Delta}{=} 1 - c_i(p)$.

In an L_{R-P} scheme, substituting $b = a$,

$$
(\Delta p_1(n))/a = f_2(p) - f_1(p) \overset{\Delta}{=} w(p)
$$

and
$$
\tag{7.21}
$$

$$
(\Delta p_2(n))/a = -w(p).
$$

Further, defining $s_i(p)$ and $\overline{s}_i(p)$ as

$$
\left.
\begin{aligned}
\overline{s}_i(p) &\overset{\Delta}{=} E[(p_i(n+1) - p_i(n))^2|p(n) = p] \\
s_i(p) &\overset{\Delta}{=} \overline{s}_i(p) - w^2(p)
\end{aligned}
\right\}
\tag{7.22}
$$

and

The process $\{p(n)\}$ defined by an L_{R-P} scheme operating in the environment defined by Eq.(7.17) is Markovian and ergodic. Hence $p(n) \to p^*$ as $n \to \infty$ where p^* is a random variable independent of $p(0)$.

From the fact that p^* is the limit of $\{p(n)\}$, we have

$$
E[\Delta p_1(n)|p = p^*] = E[w(p^*)] = 0.
$$

From Eq.(7.19) $\overline{p}$ is the zero of $w(p)$ and in general $E[w(p^*)] = 0$ will not yield $\overline{p}$. However, as seen from the following theorem, if the parameter a is chosen sufficiently small, the difference between p^* and $\overline{p}$ may be made small in a certain sense.

Theorem 7.1: The Markov process $\{p_i(n)\}_{n \geq 0}$ satisfies the following:

(a) Under assumptions (i) to (iii), $E[p_i(n) - \overline{p}_i]^2 = 0(a)$ as $n \to \infty$ (7.23)

(b) Under assumptions (i) to (iv), if $z_n^i \overset{\Delta}{=} \dfrac{p_i(n) - \overline{p}_i}{\sqrt{a}}$, (7.24) then as $a \to 0$, $na \to \infty$, z_n^i is normally distributed with mean zero and variance

$$\sigma_i^2 = \frac{s_i(\overline{p})}{2 \left| (\partial w(\overline{p}))/(\partial p_i) \right|}. \qquad (7.25)$$

For a proof of this theorem the reader is referred to Srikantakumar and Narendra (1982).

Comment 7.1: Since

$$E[w(p(n))] = E[f_2(p(n)) - f_1(p(n))] \to 0 \text{ as } n \to \infty$$

we have

$$E[f_2(p^*)] = E[f_1(p^*)].$$

Further since $[E(p_i(n) - \overline{p}_i)]^2 \le E[(p_i(n) - \overline{p}_i)^2]$, from part (a) it follows that

$$E[p_i(n)] - \overline{p}_i = 0(\sqrt{a})$$

and also as $a \to 0$,

$$E[(p_i(n) - \overline{p}_i)^2] \to 0.$$

Thus asymptotically $p(n)$ has a mean which differs from $\overline{p}$ by $0(\sqrt{a})$ and a variance $0(a)$. Hence we conclude that the asymptotic value of $p(n)$ using the L_{R-P} scheme can be approximated by $\overline{p}$ where

$$f_2(\overline{p}) = f_1(\overline{p})$$

or the two–action automaton attempts to equalize the penalty rates from the two actions.

$L_{R-\epsilon P}$ *Scheme:* As described in Chapter 5, the $L_{R-\epsilon P}$ scheme is also ergodic, and when it is used in the environment satisfying Eq.(7.17) we have

$$\Delta p_1(n) = E[p_1(n+1) - p_1(n)|p(n) = p] = p_1 p_2 [c_2(p) - c_1(p)] + 0(a)$$
$$= w(p) + 0(a).$$
$$(7.26)$$

Once again in the r.h.s. of Eq.(7.26)

$$w(p_1 = 0) = w(p_1 = 1) = 0$$

and the residual term $0(a)$ changes sign. Hence a unique $\overline{p}$ can be shown to exist such that

$$c_1(\overline{p}) = c_2(\overline{p}) \qquad (7.27)$$

Further, Theorem 7.1 applies to this case also with the new definition of $\overline{p}$ given by Eq.(7.27). Hence the $L_{R-\epsilon P}$ automaton tends to equalize the penalty probabilities of the two actions.

Learning Automata with Multiple Actions: The same results may also be extended to the multiple–action case as follows.

$$\Delta p_i(n) = E[p_i(n+1) - p_i(n)|p(n) = p]$$
$$= p_i d_i(p)[a \sum_{j\neq i} p_j] + p_i c_i(p)[-b + b \sum_{j\neq i} p_j] \qquad (7.28)$$
$$+ \sum_{j\neq i} p_j d_j(p)[-ap_i] + \sum_{j\neq i} p_j c_j(p)[\frac{b}{r-1} - bp_i].$$

In both the L_{R-P} and $L_{R-\epsilon P}$ cases the Markov process $p(n)$ is ergodic. Further, using Brouwer's fixed point theorem it can be shown that a unique $\overline{p}$ exists such that

$$\overline{p}_i c_i(\overline{p}) = \overline{p}_j c_j(\overline{p}) \qquad \forall \; i, \; j \; \in \; \{1, 2, \ldots, r\} \qquad (7.29)$$

in the case of the L_{R-P} scheme and

$$c_i(\overline{p}) = c_j(\overline{p}) \qquad \forall \; i, \; j \; \in \; \{1, 2, \ldots, r\} \qquad (7.30)$$

for an $L_{R-\epsilon P}$ scheme.
If

$$w(p) = [w_1(p), w_2(p), \ldots, w_r(p)]^T \qquad (7.31)$$

then

$$s(p) \triangleq E\{[\frac{p(n+1) - p(n)}{a} - w(p)][\frac{p(n+1) - p(n)}{a} - w(p)]^T\} \qquad (7.32)$$

and

$$z_n^i \triangleq \frac{p_i(n) - \overline{p}_i}{\sqrt{a}} \qquad (7.33)$$

$$z_n = [z_n^1, z_n^2, \ldots, z_n^r] \qquad (7.34)$$

$$A \triangleq (dw(p))/dp \Big|_{p=\overline{p}} \qquad (7.35)$$

(A is an $r \times r$ matrix).

where $\overline{p}$ is given by Eqs.(7.29) or (7.30) depending on whether L_{R-P} or $L_{R-\epsilon P}$ is used. As in Chapter 5, if $\tilde{s}(p)$ and $\tilde{A}$ represent $(r-1) \times (r-1)$ matrices, obtained from $s(p)$ and A by deleting the rth row and r^{th} column,

the following theorem can be stated which generalizes the results obtained
for the two–action case to the case of multiple actions.

Theorem 7.2: For a Markov process $\{p(n)\}_{n\geq 0}$ defined by a learning
automaton acting in an environment satisfying conditions (i) to (iv) of
Eq.(7.17),

(a)
$$E[\|p(n) - \overline{p}\|^2] = 0(a) \qquad\qquad (7.36)$$

$$E[p(n)] - \overline{p} = 0(\sqrt{a}) \text{ as } n \to \infty \qquad\qquad (7.37)$$

(b) z_n as $a \to 0$, $na \to \infty$ is normal with mean zero and covariance Σ
which is obtained as the unique solution of

$$\tilde{A}\tilde{\Sigma} + \tilde{\Sigma}\tilde{A}^T + \tilde{s}(\overline{p}) = 0 \qquad\qquad (7.38)$$

[$\overline{p}$ is the vector satisfying Eq.(7.29) for L_{R-P} and Eq.(7.30) for $L_{R-\epsilon P}$].

(c) If an $L_{R-\epsilon P}$ scheme is used and $c_k(p) > c_\ell(p)$ for all p and all $k \neq \ell$,
then as $n \to \infty$,

$$E[p_\ell(n)] - 1 = 0(\sqrt{a}) \qquad (k = 1, 2, \ldots, r) \qquad\qquad (7.39)$$

so that the learning automaton is ϵ–optimal.

Comment 7.2: In the cases considered above, $\overline{p}$ represents the value of
p satisfying $w(\overline{p}) = 0$. Using Norman's theory of Markov processes, which
evolve by small steps, it is shown that $p(n)$ can be asymptotically made
arbitrarily close to $\overline{p}$ by choosing a sufficiently small a. The sense in which
$p(n)$ is close to $\overline{p}$ is made explicit in Theorems 7.1 and 7.2. The result
implies that an automaton using the L_{R-P} scheme tends to equalize the
penalty rates of the various actions. Instead, if an $L_{R-\epsilon P}$ scheme is used,
the automaton will tend to equalize the penalty probabilities. This fact is
exploited in Chapter 9 in the context of telephone traffic routing.

7.5.3   Model C: A Dynamic Environment

In the models discussed in Sections 7.5.1 and 7.5.2, the penalty probabilities c_i $(i = 1, 2, \ldots, r)$ were assumed to be instantaneous functions of the
action probabilities. However, in many practical applications such as routing in networks, although such models are adequate to explain equilibrium

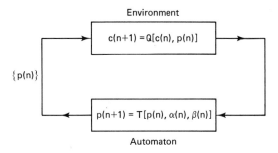

Figure 7.5: Model C.

behavior, they do not adequately describe the transient behavior of the overall system. In particular, simulation studies have shown (Nedzelnitsky and Narendra, 1987) that if $f_i[p(n)]$ assumes the same value at two instants of time n_1 and n_2 for some $i\ (=1,2,\ldots,r)$, the corresponding values $c_i(n_1)$ and $c_i(n_2)$ are not the same. This suggests the need for a dynamic model of the environment for an accurate prediction of the transient behavior. Such a model was introduced in Nedzelnitsky and Narendra (1987) and is described by a general difference equation of the form

$$c(n+1) = Q[c(n), p(n)] \tag{7.40}$$

so that the penalty probabilities can be considered as the output with the action probabilities corresponding to the input. Equation (7.40) together with the learning algorithm

$$p(n+1) = T[p(n), \alpha(n), \beta(n)] \tag{7.41}$$

constitute the state equations of the overall system. To make the model analytically tractable, the function Q is assumed to have the special form

$$Q[c(n), p(n)] = \Gamma c(n) + [I - \Gamma]f[p(n)] \tag{7.42}$$

where Γ is a diagonal matrix with elements $\gamma_i \in (0,1)$ and $f_i[p(n)]$ satisfying the conditions of Eq.(7.17). Figure 7.5 shows such a learning automaton in which both the environment and the automaton are dynamical systems. The Markov process defined by Eqs.(7.41) and (7.42) has been studied by Nedzelnitsky and Narendra (1987). Its asymptotic properties have been shown to be the same as those of Model B. However, as might be expected, the evolution of $p(n)$ and $c(n)$ are different in the two cases. Example 9.4 of network routing using learning automata, presented in Chapter 9, reveals that the

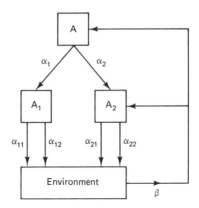

Figure 7.6: A Hierarchical System.

dynamic model predicts the transient response of the network significantly better.

According to Eq.(7.42), the action probability $p_i(n)$ affects only the penalty probability $c_i(n+1)$. More complex models can also be generated by increasing the dimensionality of the state space of the environment so that $c_i(n+1)$ depends on the past values of the action probability p_i besides $p_i(n)$. Such models can also be analyzed using the same methods described in the context of Model B and may prove more effective in predicting the transient behavior of systems more accurately.

7.6   Nonstationary Effects in a Hierarchical System

A nonstationary environment arises indirectly in connection with a hierarchical system of learning automata (Thathachar and Ramakrishnan 1981). For understanding the main ideas, consider a two–level tree hierarchy as shown in Fig. 7.6. The hierarchy consists of a single automaton with r actions at the first level, each action of which is connected to an automaton of the second level. The second–level automata interact with the environment which is assumed to be stationary. There is no restriction on the number of actions of each automaton.

The operation of the hierarchical system takes place as follows: Initially, for each automaton, the action probabilities are equal. The first–level automaton chooses an action (say α_i) based on its action probability distribution. This action triggers the automaton A_i of the second level which now chooses an action (say α_{ij}) based on its action probability distribution. The action α_{ij} interacts with the environment and elicits a response, $\beta(n)$. The penalty probability is c_{ij}. The action probabilities of both A and A_i are updated and the entire cycle is repeated.

The following notation is relevant here:

$$\beta(n) = \quad \text{response of the environment at } n$$

$$p_i(n) = \quad i^{th} \text{ action probability of the first–level automaton } A \text{ at } n$$

$$p_{ij}(n) = \quad j^{th} \text{ action probability of automaton } A_i \text{ of second level at } n$$

$$c_{ij} = \quad \text{penalty probability of the environment corresponding to the}$$
$$\text{choice of action } \alpha_{ij} \text{ at second level and } \alpha_i \text{ at first level}$$
$$= \quad Pr[\beta(n) = 1 | \alpha_i, \alpha_{ij}]$$

$$r_i = \quad \text{number of actions of automaton } A_i$$

Suppose the first–level automaton A is viewed as operating in a composite evironment consisting of the second–level automata and the environment. The equivalent penalty probabilities of the first level can be computed as follows:

$$\begin{aligned} Pr[\beta(n) = 1 | \alpha_i \text{ chosen}] &= \sum_{j=1}^{r_i} Pr[\beta(n) = 1 | \alpha_i, \alpha_{ij}] Pr[\alpha_{ij}] \\ &= \sum_{j=1}^{r_i} c_{ij} p_{ij}(n). \end{aligned} \tag{7.43}$$

Thus even when the environment is stationary (i.e., c_{ij} are constant) the equivalent penalty probabilities of the composite environment as seen by the first level keep changing with n as they are functions of $p_{ij}(n)$. The first–level automaton can thus be regarded as operating effectively in a nonstationary environment.

Reinforcement Schemes: A basic problem in the hierarchical system is to find reinforcement schemes for the individual automata in the hierarchy so the entire system has certain desirable properties. For example, one might require the hierarchical system to be ϵ–optimal and desire to find the reinforcement schemes to be used in each of the automata. An alternative way of looking at the problem is to regard the second level updating as manipulating the nonstationary environment seen by the first level to attain the desired objective.

One could attempt the problem in reverse as well. Suppose each automaton operates according to the L_{R-I} scheme. Does the entire hierarchy behave like a single equivalent automaton following the L_{R-I} scheme? Actually this question will be pursued below in a more general context with reference to reward–inaction absolutely expedient schemes.

Absolute Expediency: Let each automaton in the hierarchy use a reward–inaction absolutely expedient scheme of the form shown in Eq.(4.84). Thus the reinforcement scheme of each automaton is specified by a reward function $\lambda(\cdot)$. One can find conditions on the reward functions so that the hierarchical system is absolutely expedient.

Before attempting this problem it is necessary to clarify the concept of the hierarchical system being absolutely expedient since originally the concept was associated only with a single automaton. However, it is easy to extend the definition by considering an equivalent automaton of the hierarchical system.

The choice of action α_{ij} at the second level implies that action α_i was chosen at the first level. Hence there is a unique path from the first level to the environment connected with each action of the second level. An equivalent automaton could be thought of as having each path (α_i, α_{ij}) as an action and the product $p_i(n)p_{ij}(n)$ as the action probability associated with it. This automaton works in the same environment as the hierarchy and the definition of absolute expediency applies to it in the usual way. We say that the hierarchical system is absolutely expedient, if and only if, the equivalent automaton is absolutely expedient.

Derivation of Conditions: Let the first–level automaton A operate as follows.

$$
\left.
\begin{aligned}
\alpha_i = \quad & \text{action selected at n} \\
p_i(n+1) = \quad & p_i(n) + \lambda(p(n))(1 - p_i(n)) \quad && \text{if } \beta(n) = 0 \\
p_j(n+1) = \quad & p_j(n)(1 - \lambda(p(n))) \quad && \text{if } \beta(n) = 0 \\
& (j \neq i) \\
p_k(n+1) = \quad & p_k(n) \quad (k = 1, \ldots, r) \quad && \text{if } \beta(n) = 1
\end{aligned}
\right\}
\qquad (7.44)
$$

Similarly let the second level updating take the following form:
Let

$$\alpha_{ij} = \text{action selected at } n$$

$$\hat{p}(n) = \text{vector of all action probabilities of the hierarchy at } n$$

Automaton A_i

$$
\begin{array}{ll}
p_{ij}(n+1) = p_{ij}(n) + \lambda_i(\hat{p}(n))(1 - p_{ij}(n)) & \text{if } \beta(n) = 0 \\
p_{ik}(n+1) = p_{ik}(n)(1 - \lambda_i(\hat{p}(n))) & \text{if } k \neq j, \ \beta(n) = 0
\end{array} \Bigg\}
$$

$$(7.45)$$

Automaton A_k ($k \neq i$)

$$
p_{k\ell}(n+1) = p_{k\ell}(n) \quad (\ell = 1, \ldots, r_k) \quad \beta(n) = 0 \text{ or } 1. \quad (7.46)
$$

It is evident that the algorithm above is of the reward–inaction type. Furthermore even with a favorable response from the environment it updates only the actions of the second–level automaton which contains the selected action. The other automata in the second level are left unchanged.

The basic result concerning the absolute expediency of the hierarchical system can now be stated in the following theorem. For simplicity $\lambda(p(n))$ and $\lambda_i(\hat{p}(n))$ are represented as $\lambda(n)$ and $\lambda_i(n)$ respectively.

Theorem 7.3: The hierarchical system described by Eqs.(7.44)–(7.46) is absolutely expedient, if and only if,

$$
\lambda_i(n) = (\lambda(n))/(p_i(n+1))
$$
$$
\forall \, n, \ \forall \, p(n) \in S_r^0 \text{ and } \forall \, i = 1, \ldots, r. \quad (7.47)
$$

Proof:

Sufficiency: This part of the proof follows by showing that the equivalent automaton is absolutely expedient and also has the same reward function $\lambda(\cdot)$ as the first–level automaton.

The action probabilities of the equivalent automaton are products of the form $p_k(n)p_{k\ell}(n)$. When the selected actions are α_i, α_{ij}, considering the second–level automata not containing the selected action, [i.e., $k \neq i$, $\ell \neq j$, $\beta(n) = 0$]

$$
\begin{aligned}
p_k(n+1)p_{k\ell}(n+1) &= p_k(n)(1 - \lambda(n))p_{k\ell}(n) \\
&= p_k(n)p_{k\ell}(n)(1 - \lambda(n)).
\end{aligned} \quad (7.48)
$$

Similarly for $k \neq j$,

$$
\begin{aligned}
p_i(n+1)p_{ik}(n+1) &= [p_i(n) + \lambda(n)(1 - p_i(n))]p_{ik}(n)(1 - \lambda_i(n)) \\
&= p_i(n)p_{ik}(n)(1 - \lambda(n))
\end{aligned} \quad (7.49)
$$

using Eq.(7.47). Also, again using Eq.(7.47),

$$
\begin{aligned}
p_i(n+1)p_{ij}(n+1) &= [p_i(n) + \lambda(n)(1 - p_i(n))][p_{ij}(n) + \lambda_i(n)(1 - p_{ij}(n))] \\
&= p_i(n)p_{ij}(n) + \lambda(n)(1 - p_i(n)p_{ij}(n)).
\end{aligned}
$$
(7.50)

The action probabilities are unchanged when $\beta(n) = 1$.

Thus it is seen that the reinforcement scheme of the equivalent automaton is a reward–inaction absolutely expedient scheme with the reward function $\lambda(\cdot)$. The equivalent automaton and consequently the hierarchical system is absolutely expedient.

Necessity: The necessity follows from the fact that as seen in Chapter 4, the form of Eq.(4.84) is necessary as well for absolute expediency of the reinforcement schemes of the type being considered.

From Eq.(7.48) it is evident that for the equivalent automaton, the reward function is the same as the $\lambda(\cdot)$ of the first level. Now we want (for $k \neq j$)

$$
p_i(n+1)p_{ik}(n+1) = p_i(n)p_{ik}(n)(1 - \lambda(n)).
$$

However from Eqs.(7.44) and (7.45)

$$
\begin{aligned}
p_i(n+1)p_{ik}(n+1) &= [p_i(n) + \lambda(n)(1 - p_i(n))]p_{ik}(n)(1 - \lambda_i(n)) \\
&= p_i(n)p_{ik}(n)(1 - \lambda(n)) \\
&\quad + p_{ik}(n)[\lambda(n) - \lambda_i(n)(p_i(n) + \lambda(n)(1 - p_i(n)))].
\end{aligned}
$$
(7.51)

The second term should be identically zero i.e., for all $p_{ik}(n)$ to maintain the form of the absolutely expedient scheme. Hence

$$
\lambda_i(n) = \frac{\lambda(n)}{p_i(n+1)}.
$$
(7.52)

From the observations made earlier in Chapter 5 on absolute expediency and ϵ–optimality, the following corollary results.

Corollary: The hierarchical system of Eqs.(7.44)–(7.46) satisfying the condition of Eq.(7.47) of Theorem 7.3 is ϵ–optimal in all stationary random environments if $\lambda(p(n)) > 0$ for all $p(n)$ with the possible exception of the unit vectors.

Comment 7.3: The $\lambda_i(\cdot)$ functions of the second level are obtained by a division process which may cause concern as $p_i(n+1)$ could go to zero.

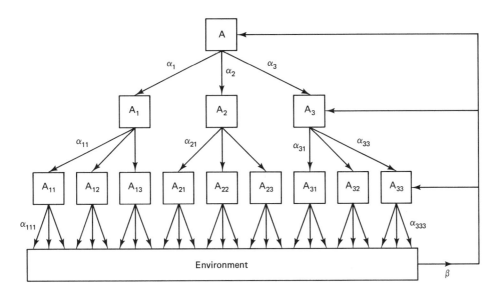

Figure 7.7: Multilevel Hierarchy.

However it is easy to see that such an event does not arise $w.p.1$ and

$$\lambda(n) < p_i(n+1) \qquad (7.53)$$

from Eq.(7.44) and hence $\lambda_i(n)$ is always bounded above by 1.

Multilevel Hierarchy: The results above can be extended to an arbitrary number of levels. For example, a three–level system with each automaton having three actions is shown in Fig. 7.7. To facilitate further discussion, the following notation is used.

Let

$$N = \quad \text{number of levels in the hierarchy}$$

$$\alpha_{i_1}, \alpha_{i_1 i_2}, \alpha_{i_1 i_2 i_3}, \ldots, \alpha_{i_1 i_2 \cdots i_N} = \quad \text{actions selected at levels } 1, 2, \ldots, N$$

respectively,

where $i_1, i_2, \ldots, i_N$ are integers ranging from 1 to the total number of actions in the corresponding automata. The actions selected are those of automata designated as $A, A_{i_1}, A_{i_1 i_2} \ldots, A_{i_1 i_2 \cdots i_{N-1}}$ respectively.

Consider the updating at the Lth level where L can take any value from 2 to N. The first level updating is the same as in Eq.(7.44). To simplify the long subscripts associated with lower levels we introduce another notation. Denote

$$i_1 i_2 \ldots i_N \text{ by } \underline{i_N}$$

thus

$$i_1 = i_1$$
$$\underline{i_2} = i_1 i_2$$
$$\underline{i_3} = i_1 i_2 i_3 \text{ and so on}$$

also

$$\underline{j_L i_{L+1}} = j_1 j_2 \ldots j_L i_{L+1} \text{ etc.}$$

<u>updating at L^{th} level</u> $(L = 2, 3 \ldots N)$

α_{i_L} = action selected at n

$A_{i_{L-1}}$ = automaton selected at $(L-1)^{th}$ level (whose action is α_{i_L})

<u>for $\beta(n) = 0$</u>

$$\underline{p_{i_L}}(n+1) = \underline{p_{i_L}}(n) + \underline{\lambda_{i_{L-1}}}(n)(1 - \underline{p_{i_L}}(n))$$
$$\underline{p_{i_{L-1} j_L}}(n+1) = \underline{p_{i_{L-1} j_L}}(n)(1 - \underline{\lambda_{i_{L-1}}}(n)) \tag{7.54}$$
$$(j_L \neq i_L)$$
$$\underline{p_{j_L}}(n+1) = \underline{p_{j_L}}(n) \text{ for all other actions.}$$

for $\beta(n) = 1$ all action probabilities are unchanged. The extension of Theorem 7.3 to the N–level automaton runs as follows.

Theorem 7.4: The N–level hierarchical system defined by Eqs.(7.44) and (7.54) is absolutely expedient, if and only if,

$$\begin{aligned}\underline{\lambda_{i_L}}(n) &= (\underline{\lambda_{i_{L-1}}}(n))/(\underline{p_{i_L}}(n+1)) \\ &= (\lambda(n))/(\underline{p_{i_1}}(n+1)\underline{p_{i_2}}(n+1) \ldots \underline{p_{i_L}}(n+1))\end{aligned} \tag{7.55}$$

for all $L = 2, 3, \ldots N$.

The proof closely follows that of Theorem 7.3. The necessity part results from an application of mathematical induction.

Comment 7.4: The previous comment on the division in Eq.(7.47) and the inequality of Eq.(7.53) applies here also and there is no computational hazard involved in Eq.(7.55).

Comment 7.5: Suppose r_L is the number of actions of each automaton at the Lth level. Since only one automaton is updated at each level in any cycle, the total number of updatings in one cycle is

$$r_1 + r_2 + \ldots + r_N.$$

The number of actions at the last level is, however, the product

$$r_1 r_2 \ldots r_N.$$

If a single automaton were used, the number of updatings in each cycle would also be the latter number. Thus the computational advantage of using a hierarchy can be seen by the magnitude of the ratio

$$\frac{r_1 r_2 \ldots r_N}{r_1 + r_2 + \ldots + r_N}.$$

The hierarchical structure is attractive for problems with large number of actions.

Comment 7.6: Given the total number of actions, one can find the optimal number of actions per automaton so that the number of updatings in each cycle is minimized. Mathematically this is the problem of minimizing

$$\sum_{i=1}^{N} r_i$$

subject to

$$\Pi_{i=1}^{N} r_i \geq K$$

where K is a given positive integer.

From a modification of the prime factor theorem, it can be shown that each r_i must be 2 or 3 for the optimum solution which may involve adding some dummy actions. For example, if $K = 75$, make

$$\Pi_{i=1}^{N} r_i = 81$$

since 81 is the nearest higher number that can be expressed as a product of 2's and 3's. As $3^4 = 81$, the solution is $r_i = 3$ $(i = 1, 2, 3, 4)$ and the number of updatings per cycle is $12 = 3 + 3 + 3 + 3$. Thus the optimal solution involves $6 = 81 - 75$ dummy actions.

Example 7.1: A hierarchical system with 128 actions arranged in seven levels was simulated. Each automaton had two actions. The penalty probabilities were all randomly selected in the interval $[0.4, 0.85]$ except for the unique minimum which had the value 0.23. An L_{R-I} updating scheme with $\lambda = 0.004$ was used for the first level.

The convergence of the action probabilities along the optimal path at various levels is shown in Fig. 7.8. The average action probability taken

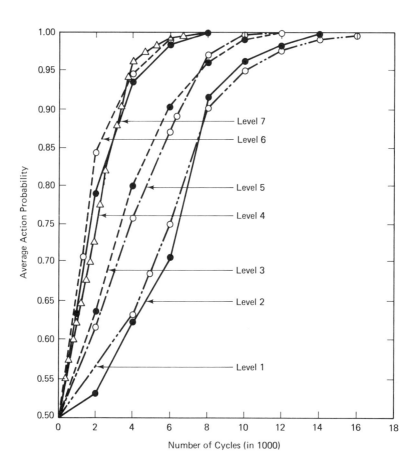

Figure 7.8: Convergence of action probabilities in hierarchical system of Example 7.1 (*Courtesy IEEE* © *1978*).

over twenty-five runs is plotted against the number of cycles in the figure. It is evident that the lower levels converge faster than the upper levels.

Comment 7.7: In the hierarchical model above, the response of the environment to the actions of the automata in the last level was used for the updating schemes of automata at all levels. In many realistic situations it appears more pertinent to model the environment to have different responses to automata at different levels. Such a model was proposed by Thathachar and Ramakrishnan (1981) who also gave an algorithm that was absolutely expedient and ϵ-optimal under certain assumptions on the optimal path. This work was further continued by Thathachar and Sastry (1987) who recognized three types of hierarchical systems based on the nature of the optimal path and gave estimator algorithms that are ϵ-optimal.

7.7 Environments with a Fixed Optimal Action

We now briefly consider another class of nonstationary environments for which analytical results are available. These are environments where one action α_ℓ continues to have the minimum penalty probability c_ℓ even though all the penalty probabilities keep changing with time. It is clear that such an environment shares a common property with stationary random environments: a single action can be called the optimal action. We have seen that absolutely expedient schemes have considerable success in converging to the optimal action in stationary environments. Similar results can also be derived for the present class of nonstationary environments (Baba and Sawaragi, 1975).

It can be shown that the procedure described in Chapter 5 for computing bounds on convergence probabilities also carries over. The conditions on penalty probabilities are however to be modified slightly as follows.

There exists a $\delta > 0$ such that

$$c_\ell(n) + \delta < c_j(n) \tag{7.56}$$

for all n and all $j \neq \ell$. Under Assumption A of Chapter 5 one can then proceed as before and conclude ϵ-optimality. Despite its seemingly obvious nature, the result is found to have wide application in many time–varying situations. In particular, the reader is referred to Chapter 8 where this result is used in a game context.

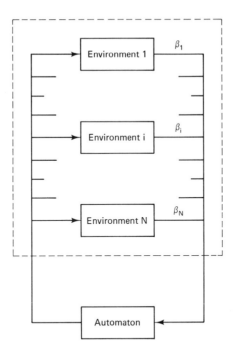

Figure 7.9: Automata acting in multiple environments.

7.8   Multiple Environments

All the learning schemes we have developed thus far dealt with a single automaton operating in a stationary random environment. Yet, much learning takes place outside this context. Students learn from many teachers; a team of doctors may be involved in diagnosing a complex disease; actions in many situations elicit different opinions. In each of the cases above learning is effected with a vector of outputs rather than a scalar output. In this section we discuss a mathematical model that describes the situations above.

Figure 7.9 shows a set of N stationary random environments denoted by $E_1, E_2, \ldots, E_N$ connected to an automaton. The environment $E_i (i = 1, 2, \ldots, N)$ is described by its action set $\underline{\alpha} = \{\alpha_1, \alpha_2, \ldots, \alpha_r\}$, the output set $\underline{\beta}^i = \{0, 1\}$ and a set of penalty probabilities $\{c_1^i, c_2^i, \ldots, c_r^i\}$ where

$$c_j^i = Pr[\beta^i(n) = 1 | \alpha(n) = \alpha_j]. \tag{7.57}$$

The action set of the automaton is also $\underline{\alpha}$ so that all the environments respond to the same action of the automaton. Considering a composite environment E to be made up of the N environments E_i in parallel, the response of the environment to an action of the automaton is an n–vector each of whose elements is a 0 or 1. The problem then is to determine how the automaton should change its strategy based on this information.

The notion of a single automaton operating in several environments was proposed independently by Koditschek and Narendra (1977) and Thathachar and Bhakthavathsalam (1977). The former considered the behavior of a fixed-structure automaton when the environments are probabilistic teachers. In the latter, the behavior of a variable-structure automaton in a two-teacher environment was analyzed. More recently Baba (1984), in a monograph, discussed the problem of a variable-structure automaton operating in many environments that are either stationary or nonstationary and obtained conditions for absolute expediency. For a detailed discussion of these problems, the reader is referred to Baba (1984).

Some difficulties are encountered while formulating a mathematical model of the learning problem in the presence of multiple environments, which are not present when only one environment exists. For example, the manner in which the outputs of the different environments are to be weighted and the precise objectives of the automaton have to be clarified. In Chapter 1 it was stated that a stationary random environment could also be viewed as a probabilistic teacher. While an environment rewards or penalizes an automaton directly, a teacher conveys information about an implicit environment by approving or disapproving the automaton's behavior. This distinction arises naturally when we address the question of whether "learning" is manifested by the capacity to gain approval from conflicting judges, or by a tendency to perform one "correct" action more often than others. The problem treated by Koditschek and Narendra (1977) considers multiple teachers and hence, to make the problem meaningful, it was postulated that the teachers "agree" on the ordering of the automaton's actions. In terms of the penalty probabilities this can be stated quantitatively as

$$c_\ell^i < c_j^i \qquad \forall\, j \neq \ell \qquad (i = 1, 2, \ldots, N) \qquad (7.58)$$

i.e., a single action α_ℓ is optimal for all the environments. The same assumption is also made by Thathachar and Bhakthavathsalam(1977) for the two environments that they consider.

Since the multiple environments provide a vector of outputs, they must be combined in some fashion to form the input to the automaton. Although this can be achieved in numerous ways, Thathachar and Bhakthavathsalam use an AND–logic in processing the two environmental responses. According to this, if the ordered pair of responses from the two environments E_1 and E_2 are respectively (1,1), (1,0), (0,1), and (0,0), only the first is considered a failure from the composite environment. According to this, the automaton receives a favorable response more often from the composite environment than from the individual environments. Using both an L_{R-P} scheme and an absolutely expedient scheme, the authors show that the automaton performs better. In the former case the optimal action is asymptotically chosen with a higher probability while in the latter case, where the automaton is ϵ–optimal, the speed of convergence is increased. These results are extended to multiple environments in Bhakthavathsalam (1987).

In contrast to the assumption of Eq.(7.58) made in the papers discussed earlier, Baba (1984) defines the optimal action of the automaton, α_ℓ, as the one corresponding to which

$$c_\ell^1 + c_\ell^2 + \ldots + c_\ell^N < c_j^1 + c_j^2 + \ldots + c_j^N \qquad j \neq \ell \qquad j = 1, 2, \ldots, r. \quad (7.59)$$

This implies that the optimal action α_ℓ is the one that minimizes the average penalty of the composite environment. In this case, if the response of the environments to an action contains M ones and $N - M$ zeros, the normalized value of the output $\beta(n)$ of the composite environment is $\beta(n) = M/N$. Using the general updating algorithm of Eq.(6.11) the probabilities of the various actions are updated as

$$p_i(n+1) = p_i(n) + (1 - \tfrac{M}{N}) \left[\sum_{j\neq i}^r g_j(p(n))\right] - \tfrac{M}{N}\left[\sum_{j\neq i}^r \quad h_j(p(n))\right]$$
$$\alpha(n) = \alpha_i$$
$$p_j(n+1) = p_j(n) - (1 - \tfrac{M}{N})g_j(p(n)) + \tfrac{M}{N}h_j(p(n)) \quad j \neq i.$$
$$(7.60)$$

In Baba (1984), it is shown that the procedure above results in absolute expediency if g_j and h_j satisfy the conditions of Eq.(6.27). It is further shown that if the outputs S_j^i of the environments are continuous variables where S_j^i denotes the response of the ith environment to α_j, and $S_j^i \in [0,1]$, the average response of the composite environment can be defined as

$$S_j = \frac{S_j^1 + S_j^2 + \ldots S_j^N}{N}. \quad (7.61)$$

In such a case the updating of probabilities at stage n is made using the algorithm

$$p_i(n+1) = p_i(n) + (1 - S_i) \left[\sum_{j\neq i}^r g_j(p(n))\right] - S_i \left[\sum_{j\neq i}^r h_j(p(n))\right]$$
$$p_j(n+1) = p_j(n) - (1 - S_i)g_j(p(n)) + S_i h_j(p(n)). \quad (7.62)$$

Baba has shown that if the action α_ℓ, as defined earlier, continues to be optimal even when the environments are nonstationary, the algorithm above yields absolute expediency under the same conditions. This can also be seen to follow directly from the result stated in Section 7.7.

In all the cases discussed above the N outputs of the environments are linearly transformed into a single scalar input to the automaton. Since the outputs of the environments are assumed to be normalized, this merely reduces to determining the average value of the outputs. In general, since the characteristics of the N environments may be quite different, normalization of the outputs may also constitute a part of the overall problem. In such a case a linear combination of $\beta^i(n)$ $(i = 1, 2, \ldots, N)$ of the N environments given by

$$\beta(n) = \theta_1 \beta^1(n) + \theta_2 \beta^2(n) + \ldots \theta_N \beta^N(n) \tag{7.63}$$

is used as the input to the automaton. The parameters θ_i $(i = 1, 2, \ldots, N)$ denote the weights attached to the different outputs and must be constrained so that $\beta(n) \in [0, 1]$. The choice of the vector $\theta = [\theta_1, \theta_2, \ldots, \theta_N]^T$ by the designer defines the performance index and in turn determines how the probabilities of the various actions are to be changed at every stage.

The results presented in this section reveal that the learning algorithms discussed in Chapters 4–6 can be extended to multiple environments with only minor modifications. Further, hierarchical structures of automata discussed in Section 7.6, acting in multiple environments as described here, can be used to model complex decision making problems. The analysis of special types of nonstationary environments discussed in earlier sections of this chapter can also be used in the context of multiple environments. Finally, while in all our discussions the outputs of the different environments were assumed to be independent, it is found that the results can also be extended to cases where dependency exists between environmental responses.

7.9   Other Nonstationary Environments

The behavior of automata in nonstationary environments, treated in Sections 7.5 and 7.6, are analytically tractable although the algebraic details for obtaining expressions of the performance may be quite involved (as for example, in Section 7.6). In contrast to these, a vast amount of qualitative information is also available in the literature regarding other specific nonstationary environments for which precise analytical results have not been obtained. In view of their practical interest, we consider them in some detail in this section.

7.9.1 Periodic Environments

Let a periodic environment consist of d stationary environments $E_1, E_2, \ldots,$ E_d. Operation of an automaton in such an environment can be considered under two different levels of available information. The simpler of these corresponds to the case where the period T ($\geq d$) is known apriori and is similar to the nonstationary case discussed in Section 7.2. The more complex case corresponds to the situation when T is unknown.

(i) *Period T Known:* Let the known period be T discrete intervals. Then we can set up T automata and a switching device that connects the automata in sequence to the environment at every instant. Thus each automaton operates in the environment once in T instants. Since the environment repeats itself every T instants, each automaton is effectively working in a stationary environment and hence converges to some desirable behavior in one of the senses considered earlier.

(ii) *Period T Unknown:* The specific problem of nonstationarity comes into play when the period is unknown. The problem is somewhat eased by assuming that an upper bound on the period is known. For this case we shall consider two solutions, one of which appears suitable for use with deterministic automata and the other with variable-structure automata. Both the solutions require a two–level organization of automata, which is, however, quite different from the hierarchy discussed in Section 7.6.

Deterministic Automata: In the first design using deterministic automata (Varshavskii, Meleshina, and Tsetlin, 1965) there are $T_{\max}$ automata in the first level where

$$T_{\max} = \quad \text{maximum possible period of the environment in terms} \\ \text{of the number of discrete intervals.}$$

There are $T_{\max}$ automata in the second level also and thus there is a one–to–one correspondence between the automata in the two levels. Let $A_i(i = 1, \ldots, T_{\max})$ and $B_i(i = 1, \ldots, T_{\max})$ represent the first– and second–level automata respectively.

Each automaton has two actions 0 and 1. If a second–level automaton B_i chooses action 1, the corresponding first–level automaton A_i is connected to the environment. Thus some of the automata in the first level are connected in sequence to the environment and elicit a response. These automata are updated in the usual manner.

A commutator moves from one of the second–level automata that has chosen action 1 to another which has chosen the same action. After the commutator completes all the second–level automata that have chosen action 1, each automaton at this level is penalized with a probability equal to the average number of penalties drawn by the first–level automata operating in that interval. The cycle repeats in this manner. The schematic diagram of the system is shown in Fig. 7.10.

The analysis of this two–level organization appears difficult and does not appear to have been made thus far. However, numerous simulations have shown that the average penalty does converge to the minimum possible value when the memory depth is sufficiently large. The time for convergence is also reasonable, being in the range of 20 to 40 times the period of the environment.

Example 7.2: The behavior of Tsetlin automata in a periodic sequence of two stationary random media whose penalty probabilities were $(c_1, 1 - c_1)$ and $(1 - c_2, c_2)$ were simulated using the two–level organization indicated above. The results are shown in Table 7.2, where N corresponds to the memory depth and τ to the number of intervals for convergence.

N	$T_{\max}$	T	c_1	c_2	$M(\infty)$	τ
10	10	5	1/8	1/8	1/8	170
10	20	6	1/8	1/8	1/8	210
10	20	7	1/4	1/4	1/4	262
10	30	10	1/4	1/3	17/60	382
15	20	11	1/8	1/8	1/8	228

Table 7.2

Variable Structure Stochastic Automata: Variable-structure stochastic automata can also be used to solve the problem of an unknown periodic environment. Although it is possible to employ the same scheme as before by replacing the deterministic automata by variable-structure automata, the results have not been found encouraging. It appears better to make use of the following arrangement shown in Fig. 7.11 (Narendra and Viswanathan, 1972).

The first level consists of a single automaton A with $T_{\max}$ actions with each action corresponding to one possible value of period and is responsible for making a decision about the value of the unknown period. The second

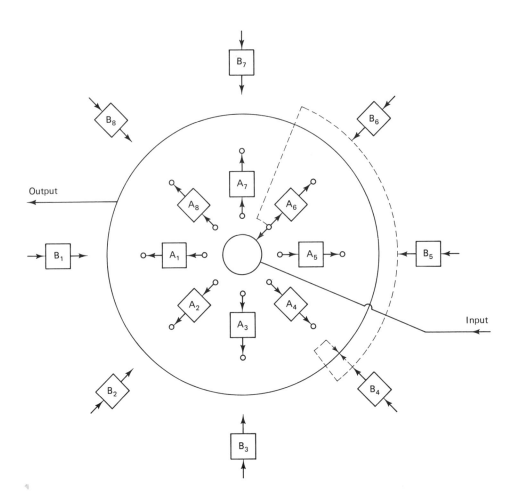

Figure 7.10: Deterministic automata in a periodic environment (*Courtesy Academic Press*).

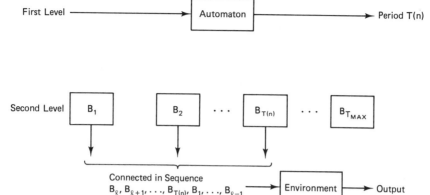

Figure 7.11: Variable-structure automata in a periodic environment.

level consists of T_{max} automata $(B_1, B_2, \ldots, B_{T_{\text{max}}})$, which are organized in such a way that if $T(n)$ is the period chosen by the first level, only $T(n)$ automata in the second level operate in a sequential manner. The arithmetic mean of the output values of the environment in these $T(n)$ operations is fed back to the first level as input for the next stage. The inputs to the second-level automata are the responses from the environment and the actions of these automata are the inputs to the environment

One can discern two time scales in the operation of the setup. The first one is the usual discrete interval that represents the rhythm of the environment and the second–level automata. The second time scale is the duration of each stage of operation of the first–level automaton, which is denoted by $1, 2, \ldots, n$. Let the number of discrete–time intervals elapsed until the end of the stage number n be t_n. It is evident that

$$t_n = \sum_{k=1}^{n} T(k) \tag{7.64}$$

and also

$$t_n = t_{n-1} + T(n). \tag{7.65}$$

Thus each stage has a variable duration depending on the value of period $T(n)$ chosen by the first–level automaton A.

In the nth stage, $T(n)$ is the period chosen and $T(n)$ members of the second–level automata are operative. Determining the first of these automata to be activated at the beginning of the nth stage is of considerable importance. If B_{ℓ_n} denotes this automaton, ℓ_n is chosen as

$$\ell_n = \{t_{n-1} - \left[\frac{t_{n-1}}{T(n)}\right] T(n) + 1\} \text{ (modulo } T(n)) \qquad (7.66)$$

where $[x]$ is the largest integer less than or equal to x. Thus the sequence of the second–level automata to be connected to the environment is

$$B_{\ell_n}, B_{\ell_n+1}, \ldots, B_{T(n)}, B_1, B_2, \ldots, B_{\ell_n-1}.$$

The expression of Eq.(7.66) for ℓ_n is obtained following the simple intuitive idea that if $T(n)$ were the exact period, $[(t_{n-1})/(T(n))]$ cycles would have elapsed by the beginning of the nth stage. The right–hand side of Eq.(7.66) indicates the number of discrete intervals "spilled over" to reach the instant $t_{n-1} + 1$ after these cycles are completed. Assuming that B_1 was the automaton connected in the first interval of the first stage, it appears natural that B_{ℓ_n} from Eq.(7.66) is to be connected at the beginning of the nth stage, at the instant $t_{n-1} + 1$.

The arithmetic mean of the responses of the environment in the nth stage lies in the closed interval $[0, 1]$ and is used directly as the input to the automaton A for the $(n + 1)^{th}$ stage. It is assumed that whenever the input to an automaton is disconnected, its action probabilities remain unchanged.

Updating Schemes: The updating schemes for the B_i automata must follow the nature of the environment. They are P–model, Q–model, or S–model schemes according to the environment in which the automata operate. We shall assume a P–model situation for simplicity. The automaton A however, must be of the S–model type for the arithmetic mean of several responses forms the input to this automaton.

Let

$$q_i(n) = Pr[\text{automaton } A \text{ chooses the output } i \text{ in the } n^{th} \text{ stage}].$$
$$i = 1, 2, \ldots, T_{\max}$$
$$p_{ij}(n) = Pr[\text{automaton } B_i \text{ chooses the action } \alpha_j \text{ in the } n^{th} \text{ stage}].$$
$$i = 1, 2, \ldots, T_{\max}$$
$$j = 1, 2.$$

It may be noted that each automaton B_i gets connected to the environment at most once in each stage. This accounts for the argument in $p_{ij}(\cdot)$ being chosen as the stage number rather than the time instant.

Automaton A. If $y(n)$ is the input to automaton A

$$y(n) = \frac{1}{T(n)} \sum_{i=1}^{T(n)} \beta(t_{n-1} + i) \qquad (7.67)$$

and if the SL_{R-I} scheme is used,

$$\left. \begin{array}{l} q_{T(n)}(n+1) = q_{T(n)}(n) + a[1 - y(n)][1 - q_{T(n)}(n)] \\ q_i(n+1) = q_i(n) - a[1 - y(n)]q_i(n) \\ \\ \qquad\qquad\qquad\qquad i = 1, 2, \ldots, T_{\max} \\ \qquad\qquad\qquad\qquad i \neq T(n) \end{array} \right\}$$

where $a \in (0,1)$.

$$(7.68)$$

Automaton B_i. The automaton B_i gets connected to the environment at most only once in the stage n. If $y_i(n)$ is its input,

$$\left. \begin{array}{ll} y_i(n) & = \beta(t_{n-1} + i - \ell_n + 1) \text{ for } i = \ell_n, \ell_n + 1, \ldots, T(n) \\ & = \beta(t_{n-1} + T(n) - \ell_n + i + 1) \text{ for } i = 1, 2, \ldots, \ell_n - 1. \end{array} \right\} \qquad (7.69)$$

For $i > T(n)$, the input is identically zero, for these automata are not connected to the environment in stage n. The index ℓ_n is given in Eq.(7.66).

When a proper choice of the period is made by the Automaton A, each B_i effectively operates in a stationary random environment and hence it appears pertinent for the B_i automata to use any ϵ-optimal scheme. For illustration, let us suppose the L_{R-I} scheme is used by all the B_i automata.

If the automaton B_i $[i = 1, 2, \ldots, T(n)]$ performs action α_j in stage n, then

$$\begin{array}{ll} p_{ij}(n+1) & = p_{ij}(n) + b[1 - y_i(n)][1 - p_{ij}(n)] \\ & \qquad i = 1, 2, \ldots, T(n) \end{array} \qquad (7.70)$$

where $b \in (0,1)$.

Since we have assumed only two actions for each automaton, the updating for the other action follows from Eq.(7.70).

Other ϵ-optimal schemes such as the one by Vorontsova (1965) can also be used here.

An improvement in the setup above is also possible. By choosing an estimate of the true period or its multiple, it is not necessary to consider all the numbers from 1 to $T_{\max}$. We can eliminate those numbers (excluding 1) which are submultiples of numbers in the range 1 to $T_{\max}$. For example, if $T_{\max} = 20$, then it is sufficient to consider the 11 numbers: 1,11,12,...,19,20. Using this procedure, the automaton A has a lesser number of actions and the convergence process may be speeded up. Also, the action that corresponds to the true period is unique because, in the original setup if $T = 7$ and $T_{\max} = 20$, the actions 7 and 14 of automaton A both correspond to the true period thus causing a nonunique answer. However, through simulations, it is known that the sum of probabilities of these two actions tends to unity with the stage number growing indefinitely large and hence the period can be recognized as 7.

As in the case of deterministic automata, the analysis of the two–level organization appears extremely difficult and much reliance must be placed on simulation results, some of which are outlined in the sequel.

Two problems are simulated here to show that practically optimal performance can be attained by the scheme described thus far.

Example 7.3: The unknown period $T = 2$ and $T_{\max} = 4$. The penalty probabilities are:

$$c_{11} = 0.125 \qquad\qquad c_{12} = 0.875$$

$$c_{21} = 0.875 \qquad\qquad c_{22} = 0.125$$

where c_{ij} = penalty probability of action α_j at time i following the beginning of a period. It is evident from the equation above that action α_1 must be performed at all odd instants and α_2 at even instants for optimal performance.

Example 7.4: Here $T = 7$, $T_{\max} = 20$. The penalty probabilities are

$$c_{i1} = 0.25 \qquad\quad c_{i2} = 0.75 \qquad\quad i = 1, 2, 3$$

$$c_{j1} = 0.75 \qquad\quad c_{j2} = 0.25 \qquad\quad j = 4, 5, 6, 7.$$

For achieving optimal performance the first action α_1 should be chosen in the first three instants and the second action α_2 for the next four instants in any period.

To evaluate the performance of such a two–level system, a quantity M_1 is defined as follows.

$$M_1(n) = \frac{1}{T(n)} \sum_{(i,k)} \sum_{j=1}^{2} p_{ij}(n) c_{kj} \qquad (7.71)$$

where $M_1(n)$ is the average performance over the nth stage. In Eq.(7.71) the indices i and k in the first summation run as follows:

$$i = \ell_n, \ell_n + 1, \ldots T(n), 1, 2, \ldots, \ell_n - 1;$$

$$k = t_{n-1} + 1, t_{n-1} + 2, \ldots, t_n$$

where t_n and ℓ_n are as defined in Eqs.(7.65) and (7.66). As in the case of any experiment involving variable-structure automata, $p_{ij}(n)$ and $M_1(n)$ are random variables and we need $E[M_1(n)]$ versus n for assessing the performance. This is obtained by running the same experiment several times and obtaining the sample mean $\tilde{M}_1(n)$.

For both the examples, the SL_{R-I} scheme was used in updating automaton A and the L_{R-I} scheme for automata B_i. The initial action probabilities were $1/T_{\max}$ for A and $1/2$ for each B_i. Each experiment was terminated when any action probability of A and some action probability of each of the B_i reached 0.98. The parameters employed and other details are given in Table 7.3. The variation of $\tilde{M}_1(n)$ with n is shown in Figs. 7.12 and 7.13 for Examples 7.3 and 7.4 respectively. Note that all the trials were successful and $\tilde{M}_1$ converged to values close to the minimum possible value.

	No. of Runs over Which Average is Taken	Parameter a of SL_{R-I} Scheme	Parameter b of L_{R-I} Scheme
Example 7.3	50	0.02	0.005
Example 7.4	10	0.003	0.001

Table 7.3

7.9.2 A Sinusoidally Varying Environment

In the previous section we discussed the possibility of using multiple automata to improve the performance in a periodic environment. We now consider the operation of a single automaton in an environment in which the penalty strengths vary sinusoidally (Chandrasekaran and Shen, 1967). Under certain assumptions, the sinusoidal penalty strengths may be considered as inputs to linear systems whose outputs are action probabilities. In such cases, frequency domain methods, which have proved so powerful in linear systems theory, can also be used for the analysis of learning automata. The general problem of an automaton operating in a nonstationary environment

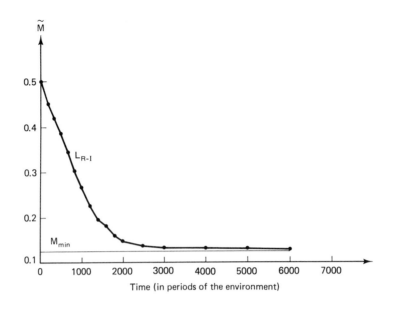

Figure 7.12: Learning curve for Example 7.3 (*Courtesy IEEE ©1972*).

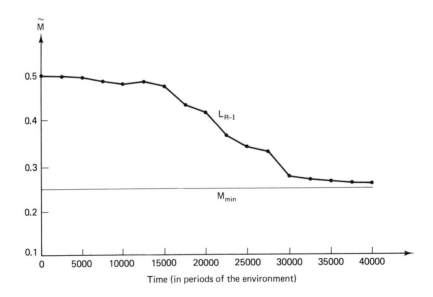

Figure 7.13: Learning curve for Example 7.4. (*Courtesy IEEE ©1972*).

was posed in Section 7.2. The results derived here provide some valuable insights regarding the type of performance that can be expected in such cases for different time variations of the penalty probabilities as well as the learning algorithms used.

For simplicity, consider a two–action automaton operating in an S–model environment according to the SL_{R-P} scheme. Thus

when $\alpha(n) = \alpha_i, (i = 1, 2)$

$$p_i(n + 1) = (1 - a)p_i(n) + a(1 - \beta(n)) \qquad (7.72)$$

$$p_j(n + 1) = (1 - a)p_j(n) + a\beta(n) \qquad (j \neq i).$$

Recall from Chapter 6 that if the environment is stationary and if the penalty strength

$$s_i = E[\beta(n)|\alpha(n) = \alpha_i], \qquad (7.73)$$

$$\lim_{n \to \infty} E[p_i(n)] = \frac{1/s_i}{\sum_{j=1}^{2} 1/s_j} \quad \text{and} \quad \lim_{n \to \infty} E[M(n)] = \frac{2}{\sum_{j=1}^{2} 1/s_j}. \qquad (7.74)$$

Now let us assume that one of the s_i varies sinusoidally with time.

$$\left.\begin{array}{rcl} s_1(n) & = & s_{10} + \epsilon_1 \cos bn \\[2mm] 0 & \leq & s_{10} \pm \epsilon_1 \leq 1. \\[2mm] s_2(n) & = & s_{20}. \end{array}\right\} \qquad (7.75)$$

Starting from Eq.(7.72) and computing the expectations in the usual manner,

$$E[p_1(n + 1)] = E[p_1(n)][k_1 - \epsilon_0 \cos bn] + k_2 \qquad (7.76)$$

where

$$\left.\begin{array}{l} k_1 = 1 - a + a(1 - s_1(n) - s_2(n)) \\[2mm] k_2 = as_2(n) \\[2mm] \epsilon_0 = a\epsilon_1. \end{array}\right\} \qquad (7.77)$$

Since only $s_1(n)$ is a function of n, k_1 is a function of n and k_2 is a constant.

Equation (7.76) is a first–order linear difference equation with a time–varying coefficient. Such an equation has the general form

$$x_{n+1} = k(n)x_n + c \qquad (7.78)$$

and its steady–state solution (where $n \gg 1$), is given by

$$E[p_1(n)] = \frac{k_2}{1 - k_{10}} - \frac{k_2\epsilon_0}{k_{10}(1 - k_{10})} \sum_{j=1}^{n-1} \cos\left[(n - j)b\right]k_{10}^j \qquad (7.79)$$

where
$$k_{10} = k_1|_{\epsilon_1=0} = (1 - a) + a(1 - s_{10} - s_{20}). \qquad (7.80)$$

The sum in Eq.(7.79) can be approximated by an integral and Eq.(7.79) has the form

$$E[p_1(n)] \cong \frac{k_2}{1 - k_{10}} - \frac{k_2\epsilon_0}{k_{10}(1 - k_{10})} \int_1^n k_{10}^j \cos[(n - j)b]\,dj. \qquad (7.81)$$

Setting [2]
$$\delta = \mathrm{Ln}(k_{10}) = \mathrm{Ln}[(1 - a) + a(1 - s_{10} - s_{20})] \qquad (7.82)$$

Equation (7.81) can be written using Eq.(7.80) as

$$E[p_1(n)] \cong \frac{s_{20}}{s_{10} + s_{20}} \left\{ 1 - a\epsilon_1 \cos\left[(n - 1)b - \tan^{-1}\frac{b}{|\delta|}\right] \right\} \qquad (7.83)$$

The second term in Eq.(7.83) is caused by the sinusoidal component of the penalty strengths of the environment and is of the same frequency b. The phase shift

$$\tan^{-1}\frac{b}{|\delta|} \qquad (7.84)$$

decreases with the frequency b and tends to zero as $b \to 0$.

The value of δ determines the maximum frequency b which assures the validity of Eq.(7.83). Let ϵ be some small positive number. Also let

$$n_0 = \frac{1}{\delta} \mathrm{Ln}(\epsilon) \qquad (7.85)$$

then if

$$\frac{1}{b} >> \frac{n_0}{2\pi} \qquad (7.86)$$

the transients disappear in a time interval that is small in comparison with a period of the environment and the previous analysis can be used with confidence. As $(1/b)$ approaches $(n_0)/(2\pi)$ the automaton starts to respond to the average of the perturbed penalty strength over one period.

Example 7.5: A two–action environment with

$$s_{10} = 0.4 + 0.1 \cos bn$$

$$s_{20} = 0.8$$

---

[2]Ln represents logarithm to base e.

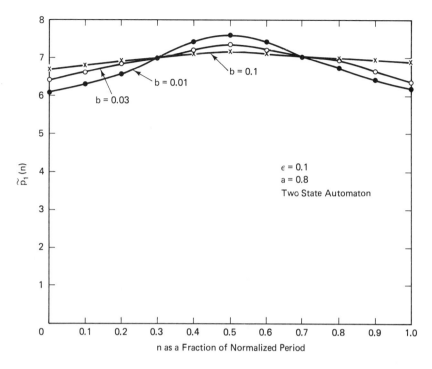

Figure 7.14: Simulation for Example 7.5.

was simulated. Three values of b (0.01, 0.03, 0.1) were used. The parameter a was set at 0.8. Fig. 7.14 shows $\tilde{p}_1(n)$, the average of $p_1(n)$, over several runs as a function of time. The abscissa shows time as a fraction of the normalized period. It is evident from the figure that for low values of b, $\tilde{p}_1(n)$ follows changes in the environment; for $b = 0.1$ however, the automaton starts averaging.

7.10   Generalizations of the Learning Automaton

In the preceding sections we encountered nonstationary environments that can be broadly classified into three categories. The first category contains environments that can assume one of a finite set of states E_i $(i = 1, 2, \ldots, d)$ and the automaton is aware of the specific state the environment is in at any instant. If the automaton is assumed to be composed of the union of d automata A_i $(i = 1, 2, \ldots, d)$, the automaton A_i is updated when the environment is in state E_i. The second category includes state-dependent nonstationary environments discussed in Section 7.5 and the hierarchical automaton described in Section 7.6. In both cases, the overall system can be described by a homogeneous Markov process so that methods described in Chapters 4 and 5 can be used to analyze their asymptotic behavior. Finally, in the third group can be included all the cases where the penalty probabilities of the environment vary according to some specific rules unknown to the automaton and the latter is designed to perform expediently. The Markovian switching environment described in Section 7.4 and the environment with sinusoidally varying parameter considered in Section 7.9.2 belong to this category.

The state E_i of the environment in the first category can be broadly characterized as the context in which the automaton acts. When the number of contexts d is small, using a separate automaton for each context is attractive, since ϵ–optimality can be achieved in a time–varying environment. However, as mentioned in Section 7.2, the procedure suffers from two principal drawbacks that are the result of d being very large in many practical problems. A large value of d implies that a large number of automata A_i have to be used and the convergence of each of them may be very slow since each context E_i occurs infrequently (even assuming that each occurs infinitely often). Hence the procedure suggested is practically infeasible unless some form of generalization is used. Recently such a generalization has been made possible by the introduction of the notion of a context vector that imposes further structure on the set $\{E_1, E_2, \ldots, E_d\}$. In this section we describe some preliminary efforts to generalize the learning automaton model, using this concept.

The Context Space (X, ℓ): Let X be a set of n–vectors together with a metric ℓ defined on it. For convenience, we shall assume that ℓ is the Euclidean metric. Any element $x \in X$ is defined as a context vector and X is called the context space. At every instant n, $x(n)$ assumes a specific value in X and the automaton is described as acting in the context $x(n)$. The response of the environment thus depends both on the context vector operative at instant n and on the action chosen. The context vector as well as the environmental response to an action are known to the automaton and the aim of the learning procedure is to evolve to either expedient or optimal learning strategies with each of the context vectors. A block diagram of the learning automaton together with the context vector $x \in X$ is shown in Figure 7.15. The process of associating an action with a context has been termed associative reinforcement learning (Barto, Sutton and Brouwer, 1981).

With the introduction of a context space X, many of the problems dis-

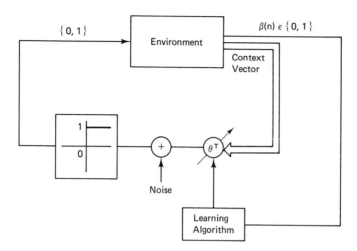

Figure 7.15: Learning automaton with a context vector.

cussed earlier can be generalized. For example, if an automaton A_i is associated with a context vector x_i, it can also be used in some neighborhood of x_i, defined by $\|x - x_i\| \leq \delta_i$. The constant δ_i is chosen, depending on the prior information available concerning the manner in which the optimal action changes with the context. Assuming that the region $D \subset X$ in which the automaton acts is bounded, D can be partitioned into d disjoint regions D_i $(i = 1, 2, \ldots, d)$ where it is assumed that the same action is optimal for all context vectors in any region D_i. This implies that a single automaton A_i can be used for the entire region D_i. Obviously the magnitude of the regions D_i will be dictated both by practical necessity as well as accuracy. Too small a region would imply that many automata have to be used while too large a region may contain context vectors for which different actions are optimal. Research in this area is still in the preliminary stages. Questions of convergence of automata acting in the different regions, methods of forming the union of regions D_i in which the same action may be optimal to achieve faster convergence and methods of dividing some of the regions D_i into subregions when necessary to improve accuracy, are currently being investigated.

So far, the manner in which the context vector $x(n)$ evolves with the stage number n has not been specified. It could either depend only on the stage number n or on the action of the automaton at stage $(n - 1)$. The mathematical description of such systems is currently in the early stages of development.

7.11   A Parametrized Stochastic Learning Unit

The aim of associative learning is to learn through experience the optimal action that is to be used in a given context x. The generalization that we have presented in the previous section attempts to accomplish this by using different automata in different regions of the context space. Since D is the union of $D_i (i = 1, 2, \ldots, d)$ this procedure yields at any stage n the probability of choosing any one of the r actions $\alpha_1, \alpha_2, \ldots, \alpha_r$ for a given context i.e. $p_i(n)$ of the preceding chapters is replaced by $p_i(x, n), x \in X$. As $n \to \infty$ a specific action is associated with each of the regions if absolutely expedient schemes are used by all the automata.

A different generalization results when one attempts to optimize the performance using a single automaton, but based on contextual information. This is best illustrated by considering an automaton with only two actions α_1 and α_2. Let $f(\theta, x)$ be a real valued function of a parameter vector θ of dimension m and the state x. Let $f(\theta^*, x) = 0$, for a particular value θ^* of θ, represent a surface in the space X, which divides the domain D in which the automaton operates into two disjoint regions and let the optimal actions in these regions be given by

$$
\begin{array}{ll}
\alpha_1 & \text{if } f(\theta^*, x) > 0 \\[2mm]
\alpha_2 & \text{if } f(\theta^*, x) \leq 0
\end{array}
\tag{7.87}
$$

Based on the context information as well as the response of the environment to an action α_i $(i = 1, 2)$, the parameter vector $\theta(n)$ is updated at every stage n and the aim is to determine this rule so that $\lim_{n \to \infty} \theta(t) = \theta^*$. In many cases, the vector θ^* satisfying Eq.(7.87) may not be unique and may belong to a set Θ. In such a case the learning algorithm should be such that

$$
\lim_{n \to \infty} \theta(n) \in \Theta.
\tag{7.88}
$$

Unlike the learning schemes described in the book thus far, where the effect of learning is contained implicitly in the vector $p(n)$ of action probabilities, it is contained in this method in the learning parameter vector $\theta(n)$. At any stage n, even assuming that learning stops, the action corresponding to any context vector x can be generated using the rule:

$$
\alpha_1 \text{ if } f(\theta(n), x) > 0 \; ; \; \alpha_2 \text{ if } f(\theta(n), x) \leq 0.
\tag{7.89}
$$

The parametrization of the context space as well as the updating of the parameter vector $\theta(n)$ is very reminiscent of methods used for optimization in many areas of systems theory and in particular pattern classification. It is not surprising that a specific form of this approach was first used in a pattern discrimination problem (Barto and Anandan, 1985).

In the introduction to Chapter 1, we referred to the research activity at the present time in parallel distributed processing networks. Such networks of neuron–like units have in recent years been shown to have intriguing computational properties and are currently of great interest to researchers in such areas as artificial intelligence and cognitive science. Of particular interest is the learning ability of the networks and it is in this context that the learning automaton and its generalizations have gained a fair amount of popularity. The new parametrized model of a learning automaton referred to earlier evolved over the past few years due to the efforts of Barto and his co–workers. Recently a generalized version of this model was proposed by Williams (1987). The advantage of these models lies in the fact that they can be considered as basic units which when interconnected could form complex networks that interact with an environment. The research related to the use of such networks to solve complex stochastic optimization problems is in the initial stages and is beyond the scope of this book. Only the basic ideas involved in the models are introduced here.

The model discussed in Barto and Anandan (1985) is restricted to the case of two actions α_1 and α_2 and the particular parametrization chosen has the form $f(\theta, x) = \theta^T x$ where $\theta, x \in \mathcal{R}^n$. It is assumed that a set of parameter vectors exists such that the hyperplane defined by $\theta^{*T} x = 0$ divides the context space X into two regions such that α_1 is the optimal action when $\theta^{*T} x > 0$ and α_2 is the optimal action when $\theta^{*T} x \leq 0$, for all $\theta^* \in \Theta$.

The learning algorithm consists of two parts (i) the choice of the action $\alpha(n)$ at stage n for a specified value of the context vector $x(n)$ and the parameter vector $\theta(n)$ and (ii) the updating of the parameter vector on the basis of the response of the environment. The former is determined as

$$
\begin{aligned}
\text{If} \quad & \theta^T(n)x(n) + \eta(n) > 0 \quad && \text{then } \alpha(n) = \alpha_1 \\
& \theta^T(n)x(n) + \eta(n) \leq 0 \quad && \text{then } \alpha(n) = \alpha_2
\end{aligned}
\tag{7.90}
$$

where $\eta(n)$ are independent identically distributed random variables with a known distribution function. The updating of the vector $\theta(n)$ is done according to the following equation where $\alpha_1 = +1$ and $\alpha_2 = -1$.

$$
\begin{aligned}
\theta(n+1) \;&=\; \theta(n) - \rho(n)\{E[\alpha(n)|\theta(n), x(n)] - \alpha(n)\}x(n) \text{ when } \beta(n) = 0 \\
&=\; \theta(n) - \lambda\rho(n)\{E[\alpha(n)|\theta(n), x(n)] - \alpha(n)\}x(n) \text{ when } \beta(n) = 1
\end{aligned}
\tag{7.91}
$$

where $0 \le \lambda \le 1$ and $\rho(n)$ satisfies the general stochastic approximation conditions

$$
\rho(n) \ge 0 \quad \sum_n \rho(n) = \infty \quad \sum_n \rho^2(n) < \infty.
$$

Under the above conditions it is shown that $\theta(n)$ tends to be the desired limit set Θ with probability 1.

The algorithm represented by equations Eq.(7.90) and (7.91) is referred to by the authors as an associative reward–penalty or A_{R-P} algorithm. According to them, if $\eta(n)$ is uniformly distributed over the interval $[-1, +1]$, the input pattern $\hat{x}$ is a constant and $\theta^T(1)\hat{x} \in [-1, +1]$, then A_{R-P} algorithm reduces to the L_{R-P} algorithm. On the other hand, when the noise η is not present and the action is chosen strictly on the basis of whether $\theta^T(n)x(n)$ is greater than or less than zero, the algorithm is similar to the deterministic, supervised learning, pattern classification algorithms. The proof of convergence of the learning algorithm in Barto and Anandan (1985) is based on an extension of the algorithm for a time–varying case given in Lakshmivarahan (1981), but the authors readily admit that a variety of other techniques may also be applicable.

The relation between stochastic approximation and stochastic automaton algorithms has been the subject of much debate in the past and efforts have been made to modify stochastic automaton algorithms to conform to the well established format used in the former (Fu and Nikolic, 1966). It is well known that stochastic approximation methods are applicable to parameter optimization problems while the methods described in the book are concerned with cases where probability distributions over finite action sets are updated. In our opinion, the model suggested by Barto to explain observed behavior in simulation studies on associative learning is very attractive, but the procedure adopted in Barto and Anandan (1985) is much closer in spirit to well known parameter optimization methods based on stochastic approximation rather than the learning procedures discussed in earlier chapters. However, the modification suggested recently by Williams (1986) while analytically equivalent to the associative learning model, captures the essential features of the learning automaton. This model is shown in Figure 7.16.

The input to the model is the context vector x while the output is the

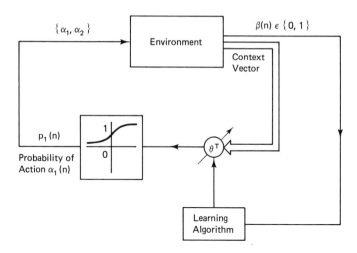

Figure 7.16: A modification of the model in Fig. 7.15.

probability p_1 with which action α_1 is chosen. The parameter vector θ is updated using the response of the environment and directly alters the probability with which the actions are chosen at the next instant. The function $f : \mathcal{R} \rightarrow [0,1]$ is strictly monotonic and analytic and possesses an inverse. It therefore appears possible to extend the algorithms developed in earlier chapters to update the parameter vector θ in the above model. In the following chapter (Section 8.7) we shall revisit this model in the context of decentralized control problems.

Chapter 8

Interconnected Automata and Games

8.1 Introduction

The discussions in the preceding chapters focused for the most part on the behavior of a single automaton operating in a random environment. Although such a model is intuitively appealing and well founded in the theory of Markov processes, it is limited in scope for both modeling and control purposes. This fact was recognized by Norman (1968) , who noted that the basic learning automata models are "...by design, simple gadgets for doing simple things." In other words, an individual automaton with a finite set of actions is attractive as a model for describing the observed behavior primarily in simple, perhaps contrived, learning situations. In addition, from a control viewpoint, while the automaton was shown to be expedient or even ϵ-optimal in many environments, it has limited applicability in view of its rapidly decreasing speed of response with increasing number of actions. In this chapter we attempt to demonstrate that the full potential of the automaton is realized in both modeling and control contexts when many automata interact in a decentralized fashion. In such situations, it is appropriate to think of a single automaton as a building block for more complex and interesting systems. It is our opinion that the principal applications of learning automata in the future will be in this area.

The first question we must address is whether automata can be interconnected in useful ways so as to exhibit group behavior that is attractive for either modeling or controlling complex systems. In the former case our interest is in determining whether a collective can possess behavior more complex than the simple sum of behaviors of its members. It is worth mentioning here that Tsetlin's interest in a single automaton was motivated primarily by its descriptive power and that he was convinced of the possibility of modeling complex self-organizing biological systems in a systematic fashion using groups of automata. From a control viewpoint the question is whether collectives of automata can be used to resolve more complex and realistic decision-making problems than those appropriate for a single automaton. Alternately, can individually "smart" automata be designed to function as a distributed yet coordinated intelligent control system? Attempts to address these questions are still in the initial stages. However, the efforts are particularly important in light of the current interest in distributed systems composed of simple but highly interconnected processing elements.

In this chapter we bring together the main results of automata formulated as mathematical games. In our opinion, these problem formulations and results provide a foundation for future research in modeling and control of complex systems using learning automata. In fact, extensions to and applications of the multi-automata models discussed below may be viewed as the rationale for the systematic study of learning automata in the future.

8.2   Decentralization, Games, and Uncertainty

Decentralization is a common and often necessary feature of complex natural and man-made systems. In both cases it arises from the reality that complete information exchange needed for centralized decision making may not be feasible. However, the coordination of decentralized decision makers is a formidable problem. Decentralization, by its very nature, introduces uncertainty into the decision process. Remote components of the same system can only have limited information about each other and the overall system. Hence, decisions must be made by individual controllers that have access only to partial information regarding the state of the system. This leads to an inevitable inconsistency between local optimality and global optimality and has been reflected in extensive studies of such systems. The theory of teams, which was developed to deal with decision rule design in decentralized systems with partial information, addresses questions which are related to the manner in which new information is to be used as well as the prior information needed by various decision makers to make rational decisions.

The mathematical foundation needed for the analysis and synthesis of problems in decentralized control is provided by game theory. The latter was established as a field in 1944 with the publication of the book <u>Theory</u> <u>of Games and Economic Behavior</u> by John von Neumann and Oscar Morgenstern. In contrast to optimization theory, which is central to methods and concepts developed for the physical sciences, game theory is particularly applicable to those problems in which different agents evaluate the objective situation differently and act in accordance with their preferences. Hence the theory is found to be particularly suited to social, economic, and political problems, where conflict of interest among decision makers is natural. The rise of game theory, as opposed to optimization theory, consequently marks an important stage in the development of mathematical methods for the analysis of complex systems. Systems involving many decision makers, acting in a decentralized manner, are best described by models taken from suitable games of strategy, which in many cases are amenable to mathematical analysis.

Any game consists of more than one player and results in some outcome (e.g. win, lose, or draw) which depends on the behavior of these players. Since, in general, each player has a different performance criterion, the outcome is valued differently by each player. The extent to which the players can communicate with one another, the information available to each player, the causal relations between the actions of the players and the outcome of the game along with any binding agreements that the players can enter into, all determine the rules of the game. Games can be played either as single-stage decision problems or repeatedly as sequential decision problems. The complexity of games can be classified in various ways depending on the number of players (2-person or N-person), the performance criterion (zero-sum or nonzero-sum), and the nature of communication used (cooperative or noncooperative).

The game theorist is interested primarily in the normative rather than the descriptive aspects of the game. In particular he or she is interested in determining how the players should play and consequently what the ultimate outcome of the game should be. Both of these are in turn related to a fundamental question of game theory, the answer to which turns out to be elusive in most situations: What is meant by rational behavior in a game? Although a vast literature exists on the subject and many plausible solutions such as min-max, equilibrium point, Pareto-optimality, and various value concepts have been proposed for different games, none seems to be universally appropriate. In fact, as the problem becomes more complex and the individual player has less control over the final outcome, it becomes even more difficult to define rational behavior. As pointed out by Morton

Davis (1973) in his excellent monograph on game theory, the perverse law "the greater the significance of the game – the more difficult it is to treat analytically" seems to have general applicability.

Game theory has advanced substantially in the last forty years and has had a profound impact on different areas of both mathematical and social sciences. A number of precise concepts such as utility, strategy, payoff, equilibrium, bargaining set, and core have been introduced by game theorists and many have become part of the general vocabulary. Some of these concepts are relevant in the context of interacting automata and we shall introduce them as they are needed.

In a game problem the uncertainty faced by an individual player is usually assumed to be entirely due to the unknown actions of the other players (i.e., endogenous uncertainty). However, in complex systems containing many decentralized controllers, generally there are also large uncertainties regarding system parameters, actions, and the frequency and nature of external events. These exogenous uncertainties add to the difficulty of the control problem and their presence motivates the use of learning theory. The use of learning schemes by the various players in repeated plays of a game does not circumvent the basic complexities of the many-player nonzero-sum games referred to earlier. Except in special cases, the notion of rational behavior is not well defined even when no exogenous uncertainty is present. Hence, the aim of using learning schemes is to seek asymptotic performance that coincides with rational behavior in those cases for which game theory provides a satisfactory concept of rationality. The two-person zero-sum game of automata and the identical payoff game of multiple automata treated in Sections 8.4 and 8.5 are two prominent examples.

In automata games, a game is played repeatedly and a large amount of uncertainty is assumed. Each individual automaton (or player) may not be aware of the number of players participating in the game, the strategies available to the other players or the responses for each possible play. In the context of games, the favorable response of the environment is referred to as success and the unfavorable response as failure. Furthermore, if the response set is $\{0,1\}$ or $\{-1,1\}$, 1 is regarded as success in contrast with earlier chapters [1]. At every stage the automaton is only aware of the strategy it has chosen and the corresponding random response (output) of the environment. Based on this information it decides on the strategy for the next play.

---

[1] The assignment of output 1 to either success or failure is arbitrary. Much of the work in automata games has adopted the success=1 convention and this will be followed in this chapter.

We note that an action of an automaton is also referred to as a *strategy* in the following sections, when the automaton is playing a game. This is not entirely consistent with game theory terminology; in general, a strategy in a repeated game denotes a decision making rule over the entire period of the play. To be precise, the updating algorithm of the automaton is its game theoretic *strategy* while a specific action chosen corresponds to a *move*.

As an illustration of the automata game setting, consider the following simple voting game, known as a Goore game (Tsetlin, 1973). Imagine a large room containing N cubicles and a raised platform. One person (voter) sits in each cubicle and a referee stands on the platform. The referee conducts a series of voting rounds as follows. On each round the voters vote yes or no (the issue is unimportant) simultaneously and independently (they do not see each other) and the referee counts the fraction θ of yes votes. The referee has a unimodal performance criterion $g(\theta)\epsilon[0,1]$, which is optimized when the fraction of yes votes is exactly θ^*. The current voting round ends with the referee awarding a dollar with probability $g(\theta)$ and assessing a dollar with probability $1 - g(\theta)$ to every voter independently. On the basis of their individual gains and losses, the voters then decide, again independently, how to cast their votes on the next round. The intriguing feature of this game is that if each voter updates according to either a Tsetlin automaton with large memory (Chapter 3) or an absolutely expedient algorithm (Chapter 4), then the entire group will asymptotically optimize the referee's performance criterion.

To formalize the qualitative ideas above, we discuss in the following section the mathematical formulation of a general automaton game. Later, we specialize these ideas to the case of two-automata zero-sum games in Section 8.4, automata games with identical payoffs in Section 8.5 and some nonzero-sum games in Section 8.6.

8.3 Mathematical Formulation of Automata Games

Let N automata $A_1, A_2, \ldots, A_N$ be assumed to take part in a game of automata. Considering a typical automaton A_j, it can be described by a quintuple $\{\beta^j, \Phi^j, F^j, \alpha^j, G^j\}$ as discussed in Chapter 2:

$$\text{The input set } \beta^j = \{\beta_1^j, \beta_2^j, \ldots, \beta_{m_j}^j\}$$
$$\text{The state set } \Phi^j = \{\phi_1^j, \phi_2^j, \ldots, \phi_{s_j}^j\}$$

The state transition function F^j such that $\phi^j(n+1) = F^j[\phi^j(n), \beta^j(n)]$

The action set $\alpha^j = \{\alpha_1^j, \alpha_2^j, \ldots, \alpha_{r_j}^j\}$

and the output function G^j such that $\alpha^j(n) = G^j[\phi^j(n)]$.

(8.1)

The definitions following are found to be useful in discussions regarding automata games.

A Play $\alpha(n)$: is a set of strategies chosen by the automata at stage n. $\alpha(n)$ can be denoted by the N-vector

$$\alpha(n) = [\alpha^1(n), \alpha^2(n), \ldots, \alpha^N(n)] \qquad (8.2)$$

Outcome of a Play $\beta(n)$: is an N-vector whose components are $\beta^1(n), \beta^2(n),$ $\ldots, \beta^N(n)$ with $\beta^j(n)$ corresponding to automaton A_j.

A Game Γ: The N automata $A_1, A_2, \ldots, A_N$ are said to participate in a game Γ, if the probability of an outcome $\beta(n)$ due to a play $\alpha(n)$.

Since automaton A_j has r_j actions there is a total of $\prod_{j=1}^{N} r_j$ possible plays. Since each component $\beta^j(n)$ of $\beta(n)$ can take on m_j values, there is a total of $\prod_{j=1}^{N} m_j$ possible outcomes corresponding to each play. Hence, to define a game completely, we need $\prod_{j=1}^{N} m_j r_j$ probabilities.

Thus far, nothing has been said about the type of automata that can take part in the game. Theoretically it is possible for A_j to correspond to different types of automata for different values of j. For example, fixed-structure automata like the Tsetlin and Krinsky automata and variable-structure automata using the L_{R-I} and L_{R-P} schemes can all participate in the same game. In fact, two-person zero-sum games were originally used by Viswanathan and Narendra (1973) to determine which of two available schemes was better from the point of view of speed of convergence and expedient behavior. For purposes of analysis, however, it is found more convenient to use identical learning algorithms for all the automata. Once the collective behavior of automata using the same algorithm has been studied in detail quantitatively, a qualitative understanding emerges regarding the behavior that can be expected when different algorithms are used.

In the next two sections, the game is described in more detail for fixed-structure automata players and variable-structure automata players. Figure 8.1 illustrates the game for the variable structure case. The game environment can be of the P-, Q-, or S-model type, as described in Chapter 2.

(a) Games of Fixed Structure Automata: Let all the automata taking part in a game be of the fixed-structure type described in Chapter 3. Then each of the automata A_j $(j = 1, 2, \ldots, N)$ can be in any one of a finite number of states. Denoting the state of automaton A_j at stage n as $\phi^j(n)$, the state of the game at that stage is determined by $\phi(n) = [\phi^1(n), \phi^2(n), \ldots, \phi^N(n)]$. If the state space Φ of the game is defined as the product space $\Phi = \Phi^1 \times \Phi^2 \times \cdots \times \Phi^N$, it follows that Φ is finite and $\phi(n) \in \Phi$.

At stage n, each automaton A_j chooses an action $\alpha^j(n)$ from its action set α^j, where $\alpha^j(n) = G^j[\phi^j(n)]$. For the play $\alpha(n) = [\alpha^1(n), \alpha^2(n), \ldots, \alpha^N(n)]$, there results the response $\beta(n) = [\beta^1(n), \beta^2(n), \ldots, \beta^N(n)]$ where $\beta^j(n)$ corresponds to automaton A_j. The responses $\beta^j(n)$ are determined by the play $\alpha(n)$ as well as the environment. Assuming that

$$\alpha(n) = \left[\alpha^1_{i_1}, \alpha^2_{i_2}, \ldots, \alpha^N_{i_N} \right],$$

i.e., the automaton A_j chooses its i_j^{th} action, and that $\beta^j(n) \in \{0, 1\}$ for all n (a P-model), let

$$Pr\left[\beta^j(n) = 1 | \alpha(n) \right] = d^j_{i_1, i_2, \ldots, i_N} \quad (j = 1, 2, \ldots, N).$$

Defining $\beta^j(n) = 1$ as a favorable response, $d^j_{i_1, i_2, \ldots, i_N}$ can be considered as the success probability of the environment corresponding to the play $\alpha(n)$. Automaton A_j observes $\beta^j(n)$ and based on its current value $\phi^j(n)$ and $\beta^j(n)$, changes its state to $\phi^j(n+1)$. Hence, the state of the overall system changes from $\phi(n)$ to $\phi(n+1)$ in Φ. Given any two states in Φ, it therefore follows that a unique transition probability exists for transferring the game from one to the other. Hence, the game of fixed-structure automata can be described by a Markov chain. If the Markov chain is ergodic then there are limiting probabilities for all the states in Φ. Denoting by $R^{i_1, i_2, \ldots, i_N}$ the stationary probability of the automata game being in state $\{\phi^1_{i_1}, \phi^2_{i_2}, \ldots, \phi^N_{i_N}\} \triangleq \phi_{i_1, i_2, \ldots, i_N}$, and assuming that the corresponding play is $\{\alpha^1_{i_1}, \alpha^2_{i_2}, \ldots, \alpha^N_{i_N}\}$, the asymptotic expected outcome (or average gain) W_j for A_j is

$$W_j = \sum_{\phi_{i_1, i_2, \ldots, i_N}} R^{i_1, i_2, \ldots, i_N} d^j_{i_1, i_2, \ldots, i_N}. \tag{8.3}$$

In the game described above, the response of the environment $\beta^j(n)$ to any automaton $A_j (j = 1, 2, \ldots, N)$ was binary. For more general environments where $\beta^j(n)$ can assume discrete or continuous values in the unit interval [0,1] (i.e., Q- and S-models) $d^j_{i_1, i_2, \ldots, i_N}$ represents the expected value

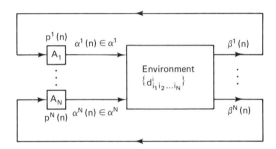

Figure 8.1: The basic automata game formulation (*Courtesy Pergamon Press*).

of the response. That is

$$E\left[\beta^j(n)|\alpha(n) = \left[\alpha_{i_1}^1, \alpha_{i_2}^2, \ldots, \alpha_{i_N}^N\right]\right] = d_{i_1,i_2,\ldots,i_N}^j.$$

Once again, W_j, the asymptotic expected outcome for A_j, is given by Eq. (8.3).

(b) Games of Variable Structure Automata: If all the automata taking part in the game use variable structure schemes, they update their probability distributions over their action sets at every instant based on the response of the environment. In this case, the analytical formulation of the game is simplified by using the notation introduced in Chapter 4. All the automata are described by the triple (α, T, β) where α and β are the action set and output set described earlier and T is the reinforcement scheme. Except in a few cases where fixed-structure automata are described for purposes of comparison, all the principal results derived in this chapter are based on variable structure schemes and hence this notation is found to be more relevant for the discussions in the sections following.

We define $p^j(n) \overset{\triangle}{=} [p_1^j(n), p_2^j(n), \ldots, p_{r_j}^j(n)]$ where $p^j(n)$ is the probability distribution governing the choice of actions of automaton A_j at the nth stage and $p_i^j(n) = Pr[\alpha^j(n) = \alpha_i^j]$. At stage n let the joint probability $Pr[\alpha(n) = [\alpha_{i_1}^1, \alpha_{i_2}^2, \ldots, \alpha_{i_N}^N]]$ be denoted by $p_{i_1,i_2,\ldots,i_N}(n)$. If the play based on this distribution is $\alpha(n) = [\alpha_{i_1}^1, \alpha_{i_2}^2 \ldots, \alpha_{i_N}^N]$ and for this play

$$E[\beta^j(n)|\alpha(n) = [\alpha_{i_1}^1, \alpha_{i_2}^2, \ldots, \alpha_N^N]] = d_{i_1,i_2,\ldots,i_N}^j,$$

then the expected outcome of the automaton A_j at stage n is given by

$$
\begin{aligned}
M^j(n) &\triangleq E[\beta^j(n)|p^1(n), p^2(n), \ldots, p^N(n)] \\
&= \sum_{i_1, i_2, \ldots, i_N} p_{i_1}^1(n) p_{i_2}^2(n) \cdots p_{i_N}^N(n) d_{i_1, i_2, \ldots, i_N}^j.
\end{aligned}
\tag{8.4}
$$

Using the definitions above, the game can now be described by a Markov process whose state space S is the product simplex space. That is

$$
S = S_{r_1}^1 \times S_{r_2}^2 \times \cdots \times S_{r_N}^N
$$

where $S_{r_i}^i$ is the r_i-dimensional simplex corresponding to automaton A_i. At every instant n, based on the probability distributions $p^1(n), p^2(n), \ldots, p^N(n)$, the automata choose a play $\alpha(n)$ and based on the response of the environment as well as the learning schemes used

$$
p(n) \triangleq \left\{ p^1(n), p^2(n), \ldots, p^N(n) \right\}
$$

evolves in S. If the automata game is such that $\lim_{n \to \infty} E[p_{i_1, i_2, \ldots, i_N}]$ exists for all $i_1, i_2, \ldots, i_N$ then the payoff function for the jth player is defined as

$$
W_j = \lim_{n \to \infty} E[M^j(n)] = \sum_{i_1, i_2, \ldots, i_N} \lim_{n \to \infty} E[p_{i_1, i_2, \ldots, i_N}] d_{i_1, i_2, \ldots, i_N}^j.
$$

W_j is the asymptotic (in the time limit) average gain of A_j.

The nature of the updating schemes (both in the deterministic and stochastic cases) determines the asymptotic behavior of the game and hence the final value W_j, when it exists.

(c) Solution Concepts in Games: In sections **(a)** and **(b)** we defined how fixed-structure and variable-structure automata participate in a game. However, the objectives of the individual automata were not specified. It was merely stated that, in a general game, each automaton has a different response from the environment at every instant that it uses to update its strategy at the next instant. Since this, in general, results in a nonzero-sum game, the problem may not always be tractable. Hence an integral part of the problem statement is the specification of the overall objective.

As mentioned in Section 8.2 the mathematical basis for the analysis of automata games comes from game theory as well as learning theory. In such games one of our principal aims is to determine conditions under which there exists some limiting behavior of the underlying Markov process and the extent to which such behavior agrees with our notions of rationality. The difficulties encountered in stating tractable problems of automata games can be traced to the fact that solution concepts in game theory that merge individual and group rationality are elusive. However, many general properties such as strategy dominance, uniqueness of the equilibrium point, and Pareto-optimality have been suggested as useful features of an optimal solution (Shubik, 1982). Some of these properties, which are quite relevant to our discussions in the sections following, are described here briefly.

Equilibrium points: In an N-person game a strategy N-tuple is said to be an equilibrium point if no player has a positive reason for changing his or her strategy, assuming that none of the other players is going to change strategies (Owen, 1982). The outcome (also called payoff) corresponding to this set of strategies is called an equilibrium outcome (payoff). For example, in the automata games described in sections (a) and (b), let

$$\alpha^o = \left[\alpha_{\underline{i_1}}^1, \alpha_{\underline{i_2}}^2, \ldots, \alpha_{\underline{i_N}}^N \right].$$

α^o is an equilibrium if

$$\max_{i_j} M^j \left(\alpha_{\underline{i_1}}^1, \alpha_{\underline{i_2}}^2, \ldots, \alpha_{i_j}^j, \ldots, \alpha_{\underline{i_N}}^N \right) = M^j \left(\alpha_{\underline{i_1}}^1, \alpha_{\underline{i_2}}^2, \ldots, \alpha_{\underline{i_j}}^j, \ldots, \alpha_{\underline{i_N}}^N \right).$$

We shall use this term synonymously with *Nash equilibrium*. Nash proved that all N-player games with finite strategy sets have at least one pure or mixed strategy equilibrium. In a two-person zero-sum game, there may be more than one equilibrium point but they have the same payoff. This is not necessarily true, however, of two-person nonzero-sum games.

Minimax (Maximin) Strategies: The worst possible payoff a player can receive with this strategy, sometimes called a strategy's security level, is at least as favorable as that of any other strategy. The fact that minimax strategies coincide with equilibrium strategies in two-person zero-sum games provides perhaps the most compelling "solution" in game theory. In this game, minimax strategies (perhaps mixed) result in a unique saddle point value for the game. Viewed in the standard matrix format, where entry $M(\alpha_i^1, \alpha_j^2)$ is the gain to row player when strategy pair (α_i^1, α_j^2) is used, row player's maximin strategy is α_{i*}^1 as defined by

$$\min_j M \left(\alpha_{i*}^1, \alpha_j^2 \right) = \max_i \min_j M \left(\alpha_i^1, \alpha_j^2 \right)$$

and column player's minimax strategy is α_{j*}^2 as defined by

$$\max_i M \left(\alpha_i^1, \alpha_{j*}^2 \right) = \min_j \max_i M \left(\alpha_i^1, \alpha_j^2 \right).$$

Dominant Strategy: A strategy dominates another when, independent of the action taken by the other players, the first strategy leads to an outcome as favorable as the second. Consequently, a case can be made for never playing a strategy that is dominated. Although this is indeed sound advice in two-person zero-sum games and in identical payoff games, in general nonzero-sum games the use of a dominated strategy can lead to a better payoff for all players (e.g., the Prisoner's Dilemma discussed in Section 8.6). In many cases in Sections 8.4 and 8.5, an automaton has a dominant strategy and converges to it rapidly. Such situations are easy to analyze and considerable simplification can be achieved by eliminating dominated strategies. As noted, however, in general nonzero-sum games, this simplification can result in a "solution" that is far from rational.

Pareto Optimality: In an N-person game, an outcome is said to be Pareto-optimal if there is no other outcome in which all players simultaneously do better. This is a modest requirement of any concept of group rationality. Unfortunately, it is not always consistent with concepts of individual rationality, such as dominance.

The importance of the definitions above as well as the relationship that exists between them will become evident in the problems discussed in the sections following. In Section 8.4 the two-person zero-sum game is discussed and it is shown that a rational solution exists. Such a solution is a Nash equilibrium and is also Pareto-optimal. In the identical payoff game, the solution can converge to any one of a finite number of equilibrium points, but only the one with the largest payoff is Pareto-optimal. If the largest payoff occurs for more than one equilibrium point, they are all Pareto-optimal. In other cases the games may have solutions that have only one of the properties defined above. In such cases our interest in using learning schemes with interconnected automata is to determine whether the corresponding properties are achieved asymptotically. Success in such cases provides some justification for studying the behavior of interconnected automata even in those situations where game theory does not provide conclusive answers.

Example 8.1: Consider three two-player games where each player has two strategies. Each game can be represented by a 2×2 matrix D whose elements are of the form $\left(d^1_{i,j}, d^2_{i,j}\right)$ where $d^1_{i,j}$ is the payoff to player 1 and $d^2_{i,j}$ the payoff to player 2 when they play strategies i and j respectively. The payoff matrices for the three cases are:

$$D_1 = \begin{bmatrix} (0,0) & (10,7) \\ (0,0) & (9,8) \end{bmatrix}; \; D_2 = \begin{bmatrix} (10,10) & (0,5) \\ (5,0) & (3,3) \end{bmatrix};$$

$$D_3 = \begin{bmatrix} (5,5) & (0,10) \\ (10,0) & (1,1) \end{bmatrix}; \; D_4 = \begin{bmatrix} (1,-1) & (2,-2) \\ (-3,3) & (0,0) \end{bmatrix}.$$

In game D_1, the first strategy of the first player (row chooser) and the second strategy of the second player (column chooser) are dominant and (10,7) is an equilibrium payoff. It is also Pareto-optimal. In game D_2, (10,10) and (3,3) are both equilibrium payoffs, but only (10,10) is Pareto-optimal. In D_3, an instance of the Prisoner's Dilemma, both players have dominant strategies but the resulting outcome (1,1), which is an equilibrium payoff, is not Pareto-optimal! In D_4, a zero-sum game, the payoff (1,-1) corresponding to the first strategy of the two players is an equilibrium payoff and is called a saddle point.

8.4   Two-Person Zero-Sum Games of Automata

Perhaps the most well known game for which rationality is well defined is the restrictive, yet extensively studied, two-person zero-sum game. In 1944, von Neumann and Morgenstern showed in their classic work that in such a game, pure or mixed minimax strategies are optimal, with the corresponding payoff defined as the von Neumann value or simply the value of the game. The years following this major advance have witnessed considerable activity in different extensions of game theory. In the method of "fictitious play" for sequential games, at each stage each player is assumed to choose the pure strategies that yield the best result against all the past choices of an opponent. In 1951 Brown conjectured that his procedure would converge to the value of the game when it is zero-sum. This was later verified by Robinson (1951). Other algorithms that exhibit similar asymptotic behavior have also been suggested by Sanghvi and Sobel (1976), but in all cases it is assumed that the payoff matrix, as well as the choice of strategy of each player at any stage, is known to the other player.

The automata version of the two-person zero-sum game was first introduced by Krylov and Tsetlin (1963) using fixed-structure automata and was later discussed by various authors from the Soviet Union. These are described well in the book by Tsetlin (1973). Chandrasekaran and Shen

(1969) and Viswanathan and Narendra (1974) studied the same problem using variable-structure automata. All these works offered solutions of varying degrees of completeness. However, it is only more recently that it was shown by Lakshmivarahan and Narendra (1981,1982), using the methods outlined in Chapter 5, that learning automata can achieve the value of the game whether or not the game has a saddle point in pure strategies. These results are presented in this section in detail.

Statement of the Problem: We consider a zero-sum game in which the outcome depends on chance as well as on the choice of the pure strategy of each of two players (automata) A_1 and A_2. A_1 has r_1 pure strategies $\alpha_i^1 (i = 1, 2, \ldots, r_1)$ and A_2 has r_2 pure strategies $\alpha_j^2 (j = 1, 2, \ldots, r_2)$. Both are allowed to use mixed strategies at any stage n. At every stage each player picks a pure strategy as a sample realization of his mixed strategy and receives a random outcome which is either a success or a failure. A success (failure) for A_1 is a failure (success) for A_2, so that the game is zero-sum. Based on the random outcome, the two players update their mixed strategies at the next stage using learning algorithms and the sequential game continues. The objective is to determine the asymptotic behavior of the two players and the conditions under which they will approach the value of the game.

The principal difference between the sequential game described above and those that have been analyzed in the literature using game theory lies in the fact that the players are not aware they are playing a game. Each is unaware of the other's strategy set and pure strategy chosen at any stage, as well as the payoff structure of the game. Based entirely on the response of the environment, which is assumed to be stationary, each player chooses an action deemed to be appropriate. In contrast to the game theoretic focus on solution concepts, the learning perspective addresses the effectiveness of simple algorithms in more complex situations than the basic environment treated in Chapters 2-7. Thus, while the two-person zero-sum game may be only of historical interest from a game theoretic viewpoint, it serves as a useful benchmark to test the group rationality of learning automata.

Assuming a binary (P-model) environment, let d_{ij} denote the probability of success to A_1 when the ith strategy α_i^1 is chosen by A_1 and the jth strategy α_j^2 is chosen by A_2. Then $c_{ij} = 1 - d_{ij}$ is the probability of success to A_2. If success and failure correspond to $\beta = +1$ and $\beta = -1$ respectively, then the expected gain of player A_1 denoted by g_{ij}, for this play, is given by

$$E\left[\beta(n) \mid \alpha^1(n) = \alpha_i^1, \alpha^2(n) = \alpha_j^2\right] = g_{ij} = d_{ij} - c_{ij} = 1 - 2c_{ij}.$$

It is obvious that $g_{ij} \in [-1, 1]$. The $(r_1 \times r_2)$ matrix G of expected gains g_{ij} is called the game matrix.

Defining

$$p_{ij}(n) \triangleq Pr[\alpha^1(n) = \alpha_i^1, \alpha^2(n) = \alpha_j^2]$$

and assuming that $\lim_{n \to \infty} p_{ij}(n) = p_{ij}$ exists, let

$$W \triangleq \sum_{i=1}^{r_1} \sum_{j=1}^{r_2} g_{ij} p_{ij}$$

W is the asymptotic expected gain of player A_1. Naturally we are interested in learning strategies under which W coincides with the value of the game.

Krylov and Tsetlin (1963): In the game introduced by Krylov and Tsetlin, the two automata are of the fixed-structure type described in Chapter 3. At each stage, depending upon their states and the output mapping, the two automata involved choose their actions $\alpha^1(n)$ and $\alpha^2(n)$. Based on the outcome, the states of the two automata are updated and the sequential game continues.

Krylov and Tsetlin first considered the simple case when player A_2 employs a constant mixed strategy. If m_j is the probability with which α_j^2 is chosen we have $\sum_{j=1}^{r_2} m_j = 1$. Since these probabilities do not depend on the strategy chosen by A_1, the probabilities of success and failure for A_1 are given by

$$d_i = \sum_{j=1}^{r_2} d_{ij} m_j, \ c_i = \sum_{j=1}^{r_2} c_{ij} m_j.$$

Hence, the expected gain for the ith strategy α_i^1 is given by

$$g_i = d_i - c_i = 1 - 2c_i.$$

This is equivalent to a single automaton operating in a stationary random environment. For a fixed-structure automaton A_1 of the $L_{2N,2}$ type, it was shown that if $g_i \geq 0$ for at least one i, the asymptotic expected gain of A_1 would be

$$W = \max_i[g_i]$$

as the number of states N of the automaton tends to infinity. Further, if A_2 uses the optimal mixed strategy, W equals the value of the game.

If all g_i are negative then

$$W = \frac{r_1}{\sum_{i=1}^{r_1} \dfrac{1}{g_i}}$$

i.e., W equals the harmonic mean of g_i.

The more interesting game situation arises when A_2 is also a learning automaton whose mixed strategy varies with time. For this case deterministic automata of a somewhat different structure than the Tsetlin automaton are used to derive the following results.

(i) If the matrix G has one and only one row of positive elements (column of negative elements) then W is the harmonic mean of the elements of that row (column).

(ii) If the conditions of (i) are not satisfied, then $W = 0$.

From the results above it is clear that the value of the game is rarely achieved by deterministic automata.

Chandrasekaran and Shen (1969): The use of variable-structure automata in games was first introduced by Chandrasekaran and Shen. For the same two-person zero-sum game problem described in the previous section they discuss the asymptotic behavior of two automata both of which use a square law reinforcement algorithm described in Chapter 4 and given below for easy reference.

If the action of the automaton at the nth stage is $\alpha(n) = \alpha_i$

$$
\begin{aligned}
p_i(n+1) &= p_i^2(n) & \beta(n) &= -1 \quad \text{failure} \\
&= 1 - \sum_{j \neq i} p_j^2(n) & \beta(n) &= +1 \quad \text{success} \\
p_j(n+1) &= p_j(n) + \frac{p_i(n) - p_i^2(n)}{r-1} & \beta(n) &= -1 \quad \text{failure} \\
&= p_j^2(n) & \beta(n) &= +1 \quad \text{success.}
\end{aligned}
\tag{8.5}
$$

With this reinforcement scheme the asymptotic performance of the automaton operating in a stationary environment is known to result in ϵ-optimality if $c_i < \frac{1}{2}$ and $c_j > \frac{1}{2}$, $j \neq i$.

The authors first discuss the game of a single automaton using the nonlinear law above against an automaton using a fixed mixed strategy. The same results as in the fixed structure case described by Krylov and Tsetlin (1963) are obtained here. When the condition $g_i \geq 0$ is not satisfied, W satisfies the inequality

$$
\max_i \min_j g_{ij} \leq W \leq \min_j \max_i g_{ij}.
\tag{8.6}
$$

When both automata use the square-law learning algorithm and only one row (one column) of the game matrix consists of all positive elements (all negative elements) then W is the harmonic mean of the elements of this row (column). Since, under the conditions above, both automata cannot be simultaneously optimal, the first automaton's winnings cannot reach the value of the game.

Viswanathan and Narendra (1974): The square law learning algorithm described by Chandrasekharan and Shen (1969) is not ϵ-optimal in all stationary environments. It is therefore not surprising that in the two-person zero-sum game context, when both the automata use the scheme, the value (corresponding to asymptotic rational behavior) is not achieved. It should be noted, that it was only around this time that the L_{R-I} scheme, discussed in Chapter 4, was first introduced and shown to be ϵ-optimal in all stationary random environments. In view of this desirable feature of the scheme, the authors suggested its use in game situations. It was argued that an L_{R-I} scheme, whose behavior in a stationary environment would be considered to be rational, would be likely to behave in a rational manner in game situations also. This conjecture has been vindicated by many of the developments in learning automata theory that followed.

As described in the preceding paragraphs, the game of an automaton against a player using a fixed mixed strategy was first considered. When the automaton uses an L_{R-I} scheme, it was shown that W achieves the value $\max_i(g_i)$ arbitrarily closely for any game matrix, by making the step size a sufficiently small. When both the automata use L_{R-I} schemes, it was shown, using an approximate stability analysis, that the saddle point of the game matrix corresponds to the only stable equilibrium of an associated difference equation. Hence, it was concluded that the automata would converge to the value of the game. This was supported by extensive simulations, some of which are presented at the end of this section.

Lakshmivarahan and Narendra (1981,1982): Although the results in the preceding sections provided an impetus to the study of two-person zero-sum games, it was only in 1981 that a complete solution to the problem was obtained by Lakshmivarahan and Narendra. The two automata use L_{R-I} schemes to update their mixed strategies at every stage based on the outcome of the game and the results are essentially those predicted by Viswanathan and Narendra (1974). However, in view of the importance of the result, as well as the fact that the method used has wider applications in learning automata theory, we present in this section the proof of the principal theorem for the pure strategy saddle point case in considerable detail. A companion result for the mixed strategy saddle-point case, using $L_{R-\epsilon P}$ schemes, is then discussed briefly.

For convenience, we shall denote the mixed strategies used by the two automata A_1 and A_2 at the nth stage by the vectors $p(n) = [p_1(n), p_2(n), \ldots, p_{r_1}(n)]^T$ and $q(n) = [q_1(n), q_2(n), \ldots, q_{r_2}(n)]^T$. The two automata use L_{R-I} schemes to update their respective probability vectors $p(n)$ and $q(n)$ based on the random outcomes and the pure strategy choices at any stage. At stage n, assuming that $\alpha^1(n) = \alpha_i^1$ and $\alpha^2(n) = \alpha_j^2$ are the pure strategies that result, the probabilities are updated as follows:

$$\left.\begin{aligned} p_i(n+1) &= p_i(n) + a[1 - p_i(n)] \\ p_s(n+1) &= p_s(n) - a\, p_s(n) \quad s \neq i \end{aligned}\right\} \text{ if } A_1 \text{ receives a success} \qquad (8.7)$$

$$p_s(n+1) = p_s(n) \qquad \text{for all } s \text{ if } A_1 \text{ receives a failure.}$$

The mixed strategy $q(n+1)$ used by A_2 on the $(n+1)^{th}$ play is defined in a similar manner. Although the same value of the step size parameter a is assumed for both players, this is not a requirement for the convergence result.

If d_{ij} denotes the probability of success to A_1 when the two automata choose the strategies α_i^1 and α_j^2 respectively, it was described earlier that $\{g_{ij}\} = G$ determines the game matrix, where $g_{ij} = d_{ij} - c_{ij}$. It is obvious that the matrix $\{d_{ij}\} = D$ is strategically equivalent to the game matrix since the linear transformation resulting in G does not alter the zero-sum property or the location of the saddle point. Hence the analysis can be carried out using either the matrix D or the matrix G. In the following sections we shall use D for convenience; further, we shall assume that d_{11} corresponds to the saddle point in pure strategies so that

$$d_{i1} < d_{11} < d_{1j} \qquad (8.8)$$

for all i and j different from 1.

We assume that both players start with arbitrary but fixed initial conditions $p(0)$ and $q(0)$ where $0 < p_i(0) < 1$ and $0 < q_j(0) < 1$ for all i and j. The mixed strategies $p(n)$ and $q(n)$ are random vectors depending on the randomly determined pure strategy choices and corresponding outcomes. It can be shown that while individually $p(n)$ and $q(n)$ are not stationary Markov sequences, jointly $\{p(n), q(n)\}$ is a stationary Markov process. The probability of success at the nth play, based on the random vectors $p(n)$ and $q(n)$ as well as the game matrix D, is $p(n)^T D q(n)$ where T denotes the transpose. Thus $M(n)$ is defined as

$$M(n) = p(n)^T D q(n). \qquad (8.9)$$

The principal contribution is contained in the following theorem.

Theorem 8.1: In the two-person zero-sum game described above, let the matrix D have a unique saddle point d_{11} in pure strategies. Then, for every $\epsilon > 0$, there exists a constant a^* (with $0 < a^* < 1$) such that if both automata use an L_{R-I} scheme with a learning parameter $a < a^*$, then

    (i) $\lim_{n \to \infty} E[M(n)]$ exists, and

    (ii) $\lim_{n \to \infty} |E[M(n)] - d_{11}| < \epsilon$.

In other words, if both players use an L_{R-I} algorithm with a sufficiently small parameter a, the average success probability asymptotically approaches the value of the game arbitrarily closely. Equivalently, the two automata will choose their first actions with a probability arbitrarily close to 1. Needless to say a^* depends on ϵ and D as well as the initial condition $(p(0), q(0))$.

The proof of the theorem is presented in six steps and is essentially the same as that given in the original paper. However, we focus our attention on the main arguments.

Step 1: In the first step we define the state space of the Markov process and show that the L_{R-I} algorithm is distance diminishing.

Let S_L denote an L-dimensional unit simplex, $\alpha^1 = \{\alpha_1^1, \alpha_2^1, \ldots, \alpha_{r_1}^1\}$, $\alpha^2 = \{\alpha_1^2, \alpha_2^2, \ldots, \alpha_{r_2}^2\}$, and $E_1 = \{$success for A_1, success for $A_2\}$. The simplex $S = S_{r_1} \times S_{r_2}$ is the state space of the Markov process $\{(p(n), q(n))\}_{n \geq 0}$. $E = \alpha^1 \times \alpha^2 \times E_1$ is known as the event space. The learning algorithm of Eq. (8.7) defines a mapping

$$T : S \times E \to S$$

such that

$$s(n+1) = T[s(n), e(n)].$$

If $d(s_1, s_2)$ refers to the Euclidean distance between s_1 and s_2 in S, a direct computation yields

$$d[s_1(n+1), s_2(n+1)] \leq d[s_1(n), s_2(n)] \text{ for all } e(n) \in E$$

and for every state $s(n)$ there exists a sequence of events $(e(n), e(n+1), \ldots, e(n+k))$ that occurs with nonzero probability such that

$$d[s_1(n+k), s_2(n+k)] \leq (1-a)d[s_1(n), s_2(n)]$$

where

$$e(n) = [\alpha^1(n), \alpha^2(n), \text{success for } A_1] \text{ and}$$

$$e(n+1) = [\alpha^1(n+1), \alpha^2(n+1), \text{success for } A_2].$$

Since S is compact, E is finite, $a \in (0,1)$, $d_{ij} \in (0,1)$ for all i, j, it follows from Appendix C that the algorithm of Eq. (8.7) is distance diminishing.

Step 2: The second step shows that the Markov process has a finite number of absorbing states to which it converges with probability 1.

Let V_{r_1} and V_{r_2} represent the vertices of the simplices S_{r_1} and S_{r_2} respectively. The elements of V_{r_1} and V_{r_2} correspond to the pure strategies of the two players. From the learning algorithms it follows that if $p(n) \in V_{r_1}$ and $q(n) \in V_{r_2}$ then $p(n+1) = p(n)$ and $q(n+1) = q(n)$ w.p.1, so that $V_{r_1} \times V_{r_2}$ constitutes the set of all absorbing states of the process $\{(p(n), q(n))\}$. If a distance diminishing model has an absorbing set A, then

$$\lim_{n \to \infty} d[s(n), A] = 0 \quad w.p.1$$

and we have for the process under consideration

$$\lim_{n \to \infty} d[(p(n), q(n)), V_{r_1} \times V_{r_2}] = 0 \quad w.p.1.$$

In other words, the Markov process converges with probability 1 to the set of all absorbing states $V_{r_1} \times V_{r_2}$. This in turn implies that $\lim_{n \to \infty} E[M(n)]$ exists.

Step 3: Our interest now is in determining the probability with which the Markov process converges to each of the $r_1 r_2$ elements of the set $V_{r_1} \times V_{r_2}$ and in particular to the element that corresponds to the optimal. Also of interest is the dependence of this probability on the step-size a in the learning algorithm. In Chapter 5 it was shown that even in the case of a single automaton operating in a stationary random environment, the determination of the probability with which the automaton converges to an action is complex. A lower bound on the probability of convergence to the optimal action could be determined in that case. A similar procedure is also used in this problem as shown below.

Let $(p^*, q^*) \in V_{r_1} \times V_{r_2}$ represent the state to which $(p(n), q(n))$ converges. Define

$$\Gamma_{ij}(p, q) \triangleq Pr[p^* = e_i^{(1)}, q^* = e_j^{(2)} | p(0) = p, q(0) = q] \quad (8.10)$$

where $e_i^{(1)}$ and $e_j^{(2)}$ are respectively unit vectors in r_1 and r_2 dimensional spaces. $\Gamma_{11}(p,q)$ denotes the probability with which the automata will converge to their optimal strategies starting from any arbitrary initial state (p,q). We are therefore interested in determining a lower bound on $\Gamma_{11}(p,q)$.

Let $D(S)$ be the space of all continuously differentiable functions with bounded derivative defined on S. Let $g(p,q)$ be an element of $D(S)$. The learning algorithm of Eq. (8.7) defines an operator U as

$$Ug(p,q) = E[g(p(n+1), q(n+1))|p(n) = p, q(n) = q]. \tag{8.11}$$

From the definition above it follows that U is linear, and preserves positive functions. The following important proposition can be proved by using the methods developed in Chapter 5.

Proposition 8.1: $\Gamma_{11}(p,q)$ is the only solution in $D(S)$ of the equation

$$U\Gamma_{11}(p,q) = \Gamma_{11}(p,q) \tag{8.12}$$

with boundary conditions

$$
\begin{aligned}
\Gamma_{11}(e_i^{(1)}, e_j^{(2)}) &= 0 \quad (i,j) \neq (1,1) \\
\Gamma_{11}(e_1^{(1)}, e_1^{(2)}) &= 1.
\end{aligned}
\tag{8.13}
$$

Equation (8.12) may be considered a generalization of Eq. (5.81) in Chapter 5. As in that simpler case of a single automaton operating in a stationary environment, the solution of the equation above is also not tractable and hence we attempt to obtain a lower bound $f_1(p,q)$ for $\Gamma_{11}(p,q)$.

Consider the function $f_1(p,q)$ defined by

$$f_1(p,q) = \frac{1 - e^{-(x/a)p_1 q_1}}{1 - e^{-(x/a)}}, \qquad x > 0. \tag{8.14}$$

It is clear that when p_1 or q_1 is zero, $f_1(p,q) = 0$ while if $p_1 = q_1 = 1$, $f_1(p,q) = 1$. Hence $f_1(p,q)$ is a function in $D(S)$, which satisfies the boundary conditions.

Using the definitions of subregular and superregular functions introduced in Chapter 5, it follows that $\Gamma_{11}(p,q)$ is a regular function. Further, if $f(p,q) \in D(S)$ and satisfies the same boundary conditions as $\Gamma_{11}(p,q)$ then

$$
\begin{aligned}
f_1(p,q) &\geq \Gamma_{11}(p,q) \quad \text{if it is superregular} \\
&\leq \Gamma_{11}(p,q) \quad \text{if it is subregular.}
\end{aligned}
\tag{8.15}
$$

Hence if $f_1(p, q)$ can be shown to be subregular, then it can be used as a lower bound on $\Gamma_{11}(p, q)$. The remaining three steps deal essentially with this problem.

Step 4: Since

$$f_1(p, q) = \frac{1 - e^{-(x/a)p_1 q_1}}{1 - e^{-(x/a)}} \qquad x > 0$$

satisfies all the boundary conditions of Eq. (8.13), our aim is to demonstrate that for some value z of x, $f_1(p, q)$ is a subregular function. In such a case a lower bound will be known for $\Gamma_{11}(p, q)$ with the step-size a as an adjustable parameter.

From the properties of superregular and subregular functions described in Chapter 5, it follows that if $f_1(p, q)$ is subregular, then so is $1 - e^{-(x/a)p_1 q_1}$ and hence $e^{-(x/a)p_1 q_1}$ must be superregular and vice versa.

Step 5: We now determine conditions under which

$$f_2(p, q) \stackrel{\triangle}{=} e^{-(x/a)p_1 q_1}$$

is superregular. If $V[u] = (e^u - 1)/u$ if $u \neq 0$ and equals 1 if $u = 0$, then

$$U f_2(p, q) - f_2(p, q) = x p_1 q_1 G[x, p, q] f_2(p, q) \tag{8.16}$$

where G can be expressed in terms of V, x, p_i, q_j and the elements of the game matrix. If $G[x, p, q] \leq 0$ for all $p_i, q_j \in (0, 1)$ and $x > 0$ then $f_2(p, q)$ is a superregular function. It can be shown that

$$\frac{1}{V[x]} \geq \frac{p^T R q}{p^T Q q} \tag{8.17}$$

where

$$R = \begin{bmatrix} 0 & c_{12} & c_{13} & \cdots & c_{1r_2} \\ d_{21} & 1 & 1 & \cdots & 1 \\ d_{31} & 1 & 1 & \cdots & 1 \\ \cdot & & & & \\ \cdot & & & & \\ \cdot & & & & \\ d_{r_1 1} & 1 & 1 & \cdots & 1 \end{bmatrix}$$

and

$$
Q = \begin{bmatrix}
0 & c_{11} & c_{11} & \cdots & c_{11} \\
d_{11} & c_{21}+d_{12} & c_{21}+d_{13} & \cdots & c_{21}+d_{1r_2} \\
d_{11} & c_{31}+d_{12} & c_{31}+d_{13} & \cdots & c_{31}+d_{1r_2} \\
\cdot & \cdot & \cdot & & \cdot \\
\cdot & \cdot & \cdot & & \cdot \\
\cdot & \cdot & \cdot & & \cdot \\
d_{11} & c_{r_11}+d_{12} & c_{r_11}+d_{13} & \cdots & c_{r_11}+d_{1r_2}
\end{bmatrix} .
$$

In view of the assumption on D every nonzero element of the matrix Q is greater than the corresponding element of the matrix R and there exists a constant η such that

$$
\eta = \max_{i,j} \left\{ \frac{R_{ij}}{Q_{ij}} \right\} < 1. \tag{8.18}
$$

$$
i \neq 1, j \neq 1
$$

Hence, the inequality (8.17) is satisfied if

$$
\frac{1}{V[x]} \geq \eta \text{ where } \eta < 1.
$$

Since $V[x]$ is a continuous function with $V[0] = 1$, a value of $x = x^*$ exists such that $1/V[x] \geq \eta$ for all $x \in (0, x^*]$.

Choosing a value $x = z = x^*$ we obtain that

$$
f_1(p,q) = \frac{1 - e^{-(z/a)p_1q_1}}{1 - e^{-(z/a)}} \tag{8.19}
$$

is a subregular function satisfying Eq. (8.15), and hence

$$
f_1(p,q) \leq \Gamma_{11}(p,q) \leq 1.
$$

Given a $\delta > 0$, it follows from Eq. (8.19) that there exists a constant $a^* < 1$ such that for all $0 < a \leq a^*$,

$$
1 - \delta \leq f_1(p,q) \leq \Gamma_{11}(p,q) \leq 1. \tag{8.20}
$$

Since

$$
\lim_{n \to \infty} E[M(n)] = \Gamma_{11}(p,q)d_{11} + [1 - \Gamma_{11}(p,q)]h[p^*, q^*, d_{ij}] \tag{8.21}
$$

where $h[., ., .]$ is a uniformly bounded nonnegative function of its arguments, from Eqs. (8.20) and (8.21) we have

$$(1 - \delta)d_{11} \leq \lim_{n \to \infty} E[M(n)] \leq d_{11} + \delta h.$$

Hence

$$\lim_{n \to \infty} |E[M(n)] - d_{11}| \leq max(\delta d_{11}, \delta h) \leq \epsilon$$

if

$$\delta = min\left(\frac{\epsilon}{d_{11}}, \frac{\epsilon}{h}\right),$$

which completes the proof.

Saddle Points in Mixed Strategies: In the discussion above, it was assumed that the game matrix has a saddle point in pure strategies and it was shown that by the proper choice of the parameter a, a linear reward-inaction scheme will converge to this state with a probability as close to one as desired. The same results can also be extended to cases where the saddle point of the game matrix is not necessarily in pure strategies; that is, it can be either in pure or mixed strategies. This was demonstrated by Lakshmivarahan and Narendra (1982) for the case of players having two actions each. Using an $L_{R-\epsilon P}$ scheme, it was shown that by the proper choice of the step sizes a and b of the reward and penalty terms, the expected value of the mixed strategy used by either player asymptotically can be made arbitrarily close to the optimal strategy dictated by game theory.

Let both players use an $L_{R-\epsilon P}$ algorithm with learning parameters b_1, a_1 and b_2, a_2 respectively. b_1 and b_2 correspond to penalty parameters of the automata A_1 and A_2 and the reward parameters a_1 and a_2 are related to b_1 and b_2 as $a_1\theta = b_1$, $a_2\theta = b_2$ where $\theta \in [0, 1]$. Once again it can be shown that $\{p(n), q(n)\}_{n \geq 0}$ is a stationary Markov process and the learning algorithm defines a mapping $T : S \times E \to S$ so that

$$(p(n+1), q(n+1)) = T[(p(n), q(n)), e(n)].$$

With the $L_{R-\epsilon P}$ schemes used by the automata, it follows that T is distance diminishing and that all states in S are nonabsorbing so the process is ergodic.

As in Chapter 5, the nature of the limiting distribution can be described more precisely by choosing the learning parameters sufficiently small. However, since two parameters a_i and b_i $(i = 1, 2)$ are involved in each of the learning schemes, the limiting behavior of the process is critically dependent on their values. For sufficiently small values of the parameters, the discrete parameter Markov process can be approximated by the solutions of a related differential equation, and the limiting distribution of the former is normal with a mean value which is approximated by the equilibrium state of the differential equation. Since the desired optimal mixed strategy corresponds to this equilibrium state, it follows that the expected gain can be made arbitrarily close to the value of the game.

Establishing the convergence of the learning algorithm essentially involves satisfaction of the conditions similar to those of Theorem 5.1. As in the case of an automaton using the $L_{R-\epsilon P}$ scheme operating in a stationary random environment analyzed in Chapter 5, the game situation also leads to nonlinear differential equations. Proving the global asymptotic stability of such equations is quite involved when each player has multiple strategies. However, the same techniques as for the two-strategy case can be used and it is expected that the results carry over to the general case also.

Computer Simulations of Two-Person Zero-Sum Games: Extensive simulations of two-person zero-sum games (Viswanathan and Narendra, 1971) have served to validate the results reported in this section. The five problems following have been chosen to emphasize specific aspects of convergence of learning automata. In Example 8.2, A_1 uses an L_{R-I} scheme while A_2 uses an L_{R-P} scheme. In Examples 8.3 and 8.4, both automata use L_{R-I} schemes and the convergence to the value of the game is seen to depend on the nature of the game matrix. In Example 8.5, both automata have three pure strategies and the game matrix has a unique saddle point. Example 8.6 has a mixed strategy saddle point equal to 0.5.

Example 8.2: With a game matrix

$$G = \begin{bmatrix} 0.2 & 0.6 \\ -0.3 & 0.75 \end{bmatrix}$$

where the entries g_{ij} represent the expected gains for automaton A_1, it is clear that (α_1^1, α_1^2) is the only saddle point. When A_1 uses an L_{R-I} scheme with step size $a = 0.05$ and A_2 uses an L_{R-P} scheme with $a = b = 0.05$, the asymptotic expected payoff to A_1 is greater than 0.2 (Fig. 8.2 top curve). If, however, A_1 uses the L_{R-P} scheme and A_2 the L_{R-I} scheme, the asymptotic payoff is less than 0.2. These results indicate that the L_{R-I} scheme outperforms the L_{R-P} scheme in a two-person zero-sum game.

Example 8.3: With the same game matrix as in Example 8.2, the au-

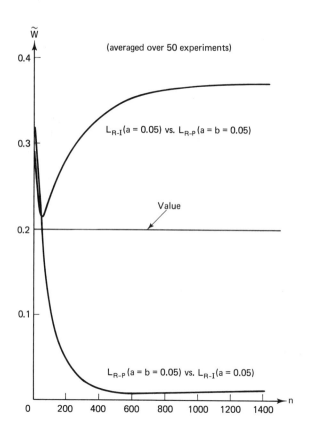

Figure 8.2: L_{R-I} vs. L_{R-P} in a two-person zero-sum game.

tomaton game was simulated with both automata using L_{R-I} schemes and $a = 0.08$. An inspection of the game matrix reveals that the player A_2 (minimizer) has a distinct advantage over A_1 (maximizer) because the first column is dominant. This is responsible for the average outcome $\widetilde{W}(n)$ converging from below to the value as shown in Fig. 8.3(b). For the same reason the average probability $\widetilde{p}_1^2(n)$ tends to unity faster than $\widetilde{p}_1^1(n)$ as seen in Fig. 8.3(a).

Example 8.4: When the game matrix has the form

$$G = \begin{bmatrix} 0.2 & 0.6 \\ -0.3 & -0.75 \end{bmatrix},$$

the first row is dominant so that A_1 has an advantage over A_2. Figure 8.4 shows that $\widetilde{p}_1^1(n)$ tends to unity faster than $\widetilde{p}_1^2(n)$ and that $\widetilde{W}(n)$ converges to the value from above.

Example 8.5: In this case both players have three pure strategies and the game matrix G is

$$G = \begin{bmatrix} 0.3 & -0.5 & 0.15 \\ 0.2 & 0.2 & 0.2 \\ 0.35 & 0.55 & -0.25 \end{bmatrix}.$$

The game matrix is seen to have a saddle point in pure strategies for (α_2^1, α_3^2). The plot of $\widetilde{W}(n)$ when both automata use L_{R-I} schemes with $a = 0.01$ is given in Fig. 8.5.

Example 8.6: All the games considered in Examples 8.2-8.5 have saddle points in pure strategies. In this example the game matrix has the form

$$D = \begin{bmatrix} 0.8 & 0.2 \\ 0.4 & 0.6 \end{bmatrix}$$

and the optimal mixed strategies for the two players A_1 and A_2 are $(p_1^1, p_2^1) = (0.25, 0.75)$ and $(p_1^2, p_2^2) = (0.5, 0.5)$ respectively, yielding a value of 0.5. Figure 8.6(a) shows the behavior of the two players when both of them use $L_{R-\epsilon P}$ algorithms. With $a = 0.002$ and $b = 0.00001$, the action probabilities oscillate around the optimal values and the value curve stays close to the optimal value of 0.5.

When both players use an L_{R-P} scheme, they tend to equalize the product of action probability and effective response failure probability. The simulation results for the case where the step sizes are $a = b = 0.002$ are shown

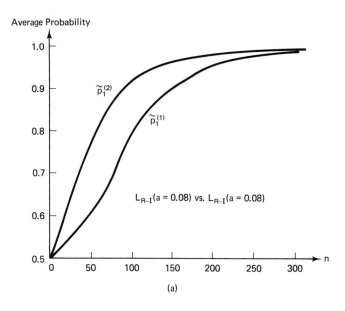

(a)

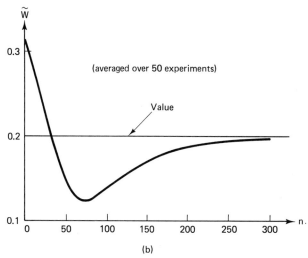

(b)

Figure 8.3: (a) Average probability vs. n; (b) $\widetilde{W}$ vs. n (*Copyright IEEE* ©*1974*).

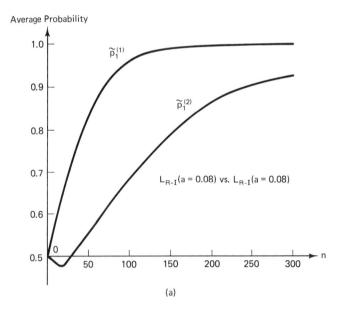

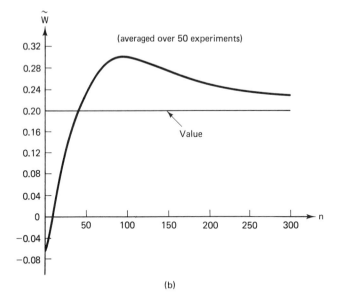

Figure 8.4: (a) Average probability vs. n; (b) $\widetilde{W}$ vs. n.

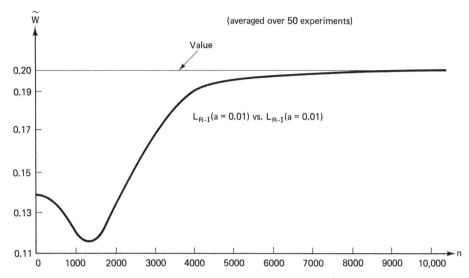

Figure 8.5: L_{R-I} vs. L_{R-I} in a two-person zero-sum game (*Copyright IEEE* ©*1974*).

in Fig. 8.6(b). The probabilities $p_1^{1*} = 0.4665$ and $p_1^{2*} = 0.4134$ can be used to approximate the stationary distributions of p_1^1 and p_1^2, and the resulting value of the game is 0.4850. This is illustrated by the plot in Fig. 8.6(b).

8.5 Games with Identical Payoffs

The two-person zero-sum game described in Section 8.4 is one notable, although limited, situation in which individual rationality agrees with group rationality. Another important special case in which rational group behavior is easily defined is the identical payoff game. In the general games of automata described in Section 8.3 this corresponds to the case where $\beta^1(n) = \beta^2(n) = \ldots = \beta^N(n)$ for all n so that the payoff $\beta(n) \in \{0, 1\}$ at every instant is identical to all the players. Hence rational behavior on the part of the various players involved in the game amounts to choosing strategies that result in the optimal payoff. Recently, Narendra and Wheeler (1983) and Thathachar and Ramakrishnan (1982,1984) have derived important results in the context of identical payoff games that form the principal topic of discussion in this section.

Ever since Krylov and Tsetlin (1963) wrote their first paper on automata games, a number of investigators have analyzed the behavior of automata

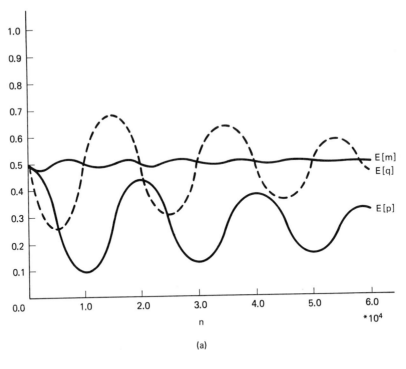

(a)

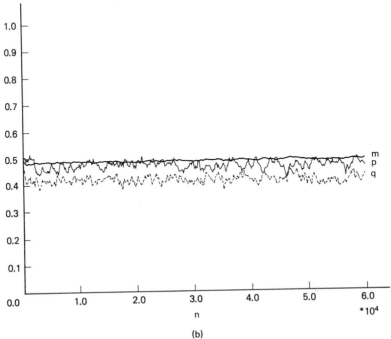

(b)

Figure 8.6: Two-person zero-sum game with optimal mixed strategies (a) $L_{R-\epsilon P}$ schemes (b) L_{R-P} schemes.

in identical payoff games. In the 1960s, work in the Soviet Union was concerned with conditions under which individual deterministic automata would play rationally in identical payoff games. Borovikov and Bryzgalov (1965), Volkonskii (1965), Ginzburg and Tsetlin (1965), Pittel (1965), Butrimenko (1967), and Vaisbord (1968) are among the many who contributed to the field. Games of voting such as the Goore game described in Section 8.2 and resource allocation problems were studied via computer simulations. The changes in the behavior of the collective were examined as the memory depth and the number of players were varied. In general, it was shown that rational behavior could be achieved with infinite memory provided the payoff structures satisfied restrictive conditions.

The behavior of variable-structure automata in two-player identical payoff games was first investigated by Viswanathan and Narendra (1971). More recently, using the same approach as that used in the previous section, Lakshmivarahan (1981) carried out a limited analysis of two-player two-action identical payoff games. In particular, for a 2 × 2 game matrix, with only one element that is maximum both in its row and column, it was shown that $L_{R-\epsilon P}$ and L_{R-I} algorithms can be chosen so that the automata can achieve a payoff that is as close to the maximum as desired. The principal contribution in Narendra and Wheeler (1983) and Thathachar and Ramakrishnan (1982, 1984) is that general results can be given for identical payoff games having an arbitrary number of players, each of whom has an arbitrary number of actions. The implications of these results, as well as simulation results of different automata games, are discussed at the end of the section.

8.5.1 Statement of the Problem

N automata, each operating independently and in total ignorance of the other automata, are involved in a game Γ as described in Section 8.3. Each player can use a learning algorithm of his or her choice which results in the selection of an action at each play. All players receive identical payoffs $\beta^i(n) = \beta(n)$ $(i = 1, 2, \ldots, N)$ as a result of the play at any stage n. The aim is to determine the asymptotic behavior of the sequential game and conditions under which the automata can receive a payoff which is arbitrarily close to the global maximum.

This section shows that by choosing the proper learning algorithms of all the automata, the expected gain increases monotonically at every stage. Under certain assumptions on the game matrix Γ this condition implies that the overall performance will be globally optimal.

Local and global maxima: The concepts of local and global maxima are important in the game with identical payoffs. A local maximum is any element of the game matrix that is simultaneously the maximum of its row and column. In an identical payoff game a local maximum is equivalent to a pure strategy equilibrium point. The global maximum is the maximum of all the local maxima and is Pareto-optimal. For instance,

$$D = \begin{bmatrix} 0.9 & 0.8 \\ 0.6 & 0.4 \end{bmatrix}$$

has only one maximum corresponding to 0.9 which is consequently the global maximum. On the other hand,

$$D = \begin{bmatrix} 0.9 & 0.5 \\ 0.6 & 0.8 \end{bmatrix}$$

has two local maxima corresponding to 0.9 and 0.8, while 0.9 is the global maximum.

The principal result of this section is applicable to an arbitrary number of automata using a class of absolutely expedient schemes and involved in the identical payoff game described earlier. However we shall first deal with the special case $N = 2$ where both automata use the L_{R-I} scheme since it permits us to focus on the theoretical questions involved. For both the specific case of $N = 2$ as well as the more general case, the following result, pertaining to a single automaton acting in a stationary environment discussed in Chapter 4, is found to be relevant.

8.5.2 Single Automaton in a Stationary Environment

Let an automaton with an action set $\alpha = \{\alpha_1, \alpha_2, \ldots, \alpha_r\}$ and an input set $\beta = \{0, 1\}$ operate in an environment defined by the success probability set $\{d_1, d_2, \ldots, d_r\}$ where $\beta = 1$ represents success and $Pr[\beta(n) = 1 | \alpha(n) = \alpha_i] = d_i$. Let the performance of the automaton be judged by the asymptotic behavior of $E[M(n)]$ where $M(n)$ is defined by $M(n) = E[\beta(n) | p(n)] = \sum_{i=1}^{r} p_i(n) d_i$. Defining $\Delta p_i(n) = E[p_i(n+1) - p_i(n) | p(n)]$, it was shown in Chapter 4 that if the automaton uses the L_{R-I} scheme, then $\Delta p_i(n) = a p_i(n) \sum_{j=1}^{r} p_j(n)(d_i - d_j)$. Using the definition of $M(n) = \sum_{i=1}^{r} p_i(n) d_i$, the conditional expectation of the change in payoff defined as

$$\Delta M(n) \overset{\triangle}{=} E[M(n+1) - M(n) | p(n)] = d^T \Delta p(n)$$

can be shown to equal $ap^T Dp/2$ where the elements of the matrix D are given by $D_{ii} = 0$, $D_{ij} = (d_i - d_j)^2$. Hence $\Delta M(n)$ is strictly positive provided that all d_i are not equal and $p_i \in (0,1)$ $i = 1, 2, \ldots, r$.

The same result is also valid when an absolutely expedient scheme is used. In this case

$$\Delta M(n) = [\lambda(p) + \mu(p)] \, p^T Dp.$$

In Chapters 4 and 5 the ϵ-optimality of the L_{R-I} algorithm was demonstrated by first showing that $M(n)$ is a supermartingale and then by showing convergence to the optimal action with a probability arbitrarily close to 1. We use the same procedure in this section for the game situation and derive an expression for $\Delta M(n)$ to demonstrate that $M(n)$ is a submartingale (since in this case we are maximizing the payoff function). The precise implications of this in terms of ϵ-optimality are discussed at the end of the section.

8.5.3 Two-Player Case

Let A_1 and A_2 be two automata involved in a stochastic sequential game with action sets $\{\alpha_1^1, \alpha_2^1, \ldots, \alpha_{r_1}^1\}$ and $\{\alpha_1^2, \alpha_2^2, \ldots, \alpha_{r_2}^2\}$ respectively. The game can be represented by an $(r_1 \times r_2)$ matrix D whose i,j^{th} element d_{ij} is the probability of success when the action pair (α_i^1, α_j^2) is chosen. To simplify the notation in the two player case we let

$$p(n)^T = \{p_1(n), p_2(n), \ldots, p_{r_1}(n)\}$$

and

$$q(n)^T = \{q_1(n), q_2(n), \ldots, q_{r_2}(n)\}$$

be the action probability vectors of the two automata at stage n. The conditional expected payoff at stage n may then be denoted by

$$M(n) = p(n)^T Dq(n)$$

and it follows that

$$\Delta M(n) = \Delta p(n)^T Dq(n) + \Delta q(n)^T D^T p(n) + E[\delta p(n)^T D \delta q(n)]$$

where

$$
\begin{aligned}
\delta p(n) &= p(n+1) - p(n) \\
\delta q(n) &= q(n+1) - q(n) \\
\Delta p(n) &= E[\delta p(n) | p(n), q(n)] \\
\Delta q(n) &= E[\delta q(n) | p(n), q(n)]
\end{aligned}
\qquad (8.22)
$$

Omitting stage index n for conciseness of notation we have for the expected incremental gain

$$\Delta M = \Delta p^T D q + \Delta q^T D^T p + E[\delta p^T D \delta q]. \tag{8.23}$$

The first two terms in Eq. (8.23) correspond to the incremental gain due to each player when the action probabilities of the other player are constant. These are equivalent to cases where each player is operating in a stationary environment discussed earlier. It therefore follows that the first two terms are of order a, where a is the algorithm step size, and are nonnegative. Hence to show that $M(n)$ is a submartingale it suffices to show that the third term is also nonnegative.

The third term can be interpreted as an interaction term, which includes the effect of the two automata acting simultaneously. It is evident that since the changes in action probabilities appear as a product in this term, it is of order a^2. Determining the sign of the third term therefore constitutes the main difficulty in demonstrating that $M(n)$ is a submartingale. We first consider the case where $r_1 = r_2 = 2$ i.e., both players have only two strategies. In this case

$$E[\delta p^T D \delta q] \triangleq \Delta \overline{M} = a^2 p_1 p_2 q_1 q_2 (d_{11} - d_{12} - d_{21} + d_{22})^2 \geq 0.$$

Following the same approach for the case when $r_1 = 3$ and $r_2 = 2$ we obtain

$$\Delta \overline{M} = a^2 [p_1 p_2 q_1 q_2 (d_{11} - d_{12} - d_{21} + d_{22})^2 + p_1 p_3 q_1 q_2 (d_{11} - d_{12} - d_{31} + d_{32})^2$$
$$+ p_2 p_3 q_1 q_2 (d_{21} - d_{22} - d_{31} + d_{32})^2] \geq 0.$$
$$\tag{8.24}$$

An expression similar to the one above can be derived for the case when r_1 and r_2 are arbitrary but finite so that $\Delta \overline{M}$ is expressed as the sum of nonnegative terms. By induction, it can be shown that if

$$\Delta \overline{M} = a^2 \sum_{\substack{i,j}}^{r_1-1, r_1-1} p_i p_j q_1 q_2 (d_{i1} - d_{j1} - d_{i2} + d_{j2})^2$$

$$(i,j) \neq (j,i)$$

for the $(r_1 - 1 \times 2)$ case, then

$$\Delta \overline{M} = a^2 \sum_{\substack{i,j}}^{r_1, r_1} p_i p_j q_1 q_2 k_{ij}$$

$$(i,j) \neq (j,i)$$

for the $(r_1 \times 2)$ case, where k_{ij} is a nonnegative constant. Hence the expression holds for arbitrary values of r_i. The same arguments readily carry over to the case where r_2 strategies are available to the second player. In such a case the expression for $\Delta \overline{M}$ contains $[r_1(r_1 - 1)][r_2(r_2 - 1)]/4$ nonnegative terms.

An identical result can be proved when general absolutely expedient schemes of the reward-inaction type are used by the two players (Thathachar and Ramakrishnan, 1982,1984). If at stage n the player A_1 chooses his or her i^{th} action, i.e., $\alpha^1(n) = \alpha^1_i$, and player A_2 chooses his or her j^{th}, i.e., $\alpha^2(n) = \alpha^2_j$, the algorithms for updating the probability vectors are given by the following:

$$\left. \begin{array}{l} p_k(n+1) = p_k(n) - \phi_k(p(n)), k \neq i \\ p_i(n+1) = p_i(n) + \sum_{k \neq i} \phi_k(p(n)) \end{array} \right\} \text{ for a success} \qquad (8.25)$$

$$p_i(n+1) = p_i(n) \quad (i = 1, 2, \ldots, r_1) \quad \text{ for a failure.}$$

Similarly

$$\left. \begin{array}{l} q_k(n+1) = q_k(n) - \psi_k(q(n)), k \neq j \\ q_j(n+1) = q_j(n) + \sum_{k \neq j} \psi_k(q(n)) \end{array} \right\} \text{ for a success} \qquad (8.26)$$

$$q_j(n+1) = q_j(n) \quad (j = 1, 2, \ldots, r_2) \quad \text{ for a failure.}$$

$\phi_k(\cdot)$ and $\psi_k(\cdot)$ are scalar valued functions of p and q respectively with $0 < \phi_k(p) < p_k$ and $0 < \psi_k(q) < q_k$ for all p_k and q_k in the interval $(0, 1)$ and satisfy the following absolute expediency conditions given in Chapter 4:

$$\begin{array}{c} \dfrac{\phi_1(p)}{p_1} = \dfrac{\phi_2(p)}{p_2} = \cdots = \dfrac{\phi_{r_1}(p)}{p_{r_1}} = \lambda_1(p) \\[2mm] \dfrac{\psi_1(q)}{q_1} = \dfrac{\psi_2(q)}{q_2} = \cdots = \dfrac{\psi_{r_2}(q)}{q_{r_2}} = \lambda_2(q). \end{array} \qquad (8.27)$$

$\Delta M(n)$ can now be expressed as

$$\begin{aligned} \Delta M(n) = {} & \lambda_1(p(n)) \sum_{i=1}^{r_1-1} \sum_{j=i+1}^{r_1} p_i(n) p_j(n) \left[\sum_{k=1}^{r_2} q_k(n)(d_{ik} - d_{jk}) \right]^2 \\ & + \lambda_2(q(n)) \sum_{i=1}^{r_2-1} \sum_{j=i+1}^{r_2} q_i(n) q_j(n) \left[\sum_{k=1}^{r_1} p_k(n)(d_{ki} - d_{kj}) \right]^2 \\ & + \mathcal{D}^T [p_{dia}(n) - p(n)p(n)^T] \otimes [q_{dia}(n) - q(n)q(n)^T] \mathcal{D} \end{aligned}$$
$$(8.28)$$

where $\mathcal{D} = [d_{11}, d_{12}, \ldots, d_{1r_2}, d_{21}, \ldots, d_{2r_2}, \ldots, d_{r_1 r_2}]^T$ is an $(r_1 r_2 \times 1)$ column vector,

$$p_{dia}(n) = \text{diag}[p_1(n), p_2(n), \ldots, p_{r_1}(n)]$$
$$q_{dia}(n) = \text{diag}[q_1(n), q_2(n), \ldots, q_{r_2}(n)]$$

and $\otimes$ is the symbol for the Kronecker product of matrices.

Each of the terms in the right-hand side of Eq. (8.28) is nonnegative so that $\Delta M(n) \geq 0$, for all n and $(p(n), q(n)) \in S_{r_1} \times S_{r_2}$. Hence $M(n)$ is a submartingale, so that irrespective of the environment, the expected payoff received by each player increases monotonically in time. Such algorithms are defined as being absolutely monotonic.

It can further be shown that a second class of algorithms also exists which has the desirable property of absolute monotonicity discussed above.

In this case, if $\alpha^1(n) = \alpha_i^1$ and $\alpha^2(n) = \alpha_j^2$, the updating is done according to the following equations:

$$
\left.
\begin{aligned}
p_i(n+1) &= p_i(n) + f_i(p(n)) \\
p_k(n+1) &= p_k(n) - \frac{1}{r_1 - 1} f_i(p(n))
\end{aligned}
\right\}
\begin{aligned}
&\text{for a success} \\
&k \neq i
\end{aligned}
\tag{8.29}
$$

$$p_i(n+1) = p_i(n) \ (i = 1, 2, \ldots, r_1) \qquad \text{for a failure}$$

and

$$
\left.
\begin{aligned}
q_j(n+1) &= q_j(n) + g_j(q(n)) \\
q_k(n+1) &= q_k(n) - \frac{1}{r_2 - 1} g_j(q(n))
\end{aligned}
\right\}
\begin{aligned}
&\text{for a success} \\
&k \neq j
\end{aligned}
$$

$$q_j(n+1) = q_j(n) \ (j = 1, 2, \ldots, r_2) \qquad \text{for a failure.} \tag{8.30}$$

$f_i(p)$ and $g_j(q)$ for all $(i = 1, 2, \ldots, r_1, j = 1, 2, \ldots, r_2)$ are scalar valued continuous functions such that

(i) $f_i(p)$ and $g_j(q)$ are nonnegative

(ii) $0 < f_i(p) < (r_1 - 1) \min_{k \neq i} p_k(n)$

   $0 < g_j(q) < (r_2 - 1) \min_{k \neq j} q_k(n)$
   for all p and q in their open simplexes.

Necessary and sufficient conditions for this class of algorithms to be absolutely monotonic are given by

$$
\begin{aligned}
f_1(p)p_1 &= f_2(p)p_2 = \cdots = f_{r_1}(p)p_{r_1} = \lambda_1(p) \\
g_1(q)q_1 &= g_2(q)q_2 = \cdots = g_{r_2}(q)q_{r_2} = \lambda_2(q)
\end{aligned}
\tag{8.31}
$$

where $\lambda_1(\cdot)$ and $\lambda_2(\cdot)$ are arbitrary functions.

8.5.4 N-Player Case

The generalization of the results above derived for the two-player case to games involving N (> 2) players can be carried out in many ways. Apart from a few basic concepts that must be understood, the difficulty is not conceptual but mainly algebraic in character. Once the number of players is fixed, changes in the number of strategies of the players can be taken into account by using the arguments given earlier. Hence, our chief concern is with the effect of introducing an additional player. This is best illustrated by considering the case of three players, each of whom have two strategies.

Three-Player Case $(2 \times 2 \times 2)$: Let $\{\alpha_1, \alpha_2\}$, $\{\beta_1, \beta_2\}$, and $\{\gamma_1, \gamma_2\}$ be the strategies available to the three players and let $(p_1(n), p_2(n))$, $(q_1(n), q_2(n))$, and $(r_1(n), r_2(n))$ be the corresponding probabilities at stage n. If the probability of success is d_{ijk} when the actions α_i, β_j, and γ_k are used by the three players, $M(n) = \sum_{i,j,k=1}^{2}[p_i(n)q_j(n)r_k(n) \ d_{ijk}]$. Assuming that all of them use the L_{R-I} scheme, the expected incremental gain $\Delta M(n)$ can be expressed as

$$\Delta M(n) = \sum_{i,j,k=1}^{2} E\left[p_i(n+1)q_j(n+1)r_k(n+1) - p_i(n)q_j(n)r_k(n)\right.$$
$$\left. \mid p_1(n), q_1(n), r_1(n)\right] d_{ijk}.$$

$\Delta M(n)$ can be shown to have terms of the form, $ap_iq_j\delta r_k$ containing a single variational term, $a^2 p_i \delta q_j \delta r_k$ containing two variational terms and $a^3 \delta p_i \delta q_j \delta r_k$ containing three variational terms. Since the solution to the two-player case is known, it follows that all terms of the first two types are nonnegative. Hence it is only necessary to show that the terms containing three variational terms are nonnegative.

For the problem under discussion it is found that

$$\Delta M_3(n) = a^3 p_1 p_2 q_1 q_2 r_1 r_2 [d_{111} - d_{112} - d_{121} - d_{211} + d_{212} + d_{221} + d_{122} - d_{222}]^2$$

where the subscript 3 in ΔM_3 refers to terms of order a^3. This result is found to generalize in a straightforward manner to both the N-player case with each player having two strategies and the more general case of N players with $r_1, r_2, \ldots, r_N$ strategies respectively (Narendra and Wheeler, 1983). In the latter case the term $\Delta M_N(n)$ of order a^N has $\Pi_{i=1}^{N} r_i(r_i - 1)/2$ terms each of which is of the form $a^N p_1 p_2 \ldots q_1 q_2 \ldots C$ where C is a perfect square and hence nonnegative.

The results above continue to hold even when more general learning algorithms are used. In fact necessary and sufficient conditions on the functions in the learning algorithm for the automata in an N-player game to be absolutely monotonic can be derived. The following development summarizes the available results (Ramakrishnan, 1982).

Let the action probability vector of automaton $A_k(k = 1, 2, \ldots, N)$ at the instant n be $p(k, n)$. Let the automata operate according to generalized nonlinear reinforcement schemes where the nonlinear functions depend both on the action chosen at n and the action probability being updated as in Eq. (4.110). The learning algorithm can be stated concisely as follows:

Let the action chosen by A_k at instant n be $\alpha_{i_k}^k$. Then for each $k = 1, 2, \ldots, N$,

$$\begin{aligned}
p(k, n+1) &= p(k, n) - [G^k]^T \left(p(k, n) \right) e_{i_k}(k) \quad \text{for a success} \\
p(k, n+1) &= p(k, n) \qquad\qquad\qquad\qquad\qquad\quad \text{for a failure}
\end{aligned} \qquad (8.32)$$

where

(i) $e_{i_k}(k)$ is the $r_k \times 1$ unit vector with unity for the i_k^{th} element and the rest zero,

(ii) $G^k(p)$ is a $r_k \times r_k$ matrix with its $(i, j)^{\text{th}}$ element given by $g_{ij}^k(p)(j \neq i)$ and the $(i, i)^{\text{th}}$ element $g_{ii}^k(p) = -\sum_{j \neq i} g_{ij}^k(p)$, $i = 1, 2, \ldots, r_k$.

Eq. (8.32) represents a nonlinear reward-inaction scheme.

We also formalize the notion of absolute monotonicity in the following definition.

Definition 8.1: A learning algorithm for the game of N automata with identical payoffs is said to be absolutely monotonic if $\Delta M(n) > 0$ for all n, all $p(k, n) \in S_{r_k}^0$ and all possible game environments.

Our attempt is now to characterize the class of absolutely monotonic learning algorithms. Using the notion of Kronecker product of matrices extensively and extending the ideas from the proof of theorems on absolutely expedient schemes (Chapter 4), we arrive at the principal result of this section, which can be stated as follows.

Theorem 8.2: In a N-automata game with identical payoffs, where each automaton employs the learning algorithm of Eq. (8.32), necessary and sufficient conditions for absolute monotonicity are given by

$$p^T(k, n) G^k(p(k, n)) = 0 \qquad (8.33)$$

for all $k = 1, 2, \ldots, N$, all $n = 0, 1, \ldots$, and all $p(k, n) \in S_{r_k}^0$.

Comment 8.1: Theorem 8.2 states that a large class of algorithms exist for which the expected payoff monotonically increases with time in arbitrary game environments.

Comment 8.2: The condition of Eq. (8.33) can be seen to be the same as the condition of Eq. (4.113) for absolute expediency of individual automata operating in stationary random environments. However, this is true only for reward-inaction schemes. In particular it holds for the L_{R-I} scheme.

Comment 8.3: The condition of Eq. (8.33) is also a generalization of the conditions of Eqs. (8.27) and (8.31) given for two-player games.

Comment 8.4: Attempts to extend Theorem 8.2 to absolutely expedient reward-penalty schemes have not been successful. In fact, a counterexample of an absolutely expedient scheme that is not absolutely monotonic is available. Thus it appears that the class of learning algorithms possessing the nonnegativity property $\Delta M(n) \geq 0$ becomes more and more restricted as the class of environments in which the automata operate becomes more complex.

8.5.5 ϵ-optimality

In an automata game of the type described above, our primary interest is in determining conditions under which the automata will be ϵ-optimal or equivalently $M(n)$ will converge to its maximum value with a probability arbitrarily close to one. In the simplest case of a single automaton operating in a stationary random environment, the property that $M(n)$ is a submartingale was adequate to demonstrate that the automaton would be ϵ-optimal. This is also the case for the (2×2) game in which the game matrix has a single element that is simultaneously maximum in both its row and column.

The generalization of this result to N players with arbitrary action sets is summarized in the following theorem.

Theorem 8.3: Let Γ be an N-player identical payoff game in which player A_i has r_i actions and all players use absolutely monotonic algorithms. If Γ has a unique pure strategy equilibrium $\alpha^* = \{\alpha_{i_1^*}^1, \alpha_{i_2^*}^2, \ldots, \alpha_{i_N^*}^N\}$ with corresponding expected success $d(\alpha^*)$, then for any $\epsilon > 0$ there exists an algorithm step size a^* such that for $0 < a < a^*$, $\lim_{n \to \infty} E[M(n)] > d(\alpha^*) - \epsilon$.

However, at present, necessary and sufficient conditions under which

$M(n)$ being a submartingale will imply ϵ-optimality of a general N-automata game are not known. As shown in the simulations at the end of this section, even in two-player games many equilibrium points (local optima) may exist. Hence, conditions under which automata will converge to local and global optima and their dependence on initial conditions are subjects of current research.

Despite the limitations described, the result above has far-reaching consequences in the decentralized control of complex systems. It implies that simple policies used independently by individual automata or decision makers with limited information can lead to desirable group behavior. The important problem of decentralized control of Markov chains discussed in Section 8.8 is based mainly on the result presented here as Theorem 8.3.

8.5.6 Simulation Studies of Identical Payoff Games

The principal result of this section as well as the discussions pertaining to local and global optimality are best illustrated by the following five simulations of games of automata. While games involving as many as six automata have been simulated, we include here typical results obtained for (2×2) and (3×3) automata games. When the game has a unique equilibrium point, the simulations reveal that the solutions converge to it with a high probability as predicted by theory. In such cases the effect of varying the step size a of the learning algorithms is of interest. Simulations of games in which the automata use the same learning algorithm but different step sizes are also included. In cases where the game matrix has more than one equilibrium point, the dependence of the solutions on the initial conditions is also revealed by these studies. Finally, some simulation results of games in which the automata use L_{R-P} and $L_{R-\epsilon P}$ schemes are also included to emphasize the nature of convergence in such cases.

Example 8.7: In this example the game matrix is

$$D = \begin{bmatrix} 0.8 & 0.6 \\ 0.3 & 0.1 \end{bmatrix}$$

so that d_{11} is the unique element that is simultaneously maximum in both its row and column and is hence a Nash equilibrium. Note that both players have a dominant first strategy. Both automata use an L_{R-I} scheme with the same step size a. Figures 8.7(a) and 8.8(a) show the evolution of the trajectories in the (p, q) space and the $(E[p], E[q])$ space respectively as the

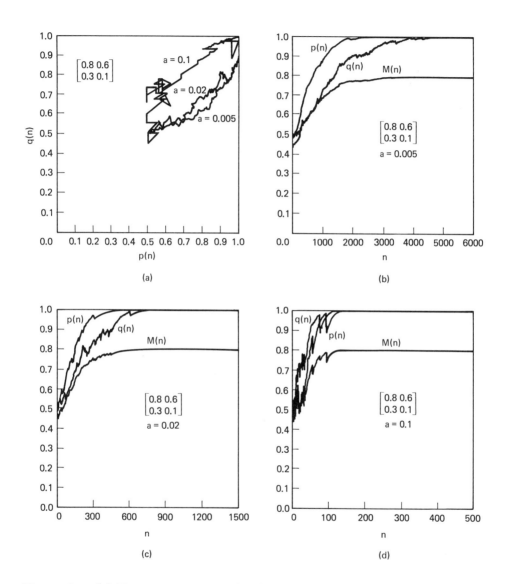

Figure 8.7: (a) Trajectories in the (p, q) space; (b)-(d) sample paths of $p(n)$, $q(n)$, and $M(n)$ for $a = 0.005$, 0.02 and 0.1.

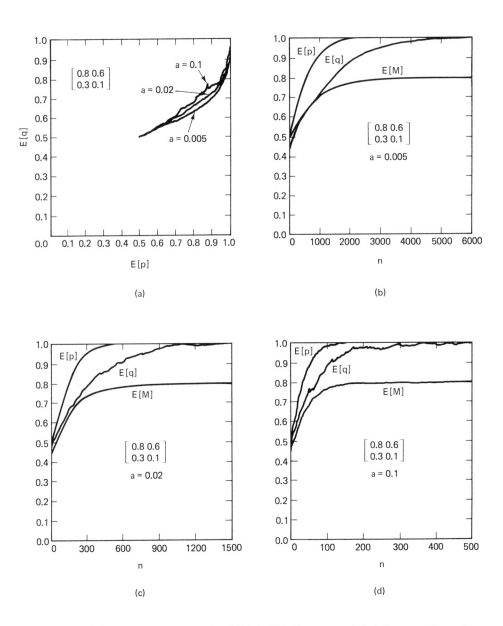

Figure 8.8: (a) Trajectories in the $(E(p), E(q))$ space; (b)-(d) mean learning curves for $a = 0.005$, 0.02 and 0.1.

step size a assumes three values $a = 0.005$, 0.02 and 0.1. The sample paths of $p(n), q(n)$, and $M(n)$ are shown in Figures 8.7(b)-(d) while mean learning curves averaged over thirty sample paths are shown in Figures 8.8(b)-(d).

Example 8.8: In this case, shown in Fig. 8.9, the game matrix is the same as in Example 8.7, except that the elements of the second row are interchanged. Now only A_1 has a dominant strategy. Both automata use L_{R-I} schemes. However, the step sizes a_1 and a_2 for the automata are assumed to be different. When $a_1 = 0.05$ while $a_2 = 0.01$ or 0.005, $E[p]$ is seen to converge to unity much faster than $E[q]$. This can be explained partly in terms of the step size and partly in terms of the game matrix since the first action of player A_1 is dominant. In the last two cases where $a_2 > a_1$ the difference in rates of convergence is found to be less pronounced (refer to Fig. 8.9).

Example 8.9: As in Examples 8.7 and 8.8, we consider a game between two automata using L_{R-I} schemes. However, the elements of the game matrix are changed so that the game has either one or two equilibrium points. Figure 8.10(a) shows the convergence of solutions from different initial conditions to a unique equilibrium (α_1^1, α_1^2) with a probability arbitrarily close to one when D has the same form as in Example 8.7. However, when

$$D = \begin{bmatrix} 0.8 & 0.1 \\ 0.3 & 0.6 \end{bmatrix}$$

both d_{11} and d_{22} are maxima in both their rows and columns and are Nash equilibria. The equilibrium point to which the solutions converge is seen to depend critically on initial conditions. This simple example reveals that suboptimality is a distinct possibility in games with identical payoffs and depends on both the initial conditions as well as the existence of more than one equilibrium point [refer to Fig. 8.10(b)].

Example 8.10: In all the preceding examples we have assumed that the automata use L_{R-I} schemes or, in general, absolutely expedient schemes. The effect of using $L_{R-\epsilon P}$ schemes with different values of reward and penalty parameters is shown in Fig. 8.11. For the same game matrix given in Example 8.8, it is assumed that both automata use identical $L_{R-\epsilon P}$ schemes with $a = 0.01$ and b assuming values 0.001, 0.003 and 0.01 respectively. The last one corresponds to a game of L_{R-P} schemes.

Figure 8.12 shows the nature of the solutions when L_{R-P} schemes are used by both automata (so that $a = b$) for different values of the parameter

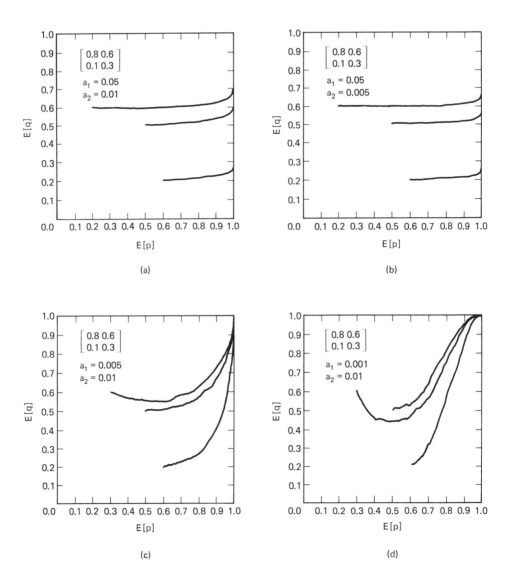

Figure 8.9: Convergence of $E(p)$ and $E(q)$ for different step sizes.

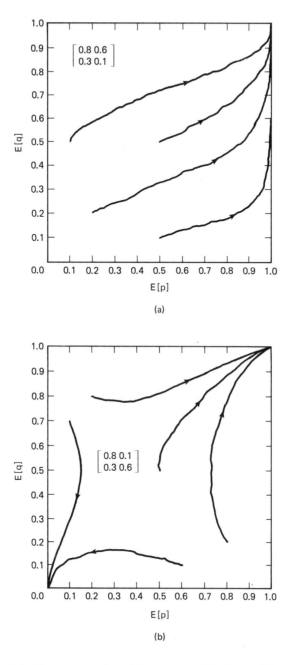

Figure 8.10: (a) Game matrix with one equilibrium; (b) game matrix with two equilibria.

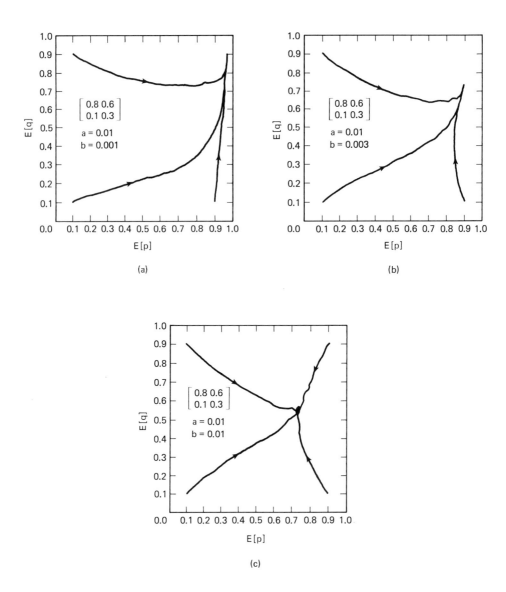

Figure 8.11: Convergence of $E[p]$ and $E[q]$ with $L_{R-\epsilon P}$ schemes.

a. Figures 8.12(a) and (b) indicate, respectively, how $(p(n), q(n))$ and $(E(p(n)), E(q(n)))$ evolve with stage number, for $a = b = 0.05$. In Fig. 8.12(c) and (d) the same quantities are depicted for $a = b = 0.005$. The convergence in these cases is in distribution and the limiting distribution is seen to depend on the value of the parameters.

Example 8.11: A (3×3) game is shown in Fig. 8.13. At $n = 0$ it is assumed that both automata choose their actions with equal probabilities [i.e., $p_i(0) = q_i(0) = \frac{1}{3}$, $i = 1, 2, 3$]. In such a case the equilibrium point to which the solutions converge depends on the game matrix. For example, when

$$D = \begin{bmatrix} 1.0 & 0.0 & 0.0 \\ 0.0 & 0.5 & 0.7 \\ 0.4 & 0.7 & 0.8 \end{bmatrix}$$

and (α_1^1, α_1^2) and (α_3^1, α_3^2) are equilibrium states, the solutions converge to the latter which does not correspond to the global optimum. In contrast to this, when

$$D = \begin{bmatrix} 1.0 & 0.8 & 0.0 \\ 0.8 & 0.5 & 0.4 \\ 0.4 & 0.4 & 0.8 \end{bmatrix}$$

the automata, starting at the same initial point in the state space, converge to the global optimum (α_1^1, α_1^2).

Comment 8.5: From the simulations above it is clear that the condition $\Delta M(n) > 0$ assured by Theorem 8.2 is not sufficient for global optimality in a game. However, it can be concluded that the convergence is to one of the equilibrium points with probability arbitrarily close to one. The state space can be partitioned in such a fashion that solutions with initial conditions in the neighborhood of an equilibrium point converge to it with a probability close to unity. In the absence of prior information it is reasonable to assume that all the automata start with equal initial probabilities for all their actions. As seen in the simulations, this ensures the convergence of the solutions to the global optimum in the (2×2) game. In contrast to this, in the (3×3) game, this condition does not assure global optimality. Hence, to achieve global optimality in identical payoff games, the reward structure must be designed in such a manner that the game matrix has a unique equilibrium point or the restriction on the type of information available to the players must be relaxed. In fact, if the actions chosen by the automata are

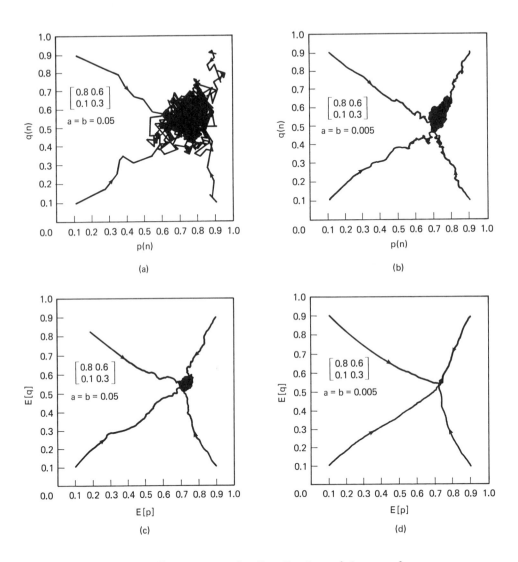

Figure 8.12: Convergence in distribution of L_{R-P} schemes.

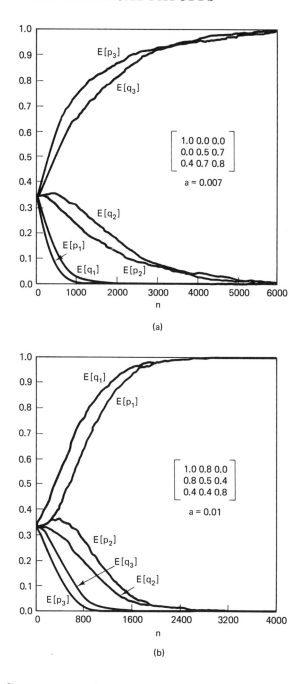

(a)

(b)

Figure 8.13: Convergence of expected values of action probabilities in games with multiple equilibria.

made known to other automata, estimator algorithms can be used and the automata will converge to the global maximum in all game environments (Thathachar and Sastry, 1987). However, this involves the increased computational burden of updating the estimates of all the elements of the game matrix.

8.6   Nonzero-Sum Games

It was mentioned in Section 8.2 that a fundamental problem of game theory is the determination of what can be considered as rational behavior in a game. The two-person zero-sum game and the identical payoff game discussed in Sections 8.4 and 8.5 respectively are two special classes of games for which rational solutions are well defined. Learning algorithms that converge to these solutions when uncertainty is present in the game matrix can therefore be considered to perform optimally.

In contrast to the games mentioned above, unique rational solutions are difficult to define for general N-person nonzero-sum games. As mentioned in Section 8.3, many different solution concepts have been proposed to reflect this diversity of situations encountered. While dealing with learning automata involved in such games, it is no longer possible to conclude from game theoretic arguments alone whether their performance is satisfactory. This in turn implies that the role of learning schemes, both in modeling and control problems, must be reevaluated in such situations. Although relatively little work currently exists in this area, the questions that arise are of fundamental importance and cannot be ignored. We devote this brief section to raising some of the issues involved by considering simple examples of nonzero-sum automata games.

The concept of an equilibrium point was defined in Section 8.3. An equilibrium point has the property that if the strategies of all the other players remain fixed, a player cannot improve his or her payoff by abandoning his or her equilibrium strategy. In Theorem 8.3 it was stated that if all the players in an identical payoff game use an L_{R-I} scheme (or more generally an absolutely expedient scheme of the reward-inaction type) and the game matrix has a unique equilibrium in pure strategies, the system will converge to this with a probability arbitrarily close to one. Alternately, if the game matrix has many equilibrium points, the system will evolve to one of these asymptotically. Using the identical procedure adopted in Section 8.5 it can be shown that the same result also applies to general N-person nonzero-sum games. That is, if the payoff structure in an N-person game has several equilibrium points and the players use an L_{R-I} scheme with an arbitrarily small step size, they will converge to one of the equilibrium points depending on the initial conditions.

In the section following, the interconnection of automata is discussed and it is shown that different interconnections lead to different nonzero-sum games. In all cases, the result above concerning the convergence of L_{R-I} schemes can be verified. In this section we shall only note the implications of the result in nonzero-sum games by considering some simple examples.

Consider the game matrix D_1 of a two-person nonzero-sum stochastic game with two learning automata as players. Let

$$D_1 = \left[\begin{array}{cc} (0.6, 0.6) & (0.4, 0.7) \\ (0.7, 0.4) & (0.1, 0.1) \end{array} \right]$$

where the pair $(0.6, 0.6)$, for example, denotes the probability of success to the two players when the strategy $(1,1)$ is played. In D_1, the strategies $(1,2)$ and $(2,1)$ are equilibria and all strategies other than $(2,2)$ are Pareto-optimal. The question that arises is which one of the strategies is to be considered a rational solution. From the point of view of the first player $(2,1)$ is optimal, while for the second player, the strategy $(1,2)$ is optimal. However, by the result described earlier, if the two players use L_{R-I} schemes the strategies would converge to either $(1,2)$ or $(2,1)$ depending upon the initial conditions.

A more interesting example is the Prisoner's Dilemma introduced in Example 8.1, which arises frequently in game theory while modeling problems in widely different fields. This game, which has been studied extensively by game theorists, leads to a fundamental paradox of nonzero-sum games. The following game matrix D_2 may be used to illustrate the nature of this paradox.

$$D_2 = \left[\begin{array}{cc} (0.2, 0.3) & (0.8, 0.2) \\ (0.1, 0.9) & (0.6, 0.8) \end{array} \right]$$

The only equilibrium in this case is the strategy $(1,1)$. However, it is the only one that is not Pareto-optimal. Since the first strategy of both players is dominant, there is no rational reason for choosing the strategy $(2,2)$, which is obviously superior. Hence, the Prisoner's Dilemma is the classic example of a situation where individual and group rationality do not concur. If both players use an L_{R-I} scheme, as in an identical payoff game, they will converge to $(1,1)$, which cannot be considered to exhibit group rationality in any sense. The convergence of the automata when both use L_{R-I} scheme is shown in Fig. 8.14. The evolution of $(p_1(n), q_1(n))$, $E[p_1(n), q_1(n)]$, and the

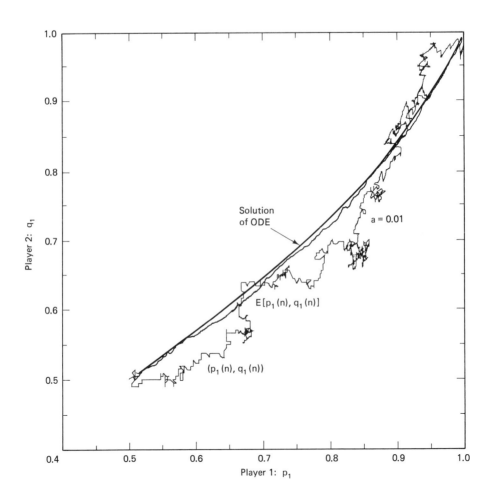

Figure 8.14: Convergence of action probabilities in nonzero-sum game.

solution of an equivalent ordinary differential equation (ODE) are all shown in the figure.

The simple examples discussed above underscore the fundamental nature of the difficulties encountered in automata games and clearly reveal that they depend more on game theoretic questions rather than on the nature of the learning algorithm used.

In a specific case, such as the Prisoner's Dilemma, the question can be asked whether the learning algorithm can be modified to converge asymptotically to a desired strategy. Recently, this problem has been studied by Thathachar and Sastry (1988) who showed that by interchanging the success and failure payoffs, automata using the L_{R-I} scheme converge to the cooperative solution (2,2). If each automaton has knowledge of the actions chosen by the other automaton after each play, then the use of estimator algorithms leads to a vastly improved rate of convergence. These results carry over to an N-person Prisoner's Dilemma.

The examples above indicate that advances in the design of learning algorithms can occur only in those cases where desired solutions can be defined from a game theoretic point of view. If different solutions are possible for a specific game, the aim of learning theory would be to generate different algorithms that converge to these solutions. In this context a second point is also worth noting. In most of the work on automata games, absolutely expedient algorithms are used since they are known to result in ϵ-optimality in two-person zero-sum games and identical payoff games. However, it might be interesting to investigate how other algorithms may perform in similar situations and whether the equilibrium points to which the automata converge have any game theoretic implications. The work by El-Fattah (1980) on market price formation, for example, uses a reinforcement scheme of the projection type (Poznyak, 1973) to demonstrate that all the automata converge in probability to a Nash solution.

8.7 Interconnected Automata

In the problems discussed thus far in this chapter, the interaction between different automata is provided by the environment. The latter reacts with a random response for a play (e.g. $\alpha(n) = [\alpha_{i_1}^1, \alpha_{i_2}^2, \ldots, \alpha_{i_N}^N]$) which is the combined effect of the actions chosen by all the participating automata. However, the automata do not interact directly with each other. It is generally recognized that the potential of learning units like the learning automaton can be increased significantly if rules can be established for their interconnection.

The very generality of the action sets $\{\alpha^j\}$ and environmental responses $\{\beta^j\}$, defined in Chapter 2, makes the definition of meaningful interconnections rather difficult. For example, the actions of an automaton can be parameter values that belong to $\mathcal{R}$, signals defined over an interval, or even instruction sets of a computer program. The response $\beta(n)$, on the other hand, is a real variable in the interval $[0,1]$ defining a measure of performance. Hence it is not an easy task to define networks of automata wherein two or more automata are connected in series or feedback as in dynamical systems.

Despite the difficulty above, it is shown in this section that different methods of interconnecting individual automaton-environment pairs is possible. In Section 8.7.1 synchronous models are defined wherein all the automata update their action probabilities synchronously based on the response of the environment. This is followed by the definition and discussion of sequential models in Section 8.7.2.

8.7.1   Synchronous Models

The methods of interconnecting individual automaton-environment pairs was introduced by Wheeler and Narendra (1985). These methods are based on plausible models of ways in which decision makers affect each other and are of interest both for modeling and control. An important consequence of this approach is that the resulting configurations can be viewed as games of automata with particular payoff structures. In specific cases, these game structures are such that results from automata game theory, which were derived in Sections 8.4 and 8.5, can be directly applied to them. In other cases the corresponding games lack the structure for which automata behavior is known and thereby provide an impetus for deriving new results in automata games. We present here only the highlights of the work contained in Wheeler and Narendra (1985) and refer the reader to the paper for further details.

The models described are such that all the automata choose their actions synchronously. For each model, the form of the interaction is stated and the corresponding game is derived. In each case the response of the environment associated with automaton A_i is denoted by $\widetilde{\beta}^i$ and the input (to A_i) by β^i, where the latter depends on the responses of all the automata. Convergence results are stated where possible by referring to results derived earlier in this chapter.

The Basic Structure: In the simplest case, two automaton environment pairs, $A_1 - E_1$ and $A_2 - E_2$, are connected in a feedback configuration as shown in Fig. 8.15(a). A_1 and A_2 are assumed to have two actions each and act into their respective environments at each time instant. The environment success probabilities are given by d_j^i, where the superscript refers to automaton i and the subscript to its jth action. In this model the response $\tilde{\beta}^i(n)$ of the pair $A_i - E_i$ is the input to the other automaton.

Figures 8.15(b)-(d) show a generalization of this idea to the case where N automata interact. The output of the automaton A_i's environment is represented by $\tilde{\beta}^i$ and an interaction matrix W is specified whose elements W_{ij} give the relative influence of the jth environment on the ith automaton. To obtain a normalized scalar input $W_{ij}\tilde{\beta}^j(n)$ to each automaton A_i, the elements W_{ij} are chosen so that $W_{ij} \geq 0$ and $\sum_{j=1}^{N} W_{ij} = 1$ for all $i = 1, 2, \ldots, N$. If an element W_{ij} is zero this implies that there is no feedback from the jth environment to the ith automaton. As will be shown, the analysis of such models reveals the importance of W_{ii} (the impact on A_i of its own environmental response) in determining the asymptotic behavior of automaton A_i. Assuming that the output of each environment is either a 0 or a 1, it follows that all the automata behave like Q-models described in Chapter 6. In the special case where all W_{ij} are equal and $W_{ij} = 1/N$, all the automata have the same performance criterion. The quantity fed back to each automaton is merely the number of successes produced by all the environments divided by N and we have an identical payoff game.

The structure described thus far can be considered as a model of a small organism (automaton) operating in a large world. The organism, responding to a feedback that is influenced by other organisms, is not aware whether or not its own actions have any influence on the measured output.

Analysis of the Basic Structure: The synchronous nature of the models described earlier makes it possible to view the interaction of the automata as a standard automaton game represented by a game matrix. In what follows, we shall analyze simple cases where two automata are involved in the game. The same concepts extend readily to feedback among N automata for $N > 2$.

In the simplest case where the input to A_1 depends on the output of A_2's environment E_2 and vice versa [Fig. 8.15(a)], the normal form of the game matrix is given directly by

$$
\Gamma = \begin{array}{cc}
 & \begin{array}{cc} \alpha_1^2 & \alpha_2^2 \end{array} \\
\begin{array}{c} \alpha_1^1 \\ \alpha_2^1 \end{array} & \left[\begin{array}{cc} (d_1^2, d_1^1) & (d_2^2, d_1^1) \\ (d_1^2, d_2^1) & (d_2^2, d_2^1) \end{array} \right]
\end{array}.
$$

The strategies of A_1 and A_2 correspond to the rows and columns of Γ.

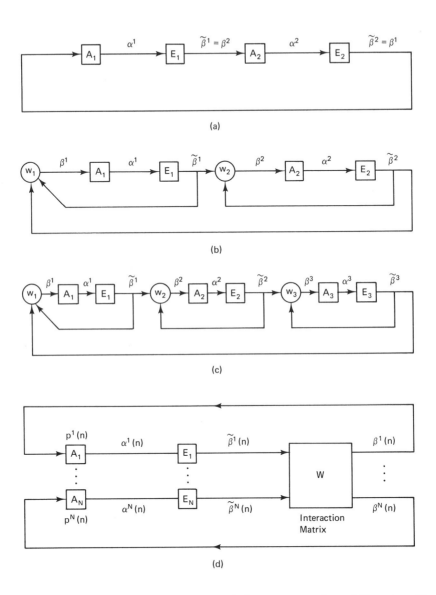

Figure 8.15: Automaton-Environment pair interconnections (*Courtesy Pergamon Press*).

Each ordered pair of Γ represents the expectation of success for A_1 and A_2 resulting from the corresponding strategy pair. From the game matrix it is evident that all four strategy pairs are equilibria. Further, for either action of A_2, A_1's actions are equally good and vice versa. Hence, as in the single automaton case, if there is no way of distinguishing between actions, on the average the automata will continue to choose each action with their initial probabilities. The same result carries over to the N-automata case where all the automata are connected in the fashion above. Simulations for two automata with success probabilities $d_1^1 = 0.6$, $d_2^1 = 0.1$, $d_1^2 = 0.7$, $d_2^2 = 0.2$ resulting in the game matrix

$$\Gamma = \begin{bmatrix} (0.7, 0.6) & (0.2, 0.6) \\ (0.7, 0.1) & (0.2, 0.1) \end{bmatrix}$$

reveal that the average probabilities $\tilde{p}_1(n)$ and $\tilde{q}_1(n)$ remain in the vicinity of their initial values independent of the step size a and number m of sample paths over which averages are taken (Table 8.1).

n	$\tilde{p}_1(n)$	$\tilde{q}_1(n)$	n	$\tilde{p}_1(n)$	$\tilde{q}_1(n)$
0	0.500	0.500	0	0.800	0.800
100	0.509	0.501	20	0.789	0.806
200	0.479	0.517	40	0.786	0.807
300	0.490	0.535	60	0.793	0.789
400	0.495	0.504	80	0.790	0.799
500	0.512	0.499	100	0.792	0.798
a=0.1	m=100		a=0.2	m=200	

Table 8.1

When an automaton receives responses from more than one environment, a more involved game results. Assuming that the two automata in Fig. 8.15(b) have success probabilities $0.8, 0.5, 0.3$ and $0.9, 0.1, 0.7$ respectively, and $W_1^1 = 0.4$, $W_2^1 = 0.6$, $W_1^2 = 0.6$, $W_2^2 = 0.4$, the game matrix has the form

$$\Gamma = \begin{bmatrix} (0.86, 0.84) & (0.38, 0.52) & (0.74, 0.76) \\ (0.74, 0.66) & (0.26, 0.34) & (0.62, 0.58) \\ (0.66, 0.54) & (0.18, 0.22) & (0.54, 0.46) \end{bmatrix}$$

In this case the first action is found to be dominant for both players so that α_1^1, α_1^2 is the globally optimal policy. The evolution of the probabilities

$\tilde{p}_i(n), \tilde{q}_i(n)$ for $i = 1, 2, 3$ shown in Table 8.2, when both automata use L_{R-I} schemes, reveals that the optimal policy is chosen asymptotically with a probability arbitrarily close to 1.

n	$\tilde{p}_1(n)$	$\tilde{p}_2(n)$	$\tilde{p}_3(n)$	$\tilde{q}_1(n)$	$\tilde{q}_2(n)$	$\tilde{q}_3(n)$
0	0.333	0.333	0.333	0.333	0.333	0.333
200	0.641	0.244	0.115	0.650	0.063	0.286
400	0.789	0.177	0.034	0.810	0.014	0.176
600	0.894	0.073	0.033	0.868	0.001	0.131
800	0.946	0.035	0.019	0.869	0.000	0.131
1000	0.961	0.026	0.012	0.913	0.000	0.087

Table 8.2

The example above indicates that the globally optimal policy can be achieved in specific cases. This is indeed the case provided no automaton has a zero weight corresponding to its own local response. In such a case the game matrix is such that each automaton chooses in the limit the action that is best in its own environment. However, the payoffs received by the automata are different from those they receive when unconnected. An interesting effect of interconnection is to redistribute the payoffs more equally. The automaton whose local environment is poorest (for its best action) improves its performance while the automaton with the best environment does worse when it is interconnected.

Other Structures of Interconnection: Many modifications of the structure described thus far are possible. We treat below four such variations and additional models can be developed easily by combining the features present in the different schemes. In contrast to the earlier model, these examples deal with changes in system structure as the automata operate.

Example 8.12: Changing Environments: In this case A_1 influences A_2 but A_2 does not influence A_1 (Fig. 8.16). Assuming that A_2 can operate in one of two stationary environments E_1^2 and E_2^2, the particular environment that it sees at any instant is determined by A_1's action. Qualitatively, one would conclude that using absolutely expedient schemes A_1 would converge to its best action so that in the limit A_2 would operate in the stationary environment determined by A_1. A_2 in turn would converge to the best action in this environment. This is confirmed by the following analysis.

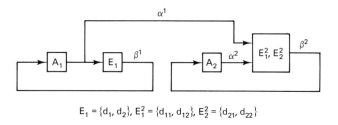

$E_1 = \{d_1, d_2\}, E_1^2 = \{d_{11}, d_{12}\}, E_2^2 = \{d_{21}, d_{22}\}$

Figure 8.16: Automaton A_1 determines A_2's environment (*Courtesy Pergamon Press*).

Analysis: The representation of the game above is particularly simple and we have

$$\Gamma = \begin{array}{c} \\ \alpha_1^1 \\ \alpha_2^1 \end{array} \begin{array}{cc} \alpha_1^2 & \alpha_2^2 \\ \left[\begin{array}{cc} (d_1, d_{11}) & (d_1, d_{12}) \\ (d_2, d_{21}) & (d_2, d_{22}) \end{array} \right] \end{array}.$$

From the game matrix it is clear that due to row dominance A_1 will converge to its best action independently of A_2, while A_2 will converge to the best action determined by A_1. The latter implies that A_2 may not receive its optimal payoff in some cases. The following simulation results are given for a typical example.

If $E_1 = \{0.8, 0.6\}$, $E_1^2 = \{0.3, 0.1\}$, $E_2^2 = \{0.1, 0.8\}$, $a = 0.03$, $m = 50$, it is obvious that the first action for A_1 and the second action for A_2 in the second environment are optimal when they are unconnected. However, since the first environment is chosen asymptotically by the actions of A_1, A_2 optimizes under the constraint by choosing its first action. The game matrix is

$$\Gamma_1 = \left[\begin{array}{cc} (0.8, 0.3) & (0.8, 0.1) \\ (0.6, 0.1) & (0.6, 0.8) \end{array} \right]$$

and the evolution of $\tilde{p}_1(n)$ and $\tilde{q}_1(n)$ is shown in Table 8.3.

n	$\tilde{p}_1(n)$	$\tilde{q}_1(n)$
0	0.500	0.500
200	0.754	0.303
400	0.915	0.400
600	0.964	0.593
800	0.992	0.754
1000	0.998	0.851

Table 8.3

In the case above A_1 acts independently and is not influenced by A_2. However, the two automata may be coordinated by giving the sum of the payoffs as the input to each player. In such a case the game matrix has the form

$$\Gamma_1^* = \begin{array}{c} \\ \alpha_1^1 \\ \alpha_2^1 \end{array} \begin{array}{cc} \alpha_1^2 & \alpha_2^2 \\ \left[\begin{array}{cc} d_1 + d_{11} & d_1 + d_{12} \\ d_2 + d_{21} & d_2 + d_{22} \end{array} \right]. \end{array}$$

If Γ_1^* has a unique equilibrium, then at least one player must have a dominant strategy and the automata will converge to the equilibrium with probability arbitrarily close to one if the step size is sufficiently small. If A_2 does not have a dominant strategy in Γ_1, then Γ_1^* may have two equilibria. In such a case, as shown in Section 8.5, the evolution of the Markov process depends critically on the initial conditions. The following examples illustrate these two cases. If $E_1 = \{0.8, 0.6\}$, $E_1^2 = \{0.8, 0.4\}, E_2^2 = \{0.1, 0.3\}$, the game matrix has the form

$$\Gamma_1^* = \left[\begin{array}{cc} 0.8 & 0.6 \\ 0.35 & 0.45 \end{array} \right]$$

when the mean value of the outputs of the two environments is fed back to the two automata. In this case both automata converge to their first actions with probabilities arbitrarily close to 1. If, however, we have the situation $E_1 = \{0.8, 0.6\}$, $E_1^2 = \{0.3, 0.1\}, E_2^2 = \{0.1, 0.8\}$, the game matrix has the form

$$\Gamma_1^* = \left[\begin{array}{cc} 0.55 & 0.45 \\ 0.35 & 0.70 \end{array} \right],$$

which has two equilibria corresponding to $\{\alpha_1^1, \alpha_1^2\}$ and $\{\alpha_2^1, \alpha_2^2\}$. Although the equilibrium point to which the automata converge in general depends on

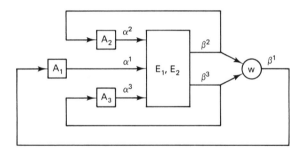

Figure 8.17: Automaton A_1 determines game for A_2 and A_3 (*Courtesy Pergamon Press*).

initial conditions, it is found that for the specific initial condition $p_1(0) = q_1(0) = 0.5$, the drift is toward the global optimum.

Example 8.13: A Coordinator. This example, shown in Fig. 8.17, generalizes the previous example by having A_1's actions determine the game A_2 and A_3 play. A_1 can be thought of as a coordinator whose input depends on the actions of A_2 and A_3. A_2 and A_3, on the other hand, are involved in a game with a time-varying matrix but are not aware of the game matrix at any instant. A_1's objective is to maximize the weighted sum of the payoffs to A_2 and A_3.

Let the environments E_1 and E_2 be represented by the game matrices

$$E_1 = \begin{bmatrix} d_{11}^{11}, d_{11}^{12} & d_{12}^{11}, d_{12}^{12} \\ d_{21}^{11}, d_{21}^{12} & d_{22}^{11}, d_{22}^{12} \end{bmatrix} ; \quad E_2 = \begin{bmatrix} d_{11}^{21}, d_{11}^{22} & d_{12}^{21}, d_{12}^{22} \\ d_{21}^{21}, d_{21}^{22} & d_{22}^{21}, d_{22}^{22} \end{bmatrix} .$$

In such a case the expected payoffs for the three players A_1, A_2, and A_3 are given by

$$M^1 = \frac{1}{2}\left(d_{jk}^{i1} + d_{jk}^{i2}\right); \; M^2 = d_{jk}^{i1}, \;\; M^3 = d_{jk}^{i2}$$

where i, j, k are the actions chosen by them.

In general, multiple equilibria can exist for this game problem and in such a case the theory is incomplete to predict the nature of convergence of the Markov process. However, it is found that if each automaton has only two actions and the automata start with equal probabilities, they will converge to the equilibrium corresponding to the global maximum.

The interconnection described above can also be considered an example in hierarchical control with nonidentical payoffs. The coordinator represents

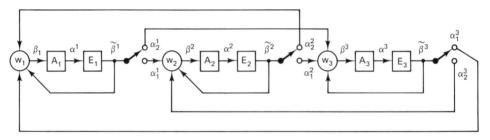

Figure 8.18: Action of automaton A_i determines who receives response of E_i (*Courtesy Pergamon Press*).

an automaton at the first level while (A_2, A_3, E_1) and (A_2, A_3, E_2), representing automata games, are located at the second level.

Example 8.14: In this case, the action of the automaton A_i determines the set of responses it is to receive. This means that the action of the automaton implicitly determines a weight vector W_{ij} $(j = 1, 2, \ldots, N)$. Or alternately, the environment changes instantaneously as a function of the action chosen.

Example 8.15: In contrast to Example 8.14, in the case shown in Fig. 8.18 the action of the automaton A_i determines which of the other automata will receive its response. Since the actions of an automaton can correspond to different physical entities, such models may arise naturally in complex systems. In each of the cases above, once the specific interconnection of the automata is known, the corresponding game matrix can be determined relatively easily. As evidenced from the examples discussed earlier, only some of these are amenable to mathematical analysis using the results of learning theory and automata games discussed in Sections 8.4 and 8.5. With increasing use of interconnected automata for both modeling and control purposes based on heuristic arguments, it is to be expected that cases will occur quite frequently when the corresponding game matrix cannot be easily analyzed. Undoubtedly these will provide motivation for further research in the area of games of automata.

8.7.2   Sequential Models

In the interconnected models described in Section 8.7.1, all the automata act synchronously. In contrast to this we describe models in this section in which only one automaton (or decision maker) acts at any time instant. The action chosen then determines the next automaton to act. The same action also generates a payoff at that instant. Such a sequential model can be viewed as a network of automata in which control passes from one automaton to another. At each instant one decision maker controls the state transitions of the decision process and the goal of all the automata is to optimize some overall performance criterion.

A Tree Structure: A simple network with a tree structure is shown in Fig. 8.19(a). In this case a definite order exists in which the automata can act. The automaton A_0 chooses an action that determines whether A_1 or A_2 is to act. This automaton in turn selects the automaton at the next lower level. This continues until an automaton at the bottom level is chosen. The action of the last automaton produces a response from a random environment, which in turn is used by all the automata on the selected path, to update their probabilities. The hierarchical structure of this form, proposed by Thathachar and Ramakrishnan (1981), was discussed in detail in Chapter 7.

In the model above it is evident that the principal aim is to choose the best action at the last level. The hierarchical structure is used mainly to improve the speed of the search procedure. The model can be extended in many ways. As stated, every automaton in a path updates its probabilities only after a complete path has been established. However, at every level there may be local responses for each automaton. In such a case a single automaton may update its probabilities both at the instant it receives a local response as well as when it receives a global response. As mentioned in Chapter 7, such problems have been considered by Thathachar and Ramakrishnan (1981) and Baba (1984).

Directed Network: Figure 8.19(b) retains the idea of local response, but dispenses with the branching property of a tree. This implies that theoretically every automaton at any level can choose any of the automata at the next level. Hence, once again, a sequenced cycle is well defined and the control passes back to automaton A_0 at the end of the cycle. Many directed flow problems have this structure and maximizing the average reward per cycle is equivalent to finding the optimal path through the network.

A General Network: The models above can be further generalized as shown in Figure 8.19(c) so that there is no ordering of an action sequence giving rise to a cycle or path through the network. Any automaton can choose any other automaton. The action of the first automaton also generates a random response that may be received by one or more automata. A possible goal of such interconnected automata may be to maximize the

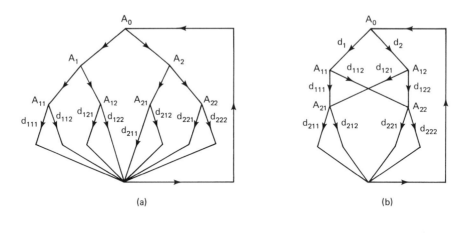

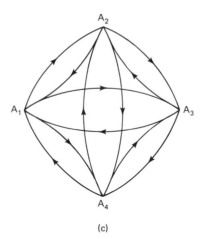

Figure 8.19: (a) tree; (b) directed network; (c) general network (*Courtesy Pergamon Press*).

average reward per time instant. However, some constraints may have to be imposed on the overall system, in order to have a well posed problem. Such a problem is discussed in detail in Section 8.8.

Random Selection of Automata: In the previous three cases considered, an action of one automaton determines deterministically the next automaton that is to act. This can be generalized by defining an action to be a probability distribution over a set of automata accessible at any instant. For example, in Fig. 8.19(b), A_0 may have three actions, each of which corresponds to a different probability distribution that A_1 or A_2 will be selected. As shown in Section 8.8 this problem formulation is equivalent to the control of Markov chains.

8.7.3 Hierarchies and Games

Both synchronous and sequential models of interconnected learning automata introduced in Sections 8.7.1 and 8.7.2 can be used for modeling as well as control purposes. The generalizations in Chapter 7 of a simple learning automaton to include multiple environments, time-varying environments, and hierarchies form the basis of these models. Each model gives rise to a game of automata. Although in some cases the game can be analyzed using known analytical results in learning theory as well as automata games, in other cases the difficulty in analyzing the corresponding automata game identifies the need for further research into automata behavior in the specific game discussed.

One general class of models that is both analytically tractable and practically attractive combines hierarchies and games and has both sequential and synchronous componenets. Models in this class are particularly well suited for representing decisions made at multiple levels using decentralized decison makers. It is well known that many complex problems in decision making can be posed as hierarchical multiobjective optimization problems. Recently, Narendra and Parthasarathy (1988) modeled such problems by several hierarchies of learning automata involved in identical payoff games at the various levels and showed that if absolutely expedient algorithms are used by all the automata the overall performance of the system will improve at every stage. Although the result was stated for an arbitrary number of hierarchies and levels, we describe briefly in this section the interaction of two hierarchies of automata at two levels. We shall denote such a collective as H_2^2 where the superscript denotes the number of hierarchies and the subscript the number of levels:

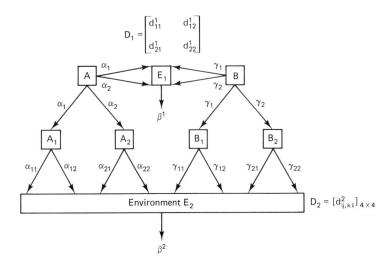

Figure 8.20: The Collective H_2^2.

The Collective H_2^2: Figure 8.20 shows a collective H_2^2 in which two automata A and B are at the highest level of the hierarchy. At any stage n automaton A performs one of two actions α_1 or α_2 with probabilities $p_1(n)$ and $p_2(n) = 1 - p_1(n)$. Similarly automaton B performs action γ_1 or γ_2 with probabilities $q_1(n)$ and $q_2(n) = 1 - q_1(n)$. Automata A_i and $B_i (i = 1, 2)$ are located at the second level and the choice of actions $\alpha_1, \alpha_2, \gamma_1$ and γ_2 by the first level automata also correspond to the choice of automata A_1, A_2, B_1, and B_2 respectively. At any instant, all the automata at a specific level play synchronously and are involved in a game. At the next instant the automata chosen at the next level play synchronously and are involved in a game at that level. After an entire cycle is completed, during which two games are played at the two levels (or N games are played, if there are N levels), all the automata update their action probabilities. The total expected payoff for all the automata can be defined as a weighted sum of the expected payoffs at the various levels. Under the conditions above the following result is given in Narendra and Parthasarathy (1988):

> Let every automaton in the collective H_2^2 described above update its action probabilities at every stage using the SL_{R-I} algorithm. If the composite response $\beta(n) \in [0, 1]$ of the overall environment to each of the automata is a weighted sum of the responses at each level and the step size of the automata in the various levels are chosen to be sufficiently small and satisfying the

conditions in Chapter 7 [Eq. (7.55)], then the expected payoff of the overall system is non-decreasing at every stage.

The result above also carries over to a collective H_N^M with M hierarchies and N levels. The model above indicates that hierarchies and automata games can be combined in novel fashions. For example, the theory can be extended readily to more general cases where each automaton operates in one or more stationary random environments while simultaneously participating in one or more games. The responses from these different environments are included as part of the normalized overall response. Models such as the one above raise new theoretical questions since the use of responses from many environments to update action probabilities leads to Q- and S- model games which have not been investigated in detail.

8.7.4   Learning in Automata Networks with Context Vectors

In Chapter 7 some methods of generalizing the learning automaton model using a context vector at every stage were suggested. In one of the methods discussed by Williams (1986) (refer to Fig. 7.16), the operation of the system consists of the following four phases:

(i) The environment picks a context input randomly.

(ii) The automaton chooses an action randomly according to a distribution determined by the context input.

(iii) Based on the action chosen and the context vector, the environment produces a random response.

(iv) The automaton changes its internal state according to some specified function of its current state, the action chosen, the context input, and the evaluation by the environment.

Such a learning automaton, which has a parametrized state and context vector, is defined as a generalized stochastic learning automaton. The advantage of such generalized automata, claimed by Williams, is that a collection of such automata can be interconnected into networks (Fig. 8.21). Actions of individual automata are treated as outputs and in turn serve as context inputs to other automata. Some automata in the network also receive a context input from the environment. If the response of the environment is treated as a reinforcement by all the automata, we have an identical payoff

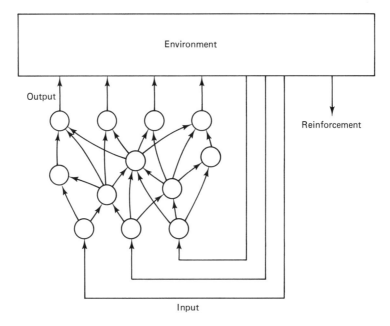

Figure 8.21: A network of generalized stochastic automata.

game similar to that considered in Section 8.5. However, the objective of the automata in the present case is to determine how the weight vectors are to be adjusted so that the performance of the system improves in some sense.

It is clear from the description above that the network of automata bears a striking resemblance to multilayered artificial neural networks or connectionist networks. In fact, it is evident that the selection of the specific form of the generalization was strongly influenced by such networks. The essential difference between the two lies in the fact that although the weights in artificial neural networks are adjusted on the basis of the error between the output of the network and some desired output, the adjustment in the network of automata described above depends on the random response of the environment and is similar in spirit to the learning schemes discussed in this book. In both cases, some performance function is improved by the adjustment of the weight vectors.

Although the suggested generalization above is interesting and certainly merits further exploration, the following comments, some of which reflect the lessons learned from the history of adaptive systems, are worth noting:

(i) Despite the practical successes of artificial neural networks as pattern recognizers, very few theoretical results exist regarding the nature of the input-output mappings that are realized by them even in deterministic situations. These difficulties are compounded in the stochastic case when generalized automata are interconnected.

(ii) In the 1960s considerable work was carried out on sensitivity methods in adaptive control. Using such methods, unknown dynamical systems were controlled by adjusting a weight vector in a controller along the gradient of a performance function using input-output measurements. Although the resulting procedure proved efficient for the case when the weight vectors were adjusted slowly, it eventually led to theoretical and practical difficulties even in a deterministic context. In particular, the stability of the overall system could not be assured when the controller was used on-line (Narendra and Annaswamy, 1988). Many of the deterministic and stochastic methods currently used in adaptive control were developed precisely to overcome these difficulties.

(iii) The powerful theorems given earlier in this chapter could be derived mainly because of the simplicity of the automaton structure. As the structure of the automaton grows more complex and begins to resemble more of a parameterized controller with actions and responses that are real variables, which permit the use of an algebra of interconnections, obtaining convergence proofs for the weight vectors becomes significantly more difficult. It is therefore not surprising that the results reported on generalized networks are considerably weaker than those given in this chapter. The analytical difficulties encountered in such cases are quite similar to those that arise while using gradient methods in stochastic dynamical systems.

The use of learning schemes in many practical problems has clearly indicated a need for generalizing the structure of the automaton. In particular, if collectives of automata are to be used as decision makers in distributed stochastic systems, the information fed back to each automaton must be increased substantially. Thus, despite the cautionary comments above, the authors feel that studies of different types of interconnected learning automata, including those described by Williams (1986), should be pursued vigorously if a viable theory is to be developed for practically attractive systems. One alternative that deserves further attention is to retain the structure of the network introduced in this section but determine the weights using the learning schemes described in earlier chapters. Since the problem can then be posed as games of automata with identical payoff, the results of this chapter can be directly applied. The drawback of such a scheme, however, would be the large number of automata that must be used and the consequent decrease in speed of convergence.

8.8   Decentralized Control of Markov Chains

As stated in Section 8.2, decentralization is called for when complete information exchange needed for centralized decision making in a system is impractical due to large spatial separation of the decision makers or limited communication channel bandwidth. In addition to system size, uncertainties regarding system parameters, control actions taken by other decision makers and external events, as well as uncertainties concerning the outcome that may result from the choice of a given action all contribute to the complexity of these problems. Even in the absence of these uncertainties it is well known that the coordination of decentralized decision makers is a formidable problem. The presence of the uncertainty introduces an additional identification problem. This feature motivates the use of an adaptive or learning approach. By using such an approach the different controllers used in the system attempt to converge to optimal strategies by improving their performance on-line, based on the response of the overall system. In this section we present a recent result due to Wheeler and Narendra (1986), which is applicable to an important class of stochastic systems: finite state Markov decision processes. The principal result derived is that, without prior knowledge of the transition probabilities or rewards, the collection of controllers will converge to the set of actions that maximizes the long-term expected reward per unit time obtained by the system.

8.8.1   Control of Markov Chains

Finite state Markov decision processes (or controlled Markov chains) have been discussed extensively in the literature. They arise when an action taken at one of the states of a Markov chain determines the transition probabilities to the other states as well as the rewards or costs that accrue from such transitions. The control problem can be stated as follows:

Let $\Phi = \{\phi_1, \phi_2, \ldots, \phi_N\}$ be the state space of a finite Markov chain $\{x_n\}_{n \geq 0}$ and $\alpha^i = \{\alpha^i_1, \alpha^i_2, \ldots, \alpha^i_{r_i}\}$ be the finite set of controls or decisions (or in the automata context, actions) available in state ϕ_i. The state transition probabilities $t_j^i(k)$ and rewards $r_j^i(k)$ depend on the starting state ϕ_i, the ending state ϕ_j and the action α_k^i used in ϕ_i. The goal is to choose the set of actions, or policy, $\alpha = [\alpha_{i_1}^1, \alpha_{i_2}^2, \ldots, \alpha_{i_N}^N] \in \mathcal{A} = \alpha^1 \times \alpha^2 \times \cdots \times \alpha^N$ that minimizes

$$J(\alpha) = \lim_{n \to \infty} \frac{1}{n} E \left[\sum_{t=0}^{n-1} r(x(t), x(t+1), \alpha) \right] \qquad (8.34)$$

where $r(x(t), x(t+1), \alpha)$ is the reward generated by a transition from $x(t)$ to $x(t+1)$ using the policy α.

In the formulation above the set of policies $\mathcal{A}$ is limited to stationary, non-randomized policies. Using the assumption that the Markov chain corresponding to each policy α is ergodic, it follows from Eq. (8.34) that the expected reward per step $J(\alpha)$ can be written in terms of the stationary probabilities $\pi_i(\alpha)$ of the states ϕ_i as

$$J(\alpha) = \sum_{i=1}^N \pi_i(\alpha) \sum_{j=1}^N t_j^i(\alpha) r_j^i(\alpha).$$

Many efforts have been reported in the literature that deal with the determination of the optimal policy α_{opt} as well as its properties when complete information concerning the transition probabilities $t_j^i(k)$ and the corresponding rewards $r_j^i(k)$ are available. A dynamic programming solution is given in (Howard 1960) but the computational cost increases dramatically with the number of states N. Methods of determining a bound on the difference in performance due to any policy α and the optimal policy α_{opt} have also been reported (White, 1963; Variaya, 1978). To get around the problem of high dimensionality, a two-layer scheme with two control algorithms operating on two time scales has been suggested but has only been partially successful (Forestier and Varaiya, 1978). In view of these difficulties, decentralization is found to be highly desirable even in cases where complete information regarding the system is available.

Quite often, the information required to solve the problem above using dynamic programming methods may not be available. In particular, the transition probabilities $t_j^i(k)$ and the corresponding rewards $r_j^i(k)$ associated with various actions may be either constant but unknown or vary with time. This leads to a problem for which adaptive solutions are required based on on-line measurements of the process. As in adaptive control theory (Narendra and Annaswamy, 1988), an indirect or a direct approach can be used to solve the optimization problem. In the former case the information about the unknown parameters must be estimated on-line even as the control action is updated. General procedures for dealing with such a situation based on the estimates of an unknown parameter vector θ (Mandl, 1974; Borkar and Varaiya, 1979; Kumar and Lin, 1982) have been reported. In contrast to this, a direct approach would involve performing an action, evaluating its effect on the performance criterion over a finite interval of time, and using the information in turn to determine the next action. In this section we use such an approach, based on learning automata, which avoids much of the computational difficulty. No specific knowledge of either $t^i_j(k)$ or $r^i_j(k)$ is assumed other than that the latter are normalized to lie in the interval $[0,1]$. Each automaton, in attempting to improve its performance, merely selects an action using a learning algorithm, waits for a response, and updates its strategy.

8.8.2   Decentralized Control Problem

The states of the controlled Markov chain $\{x(n)\}_{n \geq 0}$ where at least two actions are available are distinguished as action states. If Φ^* is the set of all action states $\Phi^* \subset \Phi$ and $|\Phi^*| = N^* \leq N$. If the Markov chain is in state $\phi_i \in \Phi^*$, an automaton A^i is used to choose an action α^i_k out of the action set α^i. This action consists of the probability vector $t^i(k)$ governing the state transition from state ϕ_i. The component $t^i_j(k)$ determines the probability of transfer to state ϕ_j under this action. As the chain moves from state ϕ_i to state ϕ_j, the reward $r^i_j(k)$ is generated. If, however, $\phi_i \notin \Phi^*$, there is only one transition vector t^i and reward vector r^i governing the chain in this state.

The principal features of the decentralized approach are:

(i)   The automaton A_i at state ϕ_i is unaware of the existence of the automata in the other states, the elements of their action sets, or the particular actions chosen by them. Even the number of states N is not needed by A_i. In this sense the scheme is very similar in spirit to the automata game discussed in earlier sections.

(ii)   Every automaton operates in the Markov chain environment exactly in the same fashion as it would if the environment were stationary. Specifically, each automaton uses an identical algorithm, which is ϵ-optimal in a stationary environment.

(iii)   The choice of the action α^i_k at any state ϕ_i is determined by the current action probabilities of the automaton at that state.

8.8.3 Choice of Action at State ϕ_i

The action set of the automaton A_i was defined as $\alpha^i = \{\alpha^i_1, \alpha^i_2, \ldots, \alpha^i_{r_i}\}$. It is assumed that the first time the Markov chain enters the state ϕ_i, the automaton A_i chooses its actions with equal probabilities. The specific action α^i_k chosen determines the new state ϕ_j from the transition probabilities $t^i_j(k)$ $(k = 1, 2, \ldots, r_i)$. Now A_j chooses an action from its action set. As the Markov chain moves from state to state, information concerning the cumulative reward generated by the process is transferred to the new state. If $x_n \neq \phi_i$, the automaton A_i does not operate.

Let the process return to state ϕ_i at time n_i, a local time scale corresponding to the $(n_i + 1)^{th}$ visit to ϕ_i $(n_i = 0, 1, 2, \ldots)$. A_i now receives the following two pieces of information from a coordinator.

(i) the cumulative reward generated up to time n

(ii) the global time n

From these, A_i computes the incremental reward $\Delta \rho^i_k(n_i)$ generated since n_i (when the chain was last in ϕ_i) and the corresponding elapsed global time $\Delta \eta^i_k(n_i)$. These increments are added to their current cumulative totals $\rho^i_k(n_i)$ and $\eta^i_k(n_i)$ resulting in new totals $\rho^i_k(n_i + 1)$ and $\eta^i_k(n_i + 1)$.

The environment response to the action of the automaton A_i is then taken to be

$$\beta^i(n_i + 1) = \frac{\rho^i_k(n_i + 1)}{\eta^i_k(n_i + 1)}.$$

Since $r^i_j(k)$ are normalized, $\beta^i(n_i)$ lies in the interval [0,1].

Algorithm: The automaton A_i uses the following updating algorithm.
If $\alpha(n) = \alpha^i_j$ then

$$p^i_j(n + 1) = \ p^i_j(n) + a\beta^i(n)[1 - p^i_j(n)] - b[1 - \beta^i(n)]p^i_j(n)$$
$$p^i_k(n + 1) = \ p^i_k(n) - a\beta^i(n)p^i_k(n) + b[1 - \beta^i(n)][\tfrac{1}{r_i - 1} - p^i_k(n)]$$
$$0 < a < 1, \quad 0 \le b < 1, \quad k \neq j$$

described in Chapter 6.

The essential features of the algorithm may be summarized as follows:

(i) If at time n, $x(n) = \phi_i \in \Phi^*$, only A_i updates its probabilities.

(ii) If $x(n) \in \Phi - \Phi^*$, no control action is taken but the reward generated and one instant of global time are added to their respective current totals.

(iii)   In the intervening time between two visits to any state ϕ_i, no knowledge of the sequence of states visited is provided to A_i. Only the current value of the total reward and the global time n are needed by A_i to update its strategy.

In Wheeler and Narendra (1986) and Wheeler (1985), it is shown that this procedure results in the convergence of the overall system to the global optimal policy α_{opt}. Although the details of the proof are found in these references we summarize below the argument used.

8.8.4   Convergence to the Optimal Policy

Since the action set of the automaton A_i at the state ϕ_i contains r_i elements ($r_i \geq 1$), there are $\prod_{i=1}^{N} r_i$ stationary policies for the control of the Markov chain. Each policy corresponds to the choice of a pure strategy at every state. Since the Markov chain is assumed to be ergodic for each control policy α, the process is not absorbed in any state or subset of states for such a policy. Hence the chain visits every state an infinite number of times.

From the assumption above it is next shown that the Markov chain control problem can be asymptotically approximated by an identical payoff game Γ of N automata. Further, Γ is shown to have a unique pure strategy equilibrium. Hence, by the results of Section 8.5, in particular Theorem 8.3, the following theorem can be stated.

Theorem 8.4: If, in the Markov chain problem discussed thus far, all the automata use an SL_{R-I} scheme, the expected gain $M(n)$ of the chain will be a submartingale. Since the corresponding game Γ has a unique pure strategy equilibrium α^* with corresponding success $d(\alpha^*)$, then for any $\epsilon > 0$ there exists a constant a^* with $0 < a^* < 1$ such that for any $0 < a < a^*$

$$\lim_{n \to \infty} E[M(n)] > d(\alpha^*) - \epsilon.$$

In other words, the group of learning algorithms is ϵ-optimal in the controlled Markov chain.

Simulation of a Controlled Markov Chain: To clarify the ideas presented in this section we present here a simple example of a Markov chain with six states described in Wheeler and Narendra (1985). The six states are denoted by $\phi_i(i = 1, 2, 3, 4, 5, 6)$ but ϕ_1 and ϕ_2 are the only action states. The transition probabilities from $\phi_i(i = 3, 4, 5,$ and $6)$ to all states of the chain are fixed while the automata A_1 and A_2, which operate when the chain is in state ϕ_1 and ϕ_2, can change these transition probabilities. We assume that A_1 has two actions corresponding to two transition probability vectors from ϕ_1 to any other state. Similarly A_2 has two actions. This implies that if T is the (6×6) transition matrix of probabilities, the last four rows of the matrix are fixed while each of the first two rows can be filled in two different ways. Hence the Markov chain can have a maximum of four stationary transition matrices corresponding to the pure strategies of the automata A_1 and A_2. Denoting these by T^{ij} $(i,j = 1,2)$ where i corresponds to the ith action of automaton A_1 and j to the jth action of A_2, in this example T^{ij} has the following form

$$
T^{ij} = \begin{bmatrix}
& & t^1(i) & & & \\
& & t^2(j) & & & \\
0.7 & 0.2 & 0.1 & 0.0 & 0.0 & 0.0 \\
0.1 & 0.1 & 0.8 & 0.0 & 0.0 & 0.0 \\
0.0 & 0.0 & 0.7 & 0.2 & 0.1 & 0.0 \\
0.0 & 0.0 & 0.0 & 0.5 & 0.1 & 0.4
\end{bmatrix}
$$

where $t^1(i)$ is the first row vector corresponding to the ith action of automaton A_1 and $t^2(j)$ is the second row vector corresponding to the jth action of A_2. Let

$$t^1(1) = (0, 0.1, 0.1, 0, 0, 0.8); \quad t^1(2) = (0.2, 0, 0, 0.2, 0.6, 0)$$
$$t^2(1) = (0.1, 0.2, 0.3, 0, 0, 0.4); \quad t^2(2) = (0, 0.9, 0, 0, 0, 0.1)$$

Corresponding to any transition from ϕ_i $(i = 3, 4, 5, 6)$ to any other state is a reward that can be denoted by a row vector r^i. However, in action states 1 and 2 the reward also depends on the action chosen and is denoted by $r^i(j)$ $i = 1, 2$, $j = 1, 2$. In the problem under consideration

$$r^1(1) = (0, 0, 0, 0, 0, 0.8) \quad r^1(2) = (0, 0, 0, 0.5, 0.1, 0)$$
$$r^2(1) = (0.9, 0.2, 0.2, 0, 0, 1) \quad r^2(2) = (0, 0.2, 0, 0, 0, 0)$$

and

$$r^3 = (1, 0, 0, 0, 0, 0)$$
$$r^4 = (0, 1, 1, 0, 0, 0)$$
$$r^5 = (0, 0, 0, 0, 1, 0)$$
$$r^6 = (0, 0, 0, 1, 1, 1).$$

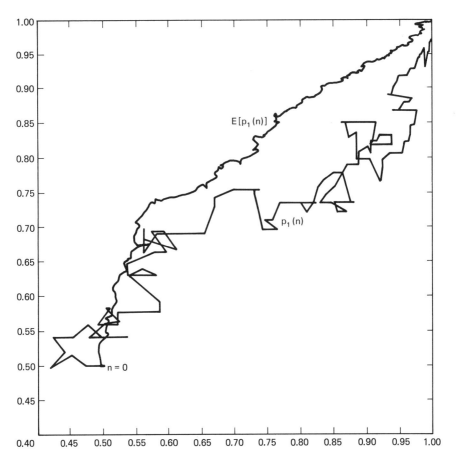

Figure 8.22: Sample path and mean path convergence of action probability $p_1(n) = [p_1^1(n), p_1^2(n)]$.

Assuming that all the transition probabilities and corresponding rewards are known, the average reward can be computed if both A_1 and A_2 choose one of their pure strategies since the corresponding Markov chain is assumed to be ergodic.

For the four stationary policies of A_1 and A_2 this computation results in the following game matrix

$$\Gamma = \left[\begin{array}{cc} 0.782 & 0.530 \\ 0.620 & 0.456 \end{array} \right].$$

Clearly the optimal policy is given by (α_1^1, α_1^2) corresponding to the first actions of both A_1 and A_2.

In the controlled Markov chain under consideration neither the transition probabilities nor the associated rewards are known to the automata, which follow the updating procedure described in this section. The convergence of the action probabilities $p_1^1(n)$ of A_1 and $p_1^2(n)$ of A_2 are shown in Fig. 8.22 when a step size $a = 0.06$ is used. A typical sample path as well as a mean learning curve averaged over 30 sample paths are included. Convergence of the mean curve to $(0.95, 0.95)$ occurred in 1900 steps of global time.

8.9 Conclusion

The behavior of learning automata in sequential stochastic games is considered in this chapter. Each automaton participating in the game operates with no information concerning the payoff structure, the number of other automata involved, the strategies available to them, or the specific actions chosen by them at any stage. Based entirely on the response of the environment it updates its action probabilities using one of the learning algorithms described in Chapters 3 and 4. In two-person zero-sum games it is shown that when the automata use L_{R-I} schemes, they converge to actions which, according to game theory, would be considered rational. In identical payoff games as well as some nonzero-sum games, it is shown that when every member of the collective of automata uses a reward-inaction absolutely expedient scheme the overall performance improves monotonically. The important point is that the learning scheme used by each automaton in these cases is precisely what it would use in a stationary environment to achieve ϵ-optimality.

When the structure of the identical payoff game is such that a unique equilibrium point exists corresponding to the global optimum, the automata converge to this value with a probability arbitrarily close to one. The important problem of controlling a Markov chain using decentralized automata discussed in Section 8.8 corresponds to this case.

The discussion in Section 8.7 centered around the problem of interconnecting automata. The fact that decentralized automata, interconnected as parts of games and hierarchies, can improve their performance as a collective bodes well for their application in complex decision-making problems in the future. Further, the structures that are evolving from such interconnections also bear close resemblance to multilayered neural networks suggesting the distinct possibility of synergism between the two fields.

Chapter 9

Applications of Learning Automata

9.1 Introduction

Although the theory of learning automata has made significant advances in the last two decades as indicated by the developments in the earlier chapters, the application of the theory to real-world problems has not kept a similar pace. Several potential applications have been suggested in the literature, but it has become increasingly clear that certain criteria must be satisfied in any specific problem if learning schemes are to be truly effective. Perhaps the most significant feature of the models of both stationary environments in Chapters 2–6 and nonstationary environments in Chapter 7 is that remarkably little is assumed about their input-output relationship. In many real applications considerably more information is generally available regarding the environment. Naturally, in such cases, the additional knowledge is incorporated in the model of the overall system to achieve more precise control. This may partially account for the fact that some of the applications suggested in the literature appear rather contrived and the results reported suffer in comparison with other standard approaches.

Learning or adaptation is generally needed in situations where the plant or environment to be controlled or identified has characteristics that are unknown or vary with time. If these time-variations are sufficiently slow and can be assumed to be constant over an interval of time T, the learning algorithms obviously have to converge over a period which is a fraction of the time interval T. Hence, the speed of adaptation becomes a critical factor in such cases. As the number of actions of an automaton increases, it was seen in the simulation studies in the previous chapters that the speed of convergence of the automaton decreases drastically and is determined by the number of events that take place in a specified interval in real time. Hence, for learning algorithms of the type discussed in this book to be viable alternatives in control problems, it is necessary that a sufficient number of events, relative to the number of actions, takes place in the interval of time over which the automata are to converge. Such questions arise in the routing problems discussed in Section 9.2. In contrast to this, in decision-making problems, where the automaton is not driven by external events but by decisions made and evaluated internally in the system, the rate of convergence of the automaton will be determined by the number of elementary operations involved per iteration of the algorithm and the execution time taken by the CPU. This in turn will determine whether the learning scheme would be effective in making decisions on-line. Such applications are discussed in Section 9.3.

As a result of the considerations above, very few practical situations exist where a single automaton with a large number of actions will prove effective without a significant generalization of the existing theory. From the results of Chapter 8 it is evident that the power of the automaton approach is best realized in complex systems when several automata operate in a distributed fashion with each automaton having a small number of actions. Such situations arise frequently in large scale systems, where practical constraints make distributed decentralized control mandatory. Traffic routing in communication networks, scheduling in computer networks, and decision making in economic networks are examples of such systems.

Essential to the operation of the automaton is the response of the environment to any of its actions. If several automata are used as controllers in a distributed system and operate in a decentralized fashion, the updating of all the automata must be based on feedback of information from the environment. In a complex system, obviously many levels of information feedback are possible. However, if the theoretical results of Chapter 8 are to be used, a random realization of a performance criterion must be available to each automaton if the mixed strategies of some or all the automata are to be updated. This poses a rather serious constraint in many applications since such feedback may be practically infeasible. Even assuming that a global performance criterion can be fed back, existing algorithms may have to be modified to achieve robustness in the presence of delays and distortions in feedback.

From the foregoing discussion, some of the desirable features of a system in which learning algorithms are to be used may be listed as follows:

(i) The system must be sufficiently complex and involve large operational uncertainties. The uncertainties must be such that a detailed mathematical model of the overall system cannot be formulated.

(ii) The system must be amenable to distributed control. Each decision maker chooses, at every stage, one out of a finite number of actions or decisions.

(iii) Feedback to every decentralized decision maker must be provided by some random realization of a performance criterion.

(iv) For the use of learning algorithms to be practically viable in large systems, the system must be such that small improvements in performance will result in significant economic returns.

How attractive learning schemes will prove to be in practical applications will depend to a large extent on how well the criteria above are satisfied. In the sections following we present several potential areas where learning schemes may have distinct advantages over existing methods. These range from the problem of routing in networks (dealt with in Section 9.2), to task scheduling in computer networks, data compression in image transmission, relaxation labeling and pattern classification (discussed in Section 9.3). Although routing problems have been simulated extensively on the computer for over a decade, some of the other problems are relatively new and their viability as applications has yet to be determined. The purpose of including all of them in this chapter is to indicate that learning schemes may prove attractive in a wide spectrum of seemingly different problems, where the amount of available information is quite limited.

In recent years researchers in areas such as image processing, image understanding, and robotics have found approaches based on learning automata theory to be particularly attractive. This may be attributed to the fact that a substantial amount of uncertainty exists in such systems rendering even a proper formulation of the design problem difficult. In the opinion of the authors, it is in such problems that the ideas developed in this book will find wide application in the future.

9.2   Routing in Networks

Recent years have witnessed revolutionary changes in the fields of computer and communication engineering. Innovations in the design and fabrication of VLSI systems and components have led to dramatic improvements in computational capabilities as well as in the speed and capacity of memory devices, while providing significant reductions in physical packaging, power dissipation and material cost. The economic utility derived from these advances has led, in turn, to the proliferation of computers — from main frames to personal computers. The requirement to interconnect these computers has given rise to innumerable network applications and architectures.

For example, telephony and circuit switching network designers have responded to these improvements in technology by specifying advanced network equipment such as digital switching machines and multi-point T1 transmission systems for deployment in public networks. Similarly, private data networks utilizing satellite, packet LAN technologies have been based on high speed multi-access VLSI components. Irrespective of the network application or architecture, the choice of the routing mechanism is almost always critical to providing an acceptable network solution. Generally, routing is viewed as a method to derive a set of rules or laws to allow any pair of nodes to communicate, while optimizing some performance criterion.

Dictated by the need for reliable communications and the need to satisfy a set of performance criteria, there has been a great deal of interest in applying adaptive routing to communication networks. Such routing schemes have been proposed for both circuit-switched and packet-switched networks. Since these networks generally involve huge investments in communication facilities, even a slight improvement in their operating efficiency results in considerable savings. By their very nature they are subject to demands over which they have very little control. In actual practice, the volume as well as the pattern of the traffic vary over wide ranges. Unusual conditions are also caused by component failures and natural disasters. Considerations such as the above underscore the need to apply adaptive network control algorithms to achieve improved performance under uncertain conditions.

Conventional techniques for the solution of routing problems usually involve some form of mathematical programming. Time-varying network conditions are approached using quasi-static algorithms with these techniques. Average load conditions are assumed to prevail in the network over a finite period and the control to be effected over that period is determined by solving a mathematical programming problem. In contrast to that, the learning approach presented in this section treats routing as a stochastic allocation problem amenable to a dynamic decentralized approach. Based on real-time feedback of network status, learning algorithms at various nodes determine how the traffic is to be routed. In view of recent advances in computer technology, the algorithms are implemented easily and hence are economically attractive.

In Section 9.2.1, routing in circuit switched networks using learning automata is considered. Following a description of the network model and the routing scheme used, simulation studies on simple networks are included. These studies are intended to serve as illustrative examples to acquaint the reader with the details of using learning automata in networks and the advantages that might result, as well as to verify some of the theoretical results given in Chapter 7. More recent efforts to improve the automaton approach are then discussed briefly and their performance is compared with existing dynamic routing schemes. In Section 9.2.2 a similar discussion of packet-switched networks is given. Finally, in Section 9.2.3, flow control in packet-switched networks is considered and the effectiveness of learning automata is discussed in this context.

9.2.1 Routing in Circuit-Switched Networks

The Network Model: The telephone traffic system, which is a typical example of a circuit-switched system, can be modeled as a set of terminals that both generates and receives calls, a connecting network which provides the physical paths or trunks over which communication takes place, and a control system that provides supervisory signals. The arriving calls generated at the terminals are modeled by a Poisson process with point–to–point traffic loads (i.e., calls per minute originating at node i destined for node j). The number of trunks, l_{ij}, in trunk group T_{ij}, as well as the calling rates $\lambda_{ij}(t)$ from node i to node j, can be conveniently collected in the form of matrices L and $\Lambda(t)$, respectively. Changes in the network conditions are therefore best described by changes in these matrices.

Routing Schemes: The specific path chosen for routing a call depends on the routing scheme. For example, if a call originating at node i and destined for node j is at node k, and there are r_1 allowable links at node k, the call will be offered to one of these links using a routing scheme. If this link is busy, the call is offered to an alternate link and the process is repeated until either a free link is found or the call is rejected.

If a fixed rule is employed, the call is offered to the r_1 links in a specific

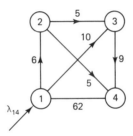

Figure 9.1: Four node network with one input.

order. If an adaptive or learning algorithm is used, the order in which the links are chosen is altered using feedback information regarding call completion or call rejection. If the choice of a sequence of links is considered as an action, the problem reduces to choosing a specific action out of a finite set of actions. Learning automata schemes as described in earlier chapters are ideally suited to accomplish this and can consequently be used to route calls through the network. Typically, if a call from a source node i, destined for node j is at node k, an automaton A_{ij}^k is used to route the calls at that node.

Example 9.1: The simple example in Fig. 9.1 is useful in explaining qualitatively why learning schemes may perform better than nonadaptive fixed rules (Narendra, Wright, and Mason, 1977). Figure 9.1 shows a four-node network with a single input λ_{14}. Calls arrive at node 1 destined for node 4. The number of trunks in the six trunk groups are given by $l_{14} = 62, l_{13} = 10$, $l_{12} = 6, l_{24} = 5, l_{23} = 5, l_{34} = 9$. Let a fixed rule, used at node 1, attempt trunk groups T_{14}, T_{13} and T_{12} in that order. Since $l_{13} = 10$ and $l_{34} = 9$, trunk group T_{13} has one free trunk even when T_{34} is busy. Hence, using the fixed rule, calls will be routed along T_{13} only to be blocked at node 3. The extra capacity along T_{12}, T_{24} is never used in this case. Using a learning rule at node 1 this is avoided since calls will be automatically routed along T_{12} when routing along T_{13} results in too many lost calls.

The example demonstrates that the fixed rule can be inefficient whenever the downchain capacity is smaller than the capacity upchain. The efficiency of a learning routing scheme on the other hand increases with additional capacity and is not sensitive to the location of such capacity in the network.

Example 9.2: The network in this case consists of four nodes and calls originating at node 1 are destined for node 3. The number of trunks in the

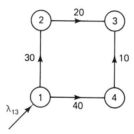

Figure 9.2: An example of a network for which a mixed strategy is optimal.

various trunk groups are $l_{12} = 30$, $l_{23} = 20$, $l_{43} = 10$ and $l_{14} = 40$. Since T_{12} is free while T_{23} is busy and similarly T_{14} is free while T_{43} is busy, calls will be lost at either node 2 or node 4. Hence if a fixed rule, denoted by (T_{12}, T_{14}) (which chooses T_{12} followed by T_{14}, when the former is busy) is used, calls will be lost at node 2 and only 20 trunks in T_{23} will be effective. Similarly if the fixed rule (T_{14}, T_{12}) is used only ten trunks are effective and calls will be lost at node 4. Hence both schemes are found to be suboptimal. If $\lambda_{13} = 5$ calls/minute the blocking probability corresponding to the second fixed rule is found to be 0.653.

For the given input, since the effective number of trunks is 30 (Fig. 9.2), a minimum blocking probability of 0.15 can be achieved theoretically by the proper choice of a routing rule. When an L_{R-I} scheme was used at node 1, after 5000 calls, the scheme resulted in a mixed strategy with action probabilities 0.673 (T_{12}, T_{14}) and 0.327 (T_{14}, T_{12}) respectively. This yielded a blocking probability of 0.186 indicating an effective use of both paths. The action probabilities are also seen to be in direct proportion to the effective trunks along the two routes.

The example above is a simple but nontrivial case of a network where a mixed rule is found to be optimal. The network described here is typical of situations in larger networks where the capacity of trunk groups is smaller down chain. In such a case, no fixed rule could utilize all the available capacity in the network under arbitrary loads and the model of time-varying networks described in Chapter 7 must be invoked to analyze the performance of the learning scheme. To verify the results presented, using the latter models requires that the calls be routed along the two available paths with different probabilities. To facilitate the study, a sequence of controlled experiments were performed by Chrystall and Mars (1981) on the network above for different call rates λ_{13} and different fixed probabilities p_1 and p_2 of routing the calls along the two trunk groups T_{14} and T_{12}. Since the action probabilities p_1 and p_2 are assumed to be constant, the values of blocking probabilities c_1 and c_2 along the two paths, as well as the total blocking probability $c_T(= c_1p_1 + c_2p_2)$, can also be computed theoretically. These values were found to correspond closely to those obtained experimentally over the entire range of the experiment.

If N represents the total number of calls at node 1 and N_1 and N_2 the number of calls attempted first along T_{14} and T_{12}, respectively, then N_1/N and N_2/N represent the estimates of the action probabilities p_1 and p_2 respectively. If N_{B_1} and N_{B_2} are respectively the blocked calls for the two actions, then N_{B_1}/N_1 and N_{B_2}/N_2 correspond to the blocking probabilities c_1 and c_2. It is important to distinguish between these blocking probabilities and the blocking probabilities along the paths 143 and 123 since these in general are not equal. This is because actions in this case do not correspond to the links T_{14} and T_{12} but to the sequences $[T_{14}, T_{12}]$ and $[T_{12}, T_{14}]$ respectively.

In Chapter 7 it was shown that when $L_{R-\epsilon P}$ schemes are used in a time-varying environment, they would tend to equalize the blocking probabilities. Similarly L_{R-P} schemes tend to equalize blocking rates i.e., $p_1c_1(p_1)$ and $p_2c_2(p_2)$. To test the validity of these theoretical predictions, both $L_{R-\epsilon P}$ and L_{R-P} schemes were used to route calls at node 1 with $\lambda_{13} = 15$ calls/minute. As predicted, the $L_{R-\epsilon P}$ scheme approximately equalized blocking probabilities yielding $c_1 = 0.507$ and $c_2 = 0.487$. The L_{R-P} scheme on the other hand resulted in action probabilities $p_1 = 0.58$ and $p_2 = 0.42$ and the corresponding blocking probabilities for the two actions were 0.44 and 0.59 respectively. This yielded $p_1c_1(p_1) = 0.255$ and $p_2c_2(p_2) = 0.248$ indicating that the blocking rates are approximately equal.

From Fig. 9.3, the action probabilities corresponding to the case $c_1 = c_2$ are seen to be $p_1 = 0.67$ and $p_2 = 0.33$. Similarly, for the case when the blocking rates are equal i.e., $p_1c_1 = p_2c_2$, the action probabilities are $p_1 = 0.58$ and $p_2 = 0.42$. These values are seen to correspond closely to the experimental values observed above. The total blocking probability is found to be relatively shallow around the optimum of 0.53 which occurs when $p_1 = 0.61$. Its values at $p_1 = 0.58$ and 0.61 as given by the L_{R-P} and $L_{R-\epsilon P}$ schemes are indistinguishable from the optimal value. The latter observation is interesting in its own right since the $L_{R-\epsilon P}$ and L_{R-P} schemes yield approximately optimal behavior in this simple example, even though the flow patterns are quite different.

In the two examples above, where only one input was present, optimal routes could be determined almost by inspection. In contrast to them, when

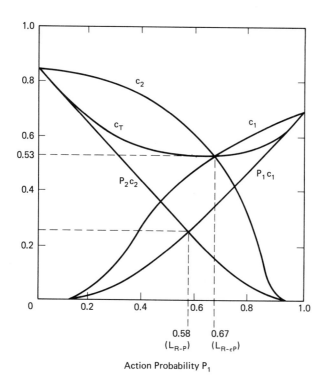

Figure 9.3: Blocking probabilities and rates versus action probabilities for 4-node network in Example 9.2.

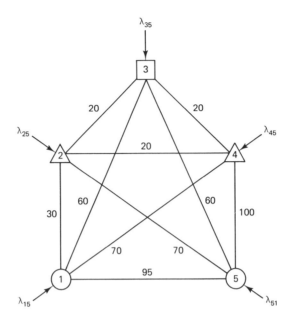

Figure 9.4: A five node network with five inputs.

several inputs are present in a network that has four or more nodes, determination of optimal routes becomes a formidable task. In Example 9.3, we consider a network with five nodes and five inputs. The inputs at nodes 1 to 4 are destined for node 5 while the input at node 5 is destined for node 1. The simulation study was carried out to compare the effectiveness of learning routing schemes with that of a fixed rule routing scheme.

Example 9.3: In the five-node network shown in Fig. 9.4 the loads are given by $\lambda_{15} = \lambda_{25} = \lambda_{35} = \lambda_{45} = \lambda_{51} = 10$ calls/minute. The fixed rule routing scheme can be described by the sequences $(T_{15}, T_{14}, T_{13}, T_{12})$, (T_{25}, T_{24}, T_{23}), (T_{35}, T_{34}), and (T_{45}) corresponding to the four nodes 1,2,3, and 4 and the sequence $(T_{51}, T_{52}, T_{53}, T_{54})$ corresponding to node 5. The sequences indicate the order in which the trunk groups are chosen at the corresponding nodes. For example $(T_{15}, T_{14}, T_{13}, T_{12})$ implies that the load at node 1 first attempts the trunk group T_{15} and when it is busy attempts T_{14} and so on. Before a proper comparison of learning schemes and fixed rule schemes can be made, the trunk groups along which the various automata at the different nodes can route the calls should be known. For the problem under consideration these are tabulated below for the different inputs λ_{ij}.

For Input $\lambda_{15} : (T_{15}, T_{14}, T_{13}, T_{12}), (T_{45}), (T_{35}, T_{34}), (T_{25}, T_{24}, T_{23})$
Input $\lambda_{25} : (T_{21}, T_{25}, T_{24}, T_{23}), (T_{15}), (T_{45}), (T_{35}, T_{34})$
Input $\lambda_{35} : (T_{32}, T_{31}, T_{35}, T_{34}), (T_{21}, T_{25}), (T_{15}), (T_{45})$
Input $\lambda_{45} : (T_{45}, T_{41}, T_{42}), (T_{15}), (T_{25})$
Input $\lambda_{51} : (T_{51}, T_{52}, T_{53}, T_{54}), (T_{21}), (T_{31}, T_{32}), (T_{41}, T_{42}, T_{43})$

For the input λ_{15} it is seen that the automaton A_{15}^1 has four choices while for the same input, the automaton at node 2 has three choices. By the process above of specifying how the various automata route for each source destination pair, the problem of looping can be avoided.

The network shown in Fig. 9.4 was engineered for the specified load to yield a blocking probability of 1.62%. When learning schemes were used to route the calls, the blocking probability was found to be 2.34%. The fact that this is greater than that resulting from a fixed rule should not be surprising since learning schemes cannot outperform fixed schemes when the latter have been designed specifically for the assumed load.

For the same loads as in the case above, the number of blocked calls (out of a total of 5000 calls) when the fixed scheme and the learning scheme were used are shown in Table 9.1 when different links failed. Since there is no extra capacity in the network, the number of blocked calls are almost equal in the two cases. However, the uniformity of service provided by the learning schemes is apparent from the simulation results.

When the total load on the network remains the same at 50 calls/minute but the individual loads vary, the robustness of the learning scheme becomes quite evident. For example, when $\lambda_{15} = 15, \lambda_{25} = 5, \lambda_{35} = 5, \lambda_{45} = 15$, and $\lambda_{51} = 10$ the fixed rule rejects 473 out of a total of 5000 calls while the learning scheme rejects only 181. Similarly, if the inputs are $\lambda_{15} = 5, \lambda_{25} = 5, \lambda_{35} = 15, \lambda_{45} = 15, \lambda_{51} = 10$ the fixed rule rejects 465 and the learning scheme 197 calls. The uniformity of service with learning schemes is evident in the two cases from Table 9.2 where the number of calls rejected in each input are given.

The simulations presented in Example 9.3 also reveal that the observed steady-state behavior of the network, where learning schemes are used for routing calls, conforms closely to that predicted by the mathematical models introduced in Chapter 7. In particular, when $L_{R-\epsilon P}$ schemes are used at the various nodes, the blocking probabilities along the routes at a specific node are equalized. Similarly, blocking rates are equalized when L_{R-P} schemes are used to route the calls.

Link Failed	Calls Rejected Fixed Rule		Calls Rejected Learning Scheme
	λ_{15}	210	235
	λ_{25}	43	141
4	λ_{35}	61	159
	λ_{45}	426	304
	λ_{51}	493	374
	λ_{15}	25	157
	λ_{25}	14	96
8	λ_{35}	603	173
	λ_{45}	121	122
	λ_{51}	24	167
	λ_{15}	217	214
	λ_{25}	113	142
10	λ_{35}	91	220
	λ_{45}	855	251
	λ_{51}	18	366

Table 9.1

	$\lambda_{15} = 15, \lambda_{25} = 5, \lambda_{35} = 5,$ $\lambda_{45} = 15, \lambda_{51} = 10$		$\lambda_{15} = 5, \lambda_{25} = 5, \lambda_{35} = 15,$ $\lambda_{45} = 15, \lambda_{51} = 10$	
	Calls Rejected		Calls Rejected	
Input	Fixed Rule	Learning Scheme	Fixed Rule	Learning Scheme
λ_{15}	74	79	1	14
λ_{25}	0	1	0	4
λ_{35}	0	13	230	65
λ_{45}	388	70	234	77
λ_{51}	11	18	0	37

Table 9.2

The simulation study of the five-node network presented in Example 9.3 is typical of extensive studies carried out at Yale University and the Robert Gordon Institute at Aberdeen in the late 1970s and early 1980s. The following conclusions were drawn from these investigations (Narendra, Wright, and Mason 1977; Narendra and Mars 1983).

(1) The $L_{R-\epsilon P}$ and L_{R-P} schemes when used in simple networks (in which the theoretical optima can be computed using mathematical programming techniques) result in a performance close to the optimum.

(2) Learning schemes do better than fixed rules in situations in which the optimum routing requires randomization.

(3) The automata at the various nodes act in such a manner as to equalize the quality of service at the different nodes as measured by the blocking probabilities corresponding to different loads.

(4) In the presence of abnormal operating conditions including link failure and node breakdown, the automata schemes result in significantly reduced blocking probabilities and node congestion, provided additional capacity is available in the network.

In Example 9.3 the action probabilities of the various automata were updated on a call-by-call basis. In practical applications this is quite unrealistic due to the size of the networks as well as the number of traffic flows. Hence, despite the superior performance exhibited by learning schemes in simulation studies, it became evident that such schemes require high real-time processing associated with each call. To avoid this, automata were updated periodically according to observations over a time interval or aperiodically after a finite number of calls N. Based on the theory developed in Chapter 7 for automata acting in multiple environments, it can be shown that these modified algorithms are also ϵ–optimal, if the environment is assumed to be stationary over the interval.

One of the drawbacks of the simple learning approach used in the examples is that the method only makes use of a limited amount of information that is available within the network. For example, when a call is blocked, all the automata involved in routing it modify their action probabilities independent of the state of the network. In recent years attempts have been made by researchers to update the automata action probabilities based on more information concerning the network (Akselrod and Langholz 1985, El-Hadidi et al. 1985, Garcia et al. 1985). These are both centralized and distributed dynamic routing methods that improve the overall grade of service over simple schemes based on call completion or rejection. Since additional information is needed for updating each automaton using such methods, common channel signaling would be required to transfer the appropriate information between nodes. In El-Hadidi et al. (1985), a routing algorithm is given, which the authors claim, combines the advantages of gradient techniques with those of the automaton method. It is asserted that the algorithm overcomes the prohibitive computational burden associated with gradient techniques while avoiding the impractical data processing required by simple learning automata schemes. Extensive computer simulations are presented to indicate that the decentralized scheme enjoys a performance close to the optimal. Inoue and Yamamoto (1988) describe a new dynamic routing scheme that uses different kinds of network status information together with learning automata. When network state information is available, well known dynamic schemes (Ash 1985, Krishnan and Ott 1986, Szybicki 1981) can be used to determine a near optimal path. However, the implementation of such schemes requires high computational power and the transfer of significant amounts of data. Learning schemes on the other hand, which are based on success and failure probabilities that are determined empirically, are easy to implement but do not include methods of preventing links from excessive overflow calls. This results in a decrease in the network throughput under overload traffic conditions. The method suggested by Inoue and Yamamoto (1988) combines the features of the two methods by using observed status information to obtain the success probability of each alternate path. It is interesting to note that this method is similar to the concept of a learning automaton using a context vector, that was described in Chapter 7. The authors claim that the procedure above results in high routing performance under time-varying traffic conditions.

In the paper by Garcia et al. (1985) traffic routing policies in telephone networks using centralized and distributed schemes are compared. In the latter category four adaptive algorithms are presented. These include

(i)   A routing algorithm with a hierarchical control structure based on two time scales

(ii) A decentralized algorithm based on the automaton approach

(iii) A centralized algorithm based on the application of the residual capacity approach (Szybicki and Bean 1979)

(iv) A distributed stochastic algorithm

On the basis of the study the authors conclude that adaptive traffic routing can improve the network performance in case of disturbances, provide robustness and equalize the losses throughout the network.

All the studies above indicate that the basic idea of a learning automaton is an attractive one that can be used effectively in the routing problem. It is also clear that the full potential of automata schemes in routing methods is yet to be realized and that by judiciously incorporating network status information in the operation of the learning automata, improved performance can be realized. Although no learning automata methods are currently proposed for implementation in any North American inter-toll network (Hurley, Seidl, and Sewell, 1987) many of the ideas included in this section have already been absorbed into schemes that have since been introduced into the telephone network.

9.2.2 Routing in Packet-Switched Networks

In the previous section the problem of routing using learning automata in circuit-switched networks and in particular the telephone network was considered. The routing algorithm in such networks operates to set up and establish paths for new calls. In contrast to this, in a packet-switched network the routing scheme transmits the packet from node to node until it reaches its destination. Adaptive techniques were first reported in connection with packet-switched networks (Boehm and Mobley 1966, Molnar 1970, and Glorioso et al. 1969) but the explicit use of learning automata was first made in connection with circuit-switched networks (Mason 1972; Narendra, Mason, and Tripathi 1974; Narendra, Wright, and Mason 1977). It was later decided that the same approach could be extended to routing in packet-switched networks. However, the actual implementation varies depending on the manner in which the messages are transmitted and on the information available concerning network status. Since the operating characteristics of packet-switched networks are significantly different from those of circuit switched networks, they give rise to quite different theoretical questions. Nevertheless, the differences in the routing problems, particularly as they pertain to the use of learning automata schemes, are easily stated and are discussed briefly in this section.

The structure of the packet-switched network is similar to that described in the previous section. It consists of a set of nodes numbered from 1 to N, and a set of links that provide communication between them. The capacity of the link connecting nodes i and j is denoted by c_{ij}. Packets from the sources enter the network at the nodes and are directed on the links to their destinations by the routing laws at each of the nodes. Packets are assumed to be generated by a traffic model described in terms of packet arrival rates and lengths. The point to point arrivals are assumed to be Poisson processes with an average arrival rate of λ_{ij} packets/sec. (pps) between nodes i and j and a message length having an exponential distribution with a mean value $1/\mu_{ij}$.

Packets are directed on the links to their destination by the routing laws at each of the nodes. At the input of each link there is a queue in which packets are placed if the link is occupied. Consequently none of the packets are blocked as in the application described in the previous section. When learning schemes are used for routing, a packet arriving at a node is directed on one of the link alternatives available at that node and transmitted to the next node. This process is repeated at the next node and the packet makes its way through the network in a node by node fasion.

Routing methods used in packet-switched networks can be classified as static, quasi-static, or adaptive, depending on the amount of current information concerning the changes in network topology and traffic conditions used in them. Analysis of adaptive routing algorithms, which continuously change with time, has been attempted by numerous research workers (Bertsekas and Gallager 1987). The problem of choosing a route for a packet reduces in such cases to the problem of determining the transition probabilities in a complex Markovian model and is generally intractable. This in turn has led to optimization techniques based on restrictive assumptions. The facts that the systems are complex, that tractable mathematical models are not available, and routing choices must be made with coarse information concerning network conditions, once again makes the automaton approach attractive in this case. Chrystall and Mars (1981), Mars et al. (1983), Nedzelnitsky and Narendra (1987), and Economides et al. (1988) have reported simulation results in this area. An analytic performance model for a packet switched network employing L_{R-I} schemes for routing packets was described by Mason (1985), and the results predicted are in close agreement with those obtained in simulation studies. Further, it was shown that the L_{R-I} schemes converge asymptotically to Nash equilibria (also referred to in this case as user equilibria). The relationship between such equilibria and the optimal strategy for the system was also described in terms of the link flow-delay models. Using these results the manner in which the link function can be modified so that the collective of L_{R-I} schemes converge to the optimal strategy, was also suggested.

Performance Criteria: Several network measurements provide convenient measures of the performance of the different routing schemes. Packet delay (defined as the time for a packet to cross from source to destination), link utilization, throughput and the average hop count (the ratio of number of packets transmitted at the nodes to the number of packets entering the network), have been used by various designers. In Chrystall and Mars (1981), Mars et al. (1983), and Nedzelnitsky and Narendra (1987), packet delay is used as the criterion of performance. In Economides et al. (1988), based on available traffic statistics, a cost is defined for every allowable path. Hence, the decision concerning the optimal path uses significantly more information in this case.

Routing Using Learning Automata: When learning schemes are used for routing at the various nodes, it is essential they all receive random realizations of the global performance criterion. From the point of view of mathematical analysis, this constitutes a major departure from the schemes described in the previous section. Although call completion or rejection could be represented by a P–model, the choice of packet delay or "network condition" as a performance criterion necessitates the use of Q– and S–models. As in the case of circuit-switched networks, it is assumed that an automaton is used at every node of the packet-switched network to route the packets to a specific destination. However, source information is not used here and hence the automaton at node m routing to node j is denoted by A_j^m. Messages entering node m are directed by A_j^m on one of the outgoing links using a probability vector p. If there are r possible outgoing links at node m, there are r corresponding queues and the elements of $p(n)$ denote the probability of a message being placed in any one of the queues at stage n, where $p(n)^T = [p_1(n), p_2(n), \ldots, p_r(n)]$.

If the automaton uses an SL_{R-P} algorithm, the action probabilities $p_i(n)$ are updated as given in Chapter 6:

If $\alpha(n) = \alpha_i$ so that the ith link is chosen for transmission at stage n then

$$
\begin{aligned}
p_i(n+1) &= p_i(n) + a(1 - \beta(n)(1 - p_i(n)) - b\beta(n)p_i(n) \\
p_j(n+1) &= p_j(n) - a(1 - \beta(n))p_j(n) + b\beta(n)\left[\tfrac{1}{r-1} - p_j(n)\right] j \neq i
\end{aligned}
\tag{9.1}
$$

where a and b are reward- and penalty- parameters, respectively, and $\beta(n)$ is the normalized failure response of the environment at stage n. When $b = 0$, the resulting algorithm is SL_{R-I} and if $b << a$ it is an $SL_{R-\epsilon P}$ algorithm. In Economides et al. (1988) different rates of adaptation are used for different network conditions. For example, the parameters are chosen so as to react quickly to large changes and slowly to small changes. Also, if the network cost is far away from the optimum, faster convergence is sought.

If learning algorithms are used in a data communicatioon network, a question that must be addressed is whether the observed behavior of the traffic coincides with the behavior predicted in Chapter 7. The following example describes a simulation study on a three-node four-link network con-

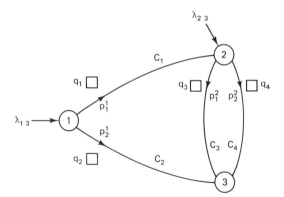

Figure 9.5: A three-node four-link network (*Courtesy IEEE © 1987*).

taining two learning automata by Nedzelnitsky and Narendra (1987).

Example 9.4: Figure 9.5 shows a three-node four-link network. The link capacities are $c_1 = c_2 = c_3 = 10$ kilobits/sec (kbps), $c_4 = 20$ kbps, where c_3 and c_4 represent the two link capacities from node 2 to node 3. An average packet length is assumed to be 1000 bits and the inputs to the network are $\lambda_{13} = 15.0$ pps, $\lambda_{23} = 12, 16$ pps. Automata located at nodes 1 and 2 are assumed to route the packets. The delay along the various paths was computed when both automata used either SL_{R-I} schemes or SL_{R-P} schemes. The delays as well as the product of delay and action probability (delay rate) along the two paths at node 1 and node 2 are shown in Table 9.3 for two values of λ_{23}. It is seen that the SL_{R-I} scheme tends to equalize delays while the SL_{R-P} scheme tends to equalize delay rates, as predicted by the theory.

Type	λ_{23}	Node	Delay Rate		Delay	
			α_1	α_2	α_1	α_2
	12.0	1	2.820	2.705	6.053	5.023
SL_{R-P}		2	1.670	1.724	2.761	4.300
	16.0	1	3.260	3.082	7.147	5.621
		2	2.374	2.405	3.819	6.226
	12.0	1	3.273	3.690	6.633	6.496
SL_{R-I}		2	2.349	1.181	3.386	3.416
	16.0	1	3.955	4.750	8.157	7.806
		2	3.474	1.956	5.082	5.256

Table 9.3: Load equalizing behavior with two automata.

Nonstationary models of environments were introduced by Narendra and Thathachar (1980) and Srikantakumar and Narendra (1982) (refer to Chapter 7) to explain the equalizing behavior described above, observed first in telephone networks and later in packet-switched networks. The models assume that the penalty probabilities $c_i(i = 1, 2, \ldots, r)$ along the links are instantaneous functions of the action probabilities p_i i.e. $c_i = f_i(p_i)$. If $f_i(p_i)$ are monotonic functions and satisfy the conditions described in Chapter 7, it was shown that the action probabilities assume values close to p_i^* where

$$f_1(p_1^*) = f_2(p_2^*) = \cdots = f_r(p_r^*) \tag{9.2}$$

when linear reward-inaction schemes are used and values close to p_i^* where

$$p_1^* f_1(p_1^*) = p_2^* f_2(p_2^*) = \cdots = p_r^* f_r(p_r^*) \tag{9.3}$$

when linear reward-penalty schemes are used.

The models imply that when $p_i(n_1) = p_i(n_2)$ at two instants of time n_1 and n_2, the penalty probability c_i must be the same at those instants. However, simulation results of network routing indicate this is not the case. For example the evolution of $p_1(n)$ for a three-node problem is shown in Figure 9.6(a).

When $\lambda_{13} = 19.0$, $p_1(54) = p_1(126)$. However, the corresponding values of $c_1(n)$ are different, indicating clearly that the network has memory. Hence a dynamic model of the environment is needed for an accurate prediction of the transient behavior (Nedzelnitsky and Narendra 1987). Figure 9.6(b) shows the simulated response of the same network for an input $\lambda_{13} = 15.0$ pps. as well as the response of a dynamic model of the environment in which the penalty probability $c_i(n)$ is related to the action probability $p_i(n)$ through a first order difference equation

$$c_i(n + 1) = \lambda_i c_i(n) + (1 - \lambda_i) f(p_i(n)). \tag{9.4}$$

The response of the dynamic model approximates the observed response closely. Better approximations of the environment can be achieved by using higher order difference equations in the place of Eq. (9.4). These results indicate that while stationary models in which $c_i(n) = f_i(p_i(n))$ are adequate to predict steady-state behavior of networks, dynamic models of the network as an environment are needed to predict the transient response.

Example 9.5: Several simulation studies on a ten-node datagram network [Fig. 9.7(a)] with 16 links, each of 9.6 kbps. capacity have been reported

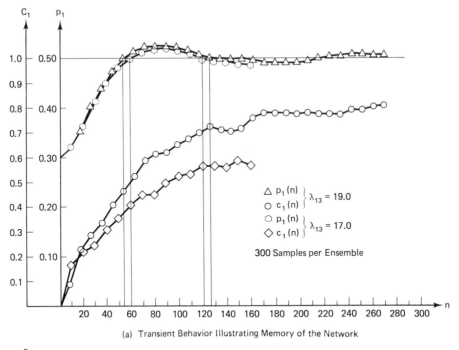

(a) Transient Behavior Illustrating Memory of the Network

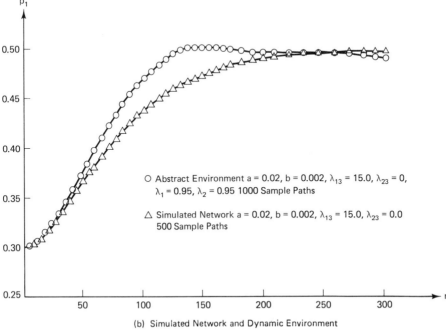

(b) Simulated Network and Dynamic Environment

Figure 9.6: Dynamic model of the environment (*Courtesy IEEE © 1987*).

by Chrystall et al. (1981). We present here one in which the network is fed from 90 sources so that each node generates data destined for all the others. The experiments studied the performance of the network over a wide range of traffic rates, the overall intensity varying from 10 to 100 pps. In all cases the packet delays, average hop count, and link utilization were measured and the performance of the learning schemes was compared with a fixed routing scheme. The fixed rule is based on the shortest path between source and destination nodes. Figures 9.7(b) shows the average packet delay as a function of packet arrival rate for the two schemes. At low packet rates the shortest path scheme outperforms the other. This is because the delay is predominantly due to the link transmission rather than queueing. However as the level of traffic increases and significant queues develop, the shortest paths have higher delays. The learning scheme on the other hand provides significantly better routing service with lower packet delays. Figures 9.7(c) and (d) show the distribution of the packet delays at low and high traffic. At low values (less than 10 pps.) the distribution plots using the two schemes are almost identical. However at high values of traffic corresponding to 90 pps. the learning automata scheme displays a significant reduction in average and maximum delays. Finally the link utilization at low and high traffic of the three schemes are shown in Figures 9.7(e) as histograms indicating the traffic on each link. The fixed routing scheme shows no alterations for different traffic conditions. In contrast to this, the learning scheme adopts a more pronounced load splitting strategy, spreading the network over any available network capacity.

Numerical studies have also been performed by Mason (1985) on the ten-node network described above. As mentioned earlier, these studies showed that L_{R-I} schemes converge to a Nash equilibrium. The relationship between this performance and the optimal performance is also described. The studies further demonstrate that the Nash strategies and the optimal system strategies differ mainly when network traffic patterns are asymmetric and the volume traffic is high. Even in the extreme cases, the difference in delay performance between the two strategies is less than 6%.

9.2.3 Flow Control in Packet-Switched Networks

Another area of active research in which new approaches using learning automata have been investigated is flow control in distributed networks. As in the previous sections, packet-switched networks are typically dimensioned to achieve delay objectives that satisfy user specific requirement, e.g. in

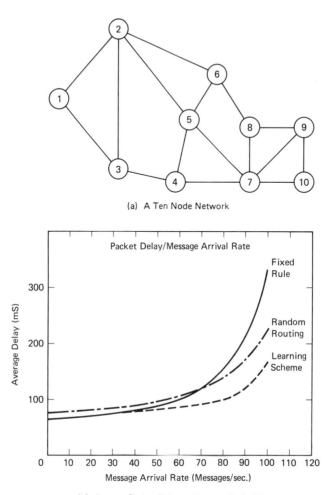

(a) A Ten Node Network

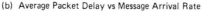

(b) Average Packet Delay vs Message Arrival Rate

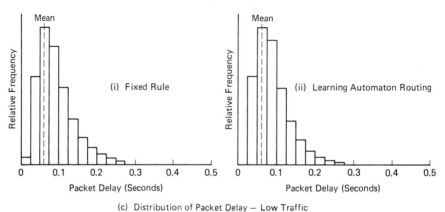

(c) Distribution of Packet Delay — Low Traffic

Figure 9.7: Simulation of a ten-node network.

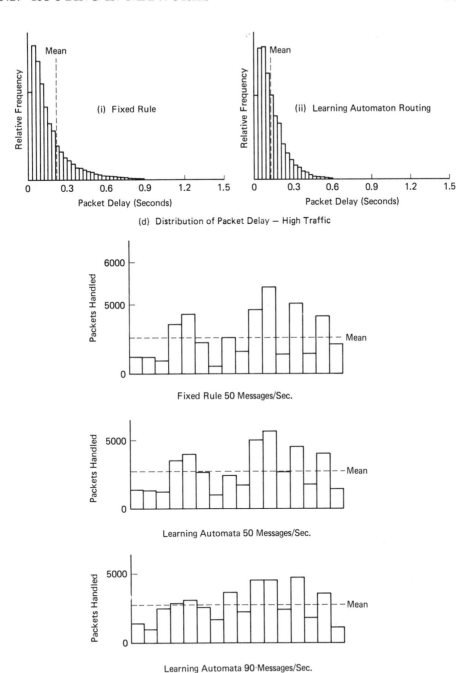

Figure 9.7: (continued).

a packet voice network, the end-to-end delay should be less than 100ms., and typically 40 ms. is specified as a threshold. However, circumstances may place excessive load on the network, which result in a severe decrease in throughput and a significant increase in transport delay. Under such conditions it is desirable to regulate the rate of traffic entry into the network. Although strictly speaking, such flow control is different from the routing problems discussed earlier, we include it here since the nature of the scheme described is such that it can also be interpreted as a problem of routing permits through the network.

Davies (1972) proposed the isarithmic scheme for regulating the total traffic offered to a packet network. The scheme requires a message to secure a permit to gain entry to the network. Limiting the number of permits consequently limits the number of packets at a given time. When the message is delivered to its destination, the permit is released and becomes available for other message arrivals. Although this approach is quite satisfactory under symmetric traffic conditions, a problem arises when the traffic flow is asymmetric, because permits collect in pools at certain nodes while not being available at others. One approach to avoid such permit collection at slow nodes involves employing an adaptive controller for permit disbursal. Such an approach using learning automata has been studied quite extensively by Mason and co-workers and is briefly reported here. For a more detailed treatment of the problem the reader is referred to the source papers.

Mason and Gu (1986) consider several isarithmic flow control architectures with both adaptive and nonadaptive control schemes. In centralized adaptive flow control, the permits are distributed to the message sources by a centralized controller that also measures the network response. To accomplish this, the controller attaches a permit to the message at the time of disbursal with the node identity to which it is routed and a permit sequence number so as to recognize it when it returns. Associating each path of the permits with an action, the automaton updates its action probabilities as the permits pass through it.

In a decentralized flow control problem, N automata are associated with the N destination nodes. Each automaton has $(N-1)$ actions, one for each of the other (source) nodes. Each individual automaton operates exactly as in the case described earlier and an automaton C_d updates its action probabilities only when a permit marked with message destination d is received. In Mason and Gu (1986) the case where N permit classes are allowed is also considered.

Control Algorithms: For the centralized scheme described earlier, if $p_i(n)$ corresponds to the probability of the ith action at stage n, the learning control scheme has the form:

$$p_i(n+1) = p_i(n)[1 + G(F_i(n) - \sum_{j=1}^{N} F_j(n)p_j(n))] \qquad (9.5)$$

where n is the stage number at which the allocation is made, $F_i(n)$ is the normalized network response strength associated with action i, and G is the adaptive loop gain parameter.

In the decentralized control scheme, N automata will be involved in a game, with each automaton attached to a destination node. In this case the action probabilities of the dth automaton are updated as follows:

$$p_{di} \quad (n+1) = p_{di}(n)[1 + G(F_{di}(n) - \sum_{j=1}^{N} F_{dj}(n)p_{dj}(n))]$$
$$i = 1, 2, \ldots, N; d = 1, 2, \ldots, N \ i \neq d. \qquad (9.6)$$

Performance Criteria: Centralized or decentralized versions of the learning schemes [i.e. Eqs. (9.5) and (9.6)] can be used to update the action probabilities only if the appropriate response is fed back to the automata. Loop delay, loop population, loop power, and path delay have been used in simulation studies. Of these, the first three can be implemented without any additional state measurements on the basis of the permit flows through the controllers. Hence we confine our attention to them in the discussion of the simulation results that follow. In the first case, loop delay corresponds to the round trip delay for the permit to cycle through the source node, the network links and back to the controller. In the second case, the reward strengths of the automata are the 1's complement of the normalized loop permit population. This can be measured on-line, since the exact loop population can be updated with each permit arrival and disbursal. In the third case of interest, the reward strength is the normalized loop power which is defined as the loop throughput delay ratio. This can be implemented in the algorithms by measuring the loop throughput and delay associated with the various control actions.

In the flow control problem, our interest is in optimizing the flow through the network. The actual flow that can be achieved naturally depends on the number of permits used, the nature of the traffic, and the specific algorithm used (i.e., the feedback) in routing the calls. Extensive computer simulations may be needed to determine flow values reasonably close to the optimal, in

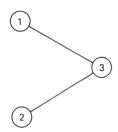

Figure 9.8: Three-node network.

order to serve as benchmarks for comparison of the effectiveness of different routing schemes. In the simulation studies it is therefore necessary to determine, under different network topologies and different load distributions, the effectiveness of the schemes assuming that the permit population is known. This in turn can be used in the selection of the learning scheme based on prior information regarding the approximate nature of the loads. Determination of the theoretical optimal flow through a network is a complex problem. Recent work by Mason and his coworkers to develop analytic performance models to evaluate the performance of routing schemes is described briefly towards the end of this section.

Centralized learning control algorithms were tested on a simple three-node network and a ten-node, thirty-two link network and these are described in Examples 9.6 and 9.7, respectively. As in the previous sections, the simple network was considered to facilitate insight into the algorithmic behavior. Since the optimal permit size and allocation can be determined in this case by exhaustive search, they can be used for evaluating algorithmic performance.

Example 9.6: Figure 9.8 shows a simple three-node network in which messages originate at nodes 1 and 2 and are destined for node 3.

We consider two cases in the simulations–the case where link capacities c_{13} and c_{23} are equal at 1.0 bps, referred to as the symmetric network and the case where $c_{13} = 1.0$ bps and $c_{23} = 2.0$ bps referred to as the asymmetric network. In Figure 9.9 the network power is plotted as a function of traffic for three different permit populations i.e., $w = 2.0, 6.0$, and 100. For a permit population of 2 the power increases monotonically with offered traffic and saturates at 9.0. For a permit population of 6 the power increases to a maximum value at an offered traffic of 4 pps and saturates at 4.5, as the traffic increases beyond 10 pps. The third case with a permit population of 100, approximates an uncontrolled network. Although the performance is

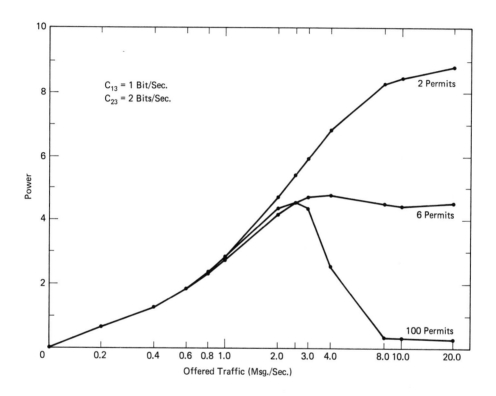

Figure 9.9: Network power vs. load.

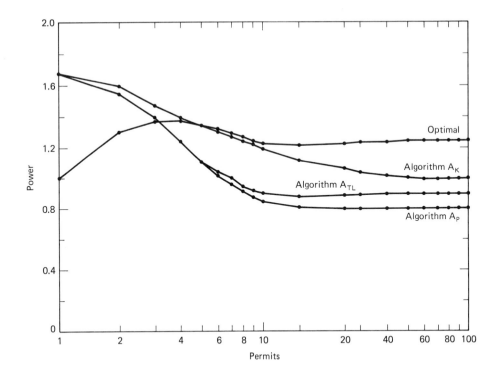

Figure 9.10: Skewed traffic (symmetric network).

slightly better for low traffic, it deteriorates rapidly for high traffic, indicating the need for controlling the entry of traffic into the network. Also, among the three permit populations considered, $w = 2.0$ is seen to be uniformly better for all offered traffic greater than 1 pps.

Figures 9.10–9.13 show the network power performance versus permit population for both symmetric and asymmetric networks with normal and skewed traffic. In each case, the performance of three different learning schemes denoted by A_{TL} (loop delay), A_K (loop population), and A_P (loop power) is shown. For comparison purposes, the optimal allocation algorithm is also included in each figure. The algorithm A_P performs reasonably well for a small permit population and degrades for a large permit population. Hence it is found to be the least attractive of the three algorithms. The algorithm A_K attempts to equalize the loop permit populations. For small permit population, its performance is significantly below the optimal level. However, it improves as the population level increases and for high populations is the best of the three algorithms. It also has a built-in fairness property, in that permit allocation cannot be deterministic even under highly

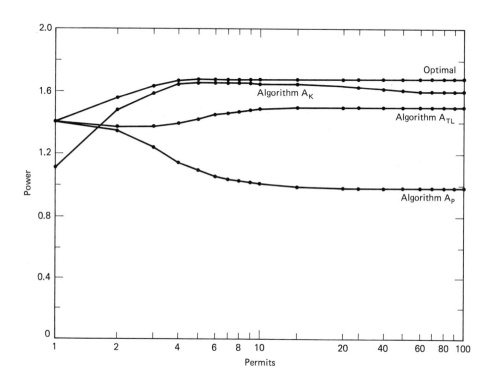

Figure 9.11: Nominal traffic (symmetric network).

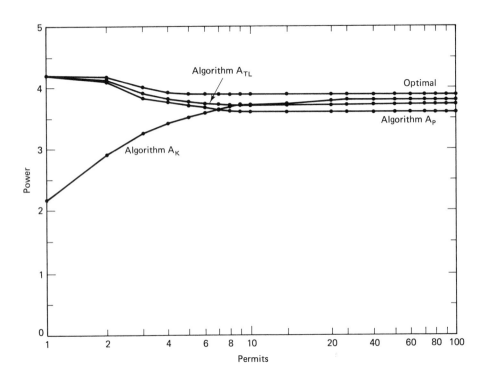

Figure 9.12: Skewed traffic (asymmetric network).

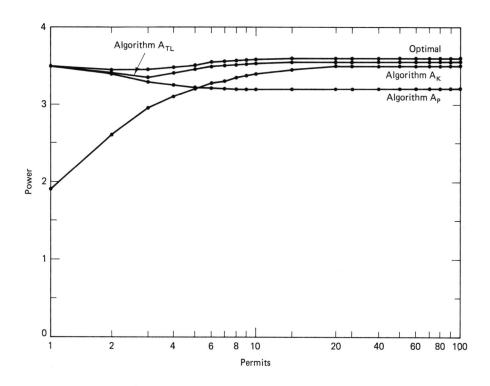

Figure 9.13: Nominal traffic (asymmetric network).

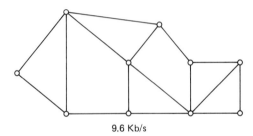

9.6 Kb/s

Figure 9.14: Ten-node network.

skewed traffic conditions. Finally, the algorithm A_{TL} performs optimally in terms of network power for highly skewed traffic distributions but the performance degrades as the permit population increases. In this sense A_{TL} and A_K are complementary.

The figures also clearly demonstrate that apart from optimally allocating the permits, there is also a need for choosing the optimal permit population to optimize the flow through the network. One method of accomplishing this is through the use of a two level automaton. Work along these lines is currently underway.

Example 9.7: For the ten-node network shown in Fig. 9.14 (which was also considered in the previous subsection) three traffic demand models were considered. For the uniform case, the arrival rate between origin destination pairs was 0.317 pps. for light traffic and 3.17 pps. for nominal traffic. For the nonuniform case, node 5 has an arrival rate of 1.217 pps. to all destination nodes while the arrival rate for all other origin destination pairs is 0.217 pps.

Figures 9.15 and 9.16 display the power performance of the three algorithms for the centralized adaptive architecture under both uniform and nonuniform traffic conditions. In the uniform traffic case, A_{TL} and A_K algorithms yield the same performance over the entire range of permit populations. A_P also yields the same performance for permit populations greater than 20. For nonuniform traffic conditions the performance of the three algorithms are different with A_K being the best, followed by A_{TL} and A_P being significantly worse. In Mason and Gu (1986) and Coderre (1988), analytic performance models were developed which are accurate and much less costly than simulations to evaluate performance. For comparison purposes, Mason and his coworkers also developed an optimal model for the flow control problem based on nonlinear programming. Network power and product of powers were used as objective criteria in this model. This enabled them to

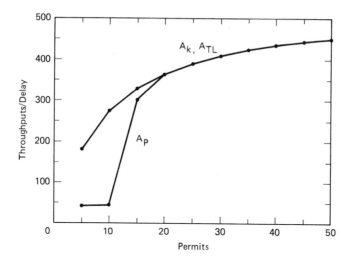

Figure 9.15: Uniform traffic, centralized control.

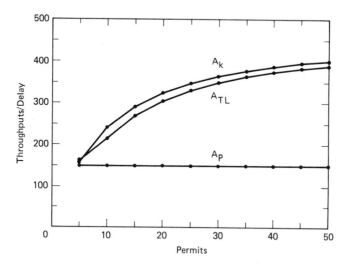

Figure 9.16: Non-uniform traffic, centralized control.

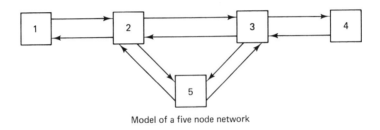

Model of a five node network

Figure 9.17: The five-node ten-link network.

them to compare the optimal flow control policy with that obtained by the adaptive procedures. The results shown in Fig. 9.18 for the five node ten link network in Fig. 9.17 reveal that the centralized adaptive flow control scheme using L_{R-I} and the A_K response give near optimal performance over a wide range of traffic conditions.

9.3   Other Applications of Learning Automata

In the previous section different applications of learning automata to routing in networks were described. Extensive simulation studies carried out on such networks lead us to believe that these represent areas where learning schemes may prove to be practically viable. However, a number of other potential areas of application have also been suggested recently by various authors, which thus far have not been experimentally tested to the same extent. We present some of these in this section to indicate that learning schemes may also prove attractive in very different contexts. Following a discussion of problems related to the optimization of queueing systems, which are quite close in spirit to those discussed in the previous section, more novel applications to data compression of images, consistent labeling problems, and pattern classification are described in this section.

9.3.1   Applications to Queueing Systems

Among the many problems that arise in the design of communication networks, only a class related to network management is amenable to solutions using learning schemes. These include routing and flow control treated in Section 9.2, priority assignment in queues, and the decentralized control of a shared communication channel. Routing, as discussed in Sections 9.2.1 and

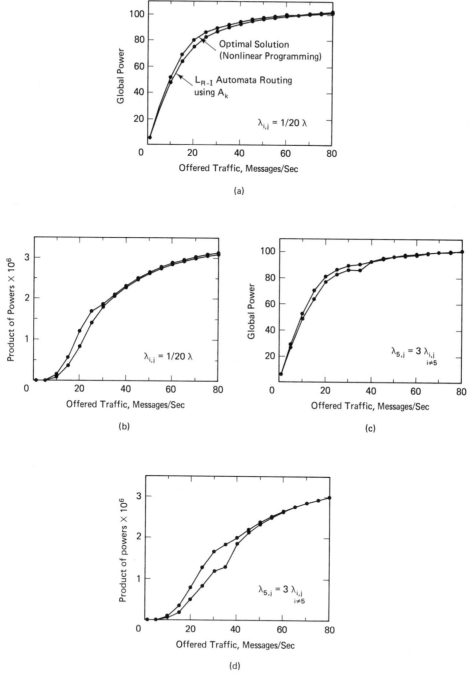

Figure 9.18: Results from the five-node ten-link network.

9.2.2 involves the selection of a path from a set of allowable paths to minimize a performance criterion such as blocking probability or mean packet delay. Flow control, treated in Section 9.2.3, deals with the restriction of traffic into a network in some form so congestion is minimized. Servicing different jobs at a processor and scheduling tasks in multiprocessor systems can be expressed in terms of priority assignments in queues. Finally, in the random access channel, the prototype of problems where a common resource is shared by many users, protocols have to be developed so that the resource is used efficiently. All of the above are in one form or another related to problems in queueing theory. When all the parameters of the system are constant and known, these problems can be solved using stochastic control theory. However, as described in Section 9.2, since system parameters are not generally known accurately and quite often vary with time, such theory cannot be applied directly and one has to resort to some form of adaptive control based on real-time measurements.

In this section several recent applications of learning automata theory are included. Although most of them are of a theoretical nature, we include them here since the basic concepts involved have general applicability in a variety of practical queueing problems that arise in networks.

Priority Assignment in a Queueing System: A prototype of many problems that arise in computer and communication networks is related to priority assignment in queues. Jobs with different priorities arrive and wait for service within different priority classes. The well known result on priority assignment states that if the highest priority is assigned to the class with shortest average service time, then the overall mean waiting time is minimized (Kleinrock 1975, Cobham 1954). Hence if the characteristics of the stochastic processes representing the different classes are known, an optimal policy can be determined. As mentioned earlier it is when such probability characteristics are not known a priori that learning schemes are found to be useful for developing meaningful priority assignments. This problem has been addressed by Meybodi and Lakshmivarahan (1983) using variable-structure automata and by Srikantakumar using fixed-structure automata (1986).

Let two classes of jobs have Poisson arrival rates λ_1 and λ_2 and exponentially distributed service times with mean values $1/\mu_1$ and $1/\mu_2$ (Fig. 9.19). Within each class the service is on a first-come-first-served basis. It is assumed that the parameters λ_i and $\mu_i (i = 1, 2)$ are not known and that all operations related to the actual implementation of an algorithm can be done

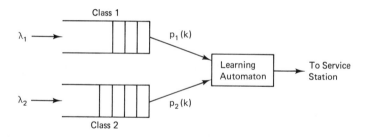

Figure 9.19: Priority assignment in a two queue system.

instantaneously. Under these conditions a learning algorithm is suggested, which asymptotically approaches the optimal fixed rule (for known values of the parameters) with a probability arbitrarily close to 1.

If $T^i(k_i)$ is defined as

$$T^i(k_i) = \frac{1}{k_i} \sum_{j=1}^{k_i} \gamma^i(j) \qquad T^i(0) = 0$$

where $\gamma^i(j)$ is the random service time for the jth job in the class i and k_i is the number of jobs from class i in the queue, then $T^i(k_i)$ can be considered as the average servicing time for class i. A dynamic threshold $T(k)$ is defined at stage k as

$$T(k) = \frac{1}{2} \left[T^1(k_1) + T^2(k_2) \right]. \tag{9.7}$$

At stage $(k + 1)$ the learning scheme chooses the $(k + 1)^{st}$ job from class i with probability $p_i(k)$ $(i = 1, 2)$ so that $p_1(k) + p_2(k) = 1$. We define $p(k) = [p_1(k), p_2(k)]^T$.

The automaton chooses one of the queues according to the distribution $p(k)$, selects the first job, services it, and notes the time $\gamma^i(k + 1)$. Using $\gamma^i(k + 1)$ the probability $p(k)$ is updated using the learning algorithm as follows:

$$\left. \begin{array}{l} p_i(k + 1) = p_i(k) + a[1 - p_i(k)] \\ p_j(k + 1) = p_j(k)[1 - a] \quad j \neq i \end{array} \right\} \text{if } \gamma^i(k + 1) \leq T(k) \tag{9.8}$$

and $p(k + 1) = p(k)$ if $\gamma^i(k + 1) < T(k)$.

In (Meybodi and Lakshmivarahan 1983), using the algorithm above it is rigorously shown that if $1/\mu_1 < 1/\mu_2$ so that the jobs in queue 1 are on the average shorter, then

$$\text{Prob}[|\lim_{k \to \infty} p_1(k) - 1|] \geq 1 - \epsilon.$$

Srikantakumar addresses the same problem using a fixed-structure automaton of Cover and Hellman described in Chapter 3. Assuming that the two queues are nonempty and defining the policies A and B as: A: choose from queue 1, B: choose from queue 2, the following procedure is used. If the automaton has $n+1$ states, in state 0 the policy A is chosen with probability $(1 - \epsilon)$. Similarly, in state n the policy B is chosen with probability $(1 - \epsilon)$. In states 1 to $n - 1$ both policies are chosen with equal probability. If the delay for the job chosen at stage k is denoted by u_k, then state transition occurs only when $u_k \in (0, \delta)$ where δ is a preassigned value. In such a case if the job chosen is from queue 1 the state of the automaton moves toward the state 0 and if it is from queue 2 it moves towards state n. Under the conditions above, it is contended that if action A is the better of the two actions it will be chosen with a probability arbitrarily close to 1. It is further argued that the deterministic scheme is superior to the variable-structure learning scheme both in terms of speed of convergence as well as the variance of the delay.

Comment 9.1: The most important aspect of applying learning schemes to practical problems lies in choosing the actions of the automaton as well as the performance criterion on which the updating is to be based. Quite often, the action set is dictated by the application, as in the two cases above. However, determining the performance criterion is not straightforward. The dynamic threshold $T(k)$ in the first case and u_k in the second determine how $p(k)$ is to be updated. The fact that widely different criteria yield ϵ–optimal response on the part of the learning automaton indicates that there may be considerable freedom in choosing the criterion function. The transient response may however be critically dependent on this choice.

Control of Service Activity: Another problem related to a single-server queueing system is considered by El Fattah et al (1985) who describe a model in which an arriving customer is either admitted or rejected. The purpose of the control is to limit the service activity to the admitted customers at a preassigned level and that level is to be maintained regardless of the customer arrival process. The implications of the results of this simple problem to flow control are readily apparent.

The most commonly used deterministic scheme is to reject an arrival if more than N customers are present in the system and maintain rejection until the number of customers drops off to a lower threshold M. Such a scheme however, will not reject a customer when the server is idle.

To permit idle time of the server for other secondary tasks, it is sug-

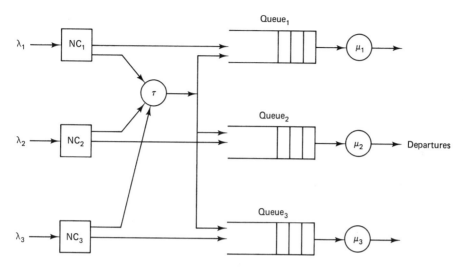

Figure 9.20: Example of task scheduling in computer networks (*Courtesy Digital Press*).

gested that a learning scheme be used to decide whether or not to accept an arrival. An automaton determines the probability $p(n)$ with which the customer is to be admitted. The r actions of the automaton correspond to r probabilities (including 0 and 1) which $p(n)$ can assume. When a customer is admitted, the internal state of the system changes, altering the probability with which the action is chosen. The state modification of the automaton is best described by a graph whose orientation depends on the number of customers present in the system.

The authors claim that the use of the automaton can be instrumental in protecting the server from saturation when the offered system load exceeds the server capacity. Furthermore, the service activity can be maintained at a preassigned level independent of the offered load so that the server has a vacation period to attend to other tasks.

Task Scheduling in Computer Networks: The problem of task scheduling in multiprocessor systems, originally suggested by Glorioso and Colon (1974), is a typical example of a queueing system in which learning schemes may prove useful. For a detailed treatment of this example the reader is referred to the book by Glorioso and Colon Osorio (1980). We present here a brief statement of the problem and some of the conclusions that can be drawn in order to relate them to the discussions in the previous sections.

Figure 9.20 represents a queueing theory counterpart of a three-processor queueing model. Three processors located at nodes 1, 2, and 3 have processing rates of μ_1, μ_2, and μ_3 respectively. The task arrival streams at the three nodes are Poisson processes with mean arrival rates λ_1, λ_2, and λ_3 respectively. Associated with each processor is a queue and the queue discipline is first-come-first-serve in the order of submittal times. The service time distributions of the processors are exponential.

The three processors are connected by a communication link to achieve higher performance and reliability through load sharing. The latter is accomplished by a task scheduler transferring tasks arriving at node i to processors at nodes $j \neq i$ on the basis of the current loads and performance of the system. The performance of the overall system is measured by the total execution time, which includes the time spent in transferring tasks from one node to another, and the time spent in a queue and the execution time of the task. It is assumed that the link connecting the processors is characterized by its mean transfer rate, τ (average number of transfers per wait time) so that $1/\tau$ represents the cost attached to the transfer of tasks between nodes.

When $\tau = 0$, the cost of transferring tasks is infinite and hence the system can be assumed to be decoupled with all the processors servicing their respective queues. When $\tau = \infty$, no cost is attached to a transfer and in this case all the loads could be lumped together to yield a single queue with a mean arrival rate equal to $\sum_{i=1}^{3} \lambda_i$. The routing scheme is then to determine how the tasks are to be routed to the different queues.

When all the parameters of the loads and processors are known, a fixed scheduling discipline (FSD) can be used to process the tasks optimally. This corresponds to the routing problem discussed in the previous section where the load is identical to that for which the network was originally designed. In such a case, as is to be expected, the task-allocation policy will be better than that of any learning scheme that has to obtain its information based on real-time measurements.

For anticipated loads, the (FSD) results in smaller mean turnaround times than an L_{R-I} scheme. In the latter a failure is defined to have occurred if the processor is busy when the call arrives. However, if the processing time of the processors is altered, corresponding to a nonstationary switching environment, the automaton adapts itself to the change and yields a smaller mean turnaround time than the FSD.

The characteristics of the automaton routing schemes observed in this context are typical of such schemes in most applications. The schemes continue to operate at close to the full capacity of the other processors when one or more processors fail or have reduced capacities. When one of the processors is idle while others are working at full capacity, the learning schemes distribute the load so there is load balancing. Such an equalization property of automata schemes has already been discussed both theoretically and practically. Finally, the discussion above also explains why the automata routing schemes can be readily extended as new processors are added to the network.

Multi-access Networks: The problem of sharing a single channel by many dispersed users arises quite often in data transmission systems. Consider a noise-free channel with a data rate of C bits per second. Users generate data packets randomly where each packet has a length of p bits. In conventional time-division multiple access (TDMA), packet slot time is assigned to each user in turn in a periodic manner. If the user traffic is low, the channel efficiency may be low using such an approach since many slots may go idle without transmission. This has led to the use of random access techniques where different users contend for the channel. This leads to simultaneous transmission on the part of different users and hence "collisions" occur with some probability, which in turn forces the users who are blocked to retransmit their packets.

The problem may be stated as follows: Each user does not have information concerning the state of the others but has access to information as to whether a packet was successfully transmitted or not and whether the channel was idle. In such a case a multi-access protocol must be devised that specifies the way the users should organize the transmissions to minimize collision or equivalently minimize the channel idle time when packets are waiting to be transmitted.

Various ad hoc rules such as exponential backoff have been proposed and analyzed for the retransmission process. If a learning scheme is used by the different users, the multi-access problem can be cast as a game of automata with identical payoffs for which the results of Chapter 8 can be applied. Srikantakumar (1983) presents a preliminary analysis of the problem. Although the approach is intriguing, considerably more theoretical analysis and simulation studies are needed to make the approach practically feasible.

9.3.2 Application to Image Data Compression

A novel approach to image data compression using stochastic learning was suggested by Hashim et al. (1986). Based more on estimation than control, the method uses automata at the transmitting and receiving ends of a communication channel to adaptively code and decode the data being sent. Like all the other applications given in this section, while initial experiments appear promising, decisions regarding the viability of this area of application can be made only after a careful comparison of the approach with well known methods of data compression.

Consider an $N \times N$ array of discrete samples or pixels obtained by sampling a continuous image at the Nyquist rate in the spatial domain. Let each pixel be represented by a finite number of quantization levels K. In the conventional pulse code modulation (PCM) technique for digital transmission and storage, such an image would require $K \times N \times N$ bits per image. This represents a large bandwidth for image transmission. Further, there is also degradation in picture quality when K is reduced to a value below 6. Many techniques have been suggested in the literature to reduce the number of bits needed for representing a pixel by exploiting the correlation between adjacent pixels. Among these, linear transformation coding and linear predictive coding are two of the important classes of compression schemes. In the first, linear transforms such as Fourier transform (Andrew and Pratt 1968, Anderson and Huang 1971), Hadamard transform (Pratt et al. 1969), Karhunen-Loeve transform (Tasb and Winta. 1971) and Slant transform (Pratt et al. 1974) have been developed based on the gray-level distribution of the image to obtain minimum mean-square error. In the second approach, classical prediction theory is used. Differential PCM first introduced by Cutler (1952) is an example of this approach and uses prior information regarding the statistics of the image source.

A learning algorithm is used by Hashim et al. (1986) to predict the conditional probability distributions of adjacent pixels. These in turn are used by a transmitter to code the gray-level values using a Huffman coder. The compression strategy is based on the classical technique of variable length coding that assigns code word lengths on the basis of pixel probability. Thus frequent pixel values are given shorter code words than less common pixel values. The receiver decodes the code words using the current estimates of the probability distributions.

Let each pixel in an image have K possible levels (or values). Let the value of the nth pixel be denoted by $g(n)$ so that $g(n) \in \{1, 2, \ldots, K\}$. The probability $Pr[g(n) = i]$ is called the pixel probability. Huffman's algorithm, which constructs an optimum code, is based on the knowledge of these pixel probabilities that can vary with both time and space. Since in practice only estimates of the probabilities can be made, the Huffman code must be based on the estimates. In the approach suggested, a learning automaton is used

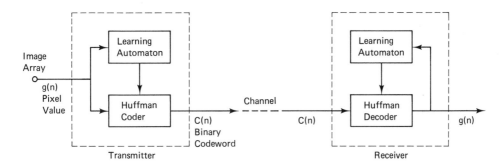

Figure 9.21: The data compression system.

to provide an estimate of the probabilities. Further, the procedure adopted is such that both transmitter and receiver can determine these estimates independently.

The data compression system consists of a transmitter and a receiver (Fig. 9.21). Two automata with identical pseudo-random generators that are synchronized are set up so that one is in the transmitter and the other in the receiver. At pixel $(n-1)$ let the vector $p(n-1)$ denote the probabilities of K levels of the pixels. It is assumed that this is the same in both the automata. Based on $p(n-1)$ and the measured value $g(n)$ of the pixel level, the Huffman coder generates the appropriate code word $c(n)$ to $g(n)$ according to the Huffman algorithm. At this stage both the automata have the same prior estimates of probabilities $p(n-1)$ and the knowledge of the gray level $g(n)$, i.e., $g(n) = i$ using the algorithm

$$
\begin{aligned}
p_i(n) &= p_i(n-1) + a(n)[1 - p_i(n-1)] \\
p_{j \neq i}(n) &= p_j(n-1)[1 - a(n)] \qquad\qquad 0 < a(n) < 1
\end{aligned}
\tag{9.9}
$$

the two automata update their probability estimates. In the algorithm $a(n) = \frac{B}{C}[C - |g(n) - \hat{g}(n)|]$ where B and C are constants and $\hat{g}(n)$ is the estimate of the gray level at stage n based on the probability distribution $p(n-1)$.

Example 9.8: The scheme presented was tested on a 256×256 image with 16 gray levels. Initially the probabilities of the gray levels were set to $1/16$ and the constants B and C were chosen to be 0.005 and 3 respectively. This implies that the minimum and maximum values $a(n)$ can assume are 0.005 and 0.02 respectively.

Using the learning automaton, the average Huffman word length was found to be 1.6925 bits/pixel. This compression was achieved without degradation of the image. Table 9.4 lists the performance of various compression schemes. The mean square error (MSE) between the actual image and the image after compression was used as a measure of degradation. The performance of the learning automata compares favorably with the best performance achieved by a DPCM.

System	No. of Quantized Levels (bits)	Entropy Compressed Image	MSE	Comment
L.A.	Use Huffman	1.695	0	No degradation
DPCM	3	1.55	12.55	Very noisy background deblared edges
DPCM	4	1.95	10.4	Noticeable noise deblared edges
DPCM	5	2.3	8.4	No noticeable noise

Table 9.4:   Data compression system performance

9.3.3   Relaxation Labeling with Learning Automata

A distinctly different area of application of learning automata theory from those considered earlier was recently proposed by Thathachar and Sastry (1986) and deals with relaxation labeling processes. In image analysis and AI many problems arise that can be formulated in terms of assigning labels to objects in a manner that is consistent with some domain-specific constraints. These are also referred to as consistent labeling problems (Haralick and Shapiro 1979). While relaxation labeling processes were initially developed to solve such labeling problems, it soon became evident that they have wider applications in such areas as image processing (Davis and Rosenfeld 1981), and character recognition (Peleg 1979). In Thathachar and Sastry (1986) the problem is posed as the interaction of a team of automata with an environment that gives noisy responses as to the consistency of the tentative labeling selected by the automata. Using weak convergence results for stochastic algorithms a local convergence result is derived and it is shown that the point of convergence depends on both the initial labeling and the constraints.

The application above of learning automata differs in two significant ways from the routing problems discussed in the preceding sections. While in the latter, the convergence of the learning automata depends on the rate at which external events take place (e.g., the rate at which calls enter the network), in the present example, the convergence of the automata is entirely determined by the computation speed of the CPU.

Further, while the use of learning automata in the routing problem can be justified primarily on the basis of economic considerations, their use in the present context is predicated on the complexity of the labeling problem and the need for a theoretically well founded method for updating probabilities. In fact this application suggests, as has been suspected for some time, that the principal areas where learning automata theory may prove particularly attractive are decision problems in complex systems with distributed processing capabilities.

Statement of the Problem: Let $\mathcal{A} = \{A_1, A_2, \ldots, A_n\}$ be a finite set of objects and let $\mathcal{C} = \{c_1, c_2, \ldots, c_m\}$ be a finite set of classes. We assume for convenience that the classes are mutually exclusive and collectively exhaustive. The problem is to assign labels to each object in a manner that is consistent with respect to a set of constraints. "Relaxation" is a method introduced by Rosenfeld et al. (1976) of using contextual information as an aid in classifying the objects A_i by allowing interactions among the possible classifications of related objects. It has been applied to pixel classification for image segmentation, image matching as well as to local feature detection. In the relaxation approach we start with a set of estimates of the probabilities $p_{ij} \geq 0$ that the object A_i belongs to class c_j $1 \leq i \leq n, 1 \leq j \leq m$ so that $\sum_{j=1}^{m} p_{ij} = 1$ for all $i = 1, 2, \ldots, n$. Also given are a set of compatibility functions $r_{ij} : \mathcal{C} \times \mathcal{C} \to \mathcal{R}$ where $r_{ij}(c_h, c_k)$ specifies the compatibility between pairs of events $A_i \in c_h$ and $A_j \in c_k$. The relaxation process then iteratively adjusts each p_{ij} based on the other $p_{jk}'^{s}$ and the compatibilities, so as to obtain the class membership probabilities that are mutually consistent. Although many algorithms have been proposed in the literature for probabilistic relaxation, our interest in this section will be entirely on how learning automata can be used to achieve this objective. We present below the notation used in Hummel and Zucker (1983).

An unambiguous labeling assignment is a function mapping $\mathcal{A}$ the set of objects to $\mathcal{C}$ the set of labels. Using an m-vector for each object as

$$p_i(c) \quad = 1 \text{ if object } A_i \text{ is mapped to } c$$
$$= 0 \text{ otherwise}$$

the space of all unambiguous labelings, K^* is the set of all mn dimensional vectors of the form $(\underline{p}_1^T, \underline{p}_2^T, \ldots, \underline{p}_n^T)^T$ where $\underline{p}_i = (p_i(1), p_i(2), \ldots, p_i(m))^T$ and only one element of $\underline{p}_i$ is 1 and all others are zero and $\sum_{s=1}^{m} p_i(c_s) = 1$. We denote the convex hull of K^* as K.

Continuous Labeling as a Team of Automata Problem: For the labeling problem a learning automaton is associated with each object $A_i(i = 1, 2, \ldots, n)$. Each automaton has m actions corresponding to the m labels. At any stage ℓ the automaton A_i assigns probabilities $[p_i^{(\ell)}(1), p_i^{(\ell)}(2), \ldots, p_i^{(\ell)}(m)] = \underline{p}_i^{(\ell)}$ to the m labels. Hence the state of the entire system at stage ℓ, denoted by the mn vector $\underline{p}^{(\ell)}$ lies in the set K. Based on the probability distributions $\underline{p}_i$ each automaton chooses an action that results in an unambiguous assignment $\underline{V} \in K^*$. The environment looks at this assignment and supplies each automaton with a response depending on the compatibility functions. The automata, in turn, use these responses to update the label probabilities and the cycle repeats. Thus the state $\underline{p}^{(\ell)}$ evolves over the state space K. It is the asymptotic behavior of this stochastic process that is of interest. It is obvious that the latter will depend on the manner in which the environment responds at any stage to the various automata as well as the specific learning algorithm used by the automata to update their probabilities. These can be described briefly as follows:

Response of Environment: At some stage let the automaton for object A_i choose action c_q. The response of the environment to this action is denoted as β_{iq} and is computed as follows from the vector p at that instant as well as the compatibility functions $r_{ij}(,)$:

$\sum_{s=1}^{m} r_{ij}(c_q, c_s)p_j(c_s)$ represents the support for label c_q of object A_i due to object A_j. The environment chooses a binary random variable X_{ij}^q such that

$$Pr[X_{ij}^q = 1] = \sum_{s=1}^{m} r_{ij}(c_q, c_s)p_j(c_s). \tag{9.10}$$

The practical realization of this consists in the environment merely sending back to A_i a response 1 with a probability $r_{ij}(c_q, c_s)$ if A_j chose the label c_s at that instant. This process is repeated for all "neighbors" c of A_i for which $r_{ij}(c_q, c) \neq 0$. If the number of neighbors is V_n then β_{iq} is computed as

$$\beta_{iq} = \frac{1}{V_n} \sum_j X_{ij}^q \tag{9.11}$$

i.e., A_i averages the responses from all its neighbors.

On the basis of the response from the environment at stage ℓ the automaton corresponding to object A_i updates its action probabilities at stage

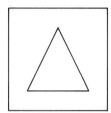

Figure 9.22: Figure for example 9.9.

$\ell + 1$ using the following scheme

$$
\begin{aligned}
p_i^{(\ell+1)}(c_q) &= p_i^{(\ell)}(c_q) + a[1 - p_i^{(\ell)}(c_q)]\beta_{iq}(\ell) \\
p_i^{(\ell+1)}(c_r) &= p_i^{(\ell)}(c_r) - a p_i^{(\ell)}(c_r)\beta_{iq}(\ell) \qquad 0 < a < 1.
\end{aligned}
\tag{9.12}
$$

Using the weak convergence methods of Kushner (1971), it is shown that the procedure above leads to the following results:

(i) For small enough value of the parameter a the asymptotic behavior of $\underline{p}^{(\ell)}$ can be approximated by the solution of an ordinary differential equation with the same initial conditions.

(ii) The n-fold m-simplex consists of corners each of which is either consistent or nonconsistent. The nonconsistent corners are strongly unstable, while the consistent corners are asymptotically stable. Hence around each of the latter corners there exists a neighborhood entering which the algorithms get absorbed. Hence convergence of the process using learning automata to label consistently depends on the initial conditions as well as the compatibility functions that determine which corners of the simplex are consistent.

Example 9.9: The algorithm described earlier was applied to the simple toy triangle problem considered earlier by Zucker et al. (1981) using standard relaxation algorithms for probability updatings and by Faugeras and Berthod (1981) using an optimization approach. Figure 9.22 shows the picture to be labeled and consists of a triangle. The objects to be labeled in this case are the sides of the triangle and the four classes are:

c_1: occluding edge, forward object above
c_2: occluding edge, forward object below
c_3: convex-fold
c_4: concave-fold

The compatibility matrix has the form

$$
R_{ij} = \begin{array}{c}
 & \begin{array}{cccc} c_1 & c_2 & c_3 & c_4 \end{array} \\
\begin{array}{c} c_1 \\ c_2 \\ c_3 \\ c_4 \end{array} & \left| \begin{array}{cccc}
.5 & 0 & 1.0 & 0 \\
0 & .5 & 0 & 1 \\
.5 & 0 & 0 & 0 \\
0 & .5 & 0 & 0
\end{array} \right.
\end{array}
$$

for $i, j = 1, 2$ and 3.

From the definitions of consistent labeling it follows that only (c_1, c_1, c_1), (c_2, c_2, c_2), and permutations of (c_1, c_1, c_3) and (c_2, c_2, c_4) correspond to consistent labelings. The results of the simulations shown in Table 9.5 indicate that the sample paths converge to the consistent labelings as predicted. The number of iterations given in the last column corresponds to the smallest iteration numbers for which all three probability vectors contain a label probability greater than .99. It is also clear that the labeling to which the process converges depends upon the initial conditions. The amount of computation done per iteration is significantly smaller than those in other methods for the general n-object m-label problem. For the specific example considered, the computational load per iteration is claimed to be one-sixth of that of Zucker et al. (1981) and less than one-tenth of that of Faugeras and Berthod (1981).

Comment 9.2: The discussions in this section, as well as the simulation results, indicate that the use of learning automata for relaxation labeling compares favorably with other known approaches for the problem. The convergence of the algorithm is critically dependent on the type of feedback that each automaton receives from the environment. One specific method of providing a response is presented here and this corresponds to a game problem with multiple payoffs – each automaton receiving a response that depends on its neighbors and the corresponding compatibility functions. In this sense it is different from the identical payoff game problems discussed in Chapter 8. It is however interesting to note that the theoretical results presented for such a problem have much in common with those presented in Chapter 8 for the identical payoff problem.

Simulation Results

Sl. No.	Initial Probabilities				Labelings L_{R-I} Converges to	Number of Iterations Needed	
						Range	Average
1)	0.25	0.25	0.25	0.25	$(c_1, c_1, c_1), (c_1, c_1, c_1)$	10–26	19.2
	0.25	0.25	0.25	0.25	$(c_1, c_1, c_1), (c_1, c_1, c_1)$		
	0.25	0.25	0.25	0.25	$(c_2, c_2, c_4), (c_2, c_4, c_2)$		
					$(c_2, c_2, c_2), (c_4, c_2, c_2)$		
2)	0.22	0.33	0.40	0.05	$(c_3, c_1, c_1), (c_1, c_1, c_1)$	12–27	17.5
	0.13	0.44	0.08	0.35	(c_2, c_2, c_2)		
	0.57	0.11	0.06	0.26	$(c_2, c_4, c_2), (c_2, c_2, c_4)$		
3)	0.5	0	0.5	0	(c_1, c_3, c_1)	9–19	14.5
	0.5	0	0.5	0	(c_3, c_1, c_1)		
	0.5	0	0.5	0	$(c_1, c_1, c_3), (c_1, c_1, c_1)$		
4)	0.5	0	0.5	0	(c_1, c_3, c_1)	9–21	14.9
	0.4	0	0.6	0	$(c_3, c_1, c_1), (c_1, c_1, c_3)$		
	0.5	0	0.5	0	(c_1, c_1, c_1)		
5)	0.3	0	0.7	0	(c_3, c_1, c_1)	7–23	14.75
	0.3	0	0.7	0	(c_1, c_3, c_1)		
	0.5	0	0.5	0	(c_1, c_1, c_1)		
6)	0.2	0	0.8	0	(c_3, c_1, c_1)	8–23	14.67
	0.3	0	0.7	0	(c_1, c_3, c_1)		
	0.5	0	0.5	0			
7)	0.51	0.49	0	0	(c_1, c_1, c_1)	9–24	16
	0.5	0	0	0.5	(c_2, c_4, c_2)		
	0	0.5	0.5	0			
8)	0.25	0.49	0.25	0.01	(c_1, c_1, c_1)	11–26	17.4
	0.33	0.33	0.33	0.01	(c_2, c_2, c_2)		
	0	0.5	0.49	0.01			
9)	0.3	0.3	0.2	0.2	(c_2, c_2, c_4)	10–23	17.1
	0.3	0.3	0.2	0.2	(c_2, c_2, c_2)		
	0.3	0.3	0.2	0.2	$(c_1, c_1, c_1), (c_1, c_1, c_1)$		

Table 9.5

Comment 9.3: At every stage, after all the automata have chosen a specific action (resulting in an unambiguous assignment) the compatibility functions $r_{ij}(c_h, c_k)$ have deterministic values. Converting these into random responses is the central feature of the approach. It is not evident whether an equivalent algorithm with identical payoffs for all the automata can be generated so that the results of Chapter 8 can be directly applied.

Comment 9.4: As mentioned in the introduction, this application represents a distinct departure from the network routing problems. It indicates how deterministic optimization problems can be cast in a stochastic format so that learning automata can be used in determining their equilibrium states. The authors feel that many of the applications of learning automata in the future will share several features with the scheme described in this section.

9.3.4 Pattern Discrimination of Context Vectors

In Chapter 7 methods of optimizing the performance of an automaton based on contextual information were discussed. In particular, in Section 7.11 the associative reward-penalty (A_{R-P}) algorithm of Barto and Anandan (1985) was presented briefly in which the action probability vector is suitably parameterized and a mapping is constructed from the environmental states to the parameter vector used. In this section, we present some simulation results that indicate how the method might perform in a practical application. Although the problem can be handled by attaching one automaton to each parameter vector, the significance of the approach as already mentioned in Chapter 7 is that it involves a novel combination of pattern classification and stochastic learning algorithms.

Recent interest in the area of neural and computational models of adaptation and learning is based on the premise that networks of interacting neuronlike processing elements can provide useful alternatives to conventional computational architectures. Such research currently goes under the name of "connectionism." The importance of the example treated in this section lies in the relation it establishes between learning automata theory and the connectionist approach to computation. The fact that attempts are being made to extend these ideas to the study of the collective behavior of interacting associative reward-penalty elements brings the ideas even closer to those of learning automata theory, as discussed in Chapter 8.

Simulation Results:

In Barto and Anandan (1985), the algorithms presented in Section 7.11 are applied to two a discrimination to be made between two vectors $x^{(1)} = (1,1)^T$ and $x^{(2)} = (1,0)^T$. The two vectors are assumed to be equally likely at each stage and the initial parameter vector $\theta(0)$ is set at zero for each run.

Example 9.10: In the first task the success probabilities with the context vector $x^{(1)}$ using the two actions $a_1 = +1$ and $a_2 = -1$ are given by

$$d(x^{(1)}, +1) = 0.1 \qquad\qquad d(x^{(1)}, -1) = 0.8$$

while those with the context vector $x^{(2)}$ are

$$d(x^{(2)}, +1) = 0.9 \qquad\qquad d(x^{(2)}, -1) = 0.2.$$

This implies that the learning algorithm should respond to $x^{(1)}$ with action a_2 and to $x^{(2)}$ with action a_1. In this case the average performance is $M_{\max} = 0.85$.

Since the success probabilities for the two patterns are widely separated and the good responses correspond to different actions, this task can be considered qualitatively to be an easy one. For this problem, the algorithm described in Section 7.11 was compared with a selective bootstrap algorithm of Widrow et al. (1973). The latter converged rapidly to the optimal value of .85 while the A_{R-P} algorithm converged to 0.8485, 0.8152 and 0.7868 respectively with $\lambda = 0.01, 0.25$ and 0.5. Figure 9.23 shows the average over 100 runs and indicates that as λ decreases, the asymptotic value increases while the speed of response decreases as described in Chapter 5.

Example 9.11: In this case, a more difficult task is chosen for the automaton and the corresponding reward probabilities are given below.

$$d(x^{(1)}, +1) = 0.4 \qquad\qquad d(x^{(1)}, -1) = 0.2$$
$$d(x^{(2)}, +1) = 0.6 \qquad\qquad d(x^{(2)}, -1) = 0.9$$

In state $x^{(1)}$ the action $a = +1$ is found to be optimal and has a reward probability of only 0.4. In the state $x^{(2)}$ even the poorer action $a = +1$ has a reward probability of 0.6. The aim of the experiment is to determine whether the actions of the automata converge to $+1$ and -1 in the two states $x^{(1)}$ and $x^{(2)}$ respectively. The mean response in such a case is $M_{\max} = 0.65$.

Figure 9.24(b) shows the results obtained in a typical run using an A_{R-P} algorithm. In this case convergence is to 0.6348 which is sufficiently close to the true optimal. In contrast to this, the algorithm of Widrow et al. (1973) oscillates for certain values of λ as in Fig. 9.24(a) while converging to wrong actions in certain other cases. Hence, in this specific case, we conclude that the A_{R-P} algorithm is distinctly better.

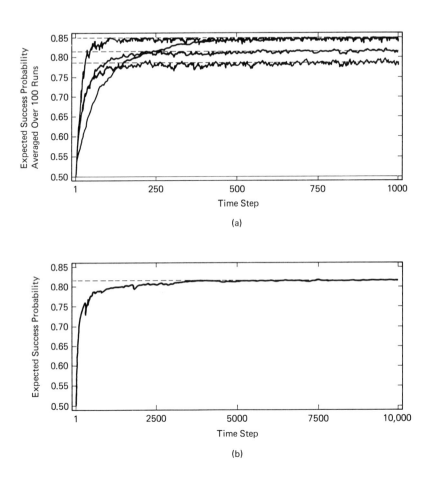

(a)

(b)

Figure 9.23: Simulation results for Example 9.10. (a) averages of M_k over 100 runs of selective bootstrap algorithm and A_{R-P} algorithm for three values of λ (b) M_k for a single run of A_{R-p} algorithm (*Courtesy IEEE* ©*1985*).

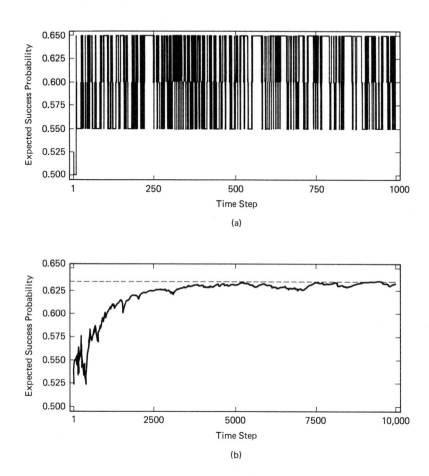

Figure 9.24: Simulation results for single runs of Example 9.11. (a) the selective bootstrap algorithm. (b) the A_{R-P} algorithm (*Courtesy IEEE* ©*1985*).

In the examples described in this section the automaton has two actions and it is not immediately obvious how the method can be generalized to the $r(> 2)$ action case. It nevertheless represents an important step since it provides for the first time a method of incorporating additional information regarding the environment to improve the performance of the automaton. On the basis of these preliminary results, it now appears worthwhile to attempt to extend the results presented in Chapter 8 to cases where partial communication may be possible between learning automata. Collectives of adaptive elements might exhibit far richer forms of behavior with such interautomaton communication. However, in view of the modified structure, the proofs of convergence are bound to be significantly more difficult than those given in Chapter 8.

9.3.5   Pattern Classification as a Game of Automata

The problem of pattern classification using supervised learning has been extensively investigated and is well documented (Duda and Hart 1973, Sklansky and Wassel 1981). Typically, in a two-class problem, patterns represented as m-dimensional vectors in a feature space X are assumed to belong to one of two classes ω_1 and ω_2. A training set of sample patterns with known classification is assumed to be available. To classify new patterns, a discriminant function $g(x) : \mathcal{R}^m \to \mathcal{R}$ is defined such that the rule

$$
\begin{aligned}
\text{if } \; & g(x) \geq 0 \qquad \text{decide } x \in \omega_1 \text{ and} \\
\text{if } \; & g(x) < 0 \qquad \text{decide } x \in \omega_2
\end{aligned}
\tag{9.13}
$$

can be used. The task is to determine the discriminant function $g(\cdot)$ which minimizes the probability of the error in the classification. No knowledge of the class-conditional densities $f(x|\omega_i)$ or the prior probabilities of the two classes $p(\omega_i)(i = 1, 2)$ is assumed.

If $Pr(\omega_i|x)$ is the probability that the feature vector x belongs to class ω_i, Bayes' decision rule

$$
x \in \omega_i \text{ if } Pr(\omega_i|x) \geq Pr(\omega_j|x)
\tag{9.14}
$$

minimizes the probability of misclassification.

Thus,

$$
g_{\text{opt}}(x) = Pr(\omega_1|x) - Pr(\omega_2|x)
\tag{9.15}
$$

is the optimal discriminant function that must be determined using the training set of sample patterns of known classification.

Some earlier approaches (Duda and Hart 1973) utilize a linear discriminant function of the form

$$g(x) = \theta^T x$$

and using the stochastic-approximation type of procedure determine the value of θ that minimizes the mean square error between $g(x)$ and $g_{\text{opt}}(x)$. However, the resulting discriminant function does not necessarily minimize the probability of misclassification. In this section we present an alternative approach suggested by Thathachar and Sastry (1987) in which the problem is posed as a game of learning automata with identical payoffs.

Let the discriminant function be expressed as a function of n real-valued parameters $\theta_1, \theta_2, \ldots, \theta_n$ so that

$$g(x) = h(\theta_1, \theta_2, \ldots, \theta_n, x). \tag{9.16}$$

The decision rule is given by Eq. (9.14). The probability of correct classification with a parameter vector θ is given by

$$\begin{aligned} J(\theta) = \quad &Pr(\omega_1)Pr(g(x) \geq 0 | x \in \omega_1) \\ &+ Pr(\omega_2)Pr(g(x) < 0 | x \in \omega_2). \end{aligned} \tag{9.17}$$

For a sample pattern x, let

$$\begin{aligned} L(x) \quad &= 1 \quad \text{if } x \text{ is properly classified} \\ &= 0 \quad \text{otherwise.} \end{aligned} \tag{9.18}$$

Then

$$J(\theta) = E[L(x)]$$

and hence maximizing $E[L(x)]$ minimizes the probability of misclassification.

The problem of pattern classification can now be posed as a game of n automata $A_1, A_2, \ldots, A_n$ each of which chooses a parameter $\theta_i (i = 1, 2, \ldots, n)$ to maximize the identical payoff $J(\theta)$. Hence, the methods outlined in Chapter 8 can be used provided each parameter θ_i is discretized and consequently belongs to a finite action set corresponding to A_i. Further, since complete communication between the automata can be assumed, estimator algorithms can be used to speed up the convergence rates.

Let $\theta_i \in \alpha^i$ where α^i is the finite action set defined by

$$\alpha^i = \{\alpha_1^i, \alpha_2^i, \ldots, \alpha_{r_i}^i\}.$$

In the game, each automaton A_i chooses a particular action (and hence a value of θ_i), and this results in a classifier with a discriminant function $g(x)$.

Any sample pattern is classified according to the rule of Eq. (9.13) and $L(x)$ is determined as given in Eq. (9.18). Thus $L(x)$ forms the payoff for all the automata that update their action probabilities according to an estimator algorithm (refer to Section 4.11). If the set of actions at any stage is $\{\alpha_{i_1}^1, \alpha_{i_2}^2, \ldots, \alpha_{i_n}^n\}$ the corresponding probability of success is $d_{i_1,i_2,\ldots,i_n}$. For using estimator algorithms it is necessary to estimate $d_{i_1,i_2,\ldots,i_n}$ and update the estimate with each pattern. As estimator algorithms enable the automata to converge to the optimal action with a probability arbitrarily close to 1, the parameter vector θ converges to its optimal value with arbitrary accuracy. The only condition needed for this is that $\max J(\theta)$ be unique.

Although L_{R-I}^θ and other absolutely monotonic algorithms could also be used for updating action probabilities, estimator algorithms are preferred for two reasons. Although they invariably converge to the global optimum, the former can converge to local maxima. Further, the former are very slow and need substantially larger training sets.

In conclusion, the automata approach learns the optimal classifier under the following assumptions:

(i)   The form of the optimal discriminant function is contained in the functional form of $g(x)$ chosen.

(ii)   The optimal values of the parameters are elements of the sets $\alpha^i (i = 1, 2, \ldots, n)$.

(iii) The maximum $J(\theta)$ after discretization is unique.

Even assuming that assumption (ii) is not satisfied, the collective of automata would learn the best classifier among the set of classifiers being considered. By choosing finer parameter sets, successively better approximations to the optimal classifier can be obtained.

Example 9.12: The following classification problem was simulated using the approach outlined in this section:

The class-conditional densities are given by

$$f_1(x|\omega_1) = N(m_1, S)$$
$$f_2(x|\omega_2) = N(m_2, S)$$

where $N(m, S)$ denotes a normal distribution with mean m and covariance matrix S. For the two-dimensional feature sets used

$$m_1 = [2.0, 2.0]^T \quad m_2 = [3.0, 3.0]^T \quad \text{and}$$

$$S = \begin{bmatrix} 1.0 & 0.25 \\ 0.25 & 1.0 \end{bmatrix}.$$

Obviously, the information above is not available to the automata.

For the automata approach the discriminant function was deliberately chosen to be nonlinear (in the parameters) and to have the form

$$g(x) = 1 - \frac{x_1}{\theta_1} - \frac{x_2}{\theta_2}$$

where θ_1 and θ_2 must be determined. Both parameters are assumed to take one of five integer values in the interval [0,10] so that each member of the collective of automata has five actions in its action set. Table 9.6 shows the evolution of the probabilities of the optimal actions α_3^1 and α_3^2 which correspond to the parameter values $\theta_1 = 5$ and $\theta_2 = 5$ respectively. The resulting discriminant function

$$g(x) = 1 - 0.2x_1 - 0.2x_2$$

is found to minimize the probability of misclassification.

n Number of Iterations	$p_3^1(n)$	$p_3^2(n)$
0	0.2	0.2
200	0.325	0.338
400	0.816	0.695
600	0.987	0.978
800	0.941	0.935
1000	0.999	0.998

Table 9.6

Although the advantages of the approach described above, such as the communication beween automata in the pattern classification problem are obvious, some of its drawbacks need to be mentioned. The use of estimator type of algorithms imply memory requirements that grow exponentially with the dimension of the feature vector space. Hence the method may not be attractive when the dimensionality of the problem is large. Further, in the example described above, five values of the parameters $\theta_i (i = 1, 2)$ were assumed to correspond to actions of the two automata. In more complex problems, the range of values of the various parameters may not be known. Despite these shortcomings, the method proposed is analytically attractive since convergence results can be derived, as indicated in Chapter 8.

9.4   Conclusion

Applications of learning automata theory to a fairly broad class of problems were considered in this chapter. A feature common to most of the problems discussed is that the systems they pertain to are complex and cannot be represented by good mathematical models. Many facts have also emerged from the numerous simulation studies presented concerning the effectiveness of automata schemes and the extent to which they can be considered as viable alternatives in practical problems.

In the various contexts discussed in Sections 9.2 and 9.3 the learning automaton approach is found to be intuitively appealing and simple to implement, provided a suitable index of performance can be measured and fed back to each constituent automaton. This may pose a serious problem since in most complex systems the quantities to be fed back are hard to determine. For example, in routing problems, the learning approach was found to perform significantly better in both circuit-switched and packet-switched networks when the response of the system is not merely call completion or average time delay but some measure of the state as well. Hence one of the principal questions to be addressed in the future is what information should be fed back for reinforcement learning and how such feedback can be achieved in practice.

The relaxation labeling problem discussed in Section 9.3.3 is typical of a large class of problems for which the learning automaton approach is particularly suited. It possesses most of the features described in Section 9.1, which are desirable in a problem, if the learning approach is to be applied successfully. The use of a context vector described in Section 9.3.4 is one method of generalizing the learning automaton, and the example described establishes the relationship between the learning approach and the connectionist approach to computation. Future efforts in this area will be directed toward the collective behavior of automata in situations where partial communication between automata is possible. The pattern classification problem treated in Section 9.3.5 reveals that many difficult problems in stochastic environments can be recast as problems of learning automata games so that the methods outlined in Chapter 8 can be applied directly.

It was mentioned in Section 9.1 that at present very few practical situations are known where automata methods have been demonstrated to be superior to existing methods. Until recently, this was true even in the routing problem, where simulation studies have been in progress for many years. Despite this, the appeal of learning schemes has continued to grow. This may be partly attributed to the increasing number of problems arising in information technology for which analytical solutions cannot be found and partly to the improvement in performance that is being realized in the solution of such problems using the learning approach with more sophisticated feedback to the automata from the environment. The authors are of the opinion that both factors mentioned above will only be more pronounced in the future, resulting in increased interest in learning automata schemes.

Epilogue

Major advances in information technology are resulting in the proliferation of distributed systems for collecting, accessing and processing data. These systems are not necessarily designed from the outset and in fact often evolve over time from the interconnection of new elements to existing systems. We are constantly made aware of how little we know about the resulting behavior of such systems and the real need that exists for new theories to guide system design and operation. The learning automaton approach provides one such conceptual framework for the design of large distributed systems, particularly when high degrees of randomness are present.

In this book, the paradigm of a learning automaton was introduced in Chapter 1 and was shown to include many interrelated concepts associated with learning. Following a quantitative definition in Chapter 2, learning schemes were introduced in Chapters 3 and 4 and were shown to perform almost optimally in stationary random environments. In Chapter 6 the same schemes were extended to environments with general outputs, and in Chapter 7 were also shown to be applicable to time–varying environments, multiple environments, and hierarchies. In Chapter 8 we discovered a major extension, especially valuable in the context of distributed systems. The simple learning schemes designed for single decision makers proved successful in game situations when individual automata act in complete ignorance of the other automata. In particular, rational behavior in two–person zero–sum games and identical payoff games was demonstrated. These results indicate that distributed systems can be designed in an optimal fashion, where game theoretic concepts are used to define optimality. The results in Chapter 8 also showed that automata organized in hierarchies, interconnected at various levels, and involved in games, can improve their performance at every stage in an expected sense. We have here a framework for understanding collectives of automata that exhibit intelligent behavior.

The simplicity of the automaton structure, the general nature of its action set, and the logic of the updating strategies make the automaton approach to modeling and control intuitively appealing. Yet, the same characteristics are also responsible for some of its serious drawbacks. Since automata, acting individually or as a part of a collective, use very little prior information, their rate of convergence in any specific situation is too slow from a practical standpoint. Although an increase in the step size results in improved speed of response, it invariably implies an increased probability of convergence to the wrong action. Hence to make the approach practically viable, new methods must be investigated in which each member of a collective of automata either shares its information with the others or uses prior information or world knowledge common to all of them. Such modifications will increase the applicability of the automaton approach beyond the simple situations in which virtually no prior information is assumed. Problems in such areas as computer vision, image understanding, and robotics are promising candidates for a learning automaton approach in which additional information is incorporated.

The need for generalizing the manner in which an individual automaton operates has been recognized for some time and has motivated numerous attempts at generalizations. Among these, the most promising are the use of estimator algorithms, in which the parameters of the environment are estimated, and the use of a context space in which the learning process takes place. In a simple automaton, the information concerning its past performance in a random environment is stored entirely in its action probability vector. This is also the case when the automaton acts as a member of a collective. In estimator algorithms, additional information concerning the effectiveness of the various actions is provided by the estimates of the failure probabilities. Although this results in improved rates of convergence, the improvement is achieved only at the expense of increased storage requirements, which quite often become prohibitively large. The second method of generalizing an individual automaton by the use of a context vector was described in Chapter 7. It is now generally recognized that the potential of groups of automata can be increased substantially by assuring that learning takes place in a context so that different optimal actions are associated with different regions in a context space. Research is still in the early stages in this intriguing area of learning automata theory.

When the actions of an automaton assume real values, it becomes possible to interconnect automata in different complex patterns to realize interesting behavior. For example, such interconnections have given rise to structures that are very similar to those of artificial neural networks. This makes it possible to use the learning automaton approach in such networks to update the weights based on the random response of the system.

In the games and hierarchies discussed in Chapter 8 it was shown only that the expected payoff is a submartingale so that on an average the collective of automata improves its behavior at every stage. However, very little could be concluded about optimality. The control of Markov chains was an exception since in this case it could be established that a unique equilibrium state existed. This indicates that the architecture of a distributed system and the performance criterion chosen may be just as important as the decision rules in order to achieve desired global behavior.

Synchronized operation of decision makers in a distributed system using identical payoffs is characteristic of engineering systems that have been designed from the outset to achieve an overall objective. In most distributed systems that evolve slowly with time, decentralized decision makers rarely conduct their analysis at the same time or use the same algorithms or have the same objectives. As a consequence, the interaction of the decision makers can be better described by N-person nonzero–sum games and well known concepts of game theory such as coalition formation, power and fair division may have to be applied. Very little work has been reported thus far in these potentially fertile areas of research.

The study of the behavior of collectives of automata in random environments invariably leads to problems in which learning theory and game theory play an important part. Game theory attempts to define rationality in specific contexts assuming that no uncertainty is present. The application of learning algorithms to these contexts has thus far attempted to assure asymptotic convergence consistent with the game theoretic concepts. New algorithms will have to be designed in the future to realize notions of rational behavior in nonzero–sum games not treated in this book. At the same time, the need to understand systems in which decision makers are interconnected in specific configurations, perhaps dictated by practical considerations, is also providing a strong impetus to research on nonzero–sum games. It is further hoped that new insights of a game theoretic nature may be achieved by a study of the asymptotic behavior of interconnected automata, using algorithms that are different from those analyzed in this book. These interactions of learning theory and game theory are bound to have a major impact on our understanding of stochastic distributed systems. The consequence of this understanding will be felt in applications of learning automata to distributed processing systems that must operate in highly uncertain environments. The learning approach can play an important role as such applications place increasing demands on information technology.

Appendix A

Markov Chains

A.1 Introduction

A stochastic process is a family of random variables $\{X(t),\ t\ \epsilon\ T\}$ defined on some sample space Ω. The set T is called the index set of the process. If T has countably many members [e.g., $T = \{0, 1, 2, \ldots\}$], the stochastic process is said to be a discrete-parameter process. If there are uncountably many members of the family [e.g., $T = \{t :\geq 0\}$], the stochastic process is said to be a continuous-parameter process. The set of distinct values assumed by a stochastic process is called the state space. The state space S of the stochastic process can be either countable or uncountable. In the former case, the stochastic process is called a chain.

Stochastic processes can therefore be classified in one of four ways depending on whether time (the index set) is discrete or continuous and the state space is discrete or continuous. In this appendix we shall be interested in discrete-time chains which further satisfy the Markovian property described below (Isaacson and Madsen 1976).

Definition A.1: A discrete-parameter stochastic process $(X(t); t = 0, 1, 2, \ldots)$ is said to be a Markov process if, for any set of n points $t_1 < t_2 < t_3, \ldots, < t_n$ in the index set, the conditional distribution of $X(t_n)$ for given values of $X(t_1), X(t_2), \ldots, X(t_{n-1})$ depends only on $X(t_{n-1})$. Or more precisely, if $x_1, x_2, \ldots, x_n$ are arbitrary real numbers,

$$Pr[X(t_n) \leq x_n \quad | \quad X(t_{n-1}) = x_{n-1}, X(t_{n-2}) = x_{n-2}, \ldots, X(t_1) = x_1]$$
$$= \quad Pr[X(t_n) \leq x_n | X(t_{n-1}) = x_{n-1}].$$
$$\text{(A.1)}$$

1	2	3
4	5	6
7	8	9

Figure A.1: Example of a Markov Chain.

A Markov process whose state space is discrete is called a Markov chain.

Transition Probabilities: Let $\phi_i(i = 1, 2, \ldots)$ denote the states of a Markov chain $\{X_n\}$ where X_n denotes $X(n)$. To specify the probability law of the Markov chain, it suffices to state at all time $n \geq m \geq 0$ and for all states ϕ_j and ϕ_k the probability

$$p_j(m) = Pr[X_m = \phi_j] \qquad (A.2)$$

and the conditional probability

$$p_{jk}(m, n) = Pr[X_n = \phi_k | X_m = \phi_j]. \qquad (A.3)$$

The function $p_{jk}(m, n)$ is called the transition probability function of the Markov chain.

Given any q instants of time $n_1, n_2, \ldots, n_q$ $(n_1 < n_2, \ldots, < n_q)$ and states $\phi_1, \phi_2, \ldots, \phi_q$,

$$Pr[X_{n_1} = \phi_1, X_{n_2} = \phi_2, \ldots, X_{n_q} = \phi_q] = p_1(n_1)p_{12}(n_1, n_2)p_{23}(n_2, n_3)$$
$$\cdots p_{q-1,q}(n_{q-1}, n_q). \qquad (A.4)$$

A Markov chain is said to be homogeneous or homogeneous in time, if $p_{jk}(m, n)$ as defined in Eq. (A.3) depends only on $n - m$. In such a case we call

$$p_{jk}^{(n)} = Pr[X_{n+m} = \phi_k | X_m = \phi_j] \text{ for } m \geq 0$$

the n-step transition probability function of the Markov chain. Then, $p_{jk}^{(n)}$ denotes the conditional probability that a homogeneous Markov chain in state ϕ_j will go to ϕ_k in n steps. When $n = 1$, the one step transition probability $p_{jk}^{(1)}$ is simply written as p_{jk}.

Consider a particle that can be in any one of nine chambers shown in Fig. A.1. Assuming that at any instant it is in one of the chambers, say 4, let us assume that it can only appear at the next instant in one of the chambers connected to it, i.e., 1, 5, and 7 with equal probability. In this case the location of the particle at instant n will depend only on its location at instant $n - 1$. Hence if X_n represents the number of the chamber occupied by the particle at time n, $\{X_n\}$ satisfies the Markov property. The matrix of transition probabilities is denoted by P, whose typical element p_{ij} represents the probability of transferring from state i to state j. For the simple example considered, we have a 9×9 transition matrix P given by

$$P = \begin{bmatrix} 0 & 1/2 & 0 & 1/2 & 0 & 0 & 0 & 0 & 0 \\ 1/3 & 0 & 1/3 & 0 & 1/3 & 0 & 0 & 0 & 0 \\ 0 & 1/2 & 0 & 0 & 0 & 1/2 & 0 & 0 & 0 \\ 1/3 & 0 & 0 & 0 & 1/3 & 0 & 1/3 & 0 & 0 \\ 0 & 1/4 & 0 & 1/4 & 0 & 1/4 & 0 & 1/4 & 0 \\ 0 & 0 & 1/3 & 0 & 1/3 & 0 & 0 & 0 & 1/3 \\ 0 & 0 & 0 & 1/2 & 0 & 0 & 0 & 1/2 & 0 \\ 0 & 0 & 0 & 0 & 1/3 & 0 & 1/3 & 0 & 1/3 \\ 0 & 0 & 0 & 0 & 0 & 1/2 & 0 & 1/2 & 0 \end{bmatrix}.$$

As seen in the example above the discrete-time Markov chain is stationary (or homogeneous) since the probability of going from one state to another in a single step is independent of time. In other words, a homogeneous Markov chain has a constant transition probability matrix associated with it. Since the elements of the matrix represent probabilities, they are all nonnegative. Further, since each state ϕ_i must be transferred to some state $\phi_j (j = 1, 2, \ldots, N)$ where N denotes the number of states, the sum of the entries in each row must be equal to one. Any square matrix that satisfies these two conditions is called a stochastic matrix. Let $a_0^T = [a_1, a_2, \ldots, a_N]$ be a row vector whose elements are nonnegative such that $\sum_{i=1}^{N} a_i = 1$. Let a_i represent the probability of finding the process in state ϕ_i at some time $t = 0$. If we now consider the row vector $a_0^T P$, the elements b_i of this vector represent the probability of finding the process in state $\phi_i (i = 1, 2, \ldots, N)$ at the instant $t = 1$. For example, $\sum_{i=1}^{N} a_i p_{i1}$ is the probability that the process will be in state ϕ_1 at $t = 1$ since

$$\sum_i a_i p_{i1} = \sum_i Pr[X(1) = \phi_1 | X(0) = \phi_i] Pr[X(0) = \phi_i]. \tag{A.5}$$

Hence post multiplication of the initial vector a_0^T by P yields the distribution of probabilities of the states of the finite Markov chain after one instant.

Similarly the distribution after n steps can be computed using the matrix P^n whose elements $p_{ij}^{(n)}$ represent the n-step transition probabilities.

Chapman-Kolmogorov Equation: A fundamental relation satisfied by the transition probability function of a Markov chain $\{X_n\}$ is the so-called Chapman-Kolmogorov equation: For all nonnegative integers m, u, and n such that $n > u > m \geq 0$ and states ϕ_i and ϕ_j

$$p_{ij}(m, n) = \sum_{\text{states } \phi_k} p_{ik}(m, u) p_{kj}(u, n) \tag{A.6}$$

where the summation is over all the states of the Markov chain.

The Chapman-Kolmogorov equation reflects the simple fact that the first $(u - m)$ steps lead from ϕ_i to ϕ_k and the subsequent transfer from ϕ_k to ϕ_j does not depend on the manner ϕ_k was reached. All the paths that go from ϕ_i to ϕ_k in $(u - m)$ steps and then from ϕ_k to ϕ_j in $(n - u)$ steps are collected together and the probability of this group of paths is given by $p_{ik}(m, u) p_{kj}(u, n)$. By summing these probabilities over all $\phi_k \, \epsilon \, S$, we get the total probability of going from ϕ_i to ϕ_j.

$$Pr[X(n) = \phi_j | X(m) = \phi_i] = \sum_{\text{states } \phi_k} Pr[X(n) = \phi_j | X(u) = \phi_k, X(m) = \phi_i]$$
$$\times Pr[X(u) = \phi_k | X(m) = \phi_i]. \tag{A.7}$$

Equation (A.6) follows directly from Eq. (A.7) and the Markov property.

In terms of the multiplication of transition probability matrices, the Chapman-Kolmogorov equations for all times $n > u > m \geq 0$ may be written as

$$P[m, n] = P[m, u] P[u, n]. \tag{A.8}$$

For a homogeneous Markov chain this in turn can be written as

$$p_{ij}^{(n-m)} = \sum_{\phi_k \epsilon S} p_{ik}^{(u-m)} p_{kj}^{(n-u)}. \tag{A.9}$$

In view of the comments made in this section it is clear that a Markov chain $\{X_n\}$ is completely determined once one knows the transition probability matrices and the unconditional probability vector $p(0)$ at time 0. A Markov chain is said to be a finite Markov chain with N states if the number of values the random variable $X(n)$ can take is finite and equal to N. The transition probability matrix of such a chain is an $N \times N$ matrix. For Markov chains with an infinite number of states the transition probability matrix is an infinite matrix whose elements are generally hard to obtain.

A.2 Definitions and Properties of Markov Chains

Given an initial vector of probabilities a_0^T and the transition matrix P of a Markov chain, we are generally interested in determining whether $a_0^T P^n$ converges to some fixed vector π as n tends to infinity, which is independent of the initial vector a_0. If such a vector π exists it is called the "long run distribution" or the "invariant distribution" or the "stationary distribution" of the Markov chain. However, not every Markov chain enjoys this property. Hence we must consider the various subclasses of processes that might occur.

(i) Decomposition of Markov Chains: Let $\phi_1, \phi_2, \ldots$ be the set of states in the state space S.

Definition A.2: A subset C of S is called closed if, for every $\phi_i \, \epsilon \, C$ and $\phi_k \, \notin \, C$, $p_{ik} = 0$. Or a closed set is one from which the state does not transfer to any state outside it. If a closed set is a single state, then that state is called an *absorbing state*.

Definition A.3: A Markov chain is called irreducible if there exists no nonempty closed set other than S itself. If S has a proper closed subset, it is called reducible.

Definition A.4: A state ϕ_j is said to be *accessible* from a state ϕ_i if for some integer $n \geq 1$, $p_{ij}^{(n)} > 0$. We denote it by $i \rightarrow j$. Two states ϕ_i and ϕ_j are said to communicate if $i \rightarrow j$ and $j \rightarrow i$ and this is denoted by $i \leftrightarrow j$.

The communication property described above is an equivalence relation since it is reflexive, symmetric, and transitive. Given a state ϕ_j of a Markov chain, its communicating class $C(j)$ is defined as the set of all states ϕ_k such that $\phi_k \leftrightarrow \phi_j$. If $C(j)$ is empty (i.e., ϕ_j does not communicate with itself) it is called a *non-return state*. If $C(j)$ is nonempty then ϕ_j communicates with itself and is called a return state.

If C_1 and C_2 are two communicating classes it follows that either $C_1 = C_2$ or C_1 and C_2 are disjoint. This in turn leads to the following important theorem.

Definition A.5: A state ϕ_j of a Markov chain has a period d if the following two conditions hold:

$$\text{(i)} \qquad p_{jj}^{(n)} = 0 \text{ unless } n = md \text{ for some integer } m \quad \text{and} \tag{A.10}$$

$$\text{(ii)} \qquad d \text{ is the largest integer with property (i).}$$

State j is called aperiodic if $d = 1$ and periodic if $d \geq 2$.

For example if $p_{jj}^{(4)}$ and $p_{jj}^{(6)}$ are nonzero the state j has a period 2. In other words the period d is the greatest common divisor of all those n's for which $p_{jj}^{(n)} > 0$.

Having discussed some of the communicating properties of the states of a Markov chain, we can now state the following theorem, which provides a method of decomposing the state space S of the chain.

Theorem A.1: The set S of states of a Markov chain can be written as the union of a finite or countably infinite family $\{C_r\}$ of disjoint set of states.

$$
\begin{aligned}
S &= C_1 \cup C_2 \ldots \cup C_r \cup \ldots \\
C_i \cap C_j &= \phi \quad i \neq j,
\end{aligned}
\tag{A.11}
$$

where each set C_r is either a communicating class of states or contains exactly one nonreturn state.

We stated earlier that a closed set in a Markov chain contains only states from which there is no transfer to any state outside it. If a Markov chain is irreducible the only nonempty closed set in S is S itself. Hence a Markov chain is *irreducible* if and only if all pairs of states communicate.

(ii) Recurrent and Nonrecurrent States: To study the evolution of a Markov chain we must classify states into two categories: those which the system visits infinitely often and those the system visits finitely often. In the long run the chain will not be at any of the latter states and we need to consider only those states the chain visits infinitely often. This leads to the concept of recurrent and nonrecurrent states. To define recurrent and nonrecurrent states precisely we introduce the following concepts.

Definition A.6: Let $f_{ij}^{(n)}$ denote the probability that the first visit occurs from a state ϕ_i to state ϕ_j at time n.

$$
\begin{aligned}
f_{ij}^{(n)} = & \; Pr[X(n+k) = \phi_j | X(n+k-1) \neq \phi_j, \\
& X(n+k-2) \neq \phi_j, \ldots, X(k+1) \neq \phi_j, X(k) = \phi_i]
\end{aligned}
\tag{A.12}
$$

If $i = j$ we refer to $f_{ii}^{(n)}$ as the probability that the first return to state ϕ_i occurs at time n. By definition $f_{ii}^{(0)} = 0$.

Definition A.7: For fixed states ϕ_i and ϕ_j let $f_{ij}^* = \sum_{n=1}^{\infty} f_{ij}^{(n)}$. The symbol f_{ij}^* then represents the probability of ever visiting state ϕ_j from state ϕ_i. If $i = j$, f_{ii}^* represent the probability of ultimately returning to state ϕ_i.

Definition A.8: A state ϕ_i is said to be recurrent if $f_{ii}^* = 1$. If $f_{ii}^* < 1$ then ϕ_i is called nonrecurrent.

If $f_{ii}^* = 1$ we are assured that the process starting at ϕ_i will continue to return to it without limit. However, if $f_{ii}^* < 1$, while there is a finite probability of returning of ϕ_i, the probability of returning an infinite number of times is zero.

When a state ϕ_i is recurrent we are interested in the mean recurrence time of ϕ_i – the time to return to ϕ_i. We define this as $\mu_i = \sum_{n=1}^{\infty} n f_{ii}^{(n)}$. A recurrent state with an infinite mean recurrence time is called null recurrent. If the mean recurrence time is finite the state is called positive recurrent.

From the definitions we have given thus far it is clear that the state space S of a Markov chain contains states that are either recurrent or nonrecurrent and the recurrent states can be further classified as null recurrent or positive recurrent. If two states ϕ_i and ϕ_j communicate they must be of the same type and must also belong to the same closed subset of S. This in turn leads to the following important lemma.

Lemma: In a finite irreducible Markov chain all states are positive recurrent.

We can now strengthen the decomposition theorem stated earlier as follows:

Theorem A.2 (Decomposition of Markov Chains): The set S of return states of a Markov chain can be written as the union of disjoint communicating classes

$$S = C_1 \cup C_2 \cup \ldots \cup C_r \cup \ldots$$

where each class C_r is either (i) a closed recurrent class, (ii) a closed nonrecurrent class or (iii) a nonclosed nonrecurrent class.

It may be noted that in a finite Markov chain there are no closed nonrecurrent communicating classes.

Relation between $p_{ij}^{(n)}$ and $f_{ij}^{(n)}$: For any states ϕ_i and ϕ_j and integers m and n (≥ 1)

$$p_{ij}^{(n)} = \sum_{m=1}^{n} f_{ij}^{(m)} p_{jj}^{(n-m)} \tag{A.13}$$

with $p_{ij}(0) = \delta_{ij}$ where δ_{ij} is the Kronecker delta $\delta_{ij} = 1 \quad i = j$ and $\delta_{ij} = 0 \quad i \neq j$. According to this equation, if the state ϕ_i goes to ϕ_j in n steps the various paths can be partitioned into mutually exclusive sets according to when they make their first visit to ϕ_j. The equation can also be written as

$$p_{ij}^{(n)} = \sum_{m=1}^{n} f_{ij}^{(n-m)} p_{jj}^{(m)}. \tag{A.14}$$

This method, known as the method of first entrance, is an alternative (compared to the Chapman-Kolmogorov equation) for expressing $p_{ij}^{(n)}$ as a sum of probabilities.

Generating Functions: Let $\{p_{ij}^{(n)}\}$ for $n \in \{0, 1, \ldots\}$ represent the sequence of n-step probabilities to visit state ϕ_j from state ϕ_i. We define the generating function $\mathcal{P}_{ij}(z) = \sum_{n=0}^{\infty} p_{ij}^{(n)} z^n$. Similarly, for the sequence $\{f_{ij}^{(n)}\}$ of n-step probabilities of first visits to state ϕ_j from state ϕ_i, we define the generating function $\mathcal{F}_{ij}(z) = \sum_{n=0}^{\infty} f_{ij}^{(n)} z^n$.

Using the generating functions, the relations of Eq. (A.13) or (A.14) can be stated as

$$\mathcal{P}_{ij}(z) = \mathcal{F}_{ij}(z)\mathcal{P}_{jj}(z) \quad z \in (-1, 1) \quad i \neq j \tag{A.15}$$

and

$$\mathcal{P}_{ii}(z) = \frac{1}{1 - \mathcal{F}_{ii}(z)} \quad z \in (-1, 1). \tag{A.16}$$

The usefulness of the generating functions lies in the fact that conditions stated in terms of $f_{ij}^{(n)}$ may be interpreted directly in terms of $p_{ij}^{(n)}$. For example, it was stated earlier that a state ϕ_k is recurrent if $f_{kk}^{*} = \sum_{n=0}^{\infty} f_{kk}^{(n)} = 1$ and nonrecurrent if $f_{kk}^{*} < 1$. It follows from the definition of $\mathcal{F}_{kk}(z)$ that $\sum_{n=0}^{\infty} f_{kk}^{(n)} < 1$ if and only if $\lim_{z \to 1-} \mathcal{F}_{kk}(z) < 1$, which from Eq. (A.16) yields the necessary and sufficient condition $\lim_{z \to 1-} \mathcal{P}_{kk}(z) < \infty$. This in turn can be expressed in terms of $\sum_{n=1}^{\infty} p_{kk}^{(n)}$ as given in the theorem below.

Theorem A.3: For any state ϕ_k in a Markov chain

$$f_{kk}^{*} < 1 \text{ if and only if } \sum_{n=1}^{\infty} p_{kk}^{(n)} < \infty$$

$$f_{kk}^{*} = 1 \text{ if and only if } \sum_{n=1}^{\infty} p_{kk}^{(n)} = \infty.$$

Thus, whether a state ϕ_k is recurrent or nonrecurrent can be determined from the behavior of $\sum_{n=1}^{\infty} p_{kk}^{(n)}$. When a Markov chain is known to be irreducible, any state can be used to classify all the states. When it is not irreducible we must first identify the various irreducible closed subsets of S. In a finite irreducible Markov chain all the states are positive recurrent. If a finite Markov chain that has both recurrent and nonrecurrent states starts in one of the nonrecurrent states, it must eventually visit one of the recurrent states with probability 1.

A.3 Ergodic and Absorbing Chains

Perhaps the most important question in the theory of Markov chains is how the chain will be distributed among the states of S after a long time. In particular, we are interested in whether or not the distribution of $\{X(n)\}$ converges to a limiting distribution as $n \to \infty$. This limiting distribution, when it exists, (defined earlier as the stationary probability distribution of $\{X(n)\}$) is of central importance (ref. Chapter 5).

Definition A.9: Let $P = \{p_{ij}\}$ be the transition matrix for a Markov chain. If $\lim_{n \to \infty} p_{ij}^{(n)} = p_j^*$ exists for all j independently of i and if $\sum_{j=1}^{\infty} p_j^* = 1$ then we say the chain is ergodic.

The conditions necessary for ergodicity are that all recurrent states are aperiodic and that there is at most one irreducible closed subset of recurrent states. Hence, if a Markov chain is irreducible, aperiodic and positive recurrent it is ergodic. While it is clear that a finite irreducible Markov chain satisfies all the above conditions, in the case of a chain with infinite states we are interested in the probability with which it stays in the nonrecurrent states. If the chain leaves the nonrecurrent states with probability 1, again the chain is ergodic. Determination of the probability with which the chain stays in the nonrecurrent states is consequently an important question.

Finite Ergodic Chains: Ergodic chains with a finite number of states occur very frequently in applications. In fact all the fixed-structure learning automata discussed in Chapter 3 are described by ergodic Markov chains. From the earlier comments it is clear that a finite chain is ergodic if (1) it is irreducible and (2) it is aperiodic. A question that often arises is how these conditions can be verified in specific cases. Assuming the transition matrix P of the Markov chain is specified, or equivalently, the transition graph is known, the following two practical methods may be adopted.

(i) If there exists a positive integer k such that the matrix P^k has no zero elements, then the chain is irreducible.

(ii) If from the transition probability matrix or the transition graph it is possible to conclude that one can go from any state to any other state with nonzero probability, then the chain is irreducible.

It was mentioned earlier that in an irreducible chain any state can be used to classify all the states. Hence to determine the period of the chain as 1 it is sufficient to verify that one of the diagonal elements of P is nonzero. This implies that the corresponding state is aperiodic so the entire chain is aperiodic. The existence of a nonzero diagonal element in P is represented in the transition graph as a self-loop.

When a finite Markov chain is ergodic, an important issue is the computation of the stationary probability distribution. In Chapter 3, this had to be carried for every learning automaton whose asymptotic behavior was studied. If p^* is the stationary state occupation probability (i.e., p_i^* denotes the probability of being in state ϕ_i) then it satisfies the vector equation

$$P^T p^* = p^*. \tag{A.17}$$

Finite Absorbing Chains: If a finite Markov chain has two or more closed sets, it may be absorbed into any one of these as $n \to \infty$. It is therefore interesting to determine the probability of being absorbed into each of the closed sets and also the mean time it takes for such an absorption. If a nonrecurrent state ϕ_i in this case is absorbed into an irreducible closed set C with probability a_i and if C is aperiodic with long run distribution $(\pi_1, \pi_2, \ldots, \pi_m)$ then $\lim_{n \to \infty} p_{ij}^{(n)} = a_i \pi_j$ for $\phi_j \in C$. If the set C is periodic such a limit will not exist.

If each closed set C defined above contains a single state, all the irreducible states are absorbing states. In such a case the probabilities a_i denote the probabilities of absorption into these states starting from an arbitrary initial state.

In nonergodic chains the general question of moving from nonrecurrent (or transient) to recurrent states is of interest. For example, if the chain has r absorbing states and starts from a transient set, a question of interest is where the chain will ultimately go to. It can be shown that it will end up in one of the absorbing states with probability 1. A second question of interest is the probability with which it will be absorbed into one of the absorbing states and what the expected time would be for such absorption. In the context of learning, similar questions were discussed in Chapter 5 for Markov processes. In the following paragraph we indicate how the absorption probabilities can be determined.

Let $\phi_1, \phi_2, \ldots, \phi_r$ correspond to the r absorbing states of a Markov chain that has N states. The transition probability P of the chain can be written as

$$
P = \left[
\begin{array}{ccc|c}
1 & & 0 & \\
 & 1 & & O \\
 & & \ddots & \\
0 & & 1 & \\
\hline
 & R & & Q \\
\end{array}
\right]
$$

where Q is an $(n-r) \times (n-r)$ matrix corresponding to the $(n-r)$ transient states and the $r \times r$ unit matrix to the absorbing states. Starting in a transient state $\phi_i (i > r)$ the probability of being absorbed in ϕ_1 in the first step is given by p_{i1}. Similarly, the probability of being absorbed in the first absorbing set in two steps can be computed by determining the probability that it remains in the transient set in the first step and the probability that it is absorbed in ϕ_1 at the second step. The same concept can be extended to determine the probability of absorption at the nth step. Denoting the probability of going from ϕ_i to ϕ_j in the transient states in n steps by $q_{ij}^{(n)}$ it is seen that this is merely the ij^{th} element of the matrix Q^n. Hence determination of the absorption probabilities involves the matrices $I, Q, Q^2, \ldots$, where I is the identity matrix. In fact it can be shown that if

$$ M = [I - Q]^{-1} = I + Q + Q^2 + \cdots \tag{A.18} $$

then the ij^{th} element of the $((n-r) \times r)$ matrix MR is the probability of absorption of the ith transient state in the jth absorbing state. The matrix M is called the fundamental matrix of an absorbing Markov chain.

Appendix B

Martingales

B.1 Introduction

A useful class of stochastic processes that finds extensive use in theoretical and applied probability is the martingale. The martingale process was first introduced by Doob and is discussed in detail in Doob (1953) and Neveu (1975). It has since developed into an important part of probability theory. Although it has found use in a variety of contexts, it is used in this book primarily in the analysis of the asymptotic behavior of learning algorithms. The results presented here are intended as preparation for some specific points discussed in Chapter 5 and not as a general introduction to martingale theory. For a detailed discussion of martingales the reader is referred to Karlin and Taylor (1975).

A simple definition of a martingale may be stated as follows.

Definition B.1: A stochastic process $\{X_n\}_{n \geq 0}$ is a martingale if for all $n \geq 0$

$$\text{(i) } E[|X_n|] < \infty \quad \text{and} \quad \text{(ii) } E[X_{n+1}|X_0, X_1, X_2, \ldots, X_n] = X_n$$

By the definition above the conditional expectation of X_{n+1} is equal to the value of X_n regardless of the values of $X_0, X_1, \ldots, X_{n-1}$. For example if X_n represents the fortune of a gambler at stage n, the martingale property implies that the game is "fair" in that the player's fortune on the average at instant $(n+1)$ is his or her fortune at stage n.

A second example of a martingale is the symmetric random walk in which the position of a particle at stage n on the real line is X_n and its position after one instant can be $X_n - 1$ or $X_n + 1$ with probability $1/2$. In such a case

$$E[X_{n+1}|X_n] = [X_n - 1]1/2 + [X_n + 1]1/2 = X_n. \tag{B.1}$$

Equation (B.1) remains true even when the conditioning is based on the previous positions of the particle. A more general definition of a martingale is given below.

Definition B.2: Let $\{X_n\}_{n \geq 0}$ and $\{Y_n\}_{n \geq 0}$ be stochastic processes. The process $\{X_n\}_{n \geq 0}$ is said to be a martingale with respect to $\{Y_n\}_{n \geq 0}$ if

(i) $E[|X_n|] < \infty$ and (ii) $E[X_{n+1}|Y_0, Y_1, \ldots, Y_n] = X_n$.

In the definition above Y_i $(i = 1, 2, \ldots)$ may be a finite or infinite dimensional vector and $\{Y_0, Y_1, \ldots, Y_n\}$ denotes the information history up to stage n which determines X_n, i.e., X_n is the function

$$X_n = E[X_{n+1}|Y_0, Y_1, \ldots, Y_n].$$

Since, from the law of total probability we have

$$E[X_n] = E[E[X_{n+1}|Y_0, \ldots, Y_n] = E[X_{n+1}]$$

it follows that

$$E[X_0] = E[X_1] = \cdots = E[X_n] \text{ for all } n$$

or in a martingale, all the random variables have the same expectation.

B.2   Supermartingales and Submartingales

For many purposes it is desirable to have available a more general concept based on an inequality.

Definition B.3: Let $\{X_n\}_{n \geq 0}$ and $\{Y_n\}_{n \geq 0}$ be stochastic processes. Then $\{X_n\}$ is called a supermartingale with respect to $\{Y_n\}$ if for all n

(i) $E[X_n^-] > -\infty$ where $x^- \overset{\triangle}{=} \min(x, 0)$.

(ii) $E[X_{n+1}|Y_1, Y_2, \ldots, Y_n] \leq X_n$.

and a submartingale if for all n

(i) $E[X_n^+] < \infty$ where $x^+ \triangleq \max(0, x)$.

(ii) $E[X_{n+1}|Y_0, Y_1, \ldots, Y_n] \geq X_n$.

In the examples following Definition B.1, if the gambler's fortune at instant $n + 1$ on the average is smaller than the fortune at stage n or if the position of the particle at stage $(n + 1)$ is $X_n - 1$ with a probability greater than $1/2$, then $\{X_n\}$ is a supermartingale.

In the definitions of both super- and submartingales X_n must be determined by the history up to time n. For both martingales as well as super- and submartingales, we will omit mention of the process $\{Y_n\}$ when it is evident from the context. We note that $\{X_n\}$ is a supermartingale with respect to $\{Y_n\}$ if and only if $\{-X_n\}$ is a submartingale with respect to $\{Y_n\}$. Further $\{X_n\}$ is a martingale with respect to $\{Y_n\}$ if and only if it is a supermartingale and a submartingale with respect to $\{Y_n\}$. Hence, if we make statements about supermartingales in the following paragraphs, equivalent statements can also be made about submartingales and martingales.

Definition B.4: A function U defined on an interval I is said to be convex, if for every $x_1, x_2 \in I$ and $0 < \alpha < 1$

$$\alpha U(x_1) + (1 - \alpha)U(x_2) \geq U(\alpha x_1 + (1 - \alpha)x_2)$$

From the definition above it follows that

$$\sum_{i=1}^{m} \alpha_i U(x_i) \geq U(\sum_{i=1}^{m} \alpha_i x_i) \tag{B.2}$$

where $x_1, x_2 \ldots, x_m \in I$.

If X is a random variable that takes values x_i in I with probability a_i $(i = 1, 2, \ldots, m)$ Eq. (B.2) can be stated as

$$E[U(x)] \geq U[E(x)].$$

Jensen's inequality states that Eq. (B.2) also applies for all real random variables X whenever U is convex on $(-\infty, \infty)$. This is also true for conditional expectations so that

$$E[U(X)|Y_0, \ldots, Y_n] \geq U[E(X|Y_0, Y_1, \ldots, Y_n)]$$

The following lemma is useful in constructing submartingales from martingales.

Lemma B.1: Let $\{X_n\}$ be a martingale with respect to $\{Y_n\}$. If U is a convex function for which $E[U(X_n)^+] < \infty$ for all n, then $U(X_n)$ is a submartingale with respect to $\{Y_n\}$. In particular $\{|X_n|\}$ is always a submartingale and $\{|X_n|^2\}$ is a submartingale whenever $E[X_n^2] < \infty$ for all n.

From the definitions above the following elementary properties of supermartingales and martingales can be obtained (the hypothesis and conclusion for the supermartingale being enclosed in parentheses).

(i) If $\{X_n\}$ is a (super)martingale with respect to $\{Y_n\}$ then

$$E[X_{n+k}|Y_0, Y_1, \ldots, Y_n](\leq) = X_n \text{ for all } k > 0.$$

(ii) If $\{X_n\}$ is a (super)martingale

$$E[X_n](\leq) = E[X_k](\leq) = E[X_0] \ 0 \leq k \leq n.$$

(iii) If g is a (nonnegative) function of $Y_0, Y_1, \ldots, Y_n$ and X_n is a (super)martingale with respect to $\{Y_n\}$ we have

$$E[g(Y_0, \ldots, Y_n)X_{n+k}|Y_0, Y_1, \ldots, Y_n](\leq) = g(Y_0, Y_1, \ldots, Y_n)X_n.$$

Examples: (i) If $Y_0 = 0$ and $Y_1, Y_2, \ldots$ are independent random variables with $E[|Y_n|] < \infty$ and $E[Y_n] = 0$ for all $n \geq 0$ and $X_n = Y_1 + Y_2 + \cdots Y_n$ for all $n \geq 1$, then $\{X_n\}_{n \geq 0}$ is a martingale with respect to Y_n. If $E[Y_n] < 0$ for all $n \geq 0$, $\{X_n\}$ is a supermartingale.
(ii) If in (i) $E[Y_k] = 0$ and $E[Y_k^2] = \sigma^2$, $(k = 1, 2, \ldots)$ and $X_0 = 0$ and $X_n = (\sum_{k=1}^n Y_k)^2 - n\sigma^2$ then $\{X_n\}_{n \geq 0}$ is a martingale with respect to $\{Y_n\}_{n \geq 0}$.

B.3 Martingales with respect to σ-fields

In the previous section the conditional expectation of X_n was of the form $E[X_n|Y_0, Y_1, \ldots, Y_n]$ where it is assumed that $X_n, Y_0, Y_1, \ldots, Y_{n-1}$ are jointly distributed random variables. However, when the results must be extended to denumerable Y_i or when Y is defined over intervals, the analysis becomes more complex. In such cases the conditional expectations of the random variables are evaluated over σ-fields of events. This suggests a definition of a martingale with respect to a sequence of σ-fields.

Let $\{X_n\}_{n \geq 0}$ be a sequence of real random variables on a probability space $(\Omega, \mathcal{F}, P)$. Let $\mathcal{F}_n$ be a sequence of sub-σ-fields of $\mathcal{F}$ with

$$\mathcal{F}_0 \subset \mathcal{F}_1 \subset \cdots \mathcal{F}_{n-1} \subset \mathcal{F}_n \cdots \subset \mathcal{F} \qquad (B.3)$$

and let X_n be measurable with respect to $\mathcal{F}_n$. $\mathcal{F}_n$, for example, can be the σ-field generated by random variables $Y_0, Y_1, \ldots, Y_n$, where the sequence $\{Y_n\}_{n \geq 0}$ is also defined on $(\Omega, \mathcal{F}, P)$. We can consider $\mathcal{F}_n$ as containing the information available at stage n. In terms of our earlier discussion X_n is measurable with respect to $\mathcal{F}_n$ if it is determined by $\{Y_0, Y_1, \ldots, Y_n\}$. The definition of a martingale in terms of σ-fields may be stated as follows.

Definition B.5: Let $\{X_n\}_{n \geq 0}$ be a sequence of random variables defined on a probability space $(\Omega, \mathcal{F}, P)$ and let $\mathcal{F}_n$ be a sequence of sub-σ-fields of $\mathcal{F}$ satisfying Eq. (B.3). Then $\{X_n\}$ is called a submartingale with respect to $\{\mathcal{F}_n\}$ if for all n

 (i) X_n is measurable with respect to $\mathcal{F}_n$,

 (ii) $E[X_n^+] < \infty$, and

 (iii) $E[X_{n+1}|\mathcal{F}_m] \geq X_m$ for $m \leq n$.

If $\{-X_n\}$ is a submartingale, then $\{X_n\}$ is a supermartingale. If both $\{-X_n\}$ and $\{X_n\}$ are submartingales, then $\{X_n\}$ is a martingale with respect to $\{\mathcal{F}_n\}$.

The various definitions and results stated earlier have their counterparts in terms of σ-fields. For example, if Z is a real-valued random variable on the probability space with an increasing family of σ-fields, $\mathcal{B}_n$, defining

$$Y_n = E[Z|\mathcal{B}_n]$$

it follows that

$$E[Y_n|\mathcal{B}_m] = E[E(Z|\mathcal{B}_n)|\mathcal{B}_m] = E[Z|\mathcal{B}_m] = Y_m \quad m < n.$$

Hence if $E[|Z|] < \infty$, the sequence $\{Y_n\}$ with the σ-fields $\mathcal{B}_n$ is a martingale.

In the context of learning, supermartingales and submartingales arise in the analysis of absolutely expedient schemes. In a two action automaton using an L_{R-I} scheme, if $c_1 < c_2$ it was shown in Chapter 4 that

$$\Delta p_1(n) = E[p_1(n+1)|p_1(0), \ldots, p_1(n)] - p_1(n) \geq 0.$$

Hence $\{p_1(n)\}_{n \geq 0}$ is a submartingale and $\{p_2(n)\}_{n \geq 0}$ is a supermartingale. More generally, if the automaton has r actions and α_ℓ and α_h correspond to actions with minimum and maximum penalty probabilities c_ℓ and c_h respectively then the sequence $\{p_\ell(n)\}_{n \geq 0}$ is a submartingale while $\{p_h(n)\}_{n \geq 0}$ is a supermartingale. This is also true if the automaton uses any absolutely expedient scheme. It can also be verified that when such a scheme is used, $M(n)$, defined as

$$M(n) = \sum_{i=1}^{r} c_i p_i(n)$$

and $p(n + 1)$ depends on only $p(n)$ and not on the earlier values such as $p(0), p(1), \ldots, p(n-1)$. It follows that

$$E[M(n + 1)|p(0), p(1), \ldots p(n)] = E[M(n + 1)|p(n)] < M(n).$$

Hence $M(n)$ is a Markovian sequence and is also a supermartingale. Similar remarks also apply to sequences $\{p_\ell(n)\}$ and $\{p_h(n)\}$. This fact makes the powerful Martingale convergence theorem given below important in the analysis of learning algorithms that are absolutely expedient.

Theorem B.1: (a) Let $\{X_n\}$ be a submartingale satisfying

$$\sup_{n \geq 0} E[|X_n|] < \infty.$$

Then there exists a random variable X_∞ to which $\{X_n\}$ converges *w.p.1*,

$$Pr[\lim_{n \to \infty} X_n = X_\infty] = 1.$$

(b) If $\{X_n\}$ is a martingale and is uniformly integrable, then in addition to part (a) $\{X_n\}$ converges in the mean, that is,

$$\lim_{n \to \infty} E[|X_n - X_\infty|] = 0$$

and

$$E[X_\infty] = E[X_n] \qquad \text{for all } n.$$

For a submartingale $\{X_n\}$,

$$\sup_{n \geq 0} E[X_n^+] < \infty \Rightarrow \sup_{n \geq 1} E[|X_n|] < \infty.$$

Hence by the theorem every nonpositive submartingale, non-negative supermartingale, or martingale that is uniformly bounded from above or from below converges with probability 1.

Convergence with probability 1 assured by Theorem B.1 does not imply convergence in the mean. However, if the sequence $\{X_n\}_{n \geq 0}$ is such that $E[|X_n|^2] \leq K < \infty$ for all n where K is a constant, convergence in the mean also prevails. This is given in the following theorem.

Theorem B.2: Let $\{X_n\}$ be a martingale with respect to $\{Y_n\}$ satisfying for some constant

$$E[X_n^2] \leq K < \infty \quad \text{for all } n.$$

Then $\{X_n\}$ converges as $n \to \infty$ to a limit random variable with probability 1 and in mean square. That is

$$Pr[\lim_{n \to \infty} X_n = X_\infty] = 1$$

and

$$\lim_{n \to \infty} E[|X_n - X_\infty|^2] = 0.$$

Since both of them imply convergence in probability the theorem implies that

$$\lim_{n \to \infty} Pr[|X_n - X_\infty| \geq \epsilon] = 0 \quad \text{for all } \epsilon > 0.$$

One handy corollary of Theorem B.1 is given below.

Corollary B.1: Under the conditions of Theorem B.1,

$$E[X_{n+1} - X_n | X_0, X_1, \ldots, X_n] \to 0 \qquad w.p.1 \text{ as } n \to \infty.$$

Appendix C

Distance Diminishing Operators

C.1 Introduction

Contraction mapping principles in both deterministic and stochastic (Bharucha-Reid, 1972) contexts have been investigated extensively in the past. The basic idea in contraction mapping is that successive applications of an operator on two different initial conditions bring them closer to each other and finally result in convergence to the solution of the equation of interest. In the context of learning, Norman (1968) developed distance diminishing operators, which are based on stochastic contraction mapping principles to prove convergence of the learning schemes. In this appendix we provide a brief introduction to this concept.

Consider a stochastic dynamic system operating in discrete time $n = 0, 1, 2, \ldots$. Let the state of the system at instant n be S_n and let S_n take values in the state space S. Let (S, d) be a metric space where d is the metric. The evolution of the state S_n is dependent on the occurrence of an associated event E_n. Thus

$$S_{n+1} = f_{E_n}(S_n) \tag{C.1}$$

where f_{E_n} is an operator that depends on E_n.

It is assumed that E_n belongs to a set E, which is finite. It is further assumed that the probabilities of various possible events at the instant n depend only on the state at n and not on any other quantity such as earlier

443

states or events or the trial number. That is,

$$Pr(E_n = e|S_n = s) = \phi_e(s) \tag{C.2}$$

where $\phi_e(s)$ is a real-valued function on $E \times S$.

We further assume that

$$(S, d) \text{ is compact.} \tag{C.3}$$

In the applications of our interest where $S \subset \mathcal{R}^k$ this assumption merely means that S is closed and bounded.

We now introduce the following notation. If ψ maps $S \rightarrow \mathcal{R}$ and g maps $S \rightarrow S$, their maximum "difference quotients" $m(\psi)$ and $\mu(g)$ are defined by

$$m(\psi) = \sup_{s \neq s'} \frac{|\psi(s) - \psi(s')|}{d(s, s')} \tag{C.4}$$

and

$$\mu(g) = \sup_{s \neq s'} \frac{d(g(s), g(s'))}{d(s, s')} \tag{C.5}$$

whether or not these are finite.

As an example, if S is an interval in the real line with $d(s, s') = |s - s'|$, and ψ is differentiable throughout S, then $m(\psi)$ is the supremum of $|\psi'(s)|$ where ψ' is the derivative of ψ.

We further assume the following:

1. $m(\psi_e) < \infty$ for all $e \in E$ $\tag{C.6}$

2. $\mu(f_e) \leq 1$ for all $e \in E$ $\tag{C.7}$

3. For any $s \in S$, there exists a positive integer k and events $e_0, e_1, \ldots, e_k$ such that
$$\mu(f_{e_0 e_1 \cdots e_k}) < 1 \text{ and } \phi_{e_0 e_1 \cdots e_k}(s) > 0 \tag{C.8}$$
where

$$\begin{aligned}
f_{e_0 e_1 \cdots e_k} &= f_{e_k}(f_{e_{k-1}} \cdots (f_{e_0}(s))) \\
\phi_{e_0 e_1 \cdots e_k}(s) &= Pr[E_0 = e_0, \ldots, E_k = e_k | S_0 = s].
\end{aligned} \tag{C.9}$$

From Eq. (C.5) we have

$$d(g(s), g(s')) \leq \mu(g)d(s, s'), \tag{C.10}$$

which suggests the terminology that an operator $g : S \to S$ be called *distance diminishing* if $\mu(g) \le 1$ and *strictly distance diminishing* if $\mu(g) < 1$.

Assumption (C.7) says that all event operators are distance diminishing while Eq. (C.8) implies that for any arbitrary initial state, some finite sequence of events with a cumulative strictly distance diminishing effect will occur on subsequent trials. In the particular case when all event operators are strictly distance diminishing, Assumption (C.8) is satisfied with $k = 1$.

In Assumption (C.8) it is understood that the integers and events associated with different states may be different.

There are two distinct types of convergence associated with such distance diminishing operators. The corresponding models are called ergodic models and absorbing models respectively. They are treated separately in what follows.

C.2   Ergodic Models

In this situation the operators are such that information on the initial state is lost eventually as the state evolves in time. For describing this situation it is convenient to have a notation for the set of values taken by S_n with positive probability corresponding to an initial state s. In other words, let

$$T_n(s) = \{\hat{s} : Pr\{S_n = \hat{s}|S_0 = s\} > 0\}. \tag{C.11}$$

Another convenient notation is $d(A, B)$ for the minimum distance between two subsets A and B of S.

$$d(A, B) = \inf_{s \in A, s' \in B} d(s, s'). \tag{C.12}$$

In the present situation we assume that asymptotic independence of the initial state is attained as follows.

$$\lim_{n \to \infty} d(T_n(s), T_n(s')) = 0 \text{ for all } s, s' \in S. \tag{C.13}$$

A system satisfying Eq. (C.13) is said to be an ergodic model. Thus, in an ergodic model the sets of states generated by different initial conditions asymptotically have common elements. The nature of convergence of the states can be made more precise and can be stated as follows.

Theorem C.1: In an ergodic model, the asymptotic distribution of S_∞ does not depend on the initial state s. Furthermore, if $\psi(\cdot)$ is any bounded continuous real-valued function on S, then

$$\lim_{n \to \infty} |E[\psi(S_n)] - E[\psi(S_\infty)]| = 0. \tag{C.14}$$

Comment C.1: The type of convergence stated in the theorem above corresponds to weak convergence of measures (Billingsley, 1968). A rigorous development of this topic is beyond the scope of this book. However, in the particular case where the state space S is a subspace of the Euclidean space $\mathcal{R}^k$, this mode of convergence is identical to convergence in distribution.

Comment C.2: The major feature of the convergence here is that asymptotic properties of the state distribution are independent of the initial state.

C.3   Absorbing Models

The distinguishing feature of these models is that there is a finite number of absorbing states $a_1, a_2, \ldots, a_N$ such that for each starting state s, there is some absorbing state $a_{j(s)}$ for which

$$\lim_{n \to \infty} d(T_n(s), a_{j(s)}) = 0. \tag{C.15}$$

A system satisfying Eq. (C.15) is said to be an absorbing model. This property is in sharp contrast with that of ergodic models because the final state here depends very much on the initial state. The only situation in which both the models have equivalent asymptotic properties is when there is only a single absorbing state.

The nature of convergence in absorbing models is almost sure convergence or convergence with probability 1. The following theorem makes this explicit.

Theorem C.2: In an absorbing model the stochastic process S_n converges *w.p.1* to a random absorbing state S_∞ where $S_\infty \in \{a_i, i = 1, 2, \ldots, N\}$.

Comment C.3: When there are a number of absorbing states, the theorem ensures that the stochastic process S_n converges to an element of the set of absorbing states *w.p.1*. There is a probability associated with convergence to each absorbing state a_i and one can define a function

$$\Gamma_i(s) = Pr\{S_\infty = a_i | S_0 = s\}. \tag{C.16}$$

Note that $\sum_{i=1}^{N} \Gamma_i(s) = 1$ where N is the number of absorbing states. Further properties of $\Gamma_i(s)$ have been explored by Norman (1968) and are used in Chapter 5.

C.4 State-Space Simplexes

Although the previous development has been described in general terms of a state space that is a compact metric space, we are mostly interested in state spaces that correspond to simplexes. This is because the state is generally the action probability vector and it takes values in a simplex. In this situation, some of the assumptions and results stated earlier can be made more explicit.

The metric $d(p, q)$ where p, q are action probability vectors defined over an r-simplex now corresponds to the Euclidean norm

$$\|p - q\| = [\sum_{i=1}^{r-1} (p_i - q_i)^2]^{1/2}.$$

The summation is taken only up to $(r - 1)$ as only $(r - 1)$ components of p and q can be independent. In the type of algorithms we have considered, the event E_n in Eq. (C.1) is made up of two components – the action selected at n and the response of the environment for this action.

The state S_n is the action probability vector $p(n)$. The updating algorithm (or reinforcement scheme) is the stochastic dynamic system represented by Eq. (C.1). The values taken by $\phi_e(s)$ in Eq. (C.2) depend on the set of penalty probabilities. The compactness assumed in Eq. (C.3) is automatically satisfied by the simplex.

In the case of ergodic models, Theorem C.1 implies that the action probability vector converges in distribution to a random vector which is independent of the initial value.

In the case of absorbing models the action probability vector converges *w.p.1* to an element of the set of absorbing states as stated in Theorem C.2.

Bibliography

Ackley, D. H., G. E. Hinton, and T. J. Sejnowski, "A Learning Algorithm for Boltzmann Machines," *Cognitive Science*, Vol. 9, 1985, pp. 147–169.

Akselrod, B. and G. Langholz, "A Simulation Study of Advanced Routing Methods in a Multiplicity Telephone Network," *IEEE Trans. Syst., Man and Cybern.*, SMC-15, 1985, pp. 730–736.

Anderson, C. B. and T. S. Huang, "Piecewise Fourier Transformation for Picture Bandwidth Compression," *IEEE Trans. Commun. Tech.*, COM–19, No. 2, April 1971, pp. 133–140.

Andrew, H. C. and W. K. Pratt, "Fourier Transform Coding of Images," Proc. Hawaii Inter. Confer. System Sci., Western, Jan. 1968, pp. 677–679.

Ash, G.R., "Use of a Trunk Status Map for Real-time DNHR," *ITC*, Vol. 11, 1985.

Aso, H. and M. Kimura, "The Structures of Automata to Adapt to an Unknown Environment," *IEEE Trans. Syst., Man and Cybern.*, SMC-6, 1976, pp. 494–504.

Aso, H. and M. Kimura, "Absolute Expediency of Learning Automata," *Inform. Sci.*, Vol. 17, 1979, pp. 91–112.

Atkinson, C. R., G. H. Bower, and E. J. Crowthers, *An Introduction to Mathematical Learning Theory*, New York: John Wiley & Sons, 1965.

Baba, N., "On the Behaviour of $SL(R-I)$ Reinforcement Scheme for Stochastic Automata," *IEEE Trans. Syst., Man and Cybern.*, SMC–6, 1976, pp. 580–82.

Baba, N., "The Absolutely Expedient Nonlinear Reinforcement Schemes under the Unknown Multi–Teacher Environment," *IEEE Trans. Syst., Man and Cybern.*, SMC-13, 1983, pp. 100–108.

Baba, N., "New Topics in Learning Automata Theory and Applications," *Lecture Notes in Control and Information Sciences*, Vol. 71, Berlin: Springer Verlag, 1984.

Baba, N., "Learning Behaviour of Hierarchical Structure Stochastic Automata Operating in a General Multi–Teacher Environment," *IEEE Trans. Syst., Man and Cybern.*, SMC–15, 1985, pp. 585–87.

Baba, N., "Learning Behaviors of the Hierarchical Structure Stochastic Automata," *IEEE Trans. Syst., Man and Cybern.*, SMC–17, 1987, pp. 868–873.

Baba, N. and Y. Sawaragi, "On the Learning Behaviour of Stochastic Automata under a Nonstationary Environment," *IEEE Trans. Syst., Man and Cybern.*, SMC–5, 1975, pp. 273–75.

Baba, N., T. Soeda, T. Shoman, and Y. Sawaragi, "An Application of Stochastic Automata to the Investment Game," *Int. J. Syst. Sci.*, Vol. 11, 1980, pp. 1447–57.

Barto, A. G., "Learning by Statistical Cooperation of Self–interested Neuron-like Computing Elements," COINS Tech. Report 81–11, Amherst: University of Massachusetts, 1985.

Barto, A. G. and P. Anandan, "Pattern–Recognizing Stochastic Learning Automata," *IEEE Trans. Syst., Man and Cybern.*, SMC–15, 1985, pp. 360–75.

Barto, A. G., R. S. Sutton, and C. W. Anderson, "Neuron-like Adaptive Elements That Can Solve Difficult Learning Control Problems," *IEEE Trans. Syst., Man and Cybern.*, SMC–13, 1983, pp. 834–46.

Barto, A. G., R. S. Sutton, and P. S. Brouwer, "Associative Search Network: A reinforcement learning associative memory," *Biological Cybernetics*, Vol. 40, 1981, pp. 201–211.

Bellman, R., *Dynamic Programming*, Princeton: Princeton University Press, 1957.

Bellman, R., *Adaptive Control Processes – A Guided Tour*, Princeton: Princeton University Press, 1961.

Bertsekas, D. and R. Gallager, *Data Networks*, Englewood Cliffs, NJ: Prentice Hall, 1987.

Bhakthavathsalam, R., Ph.D. Thesis, Dept. of Electrical Engineering, Indian Institute of Science, Bangalore, 1987.

Bhakthavathsalam, R. and M.A.L. Thathachar, "Rate of Convergence of Learning Automata," Proc. National Syst. Conf., 1977, PSG Tech., Coimbatore, India.

Bharucha–Reid, A.T., *Random Integral Equations*, New York: Academic Press, 1972.

Billingsley, P., *Convergence of Probability Measures*, New York: John Wiley & Sons, 1968.

Blum, J. R., "Multidimensional Stochastic Approximation Methods," *Annals of Mathematical Statistics*, Vol. 25, 1954, pp. 737–44.

Boehm, B. W. and R. L. Mobley, "Adaptive Routing Techniques for Distributed Communications Systems," Rand Corp., Memorandum RM–4781–PR, AD630271, Feb. 1966.

Borkar, V. and P. Varaiya, "Adaptive Control of Markov Chains I. Finite Parameter Set," *IEEE Trans. Automatic Control*, AC–24, 1979, pp. 953–58.

Borovikov, V. A. and V. I. Bryzgalov, "The Simplest Symmetric Game of Many Automata," *Avtomatika i Telemekhanika*, Vol. 26, 1965, pp. 683–87.

Bower, G. H. and E. R. Hilgard, *Theories of Learning*, New York: Appleton–Century–Crofts, 1966.

Brown, G. W., "Iterative Solutions of Games by Fictitious Play," in *Activity Analysis of Production and Allocation*, T. C. Koopmans (Ed.), Cowles Commission Monograph 13, 1951, pp. 374-6.

Burke, C. J., W. K. Estes and S. Hellyer, "Rate of Verbal Conditioning in Relation to Stimulus Variability," *Journal of Experimental Psychology*, Vol. 48, 1954, pp. 153–61.

Bush, R. R. and F. Mosteller, *Stochastic Models for Learning*, New York: John Wiley & Sons, 1958.

Butrimenko, A. V., "Games of Automata Possessing Different Activities," *Problemy Peredachi Informatsii*, Vol. 3, 1967, pp. 81–88.

Chandrasekaran, B. and K. B. Lakshmanan, "Multiple Hypothesis Testing with Finite Memory," *J. Cybernetics and Information Science, Special Issue on Learning Automata*, Vol. 1, 1977, pp. 71–81.

Chandrasekaran, B. and D.W.C. Shen, "Adaptation of Stochastic Automata in Non–Stationary Environments," Proc. Natl. Electronics Conf., Vol. 23, 1967, pp. 39–44.

Chandrasekaran, B. and D.W.C. Shen, "On Expediency and Convergence in Variable Structure Stochastic Automata," *IEEE Trans. Syst. Sci. and Cybern.*, SSC–4, 1968, pp. 52–60.

Chandrasekaran, B. and D.W.C. Shen, "Stochastic Automata Games," *IEEE Trans. Syst. Sci. and Cybern.*, SSC–5, 1969, pp. 145–49.

Chrystall, M. S. and P. Mars, "Adaptive Routing in Computer Communication Networks Using Learning Automata," Proc. IEEE Nat. Telecomm. Conf., 1981.

Chung, K. L., *Markov Chains with Stationary Transition Probabilities*, Berlin: Springer Verlag, 1960.

Cinlar, E., *Introduction to Stochastic Processes*, Englewood Cliffs, NJ: Prentice Hall, 1975.

Cleave, J. P., "The Synthesis of Finite State Homogeneous Markov Chains," *Cybernetica*, Vol. 1, 1962, pp. 38–47.

Cobham, A., "Priority Assignment in Waiting Line Problems," *Operations Research*, Vol. 2, 1954, pp. 70–76.

Coderre, J. R. J., "Modèle Optimal d'un Contrôle Global de Flux Appliqué aux Réseaux à Commutation par Paquets," Masters Thesis, University of Québec, 1988.

Cohen, P. R. and E. A. Feigenbaum, *The Handbook of Artificial Intelligence, Vol. III*, London: Pitman Books, 1981.

Cover, T. M. and M. E. Hellman, "The Two–Armed Bandit Problem with Time Invariant Finite Memory," *IEEE Trans. on Information Theory*, Vol. 16, no. 2, 1970, pp. 185–95.

Cutler, C. C., "Differential Quantization of Communication Signals," Patent No. 2, 605, 361, July 29, 1952.

Davies, D. W., "The Control of Congestion in Packet Switching Networks," *Trans. on Comm.*, COM–20, June 1972.

Davis, L. and A. Rosenfeld, "Cooperating Processes for Low–level Vision: A Survey," *Artificial Intelligence*, 17, 1981, pp. 245-63.

Davis, M.D., *Game Theory, A Nontechnical Introduction*, New York: Basic Books, 1973.

Devroye, L. P., "Probabilistic Search as a Search Selection Procedure," *IEEE Trans. Syst., Man and Cybern.*, SMC–6, 1976, pp. 315–21.

Devroye, L. P., "A Class of Performance Directed Probabilistic Automata," *IEEE Trans. on Syst., Man and Cybern.*, SMC–6, 1976, pp. 777–84.

Devroye, L. P., "An Expanding Automaton for use in Stochastic Optimization," *J. Cybern. Inform. Sci.*, 1, 1977, pp. 82–94.

Dobrovidov, A. V. and R. L. Stratonovich, "Construction of Optimal Automata Functioning in Random Media," *Automation and Remote Control*, 25, no. 10, 1964, pp. 1289–96.

Doob, J. L., *Stochastic Processes*, New York: John Wiley & Sons, 1953.

Duda, R. O. and P. E. Hart, *Pattern Classification and Scene Analysis*, New York: Wiley Interscience, 1973.

Dvoretzky, A., "On Stochastic Approximation," Proceedings of the Third Berkeley Symposium on Mathematical Statistics and Probability, California: University of California Press, 1956, pp. 39–55.

Dziong, Z., K. Liao and L. Mason, "Flow Control and Routing Methods for Wideband and Narrowband Traffic in Multislot Loss Networks," Technical Report, INRS–Telecommunications, Quebec, 1988.

Dziong, Z and L. Mason, "State-dependent Routing for a Multi-service Network," Proceedings of ConCom Conference, Baton-Rouge, La., Oct. 1988.

Economides, A.A., P.A. Ioannou, and J.A. Silvester, "Decentralized Adaptive Routing for Virtual Circuit Networks Using Stochastic Learning Automata," Proc. of IEEE INFOCOM 1988.

El–Fattah, Y. M., "Stochastic Automata Models of Certain Problems of Collective Behaviour," *IEEE Trans. Syst., Man and Cybern.*, SMC–10, 1980, pp. 304–14.

El–Fattah, Y. M., P. Boyer, A. Dupuis, and L. Romoeuf, "Use of a Learning Automaton for Control of Service Activity," Proc. Fourth Yale Workshop on Applications of Adaptive Systems Theory, Yale University, 1985, pp. 124–29.

El–Fattah, Y. M. and C. Foulard, *Learning Systems: Decision, Simulation and Control*, Berlin: Springer–Verlag, 1978.

El–Hadidi, M. T., H. M. El–Sayed, and A. Y. Bilal, "Performance Evaluation of a New Learning Automata-Based Routing Algorithm for Calls in Telephone Networks," *ITC–11*, Elsevier Science Publishers B. V. (North–Holland), 1985.

Estes, W. K., "The Statistical Approach to Learning Theory," in S. Koch (Ed.), *Psychology: A Study of a Science*, Vol. II, New York: McGraw-Hill Book Co., 1959.

Faugeras, O.D. and M. Berthod, "Improving Consistency and Reducing Ambiguity in Stochastic Labeling: An Optimization Approach," *IEEE Trans. Pattern Analysis and Machine Intelligence*, PAMI–3, July 1981, pp. 412–23.

Feldbaum, A. A., *Optimal Control Systems*, New York: Academic Press, 1965.

Forestier, J. P. and P. Varaiya, "Multilayer Control of Large Markov Chains," *IEEE Trans. Automatic Control*, AC–23, 1978, pp. 298–305.

Fu, K. S., *Sequential Methods in Pattern Recognition and Machine Learning*, New York: Academic Press, 1968.

Fu, K. S., "Learning Control Systems – Review and Outlook," *IEEE Trans. Automatic Control*, AC–15, 1970, pp. 210–21.

Fu, K. S. and R. W. McLaren, "An Application of Stochastic Automata to the Synthesis of Learning Systems," Report TR–EE–65–17, Purdue University, Lafayette, 1965.

Fu, K. S. and G.J. McMurtry, "A Study of Stochastic Automata as a Model for Learning and Adaptive Controllers," *IEEE Trans. Automatic Control*, AC–11, 1966, pp. 379–87.

Fu, K. S. and Z. J. Nikolic, "On Some Reinforcement Schemes and Their Relation to Stochastic Approximation," *IEEE Trans. Automatic Control*, AC–11, 1966, pp. 756–58.

Fu, K. S. and M. D. Waltz, "A Computer Simulated Learning Control System," *IEEE International Convention Record*, 14, Part I, 1966, pp. 190–201.

Garcia, J. M., F. Le Gall, C. Castel, P. Chemouil, P. Gauthier, G. Lechermeier, "Comparative Evaluation of Centralized/Distributed Traffic Routing Policies in Telephone Networks," *ITC–11*, Elsevier Science Publishers B. V. (North Holland), 1985.

Ginzburg, S. L. and M. L. Tsetlin, "Some Examples of Simulation of the Collective Behavior of Automata," *Problemy Peredachi Informatsii*, Vol. 1, 1965, pp. 54–62.

Glorioso, R. M. and F. C. Colon, "Cybernetic Control of Computer Networks," Fifth Annual Modeling and Simulation Conference, Pittsburgh, Pa., April 1974.

Glorioso, R. M. and F. C. Colon Osorio, *Engineering Intelligent Systems*, Bedford, MA: Digital Press, 1980.

Glorioso, R. M., G. R. Grueneich, and J. C. Dunn, "Self Organization and Adaptive Routing for Communication Networks," in Proc. EASCON 1969, IEEE publication 69C31–AES.

Haralick, R. M. and L. G. Shapiro, "The Consistent Labeling Problem – Part I," *IEEE Trans. Pattern Analysis and Machine Intelligence*, PAMI–1, 1979, pp. 173–84.

Har–El, J. and Y. Rubinstein, "Optimal Performance of Stochastic Automata and Switched Random Environments," *IEEE Trans. Syst., Man and Cybern.*, SMC–7, 1977, pp. 674–77.

Hashim, A. A., S. Amir, and P. Mars, "Application of Learning Automata to Data Compression," in *Adaptive and Learning Systems*, K. S. Narendra (Ed.), New York: Plenum Press, 1986, pp. 229–34.

Heathcote, C. R., *Probability: Elements of the Mathematical Theory*, New York: Wiley Interscience, 1971.

Herkenrath, U., D. Kalin, and S. Lakshmivarahan, "On a General Class of Absorbing Barrier Learning Algorithms," *Inform. Sci.*, Vol. 24, 1981, pp. 255–63.

Hinton, G. E. and T. J. Sejnowski, "Learning and Relearning in Boltzmann Machines," in *Parallel Distributed Processing*: Explorations in the Micro Structure of Cognition, Vol. 1: Foundations, edited by D. E. Rumelhart and J. L. McClelland, Massachusetts: M.I.T. Press, 1986, pp. 282–317.

Holland, J. H., *Adaptation in Natural and Artificial Systems*, Ann Arbor, MI: University of Michigan Press, 1975.

Hopfield, J. J. and D. W. Tank, "Neural Computation of Decisions in Optimization Problems," *Biological Cybernetics*, Vol. 52, 1985, pp. 141–52.

Howard, R. A., *Dynamic Programming and Markov Processes*, Cambridge: M.I.T. Press, 1960.

Hull, C. L., *Principles of Behaviour: An Introduction to Behaviour Theory*, New York: Appleton–Century–Crofts, 1943.

Hummel, R. A. and S. W. Zucker, "On the Foundations of Relaxation Labeling Processes," *IEEE Trans. Pattern Analysis and Machine Intelligence*, PAMI-5, May 1983, pp. 267–86.

Hurley, B. R., C.J.R. Seidl, and W. F. Sewell, "A Survey of Dynamic Routing Methods for Circuit–Switched Traffic," *IEEE Communications Magazine*, Vol. 25, no. 9, September 1987.

Inoue, A. and Yamamoto, H., "Learning Control Mechanism Using Discrete Choice Models – An Application to Nonhierarchical Routing in Telephone Networks," IN 86-107, The Institute of Electronics, Information and Communication Engineers (Japan), 1986, pp. 19–24.

Ionescu Tulcea, C. and G. Marinescu "Théorie ergodique pour des classes d'opérations non complétement continues," *Annals of Mathematics*, Vol. 52, 1950, pp. 140–47.

Iosifescu, M. and R. Theodorescu, *Random Processes and Learning*, New York: Springer Verlag, 1969.

Isaacson, D. L. and R. W. Madsen, *Markov Chains: Theory and Applications*, New York: John Wiley & Sons, 1976.

Isbell, J. R., "On a Problem of Robbins," *Annals of Mathematical Statistics*, Vol. 30, 1959, pp. 606–10.

Jarvis, R. A., "Adaptive Global Search in a Time–Variant Environment Using a Probabilistic Automaton with Pattern Recognition Supervision," *IEEE Trans. Syst. Sci. and Cybern.*, SSC–6, 1970, pp. 209–17.

Karlin, S. and H. M. Taylor, *A First Course in Stochastic Processes*, (second edition), New York: Academic Press, 1975.

Kashyap, R. L., "Application of Stochastic Approximation," in J. M. Mendel and K. S. Fu (Eds.), *Adaptive, Learning and Pattern Recognition Systems*, New York: Academic Press, 1970.

Kemeny, J. G. and J. L. Snell, *Finite Markov Chains*, Princeton: Van Nostrand, 1960.

Kiefer, J. and J. Wolfowitz, "Stochastic Estimation of the Maximum of a Regression Function," *Annals of Mathematical Statistics*, Vol. 23, 1952, pp. 462–66.

Kirkpatrick, S., C. D. Gelatt, and M. P. Vecchi, "Optimization by Simulated Annealing," *Science*, Vol. 220, 1983, pp. 671–80.

Kleinrock, L., *Queueing Systems*, Volumes I and II, New York: Wiley Interscience, 1975.

Kleinrock, L., "Distributed Systems," *Communications of the ACM*, Vol. 28, No. 11, Nov. 1985, pp. 1200–13.

Koditschek, D. E. and K. S. Narendra, "Fixed Structure Automata in a Multi–teacher Environment," *IEEE Trans. Syst., Man and Cybern.*, SMC–7, 1977, pp. 616–24.

Krinsky, V. I., "An Asymptotically Optimal Automaton with Exponential Convergence," *Biofizika*, Vol. 9, 1964, pp. 484–87.

Krishnan, K.R. and T.J. Ott, "State-dependent Routing for Telephone Traffic: Theory and Results," Proceedings of 25th CDC, Athens, Greece, Dec. 1986.

Krylov, V. Yu., "One Stochastic Automaton Which is Asymptotically Optimal in Random Medium," *Automation and Remote Control*, Vol. 24, 1964, pp. 1114–16.

Krylov, V. Yu. and M. L. Tsetlin, "Games Between Automata," *Automation and Remote Control*, Vol. 24, 1963, pp. 889–99.

Kumar, P. R. and W. Lin, "Optimal Adaptive Controllers for Unknown Markov Chains," *IEEE Trans. Automatic Control*, AC–27, 1982, pp. 765–74.

Kushner, H. J., *Approximation and Convergence Methods for Random Processes*, Cambridge: MIT Press, 1984.

Kushner, H. J., *Introduction to Stochastic Control*, New York: Holt, Rinehart, Winston, 1971.

Lakshmivarahan, S., "ϵ–Optimal Learning Algorithms – Non–absorbing Barrier Type," University of Oklahoma, Norman, School of Electrical Engineering and Computing Sciences, Technical Report EECS 7901, Feb. 1979.

Lakshmivarahan, S., *Learning Algorithms: Theory and Applications*, New York: Springer–Verlag, 1981.

Lakshmivarahan, S. and K. S. Narendra, "Learning Algorithms for Two–Person Zero–Sum Stochastic Games with Incomplete Information," *Mathematics of Operations Research*, Vol. 6, 1981, pp. 379–86.

Lakshmivarahan, S. and K. S. Narendra, "Learning Algorithms for Two–Person Zero–Sum Stochastic Games with Incomplete Information: A Unified Approach," *SIAM J. Control and Optimization*, Vol. 20, 1982, pp. 541–52.

Lakshmivarahan, S. and M.A.L. Thathachar, "Optimal Nonlinear Reinforcement Schemes for Stochastic Automata," *Inform. Sci.*, Vol. 4, 1972, pp. 121–28.

Lakshmivarahan, S. and M.A.L. Thathachar, "Absolutely Expedient Learning Algorithms for Stochastic Automata," *IEEE Trans. Syst., Man and Cybern.*, SMC–3, 1973, pp. 281–86.

Lakshmivarahan, S. and M.A.L. Thathachar, "Absolute Expediency of Q– and S–model Learning Algorithms," *IEEE Trans. Syst., Man and Cybern.*, SMC–6, 1976, pp. 222–26.

Lakshmivarahan, S. and M.A.L. Thathachar, "Bounds on the Probability of Convergence of Learning Automata," *IEEE Trans. Syst., Man and Cybern.*, SMC–6, 1976, pp. 756–63.

Langholtz, G., "Behaviour of Automata in Non–Stationary Environment," *Electronics Letter*, Vol. 7, 1971, pp. 348–49.

Langholtz, G. and E. Katz, "Learning Automata in a Three–move Zero–sum Game," *IEEE Trans. Syst., Man and Cybern.*, SMC–9, 1979, pp. 304–09.

Loéve, M., *Probability Theory*, Princeton, NJ: Van Nostrand, 1955.

Luce, R. D., *Individual Choice Behavior*, New York: John Wiley & Sons, 1959.

Luce, R. D. and H. Raiffa, *Games and Decisions*, New York: John Wiley & Sons, 1957.

Maddox, I. J., *Elements of Functional Analysis*, Cambridge University Press, 1970.

Mandl, P., "Estimation and Control in Markov Chains, *Advances in Applied Probability*, Vol. 6, 1974, pp. 40–60.

Mars, P., K. S. Narendra, and M. Chrystall, "Learning Automata Control of Computer Communications Networks," Proc. Third Yale Workshop on Applications of Adaptive Systems Theory, Yale University, 1983.

Mars, P. and E. J. Poppelbaum, *Stochastic and Deterministic Averaging Processes*, London: The Institution of Electrical Engineers, 1981.

Mason, L. G., "Self–Optimizing Allocation Systems," Ph.D. Thesis, University of Saskatchewan, 1972.

Mason, L. G., "An Optimal Learning Algorithm for S–model Environments," *IEEE Trans. Automatic Control*, AC–18, 1973, pp. 493–96.

Mason, L.G., "Equilibrium Flows, Routing Patterns and Algorithms for Store-and -forward networks," *Large Scale Systems*, Vol. 8, North-Holland, 1985, pp. 187–209.

Mason, L. G. and X. D. Gu, "Learning Automata Models for Adaptive Flow Control in Packet–Switching Networks," in *Adaptive and Learning Systems*, K. S. Narendra (Ed.), New York: Plenum Press, 1986, pp. 213–28.

McCulloch, W. S. and W. H. Pitts, "A Logical Calculus of the Ideas Immanent in Nervous Activity," *Bull. Math. Biophys.*, Vol. 5, 1943, pp. 115–33.

McLaren, R. N., "A Stochastic Automaton Model for the Synthesis of Learning Systems," *IEEE Trans. Syst. Sci. and Cybern.* SSC–2, 1966, pp. 109–14.

McMurtry, G. J. and K. S. Fu, "A Variable Structure Automaton Used as a Multimodal Searching Technique," *IEEE Trans. Automatic Control*, AC–11, 1966, pp. 379–87.

Mendel, J. M. and K. S. Fu, (Eds.), *Adaptive Learning and Pattern Recognition Systems*, New York: Academic Press, 1970.

Meybodi, M. R. and S. Lakshmivarahan, "ϵ–Optimality of a General Class of Absorbing Barrier Learning Algorithms," *Information Sciences*, 28, 1982, pp. 1–20.

Meybodi, M. R. and S. Lakshmivarahan, "A Learning Approach to Priority Assignment in a Two Class M/M/1 Queuing System with Unknown Parameters," Proc. Third Yale Workshop on Applications of Adaptive Systems Theory, Yale University, 1983, pp. 106–09.

Minsky, M. and S. Papert, *Perceptrons: An Introduction to Computational Geometry*, Cambridge: M.I.T. Press, 1969.

Molnar, I., "Recent Adaptive Trends in Telecommunications Traffic Engineering," in Proc. 6th Int. Teletraffic Cong., Munich, Sept. 1970.

Murray, F. J., "Mechanisms and Robots," *Journal of ACM*, Vol. 2, 1955, pp. 61–82.

Narendra, K. S. and A. M. Annaswamy, *Stable Adaptive Systems*, Englewood Cliffs, NJ: Prentice Hall, 1988.

Narendra, K. S. and S. Lakshmivarahan, "Learning Automata – A Critique," *J. Cybernetics and Information Science*, Vol. 1, 1977, pp. 53–65.

Narendra, K. S. and P. Mars, "The Use of Learning Algorithms in Telephone Traffic Routing – A Methodology," *Automatica*, Vol. 19, 1983, pp. 495–502.

Narendra, K. S., L. G. Mason, and S. S. Tripathi, "Application of Learning Automata to Telephone Traffic Routing Problems," Becton Center Tech. Rep. CT-60, Yale University, January 1974.

Narendra, K.S. and D.M. McKenna, "Simulation Study of Telephone Traffic Routing Using Learning Algorithms: Part I," Tech. Report 7806, Yale University, Dec. 1978.

Narendra, K. S. and K. Parthasarathy, "Learning Automata Approach to Hierarchical Multiobjective Analysis," Yale University, Center for Systems Science, Technical Report 8811, June 1988.

Narendra, K. S. and R. Viswanathan, "A Two–Level System of Stochastic Automata for Periodic Random Environments," *IEEE Transactions on Syst., Man and Cybern.,*, SMC–2, 1972, pp. 285–89.

Narendra, K. S. and M.A.L. Thathachar, "Learning Automata – A Survey," *IEEE Transactions on Syst., Man and Cybern.*, SMC–14, 1974, pp. 323–34.

Narendra, K. S. and M. A. L. Thathachar, "On the Behavior of Learning Automata in a Changing Environment with Application to Telephone Traffic Routing," *IEEE Trans. on Syst., Man and Cybern.*, SMC–10, 1980, pp. 262–69.

Narendra, K. S. and R. M. Wheeler, Jr., "An N–Player Sequential Stochastic Game with Identical Payoffs," *IEEE Trans. on Syst., Man and Cybern.*, SMC–13, 1983, pp. 1154–58.

Narendra, K. S., E. A. Wright, and L. G. Mason, "Application of Learning Automata to Teletraffic Routing and Management," *IEEE Trans. on Syst., Man and Cybern.*, SMC–7, 1977, pp. 785–92.

Nedzelnitsky, O.V. Jr., "The Application of Learning Methodology to Message Routing in Data Communication Networks," Ph. D. Thesis, Yale University, 1983.

Nedzelnitsky, O.V. Jr. and K.S. Narendra, "Simulation studies of Learning Automata Part II: Fixed Structure Automata," Tech. Report No. 7910, Yale University, 1979.

Nedzelnitsky, O. V. Jr. and K. S. Narendra, "Nonstationary Models of Learning Automata Routing in Data Communication Networks," *IEEE Trans. Syst., Man and Cybern.*, SMC–17, 1987, pp. 1004–15.

Neveu, J., *Discrete Parameter Martingales*, Amsterdam: North Holland, 1975.

Norman, M. F., "A Two–phase Model and an Application to Verbal Discrimination Learning," in R. C. Atkinson (Ed.) *Studies in Mathematical Psychology*, Stanford: Stanford University Press, 1964.

Norman, M. F., "Mathematical Learning Theory," in *Mathematics of the Decision Sciences, Part 2*, A. Dantzig, A. Veinott (Eds.), Providence, Rhode Island : American Mathematical Society, 1968, pp. 283–313.

Norman, M. F., "On Linear Models with Two Absorbing Barriers," *J. Math. Psychol.*, Vol. 5, 1968, pp. 225–41.

Norman, M. F., "Some Convergence Theorems for Stochastic Learning Models with Distance Diminishing Operators," *Journal of Mathematical Psychology*, Vol. 5, 1968, pp. 61–101.

Norman, M. F., *Markov Processes and Learning Models*, New York: Academic Press, 1972.

Norman, M. F., "A Central Limit Theorem for Markov Processes That Move by Small Steps," *The Annals of Probability*, Vol. 2, 1974, pp. 1065–74.

Norman, M. F., "Markovian Learning Process," *SIAM Review*, Vol. 16, 1974, pp. 143–62.

Oommen, B. J., "Absorbing and Ergodic Discretized Two–Action Learning Automata," *IEEE Trans. Syst., Man and Cybern.*, SMC–16, 1986, pp. 542–45.

Oommen, B. J., "Learning Automaton Solution to Stochastic Minimum–Spanning–Circle Problem," *IEEE Trans. Syst., Man and Cybern.*, SMC–16, 1986, pp. 598–603.

Oommen, B. J., "Ergodic Learning Automata Capable of Incorporating a priori Information," *IEEE Trans. Syst., Man and Cybern.*, SMC–17, 1987, pp. 717–23.

Oommen, B.J. and J.P.R. Christensen, "Epsilon-optimal Discretized Linear Reward-Penalty Learning Automata," *IEEE Trans. Syst., Man and Cybern.*, SMC–18, 1988, pp. 451–58.

Oommen, B.J. and D.C.Y. Ma, "Deterministic Learning Automata Solutions to the Equipartitioning Problem," *IEEE Trans. Computers*, Vol. 37, 1988, pp. 2–14.

Oommen, B.J., S.S. Iyengar, and N. Andrade, "On using Stochastic Automata for Trajectory Planning of Robot Manipulators in Noisy Workspaces," Proc. Fourth IEEE Conference on AI Applications, March 1988, pp. 88–94.

Owen, G., *Game Theory*, New York: Academic Press, 1982.

Paz, A., *Introduction to Probabilistic Automata*, New York: Academic Press, 1971.

Peleg, S., "Ambiguity Reduction in Handwriting with Ambiguous Segmentation and Uncertain Implementation," *Computers, Graphics and Image Processing*, Vol. 10, 1979, pp. 235–45.

Pittel, B. G., "The Asymptotic Properties of One Form of Goore Game," *Problemy Peredachi Informatsii*, Vol. 1, 1965, pp. 99–112.

Polya, G., *Mathematics and Plausible Reasoning*, Princeton, NJ: Princeton University Press, 1954.

Ponomarev, V. A., "A Construction of an Automaton Which Is Asymptotically Optimal in a Stationary Random Medium," *Biofizika*, Vol. 9, 1964, pp. 104–10.

Pontryagin, L. S., V. G. Boltyanskii, R. V. Gamkrelidze, and E. F. Mishchenko, *The Mathematical Theory of Optimal Processes*, New York: Wiley Interscience, 1962.

Poznyak, A. S., "Investigation of Convergence of Algorithms for the Functioning of Learning Stochastic Automata," *Automation and Remote Control*, 1973, pp. 77–91.

Pratt, W. K., W. H. Chen, and L. R. Welch, "Slant Transform Image Coding," *IEEE Trans. Commun. Tech.*, COM–22, 1974, pp. 1075–93.

Pratt, W. K., J. Kane, and H.C. Andrew, "Hadamard Transform Image Coding," Proc. IEEE, Vol. 57, No. 1, 1969, pp. 58–68.

Ramakrishnan, K. R., "Hierarchical Systems and Cooperative Games of Learning Automata," Ph.D. Thesis, Dept. of Electrical Engineering, Indian Institute of Science, Bangalore, 1982.

Robbins, H., "Some Aspects of the Sequential Design of Experiments," *Bulletin of American Mathematical Society*, Vol. 58, No. 5, 1952, pp. 527–35.

Robbins, H., "A Sequential Decision Problem with Finite Memory," Proc. Nat. Acad. Sci., 1956, pp. 920–23.

Robbins, H. and S. Munro, "A Stochastic Approximation Method," *Annals of Mathematical Statistics*, Vol. 22, 1951, pp. 400–07.

Robinson, J., "An Iterative Method of Solving a Game," *Annals of Mathematics*, Vol. 54, 1951, pp. 296–301.

Rosenblatt, F., "The Perceptron: A Probabilistic Model for Information Storage and Organization in the Brain," *Psychological Rev.*, Vol. 65, No. 6, 1958, pp. 386–408.

Rosenblatt, F., *Principles of Neurodynamics*, New York: Spartan, 1962.

Rosenfeld, A., R. A. Hummel, and S. W. Zucker, "Scene Labeling by Relaxation Operations," *IEEE Trans. Syst., Man and Cybern.*, SMC–6, 1976, pp. 420–33.

Samuels, S. M., "Randomized Rules for One Two–Armed Bandit Problem with Finite Memory," *Annals of Mathematical Statistics*, Vol. 39, No. 6, 1968, pp. 2103–7.

Sanghvi, A. P. and M. J. Sobel, "Bayesian Games as Stochastic Processes," *International Journal of Game Theory*, Vol. 5, 1976, pp. 1–22.

Saridis, G. N., *Self–Organizing Control of Stochastic Systems*, New York: Marcel Dekker, 1978.

Saridis, G. N., "Toward the Realization of Intelligent Controls," Proc. IEEE, Vol. 67, 1979, pp. 1115–33.

Saridis, G. N., "Intelligent Robotic Control," *IEEE Transactions on Automatic Control*, AC–28, No. 5, May 1983, pp. 547–57.

Sawaragi, Y., N. Baba, and T. Soeda, "New Topics of Learning Automata," *J. Cybern. Inform. Sci.*, Vol. 1, 1977, pp. 112–20.

Sejnowski, T. J. and C. R. Rosenberg, "NET Talk: A Parallel Network That Learns to Read Aloud," Johns Hopkins University, Department of Electrical Engineering and Computer Science Technical Report 86/01, 1986.

Sejnowski, T. J. and C. R. Rosenberg, "Parallel Networks That Learn to Pronounce English Text," *Complex Systems* Vol. 1, 1987, pp. 145–68.

Selfridge, O.G., "Tracking and Trailing: Adaptation in Movement Strategies," Unpublished draft, 1978.

Shapiro, I.J., "The Use of Stochastic Automata in Adaptive Control," Ph. D. Thesis, Yale University, 1969.

Shapiro, I. J. and K. S. Narendra, "Use of Stochastic Automata for Parameter Self–Optimization with Multi–Modal Performance Criteria," *IEEE Trans. Syst. Sci. and Cybern.*, SSC–5, 1969, pp. 352–60.

Shapley, L. S., "Stochastic Games," Proc. Nat. Acad. Sci., Vol. 39, 1953, pp. 1095–100.

Shubik, M., *Game Theory in the Social Sciences*, Cambridge, MA: MIT Press, 1982.

Sklansky, J., "Learning Systems for Automatic Control," *IEEE Trans. Automatic Control*, AC–11, 1966, pp. 6–19.

Sklansky, J. and G. N. Wassel, *Pattern Classification and Trainable Machines*, New York: Springer–Verlag, 1981.

Smith, C. V. and R. Pyke, "The Robbins–Isbell Two–Armed Bandit Problem with Finite Memory," *Annals of Mathematical Statistics*, Vol. 36, 1965, pp. 1375–86.

Srikantakumar, P. R., "Learning Models and Adaptive Routing in Telephone and Data Communication Networks," Ph.D. Thesis, Yale University, 1980.

Srikantakumar, P. R., "Application of Learning Theory to Communication Networks Control," Proc. Third Yale Workshop on Applications of Adaptive Systems Theory, Yale University, 1983, pp. 135–41.

Srikantakumar, P. R., "A Simple Learning Scheme for Priority Assignment at a Single–Server Queue," *IEEE Trans. on Syst., Man and Cybern.*, SMC–16, 1986, pp. 751–54.

Srikantakumar, P. R. and K. S. Narendra, "A Learning Model for Routing in Telephone Networks," *SIAM J. Control and Optimization*, Vol. 20, 1982, pp. 34–57.

Stefanyuk, V. L., "Example of a Problem in the Joint Behaviour of Two Automata," *Automation and Remote Control*, Vol. 24, 1963, pp. 716–19.

Suppes, P. and R. C. Atkinson, *Markov Learning Models for Multiperson Interactions*, Stanford: Stanford University Press, 1960.

Szybicki, E., "Calculation of Congestion in Trunk Networks Provided with Adaptive Traffic Routing and Automatic Network Management Systems," Proceedings of IEEE Int. Conf. Comm., Denver, Colorado, 1981.

Szybicki, E. and A.E. Bean, "Advanced Traffic Routing in Local Telephone Networks–Performance of Proposed Call Routing Algorithm," Proceedings of ITC, Vol. 9, 1979.

Tasb, M. and P. A. Winta, "Image Coding by Adaptive Block Quantization," *IEEE Trans. Commun. Tech.*, COM–19, 1971, pp. 957–72.

Thathachar, M.A.L. and R. Bhakthavathsalam, "Learning Automata Operating in Parallel Environments," *J. Cybern. Inform. Sci.*, Vol. 1, 1977, pp. 121–27.

Thathachar, M.A.L. and B. R. Harita, "Learning Automata with Changing Number of Actions," *IEEE Trans. Syst., Man and Cybern.*, SMC–17, 1987, pp. 1095–1100.

Thathachar, M.A.L. and B. J. Oommen, "Discretized Reward–Inaction Learning Automata," *J. Cybern. Inform. Sci.*, 1979, pp. 24–29.

Thathachar, M.A.L. and B. J. Oommen, "Learning Automata Possessing Ergodicity of the Mean – The Two Action Case," *IEEE Trans. Syst., Man and Cybern.*, SMC–13, 1983, pp. 1143–48.

Thathachar, M.A.L. and K. M. Ramachandran, "Asymptotic Behavior of a Learning Algorithm," *International Journal of Control*, Vol.39, 1984, pp. 827-838.

Thathachar, M.A.L. and K. M. Ramachandran, "Asymptotic Behavior of a Hierarchical System of Learning Automata," *Information Sciences*, Vol. 35, 1985, pp. 91–110.

Thathachar, M.A.L. and K. R. Ramakrishnan, "An Automaton Model of a Hierarchical Learning System," Proc. 8th IFAC World Congress, Kyoto, Japan, 1981.

Thathachar, M.A.L. and K. R. Ramakrishnan, "A Hierarchical System of Learning Automata," *IEEE Trans. Syst., Man and Cybern.*, SMC–11, 1981, pp. 236–41.

Thathachar, M.A.L. and K. R. Ramakrishnan, "On–Line Optimization with a Team of Learning Automata," Proc. IFAC Symposium on Theory and Application of Digital Control," New Delhi, India, January 1982, pp. 8–13.

Thathachar, M.A.L. and K. R. Ramakrishnan, "A Cooperative Game of a Pair of Learning Automata," *Automatica*, Vol. 20, 1984, pp. 797–801.

Thathachar, M.A.L. and P. S. Sastry, "A New Approach to the Design of Reinforcement Schemes for Learning Automata," *IEEE Trans. Syst., Man and Cybern.*, SMC–15, 1985, pp. 168–75.

Thathachar, M.A.L. and P. S. Sastry, "Relaxation Labeling with Learning Automata," *IEEE Trans. Pattern Analysis and Machine Intelligence*, PAMI–8, 1986, pp. 256–68.

Thathachar, M.A.L. and P. S. Sastry, "Estimator Algorithms for Learning Automata," Proc. Platinum Jubilee Conference on Systems and Signal Processing, Bangalore, India, 1986.

Thathachar, M.A.L. and P. S. Sastry, "A Hierarchical System of Learning Automata That Can Learn the Globally Optimal Path," *Information Sciences*, Vol. 37, 1987, pp. 143–66.

Thathachar, M.A.L. and P. S. Sastry, "Learning Optimal Discriminant Functions Through a Cooperative Game of Automata," *IEEE Trans. Syst., Man and Cybern.*, SMC–17, 1987, pp. 73–85.

Thathachar, M.A.L. and P. S. Sastry, "Learning Automata in Stochastic Games with Incomplete Information," Indo–U.S. Workshop on Systems and Signal Processing, Bangalore, India, January 1988.

Tsertsvadze, G. N., "Certain Properties of Stochastic Automata and Methods for Synthesizing Them," *Automation and Remote Control*, Vol. 24, 1963, pp. 316–26.

Tsetlin, M. L., "On the Behaviour of Finite Automata in Random Media," *Automation and Remote Control*, Vol. 22, 1962, pp. 1210–19. Originally in *Avtomatika i Telemekhanika*, Vol. 22, 1961, pp. 1345–54.

Tsetlin, M. L., *Automaton Theory and Modeling of Biological Systems*, New York: Academic Press, 1973.

Tsuji, H., M. Mizumoto, J. Toyoda, and K. Tanaka, "An Automaton in Non-Stationary Random Environment," *Information Sciences*, Vol. 6, No. 2, 1973, pp. 123–42.

Tsypkin, Ya. Z., *Adaptation and Learning in Automatic Systems*, New York: Academic Press, 1971.

Tsypkin, Ya. Z., *Foundations of the Theory of Learning Systems*, New York: Academic Press, 1973.

Tsypkin, Ya. Z. and A. S. Poznyak, "Finite Learning Automata," *Engineering Cybernetics*, Vol. 10, 1972, pp. 478–90.

Tsypkin, Ya. Z. and A. S. Poznyak, "Learning Automata," *J. Cybernetics and Information Science, Special Issue on Learning Automata*, Vol. 1, 1977, pp. 128–61.

Uhr, L., (Ed.) *Pattern Recognition*, New York: John Wiley & Sons, 1966.

Uose, H., and Y. Niitsu, "A Learning Control Approach to Dynamic Network Resource Assignments," *ITC-11*, Elsevier Science Publishers B. V. (North-Holland), 1985.

Vaisbord, E. M., "Games of Many Automata with Various Depths of Memory," *Automation and Remote Control*, Vol. 29, 1968, pp. 1938–48.

Varaiya, P., "Optimal and Suboptimal Stationary Controls for Markov Chains," *IEEE Trans. Automatic Control*, AC–23, 1978, pp. 298–305.

Varshavskii, V. I., M. V. Meleshina, and M. L. Tsetlin, "Behaviour of Automata in Periodic Random Media and the Problem of Synchronization in the Presence of Noise," *Problemi Peredachii Informatsii*, Vol. 1, No. 1, 1965, pp. 65–71.

Varshavskii, V. I. and I. P. Vorontsova, "On the Behaviour of Stochastic Automata with a Variable Structure," *Automation and Remote Control*, Vol. 24, 1963, pp. 327–33.

Viswanatha Rao, T., "Learning Solutions to Stochastic Noncooperative Games," Master's Thesis, Department of Electrical Engineering, Indian Institute of Science, 1984.

Viswanathan, R., "Learning Automaton: Models and Applications," Ph.D. Thesis, Yale University, 1972.

Viswanathan, R. and K. S. Narendra, "Simulation Studies of Stochastic Automata Models, Part I: Reinforcement Schemes," Yale University, Becton Center Technical Report CT–45, 1971.

Viswanathan, R. and K. S. Narendra, "On Variable–structure Stochastic Automata," in *Pattern Recognition and Machine Learning*, New York: Plenum Press, 1971, pp. 277–87.

Viswanathan, R. and K. S. Narendra, "Comparison of Expedient and Optimal Reinforcement Schemes for Learning Systems," *J. Cybern.*, Vol. 2, 1972, pp. 21–37.

Viswanathan, R. and K. S. Narendra, "A Note on the Linear Reinforcement Scheme for Variable Structure Stochastic Automata," *IEEE Trans. Syst., Man and Cybern.*, SMC–2, 1972, pp. 292–94.

Viswanathan, R. and K. S. Narendra, "Competitive and Cooperative Games of Variable Structure Stochastic Automata," *J. Cybern.*, Vol. 3, 1973, pp. 1–23.

Viswanathan, R. and K. S. Narendra, "Stochastic Automata Models with Application to Learning Systems," *IEEE Trans. Syst., Man and Cybern.*, SMC–3, 1973, pp. 107–11.

Viswanathan, R. and K. S. Narendra, "Games of Stochastic Automata," *IEEE Trans. Syst., Man and Cybern.*, SMC–4, 1974, pp. 131–35.

Volkonskii, V. A., "Asymptotic Properties of the Behavior of Elementary Automata in a Game," *Problemy Peredachi Informatsii*, Vol. 1, 1965, pp. 36–53.

Von Neumann, J. and O. Morgenstern, *Theory of Games and Economic Behavior*, Princeton: Princeton University Press, 1944.

Vorontsova, I. P., "Algorithms for Changing Automaton Transition Probabilities," *Problemi Peredachii Informatsii*, Vol. 1, 1965, pp. 122–26.

Waltz, M. D. and K. S. Fu, "A Heuristic Approach to Reinforcement Learning Control Systems," *IEEE Trans. Automatic Control*, AC–10, 1965, pp. 390–98.

Watanabe, S., "Learning Processes and Inverse-H Theorem," *IRE Trans. Inform. Theory*, Vol. 8, 1962, pp. 246–51.

Watanabe, S., *Knowing and Guessing*, New York: John Wiley & Sons, 1969.

Watanabe, S., "Creative Learning and Propensity Automaton," *IEEE Trans. on Syst., Man and Cybern.*, Vol. 5, 1975, pp. 603–10.

Wheeler, R. M. Jr., "Decentralized Learning in Games and Finite Markov Chains," Ph.D. Thesis, Yale University, 1985.

Wheeler, R. M. Jr. and K. S. Narendra, "Learning Models for Decentralized Decision Making," *Automatica*, Vol. 21, 1985, pp. 479–84.

Wheeler, R. M. Jr. and K. S. Narendra, "Decentralized Learning in Finite Markov Chains," *IEEE Trans. Automatic Control*, AC–31, 1986, pp. 519–26.

White, D. J., "Dynamic Programming, Markov Chains, and the Method of Successive Approximations," *Journal of Mathematical Analysis and Applications*, Vol. 6, 1963, pp. 373–76.

Widrow, B., N. K. Gupta, and S. Maitra, "Punish/Reward: Learning with a Critic in Adaptive Threshold Systems," *IEEE Trans. on Syst., Man and Cybern.*, Vol. 5, 1973, pp. 455–65.

Widrow, B. and M. E. Hoff, "Adaptive Switching Circuits," in 1960 WESCON Convention Record, Part IV, 1960, pp. 96–104.

Widrow, B. and F. W. Smith, "Pattern Recognizing Control System," in *Computer and Information Science*, J. T. Tou and R. H. Wilcox (Eds.), Cleaver Hume Press, 1964, pp. 288–317.

Wiener, N., *Cybernetics*, New York: The Technology Press John Wiley, 1948.

Williams, R. J., "Reinforcement Learning in Connectionist Networks: A Mathematical Analysis," ICS Report 8605, University of California, San Diego, 1986.

Williams, R. J., "Reinforcement–Learning Connectionist Systems," Technical Report NU–CCS–87–3, Northeastern University, 1987.

Witten, I. H., "The Apparent Conflict Between Estimation and Control – A Survey of the Two–Armed Bandit Problem," *Journal of the Franklin Institute*, 301, 1976, pp. 161–89.

Zucker, S. W., Y. G. Leclerc, and J. L. Mohammed, "Continuous Relaxation and Local Maxima Selection: Conditions for Equivalence," *IEEE Trans. Pattern Analysis and Machine Intelligence*, PAMI–3, March 1981, pp. 117–26.

Index

A

Absolute expediency, hierarchical systems, 249–50

Absolutely expedient schemes
convergence and, 168–87
bounds on $\Gamma_{i(p)}$, 173–77
computation of bounds, 173–85
convergence probabilities, 172–73
determination of $\varphi_i\,(p)$, 177–83
rate of, 187–92
Q model, 208–10
variable structures stochastic automata, 124–56

Absorbing Markov chains, 460–61

Absorbing models, distance diminishing operators, 474–75

Adaptive Control Processes—A Guided Tour (Bellman), 10

Adaptive processes, 10, 12

Automata games, *See* Games

Automata, 40–52
deterministic automaton, 41–43
feedback connection, 52–53
fixed-structure stochastic automaton, 46
in Markovian switching environment, 234–39
input of, 40
output/action of, 40

output function, 41
random inputs, 49–52
state of, 40
stochastic automaton, 43–49
transition function, 40–41
two-person zero-sum games, 292–309
variable-structure stochastic automaton, 46

B

Bayesian learning, 22–23
learning automata and, 30

C

Circuit-switched networks
routing in, 363–73
network model, 363
routing schemes, 363–73

Computer simulations, two-person zero-sum games, 304–9

Computer technology, advances in, 1–2

Connectionist architectures, 5

Context vectors
learning in automata networks with, 347–50